ZA...
Su...

ITALIAN
and
ENGLISH
Dictionary

English-Italian / Italian-English

Dictionary edited by EDIGEO

North American Edition Prepared by
the Editors of National Textbook Company

KAIBIN, XU ② COLORADO, eW

9

NTC
NTC Publishing Group

Library of Congress Cataloging-in-Publication Data

Zanichelli super-mini Italian and English dictionary : English-
    Italian, Italian-English dictionary / edited by Edigeo. —
    North-American ed. prepared by the editors of National
    Textbook Company.
        p.   cm.
        First published in 1993
        ISBN 0-8442-8447-5
        1. English language—Dictionaries—Italian.   2.
    Italian language—Dictionaries—English.   I. Edigeo.
    II. National Textbook Company.
    PC1640.Z34   1998
    453'.21—dc21
                                                    98-16233
                                                        CIP

Published by NTC Publishing Group
A division of NTC/Contemporary Publishing Group, Inc.
4255 West Touhy Avenue, Lincolnwood (Chicago), Illinois
60712-1975 U.S.A.
Copyright © 1989 by Nicola Zanichelli Editore, S.p.A.,
Bologna, Italy.
Printed in the United States of America
International Standard Book Number: 0-8442-8447-5

        03 04 05   15 14 13 12 11 10 9

Contents

Prefatory Note

The *Zanichelli Super-Mini Italian and English Dictionary* contains over 13,000 English entries and over 11,000 Italian entries. The English-Italian section is provided with pronunciations transcribed in IPA symbols. In the Italian section the stressed syllable of each poly-syllabic word is marked with a grave or an acute accent. The "open" and "closed" [e] and [o] are also marked with accents.

This convenient volume is "super" in terms of its comprehensiveness and contemporary word list, while being "mini" only in its size.

ABBREVIATIONS

Abbreviation	Italian	English
(abb.)	*abbigliamento*	clothing
(aer.)	*aeronautica*	aeronautics
agg.	*aggettivo*	adjective
(agr.)	*agricoltura*	agriculture
(alim.)	*alimentazione*	food
(anat.)	*anatomia*	anatomy
(arch.)	*architettura*	architecture
(archeol.)	*archeologica*	archeology
art.	*articolo*	article
(arte)	*arte*	art
(astr.)	*astronomia*	astronomy
attr.	*attributivo*	attributive
(autom.)	*automobilismo*	automobiles
avv.	*avverbio*	adverb
(biol.)	*biologia*	biology
(bot.)	*botanica*	botany
card.	*cardinale*	cardinal
(chim.)	*chimica*	chemistry
(cin.)	*cinema*	cinema
(comm.)	*commercio*	commerce
comp.	*comparativo*	comparative
cong.	*congiunzione*	conjunction
dif.	*difettivo*	defective
dimostr.	*dimostrativo*	demonstrative
(edil.)	*edilizia*	building
(elettr.)	*elettrotecnica*	electronics
f.	*femminile*	feminine
(fam.)	*familiare*	family
(ferr.)	*ferroviario*	railway
(fig.)	*figurato*	figurative
(fin.)	*finanza*	finance
(fis.)	*fisica*	physics
(geog.)	*geografia*	geography
(geol.)	*geologia*	geology
(geom.)	*geometria*	geometry
gramm.)	*grammatica*	grammar
impers.	*impersonale*	impersonal
indef.	*indefinito*	indefinite
(inf.)	*informatica*	information science

inter.	*interiezione*	interjection
intr.	*intransitivo*	intransitive
inv.	*invariabile*	invariable
(leg.)	*legislativo*	law
(lett.)	*letterario*	literary
(ling.)	*linguistica*	linguistics
(loc.)	*locuzione*	idiom, idiomatic
m.	*maschile*	masculine
(mat.)	*matematica*	mathematics
(mecc.)	*meccanica*	mechanics
(med.)	*medicina*	medicine
(meteor.)	*meterologia*	meterology
(mil.)	*militare*	military
(min.)	*minerario*	mining
(mus.)	*musica*	music
(naut.)	*nautica*	nautical
num.	*numerale*	numeral
ord.	*ordinale*	ordinal
part.	*partitivo*	partitive
pl.	*plurale*	plural
(pop.)	*popolare*	popular
pred.	*predicativo*	predicate
prep.	*preposizione*	preposition
pron.	*pronome*	pronoun
	pronominale	pronominal
(psic.)	*psicologia*	psychology
rel.	*relativo*	relative
(relig.)	*religione*	religion
rifl.	*riflessivo*	reflexive
s.	*sostantivo*	substantive
sing.	*singolare*	singular
(sport)	*sport*	sports
(stor.)	*storia*	history
super.	*superlativo*	superlative
(teatro)	*teatro*	theater
(tecn.)	*tecnologia*	technology
(tel.)	*televisione*	television
tr.	*transitivo*	transitive
v.	*verbo*	verb
(volg.)	*volgare*	vernacular
(zool.)	*zoologia*	zoology

ENGLISH PRONUNCIATION

Vowels

[a:]	c*ar*, f*a*ther
[æ]	*a*nd, m*a*n
[e]	b*e*d, y*e*s
[ʌ]	c*u*p, *u*p
[ə]	*a*, m*o*ther
[ə:]	g*ir*l, w*or*d
[i]	p*i*g, *i*t
[i:]	tr*ee*, pl*ea*se
[ɔ]	b*o*x, n*o*t
[ɔ:]	w*a*ll, h*or*se
[u]	b*oo*k, f*u*ll
[u:]	sh*oe*, f*oo*l

Semivowels

[j]	*y*es, *y*ou
[w]	*w*ind, a*w*ay

Diphthongs

[ai]	f*i*ve, fl*y*
[au]	h*ow*, h*ou*se
[ei]	tr*ai*n, n*a*me
[ɛə]	th*ere*, c*are*
[iə]	*ear*, h*ere*
[ou]	g*o*, b*oa*t
[ɔi]	t*oy*, *oi*l
[uə]	p*oor*, s*ure*

Consonants

[b]	*b*ook, *b*oy
[d]	*d*og, kin*d*
[tʃ]	*ch*urch, *ch*air
[k]	*c*ar, bla*ck*
[f]	*f*loor, o*ff*
[g]	*g*o, eg*g*
[ʒ]	plea*s*ure, mea*s*ure
[dʒ]	*j*udge, a*g*e
[h]	*h*at, *h*and
[l]	*l*eg, fu*ll*
[m]	*m*atch, hi*m*
[n]	*n*ame, pe*n*
[ŋ]	ri*ng*, so*ng*
[p]	*p*encil, sto*p*
[r]	*r*oom, ve*r*y
[s]	*s*un, pla*c*e
[z]	*z*oo, noi*s*e
[ʃ]	*f*i*sh*, *sh*ip
[t]	*t*rain, po*t*
[θ]	*th*in, mou*th*
[ð]	*th*is, wi*th*
[v]	*v*ery, se*v*en
[x]	lo*ch* (only in Gaelic words)

[:]	indicates that the preceding vowel is lengthened
[']	indicates that the following syllable has primary stress
[,]	indicates that the following syllable has secondary stress
[*]	stands for word final [r]
[~]	indicates a nasal vowel

Phonetic symbols in italics are optional.

INGLESE
ITALIANO

abacus ['æbəkəs] *s.* abaco *m.* (*arch.*) • pallottoliere *m.*

to abandon [ə'bændən] *v. tr.* abbandonare, lasciare

to abate [ə'beit] *v. tr.* diminuire • *intr.* placarsi

abbey ['æbi] *s.* abbazia *f.*

abbot ['æbət] *s.* abate *m.*

to abbreviate [ə'bri:vieit] *v. tr.* abbreviare

abbreviation [ə,bri:vi'eifən] *s.* abbreviazione *f.*

to abdicate [æb'dikeit] *v. tr. e intr.* abdicare

abdomen ['æbdəmen] *s.* addome *m.*

abdominal [æb'dɔminəl] *agg.* addominale

to abduct [æb'dʌkt] *v. tr.* rapire

abductor [æb'dʌktə*] *s.* rapitore *m.*

able ['eibl] *agg.* capace; **to be ~** to essere in grado di, potere, riuscire

abnormal [æb'nɔ:məl] *agg.* anormale

abode [ə'boud] *s.* dimora *f.*

to abolish [ə'bɔliʃ] *v. tr.* abolire, sopprimere

abolitionism [,æbə'liʃənizəm] *s.* abolizionismo *m.*

aboriginal [,æbə'ridʒənl] *s.* aborigeno *m.*, indigeno *m.*

to abort [ə'bɔ:t] *v. tr. e intr.* abortire

abortion [ə'bɔ:ʃən] *s.* aborto *m.*

about [ə'baut] *prep.* circa; intorno a • *avv.* intorno; circa, pressappoco; **to be ~** to accingersi, prepararsi a; **about-face** testacoda

above [ə'bʌv] *avv.* sopra, di sopra; precedentemente • *prep.* su, sopra, al di sopra; **~ all** soprattutto

abrasion [ə'breiʒən] *s.* abrasione *f.*

to abridge [ə'bridʒ] *v. tr.* riassumere; accorciare; **abridged version** compendio

abroad [ə'brɔ:d] *avv.* all'estero

to abrogate ['æbrougeit] *v. tr.* abrogare

abrupt [ə'brʌpt] *agg.* improvviso, brusco; ripido, scosceso

abscess ['æbsis] *s.* ascesso *m.*

to abscond [əb'skɔnd] *v. intr.* scappare

absconder [əb'skɔndə*] *s.* latitante *m. e f.*

absconding [əb'skɔndiŋ] *agg.* latitante

absence ['æbsəns] *s.* assenza *f.*; mancanza *f.*; contumacia *f.*

absent ['æbsənt] *agg.* assente

absent-minded ['æbsənt 'maindid] *agg.* distratto

absent-mindedly ['æbsənt 'maindidli] *avv.* distrattamente

absent-mindedness ['æbsənt 'maindidnis] *s.* distrazione *f.*

to absent oneself [æb'sent wʌn'self] *v. rifl.* assentarsi

absolute ['æbsəlu:t] *agg.* assoluto; completo, totale

absolutely ['æbsəlu:tli] *avv.* assolutamente, completamente; senz'altro

to absorb [əb'sɔ:b] *v. tr.* assorbire; assimilare

to abstain [əb'stein] *v. intr.* astenersi

abstinence ['æbstinəns] *s.* astinenza *f.*

abstract ['æbstrækt] *s.* estratto *m.*; riassunto *m.* • *agg.* astratto

to abstract [æb'strækt] *v. tr.* sottrarre, ricavare; astrarre

abstraction [æb'strækʃən] *s.* sottrazione *f.*; astrazione *f.*

abstractionism [æb'strækʃənizəm] *s.* astrattismo *m.*

abstractionist [æb'strækʃənist] *s.* astrattista *m. e f.*

absurd [əb'sə:d] *agg.* assurdo; ridicolo

abundance [ə'bʌndəns] *s.* abbondanza *f.*

abundant [ə'bʌndənt] *agg.* abbondante

abuse [ə'bju:s] *s.* abuso *m.*; insulto *m.*; maltrattamento *m.*

to abuse [ə'bju:z] *v. tr.* abusare; ingiuriare, insultare

abyss [ə'bis] *s.* abisso *m.*

acacia [ə'keiʃə] *s.* acacia *f.*

academic [,ækə'demik] *agg. e s.* accademico *m.*

academy [ə'kædəmi] *s.* accademia *f.*

acanthus [ə'kænθəs] *s.* acanto *m.*

accelerator [æk'seləreitə*] *s.* acceleratore *m.*

accent ['æksənt] *s.* accento *m.*; parlata *f.*; enfasi *f.*

to accept [ək'sept] *v. tr.* accettare; **accepted** ammesso

access ['ækses] *s.* accesso *m.*

accessory [æk'sesəri] s. accessorio m.

accident ['æksidənt] s. incidente m., infortunio m.; disgrazia f.

to acclimatize [ə'klaimətaiz]v. tr. ambientare; acclimatare; to get acclimatized ambientarsi

to accomodate [ə'kɔmədeit] v. tr. alloggiare, sistemare

accomodation [ə,kɔmə'deifən] s. alloggio m.; ricettività f.

to accompany [ə'kʌmpəni] v. tr. accompagnare; scortare

accomplice [ə'kɔmplis] s. complice m. e f.

to accomplish [ə'kɔmpliʃ] v. tr. compiere, realizzare

accomplished [ə'kɔmpliʃt] agg. compiuto; esperto

accomplishment [ə'kɔmpliʃmənt] s. realizzazione f.; impresa f.; talento m.

account [ə'kaunt] s. conto m.; acconto m.; relazione f.; current - conto corrente

accountant [ə'kauntənt] s. contabile m. e f.

accumulator [ə'kju:mjuleitə*] s. accumulatore m.

accurate ['ækjurit] agg. preciso; esatto

accusation [,ækju:(:)'zeifən] s. accusa f.; denuncia f.

to accuse [ə'kju:z] v. tr. accusare; imputare

accustomed [ə'kʌstəmd] agg. abituato

ace [eis] s. asso m.

acephalous [ə'sefələs] agg. acefalo

ache [eik] s. dolore m.

to ache [eik] v. intr. far male, dolere; aching dolorante

achievable [ə'tʃi:vəbl] agg. raggiungibile

to achieve [ə'tʃi:v] v. tr. compiere; raggiungere

achievement [ə'tʃi:vmənt] s. impresa f.; realizzazione f.

acid ['æsid] s. acido m.

acidulous [ə'sidjuləs] agg. acidulo

acinus ['æsinəs] s. acino m.

to acknowledge [ək'nɔlidʒ] v. tr. riconoscere, ammettere

acorn ['eikɔ:n] s. ghianda f.

acoustics [ə'ku:stiks] s. pl. (v. al sing.) acustica f. sing.

acquaintance [ə'kweinstəns] s. conoscente m. e f.; conoscenza f.

to acquire [ə'kwaiə*] v. tr. acquisire; entrare in possesso

to acquit [ə'kwit] v. tr. assolvere

acrobat ['ækrəb—t] s. acrobata m. e f.

acrobatics [ə'krɔ'bætiks] s. pl. acrobazia f. sing.

acropolis [ə'krɔpəlis] s. acropoli f.

across [ə'krɔs] prep. attraverso; dall'altro lato di, oltre

acrylic [ə'krilik] agg. acrilico

act [ækt] s. atto m.; decreto m.

to act [ækt] v. tr. e intr. agire, comportarsi; recitare

acting ['æktiŋ] s. recitazione f. • sostituto m.

action ['ækʃən] s. azione f.; provvedimento m.; querela f. (leg.)

active ['æktiv] agg. attivo, operoso

activity [æk'tiviti] s. attività f.

actor ['æktə*] s. attore m.

actress ['æktris] s. attrice f.

actual ['æktjuəl] agg. reale; effettivo

actually ['æktjuəli] avv. effettivamente; realmente

aculeus [ə'kju:(:)liəs] s. aculeo m.

acumen [ə'kju:men] s. acume m.

acupuncture ['ækju,pʌŋktʃə*] s. agopuntura f.

acute [ə'kju:t] agg. acuto

adamant ['ædəmənt] agg. inflessibile

to adapt [ə'dæpt] v. tr. adattare; rimaneggiare; - oneself adattarsi

adaptation [,ædæp'teifən] s. adattamento m.

to add [æd] v. tr. aggiungere; sommare

addition [ə'diʃən] s. addizione f.; aggiunta f., supplemento m.

additional [ə'diʃənəl] agg. addizionale; supplementare

additive ['æditiv] s. additivo m.

address [ə'dres] s. indirizzo m., recapito m.; - book rubrica

to address [ə'dres] v. tr. indirizzare; rivolgersi

addressee [,ædre'si:] s. destinatario m.

adequate ['ædikwit] agg. sufficiente

adherent [əd'hiərənt] agg. aderente

adhesive [əd'hi:siv] agg. adesivo

adjacent [ə'dʒeisənt] agg. adiacente, attiguo

adjective ['ædʒiktiv] s. aggettivo m.

adjoining [ə'dʒɔiniŋ] agg. adiacente, contiguo

to adjourn [ə'dʒə:n] v. tr. aggiornare, rinviare

to adjust [ə'dʒʌst] v. tr. sistemare; regolare; adattare

adjustable [ə'dʒʌstəbl] agg. adattabile; regolabile

adjustment [ə'dʒʌstmənt] s. sistemazione f.; conguaglio m.; adattamento m.

to administer [əd'ministə*] v. tr. amministrare

administration [əd,minis'streifən] s. amministrazione f.

administrator [əd'ministreitə*] s. amministratore m.

admirable ['ædmərəbl] agg. ammirevole

admiral ['ædmərəl] s. ammiraglio m.

admiration [,ædmə'reiʃən] s. ammirazione f.

to admire [əd'maiə*] v. tr. ammirare

admirer [əd'maiərə*] s. ammiratore m.

admissible [əd'misəbl] agg. ammissibile

admission [əd'miʃən] s. ammissione f.; riconoscimento m.; - **free** ingresso gratuito

to admit [əd'mit] v. tr. ammettere; riconoscere

admittance [əd'mitəns] s. ammissione f.; accesso m.; ingresso m.

adolescence [,ædou'lesns] s. adolescenza f.

adolescent [,ædou'lesnt] s. adolescente m. e f. • agg. adolescenziale

to adopt [ə'dɔpt] v. tr. adottare

adoption [ə'dɔpʃən] s. adozione f.

adoptive [ə'dɔptiv] agg. adottivo

to adore [ə'dɔ:*] v. tr. adorare

to adorn [ə'dɔ:n] v. tr. adornare, imbellire; - **oneself** ornarsi

adult ['ædʌlt] s. adulto m.

to adulterate [ə'dʌltəreit] v. tr. adulterare, contraffare

adultery [ə'dʌltəri] s. adulterio m.

advance [əd'va:ns] s. acconto m., anticipo m.; aumento m.; **in** - in acconto

to advance [əd'va:ns] v. tr. avanzare; anticipare • intr. avanzare; crescere

advanced [əd'va:nst] agg. avanzato; progredito; superiore

advantage [əd'va:ntidʒ] s. vantaggio m., profitto m.; **to take** - approfittare

advantageous [,ædvən'teidʒəs] agg. vantaggioso

adventure [əd'ventʃə*] s. avventura f.

adventurer [əd'ventʃərə*] s. avventuriero m.

adventurous [əd'ventʃərəs] agg. avventuroso

adversary ['ædvəsəri] s. avversario m.

adversity [əd'və:siti] s. avversità f.

advertising ['ædvətaiziŋ] s. pubblicità f. • agg. pubblicitario

advice [əd'vais] s. consiglio m.; consulenza f.; parere m.

advisable [əd'vaizəbl] agg. consigliabile

to advise [əd'vaiz] v. tr. e intr. avvisare; consigliare

adviser [əd'vaizə*] s. consigliere m.; consulente m. e f.

advisory [əd'vaizəri] agg. consultivo

aeration [,eiə'reiʃən] s. aerazione f.

aerial ['eəriəl] s. antenna f. • agg. aereo; - **photography** aerofotografia

aerobic [ɛər'oubik] agg. aerobico

aerodrome ['eərədroum] s. aerodromo m.

aerodynamic ['eəroudai'næmik] agg. aerodinamico

aeronautic [,eərə'nɔ:tik] agg. aeronautico

aeroplane ['eərəplein] s. aeroplano m.

aerosol ['eərə,sɔl] s. aerosol m.

aesthetic [i:s'θetik] agg. estetico

aestheticism [i:s'θetisizəm] s. estetismo m.

aesthetics [i:s'θetiks] s. pl. (v. al sing.) estetica f. sing.

afar [ə'fa:*] avv. lontano

affair [ə'feə*] s. faccenda f.; relazione f.; affare m.

to affect [ə'fekt] v. tr. incidere, influire

affectation [,æfek'teiʃən] s. affettazione f.; vezzo m.

affected [ə'fektid] agg. affettato, lezioso; affetto (med.)

affectionate [ə'fekʃnit] agg. affezionato; affettuoso; **affectionately** affettuosamente

affective [ə'fektiv] agg. affettivo

affinity [ə'finiti] s. affinità f.

to affirm [ə'fə:m] v. tr. affermare

affirmative [ə'fə:mətiv] agg. affermativo

affirmatory [ə'fə:mətəri] agg. affermativo

to affix [ə'fiks] v. tr. attaccare

to afforest [æ'fɔrist] v. tr. imboschire

affront [ə'frʌnt] s. affronto m.; insulto m.

afloat [ə'flout] avv. a galla; in mare

aforesaid [ə'fɔ:sed] agg. predetto

afraid [ə'freid] agg. pred. spaventato; **to be** - of temere

African ['æfrikən] agg. e s. africano m.

aft [a:ft] avv. a poppa

after ['a:ftə*] prep. dopo; dietro • avv. dopo, in seguito; - **lunch** dopopranzo

afternoon [,a:ftə'nu:n] s. pomeriggio m. • agg. pomeridiano

aftershave ['a:ftəʃeiv] s. dopobarba m. inv.

afterwards ['a:ftəwədz] avv. dopo, poi, quindi

again [ə'gen] avv. ancora, nuovamente

against [ə'genst] prep. contro; in senso contrario; **to be** - osteggiare

agave [ə'geivi] s. agave f.

age [eidʒ] s. epoca f., era f.; età f.; **the Middle Ages** Medioevo; **middle** - mezz'età

to age [eidʒ] v. tr. e intr. invecchiare

aged ['eidʒid] agg. dell'età di; stagionato; anziano

ageing ['eidʒiŋ] s. invecchiamento m.

11

agency ['eidʒənsi] *s.* agenzia *f.*; ente *m.*

agenda [ə'dʒendə] *s.* agenda *f.*

agent ['eidʒənt] *s.* agente *m.*; concessionario *m.*, rappresentante *m.*

agglomerate [ə'glɔmərit] *s.* agglomerato *m.*

aggressiveness [ə'gresivnis] *s.* aggressività *f.*

aggressor [ə'gresə*] *s.* aggressore *m.*

agile ['ædʒail] *agg.* agile

agility [ə'dʒiliti] *s.* agilità *f.*; scioltezza *f.*

to agitate ['ædʒiteit] *v. tr.* agitare, turbare • *intr.* agitarsi

agitation [ˌædʒi'teiʃən] *s.* agitazione *f.*

agnostic [æg'nɔstik] *agg.* agnostico

ago [ə'gou] *avv.* fa, or sono

agony ['ægəni] *s.* tormento *m.*; supplizio *m.*; angoscia *f.*

agrarian [ə'grɛəriən] *agg.* agricolo

to agree [ə'griː] *v. tr. e intr.* acconsentire; concordare; convenire

agreeable [ə'griəbl] *agg.* gradevole; simpatico

agreement [ə'griːmənt] *s.* accordo *m.*, patto *m.*; contratto *m.*

agricultural [ˌægri'kʌltʃurəl] *agg.* agricolo

agriculture ['ægrikʌltʃə*] *s.* agricoltura *f.*

aground [ə'graund] *agg.* arenato

ahead [ə'hed] *avv.* davanti, avanti; in anticipo

aid [eid] *s.* aiuto *m.*, soccorso *m.*; sovvenzione *f.*; **first** – pronto soccorso

to aid [eid] *v. tr.* aiutare

aileron ['eilərən] *s.* alettone *m.*

aim [eim] *s.* mira *f.*; scopo *m.*, finalità *f.*

to aim [eim] *v. tr. e intr.* puntare; mirare; tendere

aimless ['eimlis] *agg.* senza scopo

air [ɛə*] *s.* aria *f.*; – **conditioned** aria condizionata

to air [ɛə*] *v. tr.* arieggiare, ventilare

aircraft ['ɛə-kraːft] *s.* velivolo *m.*; **aircraft-carrier** portaerei

airplane ['ɛə-plein] *s.* aereo *m.*, aeroplano *m.*

airport ['ɛə-pɔːt] *s.* aeroporto *m.*

airy ['ɛəri] *agg.* arioso, ventilato

aisle [ail] *s.* navata *f.*; passaggio *m.*

akin [ə'kin] *agg.* consanguineo

alabaster ['æləbaːstə*] *s.* alabastro *f.*

alarm [ə'laːm] *s.* allarme *m.*; – **clock** sveglia

alarming [ə'laːmiŋ] *agg.* inquietante

alarmism [ə'laːmizm] *s.* allarmismo *m.*

albumen ['ælbjumin] *s.* albume *m.*

alcohol ['ælkəhɔl] *s.* alcol *m.*

alcoholic [ˌælkə'hɔlik] *agg.* alcolizzato

alcoholism ['ælkəhɔlizəm] *s.* alcolismo *m.*

ale [eil] *s.* birra *f.*

alert [ə'ləːt] *agg.* attento

Alexandrian [ˌælig'zaːndriən] *agg.* alessandrino

alga ['ælgə] *s.* alga *f.*

alien ['eiljən] *agg.* straniero, forestiero; alieno

alienation [ˌeiljə'neiʃən] *s.* alienazione *f.*

alight [ə'lait] *agg.* acceso

to alight [ə'lait] *v. intr.* posarsi; scendere

to align [ə'lain] *v. tr.* allineare

alike [ə'laik] *agg.* simile • *avv.* ugualmente

alimentary [ˌæli'mentəri] *agg.* alimentare

alive [ə'laiv] *agg. pred.* vivo; attivo

all [ɔːl] *agg. e pron.* tutto, tutta, tutti, tutte • *avv.* del tutto; – **but** pressoché; **not at** – niente affatto; **above** – sprattutto; **after** – dopotutto; – **right** bene, va bene

to allege [ə'ledʒ] *v. tr.* asserire, dichiarare; sostenere; **alleged** presunto

allegory ['æligəri] *s.* allegoria *f.*

allergic [ə'ləːdʒik] *agg.* allergico

allergy ['ælədʒi] *s.* allergia *f.*

to alleviate [ə'liːvieit] *v. tr.* alleviare, lenire, attenuare

alley ['æli] *s.* vicolo *m.*

alliance [ə'laiəns] *s.* alleanza *f.*; coalizione *f.*

allied ['ælaid] *agg.* alleato

alligator ['æligeitə*] *s.* alligatore *m.*

to allocate ['æləkeit] *v. tr.* distribuire, assegnare

to allot [ə'lɔt] *v. tr.* assegnare

to allow [ə'lau] *v. tr.* permettere; concedere; **to be allowed** avere il permesso

allowance [ə'lau-əns] *s.* razione *f.*

alloy ['ælɔi] *s.* lega *f.*

to allude [ə'luːd] *v. intr.* alludere

to allure [ə'ljuə*] *v. tr.* attrarre, affascinare

allurement [ə'ljuəmənt] *s.* adescamento *f.*

allusion [ə'luːʒən] *s.* allusione *f.*

alluvial [ə'luːvjəl] *agg.* alluvionale

alluvion [ə'luːvjən] *s.* alluvione *f.*

ally [ə'lai] *s.* alleato *m.*

almanac ['ɔːlmənæk] *s.* almanacco *f.*

almighty [ɔːl'maiti] *agg.* onnipotente

almond ['aːmənd] *s.* mandorla *f.*

almost ['ɔːlmoust] *avv.* pressoché, quasi

aims [aːmz] *s. inv.* carità *f.*, elemosina *f.*; **to give** – fare l'elemosina

alone [ə'loun] *agg.* solo, solitario; soltanto; **to leave** – lasciare in pace; **let** – per non parlare di

along [ə'lɔŋ] *prep.* lungo

alongside [ə'lɔŋ'said] *avv.* accanto

alphabet ['ælfəbit] *s.* alfabeto *m.*

alpine ['ælpain] *agg.* alpino

alpinism ['ælpinizəm] *s.* alpinismo *m.*

alpinist ['ælpinist] *s.* alpinista *m. e f.*

already [ɔːl'redi] *avv.* già

also ['ɔːlsou] *avv.* anche, pure

altar ['ɔːltə*] *s.* altare *m.*; **altar-piece** pala d'altare

to alter ['ɔːltə*] *v. tr. e intr.* alterare, cambiare

alteration [,ɔːltə'reiʃən] *s.* alterazione *f.*; variazione *f.*

altercation [,ɔːltə'keiʃən] *s.* diverbio *m.*

to alternate ['ɔːltəneit] *v. intr.* alternarsi; alternare

alternation [,ɔːltə'neiʃən] *s.* alternanza *f.*

alternative [ɔːl'təːnətiv] *s.* alternativa *f.* • *agg.* alternativo

alternator ['ɔːltəneitə*] *s.* alternatore *m.*

although [ɔːl'ðou] *cong.* benché, sebbene, nonostante

altitude ['æltitjuːd] *s.* altitudine *f.*

alto-rilievo ['æltourili'eivou] *s.* altorilievo *m.*

altruism ['æltruizəm] *s.* altruismo *m.*

aluminium [,ælju:minjəm] *s.* alluminio *m.*

always ['ɔːlwəz] *avv.* sempre

to amass [ə'mæs] *v. tr.* ammassare, accumulare

amateur ['æmətə:*] *agg.* dilettante

amateurish [,æmə'təːriʃ] *agg.* dilettantesco

to amaze [ə'meiz] *v. tr.* meravigliare, sorprendere

amazement [ə'meizmənt] *s.* stupore *m.*

amazing [ə'meiziŋ] *agg.* sbalorditivo

ambassador [æm'bæsədə*] *s.* ambasciatore *m.*

amber ['æmbə*] *s.* ambra *f.*; **ambergris** ambra grigia

ambience ['æmbjəns] *s.* ambiente *m.*

ambiguity [,æmbi'gjuiti] *s.* ambiguità *f.*

ambiguous [æm'bigjùəs] *agg.* ambiguo

ambition [æm'biʃən] *s.* ambizione *f.*

ambitious [æm'biʃəs] *agg.* ambizioso

ambulance ['æmbjuləns] *s.* ambulanza *f.*

ambulatory ['æmbjulətəri] *s.* ambulatorio *m.* • *agg.* ambulante

ambush ['æmbuʃ] *s.* imboscata *f.*

to amend [ə'mend] *v. tr.* emendare, correggere

amends [ə'mendz] *s. pl.* ammenda *f. sing.*

amenity [ə'miːniti] *s.* amenità *f.*

American [ə'merikən] *agg. e s.* americano *m.*

amethyst ['æmiθist] *s.* ametista *f.*

amiable ['eimjəbl] *agg.* affabile, simpatico; affettuoso

amiantus [æmi'æntəs] *s.* amianto *m.*

amicable ['æmikəbl] *agg.* amichevole

amid [ə'mid] *prep.* fra, tra, nel mezzo di

ammonia [ə'mounjə] *s.* ammoniaca *f.*

ammunition [,æmju'niʃən] *s.* munizioni *f. pl.*

amnesia [æm'niːzjə] *s.* amnesia *f.*

amnesty ['æmnesti] *s.* amnistia *f.*

among [ə'mʌŋ] *prep.* fra, tra, in mezzo a

amoral [æ'mɔrəl] *agg.* amorale

amorous ['æmərəs] *agg.* amoroso

amortization [ə,mɔːti'zeiʃən] *s.* ammortamento *m.*

to amortize [ə'mɔːtaiz] *v. tr.* ammortizzare

amount [ə'maunt] *s.* ammontare *m.*; importo *m.*; quantitativo *m.*

to amount [ə'maunt] *v. intr.* ammontare, sommare

amphetamine [æm'fetəmiːn] *s.* anfetamina *f.*

amphibian [æm'fibiən] *agg.* anfibio

amphitheatre ['æmfi,θiətə*] *s.* anfiteatro *m.*

amphora ['æmfərə] *s.* anfora *f.*

ample ['æmpl] *agg.* ampio, spazioso

amplifier ['æmplifaiə*] *s.* amplificatore *m.*

to amplify ['æmplifai] *v. tr.* aumentare; allargare

to amputate ['æmpjuteit] *v. tr.* amputare

amulet ['æmjulit] *s.* amuleto *m.*

to amuse [ə'mjuːz] *v. tr.* divertire; – **oneself** divertirsi

amusement [ə'mjuːzmənt] *s.* divertimento *m.*, svago *m.*

amusing [ə'mjuːziŋ] *agg.* divertente

anachronism [ə'nækrənizəm] *s.* anacronismo *m.*

anachronistic [ə,nækrə'nistik] *agg.* anacronistico

anaesthesia [,ænis'θiːzjə] *s.* anestesia *f.*

anaesthetic [,ænis'θetik] *s.* anestetico *m.*

to anaesthetize [æ'niːsθitaiz] *v. tr.* anestetizzare

anagram ['ænəgræm] *s.* anagramma *m.*

analgesic [,ænæl'dʒesik] *s.* analgesico *m.*, antidolorifico *m.*

analogous [ə'næləgəs] *agg.* analogo

analogy [ə'nælədʒi] *s.* analogia *f.*

to analyse ['ænəlaiz] *v. tr.* analizzare; psicanalizzare (USA); risolvere

analysis [ə'næləsis] *s.* analisi *f.*

analyst ['ænəlist] *s.* analista *m. e f.*

anarchism ['ænəkizəm] *s.* anarchia *f.*

anarchy ['ænəki] *s.* anarchia *f.*

anatomy [ə'nætəmi] *s.* anatomia *f.*

ancestor ['ænsistə*] *s.* antenato *m.*

ancestry ['ænsistri] *s.* ascendenza *f.*

anchor ['æŋkə*] s. ancora f.

to anchor ['æŋkə*] v. tr. e intr. ancorare, ancorarsi

anchorage ['æŋkəridʒ] s. ancoraggio m.

anchovy ['æntʃouvi] s. acciuga f.

ancient ['einʃənt] agg. antico; **in -** times anticamente

and [ænd, ənd] cong. e; **- so on** eccetera; **- yet** eppure

anecdote ['ænikdout] s. aneddoto m.

anemia [ə'ni:mjə] s. anemia f.

anemic [ə'ni:mik] agg. anemico

anemometer [,æni'mɔmitə*] s. anemometro m.

aneurism ['ænjuərizəm] s. aneurisma m.

angel ['eindʒəl] s. angelo m.

anger ['æŋɡə*] s. collera f., rabbia f.

angle ['æŋɡl] s. angolo m.

Anglican ['æŋɡlikən] agg. anglicano

anglicism ['æŋɡlisizəm] s. anglicismo m., inglesismo m.

Anglo-Saxon ['æŋɡlou-'sæksən] agg. e s. anglosassone m. e f.

Angora ['æŋɡərə] s. angora f.

angry ['æŋɡri] agg. arrabbiato; rabbioso; **to get -** arrabbiarsi

angular ['æŋɡjulə*] agg. angolare

animal ['æniməl] s. animale m.

animate ['ænimit] agg. animato

animated ['ænimeitid] agg. animato

animator ['ænimeitə*] s. animatore m.

anise ['ænis] s. anice m.

ankle ['æŋkl] s. caviglia f.

to annex [ə'neks] v. tr. incorporare

anniversary [,æni'və:səri] s. anniversario m.

annotation [,ænou'teiʃən] s. annotazione f., nota f.

to announce [ə'nauns] v. tr. annunciare

announcement [ə'naunsmənt] s. avviso m., annuncio m.

announcer [ə'naunsə*] s. presentatore m.

to annoy [ə'nɔi] v. tr. infastidire

annoyance [ə'nɔiəns] s. dispetto m.; seccatura f., fastidio m.

annoyed [ə'nɔid] agg. infastidito; **to get -** infastidirsi, irritarsi

annoying [ə'nɔiŋ] agg. molesto, seccante

annual ['ænjuəl] agg. annuale; **annually** annualmente

annuity [ə'njuiti] s. rendita f.; pensione f.

to annul [ə'nʌl] v. tr. annullare

annulment [ə'nʌlmənt] s. annullamento m.

anomalous [ə'nɔmələs] agg. anomalo

anonymous [ə'nɔniməs] agg. anonimo

anorak ['ænəræk] s. giacca f. a vento

anorexia [,ænou'reksiə] s. anoressia f.

another [ə'nʌðə*] agg. e pron. indef. un altro

answer ['a:nsə*] s. risposta f.; responso m.

to answer ['a:nsə*] v. tr. e intr. rispondere; **- back** controbattere; **- the telephone** rispondere al telefono

ant [ænt] s. formica f.

antagonist [æn'tæɡənist] s. antagonista m. e f., avversario m.

antagonistic [æn,tæɡə'nistik] agg. antagonistico

Antarctic [ænt'a:ktik] agg. antartico

antecedent [,ænti'si:dənt] agg. antecedente

antechamber ['ænti,tʃeimbə*] s. anticamera f.

antelope ['æntiloup] s. antilope f.

anteroom ['æntirum] s. anticamera f.

anthem ['ænθəm] s. inno m.

anthology [æn'θɔlədʒi] s. antologia f.

anthropological [,ænθrəpə'lɔdʒikəl] agg. antropologico

anthropologist [,ænθrə'pɔlədʒist] s. antropologo m.

anthropology [,ænθrə'pɔlədʒi] s. antropologia f.

anthropomorphous [,ænθrəpə'mɔ:fəs] agg. antropomorfo

antiallergic [,æntiə'lə:dʒik] agg. e s. antiallergico m.

antibiotic [,æntibai'ɔtik] s. antibiotico m.

to anticipate [æn'tisipeit] v. tr. anticipare; prevenire, precedere

anticipation [æn,tisi'peiʃən] s. anticipo m.

anticlerical [,ænti'klerikl] agg. e s. anticlericale m. e f.

anticonstitutional [,ænti,kɔnsti'tjuʃənəl] agg. anticostituzionale

anticyclone [,ænti'saikloun] s. anticiclone m.

antifreeze [,ænti'fri:z] s. antigelo m.

antifreezing [,ænti'fri:ziŋ] agg. antigelo

antineuralgic [,æntinjuə'rældʒik] agg. e s. antinevralgico m.

antiquarian [,ænti'kwɛəriən] s. antiquario m.

antique [æn'ti:k] agg. antico • s. antichità f.; **- trade** antiquariato

antiquity [æn'tikwiti] s. antichità f.

antirabic [,ænti'ræbik] agg. antirabbico

antirheumatic [,æntiru:'mætik] s. antireumatico m.

antirust [,ænti'rʌst] agg. antiruggine m.

antonomasia [,æntənou'meiʃiə] s. antonomasia f.

anus ['einəs] s. ano m.

anxiety [æŋ'zaiəti] s. ansia f.

anxious ['æŋkʃəs] agg. ansioso

any ['eni] agg. e pron. indef. qualsiasi, qualunque (in frasi afferm.); qualche, nessuno, alcuno (in frasi neg.); del, degli, qualche, un po' (in frasi interr.)

anybody ['eni,bɔdi] pron. indef. chiunque (in frasi afferm.); nessuno (in frasi neg.)

anyhow ['enihau] cong. comunque

anyone ['eniwʌn] pron. indef. chiunque (in frasi afferm.); nessuno (in frasi neg.)

anything ['eniθiŋ] pron. indef. qualunque cosa (in frasi afferm.); qualcosa, niente (in frasi neg.)

anytime ['enitaim] avv. in qualsiasi momento

anyway ['eniwei] avv. in qualsiasi modo; comunque

anywhere ['eniwɛə*] avv. dovunque (in frasi afferm.); da nessuna parte (in frasi neg.)

apart [ə'pa:t] avv. distante; da parte; separatamente

apartment [ə'pa:tmənt] s. appartamento m.; camera f.; – **building** condominio

ape [eip] s. scimmia f.

aperitif [a:(:)pari(:)'ti:f] s. aperitivo m.

aperture ['æpətjuə*] s. apertura f.

aphorism ['æfərizəm] s. aforismo m.

aphrodisiac [,æfrou'diziæk] agg. e s. afrodisiaco m.

apiculture ['eipikʌltʃə*] s. apicoltura f.

apiece [ə'pi:s] avv. a testa

apnea [æp'ni:ə] s. apnea f.

apocryphal [ə'pɔkrifəl] agg. apocrifo

to apologize [ə'pɔlədʒaiz] v. intr. scusarsi, chiedere scusa

apology [ə'pɔlədʒi] s. scusa f.

apostle [ə'pɔsl] s. apostolo m.

apostrophe [ə'pɔstrəfi] s. apostrofo m.

appalling [ə'pɔ:lŋ] agg. orrendo, terribile

apparent [ə'pærənt] agg. evidente; comprensibile

appeal [ə'pi:l] s. appello m.; supplica f.

to appeal [ə'pi:l] v. intr. fare appello; attrarre; piacere

to appear [ə'piə*] v. intr. apparire, parere; presentarsi

appearance [ə'piərəns] s. apparizione f.; comparsa f.; parvenza f.; aspetto m.

to append [ə'pend] v. tr. apporre, aggiungere; allegare; attaccare

appendicitis [ə,pendi'saitis] s. appendicite f.

appendix [ə'pendiks] s. appendice f.

appetite ['æpitait] s. appetito m.

appetizer ['æpitaizə*] s. antipasto m.

appetizing ['æpitaiziŋ] agg. appetitoso

to applaud [ə'plɔ:d] v. tr. e intr. applaudire

applause [ə'plɔ:z] s. applauso m.

apple ['æpl] s. mela f.

appliance [ə'plaiəns] s. apparecchio m.; strumento m.; **household** – elettrodomestico

applicant ['æplikənt] s. candidato m.

application [,æpli'keiʃən] s. applicazione f.; impiego m.; richiesta f.

to apply [ə'plai] v. tr. e intr. applicare; – **oneself** applicarsi, indirizzarsi

to appoint [ə'pɔint] v. tr. designare, nominare, eleggere

appointee [əpɔin'ti] s. incaricato m.

appointment [ə'pɔintmənt] s. appuntamento m.; incarico m.

appraisal [ə'preizəl] s. perizia f.; stima f.

to appraise [ə'preiz] v. tr. valutare

to appreciate [ə'pri:ʃieit] v. tr. apprezzare; gradire • intr. aumentare di valore

appreciation [ə,pri:ʃi'eiʃən] s. apprezzamento m.; rivalutazione f. (fin.)

apprehensive [,æpri'hensiv] agg. apprensivo

apprentice [ə'prentis] s. apprendista m. e f.

apprenticeship [ə'prentiʃip] s. tirocinio m., apprendistato m.

approach [ə'proutʃ] s. avvicinamento m., accesso m.

to approach [ə'proutʃ] v. intr. avvicinarsi • tr. avvicinarsi a; affrontare

appropriate [ə'proupriit] agg. appropriato, opportuno

to appropriate [ə'prouprieit] v. tr. impadronirsi di

to approve [ə'pru:v] v. tr. approvare

approximate [ə'prɔksimit] agg. approssimativo; **approximately** circa

après-ski [,aprɛʔskiː] agg. doposcì

apricot ['eiprikɔt] s. albicocca f.

April ['eiprəl] s. aprile m.

apron ['eiprən] s. grembiule m.; ribalta f. (teatro)

apse [æps] s. abside f.

apterous ['æptərəs] agg. aptero

aqualung ['ækwəlʌŋ] s. autorespiratore m. (sport)

aquamarine [,ækwəmə'ri:n] s. acquamarina f.

aquarium [ə'kwɛəriəm] s. acquario m.

Aquarius [ə'kwɛəriəs] s. acquario m. (astr.)

aquatic [ə'kwætik] agg. acquatico

aqueduct ['ækwidʌkt] s. acquedotto m.

Arab ['ærəb] *agg. e s.* arabo *m.*

arabesque [,ærə'besk] *s.* arabesco *m.*

Arabian [ə'reibjən] *agg.* arabo, arabico

Arabic ['ærəbik] *agg.* arabico • *s.* arabo *m.* (lingua)

arbiter ['a:bitə*] *s.* arbitro *m.*

arbitrary ['a:bitrəri] *agg.* arbitrario

to arbitrate ['a:bitreit] *v. tr. e intr.* arbitrare

arboreal [a:'bɔ:rfəl] *agg.* arboreo

arboriculture ['a:bərikʌltfə*] *s.* arboricoltura *f.*

arc [a:k] *s.* arco *m.*

arcade [a:'keid] *s.* arcata *f.*; galleria *f.*; portico *m.*

Arcadian [a:'keidjən] *agg.* arcadico

arcane [a:'kein] *agg.* arcano

arch [a:tf] *s.* arco *m.*; arcata *f.* • *agg.* principale; astuto

archaeologic [a:klə'lɔdʒik] *agg.* archeologico

archaeologist [,a:ki'ɔlədʒist] *s.* archeologo *m.*

archaeology [,ki'ɔlədʒi] *s.* archeologia *f.*

archaic [a:'keiik] *agg.* arcaico

archangel [a:k,eindʒəl] *s.* arcangelo *m.*

archbishop [a:tf'bifəp] *s.* arcivescovo *m.*

archer ['a:tfə*] *s.* arciere *m.*

archery [a:'tfəri] *s.* tiro *m.* con l'arco

archetype [a:kitaip] *s.* archetipo *m.*

archipelago [,:ki'peləgou] *s.* arcipelago *m.*

architect ['a:kitekt] *s.* architetto *m.*

architectonic [,a:kitek'tɔnik] *agg.* architettonico

architecture ['a:kitekfə*] *s.* architettura *f.*

architrave ['a:kitreiv] *s.* architrave *m.*

archives ['a:kaivz] *s. pl.* archivio *m. sing.*

archivolt ['a:kivoult] *s.* archivolto *m.*

Arctic ['a:ktik] *s.* Artide *f.* • *agg.* artico

ardent ['a:dənt] *agg.* ardente; appassionato, fervente

arduous [a:djuəs] *agg.* arduo, difficile

are [a:*] *s.* ara *f.* (misura)

area ['εəriə] *s.* area *f.*; zona *f.*; – **code** prefisso telefonico

arena [ə'ri:nə] *s.* arena *f.*

argil ['a:dʒil] *s.* argilla *f.*

arguable ['a:gjuəbl] *agg.* sostenibile, discutibile

to argue ['a:gju:] *v. intr.* ragionare; disputare; litigare

argument ['a:gjumənt] *s.* argomento *m.*; contesa *f.*, disputa *f.*

arid ['ærid] *agg.* arido

to arise [ə'raiz] *v. intr.* sorgere; risultare; presentarsi; alzarsi

aristocracy [,æris'tɔkrəsi] *s.* aristocrazia *f.*

aristocrat [,æristəkræt] *s.* aristocratico *m.*

aristocratic [,æristə'krætik] *agg.* aristocratico

arithmetic [,æriθ'metik] *s.* aritmetica *f.*

ark [a:k] *s.* arca *f.*

arm [a:m] *s.* braccio *m.*; bracciolo *m.*; manica *f.* • arma *f.*

to arm [a:m] *v. tr. e intr.* armare, armarsi

armament [a:'məmənt] *s.* armamento *m.*

armchair [a:m'tfεə*] *s.* poltrona *f.*

armed [a:md] *agg.* armato

armful ['a:mful] *s.* bracciata *f.*

armistice [a:'mistis] *s.* armistizio *m.*

armour ['a:mə*] *s.* armatura *f.*, corazza *f.*

to armour ['mə*]*v. tr.* corazzare, blindare; **armoured** blindato

armoury [a:'məri] *s.* armeria *f.*

armpit ['a:mpit] *s.* ascella *f.*

army [a:mi] *s.* esercito *m.*

aroma [ə'roumə] *s.* aroma *m.*

aromatic [,ærou'mætik] *agg.* aromatico

around [ə'raund] *avv.* intorno; in giro; in cerchio; in circolazione

to arouse [ə'rauz] *v. tr.* provocare, suscitare; svegliare

to arrange [ə'reindʒ] *v. tr. e intr.* ordinare, sistemare, disporre; stabilire

arrangement [ə'reindʒmənt] *s.* disposizione *f.*, ordinamento *m.*; preparativo *m.*; accordo *m.*

array [ə'rei] *s.* schieramento *m.*; esposizione *f.*

to array [ə'rei] *v. tr.* ordinare, disporre

arrear [ə'riə*] *s.* arretrato *m.*

arrest [ə'rest] *s.* arresto *m.*, cattura *f.*

to arrest [ə'rest] *v. tr.* arrestare, catturare; fermare; impedire

arrival [ə'raival] *s.* arrivo *m.*

to arrive [ə'raiv] *v. intr.* arrivare, giungere; – **at** raggiungere

arrogant ['ærəgənt] *agg.* arrogante, prepotente, tracotante

arrow ['ærou] *s.* freccia *f.*

arsenal [a:sinl] *s.* arsenale *m.*

arson ['a:sən] *s.* incendio *m.* doloso

art [a:t] *s.* arte *f.*

arterial [a:'tiəriəl] *agg.* arterioso

arteriosclerosis [a:'tiəriou-skliə'rousis] *s.* arteriosclerosi *f.*

artery [a:'təri] *s.* arteria *f.*

artful ['a:tful] *agg.* astuto; ingannevole

artichoke ['a:titfouk] *s.* carciofo *m.*

article ['a:tikl] *s.* articolo *m.*

to articulate [a:'tikjuleit] *v. tr.* scandire; articolare

articulated [a:'tikjuleitid] *agg.* articolato
artifact ['a:tifækt] *s.* manufatto *m.*
artifice ['a:tifis] *s.* stratagemma *m.*
artificial [ˌa:ti'fiʃəl] *agg.* artificiale; posticcio
artillery [a:'tiləri] *s.* artiglieria *f.*
artisan [ˌa:ti'zæn] *s.* artigiano *m.*
artist ['a:tist] *s.* artista *m. e f.*; pittore *m.*
artistic [a:'tistik] *agg.* artistico
artless ['a:tlis] *agg.* semplice; ingenuo
as [æz, əz] *avv. e cong.* come, così; poiché, giacché; mentre; quanto; – **well** anche, nonché; – **far** – fino a, per quanto; – **if** come se; – **soon** – appena; – **much** altrettanto; – **many** altrettanti
to ascend [ə'send] *v. tr.* salire; ascendere; risalire
ascending [ə'sendiŋ] *agg.* ascendente
ascent [ə'sent] *s.* ascesa *f.*, scalata *f.*, risalita *f.*; pendio *m.*
to ascertain [ˌæsə'tein] *v. tr.* appurare, constatare
asceticism [ə'setisizəm] *s.* ascetismo *m.*
ascribable [əs'kraibəbl] *agg.* attribuibile
to ascribe [əs'kraib] *v. tr.* attribuire
ash [æʃ] *s.* frassino *m.* • cenere *f.*; **–tray** portacenere
ashamed [ə'feimd] *agg.* che prova vergogna
ashlar ['æʃlə*] *s.* bugnato *m.*; **rusticated** – bugnato rustico
ashore [ə'ʃɔ:*] *agg.* a riva, a terra
Asian ['eiʃən] *agg. e s.* asiatico *m.*
Asiatic [ˌeiʃi'ætik] *agg.* asiatico
aside [ə'said] *avv.* da parte • *s.* digressione *f.*; – **from** oltre a, eccetto
to ask [a:sk] *v. tr. e intr.* domandare; informarsi (chiedere); – **for somebody** chiedere di qualcuno; – **for something** chiedere (per avere) qualcosa
askance [əs'kæns] *avv.* sospettosamente
askew [əs'kju:] *avv.* attraverso
asleep [ə'sli:p] *agg.* addormentato; **to be** – dormire
asparagus [əs'pærəgəs] *s.* asparago *m.*
aspect ['æspekt] *s.* aspetto *m.*, apparenza *f.*; esposizione *f.*
asphalt ['æsfælt] *s.* asfalto *m.*
to asphalt ['æsfælt] *v. tr.* asfaltare
to asphyxiate [æs'fiksieit] *v. intr.* asfissiare
ass [æs] *s.* asino *m.*, somaro *m.*
to assail [ə'seil] *v. tr.* assalire, attaccare
assassin [ə'sæsin] *s.* assassino *m.*
to assassinate [ə'sæsineit] *v. tr.* assassinare
assassination [əˌsæsi'neiʃən] *s.* assassinio *m.*

assault [ə'sɔ:lt] *s.* attacco *m.*, assalto *m.*, aggressione *f.*
to assault [ə'sɔ:lt] *v. tr.* assaltare, aggredire
to assemble [ə'sembl] *v. tr.* montare; riunire
assembly [ə'sembli] *s.* assemblea *f.*, riunione *f.*; montaggio *m.*
to assent [ə'sent] *v. intr.* approvare; consentire; assentire
to assert [ə'sɔ:t] *v. tr.* affermare, sostenere
assertion [ə'sɔ:ʃən] *s.* asserzione *f.*
to assess [ə'ses] *v. tr.* valutare
asset ['æset] *s.* pregio *m.*; patrimonio *m.*
assiduous [ə'sidjuəs] *agg.* assiduo
to assign [ə'sain] *v. tr.* assegnare
to assist [ə'sist] *v. tr.* assistere, aiutare
assistance [ə'sistəns] *s.* assistenza *f.*; soccorso *m.*
assistant [ə'sistənt] *s.* assistente *m. e f.*
to associate [ə'souʃiit] *agg.* consociato
to associate [ə'souʃieit] *v. tr.* associare; – **with** frequentare, associarsi
association [əˌsousi'eiʃən] *s.* associazione *f.*; connessione *f.*
assorted [ə'sɔ:tid] *agg.* assortito
to assume [ə'sju:m] *v. tr.* presupporre; assumere
assumption [ə'sʌmpʃən] *s.* supposizione *f.*; premessa *f.*
assurance [ə'ʃuərəns] *s.* assicurazione *f.*; certezza *f.*
to assure [ə'ʃuə*] *v. tr.* assicurare
asthma ['æsmə] *s.* asma *f. o m.*
asthmatic [æs'mætik] *agg.* asmatico
astigmatic [ˌæstig'mætik] *agg.* astigmatico
astir [ə'stə:*] *avv.* in piedi; in agitazione
to astonish [əs'tɔniʃ] *v. tr.* meravigliare; sorprendere; stupire
astonishing [əs'tɔniʃiŋ] *agg.* stupefacente
to astound [əs'taund] *v. tr.* sbalordire
astounding [əs'taundiŋ] *agg.* sbalorditivo
astragal ['æstrəgəl] *s.* astragalo *m.*
astragalus [æs'trægələs] *s.* astragalo *m.*
astray [əs'trei] *avv.* fuori strada; smarrito
astride [əs'traid] *avv.* a cavalcioni
astringent [əs'trindʒənt] *agg.* astringente
astrolabe ['æstrouleib] *s.* astrolabio *m.*
astrologer [əs'trɔlədʒə*] *s.* astrologo *m.*
astrologic [ˌæstro'lɔdʒik] *agg.* astrologico
astrology [əs'trɔlədʒi] *s.* astrologia *f.*
astronaut ['æstrənɔ:t] *s.* astronauta *m. e f.*
astronautical [ˌæstro'nɔ:tikəl] *agg.* astronautico
astronomer [əs'trɔnəmə*] *s.* astronomo *m.*

17

astronomical [ˌæstrə'nɔmikəl] agg. astronomico

astronomy [əs'trɔnəmi] s. astronomia f.

astute [əs'tju:t] agg. astuto

asylum [ə'sailəm] s. asilo m.; casa f. di ricovero; **lunatic** – manicomio

asymmetric [ˌæsi'metrik] agg. asimmetrico

at [æt, ət] prep. a, da, in, su; – **all** affatto; – **best** nella migliore delle ipotesi; – **first** dapprima; – **hand** a portata di mano; – **last** finalmente; – **least** almeno; – **once** subito

atavic [ə'tævik] agg. atavico

atheism ['eiθiizən] s. ateismo m.

atheist ['eiθiist] s. ateo m.

athlete ['æθli:t] s. atleta m. e f.

athletic [æθ'letik] agg. atletico

athletics [æθ'letiks] s. pl. atletica f. sing.

athwart [ə'θwɔ:t] avv. e prep. di traverso

Atlantic [ət'læntik] agg. atlantico

atlas ['ætləs] s. atlante m.

atmosphere ['ætməsfiə*] s. atmosfera f.

atmospheric [ˌætməs'ferik] agg. atmosferico

atoll [ə'tɔl] s. atollo m.

atom ['ætəm] s. atomo m.

atomic [ə'tɔmik] agg. atomico

atomizer ['ætəmaizə*] s. vaporizzatore m., nebulizzatore m.

atop [ə'tɔp] avv. e prep. in cima

atrocious [ə'trouʃəs] agg. atroce

atrocity [ə'trɔsiti] s. atrocità f.

to attach [ə'tætʃ] v. tr. attaccare

attaché [ə'tæʃei] s. addetto m.

attached [ə'tætʃt] agg. annesso; attaccato, legato

attachment [ə'tætʃmənt] s. attaccatura f.; attaccamento m.; accessorio m.

attack [ə'tæk] s. attacco m.; **heart** – attacco cardiaco

to attack [ə'tæk] v. tr. attaccare, aggredire

attacker [ə'tækə*] s. attaccante m.

to attain [ə'tein] v. tr. raggiungere • intr. pervenire

attainable [ə'teinəbl] agg. raggiungibile

attainment [ə'teinmənt] s. risultato m.; successo m.

attempt [ə'tempt] s. tentativo m., sforzo m.; attentato m.

to attempt [ə'tempt] v. tr. osare, tentare, provare

to attend [ə'tend] v. tr. e intr. frequentare, assistere, partecipare

attendance [ə'tendəns] s. frequenza f.; assistenza f.; presenza f.

attendant [ə'tendənt] s. compagno m.; addetto m.; guardiano m.

attention [ə'tenʃən] s. attenzione f.

attentive [ə'tentiv] agg. attento; **attentively** attentamente

to attest [ə'test] v. tr. attestare; testimoniare

attic ['ætik] s. attico m.; soffitta f.

attitude ['ætitju:d] s. atteggiamento m.

to attract [ə'trækt] v. tr. allettare, attirare

attraction [ə'trækʃən] s. attrattiva f.; simpatia f.; attrazione f.

attractive [ə'træktiv] agg. attraente, bello

attribute ['ætribju:t] s. attributo m.; qualità f.

to attribute [ə'tribju:)t] v. tr. attribuire, ascrivere

attrition [ə'triʃən] s. attrito m.

atypical [ə'tipikəl] agg. atipico

aubergine ['oubəʒi:n] s. melanzana f.

auction ['ɔ:kʃən] s. asta f.

audible ['ɔ:dəbl] agg. udibile

audience ['ɔ:djəns] s. pubblico m., spettatori m. pl.; udienza f.

audio ['ɔ:diou] s. audio m. inv.

audiovisual ['ɔ:diou'viʒuəl] agg. audiovisivo

auditor ['ɔ:ditə*] s. sindaco m. (di società)

auditorium [ˌɔ:di'tɔ:riəm] s. auditorio m.; sala f.

to augment [ɔ:g'ment] v. tr. aumentare

August ['ɔ:gəst] s. agosto m.

aunt [a:nt] s. zia f.

aurora [ɔ:'rɔ:rə] s. aurora f.; – **borealis** aurora boreale

auspicious [ɔ:s'piʃəs] agg. promettente

austere [ɔs'tiə*] agg. austero

austerity [ɔs'teriti] s. austerità f.

austral ['ɔ:strəl] agg. australe

Australian [ɔs'treiljən] agg. australiano

Austrian ['ɔstriən] agg. austriaco

authentic [ɔ:'θentik] agg. autentico, genuino

to authenticate [ɔ:'θentikeit] v. tr. autenticare, vidimare

authenticity [ˌɔ:θen'tisiti] s. autenticità f.

author ['ɔ:θə*] s. autore m.

authoritarian [ɔ,θɔri'teəriən] agg. autoritario

authoritative [ɔ:'θɔritətiv] agg. autorevole

authority [ɔ:'θɔriti] s. autorità f.

authorization [ˌɔ:θərai'zeiʃən] s. autorizzazione f.

to authorize ['ɔ:θəraiz] v. tr. autorizzare

auto ['ɔ:(:)tou] agg. automobilistico • s. automobile f. (USA)

autobiographical ['ɔːtouˌbaiou'græfikəl] *agg.* autobiografico

autobiography [ˌɔːtoubai'ɔgrəfi] *s.* autobiografia *f.*

autograph ['ɔːtəgraːf] *agg.* e *s.* autografo *m.*

to autograph ['ɔːtəgraːf] *v. tr.* firmare

automatic [ˌɔːtə'mætik] *agg.* automatico

autonomous [ɔː'tɔnəməs] *agg.* autonomo

autonomy [ɔː'tɔnəmi] *s.* autonomia *f.*

autumn ['ɔːtəm] *s.* autunno *m.*

autumnal [ɔː'tʌmnəl] *agg.* autunnale

auxiliary [ɔːg'ziljəri] *agg.* ausiliario; di riserva

to avail [ə'veil] *v. intr.* servire; – **oneself** valersi

available [ə'veiləbl] *agg.* disponibile, utilizzabile; libero

avalanche ['ævəlaːnʃ] *s.* valanga *f.*

avant-garde [ˌævɔːŋ'gaːd] *s.* avanguardia *f.*

to avenge [ə'vendʒ] *v. tr.* vendicare • *intr.* vendicarsi

avenue ['ævinjuː] *s.* viale *m.*, via *f.*, strada *f.* (*naut.*)

average ['ævəridʒ] *s.* media *f.* (*mat.*); avaria *f.* (*naut.*)

averse [ə'vəːs] *agg.* contrario

aversion [ə'vəːʃən] *s.* riluttanza *f.*

aviary ['eivjəri] *s.* voliera *f.*

aviation [ˌeivi'eiʃən] *s.* aviazione *f.*

aviculture ['eivikʌltʃə*] *s.* avicoltura *f.*

avifauna ['eiviˌfɔːnə] *s.* avifauna *f.*

avocado [ˌævə'kaːdou] *s.* avocado *m. inv.*

to avoid [ə'vɔid] *v. tr.* evitare, fuggire, scampare

avoidable [ə'vɔidəbl] *agg.* evitabile

avowal [ə'auəl] *s.* ammissione *f.*

to await [ə'weit] *v. tr.* aspettare, attendere

to awake o **to awaken** [ə'weik, ə'weikən] *v. tr.* e *intr.* svegliare; svegliarsi

award [ə'wɔːd] *s.* premio *m.*

to award [ə'wɔːd] *v. tr.* assegnare, attribuire, aggiudicare

aware [ə'weə*] *agg.* consapevole

awash [ə'wɔʃ] *avv.* a galla

away [ə'wei] *avv.* via, lontano; **to do** – uccidere; disfarsi; **right** – subito

awe [ɔː] *s.* timore *m.*

awesome ['ɔːsəm] *agg.* imponente

awful [ɔː'ful] *agg.* terribile, tremendo

awhile [ə'wail] *avv.* per un po'

awkward ['ɔːkwəd] *agg.* goffo

awning [ɔːniŋ] *s.* tendone *m.*

axe [æks] *s.* scure *f.*, ascia *f.*

axis ['æksis] *s.* asse *m.*

axle ['æksl] *s.* asse *f.*; **axle-shaft** semiasse (*autom.*)

azalea [ə'zeiljə] *s.* azalea *f.*

azimuth ['æziməθ] *s.* azimut *m.*

azote [ə'zout] *s.* azoto *m.*

B

baby ['beibi] *s.* neonato *m.*; bambina *f.*, bambino *m.*

bachelor ['bætʃələ•] *s.* scapolo *m.*

back [bæk] *s.* dorso *m.*, schiena *f.*; schienale *m.*; terzino *m.*; retro *m.* • *agg.* posteriore • *avv.* indietro; – **to front** alla rovescia

to back [bæk] *v. tr.* sostenere; scommettere su

backache ['bækeik] *s.* mal *m.* di schiena

backbone ['bækboun] *s.* colonna *f.* vertebrale

background ['bækgraund] *s.* sfondo *m.*; ambiente *m.*; retroterra *m. inv.*; antefatto *m.*

backstage ['bæk-'steidʒ] *s.* retroscena *f.*

back-stitch ['bæk-stitʃ] *s.* impuntura *f.*

backward ['bækwəd] *agg.* volto all'indietro; a rovescio; ritardato; sottosviluppato

backwash ['bækwɔʃ] *s.* risacca *f.*

bacon ['beikən] *s.* pancetta *f.*

bacterium [bæk'tiəriəm] *s.* batterio *m.*

bad [bæd] *agg.* cattivo; brutto; – **luck** sfortuna; – **mood** malumore; – **weather** maltempo; **too** – peccato

badge [bædʒ] *s.* distintivo *m.*; scudetto *m.*

badger ['bædʒə•] *s.* tasso *m.* (zool.)

badly ['bædli] *avv.* male, malamente

badminton ['bædmintən] *s.* volano *m.* (gioco)

bag [bæg] *s.* sacco *m.*; sacchetto *m.*; sacca *f.*, borsa *f.*; **sleeping** – sacco a pelo; **shoulder** – borsa a tracolla

to bag [bæg] *v. tr.* accaparrarsi

baggage ['bægidʒ] *s.* bagaglio *m.*; – **car** bagagliaio; – **claim** ritiro bagagli; – **room** deposito bagagli

baggy ['bægi] *agg.* gonfio, cascante

bagpipe ['bægpaip] *s.* cornamusa *f.*

bail [beil] *s.* cauzione *f.*; **to be on** – essere in libertà provvisoria (su cauzione)

bailer ['beilə•] *s.* sassola *f.*

bain-marie [ˌbã-mə'riː] *s.* bagnomaria *m.*

bait [beit] *s.* esca *f.*

to bake [beik] *v. tr.* cuocere al forno

baker ['beikə•] *s.* fornaio *m.*; – '**s (shop)** panetteria

bakery ['beikəri] *s.* panificio *m.*, panetteria *f.*

baking ['beikiŋ] *s.* cottura *f.*; **–tin** teglia, tortiera; – **pan** stampo

balance ['bæləns] *s.* bilancia *f.*; conguaglio *m.*; equilibrio *m.*; saldo *m.*

to balance ['bæləns] *v. tr.* equilibrare; pesare • *intr.* stare in equilibrio; quadrare (comm.)

balancing ['bælənsiŋ] *s.* equilibratura *f.*

balcony ['bælkəni] *s.* balcone *m.*; balconata *f.*; galleria *f.*

bald [bɔːld] *agg.* calvo, pelato

baldachin ['bɔːldəkin] *s.* baldacchino *m.*

baldly ['bɔːldli] *avv.* chiaramente

baldness ['bɔːldnis] *s.* calvizie *f. inv.*

baldric ['bɔːldrik] *s.* tracolla *f.*

ball [bɔːl] *s.* palla *f.*, pallone *m.*; sfera *f.*; gomitolo *m.* • ballo *m.*

ballast ['bæləst] *s.* zavorra *f.*; massicciata *f.*

ballet ['bælei] *s.* balletto *m.*; **–dancer** ballerino, ballerina

balloon [bə'luːn] *s.* pallone *m.*; **hot-air** – mongolfiera

ballot ['bælət] *s.* palla *f.*, scheda *f.*; voto *m.*; – **box** urna elettorale

balm [baːm] *s.* balsamo *m.*

balmy ['baːmi] *agg.* balsamico; svanito

balsam ['bɔːlsəm] *s.* balsamo *m.*

balsamic [bɔːl'sæmik] *agg.* balsamico

balustrade [ˌbæləs'treid] *s.* balaustra *f.*

bamboo [bæm'buː] *s.* bambù *m. inv.*

ban [bæn] *s.* bando *m.*, proclama *m.*

to ban [bæn] *v. tr.* proibire

banal [bə'naːl] *agg.* banale

banana [bə'naːnə] *s.* banana *f.*

band [bænd] *s.* banda *f.*; fascia *f.*; nastro *m.* • orchestra *f.*

bandage ['bændidʒ] *s.* benda *f.*, fascia *f.*

to bandage ['bændidʒ] *v. tr.* bendare, fasciare

bandaging ['bændidʒiŋ] *s.* bendaggio *m.*, fasciatura *f.*

bandit ['bændit] *s.* bandito *m.*

bang [bæŋ] *s.* colpo *m.*, scoppio *m.*

to bang [bæŋ] *v. tr.* colpire, battere • *intr.* scoppiare

banisters ['bænistəz] *s. pl.* balaustra *f. sing.*; ringhiera *f. sing.*

bank [bæŋk] *s.* argine *m.*, riva *f.*, sponda *f.*;

20

cumulo *m.*; serie *f.* • banca *f.*; banco *m.*; - robber scassinatore; - note banconota

to bank [bæŋk] *v. tr e intr.* ammucchiare; inclinare; ammassarsi; contare su; depositare in banca; avere un conto in banca

banker ['bæŋkə*] *s.* banchiere *m.*

banking ['bæŋkiŋ] *agg.* bancario

bankrupt ['bæŋkrʌpt] *agg.* fallito

bankruptcy ['bæŋkrəptsi] *s.* bancarotta *f.*, fallimento *m.*

banner ['bænə*] *s.* bandiera *f.*, stendardo *m.*; striscione *m.*, insegna *f.*

banquet ['bæŋkwit] *s.* banchetto *m.*

to banter ['bæntə*] *v. tr. e intr.* stuzzicare; canzonare

baptism ['bæptizəm] *s.* battesimo *m.*

baptismal [bæp'tizməl] *agg.* battesimale

baptistery ['bæptistəri] *s.* battistero *m.*

to baptize [bæp'taiz] *v. tr.* battezzare

bar [ba:*] *s.* barra *f.*; ostacolo *m.*; banco *m.*; bar *m.*; tavoletta *f.*; **the Bar** professione forense • *prep.* eccetto

to bar [ba:*] *v. tr.* sbarrare; vietare; escludere

barbarian [ba:'beərIən] *agg.* barbarico

barbaric [ba:'bærik] *agg.* barbaro, barbarico

barbarization [,ba:bərai'zeiʃən] *s.* imbarbarimento *m.*

barbarous ['ba:bərəs] *agg.* barbaro

barber ['ba:bə*] *s.* barbiere *m.*; - 's shop barbiere (negozio)

barbiturate [ba:'bitjurit] *s.* barbiturico *m.*

bare [beə*] *agg.* nudo; scoperto; spoglio, brullo; vuoto

to bare [beə*] *v. tr.* scoprire; rivelare

barefoot ['beəfut] *agg.* scalzo

barely ['beəli] *avv.* appena; chiaramente; poveramente

bargain ['ba:gin] *s.* affare *m.*

to bargain ['ba:gin] *v. tr e intr.* contrattare

barge [ba:dʒ] *s.* chiatta *f.*

to barge [ba:dʒ] *v. tr. e intr.* trasportare su chiatta; muoversi pesantemente

baritone ['bæritoun] *agg.* baritono

bark [ba:k] *s.* corteccia *f.* • abbaio *m.*

to bark [ba:k] *v. intr.* abbaiare

barley ['ba:li] *s.* orzo *m.*

barmaid ['ba:meid] *s.* barista *f.*

barman ['ba:men] *s.* barista *m.*

barn [ba:n] *s.* fienile *m.*, granaio *m.*

barometer [bə'rɔmitə*] *s.* barometro *m.*

baron ['bærən] *s.* barone *m.*

Baroque [bə'rouk] *s. e agg.* barocco *m.*

barrack ['bærək] *s.* caserma *f.*

barred [ba:d] *agg.* sbarrato, ostruito; vietato

barrel ['bærəl] *s.* barile *m.*; botte *f.*; - **vault** volta a botte

barren ['bærən] *agg.* arido, brullo; sterile

barrenness ['bærənnis] *s.* sterilità *f.*

barricade ['bærikeid] *s.* barricata *f.*

barrier ['bæriə*] *s.* barriera *f.*; transenna *f.*; **sound** – muro del suono

barrister ['bæristə*] *s.* avvocato *m.*

barrow ['bærou] *s.* tumulo *m.*; carriola *f.*; barella *f.*

bartender ['ba:,tendə*] *s.* barista *m. e f.*

barter ['ba:tə*] *s.* permuta *f.*

to barter ['ba:tə*] *v. tr.* barattare, scambiare

base [beis] *s.* base *f.*; zoccolo *m.*, basamento *m.* • *agg.* ignobile, vile

to base [beis] *v. tr.* basare; – oneself fondarsi, basarsi

basement ['beismənt] *s.* scantinato *m.*

to bash [bæʃ] *v. tr.* colpire con violenza

bashful ['bæʃful] *agg.* timido

basic ['beisik] *agg.* fondamentale

basically ['beisikli] *avv.* fondamentalmente

basil ['bæzl] *s.* basilico *m.*

basilica [ba'zilikə] *s.* basilica *f.*

basin ['beisn] *s.* bacino *m.*; vasca *f.*

basis ['beisis] *s.* base *f.* (*fig.*)

to bask [ba:sk] *v. intr.* crogiolarsi

basket ['ba:skit] *s.* cestino *m.*, paniere *m.*, canestro *m.*

basketball ['ba:skit,bo:l] *s.* pallacanestro *f.*

bas-relief ['bæsri,li:f] *s.* bassorilievo *m.*

bass [bæs] *s.* basso *m.*

bastard ['bæ:stəd] *agg.* bastardo

to baste [beist] *v. tr.* imbastire • ungere (*alim.*)

bastion ['bæstian] *s.* bastione *m.*

bat [bæt] *s.* pipistrello *m.* • racchetta *f.*; mazza *f.*

batch [bætʃ] *s.* infornata *f.*; gruppo *m.*; partita *f.* (di merce)

bath [ba:θ] *s.* bagno *m.*; **bubble** – bagnoschiuma; – **robe** accappatoio; – **tub** vasca da bagno; – **room** stanza da bagno

to bathe [beið] *v. tr.* bagnare • *intr.* nuotare

bather ['beiðə*] *s.* bagnante *m. e f.*

bathing ['beiðiŋ] *s.* (fare il) bagno *m.*; – **hut** cabina; – **suit** (USA) costume

baton ['bætən] *s.* sfollagente *m. inv.*; bastone *m.*; bacchetta *f.*

to batter ['bætə*] *v. tr. e intr.* battere, picchiare; **battered** malconcio

battery ['bætəri] *s.* batteria *f.*, pila *f.*

battle ['bætl] s. battaglia f.

bawdy ['bɔ:di] agg. lascivo

bawl [bɔ:l] s. urlo m.

to bawl [bɔ:l] v. tr. e intr. urlare; piangere; sgridare

bay [bei] s. baia f. • campata f. (arch.) – alloro m.; – **oak** rovere

to be [bi:, bi] v. intr. essere; esistere; stare

beach [bi:tʃ] s. spiaggia f.; lido m.; – **umbrella** ombrellone

beacon ['bi:kən] s. faro m.; boa f.; **radio** – radiofaro

bead [bi:d] s. perla f.

beak [bi:k] s. becco m.; rostro m.

beam [bi:m] s. trave f.; raggio m.

beaming ['bi:miŋ] agg. splendente

bean [bi:n] s. fagiolo m.; **French** – fagiolino

bear [bɛə*] s. orso m. • ribasso m. (Borsa)

to bear [bɛə*] v. tr. e intr. portare; reggere; tollerare; partorire; produrre; comportarsi; **to be born** nascere; – **on** influire; – **out** convalidare; – **down** premere; – **up** farsi forza; – **with** avere pazienza con

bearable ['bɛərəbl] agg. sopportabile

beard [biəd] s. barba f.

bearded ['biədəd] agg. barbuto

bearing ['bɛəriŋ] s. condotta f.; rilevamento m.; supporto m.; cuscinetto m. (mecc.)

beast [bi:st] s. bestia f., animale m.

beastly ['bi:stli] agg. abominevole

beat [bi:t] s. colpo m.; tempo m. (mus.); ritmo m.; battito m.

to beat [bi:t] v. tr. battere; colpire, percuotere

beaten ['bi:tn] agg. battuto, picchiato; sbattuto; vinto

beating ['bi:tiŋ] s. percosse f. pl.; sconfitta f.

beautician [bju:'tiʃən] s. estetista m. e f.

beautiful ['bju:təful] agg. bello

beauty ['bju:ti] s. bellezza f.

beaver ['bi:və*] s. castoro m.

because [bi'kɔz] cong. perché, poiché

to become [bi'kʌm] v. intr. diventare

bed [bed] s. letto m.; – **and board** vitto e alloggio; – **and breakfast** alloggio e prima colazione; – **cover** copriletto; – **clothes** biancheria da letto; **single** – letto a una piazza; **double** – letto matrimoniale

bedridden ['bed,ridn] agg. costretto a letto

bedside [bedsaid] s. capezzale m.; – **carpet** scendiletto; – **table** comodino

bedsitter [,bed'sitə*] s. monolocale m.

bee [bi:] s. ape f.

beech [bi:tʃ] s. faggio m.

beef [bi:f] s. manzo m.

beer [biə*] s. birra f.; **draught** – birra alla spina

beet [bi:t] s. barbabietola f.

beetle ['bi:tl] s. scarabeo m.

beetroot ['bi:tru:t] s. barbabietola f.

before [bi'fɔ:*] avv. avanti; davanti; già • prep. prima di; innanzi a; – **long** presto, prossimamente

beforehand [bi'fɔ:ænd] avv. in anticipo

to beg [beg] v. tr. e intr. pregare, supplicare; chiedere in elemosina; **I beg your pardon** chiedo scusa

beggar ['begə*] s. accattone m., mendicante m. e f.; individuo m. (fam.)

to begin [bi'gin] v. tr. e intr. cominciare, incominciare, iniziare; – **again** ricominciare; – **with** anzitutto

beginner [bi'ginə*] s. principiante m. e f.

beginning [bi'giniŋ] s. inizio m.; principio m.; esordio m.

begonia [bi'gounjə] s. begonia f.

to begrudge [bi'grʌdʒ] v. tr. dare a malincuore; invidiare

to beguile [bi'gail] v. tr. illudere

behalf [bi'ha:f] s. per conto di

to behave [bi'heiv] v. intr. comportarsi

behaviour [bi'heivjə*] s. comportamento m.; condotta f.

to behead [bi'hed] v. tr. decapitare

behind [bi'haind] avv. dietro; indietro • prep. dietro

being ['bi:iŋ] s. l'essere m.; esistenza f.

to belay [bi'lei] v. tr. legare; **belaying pin** caviglia (naut.)

belfry ['belfri] s. campanile m.

Belgian ['beldʒən] agg. e s. belga m. e f.

belief [bi'li:f] s. credenza f.; fede f.; parere m.; **beyond** – incredibile

believable [bi'li:vəbl] agg. credibile

to believe [bi'li:v] v. tr. e intr. credere; immaginare

believer [bi'li:və*] s. credente m. e f.

bell [bel] s. campana f.; campanello m.; – **tower** campanile

bellow ['belou] v. intr. muggito m.; urlo m.

belly ['beli] s. pancia f., ventre m.; – **ache** mal di pancia

bellyful ['beliful] s. mangiata f., scorpacciata f.

to belong [bi'lɔŋ] v. intr. appartenere

belongings [bi'lɔŋiŋz] s. pl. effetti m. personali

below [bi'lou] *avv.* sotto, giù • *prep.* sotto, al di sotto

belt [belt] *s.* cintura *f.*; **safety -** cintura di sicurezza

bench [bentʃ] *s.* panca *f.*, panchina *f.*; banco *m.*

bend [bend] *s.* curva *f.*

to bend [bend] *v. tr.* curvare, flettere, piegare • *intr.* piegarsi, curvarsi

beneath [bi'ni:θ] *avv. e prep.* sotto; indegno di

Benedictine [ˌbeni'diktin] *agg.* benedettino

benediction [ˌbeni'dikʃən] *s.* benedizione *f.*

benefactor [ˈbenifæktə*] *s.* benefattore *m.*

beneficence [bi'nefisəns] *s.* beneficenza *f.*

benefit ['benifit] *s.* beneficio *m.*; giovamento *m.*; utilità *f.*

to benefit ['benifit] *v. tr. e intr.* giovare a; **- by** giovarsi di, trarre vantaggio da

bent [bent] *s.* tendenza *f.*; attitudine *f.* • *agg.* piegato, curvo; disonesto; omosessuale

beret ['berei] *s.* berretto *m.*

berry ['beri] *s.* bacca *f.*; chicco *m.*

berth [bə:θ] *s.* cuccetta *f.*; ancoraggio *m.*, ormeggio *m.*

to berth [bə:θ] *v. tr. e intr.* attraccare; **berthing** attracco

to beseech [bi'si:tʃ] *v. tr.* supplicare

beside [bi'said] *prep.* presso, accanto

besides [bi'saidz] *avv.* inoltre • *prep.* oltre

to besiege [bi'si:dʒ] *v. tr.* assediare

best [best] *agg. sup. rel.* migliore; **the -** il migliore, il meglio; **- man** testimone (dello sposo); **- part** quasi tutto

bestiary ['bestiəri] *s.* bestiario *m.*

bestowal [bi'stouəl] *s.* concessione *f.*

bet [bet] *s.* scommessa *f.*; puntata *f.*

to bet [bet] *v. tr. e intr.* scommettere; puntare

to betray [bi'trei] *v. tr.* tradire

betrayal [bi'treiəl] *s.* tradimento *m.*

betrayer [bi'treiə*] *s.* traditore *m.*

better ['betə*] *agg. comp.* migliore, meglio • *avv.* meglio • *s.* scommettitore *m.*; **all the -** tanto meglio; **to get -** migliorare; **you had -** ti converrebbe; **- still** ancora meglio

to better ['betə*] *v. tr.* migliorare; superare

between [bi'twi:n] *prep.* fra, tra • *avv.* nel mezzo

beverage ['bevəridʒ] *s.* bevanda *f.*

to beware (of) [bi'weə*] *v. tr. e intr.* diffidare; stare attento a

to bewilder [bi'wildə*] *v. tr.* disorientare; confondere

bewilderment [bi'wildəmənt] *s.* confusione *f.*, perplessità *f.*

to bewitch [bi'witʃ] *v. tr.* incantare

beyond [bi'jɔnd] *prep. e avv.* oltre, al di là

bib [bib] *s.* bavaglino *m.*

Bible ['baibl] *s.* bibbia *f.*

biblical ['biblikəl] *agg.* biblico

bibliography [ˌbibli'ɔgrəfi] *s.* bibliografia *f.*

bibliophile ['biblioufail] *s.* bibliofilo *m.*

bicarbonate [bai'ka:bənit] *s.* bicarbonato *m.*

bicoloured ['bai'kʌləd] *agg.* bicolore

bicycle ['baisikl] *s.* bicicletta *f.*

bid [bid] *s.* offerta *f.*; tentativo *m.*

to bid [bid] *v. tr. e intr.* ordinare; dire; augurare

biennial [bai'eniəl] *agg.* biennale

bifocal ['bai'foukəl] *agg.* bifocale

big [big] *agg.* grande, grosso

bigamist ['bigəmist] *s.* bigamo *m.*

bigamy ['bigəmi] *s.* bigamia *f.*

bike [baik] *s.* bicicletta *f.*

bilberry ['bilbəri] *s.* mirtillo *m.*

bilge [bildʒ] *s.* sentina *f.*

bilingual [bai'liŋgwəl] *agg.* bilingue

bilingualism [bai'liŋgwəlizəm] *s.* bilinguismo *m.*

bill [bil] *s.* conto *m.*; fattura *f.*; parcella *f.*; manifesto *m.*; banconota *f.*; bolla *f.*, bolletta *f.*; **- of credit** lettera di credito

to bill [bil] *v. tr.* fatturare (*comm.*); mettere in programma

billiards ['biljədz] *s. pl.* (*v. al sing.*) biliardo *m. sing.*

billion ['biljən] *s.* bilione *m.* (UK); miliardo *m.* (USA)

billionaire [ˌbiljən'eə*] *s.* miliardario *m.* (USA)

bimonthly ['bai'mʌnθli] *agg.* bimestrale • *avv.* ogni due mesi

bin [bin] *s.* bidone *m.*; recipiente *m.*

to bind [baind] *v. tr.* legare; rilegare; saldare; fissare; impegnare; **- oneself** impegnarsi a • *intr.* grippare

binder ['baində*] *s.* rilegatore *m.*; cartella *f.*

binding ['baindiŋ] *s.* rilegatura *f.*; rilegatura *f.*; legame *m.* • *agg.* impegnativo

binoculars [bi'nɔkjuləz] *s. pl.* binocolo *m. sing.*

biochemistry ['baioʊ'kemistri] *s.* biochimica *f.*

biodegradable ['baiouːdi'greidəbl] *agg.* biodegradabile

biographer [bai'ɔgrəfə*] *s.* biografo *m.*

biographical [ˌbaiou'græfikəl] *agg.* biografico

biography [bai'ɔgrəfi] *s.* biografia *f.*

biological [ˌbaiə'lɔdʒkəl] *agg.* biologico

biologist [bai'ɔlədʒist] s. biologo m.

biology [bai'ɔlədʒi] s. biologia f.

birch [bə:tʃ] s. betulla f.

bird [bə:d] s. uccello m., volatile m.; **to be an early** - essere in anticipo

biro ['bairou] s. biro f. inv.

birth [bə:θ] s. nascita f.; origine f.; **- rate** indice di natalità

birthday ['bə:θdei] s. compleanno m.

biscuit ['biskit] s. biscotto m.

bisexual ['bai'seksjuəl] agg. bisessuale

bishop ['biʃəp] s. vescovo m.; alfiere m. (scacchi)

bishopric ['biʃəprik] s. vescovado m.

bistoury ['bisturi] s. bisturi m.

bit [bit] s. morso m., puntura f.; boccone m., pezzo m.

bitch [bitʃ] s. cagna f.; puttana f. (volg.)

bite [bait] s. morso m., puntura f.; spuntino m.

to bite [bait] v. tr. mordere; pungere • intr. abboccare

biting ['baitiŋ] agg. pungente; tagliente

bitter ['bitə*] agg. amaro; aspro; duro; gradevole; **bitter-sweet** agrodolce • s. pl. amaro m. sing.

biweekly ['bai'wi:kli] agg. bisettimanale • avv. ogni due settimane

biyearly ['bai'jiəli] agg. biennale • avv. ogni due anni

bizarre [bi'za:*] agg. bizzarro

black [blæk] agg. nero; buio, scuro

blackberry ['blækbəri] s. mora f.

blackbird ['blækbə:d] s. merlo m.

blackboard ['blækbɔ:d] s. lavagna f.

blackmail ['blækmeil] s. ricatto m.

to blackmail ['blækmeil] v. tr. ricattare

blackmailer ['blækmeilə*] s. ricattatore m.

blackout ['blækaut] s. oscuramento m.; svenimento m.; interruzione f. di corrente

blackthorn ['blækθɔ:n] s. pruno m.

bladder ['blædə*] s. vescica f.

blade [bleid] s. lama f.; lametta f.; pala f.; filo m. d'erba; **- bone** scapola f.

to blame [bleim] v. tr. incolpare

blank [blæŋk] agg. vuoto; bianco • s. lacuna f.

blanket ['blæŋkit] s. coperta f.

blare ['blɛə*] s. squillo m.

blasphemous ['blæsfiməs] agg. blasfemo

blast [bla:st] s. raffica f.

blasted ['bla:stid] agg. maledetto

blatant ['bleitənt] agg. vistoso, plateale

blaze [bleiz] s. fiammata f.

to blaze [bleiz] v. intr. ardere, bruciare

bleaching ['bli:tʃiŋ] s. candeggio m.

bleak [bli:k] agg. squallido, triste; brullo

bleeding ['bli:diŋ] s. dissanguamento m.; emorragia f.

blemish ['blemiʃ] s. macchia f.; imperfezione f.

blend [blend] s. mescolanza f., miscela f.

to blend [blend] v. tr. mescolare, fondere • intr. mescolarsi, fondersi

blending ['blendiŋ] s. miscela f., mescolanza f.

blessed ['blesid] agg. benedetto

blessing ['blesiŋ] s. benedizione f.

blind [blaind] agg. cieco • s. persiana f.

to blink [bliŋk] v. intr. lampeggiare; ammiccare

blister ['blistə*] s. vescica f., bolla f.

blizzard ['blizəd] s. bufera f. di neve

blob [blɔb] s. goccia f.; macchia f.; grumo m.

block [blɔk] s. blocco m.; ingorgo m.; intasamento m.; **- letters** stampatello m.; **- of flats** caseggiato; **road -** posto di blocco

to block [blɔk] v. tr. bloccare, ostruire

to blockade [blɔ'keid] v. tr. bloccare

blockhouse ['blɔkhaus] s. fortino m.

blond [blɔnd] agg. biondo

blood [blʌd] s. sangue m.

bloodhound ['blʌdhaund] s. segugio m.

bloody ['blʌdi] agg. sanguinante; dannato (volg.)

to bloom [blu:m] v. intr. fiorire

blooming ['blu:miŋ] agg. fiorente

blossom ['blɔsəm] s. fiore m.; fioritura f.

to blossom ['blɔsəm] v. intr. fiorire

to blot [blɔt] v. tr. macchiare; asciugare; **blotting-paper** carta assorbente

blouse [blauze] s. camicetta f.

blow [blou] s. colpo m.; percossa f.; pugno m.; soffio m.

to blow [blou] v. intr. soffiare; **- up** scoppiare; gonfiare

blue [blu] agg. azzurro; blu

bluff [blʌf] s. scogliera f.

to bluff [blʌf] v. tr. ingannare

blunder ['blʌndə*] s. errore m., strafalcione m.; cantonata f.

blunt [blʌnt] agg. ottuso; smussato, spuntato

to blush [blʌʃ] v. intr. arrossire

boar [bɔ:*] s. cinghiale m.

board [bɔ:d] s. asse f.; cartellone m.; mensa f.; vitto m.; comitato m.; bordo m. (naut.); **- and lodging** vitto e alloggio; **ironing -** asse da stiro; **on -** a bordo

to board [bɔ:d] v. tr. e intr. ospitare; imbarcarsi; stare a pensione; **boarding house** pensione; **boarding school** collegio

boast [boust] *s.* vanto *m.*

to boast [boust] *v. tr. e intr.* vantare, vantarsi

boaster ['bousta*] *s.* gradasso *m.*, spaccone *m.*, sbruffone *m.*

boat [bout] *s.* barca *f.*, battello *m.*; imbarcazione *f.*; nave *f.*; **motor** – barca a motore; **row(ing)** – barca a remi; **sail(ing)** – barca a vela; **fishing** – peschereccio; **boating** canottaggio

boatman ['boutmən] *s.* barcaiolo *m.*

body ['bɔdi] *s.* corpo *m.*; carrozzeria *f.*; giacimento *m.*; maggior parte *f.*; massa *f.*; **(dead)** – cadavere; **work** carrozzeria

bog [bɔg] *s.* acquitrino *m.*, palude *f.*

to bog [bɔg] *v. intr.* impantanarsi

boggy ['bɔgi] *agg.* paludoso

to boil [bɔil] *v. tr. e intr.* bollire, lessare; **boiled beef** lesso

boiler ['bɔilə*] *s.* caldaia *f.*; scaldabagno *m.*

boiling ['bɔiliŋ] *agg.* bollente • *s.* ebollizione *f.*

bold [bould] *agg.* baldo, audace

boldface ['bouldfeis] *s.* neretto *m.*

bollard ['bɔləd] *s.* bitta *f.*

bolt [boult] *s.* chiavistello *m.*; bullone *m.*; fulmine *m.*; balzo *m.*; rotolo *m.*

to bolt [boult] *v. tr e intr.* sprangare; scappare

bomb [bɔm] *s.* bomba *f.*

bombardment [bɔm'ba:dmənt] *s.* bombardamento *m.*

bombing ['bɔmiŋ] *s.* bombardamento *m.*

bond [bɔnd] *s.* legame *m.*, vincolo *m.*; accordo *m.*; cauzione *f.*

bone [boun] *s.* osso *m.*; **back** – spina dorsale; **bones** ossatura *f.*; **china** porcellana

bonfire ['bɔn,faiə*] *s.* falò *m.* inv.

bonnet ['bɔnit] *s.* cofano *m.*; cuffia *f.*

bony ['bouni] *agg.* osseo

to boo [bu:] *v. tr. e intr.* fischiare, disapprovare

book [buk] *s.* libro *m.*; registro *m.*; blocchetto *m.*; **mark** segnalibro; **reset** leggìo

to book [buk] *v. tr.* prenotare, fissare; **a seat on a train** prenotare un posto in treno

bookbindery ['buk,baindəri] *s.* legatoria *f.*

bookcase ['bukkeis] *s.* libreria *f.*, scaffale *m.* per libri

booking ['bukiŋ] *s.* prenotazione *f.*; **office** ufficio prenotazioni; **to cancel a** – annullare una prenotazione

bookish ['bukiʃ] *agg.* letterario

book-keeper ['buk,ki:pə*] *s.* contabile *m. e f.*

booklet ['buklit] *s.* libretto *m.*; opuscolo *m.*

bookmaker ['buk,meikə*] *s.* allibratore *m.*

bookseller ['buk,selə*] *s.* libraio *m.*

bookshop ['bukʃɔp] *s.* libreria *f.*

bookstall ['buk,stɔ:*] *s.* edicola *f.*

boom [bu:m] *s.* boma *m.*; giraffa *f.* (tel.); rimbombo *m.*; aumento *m.*

to boom [bu:m] *v. intr.* prosperare; rimbombare

boor [buə*] *agg.* maleducato, cafone

boorish ['buəriʃ] *agg.* maleducato, cafone

boost [bu:st] *s.* spinta *f.*, impulso *m.*; aumento *m.*

boot [bu:t] *s.* stivale *m.*, stivaletto *m.*; scarpone *m.*; bagagliaio *m.* (autom.)

booth [bu:ð] *s.* cabina *f.*; bancarella *f.*

booty ['bu:ti] *s.* bottino *f.*

booze [bu:z] *s.* bevanda *f.* alcolica

boozer ['bu:zə*] *s.* bevitore *m.*

border ['bɔ:də*] *s.* bordo *m.*, confine *m.*, orlo *m.*; **borderline** di confine; discutibile, marginale

to border ['bɔ:də*] *v. tr. e intr.* orlare; delimitare

bore ['bɔ:*] *s.* alesaggio *m.*; foro *m.* • scocciatore *m.*

to bore [bɔ:*] *v. tr. e intr.* trivellare; perforare; trapanare; seccare, annoiare; **to be bored** annoiarsi

boredom ['bɔ:dəm] *s.* uggia *f.*

boring ['bɔ:riŋ] *agg.* noioso, seccante

born [bɔ:n] *agg.* nato, generato

borough ['bʌrə] *s.* città *f.*

to borrow ['bɔrou] *v. tr. e intr.* prendere in prestito

bosom ['buzəm] *s.* seno *m.*

boss [bɔs] *s.* padrone *m.*

bossy ['bɔsi] *agg.* prepotente

botanic [bə'tænik] *agg.* botanico

both [bouθ] *agg. e pron.* entrambi; – ... and sia...sia

bother ['bɔðə*] *s.* disturbo *m.*; seccatura *f.*

to bother ['bɔðə*] *v. tr.* assillare; disturbare • *intr.* disturbarsi; preoccuparsi

bothersome ['bɔðəsəm] *agg.* fastidioso

bottle ['bɔtl] *s.* bottiglia *f.*; bombola *f.*; biberon *m. inv.*; **neck** strozzatura; **opener** apribottiglie

to bottle ['bɔtl] *v. tr.* imbottigliare

bottom ['bɔtəm] *s.* fondo *m.*; carena *f.*; sedere *m.* • *agg.* l'ultimo in basso

bottomless ['bɔtəmlis] *agg.* sfondato

25

bouillon ['bu:jɔ:ŋ] s. brodo m.; – **cube** dado da brodo
boulder ['bouldə*] s. ciottolo m.
boulevard ['bu:l(ə)va:d] s. viale m.
boulter ['boultə*] s. palamito m.
bound [baund] agg. legato; costretto, obbligato; rilegato • s. salto m., balzo m.; confine m.; – **for** diretto a
boundary ['baundəri] s. confine m., frontiera f.; perimetro m.
boundless ['baundlis] agg. illimitato
bouquet ['bukei] s. mazzetto m.
bourgeois ['buəʒwa:] agg. borghese
bourgeoisie [buəʒwa:'zi:] s. borghesia f.
bovine ['bouvain] agg. bovino
bow [bou] s. arco m.; fiocco m.; nodo m. • inchino m. • prua f.
to bow [bou] v. intr. chinarsi, curvarsi
bowel ['bauəl] s. intestino m.
bower ['bauə*] s. pergolato m.
bowl [boul] s. coppa f., ciotola f., scodella f. • boccia f.
bowling ['boulin] s. bowling; – **green** bocciodromo
bowman ['bouman] s. arciere m.
bowsprit ['bou-sprit] s. bompresso m.
box [bɔks] s. cassa f., cassetta f.; scatola f.; palco m.; riquadro m.; cabina f.; casella f.; televisione f. (fam.); – **office** botteghino; **letter** – cassetta per le lettere
to box [bɔks] v. tr. inscatolare • intr. fare a pugni; fare il pugile
boxer ['bɔksə*] s. pugile m.
boxing ['bɔksiŋ] s. pugilato m. • imballaggio m., inscatolamento m.
boy [bɔi] s. ragazzo m.; figlio m.; garzone m.; **little** – bambino; **old** – vecchietto; – **friend** fidanzato
to boycott ['bɔikət] v. tr. boicottare
boyhood ['bɔihud] s. gioventù f.
bra [bra:] s. reggiseno m.
brace [breis] s. sostegno m.; **braces** bretelle
to brace [breis] v. tr. sostenere; rinvigorire; – **oneself** farsi coraggio
bracelet ['breislit] s. braccialetto m.
bracket ['brækit] s. parentesi f.; supporto m.; mensola f.
bradyseism ['brædisaizəm] s. bradisismo m.
to braid [breid] v. tr. intrecciare
brain [brein] s. cervello m.; **brains** ingegno
brake [breik] s. freno m.
to brake [breik] v. tr. frenare
bramble ['bræmbl] s. rovo m.

bran [bræn] s. crusca f.
branch [bra:nʃ] s. ramo m.; diramazione f.; sezione f.; squadra f.
brand [brænd] s. marca f.; marchio m.; – **new** nuovo di zecca
to brand [brænd] v. tr. marcare
to brandish ['brændiʃ] v. tr. vibrare
brandy ['brændi] s. acquavite f.
brash [bræʃ] agg. insolente, arrogante; impetuoso
brass [bra:s] s. ottone m.
brassiere ['bræsiə*] s. reggiseno m.
brave [breiv] agg. coraggioso, valoroso
to brave [breiv] v. tr. sfidare
brawl [brɔ:l] s. rissa f., tafferuglio m.
to brawl [brɔ:l] v. intr. litigare; schiamazzare
bray [brei] s. raglio m.
breach [bri:tʃ] s. violazione f.; breccia f.
bread [bred] s. pane m.; **wholemeal** – pane integrale
to bread [bred] v. tr. impanare
breadstick ['bredstik] s. grissino m.
breadth [bredθ] s. larghezza f.
break [breik] s. rottura f.; interruzione f.
to break [breik] v. tr. rompere; spezzare; infrangere • intr. rompersi; diradarsi; diffondersi; – **off** staccare, interrompere; – **through** sfondare; – **up** distruggere
breakdown ['breikdaun] s. guasto m.; collasso m.; avaria f.
breakfast ['brekfəst] s. prima colazione f.
breakup ['breik'ʌp] s. disfacimento m.
breakwater ['breik,wɔ:tə*] s. frangiflutti m. inv.
breast [brest] s. petto m., seno m.; – **pocket** taschino
breastbone ['brestboun] s. sterno m.
breath [breθ] s. fiato m., respiro m.; soffio m.; – **taking** da togliere il respiro
to breathe [bri:ð] v. tr. e intr. respirare; – **in** inspirare; – **out** espirare
breathing ['bri:ðiŋ] s. respirazione f.
breed [bri:d] s. razza f. (zool.)
to breed [bri:d] v. tr. allevare; accoppiare; riprodurre • intr. riprodursi
breeding ['bri:diŋ] s. allevamento m.
breeze [bri:z] s. brezza f.
to brew [bru:] v. tr. fabbricare birra; preparare il tè
briar ['braiə*] s. radica f.
brick [brik] s. mattone m., laterizio m.
bricklayer ['brikleiə*] s. muratore m.
bridal ['braidl] agg. nuziale

bride [braid] *s.* sposa *f.*

bridegroom ['braidgrum] *s.* sposo *m.*

bridge [bridʒ] *s.* ponte *m.*; **swing** – ponte girevole

brief [bri:f] *agg.* breve • *s.* riassunto *m.*; memoria *f.*; direttive *f. pl.*; – **case** cartella; **briefs** mutande

to brief [bri:f] *v. tr.* riassumere

bright [brait] *agg.* luminoso, brillante; vivace; **brights** abbaglianti

to brighten ['braitn] *v. tr. e intr.* schiarire; rallegrare

brightness ['braitnis] *s.* luminosità *f.*; vivacità *f.*

brilliant ['briljənt] *agg.* brillante

brim [brim] *s.* orlo *m.*; falda *f.* (cappello)

brine [brain] *s.* salamoia *f.*

to bring [briŋ] *v. tr. e intr.* portare; causare; persuadere; condurre; – **about** effettuare; – **back** riportare; – **down** far calare; – **forward** mostrare; anticipare; – **off** portare a termine; – **round** convincere; – **up** allevare, educare, sollevare

brink [briŋk] *s.* orlo *m.*

brisk [brisk] *agg.* svelto, vivace

Britain ['britn] *s.* Gran Bretagna *f.*

British ['britiʃ] *agg.* britannico

broad [brɔːd] *agg.* largo, esteso

broadcast ['brɔːdkaːst] *s.* radiotrasmissione *f.*, trasmissione *f.*

to broadcast ['brɔːdkaːst] *v. tr.* trasmettere

broadness ['brɔːdnis] *s.* larghezza *f.*

brocade [brə'keid] *s.* broccato *m.*

broccoli ['brɔkəli] *s.* broccolo *m.*

brochure ['brouʃjuə*] *s.* opuscolo *m.*

broken ['broukən] *agg.* rotto

broker ['broukə*] *s.* mediatore *m.*

bronchitis [brɔŋ'kaitis] *s.* bronchite *f.*

bronchopneumonia ['brɔŋkouˌnjuː(ː)'mounjə] *s.* broncopolmonite *f.*

bronze [brɔnz] *s.* bronzo *m.*

brooch [broutʃ] *s.* spilla *f.*

brood [bruːd] *s.* nidiata *f.*

to brood [bruːd] *v. tr. e intr.* covare; meditare; tormentarsi

brook [bruk] *s.* ruscello *m.*

broom [brum] *s.* ginestra *f.*; ramazza *f.*, scopa *f.*

broth [brɔθ] *s.* brodo *m.*

brothel ['brɔθl] *s.* postribolo *m.*

brother ['brʌðə*] *s.* fratello *m.*; **brother-in-law** cognato

brown [braun] *agg.* bruno, castano • *s.* marrone *m.*

bruise [bruːz] *s.* ammaccatura *f.*, contusione *f.*, livido *m.*

to bruise [bruːz] *v. tr. e intr.* ammaccare; farsi un livido

brush [brʌʃ] *s.* spazzola *f.*; spazzolino *m.*; pennello *m.*; boscaglia *f.*; **shaving** – pennello da barba; **hair** – spazzola per capelli

to brush [brʌʃ] *v. tr.* spazzolare; sfiorare; – **off** rifiutare seccamente; – **up** migliorare

brusque [bru(ː)sk] *agg.* brusco

brutal ['bruːtl] *agg.* brutale

brute [bruːt] *agg.* bruto

bubble ['bʌbl] *s.* bolla *f.*

buck [bʌk] *s.* dollaro *m.* (USA, *pop.*)

bucket ['bʌkit] *s.* secchiello *m.*

buckle ['bʌkl] *s.* fibbia *f.*

buckskin ['bʌkskin] *s.* pelle *f.* di camoscio

bucolic [bjuː(ː)'kɔlik] *agg.* bucolico

bud [bʌd] *s.* bocciolo *m.*, gemma *f.*

to bud [bʌd] *v. intr.* germogliare

Buddhism ['budizəm] *s.* buddismo *m.*

to budge [bʌdʒ] *v. tr. e intr.* spostare, spostarsi

budget ['bʌdʒit] *s.* preventivo *m.*; bilancio *m.*

buffalo ['bʌfəlou] *s.* bufalo *m.*

buffer ['bʌfə*] *s.* respingente *m.*

buffoon [bʌ'fuːn] *s.* pagliaccio *m.*

bug [bʌg] *s.* cimice *f.*; insetto *m.*

build [bild] *s.* corporatura *f.*

to build [bild] *v. tr.* costruire, edificare; – **up** sviluppare

builder ['bildə*] *s.* costruttore *m.*

building ['bildiŋ] *s.* edificio *m.*; costruzione *f.* • *agg.* edificabile, edilizio

bulb [bʌlb] *s.* bulbo *m.* (*bot.*); lampadina *f.*; – **socket** portalampada

Bulgarian [bʌl'gɛəriən] *agg.* bulgaro

bulge [bʌldʒ] *s.* rigonfiamento *m.*

bulk [bʌlk] *s.* mole *f.*; maggior parte *f.*

bulkhead ['bʌlkhed] *s.* paratia *f.* (*naut.*)

bulky ['bʌlki] *agg.* massiccio, voluminoso

bull [bul] *s.* toro *m.* • editto *m.*; – **run** rialzo (Borsa)

bullet ['bulit] *s.* proiettile *m.*

bulletin ['bulitin] *s.* bollettino *f.*

bullfight ['bul-fait] *s.* corrida *f.*

bully ['buli] *agg.* prepotente

bulwark ['bulwək] *s.* baluardo *m.*; murata *f.* (*naut.*)

bump [bʌmp] *s.* urto *m.*; scossone *m.*

to bump [bʌmp] *v. tr.* urtare; tamponare

27

bumper [bʌmpə*] s. paraurti m. inv.; respingente m.

bun [bʌn] s. focaccia f.; ciambella f.; panino m. dolce

bunch [bʌntʃ] s. grappolo m.; mazzo m.

bundle [bʌndl] s. mazzetto m.; fagotto m.; fascio m.

bunk [bʌŋk] s. cuccetta f.

buoy [bɔi] s. boa f., gavitello m.

buoyancy [bɔiənsi] s. galleggiabilità f.

buoyant [bɔiənt] agg. galleggiante

burden [bə:dn] s. onere m.; peso m.

burdensome [bə:dnsəm] agg. gravoso, oneroso

bureau [bjuə'rou] s. ufficio m.; scrittoio m.; dipartimento m. (USA)

bureaucracy [bjuə'rɔkrəsi] s. burocrazia f.

bureaucratic [,bjuərou'krætik] agg. burocratico

burglar [bə:glə*] s. scassinatore m.

burglary [bə:glari] s. scasso m.; furto m.

to burgle [bə:gl] v. tr. scassinare, svaligiare

burial [berial] s. sepoltura f.

burlesque [bə:'lesk] agg. burlesco

burn [bə:n] s. scottatura f., ustione f.

to burn [bə:n] v. tr. e intr. bruciare; ustionare; scottare

burning [bə:niŋ] s. bruciore m., bruciatura f. • agg. rovente, scottante

burnt [bə:nt] agg. consumato; bruciato

burrow [bʌrou] s. tana f.

burst [bə:st] s. esplosione f., scoppio m.

to burst [bə:st] v. intr. esplodere, scoppiare, saltare in aria

to bury [beri] v. tr. seppellire

bus [bʌs] s. autobus m.; - line autolinea

bush [buʃ] s. cespuglio m.; macchia f.

business [biznis] s. affare m.; azienda f.; commercio m.; - consultant commercialista

bust [bʌst] s. busto m.

bustle [bʌsl] s. trambusto m.

busy [bizi] agg. attivo, indaffarato; occupato

but [bʌt, bət] cong. ma, però, tuttavia • prep. eccetto • avv. soltanto

butcher [butʃə*] s. macellaio m.; -'s shop macelleria

butler [bʌtlə*] s. maggiordomo m.

butt [bʌt] s. botte f. • estremità f.

butter [bʌtə*] s. burro m.

to butter [bʌtə*] v. tr. imburrare

buttercup [bʌtəkʌp] s. ranuncolo m.

butterfly [bʌt,flai] s. farfalla f.

buttock [bʌtək] s. natica f.

button [bʌtn] s. bottone m.; pulsante m.

to button [bʌtn] v. tr. abbottonare

buttonhole [bʌtnhoul] s. asola f., occhiello m.

buxom [bʌksəm] agg. formosa f.

to buy [bai] v. tr. comprare; - back ricomprare; - by instalments comprare a rate; - out rilevare; - up accaparrarsi

buyer [bai-ə*] s. compratore m.

buzzer [bʌzə*] s. cicalino m.; citofono m.

by [bai] prep. da, presso, per, con; - chance per caso; - hand a mano; - all means senz'altro; - now ormai; - the way incidentalmente; - then allora; one - one uno per volta

bye-bye [baibai] inter. ciao

bypass [bai-pa:s] s. tangenziale f.; deviazione f.

byroad [bairoud] s. strada f. secondaria

bystander [bai,stændə*] s. spettatore m.

by-work [baiwə:k] s. lavoro m. secondario

Byzantine [bi'zæntain] agg. bizantino

C

cab [kæb] *s.* taxi *m.*

cabalistic [ˌkæbəˈlistik] *agg.* cabalistico

cabaret [ˈkæbəˌrei] *s.* cabaret *m. inv.*

cabbage [ˈkæbidʒ] *s.* cavolo *m.*

cabin [ˈkæbin] *s.* cabina *f.*; capanna *f.*

cabinet [ˈkæbinit] *s.* gabinetto *m.* (in politica); mobile *m.* (per bottiglie, bicchieri...)

cable [ˈkeibl] *s.* cavo *m.*; – **car** funivia

cableway [ˈkeiblwei] *s.* teleferica *f.*

cabotage [ˈkæbətidʒ] *s.* cabotaggio *m.*

cacao [kəˈkaːou] *s.* cacao *m.*

to cackle [ˈkækl] *v. intr.* schiamazzare

cadence [ˈkeidəns] *s.* cadenza *f.*

cadet [kəˈdet] *agg.* cadetto

cadre [kaːdr] *s.* quadro *m.*, schema *m.*

cafeteria [ˌkæfiˈtiəriə] *s.* tavola *f.* calda, mensa *f.*, self-service *m. inv.*

caffeine [ˈkæfiːn] *s.* caffeina *f.*

cage [keidʒ] *s.* gabbia *f.*

cake [keik] *s.* torta *f.*; focaccia *f.*; pasticcino *m.*; tavoletta *f.*; – **of soap** saponetta

calamity [kəˈlæmiti] *s.* calamità *f.*, sciagura *f.*

calcareous [kælˈkeəriəs] *agg.* calcareo

calcium [ˈkælsiəm] *s.* calcio *m.*

to calculate [ˈkælkjuleit] *v. tr.* calcolare

calculation [ˌkælkjuˈleʃən] *s.* calcolo *m.*; congettura *f.*

calculator [ˈkælkjuleitə°] *s.* calcolatrice *f.*

calculus [ˈkælkjuləs] *s.* calcolo *m.*

calendar [ˈkælində°] *s.* calendario *m.*

calf [kaːf] *s.* vitello *m.* • polpaccio *m.*

caliber [ˈkælibə°] *s.* calibro *m.*

to calibrate [ˈkælibreit] *v. tr.* calibrare

calix [ˈkæliks] *s.* calice *m.*

call [kɔːl] *s.* chiamata *f.*; telefonata *f.*; breve visita *f.*; scalo *m.*; **trunk** –, **long distance** – (USA) telefonata interurbana; **self-dialled** – chiamata in teleselezione

to call [kɔːl] *v. tr. e intr.* chiamare; telefonare; visitare; fare scalo; – **attention** richiamare l'attenzione; – **for** passare a prendere; – **on** fare una visita a; – **back** richiamare; – **off** disdire

calligraphic [ˌkæliˈgræfik] *agg.* calligrafico

calling [ˈkɔːliŋ] *s.* vocazione *f.*

callous [ˈkæləs] *agg.* calloso; insensibile

callus [ˈkæləs] *s.* callo *m.*

calm [kaːm] *s.* calma *f.* • *agg.* calmo, tranquillo; **calmly** con calma, tranquillamente

to calm [kaːm] *v. tr.* calmare, placare; – **down** calmarsi

caloric [kəˈlɔrik] *agg.* calorico

calory [ˈkæləri] *s.* caloria *f.*

Calvinism [ˈkælvinizəm] *s.* calvinismo *m.*

Calvinist [ˈkælvinist] *s.* calvinista *m. e f.*

camel [ˈkæməl] *s.* cammello *m.*

camelia [kəˈmiːljə] *s.* camelia *f.*

cameo [ˈkæmiou] *s.* cammeo *m.*

camera [ˈkæmərə] *s.* macchina *f.* fotografica

camisole [ˈkæmisoul] *s.* maglietta *f.*

camomile [ˈkæməmail] *s.* camomilla *f.*

camouflage [ˈkæmuflaːʒ] *s.* travestimento *m.*, mimetizzazione *f.*

to camouflage [ˈkæmuflaːʒ] *v. tr.* mimetizzare; cammuffare

camp [kæmp] *s.* campo *m.*; accampamento *m.*

to camp [kæmp] *v. intr.* accamparsi; campeggiare

campaign [kæmˈpein] *s.* campagna *f.*

camper [ˈkæmpə°] *s.* campeggiatore *m.*; autocaravan *m.*

camping [ˈkæmpiŋ] *s.* campeggio *m.*

campy [ˈkæmpi] *agg.* effeminato

can [kæn, kən] *v. dif.* potere, essere in grado di, sapere, essere capace di, riuscire • *s.* barattolo *m.*; latta *f.*, lattina *f.*; tanica *f.*; scatola *f.*; – **opener** apriscatole; **cans** scatolame

to can [kæn] *v. tr.* inscatolare

canal [kəˈnæl] *s.* canale *m.*

canalization [ˌkænəlaiˈzeiʃən] *s.* canalizzazione *f.*

to canalize [ˈkænəlaiz] *v. tr.* incanalare

canasta [kəˈnæstə] *s.* canasta *f.*

to cancel [ˈkænsəl] *v. tr.* cancellare; annullare, disdire

cancellation [ˌkænseˈleiʃən] *s.* annullamento *m.*, cancellazione *f.*

candelabrum [ˌkændiˈlabrəm] *s.* candelabro *m.*

candidate [ˈkændidit] *s.* candidato *m.*

29

candidature ['kændiditʃə*] s. candidatura f.

candied ['kændid] agg. candito

candle ['kændl] s. candela f. (anche elettr.)

candlestick ['kændlstik] s. candeliere m.

candour ['kændə*] s. franchezza f.

candy ['kændi] s. caramella f.; - floss zucchero filato

cane [kein] s. canna f.; bastone m. (da passeggio)

canine ['kænain] agg. e s. canino m.

canna ['kænə] s. canna f.

canned [kænd] agg. in scatola (alim.); - food scatolame

cannibal ['kænibəl] s. cannibale m.

cannibalism ['kænibəlizəm] s. cannibalismo m.

cannon ['kænən] s. cannone m.

canoe [kə'nu:] s. canoa f.

canonical [kə'nɔnikəl] agg. canonico

canopy ['kænəpi] s. baldacchino m.

cantankerous [kən'tænkərəs] agg. irascibile, litigioso

cantata [kæn'ta:tə] s. cantata f.

to cant [kænt] v. intr. inclinarsi; canted inclinato

canteen [kæn'ti:n] s. mensa f.

cantilever ['kæntili:ve*] s. mensola f. (arch.); - roof pensilina

canvas ['kænvəs] s. tela f.

to canvass ['kænvəs] v. tr. sondare l'opinione; sollecitare (voti)

canyon ['kænjən] s. canyon m.

cap [kæp] s. berretto m.; tappo m.; cappella f. (fungo)

capable ['keipəbl] agg. capace

capacious [kə'peiʃəs] agg. spazioso

capacity [kə'pæsiti] s. capacità f.; capienza f.; portata f.

cape [keip] s. capo m., promontorio m.; mantellina f.

to caper ['keipə*] v. intr. saltellare

capillary [kə'piləri] agg. capillare

capital ['kæpitəl] agg. capitale; maiuscolo • s. capitale m. e f.; share - capitale azionario

capitalism ['kæpitəlizəm] s. capitalismo m.

capitalist ['kæpitəlist] s. capitalista m. e f.

to capitulate [kə'pitjuleit] v. intr. capitolare

caprice [kə'pri:s] s. capriccio m.

caprine ['kæprain] agg. caprino

to capsize [kæp'saiz] v. tr. e intr. capovolgere, capovolgersi, ribaltare

capsule ['kæpsju:l] s. capsula f.

captain ['kæptin] s. capitano m., comandante m.

caption ['kæpʃən] s. didascalia f.; titolo m.

captive ['kæptiv] agg. e s. prigioniero m.

capture ['kæptʃə*] s. cattura f.

to capture ['kæptʃə*] v. tr. catturare

capuchin ['kæpjuʃin] s. cappuccino m. (relig.)

car [ka:*] s. automobile f.; macchina f.; - body repairer carrozziere; - hire autonoleggio; - wash autolavaggio; - electrician elettrauto; sleeping - vagone letto

carafe [kə'ra:f] s. caraffa f.

caramel ['kærəmel] s. caramello m.; caramella f.

caravan ['kærəvæn] s. carovana f.; roulotte f. inv.

carbohydrate ['ka:bou'haidreit] s. carboidrato m.

carbon ['ka:bən] s. carbonio m.

to carbonize ['ka:bənaiz] v. tr. carbonizzare

carburettor ['ka:bjuretə*] s. carburatore m.

carcinogenic [,ka:sinou'dʒenik] agg. cancerogeno

card [ka:d] s. scheda f.; tessera f.; biglietto m. da visita; - holder schedario; identity - carta d'identità; playing cards carte da gioco; post - cartolina

cardboard ['ka:dbɔ:d] s. cartone m.

cardiac ['ka:diæk] agg. cardiaco

cardinal ['ka:dinəl] agg. e s. cardinale m.

cardiologist [,ka:di'ɔlədʒist] s. cardiologo m.

cardiopath ['ka:dioupa:θ] s. cardiopatico m.

care [keə*] s. cura f., attenzione f.; avvertenza f.; custodia f.; preoccupazione f.; to take - of curare

to care [keə*] v. intr. preoccuparsi; importare; - for prendersi cura di

career [kə'riə*] s. carriera f.

carefree ['kɛəfri:] agg. spensierato

careful ['kɛəful] agg. accurato; diligente; carefully attentamente

careless ['kɛəlis] agg. disattento; incurante; spensierato

carelessness ['kɛəlisnis] s. disattenzione f.; incuria f.

caress [kə'res] s. carezza f.

to caress [kə'res] v. tr. accarezzare

caretaker ['kɛə,teikə*] s. custode m. e f.

caricature [,kærikə'tjuə*] s. caricatura f.

caries ['kɛərii:z] s. inv. carie f.

carnation [ka:'neiʃən] s. garofano m.

carnival ['ka:nivəl] s. carnevale m.

carnivorous [ka:'nivɔ:z] agg. carnivoro

carol ['kærəl] s. canto m. (di Natale).
carpenter ['ka:pıntə*] s. falegname m., carpentiere m.
carpet ['ka:pit] s. tappeto m.; moquette f. inv.
carriage ['kærıdʒ] s. carrozza f.; trasporto m. • agg. carraio
carrier ['kæriə*] s. corriere m.; portapacchi m. inv.; veicolo m. (med.); portatore m.
carrot ['kærət] s. carota f.
to carry ['kæri] v. tr. portare; trasportare; – away asportare; – back riportare; – off rapire; – on proseguire; – out effettuare, eseguire
cart [ka:t] s. carro m., carrozzino f.
cartilage ['ka:tilidʒ] s. cartilagine f.
cartographic [ka:tɔgrəfi] agg. cartografico
carton ['ka:tən] s. stecca f. (sigarette); cartone m. (imballaggio)
cartoon [ka:'tu:n] s. fumetto m.; vignetta f.
cartoonist [ka:'tu:nist] s. vignettista m. e f.
cartridge [ka:tridʒ] s. cartuccia f.
to carve [ka:v] v. tr. incidere, intagliare; scolpire; trinciare; affettare
caryatid [ˌkæri'ætid] s. cariatide f.
cascade [kæs'keid] s. cascata f.
case [keis] s. cassa f.; astuccio m. • caso m.; fenomeno m.
cash [kæʃ] s. contante m.; moneta f.; cassa f.; – desk cassa; – dispenser bancomat
to cash [kæʃ] v. tr. incassare; riscuotere
cashier [kæ'ʃiə*] s. cassiere m.
cask [ka:sk] s. barile m., botte f.
casket [ka:skit] s. scrigno m.
casserole ['kæsəroul] s. casseruola f., tegame m.
cassette [kæ'set] s. cassetta f.
cassock ['kæsək] s. tonaca f.
cast [ka:st] s. tiro m.; cast m.
to cast [ka:st] v. tr. e intr. lanciare, buttare; assegnare una parte
castle ['ka:sl] s. castello m.; torre f. (scacchi)
to castrate [kæs'treit] v. tr. castrare
casual ['kæʒuəl] agg. casuale; occasionale; accidentale
casualty ['kæʒuəlti] s. ferito m.; vittima f.; infortunio m., incidente m.; – ward pronto soccorso
cat [kæt] s. gatto m.
cataclysm ['kætəklizəm] s. cataclisma m.
catacomb ['kætəkoum] s. catacomba f.
catalogue ['kætəlɔg] s. catalogo m.
to catalogue ['kætəlɔg] v. tr. catalogare
catamaran [ˌkætəmə'ræn] s. catamarano f.
cataract ['kætərækt] s. cateratta f.

catarrh [kə'ta:*] s. catarro m.
catastrophe [kə'tæstrəfi] s. catastrofe f.
catastrophic [ˌkætə'strɔfik] agg. catastrofico
catch [kætʃ] s. gancio m., fermo m.; pesca f.; presa f.; inganno m.
to catch [kætʃ] v. tr. prendere, afferrare; sorprendere; – a cold raffreddarsi
catching ['kætʃiŋ] agg. infettivo
catchy ['kætʃi] agg. orecchiabile
catechism ['kætikizəm] s. catechismo m.
category ['kætigəri] s. categoria f.
caterpillar ['kætəpilə*] s. bruco m.
cathedral [kə'θi:drəl] s. cattedrale f., duomo m.
Catherine-wheel ['kæθərin wi:l] s. girandola f.
Catholic ['kæθəlik] agg. cattolico; universale, aperto
Catholicism [kə'θɔlisizəm] s. cattolicesimo m.
catlike ['kætlaik] agg. felino
cattle ['kætl] s. bestiame m.
cauliflower ['kɔliflauə*] s. cavolfiore m.
causal ['kɔ:zəl] agg. causale
cause [kɔ:z] s. causa f., ragione f.
to cause [kɔ:z] v. tr. causare; procurare; produrre
caustic ['kɔ:stik] agg. caustico
caution ['kɔ:ʃən] s. avvertenza f.; cautela f.; cauzione f.
cautious ['kɔ:ʃəs] agg. prudente, cauto
cavalry ['kævəlri] s. cavalleria f.
cave [keiv] s. caverna f., grotta f.
cavern ['kævən] s. caverna f., grotta f.
caviar ['kævi:*] s. caviale m.
cavil ['kævil] s. cavillo m.
cavity ['kæviti] s. cavità f.
to cease [si:s] v. tr. e intr. cessare, smettere
cedar ['si:də*] s. cedro m.
ceiling ['si:liŋ] s. soffitto m.; tetto m. (fig.)
celebrant ['selibrənt] s. celebrante m.
to celebrate ['selibreit] v. tr. celebrare; festeggiare
celebrated ['selibreitid] agg. celebre
celebration [ˌseli'breiʃən] s. celebrazione f.; festeggiamento m.
celebrity [si'lebriti] s. celebrità f.
celery ['seləri] s. sedano m.
celestial [si'lestjel] agg. celeste
cell [sel] s. cella f.; cellula f.; pila f. (elettr.)
cellar ['selə*] s. cantina f.; sotterraneo m.
cellular ['seljulə*] agg. cellulare
Celtic ['keltik] agg. celtico
cement [si'ment] s. cemento m.
cemeterial [ˌsemi'tiəriəl] agg. cimiteriale

31

cemetery ['semitri] s. cimitero m.

censor ['sensə*] s. censore m.; censura f.

censorship ['sensəʃip] s. censura f.

census ['sensəs] s. censimento m.

cent [sent] s. centesimo m. di dollaro (USA); per - per cento

centaur ['sentɔ:*] s. centauro m.

centenarian [,senti'neəriən] s. centenario m.

centenary [sen'ti:nəri] agg. e s. centenario m.

centennial [sen'tenjəl] agg. centenario

centimetre ['senti,mi:tə*] s. centimetro m.

central ['sentrəl] agg. centrale

to centralize ['sentrəlaiz] v. tr. accentrare; centralizzare

centre ['sentə*] s. centro m.; - field centrocampo; - forward centravanti, centrattacco; - piece centrotavola

to centre ['sentə*] v. tr. centrare; incentrare

centrifugal [sen'trifjugəl] agg. centrifugo

centrifuge ['sentri,fju:dʒ] s. centrifuga f.

centring ['sentriŋ] s. centina f.; centraggio m., centratura f.

centripetal [sen'tripitəl] agg. centripeto

century ['sentʃuri] s. secolo m.

cephalalgy [,səfə'lædʒi] s. cefalea f.

ceramics [si'ræmiks] s. pl. (v. al sing.) ceramica f. sing.

ceramist [si'ræmist] s. ceramista m. e f.

cereal ['siəriəl] s. cereale m.

cerebellum [,seri'beləm] s. cervelletto m.

ceremony ['seriməni] s. cerimonia f.

certain ['sə:tn] agg. certo, sicuro

certainly ['sə:tinli] avv. certamente

certainty ['sə:tnti] s. certezza f., sicurezza f.

certificate [sə'tifikit] s. certificato m. diploma m.

certified ['sə:tifaid] agg. certificato, attestato

cervical ['sə:vikəl] agg. cervicale

to chafe [tʃeif] v. tr. e intr. logorare, sfregarsi, consumarsi

chafing-dish ['tʃeifiŋdiʃ] s. scaldavivande m. inv.

chain [tʃein] s. catena f.; collana f.

to chain [tʃein] v. tr. incatenare

chair [tʃeə*] s. sedia f.; seggio m.; cattedra f.; - lift seggiovia

chairman ['tʃeəmən] s. presidente m.

chairmanship ['tʃeəmənʃip] s. presidenza f.

chalet ['ʃælei] s. chalet m., villetta f. rustica

chalk [tʃɔ:k] s. gesso m.

challenge ['tʃælindʒ] s. sfida f.

to challenge ['tʃælindʒ] v. tr. sfidare

chamber ['tʃeimbə*] s. camera f.; salone m.; - maid cameriera d'albergo

chamois ['ʃæmwa] s. camoscio m.

champion ['tʃæmpjən] agg. e s. campione m.

championship ['tʃæmpjənʃip] s. campionato m.; scudetto m.

chance [tʃɑ:ns] s. caso m., combinazione f.; fortuna f.; occasione f.; probabilità f. • agg. casuale, fortuito, occasionale

to chance [tʃɑ:ns] v. tr. rischiare

chancellery ['tʃɑ:nsələri] s. cancelleria f. (politica)

chancellor ['tʃɑ:nsələ*] s. cancelliere m.

chandelier [,ʃændi'liə*] s. lampadario m.

change [tʃeindʒ] s. cambiamento m.; cambio m.; spiccioli m. pl.

to change [tʃeindʒ] v. tr. e intr. cambiare, modificare; scambiare

changeable ['tʃeindʒəbl] agg. variabile; instabile

channel ['tʃænl] s. canale m.; letto m. di fiume; stretto m.; English Channel la Manica

chant [tʃɑ:nt] s. canto m. liturgico

chaos [keiɔs] s. caos m.

chaotic [keɪˈɔtik] agg. caotico

chap [tʃæp] s. screpolatura f. • mascella f. • tipo m., individuo m. (fam.)

to chap [tʃæp] v. tr. screpolare

chapel ['tʃæpəl] s. cappella f.

chapter ['tʃæptə*] s. capitolo m.

character ['kæriktə*] s. carattere m.; personaggio m. (romanzo)

characteristic [,kæriktə'ristik] s. caratteristica f. • agg. caratteristico

to characterize ['kæriktəraiz] v. tr. caratterizzare

charade [ʃə'rɑ:d] s. sciarada f.

chard [tʃɑ:d] s. bietola f.

charge [tʃɑ:dʒ] s. carica f.; incarico m.; onere m.; accusa f.; spesa f.

to charge [tʃɑ:dʒ] v. tr. e intr. caricare; incaricare; addebitare; accusare

chariot ['tʃæriət] s. biga f., cocchio m.

charioteer [,tʃæriə'tiə*] s. auriga m.

charismatic [kariz'mætik] agg. carismatico

charity ['tʃæriti] s. carità f., beneficenza f.

charlatan ['ʃɑ:lətən] s. ciarlatano m.

charm [tʃɑ:m] s. incantesimo m., fascino m.; lucky - portafortuna

to charm [tʃɑ:m] v. tr. incantare, affascinare

charming ['tʃɑ:miŋ] agg. affascinante, avvincente, incantevole

chart [tʃɑ:t] s. carta f. nautica; diagramma m.

charter ['tʃa:tə*] s. noleggio m.; statuto m.; – **flight** volo charter

to charter ['tʃa:tə*] v. tr. noleggiare

charterer ['tʃa:tərə*] s. noleggiatore m.

chartreuse [ʃa:'trø:z] s. certosa f.

chase [tʃeis] s. inseguimento m.

to chase [tʃeis] v. tr. inseguire, rincorrere • intr. affrettarsi

chasm ['kæzəm] s. baratro m., voragine f.

chaste [tʃeist] agg. castigato

chastity ['tʃæstiti] s. castità f.

to chat [tʃæt] v. intr. chiacchierare

cheap [tʃi:p] agg. conveniente, economico

cheapish ['tʃi:piʃ] agg. dozzinale

cheat [tʃi:t] s. imbroglio m., fregatura f.

to cheat [tʃi:t] v. tr. e intr. imbrogliare, raggirare

check [tʃek] s. controllo m.; ispezione f.; arresto m.; assegno m.; conto m. (USA)

to check [tʃek] v. tr. controllare; frenare; contrassegnare

checkmate ['tʃek'meit] s. scaccomatto m.; to – dare scaccomatto

cheek [tʃi:k] s. guancia f.; sfacciataggine f.

cheeky ['tʃi:ki] agg. impertinente, sfacciato

to cheer ['tʃiə*] v. tr. e intr. applaudire; **cheer up!** coraggio!; – **up** rallegrarsi

cheerful ['tʃiəful] agg. allegro, contento

cheerfulness ['tʃiəfulnis] s. allegria f., contentezza f.

cheering ['tʃirin] s. applauso m.

cheese [tʃi:z] s. formaggio m.; – **factory** caseificio m.

chemical ['kemikəl] agg. chimico • s. sostanza f. chimica

chemist ['kemist] s. farmacista m. e f.; chimico m.; – **shop** farmacia

cheque [tʃek] s. assegno m.; **blank** – assegno in bianco; **uncovered** – assegno scoperto; – **book** libretto assegni

cherry ['tʃeri] s. ciliegia f.

chess [tʃes] s. scacchi m. pl. (gioco); – **board** scacchiera

chest [tʃest] s. cassa f., cassapanca f.; torace m., petto m.

chestnut ['tʃesnʌt] s. castagna f.; castagno m.

to chew [tʃu:] v. tr. masticare

chick [tʃik] s. pulcino m.

chicken ['tʃikin] s. pollo m.; **roast** – pollo arrosto; – **pox** varicella

chicory ['tʃikəri] s. cicoria f.

chief [tʃi:f] s. capo m.; comandante m. • agg. principale; – **town** capoluogo

chiefly ['tʃi:fli] avv. principalmente

child [tʃaild] (pl. **children**) bambina f.; bambino m.; – **birth** parto

childhood ['tʃaildhud] s. infanzia f.

childish ['tʃaildiʃ] agg. puerile

chill [tʃil] s. freddo m.

to chill [tʃil] v. tr. raffreddare

chilly ['tʃili] agg. freddo

chimney ['tʃimni] s. camino m., comignolo m., ciminiera f.

chimpanzee [,tʃimpən'zi:] s. scimpanzé m.

chin [tʃin] s. mento m.

china ['tʃainə] s. porcellana f.

chinaware ['tʃainəwɛə*] s. porcellana f.

Chinese ['tʃai'ni:z] agg. e s. cinese m. e f.

chip [tʃip] s. scheggia f., scaglia f.; pezzetto m.; patatina f. fritta

to chip [tʃip] v. tr. scalpellare, scheggiare • intr. scheggiarsi

chiromancer ['kaiərəmænsə*] s. chiromante m. e f.

chiropodist [ki'rɔpədist] s. pedicure m. e f. inv.; callista m. e f.

to chirrup ['tʃirəp] v. intr. cinguettare; **chirruping** cinguettio

chisel ['tʃizl] s. cesello m.; scalpello m.

to chisel ['tʃizl] v. tr. cesellare

chivalrous ['ʃivəlrəs] agg. cavalleresco

chivalry ['ʃivəlri] s. cavalleria f.

chlorine ['klɔ:ri:n] s. cloro m.

chlorophyl ['klɔrəfil] s. clorofilla f.

chocolate ['tʃɔkəlit] s. cioccolata f., cioccolatino m.; **milk** – cioccolata al latte; **plain** – cioccolata fondente

choice [tʃɔis] s. scelta f. • agg. scelto

choir ['kwaiə*] s. coro m.

to choke [tʃouk] v. tr. e intr. soffocare; ingolfare; – **up** intasare, ingorgare

choking ['tʃoukin] s. soffocamento m. • agg. soffocante

cholesterol [kɔ'lestərɔl] s. colesterolo m.

to choose [tʃu:z] v. tr. e intr. scegliere

chop [tʃɔp] s. costata f.; taglio m.; **lamb** – costata d'agnello; **pork** – costata di maiale

to chop [tʃɔp] v. tr. tagliare; tritare; – **off** recidere

chopping-board ['tʃɔpiŋ-bɔ:d] s. tagliere m.

choral ['kɔ:rəl] agg. corale

choreography [,kɔri'ɔgrəfi] s. coreografia f.

chorister ['kɔristə*] s. corista m. e f.

chorus ['kɔ:rəs] s. coro m.

to christen ['krisn] v. tr. battezzare

Christendom ['krisndəm] s. cristianità f.

Christian ['kristjən] agg. cristiano
Christianity [,kristi'æniti] s. cristianesimo m.
Christmas ['krisməs] s. natale m. • agg. natalizio; Merry – buon natale
chromatic [krə'mætik] agg. cromatico
chromium ['kroumjəm] s. cromo m.; – plating cromatura
chronic ['krɔnik] agg. cronico
chronicle ['krɔnikl] s. cronaca f., cronistoria f.
chronicler ['krɔniklə*] s. cronista m. e f.
chronologic [,krɔnə'lɔdʒik] agg. cronologico
chronometer [krə'nɔmitə*] s. cronometro m.
to chuckle ['tʃʌkl] v. intr. ridacchiare, sogghignare
chum [tʃʌm] s. compagno m.
chunk [tʃʌŋk] s. pezzo m. (grosso)
church [tʃə:tʃ] s. chiesa f.; – tower campanile
churchyard ['tʃə:tʃjɑ:d] s. cimitero m.
chute [ʃu:t] s. scivolo m.
cicada [si'kɑ:də] s. cicala f.
cicerone [,tʃitʃə'rouni] s. cicerone m.
cider ['saidə*] s. sidro m.
cigar [si'gɑ:*] s. sigaro m.
cigarette [,sigə'ret] s. sigaretta f.; – holder bocchino
cine camera ['sini'kæmərə] s. cinepresa f.
cinema ['sinimə] s. cinema m. inv.
cinematographic [,sini,mætə'græfik] agg. cinematografico
cinerary ['sinərəri] agg. cinerario
cinnabar ['sinəbɑ:*] s. cinabro m.
cinnamon ['sinəmən] s. cannella f.
circle ['sə:kl] s. cerchio m., circolo m.; galleria f. (teatro); circuito m.
to circle [sə:kl] v. tr. circondare; aggirare
circuit ['sə:kit] s. circuito m., giro m.
circuitous [s,(:)'kju:itəs] agg. tortuoso
circular ['sə:kjulə*] agg. circolare
to circulate ['sə:kjuleit] v. intr. circolare; diffondersi • v. tr. far circolare
circulation [,sə:kju'leiʃən] s. circolazione f.; diffusione f.
circumcision [,sə:kəm'siʒən] s. circoncisione f.
circumference [sə'kʌmfərəns] s. circonferenza f. (geom.)
to circumscribe ['sə:kəmskraib] v. tr. circoscrivere
circumstance ['sə:kəmstəns] s. circostanza f.
circus ['sə:kəs] s. circo m.
Cistercian [sis'tə:fjən] agg. cistercense
citadel ['sitədl] s. cittadella f.
citation [sai'teiʃən] s. citazione f.
to cite [sait] v. tr. citare

citizen ['sitizn] s. cittadino m.
citizenship ['sitiznʃip] s. cittadinanza f.
citron ['sitrən] s. cedro m.
city ['siti] s. città f. • agg. cittadino, urbano; – planner urbanista; – planning urbanistica
civic ['sivik] agg. civico
civil ['sivl] agg. civile; – servant impiegato statale; – service amministrazione civile
civility [si'viliti] s. civiltà f., educazione f.
civilization [,sivilai'zeiʃən] s. civiltà f., civilizzazione f.
claim [kleim] s. pretesa f.; reclamo m.
to claim [kleim] v. tr. pretendere; reclamare; rivendicare; sostenere
clam [klæm] s. mollusco m. (bivalve)
clamorous ['klæmərəs] agg. clamoroso
clamour ['klæmə*] s. clamore m.
to clamour ['klæmə*] v. intr. strepitare
clamp [klæmp] s. morsetto m.
clandestine [klæn'destin] s. clandestino m.
to clarify ['klærifai] v. tr. chiarire
clarinet [,klæri'net] s. clarinetto m.
clarity ['klæriti] s. chiarezza f.
clash [klæʃ] s. scontro m.
to clash [klæʃ] v. intr. scontrarsi
clasp [klɑ:sp] s. fermaglio m.
to clasp [klɑ:sp] v. tr. stringere, serrare
class [klɑ:s] s. classe f.; first – prima classe; middle – ceto medio
classic ['klæsik] agg. classico
classicism ['klæsisizəm] s. classicismo m.
classicist ['klæsisist] s. classicista m. e f.
classification [,klæsifi'keiʃən] s. classifica f., graduatoria f.
to classify ['klæsifai] v. tr. classificare
classroom ['klɑ:srum] s. aula f.
clause [klɔ:z] s. clausola f.
claustrophobia [,klɔ:strə'foubjə] s. claustrofobia f.
clavicle ['klævikl] s. clavicola f.
claw [klɔ:] s. artiglio m.; unghia f.; zampa f.
clay [klei] s. argilla f., creta f.
clean [kli:n] agg. pulito; netto • avv. completamente
to clean [kli:n] v. tr. pulire
cleaner ['kli:nə*] s. addetto m. alle pulizie
cleaning ['kli:niŋ] s. pulizia f.
cleansing ['klenziŋ] agg. detergente
clear [kliə*] agg. chiaro; limpido, nitido; palese; sgombro
to clear [kliə*] v. tr. e intr. chiarire; schiarire; discolpare; sdoganare; liberare; togliere
clearing ['kliəriŋ] s. radura f.

clearly ['kliəli] *avv.* chiaramente

clearness ['kliənis] *s.* limpidezza *f.*

cleft [kleft] *s.* crepaccio *m.*; fessura *f.*

to clench [klentʃ] *v. tr.* stringere, serrare

clepsydra ['klepsidrə] *s.* clessidra *f.*

clergy ['klə:dʒi] *s.* clero *m.*

clergyman ['klə:dʒimən] *s.* prete *m.*

cleric ['klerik] *s.* chierico *m.*

clerical ['klerikl] *agg.* clericale, ecclesiastico

clerk [kla:k] *s.* impiegato *m.* (di banca)

clever ['klevə*] *agg.* bravo, abile, intelligente

cleverness [klevənis] *s.* ingegnosità *f.*, abilità *f.*; intelligenza *f.*

click [klik] *s.* scatto *m.*

client ['klaiənt] *s.* cliente *m. e f.*

cliff [klif] *s.* falesia *f.*; rupe *f.*; scogliera *f.*

climate ['klaimit] *s.* clima *m.*

climatic [klai'mætik] *agg.* climatico

climax ['klaimæks] *s.* culmine *m.*

climb [klaim] *s.* salita *f.*, arrampicata *f.*

to climb [klaim] *v. tr. e intr.* arrampicarsi, scalare; salire

climber ['klaimə*] *s.* rampicante *m.*; scalatore *m.*, arrampicatore *m.*

climbing ['klaimiŋ] *agg.* rampicante

clinging ['kliŋiŋ] *agg.* attillato; appiccicoso (persona)

clinic ['klinik] *s.* clinica *f.*

clinical ['klinikəl] *agg.* clinico

clip [klip] *s.* fermaglio *m.*

to clip [klip] *v. tr.* tagliare; tosare

clique [kli:k] *s.* conventicola *f.*

cloak [klouk] *s.* mantello *m.*; – **room** guardaroba

clock [klɔk] *s.* orologio *m.*; **alarm** – sveglia

clog [klɔg] *s.* zoccolo *m.*

to clog [klɔg] *v. tr.* inceppare; impedire; ostruire • *intr.* intasarsi, otturarsi

cloister ['klɔistə*] *s.* chiostro *m.*

close [klous] *agg.* chiuso, serrato; nascosto; afoso; intimo • *avv.* vicino

to close [klouz] *v. tr.* chiudere • *intr.* chiudersi; finire; – **up** ostruire, serrare; **closing time** ora di chiusura

closet ['klɔzit] *s.* stanzino *m.*, bugigattolo *m.*; armadio *m.*

clot [klɔt] *s.* grumo *m.*, coagulo *m.*

cloth [klɔθ] *s.* stoffa *f.*, tela *f.*; straccio *m.*, strofinaccio *m.*

clothes [klouðz] *s. pl.* abbigliamento *m. sing.*; vestiti *m.*; biancheria *f. sing.*; – **hook** attaccapanni, – **peg** molletta per panni

clothing ['klouðiŋ] *s.* abbigliamento *m.*; vestiario *m.*

cloud [klaud] *s.* nube *f.*, nuvola *f.*; – **burst** nubifragio

to cloud [klaud] *v. intr.* annuvolarsi

cloudy ['klaudi] *agg.* nuvoloso

clove [klouv] *s.* chiodo *m.* di garofano; – **of garlic** spicchio d'aglio

clown [klaun] *s.* pagliaccio *m.*

club [clʌb] *s.* mazza *f.*, randello *m.*; circolo *m.*, associazione *f.*; **clubs** fiori (carte)

clue [klu:] *s.* indizio *m.*

clumsy ['klʌmzi] *agg.* goffo, maldestro

cluster ['klʌstə*] *s.* grappolo *m.*

clutch [klʌtʃ] *s.* frizione *f.* (*mecc.*)

to clutch [klʌtʃ] *v. tr.* afferrare

coach [koutʃ] *s.* carrozza *f.*; corriera *f.*, pullmann *m.*; vagone *m.*; vettura *f.*; allenatore *m.*

coagulant [kou'ægjulant] *s.* coagulante *m.*

coal [koul] *s.* carbone *m.*

coalition [kouə'liʃən] *s.* coalizione *f.*

coarse [kɔ:s] *agg.* grossolano

coast [koust] *s.* costa *f.*; litorale *m.*

to coast [koust] *v. intr.* costeggiare

coat [kout] *s.* giacca *f.*; mantello *m.*; rivestimento *m.*; **overcoat** cappotto; – **of arms** stemma

to coat [kout] *v. tr.* rivestire

coating ['koutiŋ] *s.* rivestimento *m.*

coauthor [kou'ɔ:θə*] *s.* coautore *m.*

cob [kɔb] *s.* pannocchia *f.*

cobble ['kɔbl] *s.* ciottolo *m.*; **cobbled paving** acciottolato

cock [kɔk] *s.* gallo *m.*

cockpit ['kɔkpit] *s.* abitacolo *m.*; cabina *f.* di pilotaggio; pozzetto *m.* (*naut.*)

cockroach ['kɔkroutʃ] *s.* scarafaggio *m.*

coconut ['koukounʌt] *s.* cocco *m.*

cod [kɔd] *s.* merluzzo *m.*

code [koud] *s.* codice *m.*; prefisso *m.*; **dialling** – prefisso telefonico

codification [ˌkɔdifi'keiʃən] *s.* codifica *f.*

coefficient [koui'fisənt] *s.* coefficiente *m.*

to coerce [kou'ə:s] *v. tr.* costringere

coeval [kou'i:vəl] *agg.* coevo

coexistent [kouig'zistənt] *agg.* coesistente

coffee ['kɔfi] *s.* caffè *m.*; – **cup** tazzina; **weak** – caffè lungo; **black** – caffè nero; **strong** – caffè ristretto; **instant** – caffè solubile

coffer ['kɔfə*] *s.* cofano *m.*, forziere *m.*, scrigno *m.*; cassettone *m.* (soffitto)

to cohabit [kou'hæbit] *v. intr.* convivere

cohabitation [ˌkouhæbi'teiʃən] s. coabitazione f.

to cohere [kou'hiə•] v. tr. aderire

coherent [kou'hiərənt] agg. coerente

coil [koil] s. rotolo m.; spirale f.

coin [koin] s. moneta f.

to coin [koin] v. tr. coniare

to coincide ['kouin'said] v. intr. coincidere; concordare

coincidence [kou'insidəns] s. coincidenza f., combinazione f.

to collaborate [kə'læbəreit] v. intr. cooperare, collaborare

collaboration [kəˌlæbə'reʃən] s. collaborazione f.

collaborator [kə'læbəreitə•] s. collaboratore m.

colander ['kʌləndə•] s. scolapasta m. inv.

cold [kould] agg. freddo • s. freddo m., gelo m.; raffreddore m.

coldly ['kouldli] avv. freddamente

colic ['kɔlik] s. colica f.

collapse [kə'læps] s. collasso m.; crollo m.

to collapse [kə'læps] v. intr. crollare, franare

collar ['kɔlə•] s. colletto m.

colleague ['kɔli:g] s. collega m. e f.

to collect [kə'lekt] v. tr. raccogliere; collezionare; riscuotere; ritirare

collection [kə'lekʃən] s. collezione f., raccolta f.; collana f.; colletta f.

collective [kə'lektiv] agg. collettivo • **collectively** collettivamente

collectivity [ˌkɔlek'tiviti] s. collettività f.

collector [kə'lektə•] s. collezionista m. e f.

college [kɔlidʒ] s. istituto m., scuola f. secondaria privata

to collide [kə'laid] v. intr. urtare; scontrarsi

collision [kə'liʒən] s. collisione f.; scontro m.; conflitto m.

colon [koulən] s. due punti m. pl. (punteggiatura); colon m.; **semi-** punto e virgola

colonial [kə'lounjəl] agg. coloniale

colonialist [kə'lounjalist] s. colonialista m. e f. • agg. colonialistico

to colonize ['kɔlənaiz] v. tr. colonizzare

colonnade [ˌkɔlə'neid] s. colonnato m.; porticato m.

colony ['kɔləni] s. colonia f.

colour ['kʌlə•] s. colore m.; - **blind** daltonico

coloured ['kʌləd] agg. colorato; di colore (detto di persona)

colourful ['kʌləful] agg. colorato; colorito, pittoresco

colt [koult] s. puledro m.

column ['kɔləm] s. colonna f.; rubrica f.

coma ['koumə] s. coma m. inv.

comb [koum] s. pettine m.

to comb [koum] v. tr. pettinare

combat ['kɔmbæt] s. combattimento m.

combination [ˌkɔmbi'neiʃən] s. combinazione f.; associazione f.

to combine [kəm'bain] v. tr. combinare; associare

to come [kʌm] v. intr. venire, giungere; provenire; - **back** ritornare; - **down** scendere; - **in** entrare; - **from** derivare; - **out** uscire, risultare; - **to** arrivare

comedian [kə'mi:djən] s. comico m.

comedy ['kɔmidi] s. commedia f.

comet ['kɔmit] s. cometa f.

comfort ['kʌmfət] s. comodità f.; conforto m., consolazione f.

to comfort ['kʌmfət] v. tr. consolare, confortare

comfortable ['kʌmfətəbl] agg. confortevole, accogliente

comforting ['kʌmfətiŋ] agg. confortevole

comic ['kɔmik] agg. e s. comico m.; **comics** fumetti

comicality [ˌkɔmi'kæliti] s. comicità f.

coming ['kʌmiŋ] s. arrivo m. • agg. prossimo; - **and going** viavai

comma ['kɔmə] s. virgola f.

command [kə'ma:nd] s. comando m.; padronanza f.

to command [kə'ma:nd] v. tr. e intr. comandare

commander [kə'ma:ndə•] s. comandante m.

to commemorate [kə'meməreit] v. tr. commemorare

commemoration [kəˌmemə'reiʃən] s. commemorazione f.

to commend [kə'mend] v. tr. lodare; raccomandare

comment ['kɔment] s. commento m.

commentary ['kɔmentəri] s. commento m.

commentator ['kɔmenteitə•] s. commentatore m.

commercial [kə'mə:ʃəl] agg. commerciale • s. annuncio m. pubblicitario

to commiserate [kə'mizəreit] v. tr. commiserare

commission [kə'miʃən] s. commissione f.

to commit [kə'mit] v. tr. commettere; affidare

commitment [kə'mitmənt] s. impegno m.; affidamento m.

committee [kə'miti] *s.* comitato *m.*, commissione *f.*

common ['kɔmən] *agg.* comune, normale, generale, condiviso

commonly ['kɔmənli] *avv.* comunemente

commonplace ['kɔmənpleis] *agg.* banale • *s.* luogo *m.* comune

to communicate [kə'mju:nikeit] *v. tr. e intr.* comunicare

communication [kə,mju:ni'keiʃən] *s.* comunicazione *f.*

communism ['kɔmjunizəm] *s.* comunismo *m.*

community [kə'mju:niti] *s.* collettività *f.*, comunità *f.*

commuter [kə'mju:(:)tə*] *s.* pendolare *m. e f.*

compact [kəm'pækt] *agg.* compatto • *s.* utilitaria *f.*

companion [kəm'pænjən] *s.* compagno *m.*

company ['kʌmpəni] *s.* compagnia *f.*; società *f.*; **insurance –** compagnia d'assicurazioni

comparable ['kɔmpərəbl] *agg.* comparabile, paragonabile

comparative [kəm'pærətiv] *agg.* comparativo

to compare [kəm'pɛə*] *v. tr.* confrontare, paragonare

comparison [kəm'pærisn] *s.* paragone *m.*

compartment [kəm'pa:tmənt] *s.* compartimento *m.*; scomparto *m.*

compass ['kʌmpəs] *s.* compasso *m.*; bussola *f.*

compassion [kəm'pæʃən] *s.* pietà *f.*

compatible [kəm'pætəbl] *agg.* compatibile; **compatibly** compatibilmente

to compel [kəm'pel] *v. tr.* costringere, forzare, obbligare

to compensate ['kɔmpenseit] *v. tr.* compensare

compensation [,kɔmpen'seiʃən] *s.* compensazione *f.*; risarcimento *m.*

to compete [kəm'pi:t] *v. intr.* competere; gareggiare

competence ['kɔmpitəns] *s.* competenza *f.*

competent ['kɔmpitənt] *agg.* competente

competition [,kɔmpi'tiʃən] *s.* competizione *f.*; concorrenza *f.*; concorso *m.*

competitive [kəm'petitiv] *agg.* competitivo; agonistico

competitiveness [kəm'petitivnis] *s.* competitività *f.*

competitor [kəm'petitə*] *s.* concorrente *m. e f.*

compilation [,kɔmpi'leiʃən] *s.* compilazione *f.*

to compile [kəm'pail] *v. tr.* redigere; compilare

to complain [kəm'plein] *v. intr.* lagnarsi, lamentarsi

complaint [kəm'pleint] *s.* lagnanza *f.*, lamentela *f.*, protesta *f.*; accusa *f.*; **to make a –** reclamare

complement ['kɔmplimənt] *s.* complemento *m.*

complementary [,kɔmplimentəri] *agg.* complementare

complete [kəm'pli:t] *agg.* completo

to complete [kəm'pli:t] *v. tr.* ultimare

completion [kəm'pli:ʃən] *s.* completamento *m.*, ultimazione *f.*

complex ['kɔmpleks] *agg. e s.* complesso *m.*

complexion [kəm'plekʃən] *s.* carnagione *f.*; colorito *m.*

complexity [kɔm'pleksiti] *s.* complessità *f.*

compliance [kəm'plaiəns] *s.* condiscendenza *f.*; sottomissione *f.*

to complicate ['kɔmplikeit] *v. tr.* complicare

complicated ['kɔmplikeitid] *agg.* complicato

compliment ['kɔmplimənt] *s.* complimento *m.*; **to pay a –** fare un complimento

complimentary [,kɔmpli'mentəri] *agg.* favorevole; complimentoso; gratuito

component [kəm'pounənt] *agg. e s.* componente *m. e f.*

to compose [kəm'pouz] *v. tr.* comporre; calmare

composer [k,m'pouzə*] *s.* compositore *m.*

composite ['kɔmpəzit] *agg.* composito

composition [,kɔmpə'ziʃən] *s.* componimento *m.*, composizione *f.*

compound [kəm'paund] *s.* miscuglio *m.*, composto *m.*; recinto *m.*

comprehension [,kɔmpri'henʃən] *s.* comprensione *f.*

comprehensive [,kɔmpri'hensiv] *agg.* complessivo; comprensivo

compress [kɔm'pres] *s.* impacco *m.*

to compress [kəm'pres] *v. tr.* comprimere

compressor [kəm'presə*] *s.* compressore *m.*

to comprise [kəm'praiz] *v. tr.* comprendere

compromise ['kɔmprəmaiz] *s.* compromesso *m.*

to compromise [kɔmprəmaiz] *v. tr.* compromettere

compulsory [kəm'pʌlsəri] *agg.* obbligatorio

to compute [kəm'pju:t] *v. tr.* calcolare

comrade ['kɔmrid] *s.* compagno *m.*, collega *m. e f.*; camerata *m.*

comradely ['kɔmridli] *agg.* cameratesco

concatenation [kɔn,kæti'neiʃən] *s.* concatenazione *f.*

concave ['kɔn'keiv] *agg.* concavo

to conceal [kən'si:l] *v. tr.* nascondere

to concede [kən'si:d] *v. tr.* concedere

conceit [kən'si:t] *s.* superbia *f.*

conceited [kən'si:tid] *agg.* presuntuoso

conceivable [kən'si:vəbl] *agg.* concepibile

to conceive [kən'si:v] *v. tr.* concepire; ideare

to concentrate ['kɔnsentreit] *v. tr. e intr.* concentrare, concentrarsi

concentration [,kɔnsen'treʃən] *s.* concentrazione *f.*

concentric [kɔn'sentrik] *agg.* concentrico

concept ['kɔnsept] *s.* concetto *m.*

conception [kən'sepʃən] *s.* concetto *m.*

conceptual [kən'septjuəl] *agg.* concettuale

concern [kən'sə:n] *s.* affare *m.*; ansietà *f.*

to concern [kən'sə:n] *v. tr.* concernere, riguardare

concert ['kɔnsət] *s.* concerto *m.*

concession [kən'seʃən] *s.* concessione *f.*

concessionaire [kən,seʃə'neə*] *s.* concessionario *m.*

conch [kɔŋk] *s.* conchiglia *f.*

to conciliate [kən'silieit] *v. tr.* conciliare

concise [kən'sais] *agg.* conciso, sintetico

to conclude [kən'klu:d] *v. tr.* concludere

conclusion [kən'klu:ʒən] *s.* conclusione *f.*

concomitant [kən'kɔmitənt] *agg.* concomitante; – **factors** fattori concomitanti

concrete ['kɔnkri:t] *agg.* concreto • *s.* calcestruzzo *m.*

concreteness [kən'kri:tnis] *s.* concretezza *f.*

to concur [kən'kə:*] *v. intr.* concorrere

to condemn [kən'dem] *v. tr.* condannare

condemnation [,kɔndem'neiʃən] *s.* condanna *f.*; – **by default** condanna in contumacia

condensation [,kɔnden'seiʃən] *s.* condensazione *f.*

to condense [kən'dens] *v. tr.* condensare

condescension [,kɔndi'senʃən] *s.* condiscendenza *f.*

condiment ['kɔndimənt] *s.* condimento *m.*

condition [kən'diʃən] *s.* condizione *f.*; **on – that** a condizione che

conditional [kən'diʃənl] *agg.* condizionale

conditioning [kən'diʃəniŋ] *s.* condizionamento *m.*

condolence [kən'douləns] *s.* condoglianze *f. pl.*

condom ['kɔndəm] *s.* preservativo *m.*

condominium ['kɔndə'miniəm] *s.* condominio *m.*; appartamento *m.* (USA)

to condone [kən'doun] *v. tr.* condonare

conduct ['kɔndʌkt] *s.* condotta *f.*; procedimento *m.*

conductor [kən'dʌktə*] *s.* direttore *m.*; bigliettaio *m.*; controllore *m.*

conduit [kən'dit] *s.* condotto *m.*, tubazione *f.*; passaggio *m.*

cone [koun] *s.* cono *m.*

confectionery [kən'fekʃnəri] *s.* confetteria *f.*, pasticceria *f.*

confederation [kən,fedə'reiʃən] *s.* confederazione *f.*

to confer [kən'fə:*] *v. tr.* conferire; – **with** consultarsi con

conference ['kɔnfərəns] *s.* rapporto *m.*; conferenza *f.*

to confess [kən'fes] *v. tr.* confessare

confessional [kən'feʃənl] *agg. e s.* confessionale *m.*

to confide [kən'faid] *v. tr. e intr.* confidare

confidence ['kɔnfidəns] *s.* fiducia *f.*; familiarità *f.*; **no-confidence** sfiducia (in politica)

confidential [,kɔnfi'denʃəl] *agg.* confidenziale, riservato

to confine [kən'fain] *v. tr.* confinare, limitare; imprigionare

confinement [kən'fainmənt] *s.* confino *m.*; prigionia *f.*

to confirm [kən'fə:m] *v. tr.* confermare, ribadire; cresimare

confirmation [,kɔnfə'meiʃən] *s.* conferma *f.*; cresima *f.*

confiscable [kən'fiskəbl] *agg.* sequestrabile

to confiscate ['kɔnfiskeit] *v. tr.* sequestrare

confiscation [,kɔnfis'keiʃən] *s.* confisca *f.*; sequestro *m.* di beni

conflict ['kɔnflikt] *s.* conflitto *m.*

confluence ['kɔnfluəns] *s.* confluenza *f.*

to conform [kən'fɔ:m] *v. tr.* adeguare, adeguarsi, conformarsi

conformism [kən'fɔ:mizəm] *s.* conformismo *m.*

to confront [kən'frʌnt] *v. tr.* affrontare; paragonare

to confuse [kən'fju:z] *v. tr.* confondere; **to get confused** confondersi

confusion [kən'fju:ʒən] *s.* confusione *f.*

to confute [kən'fju:t] *v. tr.* confutare

to congeal [kən'dʒi:l] *v. tr. e intr.* gelare; coagulare

to congest [kən'dʒest] *v. tr.* congestionare; congestionarsi

congestion [kən'dʒestʃən] *s.* congestione *f.*

to conglobate ['kɔŋgloubeit] *v. tr.* conglobare

conglomerate [kən'glɔmərit] *agg. e s.* conglomerato *m.*

to congratulate [kən'grætjuleit] *v. tr.* congratularsi, felicitarsi, complimentarsi

congratulations [kən,grætju'leiʃənz] *s. pl.* congratulazioni *f.*, felicitazioni *f.*

congregation [,kɔŋgri'geiʃən] *s.* congregazione *f.*

congress ['kɔŋgres] *s.* congresso *m.*

congruency ['kɔŋgruənsi] *s.* congruenza *f.*

conical ['kɔnikəl] *agg.* conico

conifer ['kounifə] *s.* conifera *f.*

conjecture [kən'dʒektʃə*] *s.* congettura *f.*

conjugate ['kɔndʒugit] *agg.* coniugato

to conjugate ['kɔndʒugeit] *v. tr.* coniugare

conjunctivitis [kən,dʒʌŋkti'vaitis] *s.* congiuntivite *f.*

conjurer ['kʌndʒərə*] *s.* prestigiatore *m.*

to connect [kə'nekt] *v. tr.* connettere, collegare ● *intr.* collegarsi

connected [kə'nektid] *agg.* connesso, collegato; imparentato

connection [kə'nekʃən] *s.* collegamento *m.*, connessione *f.*; contatto *m.* (*elettr.*); coincidenza *f.*; raccordo *m.*

connoisseur [,kɔni'sə:*] *s.* conoscitore *m.*, intenditore *m.*

to conquer ['kɔŋkə*] *v. tr.* conquistare

conquest ['kɔŋkwest] *s.* conquista *f.*

conscience ['kɔnʃəns] *s.* coscienza *f.*

conscious ['kɔnʃəs] *agg.* cosciente, consapevole

to consecrate ['kɔnsikreit] *v. tr.* consacrare

consecutive [kən'sekjutiv] *agg.* consecutivo

consent [kən'sent] *s.* consenso *m.*

to consent [kən'sent] *v. intr.* acconsentire

consequence ['kɔnsikwəns] *s.* conseguenza *f.*, conclusione *f.*

consequent ['kɔnsikwənt] *agg.* conseguente

conservative [kən'sə:vətiv] *agg.* conservatore

conservatory [kən'sə:vətri] *s.* conservatorio *m.*; serra *f.*

to consider [kən'sidə*] *v. tr.* considerare

considerable [kən'sidərəbl] *agg.* considerevole

considerate [kən'sidərit] *agg.* premuroso

consideration [kən,sidə'reiʃən] *s.* considerazione *f.*, riflessione *f.*

considering [kən'sidəriŋ] *prep.* in considerazione di, tenendo conto di, in vista di ● *cong.* considerato che

to consist of [kən'sist ɔv, əv] *v. intr.* consistere, constare

consistent [kən'sistənt] *agg.* coerente

consolation [,kɔnsə'leiʃən] *s.* consolazione *f.*

console ['kɔnsoul] *s.* mensola *f.* (*arch.*); quadro *m.* di comando

to console [kən'soul] *v. tr.* consolare

to consolidate [kən'sɔlideit] *v. tr. e intr.* consolidare

consolidation [kən,sɔli'deiʃən] *s.* consolidamento *m.*

consonant ['kɔnsənənt] *s.* consonante *f.*

consort ['kɔnsɔ:t] *s.* coniuge *m. e f.*, consorte *m. e f.*

conspicuous [kən'spikjuəs] *agg.* cospicuo

conspiracy [kən'spirəsi] *s.* cospirazione *f.*, congiura *f.*

conspirator [kən'spirətə*] *s.* cospiratore *m.*

constable ['kʌnstəbl] *s.* agente *m.* di polizia; conestabile *m.*, governatore *m.* (*stor.*)

constabulary [kən'stæbjulari] *s.* corpo *m.* di polizia

constant ['kɔnstənt] *agg. e s.* costante *f.*

constellation [,kɔnstə'leiʃən] *s.* costellazione *f.*

constipated ['kɔnstipeitid] *agg.* stitico

constipation [,kɔnsti'peiʃən] *s.* costipazione *f.*, stitichezza *f.*

constituency [kən'stitjuansi] *s.* collegio *m.* elettorale

constituent [kən'stitjuənt] *agg.* costituente *f.*

to constitute ['kɔnstitju:t] *v. tr.* costituire

constitution [,kɔnsti'tju:ʃən] *s.* costituzione *f.*

constitutional [,kɔnsti'tju:ʃənl] *agg.* costituzionale

to constrain [kən'strein] *v. tr.* costringere

constraint [kən'streint] *s.* costrizione *f.*

to constrict [kən'strikt] *v. tr.* restringere

constriction [kən'strikʃən] *s.* costrizione *f.*; oppressione *f.*

to construct [kən'strʌkt] *v. tr.* costruire, edificare

construction [kən'strʌkʃən] *s.* costruzione *f.*

consul ['kɔnsəl] *s.* console *m.*

consulate ['kɔnsjulit] *s.* consolato *m.*

to consult [kən'sʌlt] *v. tr.* consultare ● *intr.* consultarsi

consultant [kən'sʌltənt] *s.* consulente *m.*

to consume [kən'sju:m] *v. tr.* consumare ● *intr.* consumarsi

consumer [kən'sju:mə*] *s.* utente *m. e f.*; consumatore *m.*

consummation [,kɔnsʌ'meiʃən] *s.* completamento *m.*

consumption [kən'sʌmpʃən] *s.* consumo *m.*

contact ['kɔntækt] *s.* contatto *m.*

contagion [kən'teidʒən] *s.* contagio *m.*

contagious [kən'teidʒəs] *agg.* contagioso

to contain [kən'tein] *v. tr.* contenere; racchiudere

container [kən'teinə*] *s.* contenitore *m.*, recipiente *m.*

to contaminate [kən'tæmineit] *v. tr.* contaminare

contamination [kən'tæmi'neiʃən] *s.* contaminazione *f.*

to contemplate ['kɔntempleit] *v. tr.* contemplare

contemplative [kən'templətiv] *agg.* contemplativo

contemporary [kən'tempərəri] *agg.* contemporaneo • *s.* coetaneo *m.*

contempt [kən'tempt] *s.* disprezzo *m.*; vilipendio *m.*

to contend [kən'tend] *v. tr. e intr.* contendere; discutere

contender [kən'tendə*] *s.* contendente *m. e f.*

content ['kɔntent] *s.* contenuto *m.*; **table of contents** indice (di libro)

contention [kən'tenʃən] *s.* contesa *f.*; controversia *f.*; discordia *f.*

contest ['kɔntest] *s.* competizione *f.*; concorso *m.*; controversia *f.*

to contest [kən'test] *v. tr.* contestare; impugnare (leg.)

continent ['kɔntinənt] *s.* continente *m.*

continental [,kɔnti'nentl] *agg.* continentale

contingency [kən'tindʒənsi] *agg.* contingenza *f.*, circostanza *f.*

continual [kən'tinjuəl] *agg.* continuo

continually [kən'tinjuəli] *avv.* continuamente

continuation [kən,tinju'eiʃən] *s.* continuazione *f.*

to continue [kən'tinju(:)] *v. tr. e intr.* continuare, proseguire

continuous [kən'tinjuəs] *agg.* continuo; **continuously** continuamente

contortion [kən'tɔ:ʃən] *s.* contorcimento *m.*, contorsione *f.*

contour ['kɔntuə*] *s.* contorno *m.*

contraceptive [,kɔntrə'septiv] *agg. e s.* contraccettivo *m.*

contract ['kɔntrækt] *s.* contratto *m.*

to contract [kən'trækt] *v. tr.* contrarre

contraction [kən'trækʃən] *s.* contrazione *f.*

contractor [kən'træktə*] *s.* contraente *m. e f.*; appaltatore *m.*

to contradict [,kɔntrə'dikt] *v. tr. e intr.* contraddire; – **oneself** contraddirsi

contradiction [,kɔntrə'dikʃən] *s.* contraddizione *f.*

contraindication ['kɔntrə,indi'keiʃən] *s.* controindicazione *f.*

contraposition [,kɔntrəpə'ziʃən] *s.* contrapposizione *f.*

contrary ['kɔntrəri] *agg. e s.* contrario *m.*, opposto *m.*; **on the** – al contrario; – **to** contrariamente a

contrast ['kɔntræst] *s.* contrasto *m.*

to contrast [kən'træst] *v. tr.* contrastare

contravention [,kɔntrə'venʃən] *s.* contravvenzione *f.*

to contribute [kən'tribjut] *v. intr.* contribuire

contribution [,kɔntri'bju:ʃən] *s.* contributo *m.*; collaborazione *f.*

contrivance [kən'traivəns] *s.* espediente *m.*; congegno *m.*

to contrive [kən'traiv] *v. tr.* escogitare • *intr.* ingegnarsi

control [kən'troul] *s.* controllo *m.*

to control [kən'troul] *v. tr.* controllare

controller [kən'troulə*] *s.* controllore *m.*

controversy ['kɔntrəvə:si] *s.* controversia *f.*; vertenza *f.*

convalescence [,kɔnvə'lesns] *s.* convalescenza *f.*

convalescent [,kɔnvə'lesnt] *agg. e s.* convalescente *m. e f.*

convection [kən'vekʃən] *s.* convezione *f.*

convenience [kən'vi:njəns] *s.* comodità *f.*; convenienza *f.*

convenient [kən'vi:njənt] *agg.* conveniente, comodo

convent ['kɔnvənt] *s.* convento *m.*

convention [kən'venʃən] *s.* convenzione *f.*; convegno *m.*

conventional [kən'venʃənl] *agg.* convenzionale, comune

to converge [kən've:dʒ] *v. intr.* convergere, confluire

convergence [kən've:dʒəns] *s.* convergenza *f.*

conversation [,kɔnvə'seiʃən] *s.* conversazione *f.*; discorso *m.*

conversational [,kɔnvə'seiʃənl] *agg.* discorsivo

conversely [kən'və:sli] *avv.* invece, al contrario, per converso

conversion [kən'və:ʃən] *s.* conversione *f.*

to convert [kən'və:t] *v. tr.* convertire

convex ['kɔn'veks] *agg.* convesso

to convey [kən'vei] *v. tr.* trasmettere; trasportare

conveyance [kən'veiəns] *s.* trasporto *m.*

conveyor [kən'veiə*] s. trasportatore m.

convict ['kɔnvikt] s. condannato m.; detenuto m.

to convict [kən'vikt] v. tr. condannare

conviction [kən'vikʃən] s. convinzione f.; condanna f.

to convince [kən'vins] v. tr. convincere

convocation [ˌkɔnvə'keiʃən] s. convocazione f.

convoy ['kɔnvɔi] s. scorta f., convoglio m.

convulsion [kən'vʌlʃən] s. convulsione f.

cook [kuk] s. cuoco m., cuoca f.; – book ricettario

to cook [kuk] v. tr. e intr. cucinare; cuocere

cooker ['kukə*] s. fornello m.; cucina f.; pressure – pentola a pressione

cookery ['kukəri] s. cucina f. (gastronomia)

cookie ['kuki] s. biscotto m. (USA)

cooking ['kukiŋ] s. cottura f.; cucina f. (gastronomia)

cool [ku:l] agg. freddo; fresco; compassato

to cool [ku:l] v. tr. raffreddare; – down raffreddarsi; cool it! calma! (USA)

coolness ['ku:lnis] s. fresco m.

to cooperate [kou'ɔpəreit] v. intr. collaborare

cooperation [kouˌɔpə'reiʃən] s. collaborazione f., cooperazione f.

cooperative [kou'ɔpərətiv] s. cooperativa f.

coordination [kouˌɔːdi'neiʃən] s. coordinazione f., coordinamento m.

coordinator [kou'ɔːdineitə*] s. coordinatore m.

to cope (with) [koup] v. intr. tener testa, far fronte

copper ['kɔpə*] s. rame m.

coppice ['kɔpis] s. bosco m. ceduo

copse [kɔps] s. macchia f.

copy ['kɔpi] s. copia f.; – book quaderno

to copy ['kɔpi] v. tr. e intr. copiare; imitare; riprodurre

coral ['kɔrəl] s. corallo m. • agg. corallino

cord [kɔːd] s. corda f.

cordial ['kɔːdjəl] agg. cordiale

cordiality [ˌkɔːdi'æliti] s. cordialità f.

core [kɔː*] s. nucleo m., centro m.; torsolo m.

coriaceous [ˌkɔri'eiʃəs] agg. coriaceo

Corinthian [kə'riθiən] agg. corinzio

cork [kɔːk] s. sughero m.; tappo m.; – screw cavatappi

to cork [kɔːk] v. tr. tappare, turare

cormorant ['kɔːmərənt] s. cormorano m.

corn [kɔːn] s. cereale m.; grano m.; mais m. • callo m.; – cob pannocchia

to corn [kɔːn] v. tr. conservare (salare)

cornea ['kɔːniə] s. cornea f.

corner ['kɔːnə*] s. angolo m.; spigolo m.

to corner ['kɔːnə*] v. intr. curvare (autom.) • tr. imboscare; mettere alle strette, mettere in un angolo

cornet ['kɔːnit] s. cartoccio m.

cornice ['kɔːnis] s. cornicione m.

cornucopia [ˌkɔːnju'koupjə] s. cornucopia f.

corolla [kə'rɔlə] s. corolla f.

coronation [ˌkɔrə'neiʃən] s. incoronazione f.

corporal ['kɔːpərəl] agg. corporale • s. caporale m. (mil.)

corporation [ˌkɔːpə'reiʃən] s. compagnia f. (fin.), società f.

corpse [kɔːps] s. cadavere m.

corpuscle ['kɔːpʌsl] s. corpuscolo m.

correct [kə'rekt] agg. corretto, giusto; correctly correttamente

to correct [kə'rekt] v. tr. correggere

correction [kə'rekʃən] s. correzione f.

correlation [ˌkɔri'leiʃən] s. correlazione f.

to correspond [ˌkɔris'pɔnd] v. intr. corrispondere; concordare

correspondence [ˌkɔris'pɔndəns] s. corrispondenza f.; carteggio m.

corresponding [ˌkɔris'pɔndiŋ] agg. corrispondente

corridor ['kɔridɔː*] s. corridoio m.

to corroborate [kə'rɔbəreit] v. tr. convalidare

to corrode [kə'roud] v. tr. corrodere

corrosive [kə'rousiv] agg. corrosivo

to corrupt [kə'rʌpt] v. tr. corrompere

corruption [kə'rʌpʃən] s. corruzione f.

corset ['kɔːsit] s. busto m.

cortisone ['kɔːtizoun] s. cortisone m.

corvée ['kɔːvei] s. corvè f. inv.

cosmetic [kɔz'metik] s. cosmetico m.

cosmic ['kɔzmik] agg. cosmico

cosmopolitan [ˌkɔzmə'pɔlitən] agg. cosmopolita

cosmos ['kɔzmɔs] s. cosmo m.

cost [kɔst] s. costo m., prezzo m.

to cost [kɔst] v. intr. costare

costly ['kɔstli] agg. costoso, caro

cosy ['kouzi] agg. accogliente, confortevole

coterie ['koutəri] s. circolo m., gruppo m., cenacolo m.

cottage ['kɔtidʒ] s. casetta f., villetta f.

cotton ['kɔtn] s. cotone m.; – wool cotone idrofilo

cough [kɔf] s. tosse f.

to cough [kɔf] v. intr. tossire

could [kud, kəd] v. dif. potere, essere in grado di, riuscire

council ['kaunsl] s. consiglio m. (in politica)

counsel ['kaunsəl] s. consiglio m.

to counsel ['kaunsəl] v. tr. consigliare

counsellor ['kaunsələ*] s. consigliere m.

count [kaunt] s. conto m., conteggio m.

to count [kaunt] v. tr. e intr. contare; – on fare assegnamento

counter ['kauntə*] s. contatore m.; cassa f.; bancone m.; gettone m.; **telephone** – gettone telefonico

counteract [,kauntə'rækt] v. tr. neutralizzare, contrastare

counterclockwise ['kauntə'klɔkwais] agg. antiorario

countercurrent ['kauntə'kʌrənt] avv. controcorrente

counterfeit ['kauntəfit] s. contraffazione f., falsificazione f.

counterfoil ['kauntəfɔil] s. matrice f.

counterproductive ['kauntəprə,dʌktiv] agg. controproducente

Counter-Reformation ['kauntərefə,meiʃən] s. controriforma f.

to countersign ['kauntəsain] v. tr. controfirmare

countess ['kauntis] s. contessa f.

countless ['kauntlis] agg. innumerevole

country ['kʌntri] s. campagna f.; territorio m.; nazione f.; paese m. • agg. contadino, campestre

countryside ['kʌntri'said] s. campagna f.

county ['kaunti] s. contea f.

couple ['kʌpl] s. coppia f., paio m.

to couple ['kʌpl] v. tr. abbinare

coupon ['ku:pɔn] s. schedina f.; scontrino m.; tagliando m.

courage ['kʌridʒ] s. coraggio m.

courageous [kə'redʒəs] agg. coraggioso

courgette [,kuə'ʒet] s. zucchino m.

courier ['kuriə*] s. corriere m.

course [kɔ:s] s. corso m.; pietanza f., portata f.; **courses** mestruazioni

court [kɔ:t] s. corte f.; tribunale m.; castello m.; – **room** aula di tribunale

to court [kɔ:t] v. tr. corteggiare

courteous ['kə:tjəs] agg. cortese

courtesy ['kə:tisi] s. cortesia f.

courtyard ['kɔ:t'ja:d] s. cortile m.

cousin ['kʌzn] s. cugino m.

cover ['kʌvə*] s. coperchio m.; coperta f.; fodera f.; copertina f.; riparo m.; coperto m.; – **charge** prezzo del coperto; – **girl** fotomodella

to cover ['kʌvə*] v. tr. coprire; ricoprire; rivestire

covering ['kʌvəriŋ] s. rivestimento m.

cow [kau] s. mucca f.; – **house** stalla

coward ['kauəd] agg. vigliacco

cowl [kaul] s. cappuccio m.; cappa f.

cowslip ['kauslip] s. primula f.

coy [kɔi] agg. schivo

crab [kræb] s. granchio m.

crack [kræk] s. schianto m.; crepa f.

to crack [kræk] v. tr. incrinare, schioccare • intr. incrinarsi

cradle ['kreidl] s. culla f.; – **song** ninnananna

craft [kra:ft] s. mestiere m.; abilità f.; imbarcazione f.

craftsman ['kra:ftsmən] s. artigiano m.

crafty ['kra:fti] agg. astuto

crag [kræg] s. picco m.

cramp [kræmp] s. crampo m.

crane [krein] s. gru f.

cranial ['kreinjəl] agg. cranico

cranium ['kreinjəm] s. cranio m.

crank [kræŋk] s. manovella f.

crash [kræʃ] s. fragore m.; scontro m., collisione f.

to crash [kræʃ] v. tr. e intr. rompere; fracassarsi, schiacciarsi

crater ['kreitə*] s. cratere m.

to crave [kreiv] v. tr. desiderare fortemente; scongiurare

craving ['kreiviŋ] s. desiderio m., brama f.

crayfish ['kre-fiʃ] s. gambero m.

crayon ['kreiən] s. matita f. (pastello)

craze [kreiz] s. mania f.

crazy ['kreizi] agg. matto; stravagante; pazzesco

creak [kri:k] s. scricchiolio m.

cream [kri:m] s. panna f.; crema f.; **whipped** – panna montata

creamy ['kri:mi] agg. cremoso

to crease [kri:s] v. tr. stropicciare, spiegazzare

to create [kri:'eit] v. tr. creare

creation [kri:'eiʃən] s. creazione f.

credit ['kredit] s. credito m.

creditor ['kreditə*] s. creditore m.

creed [kri:d] s. credo m.

creek [kri:k] s. insenatura f.; torrente m.

creeper ['kri:pə*] s. rampicante m.

creeping ['kri:piŋ] agg. rampicante

to cremate [kri'meit] v. tr. cremare

cremation [kri'meiʃən] s. cremazione f.

crepuscular [kri'pʌskjulə*] agg. crepuscolare

crescendo [kri'ʃendou] s. crescendo m.

crescent ['kresnt] s. mezzaluna f.

crest [krest] s. cresta f.; crinale m.; insegna f. araldica

crevice ['krevis] s. crepa f.

crew [kru:] s. equipaggio m.

crib [krib] s. presepe m.

cricket ['krikit] s. cricket m. inv. (sport) • grillo m.

crime [kraim] s. crimine m., delitto m.

criminal ['kriminl] agg. e s. criminale m. e f.

to cringe [krindʒ] v. tr. essere servile

cripple ['kripl] s. mutilato m.; zoppo m.

crisis ['kraisis] s. crisi f.

crisp [krisp] agg. croccante

criterion [krai'ti:riən] s. criterio m.

critic ['kritik] s. critico m.

critical ['kritikəl] agg. critico

criticism ['kritisizəm] s. critica f.

criticizable ['kritisaizəbl] agg. criticabile

to criticize ['kritisaiz] v. tr. criticare

crochet ['krouʃei] s. uncinetto m.

crocodile ['krɔkədail] s. coccodrillo m.

crook [kruk] s. uncino m., gancio m.; truffatore m.

crooked ['krukid] agg. storto

crop [krɔp] s. raccolto m.

croquette [krou'ket] s. crocchetta f.

cross [krɔs] s. croce f. • agg. trasversale; arrabbiato

to cross [krɔs] v. tr. attraversare; incrociare

crossbar ['krɔsba:*] s. asticella f.

crossbow ['krɔsbou] s. balestra f.

crossbred ['krɔsbred] s. incrocio m. (di razze)

cross-country ['krɔs'kʌntri] agg. campestre

crossing ['krɔsiŋ] s. attraversamento m.; incrocio m.; traversata f.; – level – passaggio a livello

crossroad ['krɔsroud] s. traversa f.; crocevia m. inv., crocicchio m.

crosswise ['krɔswaiz] avv. attraverso

crossword ['krɔswə:d] s. cruciverba m. inv.

to crouch [krautʃ] v. intr. rannicchiarsi

crouton ['kru:tɔn] s. crostino m.

crow [krou] s. corvo m.

crowd [kraud] s. calca f., folla f., moltitudine f.

crowded ['kraudid] agg. affollato

crowding ['kraudiŋ] s. affollamento m.

crown [kraun] s. corona f.

to crown [kraun] v. tr. incoronare

crucial ['kru:ʃjəl] agg. cruciale, decisivo

cruciate ['kru:ʃieit] agg. cruciforme (bot.)

crucifix ['kru:sifiks] s. crocifisso m.

crucifixion ['kru:si'fikʃən] s. crocifissione f.

cruciform ['kru:sifɔ:m] agg. cruciforme

crude [kru:d] agg. crudo; grezzo, rozzo

cruel [kruəl] agg. crudele

cruelty ['kruəlti] s. crudeltà f.

cruise [kru:z] s. crociera f.

crumb [krʌm] s. briciola f.; mollica f.

to crumb [krʌm] v. tr. sbriciolare; impanare; scuotere la tovaglia (fam.)

to crumble [krʌmbl] v. tr. e intr. sbriciolare, sbriciolarsi

to crumple ['krʌmpl] v. tr. stropicciare

to crunch [krʌntʃ] v. tr. sgranocchiare

crusade [kru:'seid] s. crociata f.

to crush [krʌʃ] v. tr. e intr. schiacciare; stroncare

crust [krʌst] s. crosta f.

crustacean [krʌs'teifjən] s. crostaceo m.

crutch [krʌtʃ] s. gruccia f., stampella f.; biforcazione f.

cry [krai] s. grido m.

to cry [krai] v. tr. e intr. gridare; esclamare; piangere; – down svalutare

crying ['kraiiŋ] s. pianto m.

crypt [kript] s. cripta f.

cryptic ['kriptik] agg. criptico

crystal ['kristl] s. cristallo m.

crystalline ['kristəlain] agg. cristallino

to crystallize ['kristəlaiz] v. tr. cristallizzare

cube [kju:b] s. cubo m.

cubism ['kju:bizəm] s. cubismo m.

cubital ['kju:bitl] agg. cubitale (anat.)

cucumber ['kju:kʌmbə*] s. cetriolo m.

to cuddle ['kʌdl] v. tr. coccolare

cudgel ['kʌdʒəl] s. randello m.

cue [kju:] s. stecca f. (biliardo); attacco m. (teatro)

cuff [kʌf] s. schiaffo m. • polsino m.

to cuff [kʌf] v. tr. schiaffeggiare

culinary ['kʌlinəri] agg. culinario

to culminate ['kʌlmineit] v. intr. culminare

culprit ['kʌlprit] s. colpevole m. e f.

cultivable ['kʌltivəbl] agg. coltivabile

to cultivate ['kʌltiveit] v. tr. coltivare

cultivated ['kʌltiveitid] agg. coltivato; colto

cultivation [‚kʌlti'veifən] s. coltura f.

cultural ['kʌltʃərəl] agg. culturale; colturale

culture ['kʌltʃə*] s. cultura f.; coltura f.

cumbersome ['kʌmbəsəm] agg. ingombrante

cumulus ['kju:mjuləs] s. cumulo m. (meteor.)

cuneiform ['kju:niifɔ:m] agg. cuneiforme

cunning ['kʌniŋ] agg. astuto, furbo

cup [kʌp] *s.* tazza *f.*, tazzina *f.*; **paper** – bicchiere di carta
cupboard ['kʌbəd] *s.* armadio *m.*
curable ['kjuərəbl] *agg.* curabile
cure [kjuə*] *s.* cura *f.*; rimedio *m.*
to cure [kjuə*] *v. tr.* guarire; affumicare, salare • *intr.* conservarsi
curfew ['kə:fju:] *s.* coprifuoco *m.*
curia ['kjuəriə] *s.* curia *f.*
curiosity [,kjuəri'ɔsiti] *s.* curiosità *f.*
curious ['kjuəriəs] *agg.* curioso
curl [kə:l] *s.* riccio *m.*, ricciolo *m.*
to curl [kə:l] *v. tr. e intr.* arricciare, arricciarsi
curler ['kə:lə*] *s.* bigodino *m.*
currency ['kʌrənsi] *s.* valuta *f.*, moneta *f.*
current ['kʌrənt] *agg.* corrente, attuale
curse [kə:s] *s.* maledizione *f.*
to curse [kə:(:)s] *v. intr.* maledire; bestemmiare
cursed ['kə:sid] *agg.* maledetto
curt [kə:t] *agg.* breve; secco (*fig.*)
to curtail [kə:'teil] *v. tr.* accorciare, ridurre, abbreviare
curtain ['kə:tən] *s.* tenda *f.*; sipario *m.*
curve [kə:v] *s.* curva *f.*
to curve [kə:v] *v. tr. e intr.* curvare
curvilinear [,kə:vi'liniə*] *agg.* curvilineo
cushion ['kuʃən] *s.* cuscino *m.*
custard ['kʌstə] *s.* crema *f.*, dolce
custody ['kʌstədi] *s.* custodia *f.*
custom ['kʌstəm] *s.* costume *m.*; abitudine *f.*;

usanza *f.* • *agg.* su ordinazione, su misura; **customs** dogana; **customs officer** doganiere
customary ['kʌstəməri] *agg.* consueto, usuale
customer ['kʌstəmə*] *s.* cliente *m. e f.*
cut [kʌt] *s.* taglio *m.*; riduzione *f.* • *agg.* tagliato
to cut [kʌt] *v. tr.* tagliare; incidere; – **down** abbattere; – **off** troncare, recidere; – **out** ritagliare
cutaneous [kju(:)'teinjəs] *agg.* cutaneo
cute [kju:t] *agg.* carino (*fam.*)
cutis ['kju:tis] *s.* cute *f.*
cutlery ['kʌtləri] *s.* posate *f. pl.*
cutlet ['kʌtlit] *s.* costoletta *f.*; **veal** – costoletta di vitello
cutting ['kʌtiŋ] *s.* ritaglio *m.*; montaggio *m.* (*cin.*)
cuttlefish ['kʌtlfiʃ] *s.* seppia *f.*
cycle ['saikl] *s.* ciclo *m.* • bicicletta *f.*; – **track** velodromo
cyclic ['siklik] *agg.* ciclico
cycling ['saikliŋ] *s.* ciclismo *m.*
cyclist ['saiklist] *s.* ciclista *m. e f.*
cyclopean [sai'kloupjən] *agg.* ciclopico
cylinder ['silində*] *s.* cilindro *m.*; bombola *f.*
cylindrical [,si'lindrikəl] *agg.* cilindrico
cynical ['sinikl] *agg.* cinico
cynicism ['sinisizəm] *s.* cinismo *m.*
cypress ['saipris] *s.* cipresso *m.*

D

dad [dæd] s. papà m. (fam.)

Dadaism ['dadaizəm] s. dadaismo m.

daddy ['dædi] s. papà m. (fam.)

dagger ['dægə*] s. pugnale m.

daily ['deili] agg. giornaliero, quotidiano • s. quotidiano m. • avv. giornalmente, quotidianamente

daintiness ['deintinis] s. prelibatezza f.; finezza f.

dainty ['deinti] agg. delicato, fine, prelibato

dairy ['dɛəri] s. caseificio m.

dais ['deiis] s. predella f.; palco m.

daisy ['deizi] s. margherita f.

dam [dæm] s. diga f.

damage ['dæmidʒ] s. avaria f., danno m.; claim for – richiesta di risarcimento

to damage ['dæmidʒ] v. tr. danneggiare; lesionare

damask ['dæməsk] s. damasco m.

damn [dæm] inter. maledizione!

damned [dæmd] agg. insopportabile; maledetto; infame

damp [dæmp] s. umidità f., umido m. • agg. umido

to dampen ['dæmpən] v. tr. inumidire

damper ['dæmpə*] s. ammortizzatore m. (autom.)

dance [da:ns] s. ballo m., danza f.; balletto m.

to dance [da:ns] v. tr. e intr. ballare, danzare

dancer ['da:nsə*] s. ballerina f., ballerino m.

dandruff ['dændrəf] s. forfora f.

danger ['deindʒə*] s. pericolo m.

dangerous ['deindʒrəs] agg. pericoloso

to dangle ['dæŋgl] v. intr. penzolare, dondolare

dare [dɛə*] s. sfida f.

to dare [dɛə*] v. tr. e intr. osare, sfidare

daring ['dɛəriŋ] agg. ardito

dark [da:k] agg. buio; scuro • s. buio m.; to get – oscurare

to darken ['da:kən] v. tr. offuscare; scurire • intr. offuscarsi; oscurarsi

darkness [da:knis] s. buio m., oscurità f.

darling ['da:liŋ] s. caro m.

to darn [da:n] v. tr. rammendare

darnel ['da:nl] s. zizzania f.

darning ['da:niŋ] s. rammendo m.

dart [da:t] s. freccia f., dardo m.

dash [dæʃ] s. trattino m.; goccia f.

to dash [dæʃ] v. tr. lanciare • intr. precipitarsi

dashboard ['dæʃbɔ:d] s. cruscotto m.

date [deit] s. data f.; appuntamento m. • dattero m.

to date [deit] v. tr. e intr. datare; dare un appuntamento (USA, fam.)

daub [dɔ:b] s. scarabocchio m.

to daub [dɔ:b] v. tr. impiastricciare

daughter ['dɔ:tə*] s. figlia f.; daughter-in-law nuora

to dawdle ['dɔ:dl] v. intr. gingillarsi

dawn [dɔ:n] s. alba f.

day [dei] s. giorno m., giornata f.; – time diurno; by – di giorno

daybreak ['dei-breik] s. aurora f.

daylight ['deilait] s. luce f. del giorno

to daze [deiz] v. tr. stordire

to dazzle ['dæzl] v. tr. abbagliare

dead [ded] agg. morto

deadline ['dedlain] s. scadenza f.

deadly [dedli] agg. micidiale, letale

deaf [def] agg. sordo; deaf-and-dumb sordomuto

deal [di:l] s. accordo m.; quantità f.

to deal [di:l] v. tr. dare, distribuire; fornire; dare le carte • intr. fare affari; – in commerciare in; – with trattare con

dealer ['di:lə*] s. commerciante m. e f.; distributore m.

deambulatory [di'æmbjulətəri] s. deambulatorio m.

dean [di:n] s. decano m.

dear [diə*] agg. caro; costoso

dearly ['diəli] avv. ardentemente; a caro prezzo

death [deθ] s. morte f.

debate [di'beit] s. dibattito m.

to debate [di'beit] v. tr. dibattere

debauched [di'bɔ:tʃt] agg. dissoluto

debit ['debit] s. addebito m.

to debit ['debit] v. tr. addebitare

45

debris ['deibri:] *s. inv.* detrito *m.*

debt [det] *s.* debito *m.*

debtor ['deta•] *s.* debitore *m.*

debut ['deibu:] *s.* debutto *m.*

decade ['dekeid] *s.* decade *f.*, decennio *m.*

decadence ['dekədəns] *s.* decadenza *f.*

decadent ['dekədənt] *agg.* decadente

decadentism ['dekədəntizəm] *s.* decadentismo *m. (arte, lett.)*

to decaffeinate [di:'kæfineit] *v. tr.* decaffeinare

to decant [di'kænt] *v. tr.* travasare

to decapitate [di'kæpiteit] *v. tr.* decapitare

decay [di'kei] *s.* degrado *m.*; disfacimento *m.*; putrefazione *f.*

to decay [di'kei] *v. intr.* deperire; marcire

deceased [di'si:st] *agg.* defunto *m.*

deceit [di'si:t] *s.* inganno *m.*

deceitful [di'si:tful] *agg.* perfido

to deceive [di'si:v] *v. tr.* ingannare, raggirare

deceleration [di:,selə'reiʃən] *s.* decelerazione *f.*, rallentamento *m.*

December [di'sembə•] *s.* dicembre *m.*

decency ['di:snsi] *s.* decenza *f.*; pudore *m.*; decoro *m.*

decennium [di'seniəm] *s.* decennio *m.*

decent ['di:sənt] *agg.* decente, dignitoso; onesto, decoroso

decentralization [di:,sentrəlai'zeiʃən] *s.* decentramento *m.*

deceptive [di'septiv] *agg.* ingannevole

to decide [di'said] *v. tr. e intr.* decidere

deciduous [di'sidjuəs] *agg.* deciduo

decilitre ['desi,li:tə•] *s.* decilitro *m.*

decimal ['desiməl] *agg.* decimale

to decimate ['desimeit] *v. tr.* decimare

to decipher [di'saifə•] *v. tr.* decifrare

decision [di'siʒən] *s.* decisione *f.*

decisive [di'saisiv] *agg.* decisivo

deck [dek] *s.* ponte *m.*, coperta *f. (naut.)*; – **house** tuga

to deck [dek] *v. tr.* adornare

to declaim [di'kleim] *v. tr.* declamare

declaration [,deklə'reiʃən] *s.* dichiarazione *f.*

to declare [di'kleə•] *v. tr.* dichiarare, proclamare; – **oneself** dichiararsi

decline [di'klain] *s.* decadenza *f.*, declino *m.*, decadimento *m.*

to decline [di'klain] *v. intr.* declinare, decadere; deperire; rifiutare

decoction [di'kokʃən] *s.* decotto *m.*

to decode [di:'koud] *v. tr.* decifrare

decolorization [di:,kʌlərai'zeiʃən] *s.* decolorazione *f.*

decomposable [,di(:)kəm'pouzəbl] *agg.* scomponibile

to decompose [,di:-kəm'pouz] *v. tr.* decomporre; scomporre

decomposition [,di:-kɔmpə'ziʃən] *s.* decomposizione *f.*, scomposizione *f.*

to decongest [,di:kən'dʒest] *v. tr.* decongestionare

to decorate ['dekəreit] *v. tr.* decorare

decoration [,dekə'reiʃən] *s.* decorazione *f.*; ornamento *m.*

decorative ['dekərətiv] *agg.* decorativo

decorator ['dekəreitə•] *s.* decoratore *m.*

decree [di'kri:] *s.* decreto *m.*

to decree [di'kri:] *v. tr.* decretare

decrepit [di'krepit] *agg.* decrepito

to dedicate ['dedikeit] *v. tr.* dedicare

dedication [,dedi'keiʃən] *s.* dedica *f.*

deducible [di'dju:səbl] *agg.* deducibile

to deduct [di'dʌkt] *v. tr.* dedurre; detrarre

deductible [di'dʌktəbl] *agg.* deducibile

deduction [di'dʌkʃən] *s.* deduzione *f.*, detrazione *f.*

deed [di:d] *s.* atto *m.*, azione *f.*; gesto *m.*

deep [di:p] *agg.* fondo, profondo; grave (di suono)

to deepen ['di:pən] *v. tr.* approfondire

to deep-freeze ['di:p'fri:z] *v. tr.* surgelare

deer [diə•] *s.* cervo *m.*

to deface [di'feis] *v. tr.* deturpare, sfregiare; imbruttire

defacement [di'feismənt] *s.* deturpazione *f.*; sfregio *m.*

defamation [,defə'meiʃən] *s.* diffamazione *f.*

default [di'fɔ:lt] *s.* difetto *m.*; mancanza *f.*; inadempienza *f.*

defeat [di'fi:t] *s.* sconfitta *f.*

to defeat [di'fi:t] *v. tr.* sconfiggere

defect [di'fekt] *s.* difetto *m.*

defection [di'fekʃən] *s.* defezione *f.*

defective [di'fektiv] *agg.* difettoso

defence [di'fens] *s.* difesa *f.*; **self** – autodifesa

to defend [di'fend] *v. tr.* difendere

defendant [di'fendənt] *s.* imputato *m.*

defender [di'fendə•] *s.* difensore *m.*

defensive [di'fensiv] *agg.* difensivo

deferential [,defə'renʃəl] *agg.* ossequioso, rispettoso

deficiency [di'fiʃənsi] *s.* deficienza *f.*, difetto *m.*; mancanza *f.*

deficient [di'fiʃənt] *agg.* deficiente; scemo

to define [di'fain] v. tr. definire
definite ['definit] agg. definito
definition [,defi'niʃən] s. definizione f.
definitive [di'finitiv] agg. definitivo; **definitively** definitivamente
deflagration [deflə'greiʃən] s. deflagrazione f.
to deflate [di'fleit] v. tr. sgonfiare
to deflect [di'flekt] v. tr. deviare; deflettere
to deforest [di:'fɔrist] v. tr. disboscare
to deform [di'fɔ:m] v. tr. e intr. deformare, deformarsi
deformation [di:fɔ'meiʃən] s. deformazione f.
deformed [di'fɔ:md] agg. deforme
deformity [di'fɔmiti] s. deformazione f.
to defraud [di'frɔ:d] v. tr. truffare
to defrost [di:'frɔst] v. tr. sbrinare; scongelare
defroster [di'frɔstə°] s. sbrinatore m.
deft [deft] agg. abile
to defy [di'fai] v. tr. sfidare
to degenerate [di'dʒenəreit] v. intr. degenerare
degeneration [di,dʒenə'reiʃə] s. degenerazione f.
to degrade [di'greid] v. tr. degradare, declassare
degrading [di'greidiŋ] agg. degradante
to degrease [di:'gri:s] v. tr. sgrassare
degree [di'gri:] s. grado m.; laurea f.
to dehydrate [di:'haidreit] v. tr. disidratare • intr. disidratarsi
dehydration [,di:hai'dreiʃən] s. disidratazione f.
to deject [di'dʒekt] v. tr. deprimere
dejection [di'dʒekʃən] s. depressione f., sconforto m.
delation [di'leiʃən] s. delazione f.
delay [di'lei] s. indugio m.; ritardo m., dilazione f.
to delay [di'lei] v. tr. rimandare, prorogare • intr. tardare, indugiare
to delegate ['deligeit] v. tr. delegare
delegation [,deli'geiʃən] s. delegazione f.
to delete [di'li:t] v. tr. cancellare
deleterious [,deli'tiəriəs] agg. deleterio
deletion [di:'liːʃən] s. cancellatura
deliberate [di'libərit] agg. deliberato, intenzionale
to deliberate [di'libəreit] v. tr. deliberare
delicacy ['delikəsi] s. manicaretto m.
delicate ['delikit] agg. delicato
delicatessen [,delikə'tesn] s. pl. salumeria f. sing.
delicious [di'liʃəs] agg. delizioso, squisito

delight [di'lait] s. delizia f.; diletto m.
to deligth [di'lait] v. tr. deliziare, rallegrare, deliziarsi
delightful [di'laitful] agg. delizioso
to delimit [di:'limit] v. tr. delimitare
delimitation [di,limi'teiʃən] s. delimitazione f.
delinquent [di'liŋkwənt] s. delinquente m. e f., malfattore m.
delirious [di'liriəs] agg. delirante
delirium [di'liriəm] s. delirio m.
to deliver [di'livə°] v. tr. consegnare; distribuire; pronunciare • intr. partorire
delivery [di'livəri] s. consegna f.; parto m.; **cash on** – pagamento alla consegna; **home** – consegna a domicilio; – **room** sala parto
delta ['deltə] s. delta m. inv.
to delude [di'lu:d] v. tr. illudere; **oneself** illudersi
deluge ['dilju:dʒ] s. diluvio m.
delusion [di'lu:ʒən] s. illusione f.
demagogy ['deməgɔgi] s. demagogia f.
demand [di'ma:nd] s. richiesta f., domanda f.; esigenza f.
to demand [di'ma:nd] v. tr. domandare; richiedere; esigere
demanding [di'ma:ndiŋ] agg. esigente (persona); gravoso (cosa)
demented [di'mentid] agg. demente
demential [di'menʃəl] agg. demenziale (med.)
democracy [di'mɔkrəsi] s. democrazia f.
democratic [,demə'krætik] agg. democratico
demographic [,di:mə'græfik] agg. demografico
to demolish [di'mɔliʃ] v. tr. demolire
demolition [,demə'liʃən] s. demolizione f.
demon ['di:mən] s. demone m.
demonstrable ['demənstrəbl] agg. dimostrabile
to demonstrate ['demənstreit] v. tr. dimostrare; manifestare
demonstration [,demən'streiʃən] s. dimostrazione f.; manifestazione f.
to demoralize [di'mɔrəlaiz] v. tr. demoralizzare, scoraggiare
to demount [di:(·)'maunt] v. tr. smontare
demystification [di:,mistifi'keiʃən] s. demistificazione f.
den [den] s. tana f.; covo m.
denial [di'naiəl] s. negazione f.; smentita f.
to denigrate ['denigreit] v. tr. denigrare
to denote [di'nout] v. tr. denotare
to denounce [di'nauns] v. tr. denunciare
dense [dens] agg. denso

density ['densʌti] s. densità f.

dent [dent] s. ammaccatura f., tacca f.

dental ['dentl] agg. dentale

dentist ['dentist] s. dentista m. e f.

denture ['dentʃə*] s. dentiera f.

denunciation [di,nʌnsi'eiʃən] s. denuncia f.

to deny [di'nai] v. tr. negare; smentire; rinnegare; – oneself privarsi

deodorant [di:'oudərənt] agg. e s. deodorante m.

department [di'pa:tmənt] s. dipartimento m.; reparto m.

departure [di'pa:tʃə*] s. partenza f.; time of – ora di partenza

to depend [di'pend] v. intr. dipendere; – on dipendere da

dependent [di'pendənt] agg. dipendente

depilation [,depi'leiʃən] s. depilazione f.

depilatory [de'pilətəri] agg. depilatorio

to deplete [di'pli:t] v. tr. esaurire, vuotare

deplorable [di'plɔ:rəbl] agg. deplorevole

to deport [di'pɔ:t] v. tr. deportare

to depose [di'pouz] v. tr.deporre

deposit [di'pozit] s. deposito m.; caparra f.

to deposit [di'pozit] v. tr. depositare

depot ['depou] s. deposito m.; rimessa f.

depravity [di'præviti] s. depravazione f.

deprecable ['deprikəbl] agg. deprecabile

to depreciate [di'pri:ʃieit] v. tr. e intr. svalutare, ammortizzare

depreciation [di,pri:ʃi'eiʃən] s. deprezzamento m.; ammortamento m.

depressed [di'prest] agg. depresso

depression [di'preʃən] s. depressione f.

deprivation [,depri'veiʃən] s. privazione f.

to deprive [di'praiv] v. tr. privare

deprived [di'praivd] agg. privo

depth [depθ] s. profondità f.; – finder profondimetro

to depurate ['depjureit] v. tr. depurare

depurator ['depjureitə*] s. depuratore m.

deputy ['depjuti] s. deputato m.

derailment [di:'reilmənt] s. deragliamento m.

to derange [di'reindʒ] v. tr. turbare; disordinare; guastare; squilibrare

deranged [di'reindʒd] agg. squilibrato

deratization [di(:),rætai'zeiʃən] s. derattizzazione f.

deregulation ['di:'regju'leiʃən] s. liberalizzazione f.

to deride [di'raid] v. tr. deridere

derivation [,deri'veiʃən] s. derivazione f.

to derive [di'raiv] v. tr. e intr. derivare

dermatitis [,də:mə'taitis] s. dermatite f.

dermatologist [,də:mə'tɔlədʒist] s. dermatologo m.

derogation [,derə'geiʃən] s. deroga f.

desalter [di:'sɔ:ltə*] s. dissalatore m.

to descend [di'send] v. tr. e intr. scendere, discendere

descendant [di'sendənt] s. discendente m. e f.

descent [di'sent] s. discesa f.

to describe [dis'kraib] v. tr. descrivere

description [dis'kripʃən] s. descrizione f.

descriptive [dis'kriptiv] agg. descrittivo

to desecrate ['desikreit] v. tr. sconsacrare; profanare

desert [dezət] agg. e s. deserto m.

to desert [di'zət] v. tr. abbandonare

deserted [di'zə:tid] agg. abbandonato; disabitato, deserto

deserter [di'zə:tə*] s. disertore m.

desertion [di'zə:ʃən*] s. defezione f.

to deserve [di'zə:v] v. tr. meritare

deserving [di'zə:viŋ] agg. meritevole

design [di'zain] s. disegno m.; progetto m.; proposito m.; mira f.

to design [di'zain] v. tr. e intr. disegnare; progettare

to designate ['dezigneit] v. tr. designare; nominare

designer [di'zainə*] s. disegnatore m.; progettista m. f.

desinence ['desinəns] s. desinenza f.

desirable [di'zaiərəbl] agg. desiderabile

desire [di'zaiə*] s. desiderio m.

to desire [di'zaiə*] v. tr. desiderare

to desist [di'zist] v. intr. desistere

desk [desk] s. scrivania f.; banco m.; cattedra f.

desolate ['desəlit] agg. desolato

desolation [,desə'leiʃən] s. desolazione f.

to despair [dis'peə*] v. intr. disperarsi

desperate ['despərit] agg. disperato

to despise [dis'paiz] v. tr. disprezzare

despite [dis'pait] prep. malgrado; a dispetto di

despondent [dis'pondənt] agg. scoraggiato, abbattuto

despotic [des'potik] agg. dispotico

dessert [di'zə:t] s. dessert m. inv.

destination [,desti'neiʃən] s. destinazione f., meta f.

to destine ['destin] v. tr. destinare

destiny ['destini] s. destino m., sorte f.

destitute ['destitju:t] agg. destituito

to destroy [dis'trɔi] v. tr. distruggere

destruction [dis'trʌkʃən] s. distruzione f.

to detach [di'tætʃ] v. tr. distaccare

detachable [di'tætʃəbl] agg. staccabile

detached [di'tætʃt] agg. distaccato

detachment [di'tætʃmənt] s. distacco m.

detail ['di:teil] s. particolare m.; **in** – dettagliatamente

detailed ['di:teild] agg. dettagliato

to detain [di'tein] v. tr. trattenere

to detect [di'tekt] v. tr. individuare, notare, scoprire

detective [di'tektiv] s. investigatore m.

detention [di'tenʃən] s. detenzione f.

to deter [di'tə:*] v. tr dissuadere

detergent [di'tə:dʒənt] agg. e s. detergente m.

to deteriorate [di'tiəriəreit] v. tr. deteriorare

to determine [di'tə:min] v. tr. determinare; definire

detersive [di'tə:siv] s. detersivo m.

to detest [di'test] v. tr. detestare

detestable [di'testəbl] agg. detestabile, odioso

detour [di'tuə*] s. deviazione f.

detoxication [di:,tɔksi'keiʃən] s. disintossicazione f.

to detract [di'trækt] v. tr. e intr. detrarre

detraction [di'trækʃən] s. detrazione f.

devaluation [,di:,vælju'eiʃən] s. svalutazione f.

to devalue ['di:'vælju:] v. tr. svalutare

to devastate ['devəsteit] v. tr. devastare

to develop [di'veləp] v. tr. sviluppare; potenziare

development [di'veləpmənt] s. sviluppo m.; ampliamento m.

to deviate ['di:vieit] v. intr.deviare

deviation [,di:vi'eiʃən] s. deviazione f.

device [di'vais] s. congegno m., dispositivo m.; espediente m.

devil ['devl] s. diavolo m.

devious ['di:vjəs] agg. infido; tortuoso

to devise [di'vaiz] v. tr. escogitare

devoid [di'void] agg. destituito; privo

to devote [di'vout] v. tr. dedicare

devotion [di'vouʃən] s. devozione f.

to devour [di'vauə*] v. tr. divorare

dew [dju:] s. rugiada f.

dexterous ['dekstərəs] agg. destro

diabetes [,daiə'bi:ti:z] s. inv. diabete m.

diabetic [,daiə'betik] agg. diabetico

diabolical [,daiə'bɔlikəl] agg. diabolico

diadem ['daiədem] s. diadema m.

to diagnose ['daiəgnouz] v. tr. diagnosticare

diagnosis [,daiəg'nousis] s. diagnosi f.

diagonal [dai'ægənl] agg. diagonale

diagram ['daiəgræm] s. schema m., diagramma m.

dial ['daiəl] s. quadrante m. (orologio)

to dial [daiəl] v. tr. comporre (numero telefonico)

dialect ['daiəlekt] s. dialetto m.; parlata f.

dialectal [,daiə'lektl] agg. dialettale

dialectic [daiə'lektik] agg. dialettico

dialogue ['daiəlɔg] s. dialogo m.

dialysis [dai'ælisis] s. dialisi f.

diameter [dai'æmitə*] s. diametro m.

diamond ['daiəmənd] s. diamante m.; rombo m.; **diamonds** quadri (carte)

diaper ['daiəpə*] s. pannolino m.

diarrh(o)ea [,daiə'riə] s. diarrea f.

diary ['daiəri] s. diario m.; agenda f.

dice [dais] s. pl. dadi m.

to dictate [dik'teit] v. tr. dettare

dictator [dik'teitə*] s. dittatore m.

dictatorship [dik'teitəʃip] s. dittatura f.

diction ['dikʃən] s. dizione f.

dictionary ['dikʃənri] s. dizionario m., vocabolario m.

didactic [di'dæktik] agg. didattico; didascalico

didactics [di'dæktiks] s. pl. (v. al sing.) didattica f. sing.

die [dai] s. dado m.; stampo m.

to die [dai] v. intr. morire

diet ['daiət] s. dieta f.; **to be on** – essere a dieta

dietetic [,daiə'tetik] agg. dietetico

dietician [,daiə'tiʃən] s. dietologo m.

to differ ['difə*] v. intr. differire, essere diverso

difference ['difrəns] s. differenza f., diversità f.; dissapore m.

different ['difrənt] agg. diverso; **differently** diversamente

differential [,difə'renʃəl] s. differenziale m.

difficult ['difikəlt] agg. difficile; faticoso

difficulty ['difikəlti] s. difficoltà f.

diffident ['difidənt] agg. timido

to diffuse [di'fju:z] v. tr. diffondere

diffused [di'fju:zd] agg. diffuso

diffusion [di'fju:ʒən] s. diffusione f.

to dig [dig] v. tr. scavare

to digest [di'dʒest] v. tr. e intr. digerire; riassumere

digester [di'dʒestə*] s. digestivo m.

digestible [di'dʒestəbl] agg. digeribile

digestion [di'dʒestʃən] s. digestione f.

digestive [di'dʒestiv] agg. e s. digestivo m.

digger ['digə*] s. scavatrice f.

dignified ['dignifaid] agg. dignitoso

dignity ['digniti] *s.* dignità *f.*, decoro *m.*; onorificenza *f.*

dignitary ['dignitəri] *s.* dignitario *m.*

to digress [dai'gres] *v. intr.* divagare

digression [dai'grɛʃən] *s.* digressione *f.*

dike [daik] *s.* argine *m.*; diga *f.*

dilatation [,dailei'teiʃən] *s.* dilatazione *f.*

to dilate [dai'leit] *v. tr.* dilatare

dilemma [di'lemə] *s.* dilemma *m.*

dilettante [,dili'tænti] *agg.* dilettante

diligence ['dilidʒəns] *s.* diligenza *f.*

diligent ['dilidʒənt] *agg.* diligente

to dilute [dai'lju:t] *v. tr.* diluire

dim [dim] *agg.* debole, fioco (luce)

to dim [dim] *v. tr.* offuscare

dimension [di'menʃən] *s.* dimensione *f.*

to diminish [di'miniʃ] *v. tr. e intr.* diminuire

diminutive [di'minjutiv] *s.* diminutivo *m.*

din [din] *s.* fracasso *m.*

to dine [dain] *v. intr.* cenare; – out cenar fuori; **dining room** sala da pranzo

dinner ['dinə*] *s.* cena *m.*; **to have** – cenare

dinosaur ['dainəsɔ:*] *s.* dinosauro *m.*

diocese ['daiəsis] *s.* diocesi *f.*

diopter [dai'ɔptə*] *s.* diottria *f.*

dip [dip] *s.* immersione *f.*; tuffo *m.*; depressione *f.*; salsa *f.*

to dip [dip] *v. tr.* immergere; tuffare • *intr.* abbassarsi; immergersi

diploma [di'plumə] *s.* diploma *m.*

diplomacy [di'plumasi] *s.* diplomazia *f.*

diplomatic [,diplə'mætik] *agg.* diplomatico

direct [di'rekt] *agg.* diretto; – **dialling** teleselezione

to direct [di'rekt] *v. tr.* dirigere; ordinare; indirizzare

direction [di'rekʃən] *s.* direzione *f.*; istruzione *f.*; regia *f.*; **directions** avvertenze

directional [di'rekʃənl] *agg.* direzionale

directly [di'rektli] *avv.* direttamente; diritto

director [di'rektə*] *s.* direttore *m.*, dirigente *m. e f.*; regista *m. e f.*

directory [di'rektəri] *s.* elenco *m.*; **telephone** – elenco telefonico

dirt [də:t] *s.* sporcizia *f.*

dirty ['də:ti] *agg.* sporco, sudicio

to dirty ['də:ti] *v. tr.* sporcare

disability [,disə'biliti] *s.* incapacità *f.*; invalidità *f.*

disadvantage [,disəd'va:ntidʒ] *s.* svantaggio *m.*

disadvantegeous [,disædvn'teidʒəs] *agg.* svantaggioso

to disagree [,disə'gri:] *v. intr.* dissentire

disagreeable [,disə'griəbl] *agg.* sgradevole, antipatico

disagreement [,disə'gri:mənt] *s.* disaccordo *m.*; discordia *f.*

to disappear [,disə'piə*] *v. intr.* scomparire, sparire

disappearance [,disə'piərəns] *s.* sparizione *f.*, scomparsa *f.*

to disappoint [,disə'point] *v. tr.* deludere

disappointment [,disə'pointmənt] *s.* delusione *f.*, disappunto *m.*

to disapprove [,disə'pru:v] *v. tr.* disapprovare

to disarm [dis'a:m] *v. tr.* disarmare

to disassemble [,disə'sembl] *v. tr.* smontare

disassembly [,disə'sembli] *s.* smontaggio *m.*

disaster [di'za:stə*] *s.* disastro *m.*, sciagura *f.*

disastrous [di'za:strəs] *agg.* disastroso

disbandment [dis'bændmənt] *s.* sbandamento *m.*; dispersione *f.*

disbelief [,disbi'li:f] *s.* incredulità *f.*

to disbelieve [,disbi'li:v] *v. tr.* non credere

disbursement [dis'bə:smənt] *s.* esborso *m.*; pagamento *m.*

disc [disk] *s.* disco *m.*

discard ['diska:d] *s.* scarto *m.*

to discard [dis'ka:d] *v. tr. e intr.* scartare

to discern [di'sə:n] *v. tr.* discernere

discerning [di'sə:niŋ] *agg.* perspicace, oculato

discharge [dis'tʃa:dʒ] *s.* scarico *m.*; scarica *f.*; congedo *m.*

to discharge [dis'tʃa:dʒ] *v. tr.* scaricare

disciple [di'saipl] *s.* discepolo *m.*

discipline ['disiplin] *s.* disciplina *f.*

to disclose [dis'klouz] *v. tr.* scoprire, rivelare

to discolour [dis'kʌlə*] *v. tr.* scolorire

discomfort [dis'kʌmfət] *s.* scomodità *f.*

to disconcert [,diskən'sə:t] *v. tr.* sconcertare

to discontinue [,diskən'tinju:(:)] *v. tr. e intr.* cessare, interrompere

to disconnect [,diskə'nekt] *v. tr.* staccare; scollegare

disconnected [,diskə'nektid] *v. tr.* sconnesso; disinserito

disconsolate [dis'kɔnsəlit] *agg.* consolato; sconfortato

discontent [,diskən'tent] *s.* scontentezza *f.*; scontento *m.*

discontinuous [,diskən'tinjuəs] *agg.* discontinuo, saltuario; **discontinuously** saltuariamente

discord ['diskɔ:d] *s.* discordia *f.*

discordant [dis'kɔ:dənt] *agg.* discordante

discothèque ['diskəutek] *s.* discoteca *f.*

discount ['diskaunt] s. sconto m.; ribasso m.; riduzione f.

to discount ['diskaunt] v. tr. scontare; ribassare

discountable [dis'keuntəbl] agg. scontabile

to discourage [dis'karidʒ] v. tr. scoraggiare

discouragement [dis'karidʒmənt] s. sconforto m.

to discover [dis'kʌə°] v. tr. scoprire

discoverer [dis'kʌvərə°] s. scopritore m.

discovery [dis'kʌvəri] s. scoperta f.

discreet [dis'kri:t] agg. discreto

discrepancy [dis'krepənsi] s. discrepanza f.; divario m.

discretion [dis'kreʃən] s. discrezione f., moderazione f.; riserbo m.

to discriminate [dis'krimineit] v. tr. e intr. discriminare

discus ['diskəs] s. disco m. (sport)

to discuss [dis'kʌs] v. tr. discutere

discussion [dis'kʌʃən] s. discussione f.

disease [di'zi:z] s. malattia f.

diseased [di'zi:zd] agg. ammalato

to disentangle [disin'tæŋgl] v. tr. sbrogliare; - oneself districarsi

to disfigure [dis'figə°] v. tr. deturpare, sfregiare

disgrace [dis'greis] s. disonore m.; vergogna f.

disgraceful [dis'greisful] agg. disonorevole, vergognoso

disguise [dis'gaiz] s. travestimento m.

to disguise [dis'gaiz] v. tr. mascherare; - oneself mascherarsi

disgust [dis'gʌst] s. disgusto m., schifo m.; nausea f.

to disgust [dis'gʌst] v. tr. disgustare

dish [diʃ] s. piatto m.; pietanza f.; - washer lavastoviglie

disheartening [dish'haːtniŋ] agg. sconsolante

to dishevel [di'ʃevl] v. tr. scompigliare

dishonest [dis'ɔnist] agg. disonesto

dishonour [dis'ɔnə°] s. disonore m.

to disinfect [disin'fekt] v. tr. disinfettare

disinfectant [disin'fektənt] s. disinfettante m.

to disinfest [disin'fest] v. tr. disinfestare

disinhibited [disin'hibitid] agg. disinibito

to disintegrate [dis'intigreit] v. tr. disintegrare • intr. disintegrarsi

disk [disk] s. disco m.

dislike [dis'laik] s. avversione f.

to dislike [dis'laik] v. tr. non piacere

to dislocate [dis'ləkeit] v. tr. slogare

dislocation [dislə'keiʃən] s. slogatura f.

to dislodge [dis'lɔdʒ] v. tr. sloggiare

dismal ['dizməl] agg. lugubre, tetro

dismay [dis'mei] s. sgomento m.

to dismiss [dis'mis] v. tr. licenziare; - a case archiviare un processo

to dismount [dis'maunt] v. intr. smontare, scendere

to disobey [disə'bei] v. intr. disubbidire

disorder [dis'ɔːdə°] s. disordine m.

disorganization [dis,ɔːgənai'zeiʃən] s. disorganizzazione f.

disorientation [dis,ɔriən'teiʃən] s. disorientamento m.

disparaging [dis'pæridʒiŋ] agg. dispregiativo

disparate [dis'pæriti] agg. disparato

dispatch [dis'pætʃ] s. invio m.; spedizione f.; messaggio m.

to dispatch [dis'pætʃ] v. tr. spedire, mandare; espletare; sbrigare

dispenser [dis'pensə°] s. distributore m.

to disperse [dis'pəːs] v. tr. disperdere • intr. disperdersi

dispersion [dis'pəːʃən] s. dispersione f.

displacement [dis'pleismənt] s. dislocamento m. (naut.)

display [di'plei] s. manifestazione f.; visualizzazione f.

to display [di'splei] v. tr. manifestare, mostrare; visualizzare

to displease [dis'pliːz] v. tr. scontentare

disposal [dis'pouzəl] s. disposizione f.

to dispose [dis'pouz] v. tr. e intr. disporre; - of disfarsi d

disposition [dispə'ziʃən] s. disposizione f.; attitudine f.

disproportion [disprə'pɔːʃən] s. sproporzione f.

disproportionate [disprə'pɔːʃnit] agg. sproporzionato

to disprove [dis'pruːv] v. tr confutare

dispute [dis'pjuːt] s. disputa f.; vertenza f.

disqualification [dis,kwɔlifi'keiʃən] s. squalifica f.

to disqualify [dis'kwɔlifai] v. tr. squalificare

to disregard ['disri'gaːd] v. tr. trascurare

disrepute [disri'pjuːt] s. discredito m.

disrespect [disris'pekt] s. irriverenza f.

disrespectful [disris'pektful] agg. irriverente

dissatisfaction [dis,sætis'fækʃən] s. insoddisfazione f., scontentezza f.

to dissatisfy [dis'sætisfai] v. tr scontentare

to disseminate [di'semineit] v. tr. disseminare

to dissent [di'sent] v. intr. dissentire

51

dissident ['disidənt] *agg.* dissidente
dissimilar [di'similə*] *agg.* dissimile
dissimilarity [,disimi'læriti] *s.* difformità *f.*, diversità *f.*
to dissimulate [di'simjuleit] *v. tr.* dissimulare
to dissipate [di'sipeit] *v. tr.* dissipare, disperdere
to dissociate [di'souʃieit] *v. tr.* dissociare ● *intr.* dissociarsi
dissolute ['disəlu:t] *agg.* dissoluto
to dissolve [di'zɔlv] *v. tr.* dissolvere; ● *intr.* dissolversi, sciogliersi
dissonant ['disənənt] *agg.* dissonante
to dissuade [di'sweid] *v. tr.* dissuadere, distogliere
distance ['distəns] *s.* distanza *f.*, lontananza *f.*
distant ['distənt] *agg.* distante, lontano, remoto; **to be** – distare
distaste [dis'teist] *s.* disgusto *m.*
distasteful [dis'teistful] *agg.* sgradevole
to distill [dis'til] *v. tr.* distillare
distillate ['distilit] *s.* distillato *m.*
distillery [dis'tiləri] *s.* distilleria *f.*
distinct [dis'tiŋkt] *agg.* distinto
distinction [dis'tiŋkʃən] *s.* distinzione *f.*
distinctive [dis'tiŋktiv] *agg.* distintivo
to distinguish [dis'tiŋwiʃ] *v. tr.* distinguere
distinguished [dis'tiŋwiʃt] *agg.* famoso, illustre
to distort [dis'tɔ:t] *v. tr.* distorcere; travisare
distortion [dis'tɔ:ʃən] *s.* distorsione *f.*
to distract [dis'trækt] *v. tr.* distrarre
distraction [dis'trækʃən] *s.* distrazione *f.*; diversivo *m.*
to distrain [dis'trein] *v. tr.* pignorare
distress [dis'tres] *s.* pericolo *m.*; pena *f.*, angoscia *f.*
to distribute [dis'tribju(:)t] *v. tr.* distribuire; assegnare
distribution [,distri'bju:ʃən] *s.* distribuzione *f.*
distributor [dis'tribjutə*] *s.* spinterogeno *m.*
district [dis'trikt] *s.* distretto *m.*; regione *f.*; territorio *m.*
distrust [dis'trʌst] *s.* diffidenza *f.*; sfiducia *f.*
to distrust [dis'trʌst] *v. intr.* diffidare
to disturb [dis'tə:b] *v. tr.* disturbare
disturbance [dis'tə:bəns] *s.* disturbo *m.*; perturbazione *f.*
ditch [ditʃ] *s.* fossato *m.*
diuretic [,daijuə'retik] *agg. e s.* diuretico *m.*
divan [di'væn] *s.* divano *m.*
dive [daiv] *s.* tuffo *m.*; immersione *f.*
to dive [daiv] *v. intr.* tuffarsi; immergersi

diver ['daivə*] *s.* tuffatore *m.*; palombaro *m.*, sommozzatore *m.*
to diverge [dai'və:dʒ] *v. intr.* divergere
diversion [dai'və:ʃən] *s.* diversione *f.*; dirottamento *m.*
diversity [dai'və:siti] *s.* diversità *f.*
to divert [dai'və:t] *v. tr.* deviare
to divide [di'vaid] *v. tr.* dividere ● *intr.* dividersi, separarsi
divine [di'vain] *agg.* divino
divinity [di'viniti] *s.* divinità *f.*
divisible [di'vizəbl] *agg.* divisibile
division [di'viʒən] *s.* divisione *f.*; ripartizione *f.*; sezione *f.*
divorce [di'vɔ:s] *s.* divorzio *m.*
to divorce [di'vɔ:s] *v. tr.* divorziare
divorcé [di,vɔ:'sei] *s.* divorziato *m.*
divorcée [di,vɔ:'si] *s.* divorziata *f.*
to divulge [dai'vʌldʒ] *v. tr.* divulgare
to do [du:, du, də] *v. tr.* fare
dock [dɔk] *s.* bacino *m.*; molo *m.*
to dock [dɔk] *v. tr. e intr.* attraccare
docking ['dɔkiŋ] *s.* attracco *m.*
dockyard [dɔk'ja:d] *s.* arsenale *m.*; cantiere *m.* navale
doctor ['dɔktə*] *s.* dottore *m.*, medico *m.*
doctrine ['dɔktrin] *s.* dottrina *f.*
document ['dɔkjumənt] *s.* documento *m.*
to document ['dɔkjument] *v. tr.* documentare
documentary [,dɔkju'mentəri] *s.* documentario *m.*
dog [dɔg] *s.* cane *m.*; – **catcher** accalappiacani
dogma ['dɔgmə] *s.* dogma *m.*
dogmatic [dɔg'mætik] *agg.* dogmatico
doll [dɔl] *s.* bambola *f.*
dollar ['dɔlə*] *s.* dollaro *m.*
dolly ['dɔli] *s.* bambola *f.*; – **shot** carrellata (*cin.*)
dolphin ['dɔlfin] *s.* delfino *m.*
doltish ['doultiʃ] *agg.* sciocco
dome [doum] *s.* cupola *f.*
domestic [də'mestik] *agg.* domestico, casalingo; nazionale
domicile ['dɔmisail] *s.* domicilio *m.*
dominant ['dɔminənt] *agg.* dominante
to dominate ['dɔmineit] *v. tr. e intr.* dominare
domination [,dɔmi'neiʃən] *s.* dominazione *f.*
dominator ['dɔmineitə*] *s.* dominatore *m.*
dominion [də'minjən] *s.* dominio *m.*
donation [dou'neiʃən] *s.* donazione *f.*, elargizione *f.*
done [dʌn] *agg.* fatto, finito; cotto; **well** – ben cotto
donjon ['dɔndʒən] *s.* torrione *m.*

donkey ['dɔŋki] s. asino m.

donor ['douna*] s. donatore m.; **blood** - donatore di sangue

door [dɔ:°] s. porta f.; sportello m.; **- keeper** portinaio

doormat ['dɔ:mæt] s. zerbino m.

dope [doup] s. droga f. (fam.)

Doric ['dɔrik] agg. dorico

dormitory ['dɔ:mitri] s. dormitorio m.

dosage ['dousidʒ] s. dosaggio m.; posologia f.

dose [dous] s. dose f.

to dose [dous] v. tr. dosare

dot [dɔt] s. punto

to dot [dɔt] v. tr. punteggiare

double ['dʌbl] agg. doppio, duplice • avv. il doppio • s. doppio m.; controfigura f.

to double ['dʌbl] v. tr. raddoppiare

doublet ['dʌblit] s. doppione m.

doubling ['dʌbliŋ] s. raddoppio m.

doubt [daut] s. dubbio m.

to doubt [daut] v. intr. dubitare

doubtful ['dautful] agg. dubbioso

dough [dou] s. impasto m.; pasta f. per pane; quattrini m. pl. (fam.)

down [daun] avv. giù; di sotto • agg. verso il basso; discendente • s. piuma f.

downfall ['daunfɔ:l] s. caduta f.

to downgrade ['daun'greid] v. tr. esautorare

downhiller ['daun'hilə*] s. discesista m. e f.

downpour ['daunpɔ:°] s. acquazzone m.

downstairs [daun'stɛəz] avv. giù; disotto

downwind [,daun'wind] avv. sottovento

dowry ['dauəri] s. dote f.

doze [douz] s. pisolino m.

to doze [douz] v. intr. appisolarsi

dozen ['dʌzn] s. dozzina f.

drab [dræb] agg. monotono, incolore

draft [dra:ft] s. schema m.; abbozzo m.; disegno m.; tratta f. (comm.)

draftsman ['dra:ftsmən] s. disegnatore m.

drag [dræg] s. impedimento m., ostacolo m.; seccatura f.

to drag [dræg] v. tr. trascinare, tirare

dragon ['drægən] s. drago m.

drain [drein] s. fogna f.; salasso m.

to drain [drein] v. tr. prosciugare

drainage ['dreinidʒ] s. bonifica f.

draining ['dreiniŋ] s. prosciugamento m.; **- board** scolapiatti

drama ['dra:mə] s. dramma m.

dramatic [drə'mætik] agg. drammatico; sensazionale

dramatist ['dræmətist] s. drammaturgo m.

dramatization [,dræmətai'zeiʃən] s. sceneggiatura m.

to dramatize ['dræmətaiz] v. tr. sceneggiare

drapery ['dreipəri] s. drappeggio m.

drastic ['dræstik] agg. energico

draught [dra:ft] s. tiro m.; tiraggio m.; sorso m.; pescaggio m.; spiffero m.; **beer on** - birra alla spina; **draughts** dama (gioco); **- board** scacchiera

draw [drɔ:] s. sorteggio m.; pareggio m.

to draw [drɔ:] v. tr. tirare; ottenere; tracciare; disegnare; sorteggiare; **- back** indietreggiare; **- up** disporsi, redigere

drawback ['drɔ:bæk] s. inconveniente m.; svantaggio m.

drawer [drɔ:*] s. cassetto m.

drawing ['drɔ:iŋ] s. disegno m.

dread [dred] s. paura f., timore m.

to dread [dred] v. tr. temere

dreadful ['dredful] agg. terribile, spaventoso

dream [dri:m] s. sogno m.

to dream [dri:m] v. tr. e intr. sognare

dredge [dredʒ] s. draga f.

dress [dres] s. abbigliamento m.; veste f.; vestito m. (da donna); **- hanger** gruccia

to dress [dres] v. tr. e intr. vestire, vestirsi; adornare; medicare; **- oneself** vestirsi

dressing ['dresiŋ] s. medicazione f.; condimento m.; **- gown** vestaglia; **- room** spogliatoio; **salad** - condimento per insalata

dressmaker ['dres,meikə*] s. sarta f., sarto m.

dressy ['dresi] agg. elegante

to dribble ['dribl] v. tr. e intr. gocciolare, sgocciolare; sbavare

dried [draid] agg. secco

drier ['draiə*] s. essiccatore m.

drift [drift] s. moto m., spostamento m.; tendenza f.; deriva f.

drill [dril] s. trapano m.

to drill [dril] v. tr. trapanare

drink [driŋk] s. bevanda f.; bevuta f.

to drink [driŋk] v. tr. bere

drinkable ['driŋkəbl] agg. bevibile, potabile

drinker ['driŋkə*] s. bevitore m.

drip [drip] s. gocciolamento m.; sgocciolatoio m.; fleboclisi f.

to drip [drip] v. tr. e intr. gocciolare

drive [draiv] s. guida f.; trazione f.

to drive [draiv] v. tr. e intr. condurre; guidare; conficcare; **- away** scacciare; **- back** ritornare

driver ['draivə*] s. conducente m.; guidatore m.; autista m.; **screw** - cacciavite

driving ['draiviŋ] *s.* guida; **– mirror** specchietto retrovisore; **– school** scuolaguida

to drizzle ['drizl] *v. intr.* piovigginare

droll [droul] *agg.* buffo

dromedary ['drɔmədəri] *s.* dromedario *m.*

drop [drɔp] *s.* goccia *f.*; caduta *f.*; pasticca *f.*

to drop [drɔp] *v. intr.* cadere • *tr.* far cadere

dropper ['drɔpə*] *s.* contagocce *m. inv.*

drought [draut] *s.* siccità *f.*

to drown [draun] *v. tr. e intr.* affogare, annegare

drowsiness ['drauzinis] *s.* sonnolenza *f.*

drowsy ['drauzi] *agg.* sonnolento

drug [drʌg] *s.* farmaco *m.*; droga *f.*; **– addict** tossicodipendente

drugstore ['drʌgstɔ:*] *s.* farmacia *f.* (USA)

drum [drʌm] *s.* tamburo *m.*; bidone *m.*

drunk [drʌŋk] *agg.* ubriaco; **to get – sbronzarsi; dead** – ubriaco fradicio

drunkenness ['drʌŋkənnis] *s.* ubriachezza *f.*

dry [drai] *agg.* asciutto; arido, secco; **– cleaner** tintoria

to dry [drai] *v. tr.* asciugare; seccare

drying ['draiiŋ] *s.* asciugatura *f.*

dryness ['drainis] *s.* siccità *f.*

dualism ['dju(:)əlizəm] *s.* dualismo *m.*

dubber ['dʌbə*] *s.* doppiatore *m.*

dubbing ['dʌbiŋ] *s.* doppiaggio *m.*

dubious ['dju:bjəs] *agg.* dubbio, dubbioso

duchess ['dʌtʃis] *s.* duchessa *f.*

duchy ['dʌtʃi] *s.* ducato *m.*

duck [dʌk] *s.* anatra *f.*

ductile ['dʌktail] *agg.* duttile

due [dju:] *agg.* dovuto, adeguato; pagabile (*comm.*); **– register** scadenzario

duel ['dju(:)əl] *s.* duello *m.*

duet [dju(:)'et] *s.* duo *m. inv.*

duke [dju:k] *s.* duca *m.*

dukedom ['dju:kdəm] *s.* ducato *m.*

dull [dʌl] *agg.* ottuso; lento

duly ['dju:li] *avv.* regolarmente, debitamente

dumb [dʌm] *agg.* muto

dummy ['dʌmi] *agg.* falso; fittizio

dump [dʌmp] *s.* discarica *f.*

to dump [dʌmp] *v. tr.* buttare • *intr.* scaricare (rifiuti)

dune [dju:n] *s.* duna *f.*

dung [dʌŋ] *s.* letame *m.*

dungeon ['dʌndʒən] *s.* segreta *f.*, prigione *f.*

duo ['dju(:)ou] *s.* duo *m. inv.*

dupe [dju:p] *s.m.* illuso *agg. e s.*

to duplicate ['dju:plikeit] *v. tr.* raddoppiare, fare un duplicato

duplication [,dju:pli'keiʃən] *s.* duplicazione *f.*; raddoppio *m.*

durable ['djuərəbl] *agg.* durevole

duration [djuə'reiʃən] *s.* durata *f.*

during ['djuəriŋ] *prep.* durante

dust [dʌst] *s.* polvere *f.*, pulviscolo *m.*; spazzatura *f.*

to dust [dʌst] *v. tr.* spolverare

dustbin ['dʌstbin] *s.* pattumiera *f.*

duster ['dʌstə*] *s.* straccio *m.* per la polvere

dustman ['dʌstmən] *s.* netturbino *m.*

dustpan ['dʌstpæn] *s.* paletta *f.* per la spazzatura

dusty ['dʌsti] *agg.* polveroso

Dutch [dʌtʃ] *agg.* olandese

Dutchman ['dʌtʃmən] *s.* olandese *m.*

Dutchwoman ['dʌtʃ,wumən] *s.* olandese *f.*

duty ['dju:ti] *s.* dovere *m.*; compito *m.*; dazio *m.*, imposta *f.*; **harbour duties** diritti portuali

dye [dai] *s.* colorante *m.*; tinta *f.*; **hair** – tintura per capelli

to dye [dai] *v. tr.* tingere

dyeing ['daiiŋ] *s.* tintura *f.*

dyer ['daiə*] *s.* tintore *m.*

dying ['daiiŋ] *agg.* morente, moribondo

dynamic [dai'næmik] *agg.* dinamico

dynamics [dai'næmiks] *s. pl.* (*v. al sing.*) dinamica *f. sing.*

dynamism ['dainəmizən] *s.* dinamismo *m.*

dynamo ['dainəmou] *s.* dinamo *f. inv.*

dynasty ['dinəsti] *s.* dinastia *f.*

dysentery ['disntri] *s.* dissenteria *f.*

E

each [i:tʃ] *agg. e pron.* ciascuno, ogni; – **other** l'un l'altro

eager ['i:gə*] *agg.* desideroso

eagle ['i:gl] *s.* aquila *f.*

ear [iə*] *s.* orecchio *m.* • spiga *f.*; – **drum** timpano; – **ring** orecchino

early ['ə:li] *agg.* mattiniero; precoce; prematuro; anticipato • *avv.* presto

to earn [ə:n] *v. tr.* guadagnare; ottenere; meritare; – **one's living** mantenersi

earnings ['ə:niŋz] *s. pl.* guadagno *m. sing.*

earphone ['iəfoun] *s.* auricolare *m.*

earth [ə:θ] *s.* terra *f.*; massa *f.* (*elettr.*)

earthenware ['ə:θənwɛə*] *s.* terraglia *f.*

earthly ['ə:θli] *agg.* terrestre; mondano

earthquake ['ə:θkweik] *s.* terremoto *m.*

earthy ['ə:θi] *agg.* terroso

ease [i:z] *s.* agio *m.*; sollievo *m.*

easel ['i:zl] *s.* cavalletto *m.* (*arte*)

East [i:st] *s.* est *m.*, oriente *m.*

Easter ['i:stə*] *s.* pasqua *f.*; – **Monday** pasquetta; – **holidays** vacanze pasquali

eastern ['i:stən] *agg.* orientale

eastery ['i:stəli] *agg.* di levante

easy ['i:zi] *agg.* facile; disinvolto • *avv.* piano; **to make** – facilitare

to eat [i:t] *v. tr.* mangiare; corrodere

eatable ['i:təbl] *agg.* commestibile, mangiabile; – **up** divorare

ebb [eb] *s.* riflusso *m.*; – **tide** bassa marea

ebony ['ebəni] *s.* ebano *m.*

eccentric [ik'sentrik] *agg.* eccentrico

ecchymosis [,eki'mousis] *s.* ecchimosi *f.*

ecclesiastic [i,kli:zi'æstik] *agg.* ecclesiastico

echo ['ekou] *s.* eco *m. e f.*; – **sounder** ecoscandaglio *m.*

to echo ['ekou] *v. tr. e intr.* echeggiare

eclectic [ek'lektik] *agg.* eclettico

eclecticism [ek'lektisizəm] *s.* eclettismo *m.*

eclipse [i'klips] *s.* eclissi *f.*

to eclipse [i'klips] *v. tr.* eclissare

ecliptic [i'kliptik] *agg.* eclittico

ecological [,i:kə'lɔdʒikəl] *agg.* ecologico

ecology [i(:)'kɔlədʒi] *s.* ecologia *f.*

economic [,i:kə'nɔmik] *agg.* economico

economical [,i:kə'nɔmikəl] *agg.* economico

economics [,i:kə'nɔmiks] *s. pl.* (*v. al sing.*) economia *f. sing.*

economist [i'kɔnəmist] *s.* economista *m. e f.*

to economize [i'kɔnəmaiz] *v. intr.* economizzare

economy [i'kɔnəmi] *s.* economia *f.*

ecosystem ['i:kou,sistəm] *s.* ecosistema *m.*

ecstasy ['ekstəsi] *s.* estasi *f.*

eczema ['eksimə] *s.* eczema *m.*

eddy ['edi] *s.* gorgo *m.*, vortice *m.*

edge [edʒ] *s.* estremità *f.*; orlo *m.*; bordo *m.*; spigolo *m.*

edict ['i:dikt] *s.* editto *m.*

to edit ['edit] *v. tr.* correggere, rivedere

editing ['editiŋ] *s.* redazione *f.*

edition [i'diʃən] *s.* edizione *f.*

editor ['editə*] *s.* curatore *m.*; direttore *m.* (di giornale); redattore *m.*

editorial [,edi'tɔ:riəl] *agg.* editoriale, redazionale • *s.* editoriale *m.*

to educate ['edju(:)keit] *v. tr.* istruire; educare

education [,edju(:)'keiʃən] *s.* educazione *f.*; istruzione *f.*

educational [,edju(:)'keiʃənl] *agg.* educativo

eel [i:l] *s.* anguilla *f.*

effect [i'fekt] *s.* effetto *m.*

to effect [i'fekt] *v. tr.* effettuare

effective [i'fektiv] *agg.* efficace; efficiente

effectiveness [i'fektivnis] *s.* efficacia *f.*; efficienza *f.*

effeminate [i'femineit] *agg.* effeminato

efficiency [i'fiʃənsi] *s.* efficienza *f.*; rendimento *m.*

efficient [i'fiʃənt] *agg.* efficiente

effigy ['efidʒi] *s.* effigie *f.*

effluvium [e'flu:vjəm] *s.* effluvio *m.*

effort ['efət] *s.* sforzo *m.*, fatica *f.*

effusion [i'fju:ʒən] *s.* effusione *f.*

egg [eg] *s.* uovo *m.*; – **plant** melanzana; – **cup** portauovo

egocentric [,egou'sentrik] *agg.* egocentrico

egoist ['egouist] *s.* egoista *m. e f.*

Egyptian [i'dʒipʃən] *agg.* egiziano, egizio

Egyptology [,i:dʒip'tɔlədʒi] *s.* egittologia *f.*

either ['aiðə*] agg. e pron. l'uno o l'altro; entrambi; - ... or o ... o

to elapse [i'læps] v. tr. trascorrere (del tempo)

elastic [i'læstik] agg. elastico

elasticity [,i:læs'tisiti] s. elasticità f.

elbow ['elbou] s. gomito m.

elder ['eldə*] agg. più anziano, maggiore (di età)
• s. sambuco m.

elderly ['eldəli] agg. anziano, attempato

eldest ['eldist] agg. il maggiore (di età)

to elect [i'lekt] v. tr. eleggere

election [i'lekʃən] s. elezione f.

elector [i'lektə*] s. elettore m.

electoral [i'lektərəl] agg. elettorale

electric [i'lektrik] agg. elettrico

electrician [ilek'triʃən] s. elettricista m.

electricity [ilek'trisiti] s. elettricità f.

electrocardiogram [i'lektrou'ka:djougræm] s. elettrocardiogramma m.

electrocution [i,lektrə'kju:ʃən] s. folgorazione f. (elettr.)

electroencephalogram [i'lektrouen'sefəlogræm] s. elettroencefalogramma m.

electromagnetic [i'lektroumæg'netik] agg. elettromagnetico

electronic [ilek'trɔnik] agg. elettronico

electrotechnician [i'lektroutek'niʃən] s. elettrotecnico m.

elegance ['eligəns] s. eleganza f.; grazia f.; raffinatezza f.

elegant ['eligənt] agg. elegante; raffinato

elegiac [,eli'dʒaiək] agg. elegiaco

element ['elimənt] s. elemento m.

elementary [,eli'mentəri] agg. elementare

elephant ['elifənt] s. elefante m.

to elevate [i'eliveit] v. tr. sollevare

elevated [i'eliveitid] agg. elevato

elevator ['eliveitə*] s. ascensore m.

to eliminate [i'limineit] v. tr. eliminare

eligible [i'elidʒəbl] agg. adatto, che ha i requisiti; eleggibile

elitist [ei'li:tist] agg. elitario

Elizabethan [i,lizə'bi:θən] agg. elisabettiano

elk [elk] s. alce m.

elliptic [i'liptik] agg. ellittico

elm [elm] s. olmo m.

to elongate ['i:lɔŋgeit] v. tr. allungare

eloquent ['eləkwənt] agg. eloquente

else [els] agg. altro • avv. altrimenti, oppure

elsewhere ['els'wɛə*] avv. altrove

elucidation [i,lu:si'deiʃən] s. delucidazione f.

elusive [i'lu:siv] agg. elusivo

emaciated [i'meiʃieitid] agg. emaciato

to emanate ['eməneit] v. intr. emanare

emancipation [i,mænsi'peiʃən] s. emancipazione f.

to embalm [im'ba:m] v. tr. imbalsamare

embankment [im'bæŋkmənt] s. argine m.; terrapieno m.

to embark [im'ba:k] v. tr. e intr. imbarcare

embarkation [,embɑ:'keiʃən] s. imbarco m.

to embarrass [im'bærəs] v. tr. imbarazzare

embarrassing [im'bærəsiŋ] agg. imbarazzante

embarrassment [im'bærəsmənt] s. imbarazzo m.; difficoltà f.

embassy ['embəsi] s. ambasciata f.

to embed [im'bed] v. tr. incassare

to embellish [im'beliʃ] v. tr. abbellire

ember ['embə*] s. tizzone m.; **embers** brace

to embezzle [im'bezl] v. tr. impossessarsi (indebitamente)

emblematic [,embli'mætik] agg. emblematico

to embody [im'bɔdi] v. tr. incarnare

embolism ['embəlizəm] s. embolia f.

embossed [im'bɔst] agg. in rilievo; – **plate** targhetta

embrace [im'breis] s. abbraccio m., stretta f.; amplesso m.

to embrace [im'breis] v. tr. abbracciare

embroidery [im'brɔidəri] s. ricamo m.

embryo ['embriou] s. embrione m.

emerald ['emərəld] s. smeraldo m.

to emerge [i'mə:dʒ] v. intr. emergere

emergency [i'mə:dʒənsi] s. emergenza f.

emergent [i'mə:dʒənt] agg. emergente

emersion [i(:)'mə:sən] s. emersione f.

emigrant ['emigrənt] agg. e s. emigrante m. e f.

to emigrate ['emigreit] v. intr. emigrare

emigration [,emi'greiʃən] s. emigrazione f.

eminent ['eminənt] agg. eminente

emirate [e'miərit] s. emirato m.

emission [i'miʃən] s. emissione f.

emitter [i'mitə*] s. emettitore m.

emotional [i'mouʃənl] agg. emotivo

emperor ['empərə*] s. imperatore m.

emphasis ['emfəsis] s. enfasi f.

to emphasize [im'emfəsaiz] v. tr. accentuare, enfatizzare

emphatic [im'fætik] agg. enfatico

emphysema [,emfi'si:mə] s. enfisema m.

empire ['empaiə*] s. impero m.

empiric [em'pirik] agg. empirico

to employ [im'plɔi] v. tr. assumere, dar lavoro; adoperare

employee [,emplɔi'i:] s. impiegato m.; dipendente m. e f.

employment [im'plɔimənt] *s.* impiego *m.*; occupazione *f.*
empty ['empti] *agg.* vuoto
to empty ['empti] *v. tr.* vuotare
to emulate ['emiuleit] *v. tr.* emulare
emulator ['emiuleitə°] *s.* emulo *m.*
emulsion [i'mʌlʃən] *s.* emulsione *f.*
to enable [i'neibl] *v. tr.* permettere, autorizzare; mettere in grado
enamel [i'næməl] *s.* smalto *m.*
enamelling [i'næməliŋ] *s.* smaltatura *f.*
to enchant [in'tʃa:nt] *v. tr.* incantare
enchanting [in'tʃa(:)ntiŋ] *agg.* incantevole, affascinante
enchantment [in'tʃa(:)ntmənt] *s.* incanto *m.*, incantesimo *m.*
to encircle [in'sə:kl] *v. tr.* circondare
to enclose [in'klouz] *v. tr.* circondare; allegare, accludere
enclosure [in'klouʒə°] *s.* allegato *m.*; recinto *m.*, recinzione *f.*
encounter [in'kauntə°] *s.* incontro *m.*
to encounter [in'kauntə°]*v. tr.* incontrare
encouragement [in'kʌridʒmənt] *s.* incoraggiamento *m.*
encrustation [‚inkrʌs'teiʃən] *s.* incrostazione *f.*
encyclopaedia [en‚saiklou'pi:djə] *s.* enciclopedia *f.*
end [end] *s.* fine *f.*; estremità *f.*; finalità *f.*
to end [end] *v. tr. e intr.* finire, terminare, concludere
to endanger [in'deindʒə°] *v. tr.* mettere in pericolo
endemic [en'demik] *agg.* endemico
ending ['endiŋ] *s.* finale *m.*; desinenza *f.*
endless ['endlis] *agg.* infinito
endocrinologist [‚endoukri'nɔlədʒist] *s.* endocrinologo *m.*
endorsement [in'dɔ(:)smənt] *s.* approvazione *f.*, appoggio *m.*; firma *f.*
endowment [in'daumənt] *s.* dotazione *f.*; dote *f.*, lascito *m.*
endurable [in'djuərəbl] *agg.* sopportabile
to endure [in'djuə°] *v. intr.* sopportare; resistere
enemy ['enimi] *s.* nemico *m.*
energetic [‚enə'dʒetik] *agg.* energetico
energy ['enədʒi] *s.* energia *f.*
to enforce [in'fɔ:s] *v. tr.* applicare (*leg.*)
to engage [in'geidʒ] *v. tr.* impegnare; ingaggiare; ingranare (*mecc.*) • *intr.* impegnarsi
engaged [in'geidʒd] *agg.* occupato; fidanzato

engagement [in'geidʒmənt] *s.* impegno *m.*; fidanzamento *m.*
engine ['endʒin] *s.* motore *m.*; macchina *f.*
engineer [‚endʒi'niə°] *s.* ingegnere *m.*; macchinista *m.*; tecnico *m.*
engineering [‚endʒi'niəriŋ] *s.* ingegneria *f.*
English ['iŋgliʃ] *agg.* inglese
Englishman ['iŋgliʃmən] *s.* inglese *m.*
Englishwoman ['iŋgliʃ‚wumən] *s.* inglese *f.*
to engrave [in'greiv] *v. tr.* incidere
engraver [in'greivə°] *agg.* incisore
engraving [in'greiviŋ] *s.* incisione *f.*
to enhance [in'ha:ns] *v. tr.* aumentare; far risaltare
enigma [i'nigmə] *s.* enigma *m.*
enigmatic [‚enig'mætik] *agg.* enigmatico
to enjoy [in'dʒɔi] *v. tr.* godere; gustare; – oneself divertirsi
enjoyment [in'dʒɔimənt] *s.* divertimento *m.*; piacere *m.*
to enlarge [in'la:dʒ] *v. tr.* allargare; ingrandire
enlargement [in'la:dʒmənt] *s.* ingrandimento *m.*, ampliamento *m.*
to enlighten [in'laitn] *v. tr.* illuminare; rendere chiaro
enormous [i'nɔ:məs] *agg.* enorme
enough [i'nʌf] *avv.* abbastanza; assai • *agg.* bastante; **to be** – bastare
to enounce [i(:)'nauns] *v. tr.* enunciare
to enrage [in'reidʒ] *v. tr.* irritare, far infuriare
enraged [in'reidʒd] *agg.* furibondo
to enrich [in'ritʃ] *v. tr.* arricchire
to enrol(l) [in'roul] *v. tr.* iscrivere, iscriversi; registrare
enrol(l)ment [in'roulmənt] *s.* iscrizione *f.*
ensemble [ɔm'sɔmbl] *s.* complesso *m.*,
ensign ['ensain] *s.* bandiera *f.*
to ensure [in'ʃuə°] *v. tr.* assicurare
to entail [in'teil] *v. tr.* comportare, richiedere
to entangle [in'tæŋgl] *v. tr.* impigliare
to enter ['entə°] *v. tr.* entrare in; iscrivere • *intr.* entrare; iscriversi
enterprise ['entəpraiz] *s.* impresa *f.*
to entertain [‚entə'tein] *v. tr.* intrattenere; divertire
entertainment [entə'teinmənt] *s.* spettacolo *m.*; divertimento *m.*
enthusiasm [in'θju:ziæzəm] *s.* entusiasmo *m.*
enthusiastic [in‚θju:zi'æstik] *agg.* entusiasta
enthusiastically [in‚θju:zi'æstikəli] *avv.* entusiasticamente
enticement [in'taismənt] *s.* adescamento *m.*; allettamento *m.*

entire [in'taiə*] agg. intero

to entitle [in'taitl] v. tr. intitolare

entrance ['ntrəns] s. entrata f.; ingresso m.; free – ingresso libero

entrepreneur [ˌɔntrəprə'nə:*] s. imprenditore m., impresario m.

to entrust [in'trʌst] v. tr. affidare; raccomandare

entry ['entri] s. accesso m.; entrata f.; iscrizione f.; voce f. (di dizionario); **no** – vietato l'accesso

to enumerate [i'nju:məreit] v. tr. enumerare

enuresis [ˌenjuə'ri(:)sis] s. enuresi f.

envelope ['enviloup] s. busta f.; involucro m.

envious ['enviəs] agg. invidioso

environment [in'vaiərənmənt] s. ambiente m.; territorio m. circostante

environmental [in,vaiərən'mentəl] agg. ambientale

envy ['envi] s. invidia f.

ephebic [e'fi:bik] agg. efebico

ephemeral [i'femərel] agg. effimero

ephemeris [i'feməris] s. effemeride f.

epic ['epik] agg. epico • s. epopea f.

epicentre ['episntə*] s. epicentro m.

Epicureanism [ˌepikjuə'ri(:)ənizəm] s. epicureismo m.

epidemic [ˌepi'demik] agg. epidemico • s. epidemia f.

epidermic [ˌepi'də:mik] agg. epidermico

epigraph ['epigra:f] s. epigrafe f.

epilepsy ['epilepsi] s. epilessia f.

epilogue ['epilɔg] s. epilogo m.

epiphany [i'pifəni] s. epifania f.

episcopal [i'piskəpəl] agg. episcopale, vescovile

episode ['episoud] s. episodio m.

epistaxis [ˌepi'stæksis] s. epistassi f.

epitaph ['epita:f] s. epitaffio m.

epithet ['epiθet] s. epiteto m.

epoch ['i:pɔk] s. epoca f.

eponym ['epoʊnim] s. eponimo m.

eponymous [i'pɔniməs] agg. eponimo

equal ['i:kwəl] agg. uguale; pari

to equal ['i:kwəl] v. tr. uguagliare

equality [i(:)'kwɔliti] s. uguaglianza f.; parità f.

to equalize ['i:kwəlaiz] v. tr. uguagliare; pareggiare

equally ['i:(:)kwəli] avv. ugualmente

equator [i'kweitə*] s. equatore m.

equatorial [ˌekwə'tɔ:riəl] agg. equatoriale

equestrian [i'kwestriən] agg. equestre

equidistant ['i:kwi'distənt] agg. equidistante

equine ['i:kwain] agg. equino

equinox ['i:kwinɔks] s. equinozio m.

to equip [i'kwip] v. tr. equipaggiare; attrezzare

equipment [i'kwipmənt] s. attrezzatura f.; equipaggiamento m.

equivalent [i'kwivələnt] agg. equivalente

equivocal [i'kwivəkəl] agg. equivoco

era ['iərə] s. era f.

eraser [i'reiz] s. gomma f. (per cancellare)

erect [i'rekt] agg. eretto

to erect [i'rekt] v. tr. erigere

erosion [i'rouʒən] s. erosione f.

erotic [i'rɔtik] agg. erotico

erotism ['irɔtizəm] s. erotismo m.

errand ['erənd] s. commissione f.

error ['erə*] s. errore m.; colpa f.

eruption [i'rʌpʃən] s. eruzione f.

erythema [ˌeri'θi:mə] s. eritema m.

escalator ['eskəleitə*] s. scala f. mobile

escalope ['eskələp] s. scaloppina f.

escapade [ˌeskə'peid] s. scappatella f.

escape [is'keip] s. evasione f.; fuga f., scampo m.; scarico m.

to escape [is'keip] v. intr. evadere; fuggire; scappare

escarpment [is'ka:pmənt] s. scarpata f.

eschatological [ˌeskətə'lɔdʒikəl] agg. escatologico

escort ['eskɔ:t] s. scorta f.; accompagnatore m.; cavaliere m.

to escort [is'kɔ:t] v. tr. scortare

esoteric [ˌesou'terik] agg. esoterico

essay ['esei] s. saggio m.

essayist ['eseiist] s. saggista m. e f.

essence ['esns] s. essenza f.

essential [i'senʃəl] agg. essenziale

essentially [i'senʃəli] avv. essenzialmente

to establish [is'tæbliʃ] v. tr. stabilire; fondare; instaurare

establishment [is'tæbliʃmənt] s. azienda f.; stabilimento m.; istituzione f.; fondazione f.

estate [is'teit] s. patrimonio m.; proprietà f.; podere m.; – **agency** agenzia immobiliare; **real** – beni immobili

esteem [is'ti:m] s. stima f.

to esteem [is'ti:m] v. tr. stimare

estimate ['estimit] s. stima f.; preventivo m.

to estimate ['estimeit] v. tr. stimare; valutare

estimator ['estimeitə*] s. estimatore m.

estuary ['estjuəri] s. estuario m.

etching ['etʃiŋ] s. acquaforte f.

eternal [i(:)'tə:nl] agg. eterno; **eternally** eternamente eternity [i(:)'tə:niti] s. eternità f.

ethereal [i(:)'θiəriəl] agg. etereo

ethical ['eθikl] agg. etico

ethics ['eθiks] s. pl. (v. al sing.) etica f. sing.

ethnic ['eθnik] agg. etnico

ethnology [eθ'nɔlədʒi] s. etnologia f.

etiquette [eti'ket] s. galateo m.

Etruscan [i'trʌskən] agg. etrusco

etymology [ˌeti'mɔlədʒi] s. etimologia f.

euphemistic [ˌju:fi'mistik] agg. eufemistico

euphoria [ju:'fɔriəl] s. euforia f.

European [juərə'pi(:)ən] agg. europeo

Europeanism [juərə'pianizəm] s. europeismo m.

euthanasia [ju:θə'neizjə] s. eutanasia f.

to evacuate [i'vækjueit] v. tr. evacuare

to evade [i'veid] v. tr. evadere

evangelical [ˌi:væn'dʒelikəl] agg. evangelico

to evaporate [i'væpəreit] v. intr. evaporare

evaporation [iˌvæpə'reiʃən] s. evaporazione f.

evasion [i'veiʒən] s. evasione f.

evasive [i'veisiv] agg. evasivo

eve [i:v] s. vigilia f.

even ['i:vən] agg. piano; uniforme; pari (numero) • avv. perfino, addirittura; – if anche se

to even ['i:vən] v. tr. e intr. livellare, pareggiare; uguagliarsi

evening ['i:vniŋ] s. sera f.; serata f.

event [i'vent] s. evento m.; fatto m.

eventful [i'ventful] agg. movimentato

eventuality [iˌventju'æliti] s. evenienza f.

eventually [i'ventjuəli] avv. infine

ever ['evə*] avv. sempre; mai (frasi neg. e interr.); – after da allora; for – per sempre; hardly – quasi sempre; – since sin da (quando)

evergreen ['evəgri:n] agg. sempreverde

everlasting [ˌevə'la:stiŋ] agg. perenne

every ['evri] agg. ciascuno, ogni; tutti

everybody ['evribɔdi] pron. ciascuno, ognuno; tutti

everyday ['evridei] agg. giornaliero, quotidiano, comune

everyone ['evriwʌn] pron. ciascuno, ognuno; tutti

everything ['evriθiŋ] pron. tutto, ogni cosa

everywhere ['evriwɛə*] avv. dovunque

eviction [i(:)'vikʃən] s. sfratto m.

evidence ['evidəns] s. prova f., dimostrazione f.; evidenza f.

evident ['evidənt] agg. evidente, ovvio

evil ['i:vl] agg. cattivo • s. male m.

evocative [i'vɔkətiv] agg. suggestivo

evolution [ˌi:və'lu:ʃən] s. evoluzione f.

evolutive ['evəlu(:)tiv] agg. evolutivo

to exacerbate [eks'æsə(:)beit] v. tr. esacerbare

exact [ig'zækt] agg. esatto

to exact [ig'zækt] v. tr. esigere, pretendere

exacting [ig'zæktiŋ] agg. esigente

exactly [ig'zæktli] avv. precisamente; proprio

to exaggerate [ig'zædʒəreit] v. tr. e intr. esagerare

exaggeration [igˌzædʒə'reiʃən] s. esagerazione f.

to exalt [ig'zɔ:lt] v. tr. esaltare

exam [ig'zæm] s. esame m.

examination [igˌzæmi'neiʃən] s. esame m.; medical – visita medica

to examine [ig'zæmin] v. tr. esaminare; interrogare

example [ig'za:mpl] s. esempio m.

to exasperate [ig'za:spəreit] v. tr. esasperare

to excavate ['ekskəveit] v. tr. scavare

excavation [ˌekskə'veiʃən] s. scavo m.

excavator ['ekskəveitə*] s. scavatrice f.

to exceed [ik'si:d] v. tr. oltrepassare; superare • intr. eccedere

to excel [ik'sel] v. tr. superare • intr. eccellere

excellent ['eksələnt] agg. eccellente, ottimo

except [ik'sept] prep. eccetto, escluso; fuorché; – for fatta eccezione

exception [ik'sepʃən] s. eccezione f.

exceptional [ik'sepʃənl] agg. eccezionale; exceptionally eccezionalmente

excess [ik'ses] s. eccesso m. • agg. eccedente, in eccesso

excessive [ik'sesiv] agg. eccessivo

exchange [iks'tʃeindʒ] s. cambio m.; scambio m.; – rate tasso di cambio

to exchange [iks'tʃeindʒ] v. tr. cambiare; scambiare

excise [ek'saiz] s. dazio m.; imposta f.

excitable [ik'saitəbl] agg. eccitabile

to excite [ik'sait] v. tr. eccitare

exciting [ik'saitiŋ] agg. eccitante, emozionante, stimolante

to exclaim [iks'kleim] v. tr. e intr. esclamare

exclamation [ˌeksklə'meiʃən] s. esclamazione f., grido m.

to exclude [iks'klu:d] v. tr. escludere

exclusion [iks'klu:ʒən] s. esclusione f.

exclusive [iks'klu:siv] agg. esclusivo; exclusively esclusivamente

to excommunicate [ˌekskə'mju:nikeit] v. tr. scomunicare

excommunication [´ekskə‚mju:ni´keiʃən] s. scomunica f.

to excoriate [eks´kɔ:rieit] v. tr. scorticare

excoriation [eks‚kɔ:ri´eiʃən] s. escoriazione f.

to exculpate [´ekskʌlpeit] v. tr. discolpare; scagionare

excursion [iks´kə:ʃən] s. escursione f., gita f.

excursionist [iks´kə:ʃnist] s. gitante m. e f.

excuse [iks´kju:s] s. scusa f.; giustificazione f.; – me (mi) scusi; permesso

to excuse [iks´kju:z] v. tr. scusare; giustificare; perdonare; – oneself scusarsi

to execute [´eksikju:t] v. tr. eseguire, mettere in atto; giustiziare

execution [‚eksi´kju:ʃən] s. esecuzione f.

executioner [‚eksi´kju:ʃnə*] s. carnefice m.; boia m.

executive [ig´zekjutiv] agg. esecutivo • s. dirigente m. e f.

exedra [ek´si(:)drə] s. esedra f.

exemplary [ig´zempləri] agg. esemplare

exemplification [ig‚zemplifi´keiʃən] s. esemplificazione f.

exempt [ig´zempt] agg. esente

exercise [´eksəsaiz] s. esercizio m.; – book quaderno

to exercise [´eksəsaiz] v. tr. esercitare

to exert [ig´zə:t] v. tr. impiegare, esercitare

exertion [ig´zə:ʃən] s. esercizio m., sforzo m.

exhalation [‚ekshə´leiʃən] s. esalazione f.

to exhale [eks´heil] v. tr. e intr. esalare, emanare

exhaust [ig´zɔ:st] s. scappamento m.

to exhaust [ig´zɔ:st] v. tr. esaurire; **exhausting** estenuante, massacrante

exhausted [ig´zɔ(:)stid] agg. esausto; esaurito

exhaustive [ig´zɔ:stiv] agg. esauriente

to exhibit [ig´zibit] v. tr. esibire

exhibition [‚eksi´biʃən] s. esposizione f., mostra f.; salone m.

exhilarating [ig´ziləreitiŋ] agg. esilarante

exhortation [‚egzɔ:´teiʃən] s. esortazione f.

to exhume [eks´hju:m] v. tr. riesumare

exiguous [eg´zigjuəs] agg. esiguo

exile [´eksail] s. esilio m.; esule m. e f.

to exist [ig´zist] v. intr. esistere

existence [ig´zistəns] s. esistenza f.

existing [ig´zistiŋ] agg. esistente

exit [´eksit] s. uscita f.; **emergency** – uscita di sicurezza

exodus [´eksədəs] s. esodo m.

to exonerate [ig´zɔnəreit] v. tr. esonerare

exorbitant [ig´zɔ:bitənt] agg. esorbitante

to exorcize [´eksɔ:saiz] v. tr. esorcizzare

exotic [eg´zɔtik] agg. esotico

to expand [iks´pænd] v. tr. espandere; estendere; dilatare • intr. espandersi

expanse [iks´pæns] s. distesa f.

expansion [iks´pænʃən] s. espansione f.

expansive [iks´pænsiv] agg. espansivo

to expatriate [eks´pætrieit] v. intr. espatriare

to expect [iks´pekt] v. tr. aspettare; aspettarsi, prevedere

expectation [‚ekspek´teiʃən] s. aspettativa f., attesa f.

expediency [iks´pi:djənsi] s. opportunità f.; convenienza f.

expedient [iks´pi:djənt] agg. opportuno • s. espediente m.

expedition [‚ekspi´diʃən] s. spedizione f.

expeditious [‚ekspi´diʃəs] agg. sbrigativo

to expel [iks´pel] v. tr. emettere; espellere, scacciare

expense [iks´pens] s. spesa f., costo m.

expensive [iks´pensiv] agg. costoso, caro

experience [iks´piəriəns] s. esperienza f.

to experience [iks´piəriəns] v. tr. sperimentare, provare; subire, sentire

experiment [iks´perimənt] s. esperimento m.; prova f.

to experiment [iks´periment] v. tr. sperimentare

experimental [eks‚peri´mentl] agg. sperimentale

expert [´ekspə:t] agg. esperto, competente • s. perito m.

to expiate [´ekspieit] v. tr. espiare

expiration [‚ekspaiə´reiʃən] s. espirazione f.; scadenza f.

to expire [iks´paiə*] v. tr. e intr. espirare; scadere

expiry [iks´paiəri] s. termine m.

to explain [iks´plein] v. tr. spiegare, chiarire

explanation [‚eksplə´neiʃən] s. spiegazione f.

explicative [eks´plikativ] agg. esplicativo

explicit [iks´plisit] agg. esplicito; **explicitly** espressamente

to explode [iks´ploud] v. tr. e intr. esplodere

exploit [´eksplɔit] s. prodezza f.

to exploit [iks´plɔit] v. tr. sfruttare

exploiter [iks´plɔitə*] s. sfruttatore m.

exploration [‚eksplɔ:´reiʃən] s. esplorazione f.

to explore [iks´plɔ:*] v. tr. esplorare

explorer [iks´plɔ:rə*] s. esploratore m.

explosion [iks´plouʒən] s. esplosione f., scoppio m.

60

explosive [iks'plousiv] *agg. e s.* esplosivo *m.*

exponent [eks'pounənt] *s.* esponente *m. e f.*

export ['ekspɔːt] *s.* esportazione *f.*

to export [eks'pɔːt] *v. tr.* esportare

to expose [iks'pouz] *v. tr.* esporre; svelare; smascherare

exposition [,ekspə'ziʃən] *s.* esposizione *f.*

exposure [iks'pouʒə*] *s.* esposizione *f.*; – **meter** esposimetro

express [iks'pres] *agg.* espresso

to express [iks'pres] *v. tr.* esprimere

expression [iks'preʃən] *s.* espressione *f.*

expressionism [iks'preʃnizəm] *s.* espressionismo *m.*

expressive [iks'presiv] *agg.* espressivo, significativo

expressly [iks'presli] *avv.* espressamente

expropriation [eks'proupri'eiʃən] *s.* esproprio *m.*, espropriazione *f.*

expulsion [iks'pʌlʃən] *s.* espulsione *f.*

exquisite ['ekskwizit] *agg.* squisito

extemporary [iks'tempərəri] *agg.* estemporaneo

to extend [iks'tend] *v. tr.* estendere; prolungare • *intr.* estendersi

extension [iks'tenʃən] *s.* estensione *f.*; prolungamento *m.*

extensive [iks'tensiv] *agg.* esteso, vasto

to extenuate [eks'tenjueit] *v. tr.* attenuare

exterior [eks'tiəriə*] *agg.* esterno; esteriore

to exterminate [eks'tə:mineit] *v. tr.* sterminare, distruggere

extermination [eks,tə:mi'neiʃən] *s.* sterminio *m.*, distruzione *f.*

external [eks'tə:nl] *agg.* esterno; esteriore; **externally** esternamente

extinct [iks'tiŋkt] *agg.* estinto

extinction [iks'tiŋkʃən] *s.* spegnimento *m.*; estinzione *f.*

to extinguish [iks'tiŋwiʃ] *v. tr.* spegnere; estinguere

extinguisher [iks'tiŋwiʃə*] *s.* estintore *m.*

to extirpate ['ekstə:peit] *v. tr.* estirpare

to extort [iks'tɔ:t] *v. tr.* estorcere

extra ['ekstrə] *agg.* aggiuntivo

extract ['ekstrækt] *s.* estratto *m.*

to extract [iks'trækt] *v. tr.* estrarre

extractable [iks'træktəbl] *agg.* estraibile

extraction [iks'trækʃən] *s.* estrazione *f.*

extrados [eks'treidəs] *s.* estradosso *m.*

extraneous [eks'treinjəs] *agg.* estraneo

extraordinary [iks'trɔ:dənəri] *agg.* straordinario, eccezionale

extraterrestrial [,ekstrəti'restriəl] *agg.* extraterrestre

extravagance [iks'trævigəns] *s.* stravaganza *f.*; prodigalità *f.*

extravagant [iks'trævigənt] *agg.* stravagante; prodigo

extreme [iks'tri:m] *agg.* estremo; **extremely** estremamente

extremist [iks'tri:mist] *s.* estremista *m. e f.* • *agg.* estremistico

extremity [iks'tremiti] *s.* estremità *f.*

extrinsic [eks'trinsik] *agg.* estrinseco

extroverted [,ekstrou'və:tid] *agg.* estroverso

exuberant [ig'zju:bərənt] *agg.* esuberante

to exude [ig'zju:d] *v. tr. e intr.* trasudare; stillare; emanare

to exult [ig'zʌlt] *v. intr.* esultare

eye [ai] *s.* occhio *m.*; – **socket** orbita; – **shadow** ombretto; – **witness** testimone oculare; – **ball** bulbo oculare

eyebrow ['aibrau] *s.* sopracciglio *m.*

eyelash ['ailæʃ] *s.* ciglio *m.*

eyelid ['ailid] *s.* palpebra *f.*

eyesight [ai-sait] *s.* vista *f.*

F

fable ['feɪbl] s. favola f.

fabric ['fæbrɪk] s. tessuto m.

to fabricate ['fæbrɪkeɪt] v. tr. falsificare

fabrication [,fæbri'keɪʃən] s. falso m.; menzogna f.

fabulous ['fæbjʊləs] agg. favoloso

façade [fə'saːd] s. facciata f.

face [feɪs] s. faccia f., volto m.; facciata f.; – **mask** maschera di bellezza

to face [feɪs] v. tr. e intr. affrontare; fronteggiare

facilitation [fə,sɪlɪ'teɪʃən] s. facilitazione f.; agevolazione f.

facility [fə'sɪlɪtɪ] s. facilitazione f. • pl. attrezzature f.

facing ['feɪsɪŋ] agg. prospiciente • s. rivestimento m.

facsimile [fæk'sɪmɪlɪ] s. facsimile m. inv.

fact [fækt] s. fatto m.

factious ['fækʃəs] agg. fazioso

factor ['fæktə*] s. fattore m., coefficiente m.

factory ['fæktərɪ] s. fabbrica f.; stabilimento m.; manifattura f.

faculty ['fækəltɪ] s. facoltà f.

to fade [feɪd] v. intr. avvizzire; scolorire, sbiadire; svanire

fading ['feɪdɪŋ] s. dissolvenza f. (cin.); tramonto m. (fig.)

faeces ['fiːsiːz] s. pl. feci f.

to fail [feɪl] v. intr. fallire; mancare • tr. bocciare

failure ['feɪljə*] s. fallimento m.; insuccesso m.; guasto m. (mecc.)

faint [feɪnt] agg. debole, esile; pallido • s. svenimento m.

to faint [feɪnt] v. intr. svenire

fair [feə*] agg. bello; giusto; biondo • s. fiera f.; **trade** – fiera campionaria

fairly ['feəlɪ] avv. discretamente

fairy ['feərɪ] s. fata f.; – **tale** fiaba

faith [feɪθ] s. fede f.

faithful ['feɪθfʊl] agg. fedele

faithfulness ['feɪθfʊlnɪs] s. fedeltà f.

fake [feɪk] s. falsificazione f., falso m.

to fake [feɪk] v. tr. falsificare

fakir ['faːkɪə*] s. fachiro m.

fall [fɔːl] s. caduta f.; crollo m.; ribasso m.; autunno m. (USA). – **off** contrazione

to fall [fɔːl] v. intr. cadere; precipitare; discendere; riversarsi; – **asleep** addormentarsi; – **ill** ammalarsi; – **in love** innamorarsi

fallen ['fɔːlən] agg. caduto

falling ['fɔːlɪŋ] agg. cadente • s. caduta f.; decadimento m.

false [fɔːls] agg. falso; falsificato; posticcio

falsification ['fɔːlsɪfɪ'keɪʃən] s. falsificazione f.

falsifier ['fɔːlsɪfaɪə*] s. falsario m.

to falsify ['fɔːlsɪfaɪ] v. tr. falsificare, truccare

to falter ['fɔːltə*] v. intr. incespicare; balbettare; esitare

fame [feɪm] s. fama f.

familiar [fə'mɪljə*] agg. familiare, consueto, comune

to familiarize [fə'mɪljəraɪz] v. tr. rendere familiare; – **oneself** familiarizzarsi

family ['fæmɪlɪ] s. famiglia f. • agg. familiare; – **name** cognome m.

famine ['fæmɪn] s. carestia f.

famous ['feɪməs] agg. famoso

fan [fæn] s. ammiratore m.; tifoso m. • ventaglio m.; ventilatore m.; ventola f.

fanatic [fə'nætɪk] agg. fanatico; tifoso

fanaticism [fə'nætɪsɪzəm] s. fanatismo m.

fancy ['fænsɪ] s. immaginazione f.; fantasia f. • agg. speciale

to fancy ['fænsɪ] v. tr. immaginare

fang [fæŋ] s. zanna f.; dente m. (spec. di serpente)

fantastic [fæn'tæstɪk] agg. fantastico

fantasy ['fæntəsɪ] s. fantasia f.

far [faː*] agg. lontano • avv. lontano; assai; di gran lunga – **away** distante; – **from** lontano da; **as** – **as** per quanto riguarda, fino a; – **seeing** lungimirante; **so** – finora

farce [faːs] s. farsa f.

fare [feə*] s. tariffa f.

farinaceous [,færɪ'neɪʃəs] agg. farinaceo

farm [faːm] s. podere m.; fattoria f.; – **holidays** agriturismo

to farm [faːm] v. tr. coltivare

farmer ['fa:mə°] s. agricoltore m., contadino m.

farmhouse ['fa:mhaus] s. fattoria f.

farming ['fa:miŋ] s. agricoltura f.

farrier ['færiə°] s. maniscalco m.

farther ['fa:ðə°] avv. oltre; più lontano

fascinating ['fæsineitiŋ] agg. affascinante

fascination [,fæsi'neiʃən] s. fascino m.

Fascism ['fæʃizəm] s. fascismo m.

fashion ['fæʃən] s. foggia f.; moda f.; **fashionable** alla moda; **out of** - fuori moda

fast [fa:st] v. diguino m.   •   agg. veloce; fisso   •   avv. velocemente; saldamente

to fast [fa:st] v. intr. digiunare

to fasten ['fa:sn] v. tr. attaccare; fissare; allacciare

fastening ['fa:sniŋ] s. chiusura f.

fat [fæt] agg. grasso

fatal ['feitl] agg. fatidico, fatale

fatalist ['feitəlist] s. fatalista m. e f.

fatality [fə'tæliti] s. fatalità f.

fate [feit] s. fato m., sorte f.

father ['fa:ðə°] s. padre m.; **father-in-law** suocero

fatherhood ['fa:ðəhud] s. paternità f.

fatherly ['fa:ðəli] agg. paterno

fathom ['fæðəm] s. braccio m. (misura)

fatigue [fə'ti:g] s. fatica f., stanchezza f.

to fatten ['fætn] v. tr. e intr. ingrassare

fault [fɔ:lt] s. difetto m.; colpa f.; mancanza f.; errore m.

faultless ['fɔ:ltlis] agg. inappuntabile

faulty ['fɔ:lti] agg. difettoso

faun [fɔ:n] s. fauno m.

fauna ['fɔ:nə] s. fauna f.

favour ['feivə°] s. favore m.; cortesia f.

favourable ['feivərəbl] agg. favorevole, vantaggioso

favourite ['feivərit] agg. e s. favorito m., prediletto m.

favouritism ['feivəritizəm] s. favoritismo m.

fear [fiə°] s. timore m., spavento m., paura f.

to fear [fiə°] v. tr. temere

fearful ['fiəful] agg. spaventoso, pauroso

fearless ['fiəlis] agg. intrepido

feasible ['fi:zəbl] agg. fattibile

feast [fi:st] s. festa f.; banchetto m.

feat [fi:t] s. prodezza f.; atto m.

feather ['feðə°] s. penna f., piuma f.

feature ['fi:tʃə°] s. sembianza f.; **features** caratteristiche

February ['februəri] s. febbraio m.

to fecundate ['fi:kəndeit] v. tr. fecondare

federation [,fedə'reiʃən] s. federazione f.

fed up [fed ʌp] agg. stufo (fam.); **to be** - essere stufo, essere depresso

fee [fi:] s. tassa f.; compenso m., onorario m.; **school fees** tasse scolastiche

feeble ['fi:bl] agg. debole

to feed [fi:d] v. tr. e intr. cibare, nutrire; imboccare; - **oneself** nutrirsi

feeding ['fi:diŋ] s. cibo; - **bottle** poppatoio

to feel [fi:l] v. tr. e intr. percepire, sentire; provare; palpare - **blue** essere di cattivo umore

feeling ['fi:liŋ] s. sensazione f., impressione f.

feline ['fi:lain] agg. felino

fellow ['felou] s. individuo m.; tipo m.; membro m. (di associazione, accademia)   •   agg. compagno: - **citizen** concittadino m.; - **countryman** connazionale

female ['fi:meil] s. femmina f.   •   agg. femminile

feminine ['feminin] agg. femminile

femur ['fi:mə°] s. femore m.

fen [fen] s. palude f.

fence [fens] s. palizzata f., recinto m., staccionata f.

fencing ['fensiŋ] s. scherma f.

fender ['fendə°] s. parabordo m. (naut.)

fennel ['fenl] s. finocchio m.

fermentation [,fə:men'teiʃən] s. fermentazione f., fermento m.

fern [fə:n] s. felce f.

ferocious [fə'rouʃəs] agg. feroce

ferrule ['feru:l] s. puntale m.

ferry ['feri] s. traghetto m.

to ferry ['feri] v. tr. traghettare

fertile ['fə:tail] agg. fecondo, fertile

fertilizer ['fə:tilaizə°] s. fertilizzante m.

festival ['festəvəl] s. festa f.; festival m

festivity ['fe:'stiviti] s. festività f.

to fetch [fetʃ] v. tr. portare, andare a prendere

fetishism ['fi:tiʃizm] s. feticismo m.

feudal ['fju:dl] agg. feudale

feudalism ['fju:dəlizəm] s. feudalesimo m.

fever ['fi:və°] s. febbre f.; **hay** - febbre da fieno

feverish ['fi:vəriʃ] agg. febbricitante

few [fju:] agg. e pron. pochi, poche; **a** - alcuni, alcune

fiancé [fi'ã:nsei] s. fidanzato m.

fib [fib] s. bugia f.

fibre ['faibə°] s. fibra f.

fibula ['fibjulə] s. perone m.

fickle ['fikl] agg. incostante

fiction ['fikʃən] s. narrativa f.; finzione f.

fictitious [fik'tiʃəs] agg. fittizio, immaginario

63

fiddle ['fidl] *s.* violino *m.*

to fiddle ['fidl] *v. intr.* gingillarsi • suonare il violino

fiddler ['fidlə•] *s.* violinista *m. e f.*

fidelity [fi'deliti] *s.* fedeltà *f.*

fief [fi:f] *s.* feudo *m.*

field [fi:ld] *s.* campo *m.*; terreno *m.*; settore *m.*

fiend [fi:nd] *s.* demonio *m.*

fierce [fiəs] *agg.* feroce

fiery ['faiəri] *agg.* ardente

fig [fig] *s.* fico *m.*

fight [fait] *s.* combattimento *m.*

to fight [fait] *v. intr.* combattere, lottare • *tr.* combattere; opporsi a

figurative ['figjurətiv] *agg.* figurativo

figure ['figə•] *s.* figura *f.*; cifra *f.*

file [fail] *s.* archivio *m.*, schedario *m.*; lima *f.*; fila *f.*

to file [fail] *v. tr.* archiviare, schedare; limare

filibustering [filibʌstəriŋ] *s.* ostruzionismo *m.*

filiform ['filifɔ:m] *agg.* filiforme

filigree ['filigri:] *s.* filigrana *f.*

to fill [fil] *v. tr. e intr.* riempire; compilare; riempirsi; – **in** compilare un modulo

filling ['filiŋ] *s.* otturazione *f.*; compilazione *f.*

film [film] *s.* pellicola *f.*; membrana *f.*; film *m.*

to film [film] *v. tr.* filmare

filter ['filtə•] *s.* filtro *m.*

to filter ['filtə•] *v. tr. e intr.* filtrare

filth [filθ] *s.* porcheria *f.*, sporcizia *f.*

filthiness ['filθinis] *s.* sporcizia *f.*

filthy ['filθi] *agg.* lurido, sporco

fin [fin] *s.* pinna *f.*

final ['fainl] *agg.* finale; definitivo; ultimo • *s. pl.* finale *f. sing.*

finalist [fai'nəlist] *s.* finalista *m. e f.*

finally ['fainəli] *avv.* infine

finance [fai'næns] *s.* finanza *f.*

financial [fai'nænʃəl] *agg.* finanziario

financing [fai'nænsiŋ] *s.* finanziamento *m.*

find [faind] *s.* reperto *m.*; scoperta *f.*; trovata *f.*

to find [faind] *v. tr.* trovare, ritrovare, rinvenire; – **out** scoprire

finding ['faindiŋ] *s.* ritrovamento *m.*, scoperta *f.* • *pl.* conclusioni *f.*

fine [fain] *s.* multa *f.*, contravvenzione *f.* • *agg.* bello; bravo; fine, sottile

to fine [fain] *v. tr.* multare

finger ['fiŋgə•] *s.* dito *m.*; **little** – mignolo

to finger ['fiŋgə•] *v. tr.* palpare, toccare

fingerprint ['fiŋgəprint] *s.* impronta *f.* digitale

finish ['finiʃ] *s.* finale *m.*; finitura *f.*; fine *f.*

to finish ['finiʃ] *v. tr.* finire; rifinire

finishing ['finiʃiŋ] *agg.* conclusivo; – **line** traguardo; – **touch** ritocco

fiord [fjɔ:d] *s.* fiordo *m.*

fir [fə:•] *s.* abete *m.*

fire ['faiə•] *s.* fuoco *m.*; incendio *m.*

to fire ['faiə•] *v. tr.* sparare

fireman ['faiəmən] *s.* pompiere *m.*

fireplace ['faiə-pleis] *s.* caminetto *m.*, camino *m.*

fireproof ['faiə-pru:f] *agg.* ignifugo

fireworks ['faiəwə:ks] *s. pl.* fuochi *m.* d'artificio

firm [fə:m] *agg.* fermo, saldo • azienda *f.*, ditta *f.*

firmament ['fə:məmənt] *s.* firmamento *m.*; cielo *m.*

first [fə:st] *agg.* primo; principale • *avv.* innanzitutto; – **aid** pronto soccorso; **at** – dapprima; – **class** prima qualità; – **floor** pianterreno; – **born** primogenito; – **lady** consorte (del Presidente USA); – **mate** primo ufficiale (*naut.*); – **name** nome di battesimo (USA); – **night** prima teatrale; – **rate** eccellente

fiscal ['fiskəl] *agg.* fiscale

fish [fiʃ] *s.* pesce *m.*; – **bone** lisca; – **hook** amo

to fish [fiʃ] *v. tr. e intr.* pescare

fisherman ['fiʃəmən] *s.* pescatore *m.*

fishing ['fiʃiŋ] *s.* pesca *f.*; – **boat** peschereccio; – **line** lenza; – **net** rete da pesca

fishmonger ['fiʃ,mʌngə•] *s.* pescivendolo *m.*

fissure ['fiʃə•] *s.* fessura *f.*

fist [fist] *s.* pugno *m.*

fistful ['fistfəl] *s.* manciata *f.*

fit [fit] *agg.* adatto; in forma • *s.* adattamento *m.* • attacco *m.* (*med.*)

to fit [fit] *v. tr. e intr.* adattarsi; calzare

fitchew ['fitʃu:] *s.* puzzola *f.*

fitness ['fitnis] *s.* idoneità *f.*; buona salute *f.*

fitting ['fitiŋ] *s.* prova *f.* (in sartoria); montaggio *m.* • *pl.* attrezzatura *f. sing.*; arredamento *m. sing.*; accessori *m.*; – **out** allestimento (*naut.*)

fix [fiks] *s.* pasticcio *m.*

to fix [fiks] *v. tr.* fissare; stabilire; – **up** sistemare, aggiustare

fixed [fikst] *agg.* fisso

fixing ['fiksiŋ] *s.* fissazione *f.*

fizzy ['fizi] *agg.* effervescente, frizzante

flabby ['flæbi] *agg.* flaccido, molle

flag [flæg] *s.* bandiera *f.*

flagellation [,flædʒə'leiʃən] *s.* flagellazione *f.*

flageolet [,flædʒə'let] *s.* zufolo *m.*

flagon ['flægən] s. caraffa f.; fiasco m., bottiglione m.

flake [fleik] s. fiocco m.; scaglia f.; **snow** – fiocco di neve

flame [fleim] s. fiamma f.

flank [flæŋk] s. fianco m.; fiancata f.

flannel ['flænl] s. flanella f.

flap [flæp] s. falda f.; ribalta f.

flare [fleə*] s. fiammata f.; svasatura f.

flash [flæʃ] s. bagliore m., lampo m.

to flash [flæʃ] v. intr. lampeggiare, scintillare

flat [flæt] s. appartamento m.; pianura f. • agg. netto; piano, pianeggiante; sgonfio (pneumatico); scarico (elettr.)

to flatter ['flætə*] v. tr. lusingare

flattering ['flætətəriŋ] agg. lusinghiero

flavour ['fleivə*] s. aroma m., gusto m.

to flavour ['fleivə*] v. tr. aromatizzare, insaporire; condire

flavouring ['fleivəriŋ] s. condimento m.

flavourless ['fleivəlis] agg. insapore

flaw [flɔ:] s. imperfezione f., difetto m.

flax [flæks] s. lino m.

flea [fli:] s. pulce f.; – **market** mercatino

to flee [fli:] v. intr. fuggire, scappare

fleet [fli:t] s. flotta f.

Fleming ['fleming] agg. fiammingo

Flemish ['flemiʃ] agg. fiammingo

flesh [fleʃ] s. carne f.

flexibility ['fleksə'biliti] s. flessibilità f.; elasticità f.

flexible ['fleksəbl] agg. flessibile

flexuous ['fleksjuəs] agg. flessuoso

flight [flait] s. volo m.; stormo m.; traiettoria f.

flimsy ['flimzi] agg. fragile

to fling [fliŋ] v. tr. gettare; sbalzare

flint [flint] s. selce f.

flipper ['flipə*] s. pinna f.

to float [flout] v. intr. galleggiare; fluttuare

floating ['floutiŋ] agg. galleggiante; fluttuante

flock [flɔk] s. batuffolo m. • gregge m.; stormo m.

to flog [flɔg] v. tr. frustare

flogging ['flɔgiŋ] s. fustigazione f.

flood [flʌd] s. alluvione f.; diluvio m.; piena f.; marea f.

to flood [flʌd] v. tr. allagare, inondare; salire (marea); **flooding** ingolfato (carburatore)

floor [flɔ:*] s. pavimento m.; piano m.

to floor [flɔ:*] v. tr. pavimentare

flooring ['flɔ:riŋ] s. pavimentazione f.

flop [flɔp] s. insuccesso m. (fam.)

flora ['flɔ:rə] s. flora f.

floral ['flɔ:rəl] agg. floreale

floriculture ['flɔ:ri,kʌltʃə*] s. floricoltura f.

florid ['flɔrid] agg. florido

florist ['flɔrist] s. fioraio m.

flotilla [flou'tilə] s. flottiglia f.

flour ['flauə*] s. farina f.

to flourish ['flʌriʃ] v. intr. fiorire; prosperare

flourishing ['flʌriʃiŋ] agg. prosperoso

flow [flou] s. flusso m.

to flow [flou] v. intr. fluire; inondare; scorrere; circolare

flower ['flauə*] s. fiore m.; – **bed** aiuola; – **box** fioriera

to flower ['flauə*] v. intr. fiorire

flowering ['flauəriŋ] s. fioritura f.

flowing ['flouiŋ] agg. fluido; scorrevole

flu [flu:] s. influenza f.

to fluctuate ['flʌktjueit] v. intr. fluttuare; oscillare

fluctuating ['flʌktʃuətiŋ] agg. fluttuante; oscillante

fluctuation [,flʌktju'eiʃən] s. fluttuazione f.; oscillazione f.

fluency ['flu:ənsi] s. scorrevolezza f.; scioltezza f., facilità f. (di parola)

fluent ['fluənt] agg. scorrevole, fluente

fluid ['flu:id] agg. fluido

fluorescent [fluə'resənt] agg. fluorescente

fluorine ['fluəri:n] s. fluoro m.

flush [flʌʃ] s. getto m.; afflusso m.; rossore m.

to flush [flʌʃ] v. intr. scorrere; arrossire • tr. sciacquare, lavare (con un getto d'acqua)

flute [flu:t] s. flauto m.; scanalatura f. (arch.)

to flutter ['flʌtə*] v. intr. battere; fluttuare; agitarsi; tremare; sventolare

flux [flʌks] s. flusso m.

fly [flai] s. mosca f. • volo m.; – **leaf** risvolto

to fly [flai] v. intr. volare; – **across** trasvolare

foam [foum] s. schiuma f.; – **rubber** gommapiuma

foamy ['foumi] agg. schiumoso

focus ['foukəs] s. fuoco m. (fotografia)

to focus ['foukəs] v. tr. mettere a fuoco

fodder ['fɔdə*] s. foraggio m., mangime m.

fog [fɔg] s. nebbia f.; – **horn** corno da nebbia

foggy ['fɔgi] agg. nebbioso

fold [fould] s. piega f.

to fold [fould] v. tr. piegare

folder ['fouldə*] s. cartelletta f.

folding ['fouldiŋ] agg. pieghevole

foliage ['fouliidʒ] s. fogliame m.

folk [fouk] *s.* gente *f.* • *agg.* popolare, folcloristico

folklore ['fouklɔ:*] *s.* folclore *m.*

to follow ['fɔlou] *v. tr. e intr.* seguire

follower ['fɔlouə*] *s.* seguace *m. e f.*

following ['fɔlouiŋ] *agg.* seguente; successivo

fond [fɔnd] *agg.* affezionato; appassionato; **to be – of** piacere; voler bene a

to fondle ['fɔndl] *v. tr.* vezzeggiare; accarezzare

food [fu:d] *s.* cibo *m.*, nutrimento *m.*; vitto *m.*; **– grinder** tritatutto; **sea –** frutti di mare

fool [fu:l] *s.* sciocco, stupido

foolish ['fu:liʃ] *agg.* sciocco, balordo

foolishness ['fu:liʃnis] *s.* stupidità *f.*

foot [fut] *s.* piede *m.*; zoccolo *m.* (*arch.*)

football ['futbɔ:l] *s.* calcio *m.*

footballer ['futbɔ:lə*] *s.* calciatore *m.*

footboard [,futbɔ:d] *s.* pedana *f.*

footprint ['futprint] *s.* orma *f.*

fop [fɔp] *s.* vanesio *m.*

foppish ['fɔpiʃ] *agg.* vanesio

for [fɔ:*, fə*] *prep.* per; a; in modo che; perché; da; di; **to be –** servire

forage ['fɔridʒ] *s.* foraggio *m.*

to forbid [fə'bid] *v. tr.* proibire, vietare

forbidden [fə'bidn] *agg.* vietato

force [fɔ:s] *s.* forza *f.*

to force [fɔ:s] *v. tr.* forzare, costringere

forced [fɔ:st] *agg.* forzato, costretto

forcedly [fɔ:sidli] *avv.* forzatamente

ford [fɔ:d] *s.* guado *m.*

to ford [fɔ:d] *v. tr.* guadare

forearm ['fɔ:ra:m] *s.* avambraccio *m.*

to forebode [fɔ:'boud] *v. tr.* presagire

forecast ['fɔ:-ka:st] *s.* previsione *f.*

to forecast [fɔ:-ka:st] *v. tr.* prevedere

forefather ['fɔ:,fa:ðə*] *s.* antenato *m.*; progenitore *m.*

forefinger [fɔ:-fiŋgə*] *s.* indice *m.*

foregone [fɔ:'gɔ:n] *agg.* previsto, scontato

foreign ['fɔrin] *agg.* straniero, estero; estraneo

foreigner ['fɔrinə*] *s.* straniero *m.*

foreman ['fɔ:mən] *s.* caposquadra

forensic [fə'rensik] *agg.* forense

forerunner ['fɔ:rʌnə*] *s.* precursore *m.*

to foresee [fɔ:'si:] *v. tr.* presagire, prevedere

to foreshadow [fɔ:'fædou] *v. tr.* prefigurare

foreshortening [fɔ:'fɔ:təniŋ] *s.* scorcio *m.* (*arte*)

foresight ['fɔ'-sait] *s.* previdenza *f.*

forest ['fɔrist] *s.* foresta *f.*

to forestall [fɔ:'stɔ:l] *v. tr.* prevenire

to foretaste [fɔ:'teist] *v. tr.* pregustare

to foretell [fɔ:'tel] *v. tr.* predire

to forewarn [fɔ:'wɔ:n] *v. tr.* preavvisare

foreword ['fɔ:wə:d] *s.* prefazione *f.*

forfeit ['fɔ:fit] *s.* penale *f.*; penitenza *f.*

to forge [fɔ:dʒ] *v. tr.* falsificare; forgiare

forger ['fɔ:dʒə*] *s.* falsario *m.*

forgery ['fɔ:dʒəri] *s.* falsificazione *f.*

to forget [fə'get] *v. tr. e intr.* dimenticare

forgetfulness [fə'getfulnis] *s.* dimenticanza *f.*

forgivable [fə'givəbl] *agg.* perdonabile

to forgive [fə'giv] *v. tr. e intr.* perdonare

forgiveness [fə'givnis] *s.* perdono *m.*

fork [fɔ:k] *s.* forchetta *f.*; bivio *m.*, biforcazione *f.*

form [fɔ:m] *s.* forma *f.*; modulo *m.*; **bad –** maleducazione

to form [fɔ:m] *v. tr. e intr.* formare; comporre, costituire; formarsi

formal ['fɔ:məl] *agg.* formale; **– dress** abito da cerimonia

formalism ['fɔ:məlizəm] *s.* formalismo *m.*

formality [fɔ:'mæliti] *s.* formalità *f.*

formation [fɔ:'meiʃən] *s.* formazione *f.*

former ['fɔ:mə*] *agg.* anteriore; precedente; antico

formerly ['fɔ:məli] *avv.* già; in passato

formidable ['fɔ:midəbl] *agg.* formidabile

formula ['fɔ:mjulə] *s.* formula *f.*

formulary ['fɔ:mjuləri] *s.* formulario *m.*

fornix ['fɔ:niks] *s.* fornice *m.*

to forsake [fə'seik] *v. tr.* abbandonare

fort [fɔ:t] *s.* fortezza *f.*

forth [fɔ:θ] *avv.* avanti

fortification [,fɔ:tifi'keiʃən] *s.* fortificazione *f.*, rafforzamento *m.*

to fortify [fɔ:'tifai] *v. tr.* fortificare

fortnight ['fɔ:tnait] *s.* due settimane *f. pl.*

fortnightly ['fɔ:t,naitli] *agg.* quindicinale

fortress ['fɔ:tris] *s.* rocca *f.*

fortuitous [fɔ:'tju:(:)itəs] *agg.* fortuito

fortunate ['fɔ:tʃnit] *agg.* fausto

fortune ['fɔ:tʃən] *s.* fortuna *f.*, sorte *f.*; **– teller** cartomante

forum ['fɔ:rəm] *s.* foro *m.*

forward ['fɔ:wəd] *avv.* avanti

to forward ['fɔ:wəd] *v. tr.* inoltrare; inviare

forwarder ['fɔ:wədə*] *s.* spedizioniere *m.*

forwarding ['fɔ:wdiŋ] *s.* invio *m.*, spedizione *f.* (*comm.*)

fossil ['fɔsil] *s. e agg.* fossile

to fossilize ['fɔsilaiz] *v. intr.* fossilizzarsi

foster ['fɔstə*] agg. adottivo; – child figlio adottivo; – parent genitore adottivo

foul [faul] agg. brutto; schifoso

to found [faund] v. tr. fondare; istituire

foundation [faun'deiʃən] s. fondazione f.

founder ['faundə*] s. fondatore m.

founding ['faundiŋ] agg. fondatore • s. fondazione f.; fondatore m.; fusione f.

fountain ['fauntin] s. fontana f.; – pen stilografica

fox [fɔks] s. volpe f.

fraction ['frækʃən] s. frazione f.

to fractionize ['frækʃənaiz] v. tr. frazionare

fracture ['fræktʃə*] s. frattura f.

fragile ['frædʒail] agg. fragile

fragment ['frægmənt] s. frammento m.

fragmentary ['frægməntəri] agg. frammentario

fragrant ['freigrənt] agg. fragrante, odoroso

frail [freil] agg. fragile, debole

frame [freim] s. cornice f.; intelaiatura f.; struttura f.

to frame [freim] v. tr. formare; incorniciare; inquadrare

framework ['freimwɔ:k] s. intelaiatura f.

franchise ['fræntʃaiz] s. franchigia f.

Francophone ['frænkoufoun] agg. francofono

frantic ['fræntik] agg. frenetico

to fraternize ['frætənaiz] v. intr. fraternizzare

fraud [frɔ:d] s. frode f.

fraudulent ['frɔ:djulənt] agg. fraudolento

fray [frei] s. mischia f.

freckle ['frekl] s. lentiggine f.

free [fri:] agg. libero; esente; gratuito

to free [fri:] v. tr. liberare

freedom ['fri:dəm] s. libertà f.

freely ['fri:li] avv. liberamente

to freeze [fri:z] v. tr. e intr. congelare

freezer ['fri:zə*] s. congelatore m.

freezing ['fri:ziŋ] agg. ghiacciato

freight [freit] s. trasporto m.; carico m.; noleggio m.

freighter ['freitə*] s. nave f. da carico; noleggiatore m.

French [frentʃ] agg. francese; – fries patate fritte (USA)

Frenchman ['frentʃmən] s. francese m.

Frenchwoman ['frentʃ,wumən] s. francese f.

frenzied ['frenzid] agg. frenetico

frequency ['fri:kwənsi] s. frequenza f.

frequent ['fri:kwənt] agg. frequente

to frequent [fri'kwənt] v. intr. praticare

frequently ['fri:kwəntli] avv. frequentemente

fresco ['freskou] s. affresco m.

fresh [freʃ] agg. fresco

freshness ['freʃnis] s. freschezza f.

friable ['fraiəbl] agg. friabile

friar ['fraiə*] s. frate m.

friction ['frikʃən] s. frizione f.

Friday ['fraidi] s. venerdì m.

fridge [fridʒ] s. frigorifero m.

fried [fraid] agg. fritto

friend [frend] s. amico m.

friendly ['frendli] agg. amico; amichevole

friendship ['frendʃip] s. amicizia f.

frieze [fri:z] s. fregio m.

fright [frait] s. paura f., spavento m.

to frighten ['fraitn] v. tr. impaurire, spaventare, atterrire

frightful ['fraitful] agg. spaventoso, tremendo

frill [fril] s. gala f., trina f.

fringe [frindʒ] s. frangia f.

frippery ['fripəri] s. fronzolo m.

frivolous ['frivələs] agg. frivolo

frock [frɔk] s. tonaca f.

frog [frɔg] s. rana f.

frogman ['frɔgmən] s. sommozzatore m.

to frolic ['frɔlik] v. intr. folleggiare

from [frɔm, frəm] prep. da

front [frʌnt] s. fronte f.; facciata f.; in – of di fronte a

frontal ['frʌntl] agg. frontale

frontier ['frʌntjə*] s. frontiera f.

frontispiece ['frʌntispi:s] s. frontespizio m.

fronton ['frʌntən] s. frontone m.

frost [frɔst] s. gelo m.; brina f.

froth [frɔθ] s. schiuma f.

frothy ['frɔθi] agg. schiumoso

frozen ['frouzn] agg. gelato, ghiacciato

frugal ['fru:gəl] agg. frugale

fruit [fru:t] s. frutto m.; – salad macedonia

fruitful ['fru:tful] agg. fecondo, fertile

frustration [frʌs'treiʃən] s. frustrazione f.

fry [frai] s. frittura f.

to fry [frai] v. tr. friggere

frying ['fraiiŋ] agg. fritto; – pan padella

fuel [fjuəl] s. combustibile m.

fugitive ['fju:dʒitiv] agg. fuggiasco, profugo

fulcrum ['fʌlkrəm] s. fulcro m.

to fulfil [ful'fil] v. tr. esaudire

fulguration [,fʌlgju'reiʃən] s. folgorazione f.

full [ful] agg. pieno; intero; – stop punto; – up sazio

fulminant ['fʌlminənt] agg. fulminante

fumigator ['fju:migeitə*] s. zampirone m.

fun [fʌn] *s.* allegria *f.*; divertimento *m.*; – **fair** luna park

function ['fʌŋkʃən] *s.* funzione *f.*

functional ['fʌŋkʃənl] *agg.* funzionale

functionalism ['fʌŋkʃənəlizəm] *s.* funzionalismo *m.*

functionality [,fʌŋkʃə'næliti] *s.* funzionalità *f.*

functionary ['fʌŋkʃnəri] *s.* funzionario *m.*

fund [fʌnd] *s.* fondo • *pl.* capitali *m.*

fundamental [,fʌndə'mentl] *agg.* fondamentale, basilare

funeral ['fju:nərəl] *s.* funerale *m.* • *agg.* funebre; funerario

funerary ['fju:nərəri] *agg.* funerario

funereal [fju(:)'niəriəl] *agg.* funereo

fungicide ['fʌndʒisaid] *s.* fungicida *m.*

fungus ['fʌŋgəs] *s.* fungo *m.*

funicular [fju(:)'nikjulə*] *s.* funicolare *f.*

funnel ['fʌnl] *s.* imbuto *m.*; ciminiera *f.*

funny ['fʌni] *agg.* buffo, divertente; strano

fur [fə:*] *s.* pelliccia *f.*

furious ['fjuəriəs] *agg.* furioso

furnace ['fə:nis] *s.* fornace *f.*

to furnish ['fə:niʃ] *v. tr.* ammobiliare; rifornire

furnishing ['fə:niʃiŋ] *s.* arredamento *m.*

furnishings ['fə:niʃiŋz] *s. pl.* mobili *m.*; arredamento *m. sing.*

furniture ['fə:nitʃə*] *s.* arredamento *m.*

furrier ['fʌriə*] *s.* pellicciaio *m.*

furrow ['fʌrou] *s.* solco *m.*

further ['fə:ðə*] *agg.* ulteriore • *avv.* oltre; ulteriormente

fury ['fjuəri] *s.* furia *f.*

fuse [fju:z] *s.* fusibile *m.*; miccia *f.*

to fuse [fju:z] *v. tr. e intr.* fondere

fuselage [fju:zila:ʒ] *s.* fusoliera *f.*

fusible ['fju:zəbl] *agg.* fusibile

fusion ['fju:zən] *s.* fusione *f.*

to fuss [fʌs] *v. intr.* agitarsi

fussiness ['fʌsinis] *s.* agitazione *f.*

fussy ['fʌsi] *agg.* agitato

fustian ['fʌstiən] *s.* fustagno *m.*

futility [fju(:)'tiliti] *s.* futilità *f.*

future ['fju:tʃə*] *agg. e s.* futuro *m.*

futurism ['fju:tʃərizəm] *s.* futurismo *m.*

futuristic ['fju:tʃəristik] *agg.* avveniristico; futuristico (*arte*)

G

gable ['geibl] *s.* timpano *m.* (*arch.*)

gaily ['geili] *avv.* gaiamente, allegramente

gain [gein] *s.* guadagno *m.*; miglioramento *m.*

to gain [gein] *v. intr.* guadagnare; ottenere; raggiungere; migliorare

gait [geit] *s.* andatura *f.*

galaxy ['gæləksi] *s.* galassia *f.*

gale [geil] *s.* burrasca *f.*

gallant ['gælənt] *agg.* galante

galleon ['gælion] *s.* galeone *m.*

gallery ['gæləri] *s.* galleria *f.*; loggione *m.*

galley ['gæli] *s.* galera *f.*; cucina *f.* (*naut.*)

gallicism ['gælisizəm] *s.* gallicismo *m.*

gallon ['gælən] *s.* gallone *m.*

gallop ['gæləp] *s.* galoppo *m.*

to gallop ['gæləp] *v. intr.* galoppare

gallows ['gælouz] *s. pl.* forca *f. sing.*, patibolo *m. sing.*

to gamble ['gæmbl] *v. intr.* giocare d'azzardo

gambler ['gæmblə*] *s.* giocatore *m.* d'azzardo

game [geim] *s.* gioco *m.*; partita *f.*; scherzo *m.*; selvaggina *f.*

gamekeeper ['geim,ki:pə*] *s.* guardacaccia *m. inv.*

gang [gæŋ] *s.* banda *f.*

gap [gæp] *s.* apertura *f.*; divario *m.*; lacuna *f.*

garbage ['ga:bidʒ] *s.* immondizia *f.*; – can pattumiera

garden ['ga:dn] *s.* giardino *m.*; orto *m.*; – centre vivaio

gardener ['ga:dnə*] *s.* giardiniere *m.*

gardenia [ga:di:njə] *s.* gardenia *f.*

gardening ['ga:dniŋ] *s.* giardinaggio *m.*

garish ['gɛəriʃ] *agg.* sgargiante

garlic ['ga:lik] *s.* aglio *m.*

garment ['ga:mənt] *s.* indumento *m.*

garnish ['ga:niʃ] *s.* guarnizione *f.*

to garnish ['ga:niʃ] *v. tr.* guarnire

garrison ['gærisn] *s.* guarnigione *f.*

garter ['ga:tə*] *s.* giarrettiera *f.*; – belt reggicalze

gas [gæs] *s.* gas *m.*; benzina *f.* (USA); – ring fornello

gash [gæʃ] *s.* sfregio *m.*

to gash [gæʃ] *v. tr.* sfregiare

gasoline ['gæsəli:n] *s.* benzina *f.*

to gasp [ga:sp] *v. intr.* boccheggiare; ansimare

gastritis [gæs'traitis] *s.* gastrite *f.*

gastroenteric [,gæstrouen'terik] *agg.* gastrointestinale

gastronomic [,gæstrə'nɔmik] *agg.* gastronomico

gastronomy [gæs'trɔnəmi] *s.* gastronomia *f.*

gate [geit] *s.* cancello *m.*; porta *f.*

to gather ['gæðə*] *v. tr.* raccogliere; radunare

gathering ['gæðəriŋ] *s.* raduno *m.*

gaudy ['gɔ:di] *agg.* sgargiante

gauge [geidʒ] *s.* calibro *m.*; manometro *m.*; misuratore *m.*; scartamento *m.*

gauze [gɔ:z] *s.* garza *f.*

gay [gei] *agg.* omosessuale

gaze [geiz] *s.* sguardo *m.* fisso

to gaze [geiz] *v. intr.* guardare fissamente, fissare

gazebo [gə'zi:bou] *s.* gazebo *m. inv.*

gear [giə*] *s.* meccanismo *m.*; ingranaggio *m.*; cambio *m.* (*autom.*)

gel [dʒel] *s.* gelatina *f.*

gelatin(e) [,dʒelə'ti(:)n] *s.* gelatina *f.*

gem [dʒem] *s.* gemma *f.*

gender ['dʒendə*] *s.* genere *m.* (*gramm.*)

genealogy [,dʒenɪ'ælaiʒ] *v. tr.* genealogia *f.*

general ['dʒenərəl] *agg.* generale; generico; – delivery fermo posta

generality [,dʒenə'ræliti] *s.* generalità *f.*

to generalize [,dʒenərəlaiz] *v. tr.* generalizzare

generally ['dʒenərəli] *avv.* generalmente

to generate ['dʒenəreit] *v. tr.* generare

generation [,dʒenə'reiʃən] *s.* generazione *f.*

generational [,dʒenə'reiʃənəl] *agg.* generazionale

generator ['dʒenəreitə*] *s.* generatore *m.*

generic [dʒi'nerik] *agg.* generico

generous ['dʒenərəs] *agg.* generoso

genesis ['dʒenisis] *s.* genesi *f.*

genetic [dʒi'netik] *agg.* genetico

genie ['dʒi:ni] *s.* genio *m.*

genitalia [,dʒeni'teiljə] *s. pl.* genitali *m.*

genitals ['dʒenitlz] *s. pl.* genitali *m.*

genius ['dʒi:njəs] *s.* genio *m.*

gentle ['dʒentl] *agg.* gentile

gentleman ['dʒentlmən] *s.* signore *m.*

genuine ['dʒenjuin] *agg.* genuino

genuineness ['dʒenjuinnis] *s.* genuinità *f.*

genus ['dʒːnəs] *s.* genere *m.*

geographic [dʒiə'græfik] *agg.* geografico

geography [dʒi'ɔgrəfi] *s.* geografia *f.*

geology [dʒi'ɔlədʒi] *s.* geologia *f.*

geometric [dʒiə'metrik] *agg.* geometrico

geometry [dʒi'ɔmitri] *s.* geometria *f.*

georgic ['dʒɔː'dʒik] *agg.* georgico

geothermal [dʒiːouˈθəːməl] *agg.* geotermico

geranium [dʒiˈreinjəm] *s.* geranio *m.*

germ [dʒəːm] *s.* germe *m.*

German ['dʒəːmən] *agg.* tedesco

to germinate ['dʒəːmineit] *v. intr.* germogliare

gestation [dʒesˈteiʃən] *s.* gestazione *f.*

gesture ['dʒestʃəˈ] *s.* gesto *m.*; atto *m.*

to get [get] *v. tr.* prendere; ottenere; procurarsi; giungere • *intr.* diventare; – **along** andare d'accordo; – **away** scappare; – **back** riavere; – **down** scendere; – **off** scendere – on salire; – **over** superare; – **out** uscire; – **up** alzarsi, salire

ghetto ['getou] *s.* ghetto *m.*

ghost [goust] *s.* fantasma *m.*

giant ['dʒaiənt] *agg. e s.* gigante *m.*

giddiness ['gidinis] *s.* capogiro *m.*

giddy ['gidi] *agg.* stordito

gift [gift] *s.* dono *m.*, regalo *m.*; pregio *m.*

gigantic [dʒaiˈgæntik] *agg.* gigantesco

gigantism ['dʒaigæntizəm] *s.* gigantismo *m.*

to giggle ['gigl] *v. intr.* sghignazzare, ridere scioccamente

gilt [gilt] *agg.* dorato

ginger ['dʒindʒəˈ] *s.* zenzero *m.*

gipsy ['dʒipsi] *s.* gitano *m.*, zingaro *m.*

giraffe [dʒiˈraːf] *s.* giraffa *f.*

to gird [gəːd] *v. tr.* cingere

girder ['gəːdəˈ] *s.* trave *f.*

girl [gəːl] *s.* ragazza *f.*

to give [giv] *v. tr.* dare; regalare; – **back** rendere; – **in** cedere; – **up** rinunciare

giver ['givəˈ] *s.* donatore *m.*

glacial ['gleisjəl] *agg.* glaciale

glacier ['glæsjəˈ] *s.* ghiacciaio *m.*

glad [glæd] *agg.* felice, lieto

glade [gleid] *s.* radura *f.*

glamour ['glæməˈ] *s.* fascino *m.*, seduzione *f.*; incanto *m.*

glance [glaːns] *s.* occhiata *f.*, sguardo *m.*

gland [glænd] *s.* ghiandola *f.*

glare [glɛəˈ] *s.* bagliore *m.*

glass [glaːs] *s.* vetro *m.*; bicchiere *m.* • *pl.* occhiali *m.*; **sun-glasses** occhiali da sole

glassware ['glaːswɛəˈ] *s.* cristalleria *f.*

glassworks ['glaːs-wəːks] *s. pl.* (v. *al sing.*) vetreria *f. sing.*

glaze [gleiz] *s.* smalto *m.*

glide [glaid] *s.* scivolata *f.*; planata *f.*

to glide [glaid] *v. intr.* planare; scivolare

glider ['glaidəˈ] *s.* aliante *m.*

to glitter ['glitəˈ] *v. intr.* brillare, scintillare

global ['gloubl] *agg.* globale

globe [gloub] *s.* globo *m.*; mappamondo *m.*; sfera *f.*

gloom [gluːm] *s.* tristezza *f.*

gloomy [gluˈmi] *agg.* oscuro; cupo, lugubre; fosco

glorious ['glɔːriəs] *agg.* glorioso

glory ['glɔːri] *s.* gloria *f.*

gloss [glɔs] *s.* postilla *f.*, annotazione *f.*; lustro *m.*; smalto *m.*

glossary ['glɔsəri] *s.* glossario *m.*

glottology [glɔ'tɔlədʒi] *s.* glottologia *f.*

glove [glʌv] *s.* guanto *m.*

glucose ['gluːkous] *s.* glucosio *m.*

glue [gluː] *s.* colla *f.*

to glue [gluː] *v. tr.* incollare

gluteus [gluˈtiːəs] *s.* gluteo *m.*

gluttonous ['glʌtnəs] *agg.* ghiotto

glyce(a)mia [glaiˈsiːmiə] *s.* glicemia *f.*

glycerin(e) [ˌglisəˈriː(:)n] *s.* glicerina *f.*

to gnaw [nɔː] *v. tr. e intr.* rosicchiare

gnome [noum] *s.* gnomo *m.*

to go [gou] *v. intr.* andare, andarsene; – **away** andar via; – **back** ritornare; – **on** continuare; – **through** esaminare; – **in** entrare; – **out** uscire; **let's go!** andiamo!

goal [goul] *s.* meta *f.*; rete *f.* (*sport*)

goalkeeper ['goul,kiˈ(:)pəˈ] *s.* portiere *m.* (*sport*)

goat [gout] *s.* capra *f.*

goblet ['gɔblit] *s.* calice *m.*

goblin ['gɔblin] *s.* gnomo *m.*

God [Gad] *s.* Dio *m.*

goddess ['gɔdis] *s.* dea *f.*

going ['gouiŋ] *s.* andata *f.*; andatura *f.*

gold [gould] *s.* oro *m.* • *agg.* aureo; **fine –** oro zecchino; – **plated** placcato in oro

golden ['gouldən] *agg.* dorato; d'oro; biondo

goldsmith ['gouldsmiθ] *s.* orafo *m.*

golf [gɔlf] *s.* golf *m.* inv. (*sport*)

good [gud] *agg.* buono; bravo; bello • *s.* bene *m.*; – **evening** buonasera; – **looking** prestan-

te, bello; – **morning** buongiorno; – **night** buonanotte
good-bye ['gud'bai] *inter.* addio; arrivederci
goodness ['gudnis] *s.* bontà *f.*, cortesia *f.*; **my –!** accidenti!
goose [gu:s] *s.* oca *f.*
gorge [gɔ:dʒ] *s.* gola *f.* (geog.)
gorgeous ['gɔ:dʒəs] *agg.* fastoso
Gospel ['gɔspəl] *s.* vangelo *m.*
gossip ['gɔsip] *s.* chiacchiera *f.*; pettegolezzo *m.*
gossipy ['gɔsipi] *agg.* pettegolo
Gothic ['gɔθik] *agg.* gotico
gouache [gu'a:ʃ] *s.* guazzo *m.* (arte)
gourmet ['guəmei] *s.* buongustaio *m.*
to govern ['gʌvn] *v. tr. e intr.* governare
government ['gʌvnmənt] *s.* governo *m.*; amministrazione *f.*; ministero *m.*
gown [gaun] *s.* toga *f.*; veste *f.*
grace [greis] *s.* grazia *f.*
graceful ['greisful] *agg.* leggiadro
gracious ['greiʃəs] *agg.* grazioso
gradation [grə'deiʃən] *s.* gradazione *f.*
grade [greid] *s.* grado *m.*
gradient ['greidjənt] *s.* pendenza *f.*; gradiente *m.*
gradual ['grædjuəl] *agg.* graduale; **gradually** gradualmente
graduate ['grædjuit] *s.* laureato *m.*
to graduate ['grædjuit] *v. intr.* laurearsi
graffito [gra:'fi:tou] *s.* graffito *m.*
graft [gra:ft] *s.* innesto *m.*
to graft [gra:ft] *v. tr.* innestare
grain [grein] *s.* grano *m.*, granello *m.*; vena *f.* del legno
grained [greind] *agg.* granulato
gram [græm] *s.* grammo *m.*
grammar ['græmə*] *s.* grammatica *f.*
granary ['grænəri] *s.* granaio *m.*
grand [grænd] *agg.* grandioso, imponente
grandchild ['grændʧaild] *s.* nipote *m. e f.* (di nonni)
granddaughter ['græn,dɔ:tə*] *s.* nipote *f.* (di nonni)
grandeur ['grændʒə*] *s.* grandiosità *f.*
grandfather ['grænd,fa:ðə*] *s.* nonno *m.*
grandma ['grænma:] *s.* nonna *f.* (fam.)
grandmother ['græn,mʌðə*] *s.* nonna *f.* (fam.)
grandpa ['grænpa:] *s.* nonno *m.* (fam.)
grandson ['grænsʌn] *s.* nipote *m.* (di nonni)
granite ['grænit] *s.* granito *m.*
granny ['græni] *s.* nonna *f.* (fam.)
grant [gra:nt] *s.* concessione *f.*; sussidio *m.*; assegnazione *f.*

to grant [gra:nt] *v. tr.* concedere
granular ['grænjulə*] *agg.* granuloso
granulation ['grænju'leiʃən] *s.* granulazione *f.*
grape [greip] *s.* acino *m.* • *pl.* uva *f. sing.*
grapefruit ['greipfru:t] *s.* pompelmo *m.*
graphic ['græfik] *agg.* grafico • *s. pl.* grafica *f. sing.*
graphically ['græfikəli] *avv.* graficamente
to grasp [gra:sp] *v. tr.* afferrare; stringere
grass [gra:s] *s.* erba *f.*
grasshopper ['gra:s,hɔpə*] *s.* cavalletta *f.*
grassland ['gra:s-lænd] *s.* prateria *f.*
grate [greit] *s.* grata *f.*
to grate [greit] *v. tr.* grattugiare
grateful ['greitful] *agg.* grato
to gratify ['grætifai] *v. tr.* gratificare, compiacere
grating ['greitiŋ] *s.* griglia *f.*, grata *f.*
gratis ['greitis] *avv.* gratis
gratitude ['grætitju:d] *s.* gratitudine *f.*
grave [greiv] *s.* tomba *f.* • *agg.* grave; serio
gravel ['grævəl] *s.* ghiaia *f.*
gravelly ['grævəli] *agg.* ghiaioso
graveyard ['greiv-ja:d] *s.* cimitero *m.*
gravity ['græviti] *s.* gravità *f.*; serietà *f.*
gravy ['greivi] *s.* sugo *m.* (di carne); – **boat** salsiera
gray [grei] *s.* grigio *m.* (USA)
graze [greiz] *s.* escoriazione *f.*
to graze [greiz] *v. tr e intr.* pascolare • graffiare
grazing ['greiziŋ] *s.* pascolo *m.*; – **land** terreno da pascolo
grease [gri:s] *s.* grasso
to grease [gri:s] *v. tr.* ungere
greasing ['gri:siŋ] *s.* ingrassaggio *m.*
greasy ['gri:si] *agg.* untuoso
great [greit] *agg.* grande, grosso; grandioso; insigne, celebre
greatness ['greitnis] *s.* grandezza *f.*
Grecism ['gri:sizəm] *s.* grecismo *m.*
greediness ['gri:dinis] *s.* golosità *f.*
greedy ['gri:di] *agg.* goloso
Greek [gri:k] *agg.* greco
green [gri:n] *agg.* s. verde • *pl.* verdura *f. sing.*
greengrocer ['gri:n,grousə*] *s.* fruttivendolo *m.*
greenhouse ['gri:nhaus] *s.* serra *f.*
to greet [gri:t] *v. tr.* salutare
greeting ['gri:tiŋ] *s.* saluto *m.*
grenade [gri'neid] *s.* granata *f.*
grey [grei] *agg.* grigio

greyhound ['greihaund] s. leviero m.

grid [grid] s. reticolo m.

grief [gri:f] s. afflizione f., dolore m.

griffin ['grifin] s. grifone m.

grill [gril] s. griglia f., grata f.

grilled [grild] agg. alla griglia

grim [grim] agg. orribile, feroce, severo, deciso, sgradevole

grimace [gri'meis] s. smorfia f.

grin [grin] s. smorfia f., sogghigno m.

to grind [graind] v. tr. macinare; frantumare

grinding ['graindiŋ] s. macinazione f.

grip [grip] s. stretta f.

to grip [grip] v. tr. e intr. stringere

grit [grit] s. grinta f.; pietrisco m.

grizzled ['grizld] agg. brizzolato

to groan [groun] v. intr. gemere

grocery ['grousəri] s. drogheria f.

groom [gru:m] s. stalliere m.

groove [gru:v] s. scanalatura f.

gross [grous] agg. grossolano; grasso

grotesque [grou'tesk] agg. grottesco

ground [graund] s. terreno m.; terra f.; campo m.; massa f. (elettr.); – floor pianterreno

to ground [graund] v. intr. incagliarsi (naut.)

groundless ['graundlis] agg. infondato

group [gru:p] s. gruppo m.

to group [gru:p] v. tr. raggruppare

grouper ['gru:pə*] s. cernia f.

grouse [graus] s. gallo m. cedrone; pernice f.

to grow [grou] v. intr. crescere; diventare • tr. coltivare; – old invecchiare; – up diventare adulto

growth [grouθ] s. crescita f.

grudge [grʌdʒ] s. rancore m.

to grumble ['grʌmbl] v. tr. e intr. lamentarsi, brontolare

guarantee [,gærən'ti] s. garanzia f.

to guarantee [,gærən'ti] v. tr. garantire

guaranty ['gærənti] s. garanzia f.

guard [ga:d] s. guardia f.; guardiano m.

to guard [ga:d] v. tr. sorvegliare; proteggere

Guelph [gwelf] s. guelfo m.

guerilla [gə'rilə] s. guerriglia f.

to guess [ges] v. tr. e intr. indovinare; azzeccare

guest [gest] s. ospite m. e f.; invitato m.

to guffaw [gʌ'fɔ:] v. intr. sghignazzare

guidance ['gaidəns] s. guida f.

guide [gaid] s. guida f.; cicerone m.

to guide [gaid] v. tr. guidare

guild [gild] s. corporazione f.

guillotine [,gilə'ti:n] s. ghigliottina f.

guilt [gilt] s. colpa f.

guilty ['gilti] agg. colpevole

guitar [gi'ta:*] s. chitarra f.

guitarist [gi'ta:rist] s. chitarrista m. e f.

gulf [gʌlf] s. golfo m.; abisso m.

gully ['gʌli] s. calanco m.

gulp [gʌlp] s. sorso m.; boccone m.

gum [gʌm] s. gomma f.; colla f. • gengiva f.

gun [gʌn] s. fucile m.; pistola f.; arma f. da fuoco; cannone m.

to gurgle ['gə:gl] v. intr. gorgogliare

gush [gʌʃ] s. zampillo m.

to gush [gʌʃ] v. intr. sgorgare

gushing ['gʌʃiŋ] agg. zampillante

gust [gʌst] s. raffica f.

gutter ['gʌtə*] s. grondaia f.; cunetta f.

guttural ['gʌtərəl] agg. gutturale

guy [gai] s. individuo m., tipo m. (fam., USA)

gym [dʒim] s. palestra f.; ginnastica f.

gymnasium [dʒim'neizjəm] s. palestra f.

gymnastics [dʒim'næstiks] s. pl. (v. al sing.) ginnastica f. sing.

gyn(a)ecologist [,gaini'kɔlədʒist] s. ginecologo m.

H

haberdashery ['hæbədæʃəri] s. merceria f.

habit ['hæbit] s. abitudine f.; uso m; abito m.

habitual [hə'bitjuəl] agg. abituale

haemorrhage ['heməridʒ] s. emorragia f.

haemostatic [,hi:mou'stætik] agg. e s. emostatico m.

haggard ['hægəd] agg. macilento; disfatto

to haggle ['hægl] v. intr. mercanteggiare; disputare

hagiography [,hægi'ɔgrəfi] s. agiografia f.

hail [heil] s. grandine f.

to hail [heil] v. tr. e intr. grandinare; salutare • chiamare (ad alta voce)

hailstorm ['heil-stɔ:m] s. grandinata f.

hair [heə*] s. capelli m. pl.; mantello m. (di animale); pelo m.; – **cut** taglio di capelli; – **dryer** asciugacapelli; – **do** pettinatura; – **style** acconciatura; – **splitting** pedanteria

hairless ['heəlis] agg. calvo, glabro

hairy ['heəri] agg. peloso

hake [heik] s. nasello m.

half [ha:f] s. metà f.; mezzo m. • agg. mezzo; – **an hour** mezz'ora; – **moon** mezzaluna

hall [hɔ:l] s. sala f.; salone m.; vestibolo m.

hallucination [hə,lu:si'neiʃən] s. allucinazione f.

halo ['heilou] s. aureola f.

halt [hɔ:lt] s. fermata f. • inter. alt!

to halt [hɔ:lt] v. tr. fermare • intr. fermarsi

to halve [ha:v] v. tr. dimezzare

halyard ['hæljəd] s. drizza f.

ham [hæm] s. prosciutto m.; radioamatore m. (fam.)

hamlet ['hæmlit] s. borgo m.

hammer ['hæmə*] s. martello m.

to hammer ['hæmə*] v. tr. e intr. martellare, battere

hammering ['hæməriŋ] s. martellamento m.

hammock ['hæmək] s. amaca f.

hamper ['hæmpə*] s. paniere m.

to hamper ['hæmpə*] v. tr. ostacolare

hand [hænd] s. mano f.; operaio m.; lancetta f.; **at** – a portata di mano

to hand [hænd] v. tr. consegnare; porgere; dare

handbag ['hændbæg] s. borsetta f.

handball ['hændbɔ:l] s. pallamano f.

handbook ['hændbuk] s. manuale m.

handcart ['hændka:t] s. carretto m.

handcuffs ['hændkʌfs] s. pl. manette f.

handful ['hændful] s. manciata f.

handhold ['hændhould] s. appiglio m.

handicap ['hændikæp] s. ostacolo m.; vantaggio m. (sport)

handicraft ['hændikra:ft] s. artigianato m.

handkerchief ['hæŋkətʃif] s. fazzoletto m.

handle ['hændl] s. manico m.; maniglia f.; – **bar** manubrio

to handle ['hændl] v. tr. maneggiare; manipolare

handrail ['hænd-reil] s. corrimano m.

handshake ['hændʃeik] s. stretta f. di mano

handsome ['hænsəm] agg. bello; prestante, avvenente

handwork ['hænd-wə:k] s. manufatto m.

handwriting ['hænd,raitiŋ] s. calligrafia f.

handy ['hændi] agg. maneggevole, utile, destro; vicino, sottomano

handyman ['hændimæn] s. tuttofare m. inv.

to hang [hæŋ] v. tr. appendere; impiccare • intr. pendere, penzolare

hang-glider ['hæŋ-'glaidə*] s. deltaplano m.

hanging ['hæŋiŋ] agg. sospeso; pendente; pensile • s. impiccagione f.

hank [hæŋk] s. matassa f.

to happen ['hæpən] v. intr. accadere, capitare, succedere

happening ['hæpəniŋ] s. avvenimento m.

happy ['hæpi] agg. felice, contento

harbour ['ha:bə*] s. porto m.; – **office** capitaneria

hard [ha:d] agg. duro; difficile • avv. duramente; forte

hardly ['ha:dli] avv. appena; a malapena

hardness ['ha:dnis] s. durezza f.

hardship ['ha:dʃip] s. privazione f.; strapazzo m.

hardware ['ha:d-weə*] s. ferramenta f.; hardware m. inv. (inf.)

hare [heə*] s. lepre f.

harm [ha:m] s. danno m.

73

to harm [ha:m] *v. tr.* nuocere; danneggiare

harmful ['ha:mful] *agg.* nocivo

harmless ['ha:mlis] *agg.* innocuo, inoffensivo

harmonious [ha:'mounjəs] *agg.* armonioso, melodioso

harmony ['ha:məni] *s.* armonia *f.*

harp [ha:p] *s.* arpa *f.*

harpoon [ha:'pu:n] *s.* arpione *m.*; fiocina *f.*; rampone *m.*

harquebus [ha:'kwibəs] *s.* archibugio *m.*

harsh [ha:ʃ] *agg.* ostico; aspro; stridente; rigido (clima)

harvest ['ha:vist] *s.* mietitura *f.*; raccolto *m.*; vendemmia *f.*

to harvest ['ha:vist] *v. tr.* fare il raccolto; vendemmiare

haste [heist] *s.* fretta *f.*, premura *f.*

to hasten ['heisn] *v. tr.* affrettare • *intr.* affrettarsi, precipitarsi

hasty ['heisti] *agg.* frettoloso

hat [hæt] *s.* cappello *m.*; **top** – cilindro

hatch [hætʃ] *s.* boccaporto *m.* (naut.)

hatchet ['hætʃit] *s.* accetta *f.*

hate [heit] *s.* odio *m.*

to hate [heit] *v. tr.* odiare

hateful ['heitful] *agg.* odioso

hatred ['heitrid] *s.* odio *m.*

haughty ['hɔ:ti] *agg.* superbo

to have [hæv, həv, əv] *v. tr.* avere, possedere; sentire; prendere; – **something done** far fare qualcosa; – **to** dovere

haven ['heivn] *s.* porto *m.*; rifugio *m.*

haversack ['hævəsæk] *s.* bisaccia *f.*

havoc ['hævək] *s.* scempio *m.*

hawk [hɔ:k] *s.* falco *m.*

hay [hei] *s.* fieno *m.*; – **fever** febbre da fieno

hazard ['hæzəd] *s.* rischio *m.*; pericolo *m.*

hazardous ['hæzədəs] *agg.* rischioso, pericoloso

haze [heiz] *s.* caligine *f.*, foschia *f.*

hazel ['heizl] *s.* nocciola *f.*; nocciolo *m.*

hazy ['heizi] *agg.* caliginoso

head [hed] *s.* testa *f.*; capo *m.* • *agg.* principale; centrale

to head [hed] *v. tr.* capeggiare; precedere

headache ['hedeik] *s.* cefalea *f.*, mal *m.* di testa

headlight ['hedlait] *s.* faro *m.* (autom.)

headline ['hedlain] *s.* titolo *m.*

headlong ['hedlɔŋ] *agg.* precipitoso • *avv.* precipitosamente

headphone ['hedfoun] *s.* auricolare *m.* • *pl.* cuffia *f. sing.*

headrest ['hed-rest] *s.* poggiatesta *m. inv.*

to heal [hi:l] *v. tr.* e *intr.* guarire

healing ['hi:liŋ] *s.* guarigione *f.*

health [helθ] *s.* salute *f.*; **public** – **office** ufficio d'igiene

healthy ['helθi] *agg.* sano; salubre

heap [hi:p] *s.* cumulo *m.*, mucchio *m.*

to hear [hiə*] *v. tr.* sentire, udire

hearing ['hiəriŋ] *s.* udito *m.*; udienza *f.*

heart [ha:t] *s.* cuore *m.*; – **broken** desolato

hearth [ha:θ] *s.* focolare *m.*; camino *m.*

heartily ['ha:tili] *avv.* caldamente

heartless ['ha:tlis] *agg.* insensibile, crudele

hearty ['ha:ti] *agg.* cordiale, caloroso

heat [hi:t] *s.* caldo *m.*; calore *m.*

to heat [hi:t] *v. tr.* e *intr.* scaldare, riscaldare; scaldarsi

heater ['hi:tə*] *s.* calorifero *m.*, stufa *f.*, impianto *m.* di riscaldamento

heath [hi:θ] *s.* brughiera *f.*

heathenism ['hi:ðənizəm] *s.* paganesimo *m.*

heather ['heðə*] *s.* erica *f.*

heating ['hi:tiŋ] *s.* riscaldamento *m.*; **central** – riscaldamento centrale

to heave [hi:v] *v. tr.* e *intr.* sollevare; lanciare, tirare; trascinare; ansimare

heaven ['hevn] *s.* cielo *m.*; paradiso *m.*

heavenly ['hevnli] *agg.* celeste

heaviness ['hevinis] *s.* pesantezza *f.*

heavy ['hevi] *agg.* pesante, gravoso

Hebraic [hi(:)'breiik] *agg.* ebraico

Hebrew ['hi:bru:] *agg.* e *s.* ebreo *m.*

hecatomb ['hekətoum] *s.* ecatombe *f.*

hectare ['hekta:*] *s.* ettaro *m.*

hedge [hedʒ] *s.* bordo *m.*; siepe *f.*

hedgehog ['hedʒhɔg] *s.* riccio *m.*

hedonism ['hi:dənizəm] *s.* edonismo *m.*

heel [hi:l] *s.* calcagno *m.*, tallone *m.*; tacco *m.*

to heel [hi:l] *v. intr.* sbandare (naut.)

heeling ['hi:liŋ] *s.* sbandamento *m.* (naut.)

hegemony [hi(:)'geməni] *s.* egemonia *f.*

height [hait] *s.* altezza *f.*; altitudine *f.*

heir [eə*] *s.* erede *m.*

heiress ['eəris] *s.* erede *f.*

helicopter ['helikɔptə*] *s.* elicottero *m.*

heliotherapy [,hi:liou'θerəpi] *s.* elioterapia *f.*

heliport ['heli,pɔ:t] *s.* eliporto *m.*

hell [hel] *s.* inferno *m.*

Hellenic [he'li:nik] *agg.* ellenico

Hellenistic [,heli'nistik] *agg.* ellenistico

helm [helm] *s.* timone *m.*; barra *f.*

helmet ['helmit] *s.* casco *m.*; elmo *m.*

help [help] *s.* aiuto *m.*; assistenza *f.*

to help [help] v. tr. aiutare; soccorrere
helper ['helpə*] s. aiutante m. e f.
helpful ['helpful] agg. servizievole; utile
helping ['helpiŋ] s. aiuto m.; porzione f.
helpless ['helplis] agg. indifeso, impotente
hem [hem] s. orlo m., bordo m.
to hem [hem] v. tr. orlare
hemisphere ['hemisfiə*] s. emisfero m.
hemp [hemp] s. canapa f.
hen [hen] s. gallina f.; – **house** pollaio
hence [hens] avv. quindi; perciò; da ora, da ciò
henceforth ['hensfɔ:θ] avv. d'ora innanzi
hepatic [hi'pætik] agg. epatico
hepatitis [,hepə'taitis] s. epatite f.
heraldic [he'rældik] agg. araldico
herb [hə:b] s. erba f.
herbarium [hə:'beəriəm] s. erbario m.
herbicide ['hə:bisaid] s. diserbante m.
herbivorous [hə:'bivərəs] agg. erbivoro
herd [hə:d] s. mandria f.; gregge m.
here [hiə*] avv. qua, qui
hereafter [hiər'a:ftə*] avv. in avvenire
hereby ['hiə'bai] avv. con ciò
hereditary [hi'reditəri] agg. ereditario
heredity [hi'rediti] s. eredità f.
herein ['hiə'in] avv. incluso
heresy ['herəsi] s. eresia f.
heretical [hi'retikəl] agg. eretico
herewith ['hiə'wið] avv. qui accluso
heritage ['heritidʒ] s. eredità f.
hermaphrodite [hə:'mæfrədait] agg. e s. ermafrodito f.
hermit ['hə:mit] s. eremita f.
hermitage ['hə:mitidʒ] s. eremo m.
hernia ['hə:njə] s. ernia f.
hero ['hiərou] s. eroe m.
heroic [hi'rouik] agg. eroico
heron ['herən] s. airone m.
herring ['heriŋ] s. aringa f.
to hesitate ['heziteit] v. intr. esitare
heterodox ['hetərədɔks] agg. eterodosso
heterogeneous [,hetərərou'dʒi:niəs] agg. eterogeneo
heterosexual [,hetərou'seksjuəl] agg. eterosessuale
heuristic [hju:'ristik] agg. euristico
hexagonal [hek'sægənl] agg. esagonale
hi [hai] inter. ciao!
hiatus [hai'eitəs] s. iato m.
to hibernate ['haibə:neit] v. intr. svernare
hiccup ['hikʌp] s. singhiozzo m.
hidden ['hidn] agg. nascosto; ignoto
hide [haid] s. pellame m.

to hide [haid] v. tr. nascondere • intr. nascondersi
hideous ['hidiəs] agg. ripugnante, orribile
hierarchic [,haiə'ra:kik] agg. gerarchico
hierarchy ['haiə,ra:ki] s. gerarchia f.
hieratic [,haiə'rætik] agg. ieratico
hieroglyph ['haiərə,glif] s. geroglifico m.
high [hai] agg. alto, elevato • avv. in alto; – **school** scuola secondaria; – **relief** altorilievo
highway ['haiwei] s. strada f. di grande comunicazione
to hijack ['hai,dʒæk*] v. tr. dirottare
hijacking ['hai,dʒækiŋ] s. dirottamento f.
hike [haik] s. escursione f.
hiker ['haikə*] s. escursionista m. e f.
hill [hil] s. colle m., collina f.
hillock ['hilək] s. poggio m.
hilly ['hili] agg. collinoso
hind [haind] agg. posteriore
to hinder ['hində*] v. tr. inceppare; ostacolare
hindrance ['hindrəns] s. impaccio m.; ostacolo m., impedimento m.
hinge [hindʒ] s. cardine m.; cerniera f.
hint [hint] s. cenno m.; traccia f.; suggerimento m.
to hint [hint] v. tr. alludere; suggerire
hinterland ['hintəlænd] s. retroterra m. inv.
hip [hip] s. anca f.
hippo ['hipou] s. ippopotamo m.
hippocampus [,hipou'kæmpəs] s. ippocampo m.
hippodrome ['hipədroum] s. ippodromo m.
hippopotamus [,hipə'pɔtəməs] s. ippopotamo m.
hire ['haiə*] s. noleggio m.
to hire ['haiə*] v. tr. noleggiare
Hispanic [his'pænik] agg. ispanico
hiss [his] s. sibilo m.
historian [his'tɔ:riən] s. storico m.
historical [his'tɔrikəl] agg. storico
historiography [his,tɔ:ri'ɔgrəfi] s. storiografia f.
history ['histəri] s. storia f.
histrion ['histriən] s. istrione m.
hit [hit] s. colpo m.; urto m.
to hit [hit] v. tr. e intr. battere, colpire, picchiare; – **on** trovare per caso, scoprire
hitch [hitʃ] s. sobbalzo m.; disguido m.
hitchhiker ['hitʃ,haikə*] s. autostoppista m. e f.
hitchhiking ['hitʃ,haikiŋ] s. autostop m. inv.
hive [haiv] s. alveare m.
hoard [hɔ:d] s. cumulo m.; scorta f.

hoarse [hɔːs] *agg.* rauco

hoarseness ['hɔːsnis] *s.* raucedine *f.*

hobby ['hɔbi] *s.* passatempo *m.*

hoe [hou] *s.* zappa *f.*

to hoe [hou] *v. tr.* zappare

to hoist [hɔist] *v. tr.* innalzare

hold [hould] *s.* appiglio *m.*; presa *f.* • stiva *f.*

to hold [hould] *v. tr.* tenere; occupare; – **back** trattenere; – **on** aspettare, reggersi a

hole [houl] *s.* buco *m.*; apertura *f.*

to hole [houl] *v. tr.* bucare

holiday ['hɔlədei] *s.* festa *f.*; vacanza *f.* • *agg.* festivo

holiness ['houlinis] *s.* santità *f.*

hollow ['hɔlou] *s.* cavità *f.*; fossa *f.* • *agg.* cavo

holly ['hɔli] *s.* agrifoglio *m.*

holy ['houli] *agg.* sacro

homage ['hɔmidʒ] *s.* omaggio *m.*

home [houm] *s.* casa *f.*; patria *f.* • *agg.* casalingo, domestico, familiare; – **cooking** cucina casalinga

homesick ['houm-sik] *agg.* nostalgico

homesickness ['houm,siknis] *s.* nostalgia *f.*

homestead ['houm-sted] *s.* casolare *m.*

homework ['houmwɜːk] *s.* compito *m.*

homicide ['hɔmisaid] *s.* omicida *m. e f.*; omicidio *m.*

homoeopathy [,houmi'ɔpəθi] *s.* omeopatia *f.*

homoeopathic [,houmiou'pæθik] *agg.* omeopatico

homogeneity [,hɔmoudʒe'niːti] *s.* omogeneità *f.*

homogeneous [,hɔmou'dʒiːnjəs] *agg.* omogeneo

homogenized [hou'mɔdʒənaizd] *agg.* omogeneizzato

to homologate [hɔ'mɔləgeit] *v. tr.* omologare

homology [hɔ'mɔlədʒi] *s.* omologia *f.*

homonym ['hɔmənim] *s.* omonimo *m.*

homonymous [hɔ'mɔniməs] *agg.* omonimo

homosexual ['houmou'seksjuəl] *agg.* omosessuale

honest ['ɔnist] *agg.* onesto

honesty ['ɔnisti] *s.* onestà *f.*

honey ['hʌni] *s.* miele *m.*

honeyed ['hʌnid] *agg.* dolce; mellifluo

honeymoon ['hʌnimuːn] *s.* luna *f.* di miele

honorary ['ɔnərəri] *agg.* onorario

honour ['ɔnə•] *s.* onore *m.*; onorificenza *f.*

honourable ['ɔnərəbl] *agg.* onorevole

hood [hud] *s.* cappuccio *m.*

hoof [huːf] *s.* zoccolo *m.*

hook [huk] *s.* gancio *m.*; amo *m.*

hooligan ['huːligən] *s.* teppista *m. e f.*

hoopoe ['huːpuː] *s.* upupa *f.*

hoot [huːt] *s.* fischio *m.*; colpo *m.* di clacson

hop [hɔp] *s.* salto *m.* • luppolo *m.*

to hop [hɔp] *v. intr.* saltellare

hope [houp] *s.* speranza *f.*

to hope [houp] *v. tr. e intr.* sperare

hopeful ['houpful] *agg.* pieno di speranza

hopeless ['houplis] *agg.* disperato, senza speranza

horde [hɔːd] *s.* orda *f.*

horizon [hə'raizn] *s.* orizzonte *m.*

horizontal [,hɔri'zɔntl] *agg.* orizzontale

hormone ['hɔːmoun] *s.* ormone *m.*

horn [hɔːn] *s.* corno *m.*; clacson *m. inv.*

hornet ['hɔːnit] *s.* calabrone *m.*

horoscope ['hɔrəskoup] *s.* oroscopo *m.*

horrible ['hɔrəbl] *agg.* orribile

horrid ['hɔrid] *agg.* orrido, orrendo

horror ['hɔrə•] *s.* orrore *m.*

horse [hɔːs] *s.* cavallo *m.* • *agg.* equino, ippico; – **fly** tafano; – **racing** ippica

horticulture ['hɔːtikʌltʃə•] *s.* orticoltura *f.*

hospice ['hɔspis] *s.* ospizio *m.*

hospitable ['hɔspitəbl] *agg.* ospitale

hospital ['hɔspitl] *s.* ospedale *m.*

hospitality [,hɔspi'tæliti] *s.* ospitalità *f.*

to hospitalize ['hɔspitəlaiz] *v. tr.* ricoverare in ospedale

host [houst] *s.* ospite *m.* (che ospita)

hostage ['hɔstidʒ] *s.* ostaggio *m.*

hostel ['hɔstəl] *s.* ostello *m.*

hostess ['houstis] *s.* ospite *f.* (che ospita); assistente *f.* (di volo, ecc.)

hostile ['hɔstail] *agg.* ostile

hostility [hɔs'tiliti] *s.* ostilità *f.*

hot [hɔt] *agg.* caldo; bollente; piccante; – **pepper** peperoncino; – **tempered** collerico

hotchpotch ['hɔtʃpɔt] *s.* guazzabuglio *m.*

hotel [hou'tel] *s.* albergo *m.*; – **keeper** albergatore *m.*

hour ['auə•] *s.* ora *f.* • *pl.* orario *m. sing.*; **half an** – mezz'ora; **peak hours** ore di punta

house [haus] *s.* casa *f.*, abitazione *f.*

housekeeper ['haus,kiːpə•] *s.* governante *f.*; massaia *f.*

housewife ['haus-waif] *s.* casalinga *f.*

hovel ['hɔvl] *s.* baracca *f.*

how [hau] *avv.* come; in che modo; – **come?** come mai?; – **far** quanto dista; – **long** quanto tempo; – **much** quanto; – **many** quanti; – **often** quante volte

however [hau'evə°] *avv.* comunque; per quanto • *cong.* come; comunque; tuttavia
howl [haul] *s.* ululato *m.*
to howl [haul] *v. intr.* ululare; lamentarsi
huddle ['hʌdl] *s.* calca *f.*; folla *f.*
hue [hju:] *s.* tinta *f.*
to hug [hʌg] *v. tr.* abbracciare; costeggiare (*naut.*)
huge [hju:dʒ] *agg.* enorme, immenso
hull [hʌl] *s.* guscio *m.*; scafo *m.*
to hum [hʌm] *v. tr. e intr.* canticchiare
human ['hju:mən] *agg.* umano
humane [hju:'mein] *agg.* comprensivo; umano, umanitario
humanism ['hju:mənizəm] *s.* umanesimo *m.*
humanist ['hju:mənist] *s.* umanista *m. e f.*
humanitarian [hju:(,)mæni'teəriən] *agg.* umanitario
humanity [hju:(:)'mæniti] *s.* umanità *f.*
humble ['hʌmbl] *agg.* umile
humerus ['hju:mərəs] *s.* omero *m.*
humid ['hju:mid] *agg.* umido
humidifier [hju:(:)'midifaiə°] *s.* umidificatore *m.*
to humidify [hju:(:)'midifai] *v. tr.* umidificare
humidity [hju:(:)'miditi] *s.* umidità *f.*
to humiliate [hju:(:)'milieit] *v. tr.* umiliare
humiliating [hju:(:)'milieitiŋ] *agg.* umiliante
humiliation [hju:(:),mili'eiʃən] *s.* umiliazione *f.*
humor ['hju:mə°] *s.* umore *m.* (USA)
humorist ['hju:mərist] *s.* umorista *m. e f.*
humorous ['hju:mərəs] *agg.* umoristico
humour ['hju:mə°] *s.* umore *m.*, disposizione *f.* (d'animo); umorismo *m.*
hump [hʌmp] *s.* dosso *m.*; gobba *f.*; malumore *m.* (*fam.*)
hunch [hʌntʃ] *s.* gobba *f.*; sospetto *m.*
hundred ['hʌndrəd] *s. e agg.* cento
hundredth ['hʌndrədθ] *agg.* centesimo
hunger ['hʌŋgə°] *s.* fame *f.*
hungry ['hʌŋgri] *agg.* affamato; to be – aver fame
to hunt [hʌnt] *v. tr. e intr* cacciare
hunter ['hʌntə°] *s.* cacciatore *m.*
to hurl [hə:l] *v. tr.* lanciare
hurrah [hu'ra:] *inter.* evviva!
hurricane ['hʌrikən] *s.* uragano *m.*

hurried ['hʌrid] *agg.* frettoloso
hurry ['hʌri] *s.* fretta *f.*, premura *f.*; to be in a – aver fretta
to hurry ['hʌri] *v. intr.* affrettarsi
hurt [hə:t] *s.* ferita *f.*; dolore *m.*; offesa *f.* • *agg.* ferito; offeso; addolorato
to hurt [hə:t] *v. tr.* ferire, far male; – oneself ferirsi, farsi male
husband ['hʌzbənd] *s.* marito *m.*
hut [hʌt] *s.* capanna *f.*
hybrid ['haibrid] *agg.* ibrido
hydrant ['haidrənt] *s.* idrante *m.*
hydraulic [hai'drɔ:lik] *agg.* idraulico
hydraulics [hai'drɔ:liks] *s. pl.* (v. al sing.) idraulica *f. sing.*
hydrobiology ['haidroubai'ɔlədʒi] *s.* idrobiologia *f.*
hydrocarbon ['haidrou'ka:bən] *s.* idrocarburo *m.*
hydrofoil [haidrəfɔil] *s.* aliscafo *m.*
hydrogen ['haidrədʒən] *s.* idrogeno *m.*
hydrography [hai'drɔgrəfi] *s.* idrografia *f.*
hydrophobia [,haidrə'foubjə] *s.* idrofobia *f.*
hydrostatic [,haidrou'stætik] *agg.* idrostatico
hydrothermal [,haidrou'θə:məl] *agg.* idrotermale
hygiene ['haidʒi:n] *s.* igiene *f.*
hygienic [hai'dʒi:nik] *agg.* igienico
hygrometer [hai'grɔmitə°] *s.* igrometro *m.*
hymn [him] *s.* inno *m.*
hypercritical [,haipə'kritikəl] *agg.* ipercritico
hypermarket [,haipə,ma:kit] *s.* ipermercato *m.*
hypermetropia [,haipəmi'troupiə] *s.* ipermetropia *f.*
hypertension [,haipə'tenʃən] *s.* ipertensione *f.*
hyphen [haifən] *s.* trattino
to hyphenate ['haifəneit] *v. tr.* dividere in sillabe
hypocrisy [hi'pɔkrəsi] *s.* ipocrisia *f.*
hypocrite ['hipəkrit] *agg.* ipocrita
hypogeum [,haipə'dʒi:əm] *s.* ipogeo *m.*
hypothesis [hai'pɔθisis] *s.* ipotesi *f.*
hysteria [his'tiəriə] *s.* isterismo *m.*
hysteric [his'terik] *agg.* isterico
hysterical [his'terikəl] *agg.* isterico

I

ice [ais] s. ghiaccio m.; - cream gelato; - crusher tritaghiaccio; - pack banchisa
ichthyic ['ikθiik] agg. ittico
ichthyology [,ikθi'ɔlədʒi] s. ittiologia f.
icing ['aisiŋ] s. glassa f.
icon ['aikɔn] s. icona f.
iconoclast [ai'kɔnəklæst] agg. iconoclasta
iconographic [ai,kɔnə'græfik] agg. iconografico
iconography [,aikə'nɔgrəfi] s. iconografia f.
icy ['aisi] agg. gelato, gelido
idea [ai'diə] s. idea f.
ideal [ai'diəl] agg. e s. ideale
idealism [ai'diəlizəm] s. idealismo m.
to idealize [ai'diəlaiz] v. tr. idealizzare
ideation [,aidi'eiʃən] s. ideazione f.
identical [ai'dentikəl] agg. identico
identifiable [ai,denti'faiəbl] agg. identificabile
identification [ai,dentifi'keiʃən] s. identificazione f.
to identify [ai'dentifai] v. tr. identificare; riconoscere
identity [ai'dentiti] s. identità f.
ideogram ['idiougræm] s. ideogramma m.
ideological [,aidiə'lɔdʒikəl] agg. ideologico
ideology [,aidi'ɔlədʒi] s. ideologia f.
idiocy ['idiəsi] s. idiozia f.
idiom ['idiəm] s. idioma m.
idiosyncrasy [,idiə'siŋkrəsi] s. idiosincrasia f.
idiot ['idiət] s. idiota m.
idiotic [,idi'ɔtik] agg. idiota
idle ['aidl] agg. pigro, ozioso
to idle ['aidl] v. intr. oziare
idleness ['aidlnis] s. ozio m.
idol ['aidl] s. idolo m.
idolatry [ai'dɔlətri] s. idolatria f.
idyllic [ai'dilik] agg. idilliaco
if [if] cong. se, posto che, nel caso che, qualora, anche se: - anyting se mai; - not altrimenti; - so in tal caso
ignition [ig'niʃən] s. accensione f. (autom.)
ignoble [ig'noubl] agg. ignobile
ignorance ['ignərəns] s. ignoranza f.
ignorant ['ignərənt] agg. ignorante
to ignore [ig'nɔ:*] v. tr. ignorare

ilex ['aileks] s. leccio m.
ill [il] agg. malato • s. male m.; - bred maleducato; - fed denutrito; - intentioned malintenzionato
illation [i'leiʃən] s. illazione f.
illegal [i'li:gəl] agg. illegale
illegality [,ili(:)'gæliti] s. illegalità f.
illegitimate [,ili'dʒitimit] agg. illegittimo
illicit [i'lisit] agg. illecito
illiterate [i'litərit] agg. e s. analfabeta m. e f.
illness ['ilnis] s. malattia f.
illogical [i'lɔdʒikəl] agg. illogico
to illuminate [i'lju:mineit] v. tr. illuminare; chiarire
illumination [i,lju:mi'neiʃən] s. illuminazione f.
illusion [i'lu:ʒən] s. illusione f.
to illustrate ['iləstreit] v. tr. illustrare
illustrated ['iləstreitid] agg. illustrato
illustration [,iləs'treiʃən] s. illustrazione f.
image ['imidʒ] s. immagine f.; ritratto m.
imaginary [i'mædʒinəri] agg. immaginario
imagination [i,mædʒi'neiʃən] s. immaginazione f.
to imagine [i'mædʒin] v. tr. e intr. immaginare; fantasticare
imbecile ['imbisail] agg. imbecille
to imitate ['imiteit] v. tr. imitare
imitation [,imi'teiʃən] s. imitazione f.
imitator ['imiteitə*] s. imitatore m.
immanent ['imənənt] agg. immanente
immaterial [,imə'tiəriel] agg. indifferente; immateriale
immature [,imə'tjuə*] agg. immaturo
immeasurable [i'meʒərəbl] agg. smisurato
immediate [i'mi:djət] agg. immediato
immediately [i'mi:djətli] avv. immediatamente, subito
immemorial [,imi'mɔ:riəl] agg. immemorabile
immense [i'mens] agg. immenso
immensity [i'mensiti] s. immensità f.
to immerse [i'mə:s] v. tr. immergere
immersion [i'mə:ʃən] s. immersione f.
immigrant ['imigrənt] agg. e s. immigrato m.
to immigrate ['imigreit] v. intr. immigrare

immigration [,imi'greiʃən] *s.* immigrazione *f.*

imminent ['iminənt] *agg.* imminente

to immobilize [i'moubilaiz] *v. tr.* immobilizzare

immoderate [i'mɔdərit] *agg.* smodato

immodest [i'mɔdist] *agg.* impudico

immoral [i'mɔrəl] *agg.* immorale

immortal [i'mɔːtl] *agg.* immortale

immortality [,imɔː'tæliti] *s.* immortalità *f.*

to immortalize [i'mɔːtəlaiz] *v. tr.* immortalare

immovable [i'muːvəbl] *agg.* immobile; immobiliare

immune [i'mjuːn] *agg.* immune

immunity [i'mjuːniti] *s.* immunità *f.*

to immunize [i'mjuː(:)naiz] *v. tr.* immunizzare

immutable [i'mjuːtəbl] *agg.* immutabile

impact ['impækt] *s.* impatto *m.*

to impair [im'peə*] *v. tr.* danneggiare

impairment [im'peəmənt] *s.* danneggiamento *m.*; diminuzione *f.*

impalpable [im'pælpəbl] *agg.* impalpabile

impartial [im'pɑːʃəl] *agg.* imparziale, equo

impartiality ['im,pɑːʃi'æliti] *s.* imparzialità *f.*

impasse [æm'pɑːs] *s.* impasse *f. inv.*

impassioned [im'pæʃənd] *agg.* appassionato

impassive [im'pæsiv] *agg.* impassibile

impatience [im'peiʃəns] *s.* impazienza *f.*, intolleranza *f.*

impatient [im'peiʃənt] *agg.* impaziente

impeccable [im'pekəbl] *agg.* impeccabile

impediment [im'pedimənt] *s.* impedimento *m.*

impeller [im'pelə*] *s.* girante *f.*

impending [im'pendiŋ] *agg.* incombente; imminente

impenetrable [im'penitrəbl] *agg.* impenetrabile

imperceptible [,impə'septəbl] *agg.* impercettibile

imperfection [,impə'fekʃən] *s.* imperfezione *f.*

imperial [im'piəriəl] *agg.* imperiale

imperialism [im'piəriəlizəm] *s.* imperialismo *m.*; politica *f.* imperialistica

impersonal [im'pəːsənəl] *agg.* impersonale

to impersonate [im'pəːsəneit] *v. tr.* impersonare

impertinent [im'pəːtinənt] *agg.* impertinente

imperturbable [,impə(:)'təːbəbl] *agg.* imperturbabile

impetuosity [im,petju'ɔsiti] *s.* impetuosità *f.*

impetuous [im'petjuəs] *agg.* impetuoso

implacable [im'plækəbl] *agg.* implacabile

implement ['implimənt] *s.* arnese *m.*, utensile *m.*, attrezzo *m.*

to implicate ['implikeit] *v. tr.* implicare; compromettere

implication [,impli'keiʃən] *s.* implicazione *f.*; coinvolgimento *m.*

implicit [im'plisit] *agg.* implicito

implied [im'plaid] *agg.* implicito

impluvium [im'pluːvjəm] *s.* impluvio *m.*

to imply [im'plai] *v. tr.* implicare; denotare; insinuare

impolite [,impə'lait] *agg.* maleducato

import ['impɔːt] *s.* importazione *f.*

to import [im'pɔːt] *v. tr.* importare

importance [im'pɔːtəns] *s.* importanza *f.*

important [im'pɔːtənt] *agg.* importante

importation [,impɔː'teiʃən] *s.* importazione *f.*

to importune [im'pɔːtjuːn] *v. tr.* importunare

to impose [im'pouz] *v. tr.* imporre; – **oneself** imporsi

impossibility [im,pɔsə'biliti] *s.* impossibilità *f.*

impossible [im'pɔsəbl] *agg.* impossibile

imposture [im'pɔstʃə*] *s.* impostura *f.*

impotent ['impətənt] *agg.* impotente

imprecation [,impri'keiʃən] *s.* imprecazione *f.*

to impregnate [im'pregneit] *v. tr.* impregnare

to impress [im'pres] *v. tr.* imprimere; impressionare

impression [im'preʃən] *s.* impressione *f.*; impronta *f.*

impressionism [im'preʃnizəm] *s.* impressionismo *m.*

impressive [im'presiv] *agg.* impressionante; solenne

imprint ['imprint] *s.* impronta *f.*; impressione *f.*

to imprison [im'prizn] *v. tr.* imprigionare

imprisonment [im'priznmənt] *s.* prigionia *f.*; reclusione *f.*

improbable [im'prɔbəbl] *agg.* improbabile

improper [im'prɔpə*] *agg.* improprio; scorretto, sbagliato

to improve [im'pruːv] *v. tr. e intr.* migliorare

improvement [im'pruːvmənt] *s.* miglioramento *m.*; perfezionamento *m.*

to improvise ['imprəvaiz] *v. tr. e intr.* improvvisare

imprudence [im'pruːdəns] *s.* imprudenza *f.*

imprudent [im'pruːdənt] *agg.* imprudente

impudence ['impjudəns] *s.* impudenza *f.*, sfacciataggine *f.*

impudent ['impjudənt] *agg.* impudente, sfacciato

impulse ['impʌls] *s.* impulso *m.*

impulsive [im'pʌlsiv] *agg.* impulsivo

impure [im'pjuə*] *agg.* impuro

impurity [im'pjuəriti] s. impurità f.

in [in] prep. in, a • avv. dentro

inability [inə'biliti] s. inabilità f.; inattitudine f.

inaccessible [,inæk'sesəbl] agg. inaccessibile

inaccuracy [in'ækjurəsi] s. imprecisione f., inesattezza f.

inactive [in'æktiv] agg. inattivo

inactivity [,inæk'tiviti] s. inattività f.; inerzia f.

inadequate [in'ædikwit] agg. inadeguato

inadmissible [,inəd'misəbl] agg. inammissibile

inadvertence [,inəd'və:təns] s. sbadataggine f., disattenzione f.

inadvertently [,inəd'və:təntli] avv. inavvertitamente

inalienable [in'eiliənəbl] agg. inalienabile

inanimate [in'ænimit] agg. inanimato

inapt [in'æpt] agg. improprio; incapace

inattentive [,inə'tentiv] agg. disattento

inaugural [i'nɔ:gjurəl] agg. inaugurale

inauguration [i,nɔ:gju'reifən] s. inaugurazione f.

inauspicious [inɔ:s'pifəs] agg. nefasto

inborn ['in'bɔ:n] agg. innato

incalculable [in'kælkjuləbl] agg. incalcolabile

to incarnate ['inka:neit] v. tr. incarnare

incense ['insens] s. incenso m.

incentive [in'sentiv] s. incentivo m.

incest ['insest] s. incesto m.

inch [intf] s. pollice m. (misura)

incident ['insidənt] s. incidente m.

incidental [,insi,dentl] agg. incidentale

incidentally [,insi,dentli] avv. incidentalmente

incision [in'siʒən] s. incisione f.

incisive [in'saisiv] agg. incisivo

incisor [in'saizə*] s. incisivo m.

to incite [in'sait] v. tr. incitare

incivility [,insi'viliti] s. inciviltà f.

inclinable [in'klainəbl] agg. inclinabile

inclination [,inkli'neifən] s. inclinazione f.; disposizione f.

incline [in'klain] s. pendenza f.

to incline [in'klain] v. tr. inclinare • intr. propendere

to include [in'klu:d] v. tr. includere, comprendere

inclusive [in'klu:siv] agg. inclusivo, comprensivo

incoherent [,inkou'hiərənt] agg. incoerente

income ['inkəm] s. reddito m.; entrata f.; ~ tax imposta sul reddito

incomparable [in'kɔmpərəbl] agg. incomparabile

incompetent [in'kɔmpitənt] agg. incompetente, incapace

incomplete [,inkəm'pli:t] agg. incompleto

incomprehensible [in,kɔmpri'hensəbl] agg. incomprensibile

inconceivable [inkən'si:vəbl] agg. inconcepibile

inconclusive [inkən'klu:siv] agg. inconcludente

incongruous [in'kɔngruəs] agg. incongruente

inconsequent [in'kɔnsikwənt] agg. incongruente

inconsiderate [inkən'sidərit] agg. sconsiderato, avventato

inconsistent [inkən'sistənt] agg. incoerente

inconstant [in'kɔnstənt] agg. incostante

inconvenience [inkən'vi:njəns] s. disturbo m.; disagio m.

to incorporate [in'kɔ:pəreit] v. tr. incorporare • intr. fondersi

incorrect [inkə'rekt] agg. scorretto

incorrectness [inkə'rektnis] s. scorrettezza f.

incorruptible [,inkə'rʌptəbl] agg. incorruttibile

increase [in'kri:s] s. aumento m.; incremento m.; crescita f.

to increase [in'kri:s] v. tr. e intr. aumentare

incredible [in'kredəbl] agg. incredibile

incredulous [in'kredjuləs] agg. incredulo

to incriminate [in'krimineit] v. tr. incriminare

to inculcate ['inkʌlkeit] v. tr. inculcare

incunabulum [,inkju(:)'næbjuləm] s. incunabolo m.

to incur [in'kə:*] v. tr. incorrere

incurable [in'kjuərəbl] agg. incurabile

indecent [in'di:sənt] agg. indecente

indecipherable [,indi'saifərəbl] agg. indecifrabile

indecision [,indi'siʒən] s. indecisione f.

indeed [in'di:d] avv. davvero, realmente

indefatigable [,indi'fætigəbl] agg. instancabile

indefinable [,indi'fainəbl] agg. indefinibile

indefinitely [in'definitli] avv. indefinitamente

indelible [in'delibl] agg. indelebile

indemnification [in,demnifi'keifən] s. indennizzo m.

to indemnify [in'demnifai] v. tr. risarcire

to indent [in'dent] v. tr. dentellare, frastagliare • intr. essere frastagliato

independent [,indi'pendənt] agg. indipendente

indestructible [,indis'trʌktəbl] agg. indistruttibile

indeterminate [,indi'tə:minit] *agg.* indeterminato

indeterminateness [,indi'tə:minitnis] *s.* indeterminatezza *f.*

index ['indeks] *s.* indice *m.* ; - **finger** dito indice

to indicate ['indikeit] *v. tr.* indicare, mostrare

indication [,indi'keiʃən] *s.* indicazione *f.*

indicative [in'dikətiv] *agg.* indicativo

indifference [in'difrəns] *s.* indifferenza *f.*

indifferent [in'difrənt] *agg.* indifferente

indigestible [indi'dʒestəbl] *agg.* indigesto

indigestion [,indi'dʒestʃən] *s.* indigestione *f.*

indirect [,indi'rekt] *agg.* indiretto

indiscreet [,indis'kri:t] *agg.* indiscreto

indispensable [,indis'pensəbl] *agg.* indispensabile

indisposition [,indispə'ziʃən] *s.* indisposizione *f.*

indissoluble [,indi'sɔljubl] *agg.* indissolubile

indistinct [,indis'tiŋkt] *agg.* indistinto

individual [,indi'vidjuəl] *agg.* individuale • *s.* individuo *m.*

individualism [,indi'vidjualizəm] *s.* individualismo *m.*

to individualize [,indi'vidjualaiz] *v. tr.* individuare

individually [,indi'vidjuali] *avv.* individualmente

indivisible [,indi'vizəbl] *agg.* indivisibile

Indo-European ['indou,juərə'pi:ən] *agg.* indoeuropeo

indolent ['indələnt] *agg.* indolente

indoor ['in,dɔ:*] *agg.* interno; al coperto

indoors [,in'dɔ:z] *avv.* in casa, all'interno, al coperto; **to go** - entrare in casa

to induce [in'dju:s] *v. tr.* indurre; invogliare

to indulge [in'dʌldʒ] *v. tr.* appagare; assecondare

industrial [in'dʌstriəl] *agg.* industriale

industrialization [in,dʌstriəlai'zeiʃən] *s.* industrializzazione *f.*

industrious [in'dʌstriəs] *agg.* operoso

industry ['indəstri] *s.* industria *f.*; industriosità *f.*

ineffective [,ini'fektiv] *agg.* inefficace

inefficiency [,ini'fiʃənsi] *s.* inefficienza *f.*

inefficient [,ini'fiʃənt] *agg.* inefficace

ineluctable [,ini'lʌktəbl] *agg.* ineluttabile

inequality [,ini(:)'kwɔliti] *s.* disuguaglianza *f.*

inertia [i'nə:ʃjə] *s.* inerzia *f.* (*fis.*)

inertness [i'nə:tnis] *s.* inerzia *f.*

inevitable [in'evitəbl] *agg.* inevitabile

inexact [,inig'zækt] *agg.* inesatto

inexactitude [,inig'zæktitju:d] *s.* inesattezza *f.*

inexhaustible [,inig'zɔ:stəbl] *agg.* inesauribile

inexistent [,inig'zistənt] *agg.* inesistente

inexpensive [,iniks'pensiv] *agg.* economico, a buon mercato

inexperienced [,iniks'piəriənst] *agg.* inesperto

inexpert [,ineks'pə:t] *agg.* inesperto

inexplicable [in'eksplikəbl] *agg.* inspiegabile

inexpugnable [,iniks'pʌgnəbl] *agg.* inespugnabile

infallible [in'fæləbl] *agg.* infallibile

infancy ['infənsi] *s.* infanzia *f.*

infantile ['infəntail] *agg.* infantile

infantry ['infəntri] *s.* fanteria *f.*

infarct [in'fa:kt] *s.* infarto *m.*

to infect [in'fekt] *v. tr.* contagiare

infected [in'fektid] *agg.* infetto

infection [in'fekʃən] *s.* infezione *f.*

infectious [in'fekʃəs] *agg.* infettivo

to infer [in'fə:*] *v. tr.* desumere

inference ['infərəns] *s.* illazione *f.*

inferior [in'fiəriə*] *agg.* inferiore

inferiority [in,fiəri'ɔriti] *s.* inferiorità *f.*

to infest [in'fest] *v. tr.* infestare

to infiltrate [in'filtreit] *v. intr.* infiltrarsi

infinite ['infinit] *agg.* infinito

infinitesimal [,infini'tesiməl] *agg.* infinitesimale

infinity [in'finiti] *s.* infinità *f.*; infinito *m.*

infirmary [in'fə:məri] *s.* infermeria *f.*

infirmity [in'fə:miti] *s.* infermità *f.*; malanno *m.*

inflammable [in'flæməbl] *agg.* infiammabile

inflammation [,inflə'meiʃən] *s.* infiammazione *f.*

to inflate [in'fleit] *v. tr. e intr.* gonfiare

inflated [in'fleitid] *agg.* gonfio

inflation [in'fleiʃən] *s.* inflazione *f.*

inflexible [in'fleksəbl] *agg.* inflessibile

to inflict [in'flikt] *v. tr.* infliggere

influence [in'fluəns] *s.* influenza *f.*; influsso *m.*

to influence ['influəns] *v. tr.* influire

influential [,influ'enʃəl] *agg.* influente

influenza [,influ'enzə] *s.* influenza *f.* (*med.*)

to inform [in'fɔ:m] *v. tr.* informare; avvertire • *intr.* dare informazioni

informal [in'fɔ:ml] *agg.* informale

informally [in'fɔ:məli] *avv.* senza formalità

informatics [,infə'mætiks] *s. pl.* (*v. al sing.*) informatica *f. sing.*

information [,infə'meiʃən] *s.* informazioni *f. pl.*

infringement [in'frindʒmənt] *s.* trasgressione *f.*

to infuse [in'fju:z] *v. tr.* infondere

infusion [in'fju:ʒən] *s.* infusione *f.*

81

ingenious [in'dʒiːnjəs] *agg.* geniale; ingegnoso

ingeniousness [in'dʒenjuəsnis] *s.* genialità *f.*

ingenuity [,indʒi'njuːiti] *s.* ingegnosità *f.*

ingenuous [in'dʒenjuəs] *agg.* ingenuo

ingenuousness [in'dʒenjuəsnis] *s.* ingenuità *f.*

to ingest [in'dʒest] *v. tr.* ingerire

ingrained [in'greind] *agg.* impregnato

ingratitude [in'grætitjuːd] *s.* ingratitudine *f.*

ingredient [in'griːdjənt] *s.* ingrediente *m.*

to inhabit [in'hæbit] *v. tr.* abitare

inhabitant [in'hæbitənt] *s.* abitante *m. e f.*

to inhale [in'heil] *v. tr. e intr.* inalare

inherent [in'hiərənt] *agg.* inerente

to inherit [in'herit] *v. tr. e intr.* ereditare

inheritance [in'heritəns] *s.* eredità *f.*

to inhibit [in'hibit] *v. tr.* inibire

inhibition [,inhi'biʃən] *s.* inibizione *f.*

inhospitable [in'hɔspitəbl] *agg.* inospitale

inhuman [in'hjuːmən] *agg.* disumano

inimitable [i'nimitəbl] *agg.* inimitabile

initial [i'niʃəl] *agg.* iniziale

initiate [i'niʃiit] *s.* iniziato *m.*

initiative [i'niʃiətiv] *s.* iniziativa *f.*

initiator [i'niʃieitə*] *s.* iniziatore *m.*

to inject [in'dʒekt] *v. tr.* iniettare

injection [in'dʒekʃən] *s.* iniezione *f.*

injector [in'dʒektə*] *s.* iniettore *m.*

injunction [in'dʒʌŋkʃən] *s.* ingiunzione *f.*

to injure ['indʒə*] *v. tr.* danneggiare; ferire

injury ['indʒəri] *s.* danno *m.*; ferita *f.*

injustice [in'dʒʌstis] *s.* ingiustizia *f.*

ink [iŋk] *s.* inchiostro *m.*

inland ['inlənd] *s.* retroterra *m. inv.*

inlay ['inlei] *s.* intarsio *m.*

inlet ['inlet] *s.* insenatura *f.*; immissione *f.* (mecc.)

inn [in] *s.* locanda *f.*, taverna *f.*

innate ['i'neit] *agg.* innato

inner ['inə*] *agg.* interno; interiore

innkeeper ['in,kiːpə*] *s.* locandiere *m.*

innocence ['inəsəns] *s.* innocenza *f.*

innocent ['inəsənt] *agg.* innocente

innocuous [i'nɔkjuəs] *agg.* innocuo

innovator ['inouveitə*] *s.* innovatore *m.*

innumerable [i'njuːmərəbl] *agg.* innumerevole

inoffensive [,inə'fensiv] *agg.* inoffensivo

inopportune [in'ɔpətjuːn] *agg.* inopportuno

inorganic [,inɔː'gænik] *agg.* inorganico

in-patient [in,peiʃənt] *s.* degente *m. e f.*

inquest ['inkwest] *s.* inchiesta *f.* giudiziaria

to inquire [in'kwaiə*] *v. intr.* indagare; informarsi • *tr.* chiedere

inquiry [in'kwaiəri] *s.* indagine *f.*

inquisition ['inkwi'ziʃən] *s.* inquisizione *f.*

insane [in'sein] *agg.* demente, matto

insanity [in'sæniti] *s.* demenza *f.*

insatiable [in'seiʃjəbl] *agg.* insaziabile

to inscribe [in'skraib] *v. tr.* iscrivere

inscription [in'skripʃən] *s.* iscrizione *f.*

insect ['insekt] *s.* insetto *m.*

insecticide [in'sektisaid] *s.* insetticida *m.*

insecurity [,insi'kjuəriti] *s.* insicurezza *f.*

insensitive [in'sensitiv] *agg.* insensibile

inseparable [in'sepərəbl] *agg.* inseparabile

to insert [in'səːt] *v. tr.* inserire

insertion [in'səːʃən] *s.* inserzione *f.*

inside [in'said] *s.* interno *m.* • *avv. e prep.* dentro, in casa

insidious [in'sidiəs] *agg.* insidioso

insignificant [,insig'nifikənt] *agg.* insignificante

to insinuate [in'sinjueit] *v. tr.* insinuare; – oneself insinuarsi

insipid [in'sipid] *agg.* insipido

to insist [in'sist] *v. intr.* insistere

insistent [in'sistənt] *agg.* insistente

insolation [,insou'leiʃən] *s.* insolazione *f.*

insolence ['insələns] *s.* insolenza *f.*

insoluble [in'sɔljubl] *agg.* insolubile

insolvent [in'sɔlvənt] *agg.* insolvente

insomnia [in'sɔmniə] *s.* insonnia *f.*

to inspect [in'spekt] *v. tr.* ispezionare

inspection [in'spekʃən] *s.* ispezione *f.*

inspector [in'spektə*] *s.* ispettore *m.*

inspiration [,inspə'reiʃən] *s.* ispirazione *f.*

to inspire [in'spaiə*] *v. tr.* ispirare; inspirare

inspirer [in'spaiərə*] *s.* ispiratore *m.*

to install [in'stɔːl] *v. tr.* installare

installation [,instə'leiʃən] *s.* installazione *f.*

instal(l)ment [in'stɔːlmənt] *s.* rata *f.*; puntata *f.*; lotto *m.*

instance ['instəns] *s.* esempio *m.*; caso *m.*; **for** – per esempio

instant ['instənt] *s.* istante *m.*

instantaneous [,instən'teinjəs] *agg.* istantaneo

instantly ['instəntli] *avv.* istantaneamente

instead [in'sted] *avv.* invece

instinct ['instiŋkt] *s.* istinto *m.*

instinctive [in'stiŋktiv] *agg.* istintivo

institute ['institjuːt] *s.* istituto *m.*

to institute ['institjuːt] *v. tr.* istituire

institution [,insti'tjuːʃən] *s.* istituzione *f.*

institutional [,insti'tjuːʃənl] *agg.* istituzionale

to instruct [in'strʌkt] *v. tr.* istruire

instruction [in'strʌkʃən] *s.* istruzione *f.*

instructive [in'strʌktiv] *agg.* istruttivo

instructor [in'strʌktə*] s. istruttore m.

Instrument ['instrumənt] s. strumento m., apparecchio m.

instrumentalist [,instru'mentəlist] s. strumentista m. e f.

insubstantial [,in-səb'stænʃəl] agg. inconsistente

insufficient [,insə'fiʃənt] agg. insufficiente, scarso

insular ['insjulə*] agg. insulare

to insulate ['insjuleit] v. tr. isolare

insulated ['insjuleitid] agg. isolato

insulating ['insjuleitiŋ] s. isolante m.

insulation [,insju'leiʃən] s. isolamento m.

insult ['insʌlt] s. insulto m.

to insult [in'sʌlt] v. tr. insultare

insulting [in'sʌltiŋ] agg. offensivo

insurance [in'ʃuərəns] s. assicurazione f.; - policy polizza di assicurazione; life - assicurazione sulla vita

to insure [in'ʃuə*] v. tr. assicurare

insurrection [,insə'rekʃən] s. insurrezione f., sommossa f.

intact [in'tækt] agg. intatto

intake ['in-teik] s. presa f. (d'acqua, ecc.)

integral ['intigrəl] agg. integrale

integrant ['intigrənt] agg. integrante

intellectual [,inti'lektjuəl] agg. intellettuale

intellectualism [,inti'lektjuəlizəm] s. intellettualismo m.

intelligence [in'telidʒəns] s. intelligenza f.

intelligent [in'telidʒənt] agg. intelligente

intelligible [in'telidʒibl] agg. intelligibile

to intend [in'tend] v. tr. e intr. intendere, avere intenzione di

intense [in'tens] agg. intenso

to intensify [in'tensifai] v. tr. intensificare

intensity [in'tensiti] s. intensità f.

intention [in'tenʃən] s. intenzione f.; proposito m., intento m.

intentional [in'tenʃənl] agg. intenzionale

interaction [,intər'ækʃən] s. interazione f.

to intercept [,intə(:)'sept] v. tr. intercettare

intercession [,intə'seʃən] s. intercessione f.

interchange ['intə(:)'tʃeindʒ] s. svincolo m.; interscambio m.

intercolumn [,intə'kɔləm] s. intercolunnio m.

intercom ['intəkɔm] s. interfono m.

intercontinental [,intə,kɔnti'nentl] agg. intercontinentale

intercourse ['intə(:)kɔːs] s. rapporto m.

interdisciplinary [,intə'disiplinəri] agg. interdisciplinare

interest ['intrist] s. interesse m.

to interest ['intrist] v. tr. interessare

interested ['intristid] agg. interessato

interesting ['intristiŋ] agg. interessante

to interfere [,intə'fiə*] v. intr. interferire; immischiarsi

interference [,intə'fiərəns] s. interferenza f.; ingerenza f.

interior [in'tiəriə*] agg. interiore • s. interno m.; entroterra m.

interlocutor [,intə(:)'lɔkjutə*] s. interlocutore m.

intermediate [,intə(:)'miːdjət] agg. intermedio

intermezzo [,intə(:)'metsou] s. intermezzo m.

interminable [in'tə:minəbl] agg. interminabile

intermittent [,intə'mitənt] agg. intermittente

internal [in'tə:nl] agg. interno; **internally** internamente

international [,intə(:)'næʃənl] agg. internazionale

interphone ['intəfoun] s. citofono m.

to interpolate [in'tə:pouleit] v. tr. interpolare

to interpose [,intə(:)'pouz] v. tr. frapporre, interporre • intr. intromettersi

to interpret [in'tə:prit] v. tr. interpretare

interpretation [in,tə:pri'teiʃən] s. interpretazione f.

interpreter [in'tə:pritə*] s. interprete m. e f.

to interrupt [,intə'rʌpt] v. tr. interrompere

intersection [,intə'sekʃən] s. intersezione f.

interstice [in'tə:stis] s. interstizio m.

to intertwine [,intə(:)'twain] v. tr. intrecciare • intr. attorcigliarsi

intertwinement [,intə(:)'twainmənt] s. intreccio m.

interurban [,intər'ə:bən] agg. interurbano

interval ['intəvəl] s. intervallo m.

to intervene [,intə(:)'viːn] v. intr. intervenire

intervention [,intə(:)'venʃən] s. intervento m.

interview ['intəvjuː] s. intervista f.; colloquio m., udienza f.

to interview ['intəvjuː] v. tr. intervistare

intestinal [in'testinl] agg. intestinale

intestine [in'testin] s. intestino m.

intimacy ['intiməsi] s. intimità f.

intimate ['intimit] agg. intimo

into ['intu, 'intə] prep. in, dentro

intolerable [in'tɔlərəbl] agg. intollerabile

intolerant [in'tɔlərənt] agg. intollerante

intoxication [in,tɔksi'keiʃən] s. intossicazione f.; ebbrezza f.

intrados [in'treidɔs] s. intradosso m.

intransigent [in'trænsidʒənt] agg. e s. intransigente m.

intricate ['intrikit] agg. intricato; macchinoso

intrigue [in'tri:g] s. intrigo m.

to introduce [,intrə'dju:s] v. tr. introdurre; presentare

introduction [,intrə'dʌkʃən] s. introduzione f.; presentazione f.

introspective [,introu'spektiv] agg. introspettivo

introvert ['introuvə:t] agg. introverso

to intrude [in'tru:d] v. intr. disturbare; introdurre

intruder [in'tru:də*] s. intruso m.

intrusion [in'tru:ʒən] s. intrusione f.

intrusive [in'tru:siv] agg. importuno

intuition [,intju:'iʃən] s. intuizione f.

intuitive [in'tju:itiv] agg. intuitivo

inundation [,inʌn'deiʃən] s. inondazione f.

inurement [i'njuəmənt] s. assuefazione f., abitudine f.

to invade [in'veid] v. tr. invadere

invader [in'veidə*] s. invasore m.

invalid ['invəli:d] e. agg. invalido m.; infermo m.

invalidity [,invə'liditi] s. invalidità f.

invaluable [in'væljuəbl] agg. inestimabile

invasion [in'veiʒən] s. invasione f.

to invent [in'vent] v. tr. inventare

invention [in'venʃən] s. invenzione f.

inventiveness [in'ventivnis] s. inventiva f.

inventor [in'ventə*] s. inventore m.

inventory ['inventri] s. inventario m.

inversion [in'və:ʃən] s. inversione f.

to invert [in'və:t] v. tr. invertire

invertebrate [in'və:tibrit] agg. invertebrato

to invest [in'vest] v. tr. investire

to investigate [in'vestigeit] v. tr. e intr. investigare

investigation [in,vesti'geiʃən] s. indagine f., investigazione f.; **the - of a crime** le indagini su un delitto

investment [in'vestmənt] s. investimento m.

investor [in'vestə*] s. investitore m. (fin.)

invincible [in'vinsəbl] agg. invincibile

invisible [in'vizəbl] agg. invisibile

invitation [,invi'teiʃən] s. invito m.; richiamo m.; **- card** biglietto d'invito

to invite [in'vait] v. tr. invitare

invoice ['invois] s. fattura f.

involuntary [in'vɔləntəri] agg. involontario

involution [,invə'lu:ʃən] s. involuzione f.

to involve [in'vɔlv] v. tr. coinvolgere

inward ['inwəd] agg. interno, interiore • avv. verso l'interno

Ionian [ai'ounjən] agg. ionico

Ionic [ai'ɔnik] agg. ionico

irascible [i'ræsibl] agg. irascibile

Irish ['aiəriʃ] agg. irlandese

Irishman ['aiəriʃmən] s. irlandese m.

Irishwoman ['aiəriʃ,wumən] s. irlandese f.

iron ['aiən] s. ferro m.; **steam –** ferro a vapore

to iron ['aiən] v. tr. stirare

ironical [ai'rɔnikəl] agg. ironico

ironing ['aiəniŋ] s. stiratura f.

ironmongery ['aiən,mʌŋgə*] s. negozio m. di ferramenta

irony ['aiərəni] s. ironia f.

irrational [i'ræʃənl] agg. irrazionale • s. numero m. irrazionale (mat.)

irredentism [,iri'dentizəm] s. irredentismo m.

irregular [i'regjulə*] agg. irregolare

irrelevant [i'relivənt] agg. non pertinente

irremediable [,iri'mi:djəbl] agg. irrimediabile

irreparable [i'repərəbl] agg. irreparabile

irreplaceable [,iri'pleisəbl] agg. insostituibile

irresistible [,iri'zistəbl] agg. irresistibile

irrespirable [i'respirəbl] agg. irrespirabile

irresponsible [,iris'pɔnsəbl] agg. irresponsabile, non responsabile

to irrigate ['irigeit] v. tr. irrigare

irrigation [,iri'geiʃən] s. irrigazione f.

irritable ['iritəbl] agg. irritabile

to irritate ['iriteit] v. tr. irritare

irritating ['iriteitiŋ] agg. irritante

irritation [,iri'teiʃən] s. irritazione f.

irruption [i'rʌpʃən] s. irruzione f.

Islamic [iz'læmik] agg. islamico

island ['ailənd] s. isola f.

isle [ail] s. isola f.

isobar ['aisouba:*] s. isobara f.

isobath ['aisouba:θ] s. isobata f.

to isolate ['aisəleit] v. tr. isolare

isolated ['aisəleitid] agg. isolato

isolation [,aisə'leiʃən] s. isolamento m.

Israelite ['izriəlait] agg. israelitico

issue ['isju:] s. emissione f.; pubblicazione f.; fuoriuscita f.

to issue ['isju:] v. tr. emettere; pubblicare; **to - tickets** rilasciare biglietti

isthmus ['isməs] s. istmo m.

Italian [i'tæljən] agg. italiano

Italic [i'tælik] agg. italico

italic [i'tælik] agg. corsivo m.

itch [itʃ] s. prurito m.

to itch [itʃ] v. intr. prudere

item ['aitəm] *s.* articolo *m.*; elemento *m.*; notizia *f.*

iterative ['itərətiv] *agg.* iterativo

itinerant [i'tinərənt] *agg.* ambulante

itinerary [ai'tinərəri] *s.* itinerario *m.*

itself [it'self] *pron.* esso stesso, se stesso

ivory ['aivəri] *s.* avorio *m.* • *agg.* eburneo

ivy ['aivi] *s.* edera *f.*

J

jack [dʒæk] s. boccino m.; cric m.; fante m. (carte)

jacket ['dʒækit] s. giubbotto m.; copertina f.; **life** - giubbotto di salvataggio; **blue** - marinaio; **dinner** - smoking

Jacobin ['dʒækəbin] agg. giacobino

jail [dʒeil] s. carcere m.

to jail [dʒeil] v. tr. imprigionare

jailer ['dʒeilə*] s. secondino m.

jam [dʒæm] s. confettura f. • blocco m.

to jam [dʒæm] v. tr. bloccare • intr. bloccarsi, incepparsi

jamb [dʒæm] s. stipite m.

janitor ['dʒænitə*] s. portinaio m.

January ['dʒænjuəri] s. gennaio m.

Japanese [,dʒæpə'ni:z] agg. giapponese

jar [dʒɑ:] s. barattolo m.

jargon ['dʒɑ:gən] s. gergo m.

jasmin ['dʒæsmin] s. gelsomino m.

javelin ['dʒævlin] s. giavellotto m.

jaw [dʒɔ:] s. mascella f.

jazzman ['dʒæzmæn] s. jazzista m.

jealous ['dʒeləs] agg. geloso

jealousy ['dʒeləsi] s. gelosia f.; invidia f.

jelly ['dʒeli] s. gelatina f.; – **fish** medusa

jerk [dʒə:k] s. sobbalzo m.

to jerk [dʒə:k] v. intr. sobbalzare

jersey ['dʒə:zi] s. maglia f.

jest [dʒest] s. scherzo m.

to jest [dʒest] v. intr. scherzare

jester ['dʒestə*] s. giullare m.

Jesuit ['dʒezjuit] s. gesuita m.

jet [dʒet] s. getto m.; zampillo m.

jewel ['dʒu:əl] s. gioiello m.; gemma f.

jeweller ['dʒu:ələ*] s. gioielliere m.

jewel(le)ry ['dʒu:əlri] s. gioielleria f.

Jewish ['dʒu:iʃ] agg. ebraico

jib [dʒib] s. fiocco m. (naut.)

job [dʒɔb] s. lavoro m.; impiego m.

to join [dʒɔin] v. tr. collegare; raggiungere • intr. congiungersi; associarsi

joint [dʒɔint] s. giunto m.; articolazione f.

to joint [dʒɔint] v. tr. collegare

jointed ['dʒɔintid] agg. snodabile

joke [dʒouk] s. barzelletta f.; scherzo m.; **in** - per scherzo; **no** - senza scherzi

to joke [dʒouk] v. intr. scherzare

joker ['dʒoukə*] s. jolly m. inv.

jolly ['dʒɔli] agg. gioviale

jolt [dʒoult] s. sobbalzo m.

to jolt [dʒoult] v. intr. sobbalzare

journal ['dʒə:nl] s. giornale m.; diario m.

journalism ['dʒə:nəlizəm] s. giornalismo m.

journalist ['dʒə:nəlist] s. giornalista m. e f.

journey ['dʒə:ni] s. viaggio m.; tragitto m.; **the** - **out** il viaggio d'andata

jovial ['dʒouvjəl] agg. gioviale

joy [dʒɔi] s. gioia f.

jubilee ['dʒu:bili:] s. giubileo m.

judge [dʒʌdʒ] s. giudice m. e f.

to judge [dʒʌdʒ] v. tr. e intr. giudicare

judgment ['dʒʌdʒmənt] s. giudizio m.

judicial [dʒu(:)'diʃəl] agg. giudiziario

judiciary [dʒu(:)'diʃiəri] agg. giudiziario

jug [dʒʌg] s. brocca f.

juggler ['dʒʌglə*] s. giocoliere m.

juice [dʒu:s] s. succo m.

July [dʒu(:)'lai] s. luglio m.

jumble ['dʒʌmbl] s. miscuglio m.

jump [dʒʌmp] s. salto m.

to jump [dʒʌmp] v. tr. e intr. saltare, balzare; trasalire

jumper ['dʒʌmpə*] s. pullover m. inv.

junction ['dʒʌŋkʃən] s. giunzione f.

June [dʒu:n] s. giugno m.

jungle ['dʒʌŋgl] s. giungla f.

junk [dʒʌŋk] s. cianfrusaglie f. pl.

Junoesque [,dʒu:nou'esk] agg. giunonico

juridical [dʒuə'ridikəl] agg. giuridico

jurisdictional [,dʒuəris'dikʃənl] agg. giurisdizionale

jurisprudence ['dʒuəris,pru:dəns] s. giurisprudenza f.

jurist ['dʒuərist] s. giurista m. e f.

jury ['dʒuəri] s. giuria f.

just [dʒʌst] agg. giusto; onesto • avv. esattamente; proprio; appena; – **about** quasi; – **after** subito dopo; – **in case** caso mai; – **now** poco fa; – **over** poco più

justice ['dʒʌstis] *s.* giustizia *f.*
justifiable ['dʒʌstifaiəbl] *agg.* giustificabile
justification [ˌdʒʌstifi'keiʃən] *s.* giustificazione *f.*

to justify ['dʒʌstifai] *v. tr.* giustificare; – **oneself** giustificarsi
juxtaposition [ˌdʒʌkstəpə'ziʃən] *s.* giustapposizione *f.*

K

kaleidoscope [kə'laidəskoup] s. caleidoscopio m.
kangaroo [,kæŋgə'ru:] s. canguro m.
keel [ki:l] s. chiglia f. (naut.)
keen [ki:n] agg. affilato, tagliente, acuto
keep [ki:p] s. torrione m.
to keep [ki:p] v. tr. tenere; conservare; mantenere • intr. mantenersi; – away stare lontano
keeper ['ki:pə°] s. guardiano m.
kennel ['kenl] s. canile m.
key [ki:] s. chiave f.; tasto m.
keyboard ['ki:bɔ:d] s. tastiera f.
keyhole ['ki:houl] s. toppa f. (serratura)
kick [kik] s. calcio m.; corner – calcio d'angolo; penalty – calcio di rigore
to kick [kik] v. intr. tirare calci
kid [kid] s. bambino m.; capretto m.
to kidnap ['kidnæp] v. tr. rapire
kidnapper ['kid,næpə°] s. rapitore m.
kidnapping ['kid,næpiŋ] s. rapimento m.
kidney ['kidni] s. rene m., rognone m. (alim.)
to kill [kil] v. tr. uccidere
killing ['kiliŋ] s. uccisione f.
kiln [kiln] s. fornace f.
kilogram ['kiləgræm] s. chilogrammo m.
kilometre ['kilə,mi:tə°] s. chilometro m.
kilometric [,kilou'metrik] agg. chilometrico
kind [kaind] s. genere m.; qualità f. • agg. gentile
kindergarten ['kində,ga:tn] s. asilo m.
kindness ['kaindnis] s. gentilezza f., cortesia f.
kinetic [kai'netik] agg. cinetico

king [kiŋ] s. re m. inv.
kingdom ['kiŋdəm] s. regno m.
kinship ['kinʃip] s. parentela f.
kinsman ['kinzmən] agg. consanguineo
kiss [kis] s. bacio m.
to kiss [kis] v. tr. baciare
kitchen ['kitʃin] s. cucina f.
kite [kait] s. aquilone m.
kitten ['kitn] s. gattino m.
knapsack ['næpsæk] s. zaino m.
to knead [ni:d] v. tr. impastare
kneading ['ni:diŋ] s. impastatura f.; – trough madia
knee [ni:] s. ginocchio m.
to kneel [ni:l] v. intr. inginocchiarsi
knickknack ['niknæk] s. soprammobile m.
knife [naif] s. coltello m.
knitting ['nitiŋ] s. lavoro m. a maglia; – needle ferro da calza
knob [nɔb] s. maniglia f.; manopola f., pomello m.
to knock [nɔk] v. tr. picchiare, battere • intr. (– at) bussare
knocker ['nɔkə°] s. battente m.
knoll [noul] s. poggio m.
knot [nɔt] s. nodo m.; capannello m.
to knot [nɔt] v. tr. annodare
knotty ['nɔti] agg. nodoso
to know [nou] v. tr. sapere; conoscere
knowledge ['nɔlidʒ] s. conoscenza f.
known [noun] agg. noto

L

lab [læb] s. laboratorio m. (fam.)

label ['leibl] s. cartellino m.; etichetta f.

laboratory [lə'bɔrətəri] s. laboratorio m.

labour ['leibə*] s. lavoro m.; fatica f.; travaglio m.

labourer ['leibərə*] s. manovale m.

labyrinth ['læbarinθ] s. labirinto m.

lace [leis] s. pizzo m.; stringa f.

to lace [leis] v. tr. allacciare

laceration [,læsə'reifən] s. lacerazione f.

lack [læk] s. mancanza f.; difetto m.

to lack [læk] v. tr. mancare di

laconic [lə'kɔnik] agg. laconico

lacquer ['læka*] s. lacca f.

lad [læd] s. ragazzo m.; garzone m.

ladder ['lædə*] s. scala f.; smagliatura f. (calze)

laden ['leidn] agg. carico

ladle ['leidl] s. mestolo m.

lady ['leidi] s. signora f.

lagoon [lə'gu:n] s. laguna f.

laicism ['leiisizəm] s. laicismo m.

lair [lɛə*] s. covo m.

lake [leik] s. lago m.

lamb [læm] s. agnello m.; – **chop** costata d'agnello

lame [leim] agg. zoppo, storpio

to lament [lə'ment] v. tr. e intr. lamentare

lamina ['læminə] s. lamina f.

lamp [læmp] s. lampada f.; lampione m.; – **post** lampione; – **shade** paralume

lance [la:ns] s. lancia f.

lancinating ['la:nsineitiŋ] agg. lancinante

land [lænd] s. terra f.; paese m.; suolo m.; terreno m.   •   agg. terrestre; fondiario

to land [lænd] v. intr. sbarcare; approdare; atterrare

landed ['lændid] agg. fondiario

landing ['lændiŋ] s. approdo m.; atterraggio m.; scalo m.; pianerottolo m.; – **strip** pista di atterraggio

landlady ['læn,leidi] s. padrona f. di casa; affittacamere f. inv.

landlord ['lænlɔ:d] s. padrone m. di casa; affittacamere m. inv.

landscape ['lændskeip] s. paesaggio m.

landslide ['lændslaid] s. frana f.

lane [lein] s. corsia f.; pista f.; sentiero m., viottolo m.; vicolo m.

language ['læŋgwidʒ] s. lingua f.; linguaggio m.

languor ['læŋgə*] s. languore m.

lantern ['læntən] s. lanterna f.

lap [læp] s. grembo m.; giro m.   •   leccata f.

to lap [læp] v. tr. leccare   •   ripiegare; dare un giro di distacco

lapel [lə'pel] s. risvolto m.

lapidary ['læpidəri] agg. lapidario

to lapidate ['læpideit] v. tr. lapidare

lapse [læps] s. errore m.; lapsus m. inv.

lard [la:d] s. strutto m.

large [la:dʒ] agg. grande, grosso, vasto

largeness ['la:dʒnis] s. ampiezza f.; grandezza f.; larghezza f.

larval ['la:vəl] agg. larvale

laryngitis [,lærin'dʒaitis] s. laringite f.

larynx ['læriŋks] s. laringe f.

lash [læʃ] s. sferza f.; sferzata f.; **eye** – ciglio

to lash [læʃ] v. tr. sferzare, battere; legare

last [la:st] agg. ultimo; finale; scorso

to last [la:st] v. intr. durare

lasting ['la:stiŋ] agg. duraturo, durevole

late [leit] agg. tardo; defunto; recente   •   avv. tardi, in ritardo; recentemente; **to be** – essere in ritardo

latch [lætʃ] s. chiavistello m.

lately ['leitli] avv. recentemente

latent ['leitənt] agg. latente

later ['leitə*] agg. posteriore   •   avv. più tardi, dopo

lateral ['lætərəl] agg. laterale

latest ['leitist] agg. ultimo

lathe [leið] s. tornio m.

lather ['la:ðə*] s. schiuma f.

lathery ['la:ðəri] agg. schiumoso

Latin ['lætin] agg. latino

Latinism ['lætinizəm] s. latinismo m.

Latinist ['lætinist] s. latinista m. e f.

Latinity [lə'tiniti] s. latinità f.

latitude ['lætitju:d] s. latitudine f.

latter ['lætə*] agg. secondo (di due); (quest') ultimo • pron. il secondo; l'ultimo (di due)
lattice ['lætis] s. traliccio m.
laugh [la:f] s. risata f.
to laugh [la:f] v. intr. ridere
laughter ['la:ftə*] s. risata f.
launch [lɔ:ntʃ] s. varo m.
to launch [lɔ:ntʃ] v. tr. lanciare; varare (naut.)
launching [lɔ:ntʃiŋ] s. lancio m.; varo m.
launderette [,lɔ:ndə'ret] s. lavanderia f. automatica
laundry ['lɔ:ndri] s. lavanderia f.
laurel ['lɔrəl] s. alloro m.
lava ['la:və] s. lava f.
lavage [læ'vidʒ] s. lavanda f. gastrica
lavatory ['lævətəri] s. gabinetto m.
lavender ['lævində*] s. lavanda f.
lavish ['læviʃ] agg. generoso; sontuoso, sfarzoso
law [lɔ:] s. legge f.; diritto m.
lawful ['lɔ:ful] agg. lecito; legale
lawn [lɔ:n] s. prato m.
lawsuit ['lɔ:-sju:t] s. causa f., processo m.
lawyer ['lɔ:jə*] s. avvocato m.
laxative ['læksətiv] agg. lassativo
lay [lei] agg. laico • s. disposizione f.
to lay [lei] v. tr. e intr. posare; porre; progettare; – out tracciare
layer ['leiə*] s. strato m.
layout ['leiaut] s. pianta f.; tracciato m.; progetto m., bozzetto m.
to laze [leiz] v. intr. oziare
laziness ['leizinis] s. pigrizia f.
lazy ['leizi] agg. pigro
lead [li:d] s. piombo m.; comando m.; vantaggio m.; avanguardia f.; guinzaglio m.
to lead [li:d] v. tr. condurre, guidare
leaden ['ledn] agg. plumbeo
leader ['li:də*] s. capo m.; direttore m.
leadership ['li:dəʃip] s. guida f.; direzione f.; comando m.
leaf [li:f] s. foglia f.
leaflet ['li:f-lit] s. volantino m.
league [li:g] s. lega f.; alleanza f.
leak [li:k] s. falla f.; fessura f.
to leak [li:k] v. intr. perdere (liquidi); penetrare; fare acqua (naut.)
lean [li:n] agg. magro
to lean [li:n] v. intr. pendere; inclinarsi; appoggiarsi
leaning ['li:niŋ] agg. pendente
leanness ['li:nnis] s. magrezza f.
leap [li:p] s. salto m.; – year anno bisestile

to leap [li:p] v. tr. saltare
to learn [lə:n] v. tr. e intr. imparare
learned ['lə:nid] agg. colto
learning ['lə:niŋ] s. cultura f.; apprendimento m.
lease [li:s] s. affitto m., contratto m. d'affitto
to lease [li:s] v. tr. affittare
leash [li:ʃ] s. guinzaglio m.
least [li:st] agg. minimo; il più piccolo • avv. meno (di tutti); at – almeno; – of all tanto meno; to say the – a dir poco
leather ['leðə*] s. cuoio m.; pelle f.; – goods shop pelletteria; shammy – pelle di camoscio
leatherwear ['leðəweə*] s. pelletteria f.
leave [li:v] s. permesso m.; congedo m.
to leave [li:v] v. tr. lasciare; abbandonare • intr. partire; – off smettere; – out tralasciare; leaving partenza
lecture ['lektʃə*] s. conferenza f.; predica f.; lezione f.
to lecture ['lektʃə*] v. tr. e intr. fare lezione; tenere una conferenza
lecturer ['lektʃərə*] s. conferenziere m.; lettore m. (universitario); professore m. (universitario) (USA)
ledge [ledʒ] s. sporgenza f.; ripiano m.; window – davanzale
lee [li:v] s. ridosso m.
leeward ['li:wəd] agg. e avv. sottovento
leeway ['li:wei] s. scarroccio m. (naut.)
leek [li:k] s. porro m.
left [left] agg. sinistro • s. sinistra f.; – handed mancino
leg [leg] s. gamba f.; zampa f.
legal ['li:gəl] agg. legale
to legalize ['li:gəlaiz] v. tr. legalizzare
legend ['ledʒənd] s. leggenda f.
legendary ['ledʒəndəri] agg. leggendario
legion ['li:dʒən] s. legione f.
legislation [,ledʒis'leiʃən] s. legislazione f.
legislative ['ledʒislətiv] agg. legislativo
legitimate [li'dʒitimit] agg. legittimo
to legitimate [li'dʒitimit] v. tr. legittimare
legume ['legju:(:)m] s. legume m.
leisure ['leʒə*] s. tempo m. libero; agio m.
leisurely ['leʒəli] avv. con comodo
lemon ['lemən] s. limone m.
lemonade [,lemə'neid] s. limonata f.
to lend [lend] v. tr. prestare; – oneself prestarsi
length [leŋθ] s. lunghezza f.; durata f.; at – per esteso
to lengthen ['leŋθən] v. tr. allungare
leniency ['li:njənsi] s. mitezza f.

lenient ['li:njənt] agg. mite

lenitive ['lenitiv] agg. lenitivo

lens [lenz] s. lente f.; **contact** – lente a contatto

Lent [lent] s. quaresima f.

lentil ['lentil] s. lenticchia f.

leopard ['lepəd] s. leopardo m.

leotard ['li:əta:d] s. calzamaglia f.

leper ['lepə*] agg. lebbroso

leprosy ['leprəsi] s. lebbra f.

lesion ['li:ʒən] s. lesione f.

less [les] agg. meno; minore • avv. meno, di meno

lesser ['lesə*] agg. minore

lesson ['lesn] s. lezione f.

let [let] s. affitto m.; **rooms to** – si affittano camere

to let [let] v. tr. lasciare; permettere; affittare

lethal ['li:əəl] agg. letale

lethargy ['leθədʒi] s. letargo m.

letter ['letə*] s. lettera f.; **registered** – raccomandata; – **box** buca delle lettere

lettered ['letəd] agg. letterato

lettuce ['letis] s. lattuga f.

leuk(a)emia [lju:'ki:miə] s. leucemia f.

level ['levl] s. livello m.; piano m. • agg. piatto; equilibrato

to level ['levl] v. tr. livellare; pareggiare; uguagliare; – **crossing** passaggio a livello

lever ['li:və*] s. leva f.

levy ['levi] s. leva f. (mil.); imposta f.

lexicon ['leksikən] s. lessiço m.

liability [,laiə'biliti] s. responsabilità f.; svantaggio m.

liable ['laiəbl] agg. responsabile; soggetto

liar ['laiə*] s. bugiardo m.

liberal ['libərəl] agg. generoso; liberale

liberalism ['libərəlizəm] s. liberalismo m.

liberalization [,libərəlai'zeiʃən] s. liberalizzazione f.

to liberate ['libəreit] v. tr. liberare

libertine ['libə:tain] agg. libertino

liberty ['libəti] s. libertà f.

librarian [lai'breəriən] s. bibliotecario m.

library ['laibrəri] s. biblioteca f.

librettist [li'bretist] s. librettista m. e f.

libretto [li'bretou] s. libretto m. (mus.)

licence ['laisəns] s. licenza f.; autorizzazione f.; patente f.; **gun** – licenza di caccia; **driving** – patente

licentious [lai'senʃəs] agg. licenzioso·

licit ['lisit] agg. lecito

lick [lik] s. leccata f.

to lick [lik] v. tr. leccare

licorice ['likəris] s. liquirizia f.

lid [lid] s. coperchio m.

lie [lai] s. bugia f. • configurazione f.

to lie [lai] v. intr. mentire • giacere; rimanere; – **down** sdraiarsi

lieutenant [lef'tenənt] s. tenente m.

life [laif] s. vita f.; – **annuity** vitalizio; **still** – natura morta

lifebelt ['laifbelt] s. salvagente m.

lifeboat ['laifbout] s. battello m. di salvataggio

lifeless ['laif-lis] agg. inanimato

lifelike ['laif-laik] agg. realistico

lifelong ['laif-lɔŋ] agg. di tutta una vita

lifesize ['laif-saiz] agg. a grandezza naturale

lift [lift] s. ascensore m.

to lift [lift] v. tr. sollevare; alzare

light [lait] s. luce f.; lampada f.; fuoco m.; faro m. • agg. chiaro; leggero; **parking lights** luci di posizione

to light [lait] v. tr. accendere; illuminare

to lighten ['laitŋ] v. tr. illuminare; lampeggiare • alleggerire

lighter ['laitə*] s. accendino m.

lighthouse ['laithaus] s. faro m.

lighting ['laitiŋ] s. illuminazione f.

lightness ['laitnis] s. luminosità f. • leggerezza f.

lightning ['laitniŋ] s. lampo m.; fulmine m.; – **conductor** parafulmine

like [laik] agg. simile; uguale • prep. come; tipico di • avv. e cong. come; **to be** – assomigliare

to like [laik] v. tr. piacere; gradire

likely ['laikli] agg. probabile; verosimile • avv. probabilmente

likeness ['laiknis] s. somiglianza f.

likewise ['laik-waiz] avv. similmente; altrettanto

liking ['laikiŋ] s. simpatia f.; predilezione f.; gradimento m.

lilac ['lailək] agg. lilla

lily ['lili] s. giglio m.; – **of the valley** mughetto

limb [lim] s. membro m., arto m.

lime [laim] s. tiglio m. (bot.); lime m. (bot.); calce f.

limelight ['laimlait] s. ribalta f.

limestone ['laimstoun] s. calcare m.

limit ['limit] s. limite m.

to limit ['limit] v. tr. limitare

limitation [,limi'teiʃən] s. limitazione f.

limousine ['limu(:)zi:n] s. berlina f. (autom.)

to limp [limp] v. intr. zoppicare

limpid ['limpid] agg. limpido

line [lain] s. linea f., riga f.; fila f.; fune f.; lenza f.; **shipping** – compagnia di navigazione

to line [lain] v. tr. fiancheggiare • foderare; rivestire

linear ['liniə*] agg. lineare

linearity [,lini'æriti] s. linearità f.

linen ['linin] s. lino m.; biancheria f.

linesman ['lainzmən] s. segnalinee m. inv.

line-up ['lainʌp] s. schieramento m.

linguistic [liŋ'gwistik] agg. linguistico

lining ['lainiŋ] s. fodera f.; rivestimento m.; pastiglia f. (autom.)

link [liŋk] s. collegamento m.; legame m.

to link [liŋk] v. tr. collegare

lint [lint] s. garza f.

lintel ['lintl] s. architrave m.

lion ['laiən] s. leone m.

lioness ['laiənis] s. leonessa f.

lip [lip] s. labbro m.

lipid ['lipid] s. lipide m.

lipstick ['lip-stik] s. rossetto m.

to liquefy ['likwifai] v. tr. e intr. liquefare, liquefarsi

liquid ['likwid] agg. liquido

to liquidate ['likwideit] v. tr. liquidare

liquidation [,likwi'deiʃən] s. liquidazione f.; eliminazione f.

liquidity [li'kwiditi] s. liquidità f.

liquor ['likə*] s. liquore m.

list [list] s. lista f.; elenco m.; **price** – listino

to list [list] v. tr. elencare

to listen (to) ['lisn] v. intr. ascoltare

listener ['lisnə*] s. ascoltatore m.

litany ['litəni] s. litania f.

literal ['litərəl] agg. letterale

literally ['litərəli] avv. letteralmente

literary ['litərəri] agg. letterario

literature ['litəritʃə*] s. letteratura f.

lithograph ['liθəgra:f] s. litografia f.

lithography [li'θɔgrəfi] s. litografia f.

litre ['li:tə*] s. litro m.

litter ['litə*] s. nidiata f.; rifiuti m. pl.; – **bin** cestino per i rifiuti

little ['litl] agg. piccolo; poco; **a** – un po', poco

liturgical [li'tə:dʒikəl] agg. liturgico

liturgy ['litə(:)dʒi] s. liturgia f.

live [laiv] agg. vivo; in diretta (tel.)

to live [liv] v. intr. vivere; abitare

liveliness ['laivlinis] s. vivacità f.

lively ['laivli] agg. vivace; animato

liver ['livə*] s. fegato m.

livery ['livəri] s. livrea f.

livestock ['laivstɔk] s. bestiame m.

livid ['livid] agg. livido, paonazzo

living ['liviŋ] agg. vivente, vivo

lizard ['lizəd] s. lucertola f.

load [loud] s. carico m.; peso m.

to load [loud] v. tr. caricare

loaded ['loudid] agg. carico

loaf [louf] s. pagnotta f.

to loaf [louf] v. intr. bighellonare

loan [loun] s. prestito m.

to loan [loun] v. tr. prestare

loath [louθ] agg. restio, schivo

to loathe [louð] v. tr. odiare

lobby ['lɔbi] s. atrio m.

lobster ['lɔbstə*] s. aragosta f.

local ['loukəl] agg. locale

locality [lou'kæliti] s. luogo m.

to localize ['loukəlaiz] v. tr. localizzare

to locate [lou'keit] v. tr. individuare; localizzare

location [lou'keiʃən] s. ubicazione f.; set m. esterno (cin.)

lock [lɔk] s. serratura f.; chiusa f.

to lock [lɔk] v. tr. chiudere (a chiave); serrare; – **in** rinchiudere; – **out** chiudere fuori; – **up** imprigionare

locket ['lɔkit] s. medaglione m.

locomotive ['loukə'moutiv] s. locomotiva f.

lodge [lɔdʒ] s. casetta f.; loggia f.

to lodge [lɔdʒ] v. tr. alloggiare; ospitare

lodging ['lɔdʒiŋ] s. alloggio m.; **board and** – vitto e alloggio

loft [lɔft] s. soffitta f.; magazzino m. (USA)

log [lɔg] s. tronco m. • giornale m. di bordo

loggia ['lɔdʒiə] s. loggia f.

logic ['lɔdʒik] s. logica f.

logical ['lɔdʒikəl] agg. logico

logically ['lɔdʒikəli] avv. logicamente

Londoner ['lʌndənə*] s. londinese m. e f.

lonely ['lounli] agg. solitario

long [lɔŋ] agg. lungo • avv. molto; molto tempo; **as** – **as** per tutto il tempo che, finché, se; **at** – **last** finalmente; – **lived** longevo; **no longer** non più; – **sighted** presbite

longing ['lɔŋiŋ] s. voglia f.

longitude ['lɔn d ʒitju:d] s. longitudine f.

longitudinal [,lɔndʒi'tju:dinl] agg. longitudinale

loo [lu:] s. gabinetto m. (fam.)

look [luk] s. occhiata f.; sguardo m.; aspetto m.

to look [luk] v. intr. parere, sembrare • tr. guardare; – **after** curare, curarsi di; – **for** cercare; – **like** assomigliare; – **up** recare (informazioni)

loom [lu:m] *s.* telaio *m.*
loop [lu:p] *s.* anello *m.*; ansa *f.*; cappio *m.*
loose [lu:s] *agg.* sciolto; largo
to loose [lu:s] *v. tr.* sciogliere
to loosen ['lu:sn] *v. tr.* slacciare
loot [lu:t] *s.* refurtiva *f.*, bottino *m.*
to loot [lu:t] *v. tr.* saccheggiare
loquacious [loʊ'kweiʃəs] *agg.* loquace
lord [lɔ:d] *s.* padrone *m.*; lord *m.*; **The Lord** il Signore
lorry ['lɔri] *s.* camion *m. inv.*
to lose [lu:z] *v. tr. e intr.* perdere; – **oneself** perdersi
loss [lɔs] *s.* perdita *f.*; sconfitta *f.*
lost [lɔst] *agg.* smarrito, perduto; **to be** – essere perduto
lot [lɔt] *s.* sorte *f.*; lotto *m.* (*comm.*)
lotion ['loʊʃən] *s.* lozione *f.*
lottery ['lɔtəri] *s.* lotteria *f.*
lotting ['lɔtiŋ] *s.* lottizzazione *f.*
loud [laud] *agg.* forte, alto (suono); **loudly** forte, a voce alta; **loud-speaker** altoparlante
lounge [laundʒ] *s.* salone *m.*
to lounge [laundʒ] *v. intr.* bighellonare; poltrire
lounger ['laundʒə*] *s.* fannullone *m.*
louse [laus] *s.* pidocchio *m.*
love [lʌv] *s.* amore *m.*
to love [lʌv] *v. tr.* amare; voler bene
lovely ['lʌvli] *agg.* bello; piacevole
lover ['lʌvə*] *s.* innamorato *m.*; amante *m. e f.*
loving ['lʌviŋ] *agg.* affettuoso
low [loʊ] *agg.* basso; – **beam headlights** anabbaglianti
to lower ['loʊə*] *v. tr.* abbassare; calare
lower ['loʊə*] *agg.* inferiore; – **case** minuscolo (carattere tipografico)
lowest ['loʊist] *agg.* infimo; minimo; – **gear** minimo (*autom.*)
lowland ['loʊlənd] *s.* bassopiano *m.*; pianura *f.*
loyal ['lɔiəl] *agg.* leale
loyalty ['lɔiəlti] *s.* lealtà *f.*
lozenge ['lɔzindʒ] *s.* losanga *f.*; pasticca *f.*

lubricant ['lu:brikənt] *s.* lubrificante *m.*
to lubricate ['lu:brikeit] *v. tr.* lubrificare
lubrication [,lu:bri'keiʃən] *s.* lubrificazione *f.*
lucid ['lu:sid] *agg.* lucido
lucidity [lu:'siditi] *s.* lucidità *f.*
luck [lʌk] *s.* fortuna *f.*
lucky ['lʌki] *agg.* fortunato
lucre ['lu:kə*] *s.* lucro *m.*
luggage ['lʌgidʒ] *s.* bagaglio *m.*; **hand** – bagaglio a mano; **left** – **office** deposito bagagli
lukewarm ['lu:k-wɔ:m] *agg.* tiepido
lullaby ['lʌləbai] *s.* ninnananna *f.*
lumbago [lʌm'beigou] *s.* lombaggine *f.*
lumber ['lʌmbə*] *s.* legname *m.* (USA); cianfrusaglie *f. pl.*; – **room** ripostiglio
luminosity [,lu:mi'nɔsiti] *s.* luminosità *f.*
luminous ['lu:minəs] *agg.* luminoso
lump [lʌmp] *s.* zolletta *f.*
lunacy ['lu:nəsi] *s.* demenza *f.*
lunar ['lu:nə*] *agg.* lunare
lunatic ['lu:nətik] *agg. e s.* pazzo *m.*
lunch [lʌnʃ] *s.* pranzo *m.*; **to have** – pranzare
to lunch [lʌnʃ] *v. intr.* pranzare
lunette [lu:'net] *s.* lunetta *f.*
lush [lʌʃ] *agg.* lussureggiante
lust [lʌst] *s.* libidine *f.*
lustful ['lʌstful] *agg.* lussurioso
lustre ['lʌstə*] *s.* lustro *m.*
lute [lu:t] *s.* liuto *m.*
Lutheranism ['lu:θərənizəm] *s.* luteranesimo *m.*
lutist ['lu:tist] *s.* liutaio *m.*
luxuriant [lʌg'zjuəriənt] *agg.* lussureggiante, rigoglioso
luxurious [lʌg'zjuəriəs] *agg.* lussuoso
luxury ['lʌkʃəri] *s.* lusso *m.*
lycée [li:sei] *s.* liceo *m.*
lying ['laiiŋ] *agg.* bugiardo
lymph [limf] *s.* linfa *f.*
lynching ['linʃiŋ] *s.* linciaggio *m.*
lyre ['laiə*] *s.* lira *f.* (*mus.*)
lyric ['lirik] *agg.* lirico
lyricism ['lirisizəm] *s.* lirismo *m.*

M

ma [ma:] s. mamma f. (fam.)

macabre [mə'ka:br] agg. macabro

to macerate ['mæsəreit] v. tr. macerare

machination [,mæki'neiʃən] s. macchinazione f., complotto m.

machine [mə'ʃi:n] s. macchina f.; **answering –** segreteria telefonica; **– shop** officina meccanica

machinery [mə'ʃi:nəri] s. macchinario m.; meccanismo m.

mackerel ['mækrəl] s. sgombro m.; **– sky** cielo a pecorelle

mackintosh ['mækintɔʃ] s. impermeabile m.

macrobiotic [,mækroubai'ɔtik] agg. macrobiotico

macroscopic [,mækrou'skɔpik] agg. macroscopico

mad [mæd] agg. folle, matto; maniaco; entusiasta

madam ['mædəm] s. signora f. (vocat. senza nome proprio)

made [meid] agg. fatto, fabbricato; **a self– man** uno che si è fatto da sé; **to be – of something** constare

madhouse ['mædhaus] s. manicomio m.

madman ['mædmən] s. pazzo m.

madness ['mædnis] s. follia f., pazzia f.

madrigal ['mædrigəl] s. madrigale m.

Maecenas [mi(:)'si:næs] s. mecenate m. e f.

magazine [,mægə'zi:n] s. periodico m., rivista f.; caricatore m. (fotografico e militari)

maggoty ['mægəti] agg. bacato

magic ['mædʒik] s. magia f. • agg. magico

magician [mə'dʒiʃən] s. mago m.

magistrate ['mædʒistrit] s. magistrato m.; giudice m. di pace (USA)

magnanimous [mæg'næniməs] agg. magnanimo

magnate ['mægneit] s. magnate m.

magnet ['mægnit] s. calamita f., magnete m.

magnetic [mæg'netik] agg. magnetico

magnetism ['mægnitizəm] s. magnetismo m.

magnificence [mæg'nifisns] s. grandiosità f.; sfarzo m.

magnificent [mæg'nifisənt] agg. magnifico, superbo; **magnificently** magnificamente

to magnify ['mægnifai] v. tr. ingrandire

magnolia [mæg'nouljə] s. magnolia f.

mahogany [mə'hɔgəni] s. mogano m.

maid [meid] s. cameriera f., donna f. di servizio

maidenhood ['meidnhud] s. giovinezza f. (di ragazza); verginità f.

mail [meil] s. posta f.; **by air –** per posta aerea

to mail [meil] v. tr. impostare, imbucare; **mailing list** indirizzario

mailman ['meilmæn] s. postino m.

main [mein] agg. principale; **– course** portata principale; **– entrance** portone; **gas, water mains** conduttura del gas, dell'acqua; **mainly** perlopiù, principalmente

mainland ['meinlənd] s. terraferma f.

mainsail ['meinseil] s. randa f.

to maintain [men'tein] v. tr. mantenere, conservare; affermare; curare la manutenzione

maintenance ['meintinəns] s. manutenzione f.; sostentamento m.; alimenti m. pl. (leg.)

maize [meiz] s. granturco m.

majestic [mə'dʒestik] agg. maestoso

majesty ['mædʒisti] s. maestà f.; **Her Majesty** Sua Maestà (la Regina)

majolica [mə'jɔlikə] s. maiolica f.

major ['meidʒə*] agg. maggiore, principale • s. maggiorenne m. e f.

majority [mə'dʒɔriti] s. prevalenza f., maggioranza f.

make [meik] s. fabbricazione f.; marca f.

to make [meik*] v. tr. e intr. fare; costruire; rendere; **– up** riconciliare; truccare; **– up for** rimediare; **– for** dirigersi; **– out** mettere insieme (fig.); intravedere

make-believe ['meikbi,li:v] s. finzione f.

maker ['meikə*] s. creatore m., fabbricante m.

makeshift ['meikʃift] s. ripiego m.

make-up ['meikʌp] s. formazione f.; trucco m.; temperamento m.

malaise [mæ'leiz] s. malessere m.

malaria [mə'lɛəriə] s. malaria f.

male [meil] agg. maschile • s. maschio m.; **– chauvinist** maschilista; **– nurse** infermiere

94

malediction [,mæli'dikʃən] s. maledizione f.

malefic [mə'lefik] agg. dannoso, malefico

malevolent [mə'levələnt] agg. maligno

malformation [mælfɔ:'meiʃən] s. malformazione f. (med.)

malice ['mælis] s. malizia f.

malicious [mə'liʃəs] agg. maligno, malizioso

to malign [mə'lain] v. tr. calunniare

malignant [mə'lignənt] agg. maligno (med.)

malignity [mə'ligniti] s. malignità f.

malleable ['mæliəbl] agg. malleabile

malleolus [mə'li:oʊləs] s. malleolo m.

mallow ['mæləu] s. malva f.

malt [mɔ:lt] s. malto m.

to maltreat [mæl'tri:t] v. tr. maltrattare

mammal ['mæməl] s. mammifero m.; **the Mammalia** i mammiferi

mammalian [mæ'meiljən] agg. e s. mammifero m.

man [mæn] s. uomo; dipendente m.; pedina f. (nella dama); – **made** artificiale

to manage ['mænidʒ] v. tr. e intr. amministrare, gestire; riuscire; arrangiarsi, districare; – **by oneself** cavarsela

management ['mænidʒmənt] s. amministrazione f., gestione f.

manager ['mænidʒə*] s. direttore m., gestore m.; dirigente m. e f.

mandatory ['mændətəri] agg. obbligatorio

mandible ['mændibl] s. mandibola f.

mandolin(e) [,mændə'li:n] s. mandolino m.

mandrel ['mændrəl] s. mandrino m.

mane [mein] s. criniera f.

manège [mæ'neiʒ] s. maneggio m.

manhole ['mænhoul] s. botola f.; – **cover** tombino

mania ['meinjə] s. mania f.

maniac ['meiniæk] agg. maniaco

manicure ['mænikjuə*] s. manicure f.; – **set** necessario da unghie

manifest ['mænifest] agg. palese

to manifest ['mænifest] v. tr. manifestare, dichiarare; – **oneself** manifestarsi

manifestation [,mænifes'teiʃən] s. manifestazione f.

manifold ['mænifould] agg. molteplice, vario

to manipulate [mə'nipjuleit] v. tr. manipolare

manipulation [mə,nipju'leiʃən] s. manipolazione f.

mankind [mæn'kaind] s. genere m. umano

manliness ['mænlinis] s. virilità f.

manly ['mænli] agg. maschile, virile

manna ['mænə] s. manna f.

manner ['mænə*] s. foggia f.; maniera f. • pl. usanze f., educazione f. sing.; galateo m. sing.

mannerism ['mænərizəm] s. manierismo m.

manoeuvre [mə'nu:və*] s. manovra f.

to manoeuvre [mə'nu:və*] v. tr. e intr. manovrare

manometer [mə'nɔmitə*] s. manometro m.

manor ['mænə*] s. feudo m.; villa f.; residenza f. di campagna

manpower ['mæn,pauə*] s. manodopera f.

mansard ['mænsa:d] s. mansarda f.

mansion ['mænʃən] s. palazzo m.; casa f. signorile

mantle ['mæntl] s. mantello m., manto m.

manual ['mænjuəl] agg. e s. manuale m.; – **dexterity** manualità; **manually** manualmente

manufacture [,mænju'fæktʃə*] s. manifattura f.; fabbricazione f.

to manufacture [,mænju'fæktʃə*] v. tr. fabbricare

manumission [,mænju'miʃən] s. manomissione f. (stor.)

manure [mə'njuə*] s. concime m., letame m.

manuscript ['mænjuskript] s. manoscritto m.

many ['meni] agg. e pron. pl. molti; **too** – troppi; – **coloured** variopinto; – **sided** multiforme

map [mæp] s. carta f. geografica, mappa f.

maple ['meipl] s. acero m.

marathon ['mærəθən] s. maratona f.

marble ['ma:bl] s. marmo m.

March [ma:tʃ] s. marzo m.

march [ma:tʃ] s. marcia f.

to march [ma:tʃ] v. intr. marciare

margarine [,ma:dʒə'ri:n] s. margarina f.

margin [ma:dʒin] s. margine m.

marginal ['ma:dʒnəl] agg. marginale; – **note** postilla

to marginalize ['ma:dʒinəlaiz] v. tr. emarginare

marina [mə'ri:nə] s. marina m. (naut.)

marine [mə'ri:n] agg. marino

mariner ['mærinə*] s. marinaio m.

maritime ['mæritaim] agg. marittimo

mark [ma:k] s. marca f.; marchio m.; impronta f.; voto m.

to mark [ma:k] v. tr. segnare; contraddistinguere; – **out** tracciare

market ['ma:kit] s. mercato m.; **to play the** – giocare in Borsa; – **place** mercato (luogo)

marketable ['ma:kitəbl] agg. vendibile

marmalade ['ma:məleid] s. marmellata f. di agrumi

marmot ['ma:mət] s. marmotta f.

marquee [ma:'ki:] s. tendone m.

marquess ['ma:kwis] s. marchese m.

marquis ['ma:kwis] s. marchese m.

marriage ['mæridʒ] s. matrimonio m. • agg. matrimoniale; **to take in** - prendere per marito (o per moglie)

married ['mærid] agg. coniugato; **to get** - sposarsi

marrow ['mærou] s. midollo m.

marrowbone ['mærouboun] s. ossobuco m.

to marry ['mæri] v. tr. sposare • intr. sposarsi; **to** - **again** risposarsi

marsh [ma:ʃ] s. acquitrino m., palude f.

marshy ['ma:ʃi] agg. paludoso

martial ['ma:ʃəl] agg. marziale: - **court** corte marziale; - **law** legge marziale

Martian ['ma:ʃjən] s. marziano m.

martyr ['ma:tə*] s. martire m. e f.

martyrodom ['ma:tədəm] s. martirio m.

marvel ['ma:vəl] s. meraviglia f.; prodigio m.

marvellous ['ma:viləs] agg. meraviglioso, stupendo

Marxism ['ma:ksizəm] s. marxismo m.

marzipan [,ma:zi'pæn] s. marzapane m.

mascara [mæs'ka:rə] s. mascara m. inv.

mascot ['mæskət] s. mascotte f. inv.

masculine ['mæ:skjulin] agg. maschile

mash [mæʃ] s. poltiglia f.; purè m.

to mash [mæʃ] v. tr. schiacciare; macerare

mask [ma:sk] s. maschera f.

to mask [ma:sk] v. tr. mascherare • intr. mascherarsi

masochism ['mæsəkizəm] s. masochismo m.

masonry ['meisənri] s. massoneria f.

to masquerade [,mæskə'reid] v. intr. mascherarsi

mass [mæs] s. massa f., folla f.

Mass [mæs] s. messa f.; **to attend** - andare a messa; - **book** messale

massacre ['mæsəke*] s. massacro m.

massage ['mæsa:ʒ] s. massaggio m.

to massage ['mæsa:ʒ] v. tr. massaggiare

massive ['mæsiv] agg. massiccio

mast [ma:st] s. albero m. (naut.)

master ['ma:stə*] s. maestro m.; padrone m., datore m. di lavoro

to master ['ma:stə*] v. tr. e intr. dominare; impadronirsi

masterly ['ma:stəli] agg. magistrale

masterpiece ['ma:stəpi:s] s. capolavoro m.

mastery ['ma:stəri] s. dominio m., padronanza f.; perizia f.

mastic ['mæstik] s. mastice m.

to masticate ['mæstikeit] v. tr. masticare

mastodontic [,mæstə'dɔntik] agg. mastodontico

mat [mæt] s. stuoia f., zerbino m.; groviglio m. • agg. opaco

match [mætʃ] s. fiammifero m. • incontro m., partita f. (sport)

to match [mætʃ] v. tr. accordare; pareggiare • intr. accoppiarsi

mate [meit] s. compagno m., coniuge m. e f.; aiutante m. e f.; ufficiale m. in seconda (naut.); **check** - scacco matto

material [mə'tiəriəl] agg. materiale • s. sostanza f.; materiale m., stoffa f.; **materially** materialmente

materialism [mə'tiəriəlizəm] s. materialismo m.

maternal [mə'tə:nl] agg. materno

maternity [mə'tə:niti] s. maternità f.; - **leave** congedo per maternità

mathematical [,məθi'mætikəl] agg. matematico; esatto

mathematics [,mæθi'mætiks] s. pl. (v. al sing.) matematica f. sing.

maths [mæθs] s. pl. (v. al sing.) matematica f. sing. (fam.)

matriarchal [,meitri'a:kəl] agg. matriarcale

to matriculate [mə'trikjuleit] v. intr. iscriversi all'università

matrimonial [,mætri'mounjəl] agg. matrimoniale

matrix ['meitriks] s. matrice f.

matron ['meitrən] s. infermiera f. capo; governante f.; matrona f.

matter ['mætə*] s. argomento m.; motivo m.; materia f.

to matter ['mætə*] v. intr. interessare

mattock ['mætək] s. zappa f.

mattress ['mætris] s. materasso m.

maturation [,mætjuə'reiʃən] s. maturazione f.

mature [mə'tjuə*] agg. maturo

to mature [mə'tjuə*] v. tr. e intr. maturare; scadere (di obbligazioni)

maturity [mə'tjuəriti] s. maturità f.

mausoleum [,mɔ:sə'liəm] s. mausoleo m.

mauve [mouv] agg. malva

maximalism ['mæksiməlizəm] s. massimalismo m.

maximum ['mæksiməm] agg. e s. massimo m.

may [mei] v. dif. potere, essere possibile; **may I speak?** posso parlare?; **it may be** può darsi

May [mei] s. maggio m.

maybe ['meibi:] avv. forse, probabilmente

mayonnaise [ˌmeiə'neiz] s. maionese f.

mayor [mɛə*] s. sindaco m.

maze [meiz] s. dedalo m., labirinto m.

meadow ['medou] s. prato m.

meagre ['miːgə*] agg. magro, smunto

meal [miːl] s. farina f. • pasto m.; - **ticket** buono pasto

mean [miːn] agg. gretto, meschino; medio • s. mezzo m., maniera f.; media f. (mat.) • pl. mezzi m., sostanze f.; **economical** - possibilità economiche; - **of transport** mezzi di trasporto

to mean [miːn] v. tr. e intr. significare, intendere

meander [mi'ændə*] s. meandro m.

meaning ['miːniŋ] s. significato m., senso m.; proposito m.

meaningless ['miːniŋlis] agg. senza senso; senza scopo

meantime ['miːn'taim] avv. mentre; **in the** - nel frattempo

meanwhile ['miːn'wail] avv. frattanto, intanto

measles ['miːzlz] s. pl. (v. al sing.) morbillo m. sing.

measurable ['meʒərəbl] agg. misurabile

measure ['meʒə*] s. misura f.; provvedimento m.; **to a great** - abbondantemente; **small** - misurino

to measure ['meʒə*] v. tr. e intr. misurare; - **out** dosare

measured ['meʒəd] agg. compassato

meat [miːt] s. carne f. ; - **ball** polpetta; - **grinder** tritacarne; - **skewer** spiedino di carne

mechanical [mi'kænikəl] agg. meccanico; **mechanically** meccanicamente

mechanics [mi'kæniks] s. pl. (v. al sing.) meccanica f. sing.

mechanism ['mekənizəm] s. meccanismo m.

mechanization [ˌmekənai'zeiʃən] s. meccanizzazione f.

medal ['medl] s. medaglia f.

medallion [mi'dæljən] s. medaglione m.

to meddle (in) ['medl] v. intr. immischiarsi

media ['miːdjə] s. pl. mezzi m. di comunicazione di massa

mediator ['miːdieitə*] s. mediatore m.

medical ['medikəl] agg. medico

medicament [me'dikəmənt] s. medicazione f.

to medicate ['medikeit] v. tr. medicare

medicinal [me'disinl] agg. medicinale

medicine ['medisin] s. medicina f.

mediocre ['miːdioukə*] agg. mediocre

mediocrity [ˌmiːdi'ɔkriti] s. mediocrità f.

medioeval [ˌmedi'iːvəl] agg. medievale

to meditate ['mediteit] v. tr. e intr. meditare

meditation [ˌmedi'teiʃən] s. meditazione f.

Mediterranean [ˌmeditə'reinjən] agg. e s. mediterraneo m.

medium ['miːdjəm] agg. medio

medlar ['medlə*] s. nespola f.

medley ['medli] s. mescolanza f.

medusa [mi'djuːzə] s. medusa f.

meek [miːk] agg. mite

to meet [miːt] v. tr. incontrare, fare conoscenza; soddisfare, combaciare (mecc.); • intr. incontrarsi, vedersi

meeting ['miːtiŋ] s. ritrovo m., riunione f.; incontro m. (sport); - **point** rendez-vous

megalithic [ˌmega'liθik] agg. megalitico

megalomaniac [ˌmegəlo'meiniæk] agg. e s. megalomane m. e f.

megaphone ['megəfoun] s. megafono m.

melancholic [melən'kɔlik] agg. malinconico

melancholy ['melənkəli] s. malinconia f.

mellow ['melou] agg. maturo

melodious [mi'loudjəs] agg. melodioso

melodramatic [ˌmeloudrə'mætik] agg. melodrammatico

melody ['melədi] s. melodia f.

melon ['melən] s. melone m.

to melt [melt] v. tr. e intr. fondere, liquefare, sciogliere

melting ['meltiŋ] agg. fondente; struggente • s. fusione f.

member ['membə*] s. membro m.; elemento m.; socio m.

membership ['membəʃip] s. appartenenza f. (a un club)

membrane ['membrein] s. membrana f.

memo ['memou] s. promemoria m. inv.

memorable ['memərəbl] agg. memorabile

memorandum [ˌmemə'rændəm] s. promemoria m. inv.

memorial [mi'mɔːriəl] agg. commemorativo; - **tablet** lapide

memory ['meməri] s. memoria f.; ricordo m.; rievocazione f.

menace ['menəs] s. minaccia f.

to menace ['menəs] v. tr. minacciare

menacing ['menəsiŋ] agg. minaccioso

to mend [mend] v. tr. aggiustare, rammendare

mendable ['mendəbl] agg. aggiustabile, riparabile

mending ['mendiŋ] s. rammendo m.

menial ['miːnjəl] agg. servile, umile

meningitis [ˌmenin'dʒaitis] s. meningite f.

meniscus [mi'niskəs] s. menisco m.
menopause ['menoupɔːz] s. menopausa f.
menses ['mensiːz] s. pl. mestruazioni f.
menstruation [,menstru'eiʃən] s. mestruazione f.
mental ['mentl] agg. mentale, psichico; – **hospital** manicomio; **mentally** mentalmente
mentality [men'tæliti] s. mentalità f.
to mention ['menʃən] v. tr. nominare, menzionare; **above mentioned** sopracitato; **don't – it!** non c'è di che!
menu ['menjuː] s. menu m. inv.
mercantile ['məːkantail] agg. mercantile
mercantilism ['məːkəntilizəm] s. mercantilismo m.
mercenary ['məːsinəri] agg. e s. mercenario m.
merchandise ['məːtʃəndais] s. merce f.
merchant ['məːtʃənt] s. mercante m. • agg. mercantile
merciful ['məːsiful] agg. misericordioso, clemente, pietoso
mercury ['məːkjuri] s. mercurio m.
mercy ['məːsi] s. misericordia f., pietà f.
mere [miə*] agg. puro, semplice
to merge [məːdʒ] v. tr. e intr. fondere, incorporare
meridian [mə'ridiən] s. meridiano m.
meringue [mə'ræŋ] s. meringa f.
merit ['merit] s. merito m., pregio m.
merlon ['məːlən] s. merlo m. (arch.)
merry ['meri] agg. allegro, giocoso; – **go-round** giostra; – **Christmas** buon natale
mesh [meʃ] s. maglia f. (di rete); **in –** inserito; **out of –** disinserito
mess [mes] s. confusione f., scompiglio m.; sporcizia f.; mensa f., rancio m.; **a – up in** casino; **to make a – of something** rovinare qualcosa; **to get oneself in a –** mettersi nei guai
to mess (up) [mes] v. tr. mettere in disordine; mandare a monte
message ['mesidʒ] s. messaggio m., ambasciata f.
messenger ['mesindʒə*] s. messaggero m.
metal ['metl] s. metallo m.
metallic [mi'tælik] agg. metallico
metallurgic(al) [,metə'ləːdʒik(əl)] agg. metallurgico
metamorphism [,metə'mɔːfizəm] s. metamorfismo m.
metamorphosis [,metə'mɔːfəsis] s. metamorfosi f.
metaphor ['metəfə*] s. metafora f.

metaphoric(al) [,metə'fɔrik(əl)] agg. metaforico
metaphysical [,metə'fizikəl] agg. metafisico
métayage ['meтədʒːʒ] s. mezzadria f.
meteor ['miːtjə*] s. meteora f.
meteorologic(al) [,miːtjərə'lɔdʒik(əl)] agg. meteorologico
meteorology [,miːtjə'rələdʒi] s. meteorologia f.
meter ['miːtə*] s. misuratore m., contatore m.; tassametro m.; metro m. (unità di misura) (USA); **parking –** parchimetro
methane ['meθein] s. metano m.
method ['meθəd] s. metodo m.; sistema m.
methodic(al) [mi'θɔdik(əl)] agg. metodico
Methodist ['meθədist] agg. e s. metodista m. e f.
methodological [,meθədə'lɔdʒikəl] agg. metodologico
meticulous [mi'tikjuləs] agg. meticoloso
metope ['metoup] s. metopa f.
metre ['miːtə*] s. metro m.; **cubic –** metro cubo; **square –** metro quadrato
metric ['metrik] agg. metrico
metrical ['metrikəl] agg. metrico
metropolitan [,metrə'pɔlitən] agg. metropolitano • s. metropolita m.
mettle ['metl] s. coraggio m., fegato m. (fig.)
mezzanine ['mezəniːn] s. ammezzato m.; – **floor** soppalco
to miaow [miː'au] v. intr. miagolare
microbe ['maikroub] s. microbo m.
microcosm ['maikroukɔzəm] s. microcosmo m.
microfilm ['maikroufilm] s. microfilm m. inv.
microorganism ['maikruˈɔːgənizəm] s. microrganismo m.
microphone ['maikrəfoun] s. microfono m.
microscope ['maikrəskoup] s. microscopio m.
mid [mid] agg. medio, di mezzo; – **August holiday** ferragosto; **in – winter** nel cuore dell'inverno
midday ['middei] s. mezzogiorno m.
middle [midl] agg. medio, di mezzo • s. mezzo m., centro m.; – **age** mezza età; – **class** borghesia; – **school** scuola media inferiore; **the Middle Ages** il medioevo
middleman ['midlmæn] s. mediatore m., intermediario m.
midge [midʒ] s. moscerino m.
midget ['midʒit] agg. minuscolo • s. nano m.
midnight ['midnait] s. mezzanotte f.
midway ['mid'wei] avv. a metà strada
midwife ['midwaif] s. levatrice f., ostetrica f.

might [mait] *s.* potenza *f.*, forza *f.*

mighty ['maiti] *agg.* poderoso, forte • *avv.* estremamente

migraine [mi'grein] *s.* emicrania *f.*

migrant ['maigrənt] *agg.* migratorio

to migrate [mai'greit] *v. intr.* migrare, emigrare

migratory ['maigrətəri] *agg.* migratorio

mike [maik] *s.* microfono *m.*

mild [maild] *agg.* mite; dolce; leggero

mile [mail] *s.* miglio *m.*; **nautical** – miglio marino

mileometer [mai'lɔmitə*] *s.* contamiglia *m.*

militant ['militənt] *agg.* militante

military ['militəri] *s.* militare *m.*

to militate ['militeit] *v. intr.* militare

milk [milk] *s.* latte *m.*; **curdled** – latte cagliato; **powdered** – latte in polvere; **skimmed** – latte scremato

to milk [milk] *v. tr.* mungere

mill [mil] *s.* mulino *m.*; cartiera *f.*; tessitura *f.*

to mill [mil] *v. tr.* macinare; **milled** zigrinato (di monete)

millenary [mi'lenəri] *agg.* millenario

millennium [mi'leniəm] *s.* millennio *m.*

millesimal [mi'lesiməl] *agg. e s.* millesimo *m.*

millet ['milit] *s.* miglio *m.* (*bot.*)

milliard ['miljɑːd] *s.* miliardo *m.*

millimetre ['mili,miːtə*] *s.* millimetro *m.*

million ['miljən] *s.* milione *m.*

millionaire [,miljə'nɛə*] *agg. e s.* milionario *m.*

millstone ['mil-stoun] *s.* macina *f.*

mime [maim] *s.* mimo *m.*

mimetic [mi'metik] *agg.* mimetico

mimic ['mimik] *s.* imitatore *m.*

minaret ['minəret] *s.* minareto *m.*

to mince [mins] *v. tr.* tritare

mincer ['minsə*] *s.* tritatutto *m. inv.*

mind [maind] *s.* mente *f.*, intelligenza *f.*; pensiero *m.*, opinione *f.*; – **bending** di difficile comprensione; **out of** – matto; **to have in** – avere in mente; **to make up one's** – decidere

to mind [maind] *v. tr. e intr.* badare, fare attenzione; rincrescere; **mind the step!** attenzione al gradino; **never mind** non importa

mine [main] *s.* miniera *f.*; mina *f.*

to mine [main] *v. tr.* estrarre, scavare; minare

miner ['mainə*] *s.* minatore *m.*

mineral ['minərəl] *agg. e s.* minerale *m.*

mineralogy [,minə'rælədʒi] *s.* mineralogia *f.*

to mingle ['miŋgl] *v. tr. e intr.* mescolare

miniature ['minjətʃə*] *s.* miniatura *f.*

miniaturist ['minjətjuərist] *s.* miniaturista *m. e f.*

minimize ['minimaiz] *v. tr.* minimizzare

minimum ['miniməm] *agg. e s.* minimo *m.*

mining ['mainiŋ] *agg.* minerario • *s.* estrazione *f.*

miniskirt ['miniskəːt] *s.* minigonna *f.*

minister ['ministə*] *s.* ministro *m.*

ministry ['ministri] *s.* ministero *m.*

mink [miŋk] *s.* visone *m.*

minor ['mainə*] *agg.* minore, meno importante • *s.* minorenne *m. e f.*

minority [mai'nɔriti] *s.* minoranza *f.*

mint [mint] *s.* menta *f.*; zecca *f.*

to mint [mint] *v. tr.* coniare

minuet [,minju'et] *s.* minuetto *m.*

minus ['mainəs] *prep. e avv.* meno

minute ['minit] *agg.* minuscolo • *s.* minuto *m.*

to minute ['minit] *v. tr.* verbalizzare (*leg.*); cronometrare

miracle ['mirəkl] *s.* miracolo *m.*

miraculous [mi'rækjuləs] *agg.* miracoloso

mirage ['mirɑːʒ] *s.* miraggio *m.*

mire [maiə*] *s.* melma *f.*

mirror ['mirə*] *s.* specchio *m.*

mirth [mɔːθ] *s.* allegria *f.*

miry ['maiəri] *agg.* melmoso

misadventure ['misəd'ventʃə*] *s.* disavventura *f.*, incidente *m.*

misanthrope ['mizənθroup] *s.* misantropo *m.*

misanthropic(al) [,mizən'θrɔpik(əl)] *agg.* misantropo

to misbehave ['misbi'heiv] *v. intr.* comportarsi male

misbeliever ['misbi'liːvə*] *s.* miscredente *m. e f.*, empio *m.*

misbelieving ['misbi'liːviŋ] *agg.* miscredente

miscarriage ['mis'kæridʒ] *s.* aborto *m.*; fallimento *m.*; smarrimento *m.* (di una lettera)

to miscarry ['mis'kæri] *v. intr.* abortire

miscellaneous [,misi'leinjəs] *agg.* eterogeneo

miscellany [mi'seləni] *s.* miscellanea *f.*

mischief ['mis-tʃif] *s.* danno *m.*; malizia *f.*; birichinata *f.*

misdeed ['mis'diːd] *s.* misfatto *m.*

miser ['maizə*] *s.* tirchio *m.*

miserable ['mizərəbl] *agg.* miserabile, misero

miserly ['maizəli] *agg.* taccagno

misery ['mizəri] *s.* miseria *f.*; infelicità *f.*

misfit ['misfit] *s.* disadattato

misfortune [mis'fɔːtʃən] *s.* disgrazia *f.*, sventura *f.*

99

misgiving [mis'givin] s. timore m.; dubbio m.

mishap ['mishæp] s. contrattempo m.; disavventura f.

to misinterpret ['misin'tə:prit] v. tr. travisare

to misjudge ['mis'dʒʌdʒ] v. tr. valutare male

to mislead [mis'li:d] v. tr. mettere fuori strada, ingannare

misleading [mis'li:diŋ] agg. ingannevole

misogynic [mai'zɔdʒənik] agg. misogino

misogynist [mai'sɔdʒinist] s. misogino m.

misprint ['mis'print] s. refuso m.

Miss [mis] s. signorina f. (davanti al nome proprio)

miss [mis] s. colpo m. mancato

to miss [mis] v. tr. e intr. fallire, sbagliare; mancare, lasciarsi sfuggire; – **the train** perdere il treno

missal ['misəl] s. messale m.

misshapen ['mis'ʃeipən] agg. malfatto

missile ['misail] s. missile m.

mission ['miʃən] s. missione f.

missionary ['miʃnəri] s. missionario m.

mist [mist] s. foschia f.

mistake [mis'teik] s. errore m., sbaglio m.; **to make a** – sbagliare

to mistake [mis'teik] v. tr. e intr. equivocare, sbagliare; confondere; **to be mistaken** aver torto

mistaken [mis'teikən] agg. erroneo

mister ['mistə*] s. signore (davanti al nome proprio, abbr. in **Mr**)

mistletoe ['misltou] s. vischio m.

mistress ['mistris] s. padrona f.

mistrust ['mis'trʌst] s. sfiducia f.

misty ['misti] agg. nebbioso

to misunderstand ['misʌndə'stænd] v. tr. e intr. equivocare, fraintendere

misunderstanding ['misʌndə'stændiŋ] s. equivoco m., malinteso m.

mite [mait] s. obolo m.

to mitigate ['mitigeit] v. tr. mitigare

mitre ['maitə*] s. mitra f.

to mix [miks] v. tr. e intr. mescolare; – **up** confondere, imbrogliare

mixed [mikst] agg. misto; – **up** confuso; **to get** – **up** confondersi

mixer ['miksə*] s. miscelatore m.

mixing ['miksiŋ] s. mescolanza f.

mixture ['mikstʃə*] s. impasto m., miscela f.

mnemonic [ni:'mɔnik] agg. mnemonico

moan [moun] s. gemito m., lamento m.

to moan [moun] v. intr. gemere, lamentarsi

moat [mout] s. fossato m.

mob [mɔb] s. folla f.

mobile ['moubail] agg. mobile, instabile

mobility [mou'biliti] s. mobilità f.

mobilization [,moubilai'zeiʃən] s. mobilitazione f.

moccasin ['mɔkəsin] s. mocassino m.

to mock [mɔk] v. tr. deridere

mockery ['mɔkəri] s. scherno m.

modality [mou'dæliti] s. modalità f.

mode [moud] s. modo m.

model ['mɔdl] agg. esemplare • s. modello m., fotomodella f.

to model ['mɔdl] v. tr. e intr. modellare

modelling ['mɔdliŋ] s. modellismo m.

moderate ['mɔdərit] agg. moderato, modico, discreto

to moderate ['mɔdəreit] v. tr. e intr. moderare

moderation [,mɔdə'reʃən] s. discrezione f., moderazione f.

modern ['mɔdən] agg. moderno

modernism ['mɔdənizəm] s. modernismo m.

modernity [mɔ'də:niti] s. modernità f.

to modernize ['mɔdənaiz] v. tr. modernizzare

modest ['mɔdist] agg. modesto

modesty ['mɔdəsti] s. pudore m.

modifiable ['mɔdifaiəbl] agg. modificabile

modification [,mɔdifi'keiʃən] s. modifica f., modificazione f.

to modify ['mɔdifai] v. tr. modificare

modular ['mɔdjulə*] agg. componibile, modulare

module ['mɔdjul] s. modulo m.

Mohammedan [mou'hæmidən] agg. maomettano

moist [mɔist] agg. umido

to moisten ['mɔisn] v. tr. e intr. inumidire

moisture ['mɔistʃə*] s. umidità f.

to moisturize ['mɔistʃəraiz] v. tr. umidificare

moisturizing ['mɔistʃəraiziŋ] agg. idratante

mole [moul] s. neo m. • talpa f.

molecule ['mɔlikju:l] s. molecola f.

to molest [mou'lest] v. tr. molestare

molten ['moultən] agg. fuso

mom [mɔm] s. mamma f. (USA, fam.)

moment ['moumənt] s. momento m.; **at the** – momentaneamente

momentary ['mouməntəri] agg. momentaneo

momentous [mou'mentəs] agg. molto importante

monachism ['mɔnəkizəm] s. monachesimo m.

monarch(al) [mɔ'na:kik(əl)] agg. monarchico

monarchy ['mɔnəki] s. monarchia f.

monastery ['mɒnəstəri] s. monastero m.

monastic [mə'næstik] agg. monastico

Monday ['mʌndi] s. lunedì m.

monetary ['mʌnitəri] agg. monetario

money ['mʌni] s. denaro m., moneta f., quattrini m. pl.; – **box** salvadanaio; – **changer** cambiavalute; – **order** vaglia; **for** – in contanti

monitor ['mɒnitə*] s. dispositivo m. di controllo; monitor m. inv.

to monitor ['mɒnitə*] v. tr. controllare (con un dispositivo)

monk [mʌŋk] s. frate m., monaco m.

monkey ['mʌŋki] s. scimmia f.

monochrome ['mɒnəkroum] agg. monocromatico

monogamy [mɒ'nɒgəmi] s. monogamia f.

monograph ['mɒnəgra:f] s. monografia f.

monolithic [,mɒnəʊ'liθik] agg. monolitico

monologue ['mɒnəlɔg] s. monologo m.

monomaniac [,mɒnəʊ'meinjæk] agg. monomaniaco

monopoly [mə'nɒpəli] s. monopolio m.

monosyllable ['mɒnə,siləbl] s. monosillabo m.

monotheism ['mɒnəʊθi:,izəm] s. monoteismo m.

monotonous [mə'nɒtnəs] agg. monotono, uniforme

monotony [mə'nɒtni] s. monotonia f.

monsoon [mɒn'su:n] s. monsone m.; **dry** – monsone invernale; **wet** – monsone estivo

monster ['mɒnstə*] s. mostro m.

monstrous ['mɒnstrəs] agg. mostruoso

month [mʌnθ] s. mese m.

monthly ['mʌnθli] agg. e s. mensile f. • avv. mensilmente

monument ['mɒnjumənt] s. monumento m.

monumental [,mɒnju'mentl] agg. monumentale

mood [mu:d] s. umore m., stato m. d'animo

moody ['mu:di] agg. lunatico; malinconico

moon [mu:n] s. luna f.; **moonlight** chiaro di luna

moor [muə*] s. brughiera f.

to moor [muə*] v. tr. e intr. ormeggiare

mooring ['muəriŋ] s. ormeggio m. • pl. cavi m. d'ormeggio

mop [mɒp] s. spazzolone m.; zazzera f.

moped ['mouped] s. motorino m.

moquette [mɒ'ket] s. moquette f. inv.

moraine [mɒ'rein] s. morena f.

moral ['mɒrəl] agg. e s. morale f. • pl. moralità f. sing.

morale [mɒ'ra:l] s. stato m. d'animo

moralism ['mɒrəlizm] s. moralismo m.

to moralize ['mɒrəlaiz] v. tr. moralizzare

morally ['mɒrəli] avv. moralmente

moray ['mourei] s. murena f.

morbid ['mɔ:bid] agg. morboso

more [mɔ:*] agg. e pron. più; altro (in aggiunta) • avv. di più; oltre (temporale); ancora; – **or less** pressappoco; **once** – ancora una volta; **no** – non più

moreover [mɔ:'rouvə*] avv. inoltre, peraltro

moribund ['mɒribʌnd] agg. e s. moribondo m.

morning ['mɔ:niŋ] s. mattino m. • agg. mattutino; – **performance** spettacolo pomeridiano a teatro; **good** – buon giorno (di mattina); **in the** – di mattina

morphological [,mɔ:fə'lɔdʒikəl] agg. morfologico

morphology [mɔ:'fɔlədʒi] s. morfologia f.

morsel ['mɔ:səl] s. boccone m.

mortal ['mɔ:tl] agg. e s. mortale m.

mortality [mɔ:'tæliti] s. mortalità f.

mortar ['mɔ:tə*] s. mortaio m.

mortgage ['mɔ:gidʒ] s. ipoteca f.; mutuo m.

mortification [,mɔ:tifi'keiʃən] s. mortificazione f.

to mortify ['mɔ:tifai] v. tr. mortificare

mortuary ['mɔ:tjuəri] s. obitorio m., camera f. mortuaria

mosaic [mə'zeiik] s. mosaico m.

mosque [mɔsk] s. moschea f.

mosquito [məs'ki:tou] s. zanzara f.; – **net** zanzariera

moss [mɒs] s. muschio m.

most [moust] agg., avv. e pron. più, di più; la maggior parte; **at (the)** – tutt'al più; **at most** sì massimo

mostly ['moustli] avv. soprattutto

moth [mɔθ] s. tarma f.; – **killer** tarmicida

mother ['mʌðə*] s. madre f., mamma f. • agg. materno; **mother-in-law** suocera; **step** – matrigna; – **to-be** donna incinta; – **country** madrepatria; – **of-pearl** madreperla

motherhood ['mʌðəhud] s. maternità f.

motherland ['mʌðələnd] s. madrepatria f.

motherly ['mʌðəli] agg. materno

motif [mou'ti:f] s. motivo m., tema m. (mus., lett., arte)

motion ['mouʃən] s. movimento m.; – **picture film library** cineteca

motive [moutiv] s. motivo m.; movente f.

motocross ['mɒtəkrɔs] s. motocross m. inv.

motor ['moutə*] s. motore m. • agg. a motore; automobilistico; autostradale; motorio (*med.*); – **scooter** motorino; – **bike**, – **cycle** motocicletta; – **boat** motoscafo; – **sled** motoslitta

motorway ['moutəwei] *s.* autostrada *f.*, superstrada *f.*; **toll** – autostrada a pedaggio

mould [mould] *s.* calco *m.*, stampo *m.* • muffa *f.*

to mould [mould] *v. tr.* forgiare, modellare

moulding ['mouldiŋ] *s.* modanatura *f.*

mouldy ['mouldi] *agg.* ammuffito

moult [moult] *s.* muta *f.* (della pelle o del pelo)

mound [maund] *s.* tumulo *m.*

mount [maunt] *s.* monte *m.* (davanti a nome proprio)

to mount [maunt] *v. tr. e intr.* montare; salire

mountain ['mauntin] *s.* montagna *f.*; – **climber** alpinista; – **pass** valico

mountainous ['mauntinəs] *agg.* montagnoso

mountbank ['mauntibæŋk] *s.* ciarlatano *m.*

to mourn [mɔ:n] *v. tr. e intr.* lamentare, piangere; portare il lutto

mournful ['mɔ:nful] *agg.* funebre, luttuoso

mourning ['mɔ:niŋ] *s.* lutto *m.*

mouse [maus] *s.* topo *m.*

moustache [məs'ta:ʃ] *s.* baffo *m.*

mouth [mauθ] *s.* bocca *f.*; foce *f.*; imboccatura *f.*, apertura *f.*

mouthful ['mauθful] *s.* boccone *m.*

mouthpiece ['mauθpi:s] *s.* bocchino *m.*; boccaglio *m.*

mouthwash ['mauθwɔʃ] *s.* collutorio *m.*

movable ['mu:vəbl] *agg.* mobile

move [mu:v] *s.* mossa *f.* (in un gioco); trasloco *m.*

to move [mu:v] *v. tr. e intr.* muovere, spostare, traslocare; commuovere; – **on** circolare; – **up** anticipare; **moved** commosso; spostato

movement ['mu:vmənt] *s.* mossa *f.*, movimento *m.*

movie ['mu:vi] *s.* film *m. inv.*; • *agg.* cinematografico

moving ['mu:viŋ] *agg.* commovente

Mr ['mistə*] *s.* signore *m.* (davanti al nome proprio)

Mrs ['misiz] *s.* signora *f.* (davanti al nome proprio)

Ms [miz] *s.* signora *f.*, signorina *f.* (davanti al nome proprio)

much [mʌtʃ] *agg. indef.*, *avv. e pron.* molto, assai; **too** – troppo

muck [mʌk] *s.* letame *m.*; porcheria *f.* (*fam.*)

mucous ['mju:kous] *s.* mucosa *f.*

mud [mʌd] *s.* fango *m.*, melma *f.*

muddle ['mʌdl] *s.* confusione *f.*, scompiglio *m.*

to muddle ['mʌdl] *v. tr.* scompigliare, confondere

muddler ['mʌdlə*] *agg. e s.* confusionario *m.*

muddy ['mʌdi] *agg.* limaccioso, torbido, fangoso

mug [mʌg] *s.* boccale *m.*, tazza *f.*

mulberry ['mʌlbəri] *s.* gelso *m.*; mora *f.*

mule [mju:l] *s.* mulo *m.*; – **track** mulattiera

mullet ['mʌlit] *s.* muggine *m.*; **red** – triglia; **gray** – cefalo

multiannual [,mʌlti'ænjuəl] *agg.* poliennale

multicoloured [,mʌlti'kʌləd] *agg.* multicolore

multiform ['mʌltifɔ:m] *agg.* multiforme

multimillionaire ['mʌltimiljə'nɛə*] *agg. e s.* miliardario *m.*

multinational [,mʌlti'næʃənl] *agg. e s.* multinazionale *f.*

multiple ['mʌltipl] *agg. e s.* multiplo *m.*

multiplication [,mʌltipli'keiʃən] *s.* moltiplicazione *f.*

to multiply ['mʌltiplai] *v. tr. e intr.* moltiplicare • *intr.* moltiplicarsi

multitude ['mʌltitju:d] *s.* moltitudine *f.*

mum [mʌm] *agg.* muto (*fam.*)

to mumble ['mʌmbl] *v. tr. e intr.* borbottare

mummy ['mʌmi] *s.* mummia *f.*; mamma *f.* (*fam.*)

mumps [mʌmps] *s.* parotite *f.*, orecchioni *m. pl.*

mundane ['mʌndein] *agg.* mondano

municipal [mju(:)'nisipəl] *agg.* comunale, municipale

municipality [mju(:)nisi'pæliti] *s.* municipio *m.*, comune *m.*

munificence [mju(:)'nifisns] *s.* munificenza *f.*

munition [mju(:)'niʃən] *s.* munizioni *f. pl.*

mural ['mjuərəl] *s.* murale *m.*

murder ['mə:də*] *s.* assassinio *m.*

to murder ['mə:də*] *v. tr.* assassinare

murderer ['mə:dərə*] *s.* assassino *m.*; omicida *m. e f.*

murmur ['mə:mə*] *s.* sussurro *m.*; soffio *m.* (*med.*)

to murmur ['mə:mə*] *v. tr. e intr.* mormorare

muscle ['mʌsl] *s.* muscolo *m.*

muscular ['mʌskjulə*] *agg.* muscolare (*med.*); muscoloso

muse [mju:z] *s.* musa *f.*

to muse [mju:z] *v. tr. e intr.* rimuginare; – **over/upon something** meditare su qualcosa

museum [mju(:)'ziəm] *s.* museo *m.*

mushroom ['mʌʃruːm] *s.* fungo *m.*

music ['mjuːzik] *s.* musica *f.*; – **stand** leggio

musical ['mjuːzikəl] *s.* commedia *f.* musicale
 • *agg.* melodioso, musicale

musicassette ['mjuːzikæ,set] *s.* musicassetta *f.*

musician [mju(:)'ziʃən] *s.* musicista *m.* e *f.*;
 street – suonatore ambulante

musk [mʌsk] *s.* muschio *m.* (in profumeria)

Muslim ['muslim] *agg.* e *s.* mussulmano *m.*

mussel ['mʌsl] *s.* cozza *f.*, mitilo *m.*

Mussulman ['mʌslmən] *agg.* mussulmano

must [mʌst, məst] *v. dif.* dovere • *s.* ciò di cui
 non si può fare a meno

mustard ['mʌstəd] *s.* senape *f.*

muster ['mʌstə•] *s.* adunata *f.*; ispezione *f.*

mute [mjuːt] *agg.* e *s.* muto *m.*

mutilation [,mjuːti'leiʃən] *s.* mutilazione *f.*

mutineer [,mjuːti'niə•] *s.* ammutinato *m.*

mutinous ['mjuːtinəs] *agg.* ribelle, sovversivo

mutiny ['mjuːtini] *s.* ammutinamento *m.*, ribellione *f.*

to mutiny ['mjuːtini] *v. intr.* ammutinarsi, ribellarsi

mutism ['mjuːtizəm] *s.* mutismo *m.*

to mutter ['mʌtə•] *v. tr.* e *intr.* borbottare

mutton ['mʌtn] *s.* carne *f.* di montone

mutual ['mjuːtjuəl] *agg.* mutuo, reciproco

muzzle ['mʌzl] *s.* museruola *f.*; muso *m.*; bocca
 f. di arma da fuoco

Mycenaean [mai'siːniən] *agg.* miceneo

myopic [mai'ɔpik] *agg.* miope

myriad ['miriəd] *s.* miriade *f.*

mysterious [mis'tiəriəs] *agg.* arcano, misterioso

mystery ['mistəri] *s.* mistero *m.*

mystical ['mistikəl] *agg.* mistico

mysticism ['mistisizəm] *s.* misticismo *m.*

mystifier ['mistifaə•] *s.* mistificatore *m.*

myth [miθ] *s.* mito *m.*

mythical ['miθikəl] *agg.* mitico

to mythicize ['miθisaiz] *v. tr.* mitizzare

mythologic(al) [,miθə'lɔdʒik(əl)] *agg.* mitologico

mythology [mi'θɔlədʒi] *s.* mitologia *f.*

mythomaniac [,miθə'meiniæk] *agg.* mitomane

N

nabob ['neibɔb] s. nababbo m.

nacelle [nə'sel] s. carlinga f.

nagging ['nægiŋ] agg. insistente, fastidioso

naiad ['naiæd] s. naiade f.

nail [neil] s. chiodo m.; unghia f.; – **polish** smalto da unghie; – **file** limetta

to nail [neil] v. tr. inchiodare

naïve [na:'i:v] agg. ingenuo, naif

naïvety [na:'i:vti] s. ingenuità f.

naked ['neikid] agg. nudo

name [neim] s. nome m.; – **day** onomastico; **pen** – pseudonimo; **Christian** – (UK), **first** – (USA) nome di battesimo; **family** – cognome; **full** – nome e cognome; **my** – **is** ... mi chiamo ...; **what's your** – ? come ti chiami?

to name [neim] v. tr. chiamare, denominare

namely ['neimli] cong. ossia, cioè

nap [næp] s. pisolino m., siesta f.; **to take a** – schiacciare un pisolino

nape [neip] s. nuca f.

napkin ['næpkin] s. pannolino m.; **table** – tovagliolo

nappy ['næpi] s. pannolino m.

narcissist [na:'sisist] s. narcisista m. e f.

narcotic [na:'kɔtik] agg. e s. narcotico m.; – **addiction** tossicodipendenza

to narrate [næ'reit] v. tr. narrare

narration [næ'reiʃən] s. narrazione f.

narrator [næ'reitə*] s. narratore m.

narrow ['nærou] agg. ristretto, stretto, limitato • s. stretto m.; – **minded** gretto

narthex ['na:θeks] s. nartece m.

nasal ['neizəl] agg. nasale

nasty ['na:sti] agg. sporco, osceno, schifoso; – **smell** puzza

natality [nei'tæliti] s. natalità f.

nation ['neiʃən] s. nazione f.

national ['næʃənl] agg. nazionale

nationalism ['næʃnəlizəm] s. nazionalismo m.

nationality [,næʃə'næliti] s. nazionalità f.

native ['neitiv] agg. natale, originario • s. indigeno m.; – **land** patria

nativity [nə'tiviti] s. natività f.

natural ['nætʃrəl] agg. naturale, schietto, spontaneo; bequadro (mus.)

naturalism ['nætʃrəlizəm] s. naturalismo m.

naturalist ['nætʃrəlist] s. naturalista m. e f.

to naturalize ['nætʃrəlaiz] v. tr. naturalizzare

naturally ['nætʃrəli] avv. naturalmente

nature ['neitʃə*] s. natura f., carattere m.

naturism ['neitʃərizəm] s. naturismo m.

naturist ['neitʃərist] s. naturista m. e f.

naughtiness ['nɔ:tinis] s. cattiveria f.

naught [nɔ:t] s. zero m.; nulla m.

naughty ['nɔ:ti] agg. capriccioso, cattivo

naumachia [nɔ:'meikjə] s. naumachia f.

nausea ['nɔ:sjə] s. nausea f.

to nauseate ['nɔ:sieit] v. tr. e intr. nauseare

nauseating ['nɔ:sieitiŋ] agg. nauseabondo

nautical ['nɔ:tikəl] agg. nautico; – **mile** miglio marino; – **almanac** effemeridi

naval ['neivəl] agg. marittimo, nautico, navale

nave [neiv] s. navata f. centrale

navel ['neivəl] s. ombelico m.

navigability [,nævigə'biliti] s. navigabilità f.

navigable ['nævigəbl] agg. navigabile

navigation [,nævi'geiʃən] s. navigazione f.

navy ['neivi] s. marina f.

Nazi(i)sm ['na:tsi(i)zəm] s. nazismo m.

near [niə*] agg., avv. e prep. vicino, presso; quasi (nei composti); – **friend** amico intimo; – **miss** mancato per poco; – **sighted** miope

nearby ['niəbai] agg. e avv. accanto, nelle vicinanze

nearly ['niəli] avv. quasi, per poco

neat [ni:t] agg. lindo, ordinato

nebula ['nebjulə] s. nebulosa f.

nebulous ['neibjuləs] agg. nebuloso, vago, indistinto

necessarily ['nesisərili] avv. necessariamente

necessary ['nesisəri] agg. necessario, inevitabile

necessity [ni'sesiti] s. necessità f.; **of** – necessariamente

neck [nek] s. collo m.

necklace ['neklis] s. collana f.

necklet ['neklit] s. colletto m.

neckline ['neklain] s. scollatura f.

necktie ['nek-tai] s. cravatta f. (USA)

necropolis [ne'krɔpəlis] s. necropoli f.

nectar ['nektə*] s. nettare m.
need [ni:d] s. bisogno m., esigenza f. • pl. fabbisogno m. sing.
to need [ni:d] v. tr. aver bisogno
needle ['ni:dl] s. ago m.
negation [ni'geiʃən] s. negazione f.
negative ['negətiv] agg. negativo • s. negazione f.
neglect [ni'glekt] s. omissione f.
to neglect [ni'glekt] v. tr. trascurare
negligence ['neglidʒəns] s. negligenza f.
negligible ['neglidʒəbl] agg. trascurabile, insignificante
to negotiate [ni'gouʃieit] v. tr. e intr. contrattare, negoziare
negotiation [ni,gouʃi'eiʃən] s. trattativa f.
neigh [nei] s. nitrito m.
neighbour ['neibə*] s. vicino m. di casa
neighbourhood ['neibəhud] s. vicinato m., quartiere m.
neighbouring ['neibəriŋ] agg. confinante, limitrofo
neither ['naiðə*] avv. e cong. neanche, né • agg. e pron. nessuno dei due; – ... nor ... né ... né ...
neoclassic(al) [,ni:ou'klæsik(əl)] agg. neoclassico
neoclassicism [,ni:ou'klæsisizəm] s. neoclassicismo m.
Neolithic [,ni:ou'liθik] agg. neolitico
neologism [ni'(:)olədʒizəm] s. neologismo m.
neophyte ['ni:oufait] s. neofita m. e f.
neorealism [,ni:ou'ri:lizəm] s. neorealismo m.
nephew ['nevju:] s. nipote m. (di zii)
nepotism ['nepətizəm] s. nepotismo m.
nervation [nə:(')veiʃən] s. nervatura f. (bot.)
nerve [nə:v] s. nervo m.; forza f. (fig.); **to get on somebody's nerves** innervosire
nervous ['nə:vəs] agg. nervoso; timido
nervousness ['nə:vəsnis] s. nervosismo m.
nest [nest] s. nido m.
to nest [nest] v. intr. nidificare
to nestle ['nesl] v. intr. annidarsi
net [net] s. netto • s. rete f.
nettle ['netl] s. ortica f.
network ['net:wə:k] s. rete f. (di comunicazione); sistema m.
neuralgia [njuə'rældʒə] s. nevralgia f.
neurologist [njuə'rolədʒist] s. neurologo m.
neurosis [njuə'rousis] s. nevrosi f.
neurotic [njuə'rɔtik] agg. e s. complessato m., nevrotico m.
neuter ['nju:tə*] agg. neutro (gramm.)

neutral ['nju:trəl] agg. neutrale, neutro • s. folle m. (autom.)
neutrality [nju:'træliti] s. neutralità f.
to neutralize ['nju:tralaiz] v. tr. neutralizzare
never ['nevə*] avv. mai; – **again** mai più; – **ending** incessante; **you – know** non si sa mai; – **mind** non importa, pazienza; **well, I – !** ma guarda un po'!, chi l'avrebbe detto!
nevertheless [,nevəðə'les] cong. tuttavia
new [nju:] agg. nuovo, recente, altro; – **year's day** capodanno • avv. appena, di recente
news [nju:z] s. pl. (v. al sing.) novità f.; notizia f. sing. e pl.; cronaca f. sing.; **the** – notiziario, telegiornale; – **agent** giornalaio; – **letter** volantino (comm.); – **reel** cinegiornale, telecronaca; **society** – cronaca mondana; **crime** – cronaca nera; **a piece of** – una notizia
newspaper ['nju:s,peipə*] s. giornale m.
next [nekst] agg. prossimo, seguente • avv. dopo, in seguito; – **to** vicino a, presso; – **door** vicino
nexus ['neksəs] s. nesso m.
nib [nib] s. pennino m.
nice [nais] agg. bello, simpatico, gentile, grazioso
niche [nitʃ] s. nicchia f.
nickname ['nikneim] s. soprannome m.
nicotine ['nikəti:n] s. nicotina f.
niece [ni:s] s. f. nipote f. (di zii)
night [nait] agg. notturno • s. notte f., serata f.; **tonight** stanotte; **last** – ieri notte; **good** – buona notte; **at** –, **by** – di notte; – **gown** camicia da notte
nightie ['naiti] s. camicia f. da notte
nightingale ['naitiŋ,geil] s. usignolo m.
nightmare ['naitmeə*] s. incubo m.
nihilism ['naiilizəm] s. nichilismo m.
nimble ['nimbl] agg. agile, lesto
nimbleness ['nimblnis] s. agilità f.
nipper ['nipə*] s. pinza f.; **cutting nippers** tronchese
nitrogen ['naitridʒən] s. azoto m.
no [nou] avv. no, non • agg. nessuno, niente; – **one** nessuno
nobiliary [nou'biljəri] agg. nobiliare
nobility [nou'biliti] s. nobiltà f.
noble ['noubl] agg. magnanimo, nobile
nobody ['noubədi] pron. indef. nessuno
nocturnal [nɔk'tə:nl] agg. notturno
nod [nɔd] s. cenno m.
to nod [nɔd] v. intr. annuire, accennare col capo
noise [nɔiz] s. rumore m., schiamazzo m.; scalpore m.

noisy ['nɔizi] *agg.* rumoroso

nomad(e) ['nəmæd] *s.* nomade *m. e f.*

nomination [,nɔmi'neiʃən] *s.* incarico *m.*

nominative ['nɔminətiv] *agg.* nominativo

non-acceptance ['nɔnək'septəns] *s.* mancata accettazione *f.* (*comm.*)

non-addicting ['nɔnə'diktiŋ] *agg.* che non causa assuefazione

non-alcoholic ['nɔn,ælkə'hɔlik] *agg.* analcolico

non-chalance ['nɔnʃələns] *s.* noncuranza *f.*

non-compliance ['nɔnkəm'plaiəns] *s.* inadempienza *f.* (*leg.*)

nonconformism ['nɔnkən'fɔ:mizəm] *s.* anticonformismo *m.*

nondenominational ['nɔndi,nɔmi'neiʃənəl] *agg.* aconfessionale

non-drinker ['nɔn'driŋkə*] *s.* astemio *m.*

none [nʌn] *pron. indef.* nessuno, niente • *avv.* non, per niente

nonplus ['nɔn'plʌs] *s.* imbarazzo *m.*; perplessità *f.*

nonsense ['nɔnsəns] *s.* controsenso *m.*, sciocchezza *f.*

non-smoker [,nɔn'smoukə*] *s.* non fumatore *m.*

non-stop ['nɔn'stɔp] *agg.* ininterrotto

non-violence ['nɔn'vaiələns] *s.* non-violenza *f.*

noon [nu:n] *s.* mezzogiorno *m.*

noose [nu:s] *s.* laccio *m.*

nor [nɔ:, nə*] *cong.* né, neanche; **neither this - that** né questo né quello

Nordic ['nɔ:dik] *agg. e s.* nordico *m.*

norm [nɔ:m] *s.* norma *f.*

normal ['nɔ:məl] *agg.* normale

normality [nɔ:'mæliti] *s.* normalità *f.*

Norman ['nɔ:mən] *agg. e s.* normanno *m.*

north [nɔ:θ] *s.* nord *m.* • *agg.* settentrionale; **the - star** la stella polare

northern ['nɔ:ðən] *agg.* settentrionale

nose [nouz] *s.* naso *m.*

nostalgic [nɔs'tældʒik] *agg.* nostalgico

nostril ['nɔstril] *s.* narice *f.*

not [nɔt] *avv.* non, no; **- even** neanche, neppure; **- any**, **- any (of)**, **- anybody**, **- anything** nessuno, niente

notable ['noutəbl] *agg.* notevole, importante • *s.* notabile *m.*

notary ['noutəri] *s.* notaio *m.*

notation [nou'teiʃən] *s.* notazione *f.*; numerazione *f.* (*mat.*)

notch [nɔtʃ] *s.* tacca *f.*

note [nout] *s.* annotazione *f.*; bolla *f.* (*comm.*); nota *f.* (*mus.*)

to note [nout] *v. tr.* notare, constatare

notebook ['noutbuk] *s.* taccuino *m.*

nothing ['nʌθiŋ] *pron. indef.* niente, nulla • *avv.* per nulla

notice ['noutis] *s.* avviso *m.*, preavviso *m.*; scritta *f.* (su di un cartello); **- board** tabellone

to notice ['noutis] *v. tr.* osservare • *intr.* stare attento

noticeable ['noutisəbl] *agg.* osservabile; notevole; percettibile

to notify ['noutifai] *v. tr.* avvisare

notion ['nouʃən] *s.* concetto *m.*; nozione *f.*

notoriety [,noutə'raiəti] *s.* notorietà *f.*

notwithstanding [,nɔtwið'stændiŋ] *prep.* nonostante • *avv.* tuttavia

nought [nɔ:t] *s.* zero *m.*, nulla *m.* • *avv.* niente

noun [naun] *s.* sostantivo *m.*

to nourish ['nʌriʃ] *v. tr.* nutrire

nourishing ['nʌriʃiŋ] *agg.* nutriente

nourishment ['nʌriʃmənt] *s.* nutrimento *m.*, alimento *m.*

novel ['nɔvəl] *s.* romanzo *m.* • *agg.* nuovo; **the -** la narrativa

novelist ['nɔvəlist] *s.* romanziere *m.*

novelty ['nɔvəlti] *s.* novità *f.*

November [nou'vembə*] *s.* novembre *m.*

now [nau] *avv. e cong.* adesso, ora

nowadays ['nauədeiz] *avv.* oggigiorno • *s.* oggi *m.*, presente *m.*

nowhere ['nouweə*] *avv.* da nessuna parte

noxious ['nɔkʃəs] *agg.* nocivo

nozzle ['nɔzl] *s.* ugello *m.*

nth [enθ] *agg.* ennesimo

nuclear ['nju:kliə*] *agg.* nucleare

nucleus ['nju:kliəs] *s.* nucleo *m.*

nude [nju:d] *agg. e s.* nudo *m.*

nudism ['nju:dizəm] *s.* nudismo *m.*

nudist ['nju:dist] *s.* nudista *m. e f.*

nuisance ['nju:sns] *s.* scocciatura *f.*; rompiscatole *m. e f. inv.*; fastidio *m.*

null [nʌl] *agg.* nullo

number ['nʌmbə*] *s.* numero *m.*

to number ['nʌmbə*] *v. tr.* numerare

numbering ['nʌmbəriŋ] *s.* numerazione *f.*

numbness ['nʌmnis] *s.* torpore *m.*

numeral ['nju:mərəl] *agg.* numerale • *s.* numero *m.*, cifra *f.*

numeration ['nju:mə'reiʃən] *s.* numerazione *f.* (*mat.*)

numeric(al) [nju(:)'merik(ǝl)] *agg.* numerico; **numerically** numericamente

numerous ['nju:mǝrǝs] *agg.* numeroso; **a – acquaintance** un largo giro di conoscenze

numismatics [,nju:miz'mætiks] *s. pl.* (*v. al sing.*) numismatica *f. sing.*

nun [nʌn] *s.* suora *f.*; **cloistered –** suora di clausura

nuptial ['nʌpʃǝl] *agg.* nuziale

nurse [nǝ:s] *s.* balia *f.*, bambinaia *f.*; infermiera *f.*, infermiere *m.*

to nurse [nǝ:s] *v. tr.* allattare; aver cura di, curare; **nursing home** casa di cura

nursery ['nǝ:sri] *s.* vivaio *m.*; stanza *f.* dei bambini; **– school** asilo infantile

nut [nʌt] *s.* noce *f.* (*bot.*); dado *m.* (*mecc.*); **nuts** pazzo (*fam.*); **to go nuts** impazzire

nutcrackers ['nʌt,krækǝ*] *s. pl.* schiaccianoci *m. sing.*

nutritionist [nju(:)'triʃǝnist] *s.* dietologo *m.*

nymph [nimf] *s.* ninfa *f.*

nymphaeum [nim'fi:ǝm] *s.* ninfeo *m.*

O

oak [ouk] s. quercia f.; **bay** – rovere
oar [ɔ:*] s. remo m.; **oarsman** rematore
oasis [ou'eisis] s. oasi f.
oat [out] s. avena f.; **oatmeal** farina d'avena
oath [ouθ] s. giuramento m.
obedience [ə'bi:djəns] s. ubbedienza f.
obedient [ə'bi:djənt] agg. ubbidiente
obelisk ['ɔbilisk] s. obelisco m.
obese [ou'bi:s] agg. obeso
obesity [ou'bi:siti] s. obesità f.
to obey [ə'bei] v. tr. e intr. ubbidire
obituary [ə'bitjuəri] s. necrologio m.
object ['ɔbdʒikt] s. oggetto m.; scopo m.; – lesson dimostrazione pratica
to object [ab'dʒekt] v. tr. e intr. obiettare, opporsi; – to disapprovare
to objectify [ɔb'dʒektifai] v. tr. oggettivare
objection [əb'dʒekʃən] s. obiezione f.
objective [ɔb'kʒektiv] agg. obiettivo, oggettivo
objectivity [,ɔbdʒek'tiviti] s. obiettività f.
obligation [,ɔbli'geiʃən] s. obbligo m.; impegno m. (comm.)
to oblige [ə'blaidʒ] v. tr. obbligare
oblique [ə'bli:k] agg. obliquo
oblivion [ə'blivian] s. oblio m.
oblong ['ɔblɔŋ] agg. oblungo
obnoxious [əb'nɔkʃəs] agg. ripugnante
obscene [əb'si:n] agg. osceno
obscenity [əb'si:niti] s. oscenità f., indecenza f.
obscurantism [,ɔbskjuə'ræntizəm] s. oscuran-
tismo m.
obscure [əb'skjuə*] agg. oscuro, ignoto
to obscure [əb'skjuə*] v. tr. oscurare
obscurity [əb'skjuəriti] s. oscurità f.
observation [,ɔbzə(:)'veiʃən] s. osservazione f.,
spirito m. d'osservazione
observatory [əb'zə:vatri] s. osservatorio m.
to observe [əb'zə:v] v. tr. e intr. osservare
observer [əb'zə:və*] s. osservatore m.
obsession [əb'seʃən] s. ossessione f., fissazione f.
obsessive [əb'sesiv] agg. ossessivo
obsolete ['ɔbsəli:t] agg. obsoleto
obstacle ['ɔbstəkl] s. ostacolo m.

obstetrician [,ɔbste'triʃən] s. ostetrico m.
obstinacy ['ɔbstinasi] s. ostinazione f.
obstinate ['ɔbstinit] agg. ostinato
to obstruct [əb'strʌkt] v. tr. ostruire, impedire
obstruction [əb'strʌkʃən] s. ostruzione f.,
ostacolo m.
obstructionism [əb'strʌkʃənizəm] s. ostruzionismo m.
to obtain [əb'tein] v. tr. ottenere • intr. essere in voga
obturator ['ɔbtjuəreitə*] s. otturatore m.
obtuse [əb'tju:s] agg. ottuso
to obviate ['ɔbvieit] v. intr. ovviare
obvious ['ɔbvias] agg. ovvio, logico; **obviously**
ovviamente
occasion [ə'keiʒən] s. occasione f.; motivo m.;
pretesto m.; **on** – occasionalmente
occasional [ə'keiʒənl] agg. accidentale; **occasionally** occasionalmente
occidental [,ɔksi'dentl] agg. occidentale
to occlude [ɔ'klu:d] v. tr. occludere
occlusion [ɔ'klu:ʒən] s. occlusione f.
to occult [ɔ'kʌlt] v. tr. occultare
occupation [,ɔkju'peiʃən] s. occupazione f.;
professione f.
to occupy ['ɔkjupai] v. tr. occupare; – oneself
occuparsi
to occur [ə'kə:*] v. intr. accadere, succedere;
esserci
ocean ['ouʃən] s. oceano m.
oceanic [,ouʃi'ænik] agg. oceanico
oceanography [,ouʃə'nɔgrəfi] s. oceanogra-
fia f.
ochre ['oukə*] agg. ocra
octagonal [ɔk'tægənl] agg. ottagonale
October [ɔk'toubə*] s. ottobre m.
octopus ['ɔktəpəs] s. polpo m.
ocular ['ɔkjulə*] agg. oculare
oculist ['ɔkjulist] s. oculista m. e f.
odd [ɔd] agg. dispari; scompagnato; casuale;
bizzarro; **one pound** – una sterlina e rotti
odds [ɔdz] s. pl. disparità f. sing.; svantaggio m.
sing.; quotazione f. sing. (di scommesse)
odometer [ou'dɔmitə*] s. contachilometri m.
(USA)

odontologist [,ɔdɔn'tɔlədʒist] *s.* odontoiatra *m.* e *f.*

odour ['oudə*] *s.* odore *m.* (piacevole), profumo *m.*

Odyssey ['ɔdisi] *s.* odissea *f.*

oecumenical [,i:kju'menikəl] *agg.* ecumenico

oedema [i(:)'di:mə] *s.* edema *m.*

oenological [,i:nou'lɔdʒikəl] *agg.* enologico

of [ɔv, əv] *prep.* di, fra (*part.*); – **course** certamente

off [ɔ:f] *avv.* via, lontano • *prep.* da, lontano da; – **and on** di tanto in tanto

offence [ə'fens] *s.* offesa *f.*; reato *m.*; **to take** – offendere

to offend [ə'fend] *v. tr.* offendere

offender [ə'fendə*] *s.* colpevole *m.* e *f.* (*leg.*)

offensive [ə'fensiv] *s.* offensiva *f.* • *agg.* offensivo

offer ['ɔfə*] *s.* offerta *f.*

to offer ['ɔfə*] *v. tr.* e *intr.* offrire, porgere

office ['ɔfis] *s.* ufficio *m.*; funzione *f.*; – **hours** orario d'ufficio; **post** – ufficio postale; **tourist** – ufficio turistico; – **boy** fattorino

officer ['ɔfisə*] *s.* ufficiale *m.*; agente *m.* di polizia

official [ə'fiʃəl] *s.* funzionario *m.* • *agg.* ufficiale; – **character** ufficialità

offshoot ['ɔ:fʃu:t] *s.* germoglio *m.*

offspring ['ɔ:spriŋ] *s.* discendente *m.* e *f.*

often ['ɔ:fn] *avv.* frequentemente, spesso

ogive ['oudʒaiv] *s.* ogiva *f.*

oil [ɔil] *s.* olio *m.*; petrolio *m.* • *agg.* petrolifero; **in** – sott'olio; – **mill** frantoio

to oil [ɔil] *v. tr.* lubrificare, oliare

oiler ['ɔilə*] *s.* oliatore *m.*

oily ['ɔili] *agg.* oleoso, unto

ointment ['ɔintmənt] *s.* pomata *f.*

okay, OK ['ou'kei] *agg.* corretto • *avv.* bene • *inter.* va bene!

old [ould] *agg.* vecchio; **to become older** invecchiare; – **fashions** moda antiquata; – **fashioned** superato; **how** – **are you?** quanti anni hai?; – **age** vecchiaia

olfaction [ɔl'fækʃən] *s.* olfatto *m.*

oligarchy ['ɔliga:ki] *s.* oligarchia *f.*

olive ['ɔliv] *s.* oliva *f.*; – **tree** olivo

Olympiad [ou'limpiæd] *s.* olimpiade *f.*

Olympic [ou'limpik] *agg.* olimpico; – **games** olimpiadi

omelette ['ɔmlit] *s.* frittata *f.*

omen ['oumen] *s.* presagio *m.*

ominous ['ɔminəs] *agg.* di malaugurio

omission [ou'miʃən] *s.* omissione *f.*

to omit [ou'mit] *v. tr.* omettere

omnipotent [ɔm'nipətənt] *agg.* onnipotente

omnipresent ['ɔmni'prezənt] *agg.* onnipresente

omnivorous [ɔm'nivərəs] *agg.* onnivoro

on [ɔn] *avv.* addosso; avanti; acceso, in funzione • *prep.* sopra, su, a; **go –! avanti!**; – **Saturdays** di sabato; – **board** a bordo; – **foot** a piedi

once [wʌns] *avv.* una volta; un tempo • *cong.* quando, una volta che; **at** – subito; **all at** – improvvisamente

one [wʌn] *agg.* e *pron. indef.* uno, un solo • *pron. dimostr.* quello; – **by** – uno alla volta; **no** – nessuno

onerous ['ɔnərəs] *agg.* oneroso

oneself [wʌn'self] *pron. rifl.* sé, se stesso; **by** – da solo

onion ['ʌnjən] *s.* cipolla *f.*

only ['ounli] *agg.* unico • *cong.* solo, ma

onward ['ɔnwəd] *avv.* avanti, oltre

onyx ['ɔniks] *s.* onice *f.*

opal ['oupəl] *s.* opale *m.*

opalescent [,oupə'lesənt] *agg.* opalescente

opaque [ou'peik] *agg.* opaco

open ['oupən] *agg.* aperto

to open ['oupən] *v. tr.* e *intr.* aprire; inaugurare

opening ['oupniŋ] *s.* apertura *f.*; varco *m.*; inaugurazione *f.*; esordio *m.* • *agg.* apribile; inaugurale

openly ['oupənli] *avv.* francamente

opera ['ɔpərə] *s.* opera *f.* lirica (*mus.*); **comic** – opera buffa

to operate ['ɔpəreit] *v. tr.* e *intr.* operare, funzionare

operatic [,ɔpə'rætik] *agg.* melodrammatico

operation [,ɔpə'reiʃən] *s.* funzionamento *m.*; intervento *m.*; operazione *f.*

operative ['ɔpərətiv] *agg.* operativo, efficace

operator ['ɔpəreitə*] *s.* operatore *m.* e *f.*; centralinista *m.* e *f.*

operetta [,ɔpə'retə] *s.* operetta *f.*

ophthalmology [,ɔfθæl'mɔlədʒi] *s.* oftalmologia *f.*

opinion [ə'pinjən] *s.* opinione *f.*

opponent [ə'pounənt] *s.* avversario *m.*

opportune ['ɔpətju:n] *agg.* opportuno; tempestivo

opportunism [,ɔpə'tju:nizəm] *s.* opportunismo *m.*

opportunity [,ɔpə'tju:niti] *s.* occasione *f.*, possibilità *f.*

to oppose [ə'pəuz] *v. tr.* opporre, osteggiare; **–
oneself** opporsi
opposite ['ɔpəzit] *agg. e s.* opposto *m.*, contrario *m.* • *avv. e prep.* davanti, di fronte
opposition [,ɔpə'ziʃən] *s.* opposizione *f.*
to oppress [ə'pres] *v. tr.* opprimere
oppression [ə'preʃən] *s.* oppressione *f.*
oppressive [ə'presiv] *agg.* opprimente
oppressor [ə'presə*] *s.* oppressore *m.*
to opt [ɔpt] *v. intr.* optare
optic ['ɔptik] *agg.* ottico
optical ['ɔptikəl] *agg.* ottico
optician [ɔp'tiʃən] *s.* occhialaio *m.*
optics ['ɔptiks] *s. pl.* (*v. al sing.*) ottica *f. sing.*
optimal ['ɔptiməl] *agg.* ottimale
optimism ['ɔptimizəm] *s.* ottimismo *m.*
optimist ['ɔptimist] *agg.* ottimista
to optimize ['ɔptimaiz] *v. tr.* ottimizzare
optimum ['ɔptiməm] *agg.* ottimale
optional ['ɔpʃənl] *agg.* facoltativo
opulence ['ɔpjuləns] *s.* opulenza *f.*
or [ɔ:*, ə*] *cong.* o, oppure; **either ... – ... o** ...
o ...; **– else** altrimenti
oracle ['ɔrəkl] *s.* oracolo *m.*
oral ['ɔːrəl] *agg.* orale
orange ['ɔrindʒ] *s.* arancia *f.* • *agg.* arancione, arancio
orangeade ['ɔrindʒ'eid] *s.* aranciata *f.*
orator ['ɔrətə*] *s.* oratore *m.*
oratory ['ɔrətəri] *s.* oratorio *m.*
orbit ['ɔːbit] *s.* orbita *f.*
orchard ['ɔːtʃəd] *s.* frutteto *m.*
orchestra ['ɔːkistrə] *s.* orchestra *f.*
orchid ['ɔːkid] *s.* orchidea *f.*
order ['ɔːdə*] *s.* ordine *m.*; commessa *f.*; ordinamento *m.*; **postal –** vaglia postale; **telegraphic money –** vaglia telegrafico; **out of –** fuori servizio
to order ['ɔːdə*] *v. tr.* ordinare, disporre •
intr. comandare
ordinal ['ɔːdinl] *agg.* ordinale
ordinance ['ɔːdinəns] *s.* ordinanza *f.*
ordinary ['ɔːdnri] *agg.* mediocre; ordinario
ordination [,ɔːdi'neiʃən] *s.* ordinazione *f.* (*relig.*)
ore [ɔː*] *s.* minerale *m.*
organ ['ɔːgən] *s.* organo *m.*
organic [ɔː'gænik] *agg.* organico
organism ['ɔːgənizəm] *s.* organismo *m.*
organization [,ɔːgənai'zeiʃən] *s.* ordinamento
m.; organizzazione *f.*
to organize ['ɔːgənaiz] *v. tr.* organizzare •
intr. organizzarsi

orgy ['ɔːdʒi] *s.* orgia *f.*
orient ['ɔːriənt] *s.* oriente *m.*; **the Orient** i paesi
orientali
Oriental [,ɔːri'entl] *agg.* orientale
to orientate ['ɔːrienteit] *v. tr.* orientare; **– oneself** orientarsi
orientation [,ɔːrien'teiʃən] *s.* orientamento *m.*
origin ['ɔridʒin] *s.* origine *f.*, principio *m.*; nascita *f.*
original [ə'ridʒənl] *agg.* originale, autentico;
originario • *s.* originale *m.*
originality [ə,ridʒi'næliti] *s.* originalità *f.*
to originate [ə'ridʒineit] *v. tr.* dare origine •
intr. nascere, provenire
ornament ['ɔːnəmənt] *s.* ornamento *m.*, addobbo *m.*
ornamental [,ɔːnə'mentl] *agg.* ornamentale
ornithology [,ɔːni'θɔlədʒi] *s.* ornitologia *f.*
orography [ɔ'rɔgrəfi] *s.* orografia *f.*
orphan ['ɔːfən] *agg. e s.* orfano *m.*
orthodox ['ɔːθədɔks] *agg.* ortodosso
orthodoxy ['ɔːθədɔksi] *s.* ortodossia *f.*
orthogonal [ɔː'θɔgənl] *agg.* ortogonale
orthography [ɔː'θɔgrəfi] *s.* ortografia *f.*
orthopaedist [,ɔːθou'piːdist] *s.* ortopedico *m.*
to oscillate ['ɔsileit] *v. intr.* oscillare
oscillation [,ɔsil'leiʃən] *s.* oscillazione *f.*
osseous ['ɔsiəs] *agg.* osseo
ostensory [ɔs'tensəri] *s.* ostensorio *m.*
ostentation [,ɔsten'teiʃən] *s.* ostentazione *f.*;
esibizione *f.*
ostrich ['ɔstritʃ] *s.* struzzo *m.*
other ['ʌðə*] *agg. e pron. indef.* altro; **any –**
qualche altro; **every –** ogni altro; **none – than**
proprio, non altri che; **– people** altri; **– 's, –
people's** altrui; **– than** tranne
otherwise ['ʌðəwaiz] *avv.* diversamente •
cong. altrimenti
otitis [ou'taitis] *s.* otite *f.*
Ottoman ['ɔtəmən] *agg. e s.* ottomano *m.*
out [aut] *agg.* esterno, spento • *avv.* fuori, finito; **– of** fuori da; **– here** qui fuori; **– and –**
vero; **– loud** a voce alta; **– there** laggiù
outboard ['autbɔːd] *s.* fuoribordo *m. inv.*
outcast ['autkɑːst] *s.* reietto *m.*
outcome ['autkʌm] *s.* esito *m.*, risultato *m.*
outdoor ['autdɔː*] *agg.* esterno, all'aria aperta
outdoors ['aut'dɔːz] *avv.* all'aria aperta
outer ['autə*] *agg.* esteriore, esterno
outfit ['autfit] *s.* equipaggiamento *m.*, attrezzatura *f.*
outing ['autiŋ] *s.* gita *f.*, escursione *f.*
outlaw ['aut-lɔː] *s.* bandito *m.*

outlet ['aut-let] *s.* sbocco *m.*, sfogo *m.*; presa *f.* elettrica

outline ['aut-lain] *s.* profilo *m.*; schema *m.*

to outline ['aut-lain] *v. tr.* delineare, disegnare

outlook ['aut-luk] *s.* veduta *f.*; prospettiva *f.*; modo *m.* di vedere

outpost ['autpoust] *s.* avamposto *m.*

output ['autput] *s.* produzione *f.*, rendimento *m.*

outrage ['aut-reidʒ] *s.* oltraggio *m.*

outrageous [aut'reidʒəs] *agg.* atroce

outside [aut'said] *agg.* e *s.* esterno *m.* • *avv.* fuori

outsider [aut'saidə*] *s.* estraneo *m.* (escluso da un gruppo)

outskirts ['aut-skə:ts] *s. pl.* periferia *f. sing.*

outstanding [aut'stændiŋ] *agg.* notevole, sporgente

outward ['autwəd] *agg.* esteriore

ouzel ['u:zl] *s.* merlo *m.* (zool.)

oval ['ouvəl] *agg.* ovale

oven ['ʌvn] *s.* forno *m.*

over ['ouvə*] *prep.* sopra, su; nel corso di (temporale); oltre, più • *avv.* al di sopra; – **tired** stanchissimo; – **again** daccapo; – **there** laggiù; **all** – dappertutto

overall ['ouverəl] *agg.* complessivo • *s. pl.* tuta *f. sing.*

to overburden [,ouvə'bə:dn] *v. tr.* sovraccaricare

overcast ['ouvə'ka:st] *agg.* nuvoloso

overcoat ['ouvəkout] *s.* soprabito *m.*

to overcome [,ouvə'kʌm] *v. tr.* superare, sopraffare

overcooked ['ouvə'kukt] *agg.* troppo cotto

to overdo [,ouvə'du:] *v. tr.* eccedere, esagerare

to overestimate ['ouvər'estimeit] *v. tr.* sopravvalutare

to overexpose ['ouvəriks'pouz] *v. tr.* sovraesporre

to overflow [,ouvə'flou] *v. intr.* traboccare

overflowing [,ouvə'flouiŋ] *s.* straripamento *m.*

overhang ['ouvəhæŋ] *s.* sporgenza *f.*, strapiombo *m.*

overhaul ['ouvə:hɔ:l] *s.* revisione *f.* (mecc.)

overheated [,ouvə'hi:tid] *agg.* surriscaldato

overland ['ouvə'lænd] *agg.* e *avv.* per via di terra; **the** – **route** l'itinerario

to overload [,ouvə'loud] *v. tr.* sovraccaricare

to overlook [,ouvə'luk] *v. tr.* e *intr.* sorvolare; trascurare, non rilevare

overnight ['ouvə'nait] *avv.* di notte; – **stay** pernottamento

overpass ['ouvə,pa:s] *s.* cavalcavia *m. inv.*

to overrate [,ouvə'reit] *v. tr.* stimare eccessivamente

overseas ['ouvə'si:(z)] *avv.* oltremare

oversight [,ouvəsait] *s.* disattenzione *f.*, svista *f.*; sorveglianza *f.*

to oversleep [,ouvə'sli:p] *v. tr.* e *intr.* dormire troppo

to overstep [,ouvə'step] *v. tr.* oltrepassare

to overtake [,ouvə'teik] *v. tr.* raggiungere, sorpassare; **overtaking** sorpasso; **no overtaking** divieto di sorpasso

to overthrow [,ouvə'θrou] *v. tr.* rovesciare

overturn [,ouvə'tə:n] *s.* ribaltamento *m.*

to overturn [,ouvə'tə:n] *v. tr.* ribaltare • *intr.* ribaltarsi

to overwhelm [,ouvə'welm] *v. tr.* sopraffare, travolgere

overwhelming [,ouvə'welmiŋ] *agg.* opprimente, travolgente

ovine ['ouvain] *agg.* ovino

oviparous [ou'vipərəs] *s.* oviparo *m.*

ovoid ['ouvɔid] *agg.* ovoidale

to owe [ou] *v. tr.* e *intr.* essere debitore

owl [aul] *s.* gufo *m.*

own [oun] *agg.* proprio; – **goal** autogoal

to own [oun] *v. tr.* possedere, avere

owner ['ounə*] *s.* proprietario *m.*, padrone *m.*

ox [ɔks] *s.* bue *m.*

oxide ['ɔksaid] *s.* ossido *m.*

to oxidize ['ɔksidaiz] *v. tr.* ossidare • *intr.* ossidarsi

oxygen ['ɔksidʒən] *s.* ossigeno *m.*

oyster ['ɔistə*] *s.* ostrica *f.*

ozone ['ouzoun] *s.* ozono *m.*

P

pa [pa:] s. babbo m., papà m. (fam.)
pace [peis] s. andatura f., passo m.
pacific [pə'sifik] agg. pacifico
pacification [,pæsifi'keiʃən] s. pacificazione f.
pacifism ['pæsifizəm] s. pacifismo m.
pack [pæk] s. pacco m., imballaggio m.
to pack [pæk] v. tr. imballare; – up fare le valigie; smettere di lavorare; spegnersi (di un motore)
package ['pækidʒ] s. pacco m.
packet ['pækit] s. pacchetto m.
packing ['pækiŋ] s. imballaggio m.
pact [pækt] s. patto m.
pad [pæd] s. cuscinetto m.; rampa f. (di missile)
to pad [pæd] v. tr. imbottire
padding ['pædiŋ] s. imbottitura f.
paddle ['pædl] s. pagaia f., remo m.; spatola f.
padlock ['pædlɔk] s. lucchetto m.
paediatrist [,pi:di'ætrist] s. pediatra m. e f.
paganism ['peigənizəm] s. paganesimo m.
page [peidʒ] s. pagina f. • paggio m.; fattorino m.
pagoda [pə'goudə] s. pagoda f.
pail [peil] s. secchio m.
pain [pein] s. dolore m., male m., pena f.; – killer antidolorifico
painful ['peinful] agg. doloroso, penoso
painless ['peinlis] agg. indolore
paint [peint] s. pittura f., vernice f., tinta f.; wet – vernice fresca
to paint [peint] v. tr. e intr. dipingere, tingere, verniciare
painter ['peintə*] s. pittore m.
painting ['peintiŋ] s. dipinto m., quadro m.
pair [peə*] s. coppia f.; paio m.
palace ['pælis] s. reggia f., palazzo m.
paladin ['pælədin] s. paladino m.
palaeography [,pæli'ɔgrəfi] s. paleografia f.
Palaeolithic [,pæliou'liθik] agg. paleolitico
palafitte ['pæləfit] s. palafitta f.
palate ['pælit] s. palato m.
pale [peil] agg. pallido • s. picchetto m., palo m.
to pale [peil] v. intr. impallidire

palette ['pælit] s. tavolozza f.
palliative ['pæliətiv] s. palliativo m.
palm [pa:m] s. palmo m. (anat.); palma f. (bot.); – grove palmizio; date – palma da datteri
palmiped ['pælmiped] s. palmipede m.
to palpate ['pælpeit] v. tr. palpare
palpitation [,pælpi'teiʃən] s. palpitazione f.
paltry ['pɔ:ltri] agg. meschino, ridicolo
to pamper ['pæmpə*] v. tr. vezzeggiare
pamphlet ['pæmflit] s. opuscolo m.
pan [pæn] s. pentola f.; sauce – casseruola; frying – padella; baking – teglia
pancake ['pænkeik] s. frittella f.
panda ['pændə] s. panda m. inv.; – car pantera della polizia
pandemonium [,pændi'mounjəm] s. pandemonio m.
panegyric [,pæni'dʒirik] s. panegirico m.
panel ['pænl] s. pannello m.; quadro m. (cin.); – doctor medico della mutua
Panhellenism [,pæn'helinizəm] s. panellenismo m.
panic ['pænik] s. panico m.
panicle ['pænikl] s. pannocchia f.
panning ['pæniŋ] s. panoramica f. (cin.)
panorama [,pænə'ra:mə] s. paesaggio m.
panoramic [,pænə'ræmik] agg. panoramico
pantagruelian ['pæntəgru'eliən] agg. pantagruelico
pantheism ['pænθi:izəm] s. panteismo m.
panties ['pæntiz] s. pl. mutande f. (da donna)
pantomime ['pæntəmaim] s. pantomima f.; mimica f.
pants [pænts] s. pl. pantaloni m. (USA); mutande f.
papa [pə'pa:] s. papà m. (fam.)
papacy ['peipəsi] s. papato m.
papal ['peipəl] agg. papale, pontificio
paper ['peipə*] s. carta f.; giornale m. • agg. cartaceo; heap of – scartoffia; sheet of – foglio di carta; toilet – carta igienica; writing – carta da lettere; papers documento di identità; morning – giornale del mattino
papiermaché ['pæpjma:ʃei] s. cartapesta f.

papism ['peipizəm] *s.* papismo *m.*

paprika ['pæprikə] *s.* paprica *f.*, pepe *m.* rosso

papyrus [pə'paiərəs] *s.* papiro *m.*

parable ['pærəbl] *s.* parabola *f.* (*lett.*)

parabola [pə'ræbələ] *s.* parabola *f.* (*geom.*)

parachute ['pærəʃu:t] *s.* paracadute *m. inv.*; **parachuting** paracadutismo

parade [pə'reid] *s.* parata *f.*; rivista *f.* (*mil.*)

to parade [pə'reid] *v. tr.* ostentare

paradise ['pærədais] *s.* paradiso *m.*

paradox ['pærədɔks] *s.* paradosso *m.*

paradoxical [,pærə'dɔksikəl] *agg.* paradossale

paragraph ['pærəgra:f] *s.* trafiletto *m.*

parallel ['pærələl] *agg. e s.* parallelo *m.*

parallelepiped [,pærəle'lepiped] *s.* parallelepipedo *m.*

parallelism ['pærə'lelizəm] *s.* parallelismo *m.*

to paralyse ['pærəlaiz] *v. tr.* paralizzare

paralysis [pə'rælisis] *s.* paralisi *f.*

parameter [pə'ræmitə*] *s.* parametro *m.*

paranoia [,pærə'nɔjə] *s.* paranoia *f.*

parapet ['pærəpit] *s.* parapetto *m.*

paraphrase ['pærəfreiz] *s.* parafrasi *f.*

parapsychology [,pærəsai'kɔlədʒi] *s.* parapsicologia *f.*

parasite ['pærəsait] *s.* parassita *m.*

parasol ['pærə'sɔl] *agg. inv.* parasole

parcel ['pa:sl] *s.* pacco *m.*

to parch [pa:tʃ] *v. tr.* essiccare; **parching thirst** arsura

parchment ['pa:tʃmənt] *s.* pergamena *f.*

pardon ['pa:dn] *s.* perdono *m.*; **pardon?** prego? (per invitare a ripetere); **I beg your** – mi scusi

to pardon ['pa:dn] *v. tr. e intr.* perdonare, scusare; graziare

pardonable ['pa:dnəbl] *agg.* perdonabile

parent ['pεərənt] *s.* genitore *m.*

parenthesis [pə'renθisis] *s.* parentesi *f.*

parish ['pæriʃ] *s.* parrocchia *f.* • *agg.* parrocchiale; – **priest** parroco (cattolico)

Parisian [pə'rizjən] *agg.* parigino

parity ['pæriti] *s.* parità *f.*

park [pa:k] *s.* parco *m.*

to park [pa:k] *v. tr. e intr.* parcheggiare

parking ['pa:kiŋ] *s.* parcheggio *m.*, posteggio *m.*; **no** – divieto di sosta; – **meter** parchimetro

parliament ['pa:ləmənt] *s.* parlamento *m.*; **the Houses of** – le Camere (UK)

parliamentary [,pa:lə'mentəri] *agg.* parlamentare

parlour ['pa:lə*] *s.* parlatorio *m.*; **beauty** – istituto di bellezza

parochial [pə'roukjə] *agg.* parrocchiale, provinciale

parochialism [pə'roukjəlizəm] *s.* campanilismo *m.*

parody ['pærədi] *s.* parodia *f.*

paroxysmal [,pærək'sizməl] *agg.* parossistico

parricide ['pærisaid] *s.* parricidio *m.*

parrot ['pærət] *s.* pappagallo *m.*

to parry ['pæri] *v. tr.* scansare

parsimonious [,pa:si'mounjəs] *agg.* parsimonioso

parsley ['pa:sli] *s.* prezzemolo *m.*

parson ['pa:sn] *s.* parroco *m.* (anglicano); pastore *m.* (protestante)

part [pa:t] *s.* parte *f.*

partial ['pa:ʃəl] *agg.* parziale

to participate [pa:'tisipeit] *v. intr.* partecipare

participation [pa:,tisi'peiʃən] *s.* partecipazione *f.*

particle ['pa:tikl] *s.* particella *f.*

particular [pə'tikjulə*] *agg. e s.* particolare *m.*

particularity [pə,tikju'læriti] *s.* particolarità *f.*

parting ['pa:tiŋ] *s.* distacco *m.*, partenza *f.*, separazione *f.*; scriminatura *f.* (nei capelli)

partisan [,pa:ti'zæn] *agg.* partigiano

partition [pa:'tiʃən] *s.* partizione *f.*

partly ['pa:tli] *avv.* parzialmente

partner ['pa:tnə*] *s.* socio *m.*, compagno *m.*

partnership ['pa:tnəʃip] *s.* società *f.*, associazione *f.*

partridge ['pa:tridʒ] *s.* pernice *f.*

party ['pa:ti] *s.* festa *f.*, ricevimento *m.*; partito *m.*; comitiva *f.*; parte *f.* (*leg.*)

pass [pa:s] *s.* tessera *f.*, lasciapassare *m.*; passo *m.* (*geog.*)

to pass [pa:s] *v. tr.* passare, oltrepassare, superare; promuovere • *intr.* passare; trascorrere; – **by** passare oltre, vicino; – **over** scavalcare

passage ['pæsidʒ] *s.* passaggio *m.*; corridoio *m.*; tragitto *m.*; traversata *f.* (*naut.*); brano *m.*

passenger ['pæsindʒə*] *s.* passeggero *m.*, viaggiatore *m.*

passing ['pa:siŋ] *agg.* passeggero, di passaggio

passion ['pæʃən] *s.* passione *f.*

passional ['pæʃənl] *agg.* passionale

passionate ['pæʃənit] *agg.* appassionato

passive ['pæsiv] *agg.* passivo

passport ['pa:s-pɔ:t] *s.* passaporto *m.*

past [pa:st] *agg.* scorso • *s.* passato *m.* • *prep.* dopo, oltre

pasta ['pæstə] *s.* pastasciutta *f.*

paste [peist] s. pasta f.; colla f.; **tooth** – dentifricio

pastille [pæs'ti:l] s. pastiglia f.

pastime ['pa:s-taim] s. passatempo m.

pastor ['pa:stə*] s. pastore m. (relig.)

pastoral ['pa:stərəl] agg. pastorale

pastry ['peistri] s. pasta f. (per dolci); pasticcino m.; – **shop** pasticceria

pasture ['pa:stʃə*] s. pascolo m.

pasty ['peisti] agg. pastoso

patch [pætʃ] s. toppa f.

to patch [pætʃ] v. tr. rattoppare

paté ['pætei] s. paté m. inv.

patent ['peitənt] s. brevetto m.

to patent ['peitənt] v. tr. brevettare

paternal [pə'tə:nl] agg. paterno

paternalism [pə'tə:nəlizəm] s. paternalismo m.

paternity [pə'tə:niti] s. paternità f.

path [pa:θ] s. sentiero m.; traiettoria f.

pathetic [pə'θetik] agg. patetico

pathologic(al) [,pæθə'lɔdʒk(əl)] agg. patologico, morboso

pathology [pə'θɔlədʒi] s. patologia f.

pathos ['peiθɔs] s. pathos m.

patience ['peiʃəns] s. pazienza f.

patient ['peiʃənt] agg. paziente; **to be** – pazientare

patina ['pætinə] s. patina f.

patriarch ['peitria:k] s. patriarca m.

patriarchate ['peitria:kit] s. patriarcato m.

patrician [pə'triʒən] agg. patrizio

patrimonial [,pætri'mounjəl] agg. patrimoniale

patrimony ['pætriməni] s. patrimonio m.

patriot ['pætriət] s. patriota m. e f.

patrol [pə'troul] s. pattuglia f., perlustrazione f., ronda f.; – **boat** vedetta della guardia costiera; – **car** gazzella della polizia

patron ['peitrən] s. mecenate m. e f.; protettore m.

patronage ['pætrənidʒ] s. mecenatismo m.; protezione f.

patronymic [,pætrə'nimik] s. patronimico m.

to patter ['pætə*] v. tr. borbottare • intr. picchiettare

pattern ['pætən] s. modello m., motivo m.; disegno m.

paunch [pɔ:ntʃ] s. pancione m.

pause [pɔ:z] s. pausa f., sosta f., tregua f.

to pause [pɔ:z] v. intr. sostare; fare una pausa

to pave [peiv] v. tr. pavimentare (una strada)

pavement ['peivmənt] s. selciato m.; marciapiede m.

pavilion [pə'viljən] s. padiglione m.

pawn [pɔ:n] s. pegno m., garanzia f.; pedina f. (scacchi e fig.)

to pawn [pɔ:n] v. tr. impegnare (al monte di pietà)

pay [pei] s. paga f., compenso m.

to pay [pei] v. tr. pagare; – **back** restituire; – **off** saldare; dirigere sottovento (naut.); – **up** estinguere

payable ['peiəbl] agg. pagabile

payment ['peimənt] s. pagamento m.; – **in full** saldo; **terms of** – condizioni di pagamento

pea [pi:] s. pisello m.

peace [pi:s] s. pace f.

peaceful ['pi:sful] agg. pacifico, tranquillo

peach [pi:tʃ] s. pesca f. (frutto); pesco m.

peacock [pi:kɔk] s. pavone m.

peak [pi:k] s. vetta f., picco m.; punta f.; visiera f. • agg. di punta

peal [pi:l] s. scampanio m.

peanut ['pi:nʌt] s. arachide f.

pear [pɛə*] s. pera f.; – **tree** pero

pearl [pə:l] s. perla f.

pearly ['pə:li] agg. perlaceo

peasant ['pezənt] s. villico m., contadino m. (stor.)

peat [pi:t] s. torba f.

pebble ['pebl] s. ciottolo m.; **pebbly shore** greto

peculiar [pi'kju:liə*] agg. singolare, particolare, caratteristico

peculiarity [pi,kju:li'æriti] s. peculiarità f.; caratteristica f.

pedagogy ['pedəgɔgi] s. pedagogia f.

pedal ['pedl] s. pedale m.

to pedal ['pedl] v. intr. pedalare

pedant ['pedənt] s. pedante m. e f., pignolo m.

pedantic [pi'dæntik] agg. pedante

pedantry ['pedəntri] s. pedanteria f., pignoleria f.

to peddle ['pedl] v. tr. fare il venditore ambulante; spacciare (droga)

pedestal ['pedistl] s. piedistallo m.

pedestrian [pi'destriən] agg. pedestre; pedonale • s. pedone m.

pedicure ['pedikjuə*] s. pedicure m. e f. inv.

pediment ['pedimənt] s. frontone m.

pee [pi:] s. pipì f. (fam.)

to pee [pi:] v. intr. fare pipì (fam.)

peel [pi:l] s. buccia f., scorza f.

to peel [pi:l] v. tr. pelare, sbucciare

to peep [pi:p] v. intr. occhieggiare

peerless ['piəlis] agg. impareggiabile

peevish ['pi:viʃ] *agg.* permaloso

peg [peg] *s.* piolo *m.*, spinotto *m.*; appiglio *m.* (*fig.*)

pejorative ['pi:dʒərətiv] *agg.* spregiativo

to pelt [pelt] *v. intr.* scrosciare

pen [pen] *s.* penna *f.*; recinto *m.*; **balipoint** – penna a sfera; **fountain** – stilografica

penal ['pi:nl] *agg.* penale

to penalize ['pi:nəlaiz] *v. tr.* penalizzare

penalty [penlti] *s.* pena *f.*; penalità *f.*; punizione *f.* (*sport*)

penance ['penəns] *s.* penitenza *f.*

pencil ['pensl] *s.* matita *f.*; – **harpener** temperamatite

pendant ['pendənt] *s.* ciondolo *m.*

pending ['pendiŋ] *agg.* pendente (*leg.*); indeciso (*fig.*)

pendular ['pendjulə*] *agg.* pendolare

pendulum ['pendjuləm] *s.* pendolo *m.*

to penetrate ['penitreit] *v. tr. e intr.* penetrare

penetration [,peni'treiʃən] *s.* penetrazione *f.*; acume *m.*

penguin ['peŋgwin] *s.* pinguino *m.*

penicillin [,peni'silin] *s.* penicillina *f.*

peninsula [pi'ninsjula] *s.* penisola *f.*

peninsular [pi'ninsjulə*] *agg.* peninsulare

penis ['pi:nis] *s.* pene *m.*

penitence ['penitəns] *s.* penitenza *f.*, pentimento *m.*

penitent ['penitənt] *s.* penitente *m. e f.*

penitentiary [,peni'tenʃəri] *s.* penitenziario *m.*

penknife ['pennaif] *s.* temperino *m.*

pennant ['penənt] *s.* gagliardetto *m.*

penny ['peni] *s.* un centesimo *m.* di sterlina

pensile ['pensail] *agg.* pensile

pension ['penʃən] *s.* pensione *f.*

pensioner ['penʃənə*] *s.* pensionato *m.*

pensive ['pensiv] *agg.* pensieroso

pentagonal [pen'tægənl] *agg.* pentagonale

Pentecost ['pentikɔst] *s.* pentecoste *f.*

penultimate [pi'nʌltimit] *agg.* penultimo

penury ['penjuri] *s.* penuria *f.*, miseria *f.*

people ['pi:pl] *s.* popolo *m.*, gente *f.* • *pl.* (*v. al sing.*) persone *f.*, folla *f. sing.*; **a lot of** – un mucchio di gente

to people ['pi:pl] *v. tr.* popolare

peplos ['peplɔs] *s.* peplo *m.*

pepper ['pepə*] *agg.* pepato • *s.* pepe *m.*; peperone *m.*; – **mill** macinapepe; **Red** – peperoncino; **Green** – peperone

peppermint ['pepəmint] *s.* menta *f.*

peppery ['pepəri] *agg.* pepato

to perceive [pəsi:v] *v. tr.* percepire

percent [pə'sent] *agg.* percentuale

percentage [pə'sentidʒ] *s.* percento *m. inv.*

perceptible [pə'septəbl] *agg.* sensibile

perception [pə'sepʃən] *s.* percezione *f.*

perch [pə:tʃ] *s.* pesce *m.* persico • pertica *f.*, bastone *m.*

peregrination [,perigri'neiʃən] *s.* peregrinazione *f.*

peremptory [pə'remptəri] *agg.* perentorio

perennial [pə'renjəl] *agg.* perenne

perfect [pə'fikt] *agg.* perfetto; **perfectly** perfettamente

to perfect [pə'fekt] *v. tr.* perfezionare; – **oneself** perfezionarsi

perfection [pə'fekʃən] *s.* perfezione *f.*

perfectionist [pə'fekʃənist] *s.* perfezionista *m. e f.*

perfidious [pə:'fidiəs] *agg.* perfido

perforation [,pə:fə'reiʃən] *s.* perforazione *f.*, traforo *m.*

to perform [pə'fɔ:m] *v. tr.* eseguire; recitare, rappresentare (*teatro*) • *intr.* funzionare; – **oneself** esibirsi

performance [pə'fɔ:məns] *s.* esecuzione *f.*; rappresentazione *f.*, spettacolo *m.*

performer [pə'fɔ:mə*] *s.* artista *m. e f.*, attore *m.*, esecutore *f.*, suonatore *m.*

perfume [pə'fju:m] *s.* profumo *m.*; – **shop** profumeria

to perfume [pə'fju:m] *v. tr.* profumare

pergola ['pə:gələ] *s.* pergolato *m.*

perhaps [pə'hæps] *avv.* forse

peril ['peril] *s.* pericolo *m.*

perimeter [pə'rimitə*] *s.* perimetro *m.*

perimetric(al) [,peri'metrik(əl)] *agg.* perimetrale

period ['piəriəd] *s.* periodo *m.*; punto *m.*; termine *m.* (*fig.*)

periodical [,piəri'ɔdikəl] *agg.* periodico; **periodically** periodicamente

periodicity [,piəriə'disiti] *s.* periodicità *f.*

periphrasis [pə'rifrəsis] *s.* perifrasi *f.*

periscope ['periskoup] *s.* periscopio *m.*

to perish ['periʃ] *v. intr.* perire; deperire (di cose)

perishable ['periʃəbl] *agg.* deteriorabile

peritonitis [,peritə'naitis] *s.* peritonite *f.*

permanent ['pə:mənənt] *agg.* permanente, stabile • *s.* permanente *f.*

to permeate [pə:mieit] *v. tr.* permeare

permission [pə'miʃən] *s.* permesso *m.* • *agg.* permissivo

permit ['pə:mit] *s.* permesso *m.*, nullaosta *m. inv.*

to permit [pə'mit] *v. tr.* permettere

permutation [,pə:mju:'teiʃən] *s.* permuta *f.*

pernicious [pə:'niʃəs] *agg.* pernicioso

perpendicular [,pə:pən'dikjulə*] *agg. e s.* perpendicolare *f.*

perpetual [pə'petjuəl] *agg.* perpetuo, perenne

perplexed [pə'plekst] *agg.* perplesso

perplexity [pə'pleksiti] *s.* perplessità *f.*

persecution [,pə:si'kju:ʃən] *s.* persecuzione *f.*

perseverance [,pə:si'viərəns] *s.* perseveranza *f.*

to persevere [,pə:si'viə*] *v. intr.* insistere

to persist [pə'sist] *v. intr.* persistere

person ['pə:sn] *s.* persona *f.* • *pron. indef.* tale; **in –** personalmente

personage [pə'snidʒ] *s.* personaggio *m.*

personal ['pə:snl] *agg.* personale; **personally** personalmente

personality [,pə:sə'næliti] *s.* personalità *f.*; personaggio *m.*

to personalize ['pə:sənəlaiz] *v. tr.* personalizzare

personification [pə:,sɔnifi'keiʃən] *s.* personificazione *f.*

perspective [pə'spektiv] *s.* prospettiva *f.* • *agg.* prospettico

perspicacity [,pə:spi'kæsiti] *s.* perspicacia *f.*, sagacia *f.*

perspiration [,pə:spə'reiʃən] *s.* sudore *m.*, traspirazione *f.*

to perspire [pəs'paiə*] *v. intr.* sudare

to persuade [pə'sweid] *v. tr.* persuadere; **– oneself** persuadersi

persuasion [pə'sweiʒən] *s.* persuasione *f.*, convincimento *m.*

persuasive [pə'sweiziv] *agg.* persuasivo

pertinent ['pə:tinənt] *agg.* pertinente, relativo

perturbation [,pə:tə:'beiʃən] *s.* perturbazione *f.*

to pervade [pə'veid] *v. tr.* pervadere

perverse [pə'və:s] *agg.* perverso, iniquo

perversion [pə'və:ʃən] *s.* perversione *f.*

pervert ['pə:və:t] *s.* pervertito *m.*

pessimism ['pesimizəm] *s.* pessimismo *m.*

pessimist ['pesimist] *s.* pessimista *m. e f.*

pest [pest] *s.* insetto *m.* nocivo; persona *f.* fastidiosa; peste *f.*

to pester ['pestə*] *v. tr.* seccare, importunare

pestiferous [pes'tifərəs] *agg.* pestifero

pestilence ['pestiləns] *s.* pestilenza *f.*

pet [pet] *s.* animale *m.* domestico; beniamino *m.*

petal ['petl] *s.* petalo *m.*

petard [pə'ta:d] *s.* petardo *m.*

petition [pi'tiʃən] *s.* ricorso *m. (leg.)*

to petrify ['petrifai] *v. tr.* sbalordire • *intr.* impietrire

petrol ['petrəl] *s.* benzina *f.*

petroleum [pi'trouljəm] *s.* petrolio *m.*

petticoat ['petikout] *s.* sottoveste *f.*

petty ['peti] *agg.* meschino

pew [pju:] *s.* panca *f.* (di una chiesa)

pewter ['pju:tə*] *s.* peltro *m.*

to phagocytize [fə'gousitaiz] *v. tr.* fagocitare

phalanstery ['fælənstəri] *s.* falansterio *m.*

phalanx ['fælæŋks] *s.* falange *f.*

phantom ['fæntəm] *s.* fantasma *m.*

pharaonic [,feə'rɔnik] *agg.* faraonico

pharmacy ['fa:məsi] *s.* farmacia *f.*

pharyngitis [,færin'dʒaitis] *s.* faringite *f.*

phase [feiz] *s.* fase *f.*; **– displacement** sfasamento *(elettr.)*

pheasant ['feznt] *s.* fagiano *m.*

phenomenal [fi'nɔminl] *agg.* fenomenale

phenomenon [fi'nɔminən] *s.* fenomeno *m.*

philanthropist [fi'lænθrəpist] *s.* filantropo *m.*

philately [fi'lætəli] *s.* filatelia *f.*

philharmonic [,fila:'mɔnik] *agg. e s.* filarmonica *f.*

philology [fi'lɔlədʒi] *s.* filologia *f.*

philosopher [fi'lɔsəfə*] *s.* filosofo *m.*

philosophic [,filə'sɔfik] *agg.* filosofico

philosophy [fi'lɔsəfi] *s.* filosofia *f.*

phleboclysis [,flebou'klaisis] *s.* flebo *f.*

phlegm [flem] *s.* flemma *f.*; muco *m.*, catarro *m. (med.)*

phlegmatic [fleg'mætik] *agg.* flemmatico

phlogosis [flə'gousis] *s.* flogosi *f.*

phobia ['foubjə] *s.* fobia *f.*

Phoenician [fi'niʃən] *agg.* fenicio

phone [foun] *s.* telefono *m. (fam.)*; **over the –** al telefono; **– book** rubrica telefonica

to phone [foun] *v. tr. e intr.* telefonare

phonetic [fə'netik] *agg.* fonetico

phosphorescent [,fɔsfə'resənt] *agg.* fosforescente

photo ['foutou] *s.* fotografia *f.*

photocopy ['foutou'kɔpi] *s.* fotocopia *f.*

photogenic [,foutou'dʒenik] *agg.* fotogenico

photograph ['foutəgra:f] *s.* fotografia *f.*

to photograph ['foutəgra:f] *v. tr.* fotografare

photographer [fə'tɔgrəfə*] *s.* fotografo *m.*

photographic [,foutə'græfik] *agg.* fotografico

phrase [freiz] *s.* frase *f. (gramm.)*

phraseologic [,freiziə'lɔdʒikəl] *agg.* fraseologico

physical ['fizikəl] *agg.* fisico

physician [fi'ziʃən] s. dottore m., medico m.

physics ['fiziks] s. fisica f.

physiognomist [ˌfizi'ɔnəmist] s. fisionomista m. e f.

physiological [ˌfiziə'lɔdʒikəl] agg. fisiologico

physiotherapist [ˌfiziou'θerəpist] s. fisioterapista m. e f.

physiotherapy [ˌfiziou'θerəpi] s. fisioterapia f.

pianist ['piænist] s. pianista m. e f.

piano ['pjænou] s. pianoforte m.

pick [pik] s. piccone m.

to pick [pik] v. tr. cogliere; scegliere; – **up** raccogliere, estrarre (a caso); – **out** scegliere

pickle ['pikl] s. salamoia f.; **pickles** cetrioli sottaceto

pickpocket ['pik,pokit] s. borseggiatore m.

picnic ['piknik] s. scampagnata f.

pictorial [pik'tɔ:riəl] agg. pittorico

picture ['piktʃə*] s. figura f., illustrazione f., immagine f., fotogramma m., dipinto m., quadro m.; ritratto m.

picturesque [ˌpiktʃə'resk] agg. pittoresco

pie [pai] s. timballo m., torta f.; **apple** – torta di mele

piece [pi:s] s. pezzo m.; moneta f.; – **of news** notizia

pier [piə*] s. banchina f., molo m.; pilone m.

to pierce [pias] v. tr. e intr. forare; trapassare

piercing ['piasiŋ] s. foratura f. • agg. penetrante, pungente

pig [pig] s. maiale m., porco m.; **Guinea** – porcellino d'India, cavia

pigeon ['pidʒin] s. piccione m.; **carrier** – piccione viaggiatore

pigmentation [ˌpigmən'teiʃən] s. pigmentazione f.

pigsty ['pigstai] s. porcile m.

pile [pail] s. pila f., mucchio m., sacco m. • pl. emorroidi f.

pilgrim ['pilgrim] s. pellegrino m.

pilgrimage ['pilgrimidʒ] s. pellegrinaggio m.

pill [pil] s. pillola f.

pillage ['pilidʒ] s. saccheggio m.

to pillage ['pilidʒ] v. tr. e intr. saccheggiare

pillager ['pilidʒə*] s. saccheggiatore m.

pillar ['pilə*] s. pilastro m., colonna f.

pillow ['pilou] s. guanciale m.; – **case** federa

pilot ['pailət] s. pilota m. e f.; – **book** portolano

to pilot ['pailət] v. tr. pilotare

pin [pin] s. spillo m.; perno m.

pinafore ['pinəfɔ*] s. grembiule m. (da bambino)

pincers ['pinsəz] s. pl. pinze f., tenaglie f.

pinch [pintʃ] s. pizzicotto m.

to pinch [pintʃ] v. tr. pizzicare

pine [pain] s. pino m.; – **cone** pigna f.; – **seed** pinolo; – **wood** pineta

pineapple ['pain,æpl] s. ananas m. inv.

pink [piŋk] agg. rosa

pinnacle ['pinəkl] s. pinnacolo m.

pint [paint] s. pinta f.

pioneer [ˌpaiə'niə*] s. pioniere m.

pip [pip] s. seme m. (di frutti)

pipe [paip] s. pipa f.; canna f. (dell'organo); tubo m.; – **exhaust** – tubo di scappamento

piper ['paipə*] s. zampognaro m.

piping ['paipiŋ] s. condotta f., tubazione f.

pique [pi:k] s. irritazione f.

piracy ['paiərəsi] s. pirateria f.

pirate ['paiərit] s. pirata m.

pisciculture ['pisikʌltʃə*] s. piscicoltura f.

pistachio [pis'ta:ʃiou] s. pistacchio m.

pistol ['pistl] s. pistola f.

piston ['pistən] s. pistone m.

pit [pit] s. fossa f.; nocciolo m.

pitch [pitʃ] s. lancio m.; inclinazione f., beccheggio m. (naut.); campo m. da gioco

pitcher ['pitʃə*] s. brocca f. • lanciatore m. (di baseball)

pitiless ['pitilis] agg. impietoso

pity ['piti] s. pietà f., compassione f., peccato m.; **what a** – ! che peccato!

to pity ['piti] v. tr. compiangere

pivot ['pivət] s. cardine m., perno m.

placard ['plækəd] s. manifesto m.; cartello m.

place [pleis] s. località f., luogo m., posto m.; – **card** segnaposto; **to take** – accadere; **birth** – luogo di nascita

to place [pleis] v. tr. collocare, disporre, mettere; – **before** preporre; – **oneself** mettersi, porsi

placement ['pleismənt] s. piazzamento m., collocamento m.

placid ['plæsid] agg. placido

plagiarism ['pleidʒiərizəm] s. plagio m.

to plagiarize ['pleidʒiəraiz] v. tr. plagiare

plague [pleig] s. peste f.; flagello m.

plain [plein] agg. evidente; semplice; ordinario • s. pianura f.; mappa f.; progetto m.

plait [plæt] s. treccia f.

plan [plæn] s. piano m., progetto m.; pianta f.

to plan [plæn] v. tr. impostare, progettare, pianificare

plane [plein] s. aereo m.; pialla f.; piano m. (geom.); planata f. • platano m.

to plane [plein] v. intr. planare

planet ['plænit] *s.* pianeta *m.*, astro *m.*
planimetry [plæ'nimitri] *s.* planimetria *f.*
planisphere ['plænisfiə*] *s.* planisfero *m.*
plank [plæŋk] *s.* asse *f.*, tavola *f.*
planner ['plænə*] *s.* progettista *m.* e *f.*
planning ['plæniŋ] *s.* progettazione *f.*
plant [pla:nt] *s.* impianto *m.*, stabilimento *m.*; pianta *f.*
to plant [pla:nt] *v. tr.* piantare
plantation [plæn'teiʃən] *s.* piantagione *f.*
plaster ['pla:stə*] *s.* cerotto *m.*; gesso *m.*, intonaco *m.*
to plaster ['pla:stə*] *v. tr.* ingessare
plastic ['plæstik] *agg.* plastico • *s.* plastica *f.*
plasticity [plæs'stisiti] *s.* plasticità *f.*
to plasticize ['plætisaiz] *v. tr.* plastificare
plate [pleit] *s.* lamiera *f.*, lastra *f.*; piatto *m.*; targa *f.*; tavola *f.*; **number** - targa automobilistica
plateau ['plætou] *s.* altopiano *m.*
platform ['plætfɔːm] *s.* piattaforma *f.*, palco *m.*; marciapiede *m.* (*ferr.*); **roof** - pensilina
platinum ['plætinəm] *s.* platino *m.*
Platonic [plə'tɔnik] *agg.* platonico
platonically [plə'tɔnikali] *avv.* platonicamente
plausible ['plɔːzəbl] *agg.* plausibile
play [plei] *s.* commedia *f.*, dramma *m.*, spettacolo *m.*; gioco *m.*; **- off** spareggio
to play [plei] *v. tr.* e *intr.* giocare; suonare; impersonare; recitare
playbill ['pleibil] *s.* locandina *f.*
player ['pleiə*] *s.* giocatore *m.*, suonatore *m.*
playful ['pleiful] *agg.* giocoso
playwright ['pleirait] *s.* commediografo *m.*; drammaturgo *m.*
plea [pli:] *s.* scusa *f.*; supplica *f.*; lite *f.*; causa *f.*
pleasant ['pleznt] *agg.* piacevole, ameno; gradito
please [pli:z] *inter.* per favore!; prego!
to please [pli:z] *v. tr.* e *intr.* piacere, essere gradito a; soddisfare
pleased [pli:zd] *agg.* contento, compiaciuto
pleasing ['pli:ziŋ] *agg.* piacevole
pleasure ['pleʒə*] *s.* piacere *m.*; godimento *m.*; **to take - in** compiacersi, divertirsi
plebs [plebz] *s.* plebe *f.* (*stor.*)
plectrum ['plektrəm] *s.* plettro *m.*
pledge [pledʒ] *s.* pegno *m.*
to pledge [pledʒ] *v. tr.* impegnare; **- oneself** promettersi
plentiful ['plentiful] *agg.* abbondante
plenty ['plenti] *s.* abbondanza *f.*
pleonastic ['pliə'næstik] *agg.* pleonastico

pleurisy ['pluərisi] *s.* pleurite *f.*
pliable ['plaiəbl] *agg.* duttile, flessibile
pliant ['plaiənt] *agg.* pieghevole
pliers ['plaiəz] *s. pl.* pinze *f.*
plinth [plinθ] *s.* plinto *m.*, base *f.*, zoccolo *m.* (di colonna)
plot [plɔt] *s.* intreccio *m.*, trama *f.*; macchinazione *f.*, complotto *m.*
to plot [plɔt] *v. tr.* disegnare, tracciare • *intr.* complottare
plough [plau] *s.* aratro *m.*
to plough [plau] *v. tr.* arare
plug [plʌg] *s.* spina *f.* (*elettr.*); tappo *m.* (idraulico)
to plug [plʌg] *v. tr.* turare; **- in** innestare (la spina)
plum [plʌm] *s.* prugna *f.*, susina *f.*
plumber ['plʌmə*] *s.* idraulico *m.*
plumbing ['plʌmiŋ] *s.* conduttura *f.*
plump [plʌmp] *agg.* carnoso, grasso
to plump [plʌmp] *v. intr.* piombare, cadere
plunder ['plʌndə*] *s.* saccheggio *m.*
to plunder ['plʌndə*] *v. tr.* e *intr.* saccheggiare
plunge [plʌndʒ] *s.* immersione *f.*; tuffo *m.*
to plunge [plʌndʒ] *v. tr.* e *intr.* immergere; tuffare, tuffarsi; **- oneself** immergersi, tuffarsi; **- into** precipitarsi
plural ['pluərəl] *agg.* plurale
pluralism ['pluərəlizəm] *s.* pluralismo *m.*
plurality [pluə'ræliti] *s.* pluralità *f.*
pluriannual ['pluəri'ænjuəl] *agg.* pluriennale
plus [plʌs] *prep.* più
plush [plʌʃ] *s.* felpa *f.*
plutocracy [plu:'tɔkrəsi] *s.* plutocrazia *f.*
pluvial ['plu:vjəl] *agg.* pluviale
to ply [plai] *v. tr.* maneggiare, adoperare
pneumonia [nju:(:)'mounjə] *s.* polmonite *f.*
pocket ['pɔkit] *s.* tascabile • *s.* tasca *f.*
to pocket ['pɔkit] *v. tr.* intascare
pod [pɔd] *s.* baccello *m.*, buccia *f.* (di legumi)
podium ['poudiəm] *s.* podio *m.*
poem ['pouim] *s.* poema *m.*; poesia *f.*
poet ['pouit] *s.* poeta *m.*
poetic [pou'etik] *agg.* poetico
poetics [pou'etiks] *s. pl.* (*v. al sing.*) poetica *f. sing.*
poetry ['pouitri] *s.* poesia *f.*
point [point] *s.* punta *f.*; punto *m.*; **- of view** punto di vista
to point [point] *v. tr.* puntare; **- to/at** indicare; **- out** avvertire, segnalare
pointillism ['pwæntilizəm] *s.* divisionismo *m.*
poison ['pɔizn] *s.* veleno *m.*

to poison ['pɔizn] v. tr. avvelenare

poisoning ['pɔizniŋ] s. avvelenamento m.

poisonous ['pɔiznəs] agg. velenoso

polar ['poulə*] agg. polare

to polarize ['poularaiz] v. tr. polarizzare

pole [poul] agg. polare • s. asta f., palo m.; polo m.

Pole [poul] s. polacco m.

polecat ['poulkæt] s. puzzola f.

polemic [pə'lemik] agg. polemico • s. polemica f.

police [pə'li:s] agg. poliziesco • s. polizia f.; – **commissioner** questore; – **station** stazione di polizia

policeman [pə'li:smən] s. poliziotto m.

policy ['pɔlisi] s. polizza f.; politica f. (indirizzo politico)

Polish ['pouliʃ] s. polacco m. (lingua)

polish ['pɔliʃ] s. cera f., lucido m.

to polish ['pɔliʃ] v. tr. levigare, lucidare

polished ['pɔliʃt] agg. lucido

polite [pə'lait] agg. cortese, garbato

politeness [pə'laitnis] s. cortesia f., educazione f.

political [pə'litikəl] agg. politico

politics ['pɔlitiks] s. pl. (v. al sing.) politica f. sing.; **home** – politica interna; **foreign** – politica estera

poll [poul] s. sondaggio m.; elezione f.

to poll [poul] v. tr. sondare (l'opinione); scrutinare

pollen ['pɔlin] s. polline m.

pollination [,pɔli'neiʃən] s. impollinazione f.

to pollute [pə'lu:t] v. tr. inquinare

pollution [pə'lu:ʃən] s. inquinamento m.

polychromatic [,pɔlikrou'mætik] agg. policromatico

polyclinic [,pɔli'klinik] s. policlinico m.

polygamist [pɔ'ligəmist] s. poligamo m.

polygamous [pɔ'ligəməs] agg. poligamo

polyglot ['pɔliglɔt] agg. e s. poliglotta m. e. f.

polygon ['pɔligən] s. poligono m.

polygonal [pɔ'ligənl] agg. poligonale

polyhedric [,pɔli'hedrik] agg. poliedrico

polymorphous [,pɔli'mɔːfəs] agg. polimorfo

polyp ['pɔlip] s. polipo m.

polyphonic [,pɔli'fɔnik] agg. polifonico

polyptych ['pɔliptik] s. polittico m.

polytechnic [,pɔli'teknik] agg. politecnico

polytheism ['pɔliθi:izəm] s. politeismo m.

polyvalent ['pɔli'veilənt] agg. polivalente

pomade [pə'ma:d] s. pomata f.

pomegranate ['pɔm,grænit] s. melagrana f.

pomp [pɔmp] s. sfarzo m.

pompous ['pɔmpəs] agg. pomposo

pond [pɔnd] s. stagno m., laghetto m.

to ponder ['pɔndə*] v. tr. e intr. meditare, ponderare

pontiff ['pɔntif] s. pontefice m.

pontifical [pɔn'tifikəl] agg. pontificio

pontificate [pɔn'tifikit] s. pontificato m.

poodle ['pu:dl] s. cane m. barbone

pool [pu:l] s. stagno m., laghetto m., pozza f.; posta f., piatto m. (giochi di carte); biliardo m. (USA); consorzio m.; **swimming** – piscina; **pools** totocalcio

poor [puə*] agg. povero, miserabile, scadente; – **figure** figuraccia; **the** – , – **people** i poveri

pop [pɔp] s. schiocco m., botto m.

pope [poup] s. papa m., pontefice m.

poplar ['pɔplə*] s. pioppo m.

poppy ['pɔpi] s. papavero m.

populace ['pɔpjuləs] s. plebe f.

popular ['pɔpjulə*] agg. divulgativo, popolare

popularity [,pɔpju'læriti] s. popolarità f.

to populate ['pɔpjuleit] v. tr. popolare

population [,pɔpju'leiʃən] s. popolazione f.

populism ['pɔpjulizəm] s. populismo m.

populous ['pɔpjuləs] agg. popoloso

porcelain ['pɔːslin] s. porcellana f.

pore [pɔː*] s. poro m.

pork [pɔːk] s. maiale m., porco m.

pornographic [,pɔː'nɔgrafik] agg. pornografico

porphyry [pɔːfiri] s. porfido m.

porpoise ['pɔːpəs] s. focena f., delfino m.

porridge ['pɔridʒ] s. zuppa f. d'avena

port [pɔːt] agg. portuale; sinistro (naut.) • s. porto m.; – **of call** scalo

portable ['pɔːtəbl] agg. portabile

portal ['pɔːtl] s. portale m.

portent ['pɔːtent] s. portento m.

portentous [pɔː'tentəs] agg. prodigioso

porter ['pɔːtə*] s. custode m. e f., portinaio m; facchino m.; – **'s lodge** portineria

portfolio [pɔːt'fouljou] s. cartella f.; portafoglio m. (in politica ed economia)

portico ['pɔːtikou] s. loggiato m., portico m.

portion ['pɔːʃən] s. porzione f., quota f.

portrait ['pɔːtrit] s. ritratto m.

to portray [pɔː'trei] v. tr. ritrarre, descrivere

to pose [pouz] v. intr. posare

position [pə'ziʃən] s. posizione f.

to position [pə'ziʃən] v. tr. posizionare

positive ['pɔzətiv] agg. positivo; preciso

positivism ['pɔzitivizəm] s. positivismo m.

posology [pou'sɔlədʒi] s. posologia f.

to possess [pə'zes] *v. tr.* possedere, avere

possession [pə'zeʃən] *s.* possesso *m.*

possessive [pə'zesiv] *agg.* possessivo

possibility [,pɔsə'biliti] *s.* possibilità *f.*

possible ['pɔsəbl] *agg.* eventuale; possibile

possibly ['pɔsibli] *avv.* forse; in alcun modo

post [poust] *agg.* postale • *s.* posto *m.* (di lavoro); palo *m.*; posta *f.*; – **office** ufficio postale

to post [poust] *v. tr.* impostare; – **up** affiggere

postage ['poustidʒ] *s.* affrancatura *f.*

postal ['poustəl] *agg.* postale

postcard ['pouskɑ:d] *s.* cartolina *f.*

to postdate ['poust'deit] *v. tr.* postdatare

poster ['poustə*] *s.* cartellone *m.*, manifesto *m.*

posterior [pɔs'tiəriə*] *agg.* posteriore

posterity [pɔs'teriti] *s.* posterità *f.*

posthumous ['pɔstjuməs] *agg.* postumo

postman ['poustmən] *s.* postino *m.*

postmark ['poustmɑ:k] *s.* timbro *m.* (postale)

post-modern ['poust'mɔdən] *agg.* postmoderno

to postpone [poust'poun] *v. tr.* posporre, posticipare

postponement [poust'pounmənt] *s.* rinvio *m.*

postulate ['pɔstjulilt] *s.* postulato *m.*

posture ['pɔstʃə*] *s.* posizione *f.*, atteggiamento *m.*

post-war ['poust'wɔ:*] *agg.* postbellico

pot [pɔt] *s.* pentola *f.*, vaso *m.*, barattolo *m.*

potable ['poutəbl] *agg.* bevibile

potato [pə'teitou] *s.* patata *f.*; – **flour** fecola *f.*

potency ['poutənsi] *s.* efficacia *f.*

potent ['poutənt] *agg.* potente

potential [pə'tenʃəl] *agg.* potenziale

to potentiate [pə'tenʃieit] *v. tr.* potenziare

pottery ['pɔtəri] *s.* ceramica *f.*

poultry ['poultri] *s.* pollame *m.*

pound [paund] *s.* libbra *f.*; sterlina *f.*

to pour [pɔ:*] *v. tr.* versare; – **off** travasare • *intr.* diluviare, piovere

pout [paut] *s.* broncio *m.*

poverty ['pɔvəti] *s.* miseria *f.*, povertà *f.*

powder ['paudə*] *s.* polvere *f.*; cipria *f.*

power ['pauə*] *s.* energia *f.*, potenza *f.*; potere *m.*, facoltà *f.*; – **boat** barca a motore; – **station** centrale elettrica; – **steering** servosterzo

powerful ['pauəful] *agg.* poderoso, potente

powerless ['pauəlis] *agg.* impotente

practicable ['præktikəbl] *agg.* praticabile

practical ['præktikəl] *agg.* pratico

practicality [,prækti'kæliti] *s.* praticità *f.*

practically ['præktikəli] *avv.* praticamente

practice ['præktis] *s.* esercizio *m.* (di una professione); prassi *f.*; **to get** – impratichirsi

to practise ['præktis] *v. tr.* esercitare, praticare • *intr.* esercitarsi, impraticticirsi

practising ['præktisiŋ] *agg.* praticante

praetor [pri:tə*] *s.* pretore *m.* (stor.)

pragmatic [præg'mætik] *agg.* pragmatico

prairie ['preəri] *s.* prateria *f.*

praise [preiz] *s.* elogio *m.*, lode *f.*

to praise [preiz] *v. tr.* lodare

praiseworthy ['preiz,wə:ði] *agg.* encomiabile

pram [præm] *s.* carrozzina *f.*; battellino *m.* (naut.)

prank [præŋk] *s.* scappatella *f.*

praxis ['præksis] *s.* prassi *f.*

prawn [prɔ:n] *s.* gamberetto *m.*

to pray [prei] *v. tr. e intr.* pregare

prayer [preə*] *s.* preghiera *f.*

preach [pri:tʃ] *s.* predica *f.*

to preach [pri:tʃ] *v. tr. e intr.* predicare

preacher [pri:tʃə*] *s.* predicatore *m.*

preaching [pri:tʃiŋ] *s.* predicazione *f.*

preamble [pri:'æmbl] *s.* preambolo *m.*

precarious [pri'keəriəs] *agg.* precario

precariousness [pri'keəriəsnis] *s.* precarietà *f.*

precaution [pri'kɔ:ʃən] *s.* precauzione *f.*

to precede [pri(:)'si:d] *v. tr. e intr.* precedere; prevenire

precedence [pri(:)'si:dəns] *s.* precedenza *f.*, priorità *f.*

preceding [pri(:)'si:diŋ] *agg.* precedente

precept ['pri:sept] *s.* precetto *m.*

preciosity [,preʃi'ɔsiti] *s.* preziosismo *m.*

precious ['preʃəs] *agg.* prezioso

to precipitate [pri'sipiteit] *v. tr. e intr.* precipitare

precipitation [pri,sipi'teiʃən] *s.* precipitazione *f.*; fretta *f.*

precipitous [pri'sipitəs] *agg.* precipitoso

precise [pri'sais] *agg.* preciso

precisely [pri'saisli] *avv.* precisamente

precision [pri'siʒən] *s.* precisione *f.*

precocious [pri'kouʃəs] *agg.* precoce

preconception ['pri:kən'sepʃən] *s.* preconcetto *m.*

precursor [pri:'kə:sə*] *s.* precursore *m.*

predatory ['predətəri] *agg.* predatorio

to predecease ['pri:di'si:s] *v. tr.* premorire

to predestinate [pri:'destineit] *v. tr.* predestinare

predestination [pri:,desti'neiʃən] *s.* predestinazione *f.*

to predetermine ['pri:di'tə:min] v. tr. predeterminare

predicament [pri'dikəmənt] s. frangente m.; situazione f. difficile

to predict [pri'dikt] v. tr. predire

prediction [pri'dikʃən] s. profezia f.

predictable [pri'diktəbl] agg. prevedibile

to predispose ['pri:dis'pouz] v. tr. predisporre

predominance [pri'dɔminəns] s. predominio m., prevalenza f.

predominant [pri'dɔminənt] agg. predominante, prevalente

to predominate [pri'dɔmineit] v. intr. predominare

pre-eminent [pri'eminənt] agg. preminente

to pre-exist ['pri:ig'zist] v. intr. preesistere

pre-existent ['pri:ig'zistənt] agg. preesistente

preface ['prefis] s. prefazione f.

prefecture [pri'fektjuə*] s. prefettura f.

to prefer [pri'fə:*] v. tr. prediligere, preferire

preferable ['prefərəbl] agg. preferibile; **preferably** preferibilmente

preference ['prefərəns] s. preferenza f.

to prefigure [pri'figə*] v. tr. prefigurare

prefix ['pri:fiks] s. prefisso m.

to prefix [pri:'fiks] v. tr. premettere

pregnancy ['pregnənsi] s. gestazione f., gravidanza f.

pregnant ['pregnənt] agg. pregnante; incinta

prehistoric ['pri:his'tɔrik] agg. preistorico

prehistory ['pri:'histəri] s. preistoria f.

prejudice ['predʒudis] s. pregiudizio m.

prejudiced ['predʒudist] agg. prevenuto

prelate ['prelit] s. prelato m.

preliminary [pri'liminəri] agg. preliminare

prelude ['prelju:d] s. preludio m.

premarital [pri:'mærital] agg. prematrimoniale

premature [,premə'tjuə*] agg. prematuro

premeditation [pri(:),medi'teiʃən] s. premeditazione f.

premise ['premis] s. premessa f. • pl. fabbricati m.; sede f. sing.

to premise [pri'maiz] v. tr. e intr. premettere

premonitory [pri'mɔnitəri] agg. premonitore

preparation [,prepə'reiʃən] s. preparazione f.; preparativi m. pl.

to prepare [pri'pɛə*] v. tr. preparare; **- oneself** prepararsi

preponderant [,pri'pɔndərənt] agg. preponderante

Pre-Raphaelite ['pri:'ræfiəlait] agg. preraffaellita

prerogative [pri'rɔgətiv] s. prerogativa f.

presage ['presidʒ] s. presagio m.

to presage ['presidʒ] v. intr. presagire

Presbyterian [,prezbi'tiəriən] agg. presbiteriano

presbytery ['prezbitəri] s. presbiterio m.

to prescind [pri'sind] v. intr. prescindere

to prescribe [pris'kraib] v. tr. prescrivere

prescription [pris'kripʃən] s. prescrizione f.; ricetta f. (med.)

presence ['prezns] s. presenza f., partecipazione f.

present ['preznt] agg. presente, attuale • s. dono m., regalo m.; **the -** il presente; **at -** momentaneamente; **to be -** presenziare, assistere

to present [pri'zent] v. tr. presentare; regalare

presentable [pri'zentəbl] agg. presentabile

presentation [,prezent'eiʃən] s. presentazione f.; rappresentazione f.

presentiment [pri'zentimənt] s. presentimento m.

preservation [,prezə(:)'veiʃən] s. preservazione f., mantenimento m.

preservative [pri'zə:vətiv] s. conservante m.

preserve [pri'zə:v] s. conserva f.; riserva f.

to preserve [pri'zə:v] v. tr. conservare, custodire

to preside [pri'zaid] v. tr. presiedere

presidency ['prezidənsi] s. presidenza f.

president ['prezidənt] s. presidente m.

presidential [,prezi'denʃal] agg. presidenziale

press [pres] s. stretta f., ressa f.; stampa f.

to press [pres] v. tr. comprimere, premere; incalzare

pressing ['presiŋ] agg. prepotente, urgente, incalzante

pressure ['preʃə*] s. pressione f. (anche fig.); **- cooker** pentola a pressione; **blood -** pressione sanguigna

prestige [pres'ti:ʒ] s. autorità f., prestigio m.

prestigious [pres'tidʒəs] agg. prestigioso

to presume [pri'zju:m] v. tr. presumere

presumptuous [pri'zʌmptjuəs] agg. presuntuoso

to presuppose [,pri:sə'pouz] v. tr. presupporre

presupposition [,pri:sʌpə'ziʃən] s. presupposto m.

pretence [pri'tens] s. finzione f., simulazione f.; pretesto m.

to pretend [pri'tend] v. tr. fingere; pretendere • intr. pretendere

pretender [pri'tendə*] s. pretendente m. e f.

pretension [pri'tenʃən] s. pretesa f.

pretext ['pri:tekst] s. pretesto m.

pretty ['priti] agg. carino, grazioso, gradevole

to prevail [pri'veil] v. intr. prevalere

prevailing [pri'veiliŋ] agg. dominante

prevalence ['prevələns] s. prevalenza f.

to prevent [pri'vent] v. tr. impedire, vietare; prevenire

prevention [pri'venʃən] s. prevenzione f.

preview ['pri:vju:] s. anteprima f.

previous ['pri:vjəs] agg. anteriore, precedente; antecedente

prevision [pri(:)'viʒən] s. previsione f.

pre-war ['pri:'wɔ:'] agg. prebellico

prey [prei] s. preda f.

price [prais] s. prezzo m.; valore m.; – list tariffario

priceless ['praislis] agg. inestimabile, d'incalcolabile valore

prick [prik] s. spina f.; stimolo m.

to prick [prik] v. tr. pungere

pride [praid] s. orgoglio m., superbia f.

priest [pri:st] s. prete m., sacerdote m.

priesthood ['pri:sthud] s. sacerdozio m.

primary ['praiməri] agg. primario, originario

prime [praim] agg. primario, primo (mat.)

primitive ['primitiv] agg. primitivo

primordial [prai'mɔ:djəl] agg. primordiale

primrose ['primrouz] s. primula f.

prince [prins] s. principe m.; – Charming il principe azzurro

princedom ['prinsdəm] s. principato m.

princess [prin'ses] s. principessa f.

principal ['prinsəpəl] agg. principale; **principally** principalmente

principality [,prinsi'pæliti] s. principato m.

principate ['prinsipit] s. principato m. (stor.)

principle ['prinsipl] s. principio m., regola f., norma f.

print [print] s. impronta f.; stampa f.; **out of** – esaurito (libro); **off-print** estratto

to print [print] v. tr. stampare

printer ['printə'] s. stampante f.; tipografo m.

printing ['printiŋ] s. stampa f.; tiratura f.

printout ['print,aut] s. tabulato m.

prior ['praiə'] s. priore m. • agg. precedente

priority [prai'ɔriti] s. precedenza f., priorità f.

prism ['prizm] s. prisma m.

prison ['prizn] agg. carcerario • s. prigione f.

prisoner ['priznə'] s. prigioniero m.

private ['praivit] agg. privato, personale; **in** – privatamente

privilege ['prividʒ] s. privilegio m.

to privilege ['prividʒ] v. tr. privilegiare

prize [praiz] s. premio m.; – **giving** premiazione

probability [,probə'biliti] s. probabilità f.

probable ['probəbl] agg. probabile; **probably** probabilmente

problem ['probləm] s. problema m. • agg. problematico

problematic [,probli'mætik] agg. problematico, incerto

procedure [prə'si:dʒə'] s. procedura f., trafila f., procedimento m.

to proceed [prə'si:d] v. intr. procedere; provenire; **proceedings** procedimento (leg.); atti (di un convegno)

proceeds ['prousi:dz] s. pl. ricavo m. sing.; incasso m. sing.

process ['prouses] s. procedimento m.; processo m. (tecn.)

to process ['prouses] v. tr. elaborare (dei dati); **processing** metodo di elaborazione

procession [prə'seʃən] s. corteo m., processione f.

to proclaim [prə'kleim] v. tr. proclamare

proclamation [,proklə'meiʃən] s. proclamazione f.

to procreate ['proukrieit] v. tr. generare, procreare

to procure [prə'kjuə'] v. tr. procacciare, procurare

prodigality [,prodi'gæliti] s. prodigalità f., generosità f.

prodigious [prə'didʒəs] agg. prodigioso

prodigy ['prodidʒi] s. prodigio m., portento m.

produce ['prodju:s] s. prodotto m., produzione f.; risultato m.

to produce [prə'dju:s] v. tr. produrre, fabbricare, generare; presentare

producer [prə'dju:sə'] s. produttore m., impresario m.

product ['prodʌkt] s. prodotto m.

production [prə'dʌkʃən] s. produzione f.; messa f. in scena

productivity [,prodʌk'tiviti] s. produttività f., rendimento m.

profane [prə'fein] agg. profano

profession [prə'feʃən] s. professione f.

professional [prə'feʃənl] agg. professionale • s. professionista m. e f.

professionalism [prə'feʃnəlizəm] s. professionismo m.

professor [prə'fesə'] s. cattedratico m., professore m.

profile ['proufail] s. profilo m.

profit ['prɔfit] s. profitto m., beneficio m., lucro m.

to profit ['prɔfit] v. tr. giovare a • intr. beneficiare, approfittare

profitability [,prɔfitə'biliti] s. redditività f., profitto m.

profitable ['prɔfitəbl] agg. proficuo, redditizio

progenitor [prou'dʒenitə*] s. progenitore m.

prognosis [prɔg'nousis] s. prognosi f.

prognostic [prɔg'nɔstik] s. pronostico m.

program ['prougræm] s. programma m. (USA)

to program ['prougræm] v. tr. programmare

programme ['prougræm] s. programma m.

programming ['prougræmiŋ] s. programmazione f.

progress ['prougres] s. progresso m.; rendimento m. (scol.)

to progress [prə'gres] v. intr. progredire, avanzare

progression [prə'greʃən] s. progressione f.

progressive [prə'gresiv] agg. progressivo

to prohibit [prə'hibit] v. tr. proibire

prohibition [,proui'biʃən] s. divieto m., proibizione f.

project ['prɔdʒekt] s. piano m., progetto m.

to project [prə'dʒekt] v. tr. proiettare

projection [prə'dʒekʃən] s. sporgenza f.; proiezione f.

projector [prə'dʒektə*] s. proiettore m.

to proliferate [prou'lifəreit] v. intr. proliferare

prolific [prə'lifik] agg. fecondo, prolifico

prolix ['prouliks] agg. prolisso

prologue [proulɔg] s. prologo m.

to prolong [prə'lɔŋ] v. tr. allungare

prolongation [,proulɔŋ'geiʃən] s. prolungamento m.

promenade [,prɔmi'na:d] s. lungomare m., passeggiata f.

prominence ['prɔminəns] s. sporgenza f., prominenza f.; importanza f.

prominent ['prɔminənt] agg. eminente, notevole

promiscuity [,prɔmis'kju(:)ti] s. promiscuità f.

promise ['prɔmis] s. promessa f.

to promise ['prɔmis] v. tr. e intr. promettere

to promote [prə'mout] v. tr. promuovere

promoter [prə'moutə*] s. promotore m.

promotion [prə'mouʃən] s. promozione f.

prompt [prɔmpt] agg. immediato, pronto, sollecito • s. suggerimento m.

to prompt [prɔmpt] v. tr. suggerire, provocare, incitare

prompter ['prɔmptə*] s. suggeritore m.

pronaos [prou'neios] s. pronao m.

prone [proun] agg. disposto, incline, prono

pronoun ['prounaun] s. pronome m.

to pronounce [prə'nauns] v. tr. e intr. pronunciare

pronunciation [prə,nʌnsi'eiʃən] s. pronuncia f.

proof [pru:f] s. prova f., dimostrazione f., bozza f.; (nei composti) resistente; **water-proof** impermeabile

prop [prɔp] s. sostegno m.

to prop [prɔp] v. tr. puntellare

propaganda [,prɔpə'gændə] s. propaganda f.

to propagate ['prɔpəgeit] v. tr. e intr. propagare

propeller [prə'pelə*] s. elica f.

proper ['prɔpə*] agg. proprio; appropriato, corretto

properly ['prɔpəli] avv. opportunamente

property ['prɔpəti] s. patrimonio m.; proprietà f.; qualità f.

prophecy ['prɔfisi] s. profezia f.

prophet ['prɔfit] s. profeta m.

prophetic [prə'fetik] agg. profetico

prophylactic [,prɔfi'læktik] s. preservativo m.

prophylaxis [,prɔfi'læksis] s. profilassi f.

to propitiate [prə'piʃieit] v. tr. propiziare

propitious [prə'piʃəs] agg. propizio

proportion [prə'pɔ:ʃən] s. proporzione f.

proportional [prə'pɔ:ʃənl] agg. proporzionale

proposal [prə'pouzəl] s. proposta f.

to propose [prə'pouz] v. tr. e intr. proporre, presentare

proprietor [prə'praiətə*] s. proprietario m.; titolare m.

propulsion [prə'pʌlʃən] s. propulsione f.

propylaeum [,prɔpi'li:əm] s. propileo m.

prose [prouz] s. prosa f.

to prosecute ['prɔsikju:t] v. tr. proseguire; perseguire (leg.)

prosecution [,prɔsi'kju:ʃən] s. prosecuzione f.

prospect ['prɔspekt] s. prospettiva f.

prospective [prəs'pektiv] agg. potenziale; futuro

to prosper ['prɔspə*] v. intr. prosperare

prosperous ['prɔspərəs] agg. prosperoso

prosthesis ['prɔsθisis] s. protesi f.

prostitute ['prɔstitju:t] s. prostituta f.

prostyle ['proustail] s. prostilo m.

protagonist [prou'tægənist] s. protagonista m. e f.

to protect [prə'tekt] v. tr. difendere, proteggere

protection [prə'tekʃən] s. protezione f., difesa f., riparo m.

protectionism [prə'tekʃənizəm] s. protezionismo m.

protein ['prouti:n] s. proteina f.

protest ['proutest] s. protesta f.

to protest [prə'test] v. intr. protestare, reclamare

Protestant ['protistənt] agg. e s. protestante m. e f.

Protestantism ['protistəntizəm] s. protestantesimo m.

protocol ['proutəkɔl] s. protocollo m.

protomartyr ['proutou,ma:tə*] s. protomartire m.

prototype ['proutətaip] s. prototipo m.

to protrude [prə'tru:d] v. tr. sporgere

protruding [prə'tru:diŋ] agg. sporgente

protuberance [prə'tju:bərəns] s. protuberanza f.

protuberant [prə'tju:bərənt] agg. sporgente

proud [praud] agg. orgoglioso; superbo

to prove [pru:v] v. tr. provare; dimostrare • intr. rivelarsi

provenance ['provinəns] s. provenienza f., origine f.

Provençal [,provã:n'sa:l] agg. e s. provenzale m. e f.

proverb ['provəb] s. proverbio m.

proverbial [prə'və:bjəl] s. proverbiale m.

to provide [prə'vaid] v. tr. e intr. fornire, procurare

provided [prə'vaidid] cong. purché, sempre che, a condizione che

providence ['providəns] s. previdenza f., provvidenza f.

provident ['providənt] agg. previdente

providential [,provi'denʃəl] agg. provvidenziale, opportuno

province ['provins] s. provincia f.

provincial [prə'vinʃəl] agg. provinciale

provincialism [prə'vinʃəlizəm] s. provincialismo m.

provision [prə'viʒən] s. provvista f. • pl. viveri m.

provisional [prə'viʒənl] agg. provvisorio

provocation [,provə'keiʃən] s. provocazione f.

provocative [prə'vɔkətiv] agg. provocante

to provoke [prə'vouk] v. tr. provocare

provoking [prə'voukiŋ] agg. provocante

proximity [prɔk'simiti] s. prossimità f., vicinanza f.

proxy ['prɔksi] s. delega f.

prudence ['pru:dəns] s. prudenza f.

prudent ['pru:dənt] agg. prudente

prune [pru:n] s. prugna f. secca

to prune [pru:n] v. tr. potare

to pry [prai] v. intr. curiosare

psalm [sa:m] s. salmo m.

pseudonym ['sju:dənim] s. pseudonimo m.

psychiatrist [sai'kai-ətrist] s. psichiatra m. e f.

psychic(al) ['saikik(əl)] agg. psichico

psychoanalysis [,saikouə'næləsis] s. psicoanalisi f.

psychologic [,saikə'lɔdʒik] agg. psicologico

psychology [sai'kɔlədʒi] s. psicologia f.

psychosis [sai'kousis] s. psicosi f.

pub [pʌb] s. osteria f.

puberty ['pju:bəti] s. pubertà f.

public ['pʌblik] agg. e s. pubblico m. ; – **house** taverna

publican ['pʌblikən] s. oste m.

publication [,pʌbli'keiʃən] s. pubblicazione f.

publicity [pʌb'lisiti] s. pubblicità f.

to publicize ['pʌblisaiz] v. tr. pubblicizzare

to publish ['pʌbliʃ] v. tr. pubblicare

publisher ['pʌbliʃə*] s. editore m.

pudding ['pudiŋ] s. budino m.

puddle ['pʌdl] s. pozzanghera f.

puff [pʌf] s. soffio m.

pull [pul] s. maniglia f.; strappo m., tiro m.

to pull [pul] v. tr. tirare, trainare; – **up** fermarsi

pulley ['puli] s. carrucola f.

pullover ['pul,ouvə*] s. pullover m. inv.

pulmonary ['pʌlmənəri] agg. polmonare

pulp [pʌlp] s. polpa f.; polpastrello m.

pulpit ['pulpit] s. pulpito m.

pulsation [pʌl'seiʃən] s. pulsazione f.

pulse [pʌls] s. polso m. (med.); impulso m.

to pulverize ['pʌlvəraiz] v. tr. polverizzare • intr. polverizzarsi

pump [pʌmp] s. pompa f.; distributore m. di benzina

to pump [pʌmp] v. tr. pompare

pumpkin ['pʌmpkin] s. zucca f.

punch [pʌntʃ] s. cazzotto m., pugno m.; perforatrice f.; punzone m.

to punch [pʌntʃ] v. tr. forare, perforare; dare un pugno, pestare

punctual ['pʌŋktjuəl] agg. puntuale

punctuality ['pʌŋktjuˈæliti] s. puntualità f.

to punctuate ['pʌŋktjueit] v. tr. punteggiare

puncture ['pʌŋktʃə*] s. foratura f. (di una gomma); puntura f.; **to get a –** forare

to punish ['pʌniʃ] v. tr. punire, infliggere una punizione

punishment ['pʌniʃmənt] s. castigo m., pena f., punizione f.

pupil ['pju:pl] s. allievo m., scolaro m.; pupilla f. (anat.)

puppet ['pʌpit] s. burattino m., pupazzo m.

puppeteer [,pʌpi'tiə*] s. burattinaio m.

puppy ['pʌpi] s. cucciolo m.

purchase ['pə:tʃəs] s. acquisto m.

to purchase ['pə:tʃəs] v. tr. comprare

purchaser ['pə:tʃəsə*] s. acquirente m. e f., compratore m.

pure [pjuə*] agg. puro

purée ['pjuarei] s. purè m.

purgative ['pə:gətiv] agg. e s. purgante m.

purgatory ['pə:gətəri] s. purgatorio m.

purge [pə:dʒ] s. purga f., purgante m.; epurazione f. (politica)

to purge [pə:dʒ] v. tr. purgare, purificare

purging ['pə:dʒiŋ] s. purificazione f.

to purify ['pjuərifai] v. tr. purificare

purism ['pjuərizəm] s. purismo m.

Puritanism ['pjuəritənizəm] s. puritanesimo m.

to purloin [pə:'lɔin] v. tr. trafugare

purple ['pə:pl] agg. purpureo, violaceo • s. porpora f.

purpura ['pə:pjuərə] s. porpora f. (med.)

purpose ['pə:pəs] s. finalità f., proposito m., scopo m.; **on** – appositamente; **to no** – invano

purse [pə:s] s. borsellino m.; borsa f. (USA)

pursuance [pə'sju:əns] s. proseguimento m.

to pursue [pə'sju:] v. tr. inseguire; perseguire • intr. proseguire

pus [pʌs] s. pus m.

push [puʃ] s. spinta f.; – **button** pulsante; – **cart** passeggino

to push [puʃ] v. tr. e intr. pigiare, spingere; – **about** sballottare; – **aside** scostare; – **up** alzare; – **along** continuare; – **drugs** spacciare droga

pusher ['puʃə*] s. spacciatore m.

pussycat ['pusikæt] s. micio m.

to put [put] v. tr. mettere; – **away** mettere via; – **back** riporre; – **before** premettere; – **by** risparmiare; – **down** sopprimere, posare; – **in** inserire, infilare; – **off** posticipare, rinviare; – **on** indossare; – **out** spegnere (un fuoco); – **up with** sopportare

putrefaction [,pju:tri'fækʃən] s. putrefazione f., marciume m.

to putrefy ['pju:trifai] v. intr. imputridire

putty ['pʌti] s. stucco m., mastice m.

to putty ['pʌti] v. tr. stuccare

puzzle ['pʌzl] s. rompicapo m.

to puzzle ['pʌzl] v. tr. confondere • intr. essere perplesso

puzzling ['pʌzliŋ] agg. concertante

pyjamas [pə'dʒa:məz] s. pl. pigiama m. sing.

pylon ['pailən] s. traliccio m., pilone m.

pyramid ['pirəmid] s. piramide f.

pyramidal [pi'ræmidl] agg. piramidale

pyre [paiə*] s. rogo m.

pyromaniac [,pairou'meinjæk] s. piromane m. e f.

pyrotechnic(al) [,pairou'teknik(əl)] agg. pirotecnico

python ['paiθən] s. pitone m.

Q

quack [kwæk] s. ciarlatano m.

quadrangular [kwɔ'dræŋgjulə*] agg. quadrangolare

quadrant ['kwɔdrənt] s. quadrante m.

quadrennial [kwɔ'drenjəl] agg. quadriennale

quadruped ['kwɔdruped] agg. quadrupede

quadruple ['kwɔdrupl] agg. quadruplo

quagmire ['kwægmaiə*] s. pantano m.

quail [kweil] s. quaglia f.

to quail [kweil] v. intr. sgomentarsi

quaint [kweint] agg. bizzarro

quake [kweik] s. tremito; **earth–** terremoto

to quake [kweik] v. intr. tremare

Quaker ['kweikə*] s. quacchero m.

qualification [,kwɔlifi'keiʃən] s. qualifica f., titolo m.

to qualify ['kwɔlifai] v. tr. abilitare; qualificare

quality ['kwɔliti] s. qualità f., pregio m.

quantity ['kwɔntiti] s. quantità f., quantitativo m.

quantum ['kwɔntəm] s. quanto m.

quarantine ['kwɔrənti:n] s. quarantena f.

quarrel ['kwɔrəl] s. disputa f., lite f., litigio m., contrasto m.

to quarrel ['kwɔrəl] v. intr. bisticciare, litigare

quarrelsome ['kwɔrəlsəm] agg. litigioso, rissoso

quarry ['kwɔri] s. cava f.; preda f.

quart [ka:t] s. quarto m. di gallone

quarter ['kwɔːtə*] s. rione m.; quarto m. (mat.); **– light** deflettore (autom.)

quarterly ['kwɔːtəli] agg. trimestrale

quartet [kwɔː'tet] s. quartetto m.; **string –** quartetto d'archi

quartz [kwɔːts] s. quarzo m.

quatrain ['kwɔtrein] s. quartina f.

quatrefoil ['kætrəfɔil] s. quadrifoglio m.

quay [ki:] s. banchina f., molo m.

queen [kwi:n] s. regina f.

queer [kwiə*] agg. originale, strano; omossessuale (fam.)

to quench [kwentʃ] v. tr. estinguere, spegnere; **– one's thirst** dissetarsi

query ['kwiəri] s. domanda f., quesito m.

to query ['kwiəri] v. tr. investigare

question ['kwestʃən] s. domanda f., questione f., problema m.

to question ['kwestʃən] v. tr. interrogare; dubitare di • intr. fare domande

questionable ['kwestʃənəbl] agg. dubbio

questionnaire [,kwestiə'nɛə*] s. questionario m.

queue [kju:] s. coda f., fila f.

to queue up [kju:ʌp] v. intr. fare la coda

quick [kwik] agg. svelto, veloce; **quickly in** fretta, prontamente

quickness ['kwiknis] s. sveltezza f.

quicksilver ['kwik,silvə*] s. mercurio m.

quiet ['kwaiət] agg. quieto, tranquillo • s. quiete f., tranquillità f.

quilt [kwilt] s. strapuntino m., trapunta f., piumino m.

quince [kwins] s. mela f. cotogna

quintal ['kwintl] s. quintale m.

quintet(te) [kwin'tet] s. quintetto m.

to quit [kwit] v. tr. abbandonare • intr. andarsene

quite [kwait] avv. proprio, del tutto, completamente; abbastanza; certo! **– a bit, – a lot** abbastanza (di quantità); **– a while** abbastanza (tempo); **– right** giustissimo

quittance ['kwitəns] s. quietanza f., ricevuta f.

to quiver ['kwivə*] v. intr. fremere, tremare

quiver ['kwivə*] s. faretra f. • tremito m.

quota ['kwoutə] s. aliquota f.

quotation [kwou'teiʃən] s. citazione f.; quotazione f.

to quote [kwout] v. tr. citare; quotare (fin.)

quotient ['kwouʃənt] s. quoziente m.

rabbi ['ræbai] s. rabbino m.

rabbin ['ræbin] s. rabbino m.

rabbit ['ræbit] s. coniglio m.

rabid ['ræbid] agg. rabbioso (animali)

rabies ['reibi:z] s. rabbia f. (med.)

race [reis] s. gara f., corsa f., regata f.; razza f.

to race [reis] v. intr. gareggiare; **racing stable** scuderia

racism ['reisizəm] s. razzismo m.

racist ['reisist] agg. razzista

rack [ræk] s. rastrelliera f.; **luggage** – portabagagli

racket ['rækit] s. baccano m., fracasso m.; racket m. • racchetta f.

racoon [rə'ku:n] s. procione m.

radiant ['reidjənt] s. radiante m.

radiator ['reidieitə*] s. calorifero m., radiatore m.

radical ['rædikəl] s. radicale m. e f.

radio ['reidiou] s. radio f.; – **amateur** radioamatore

radioactive ['reidiou'æktiv] agg. radioattivo

radioactivity ['reidiouæk'tiviti] s. radioattività f.

radiography [,reidi'ɔgrəfi] s. radiografia f.

radiologist [,reidi'ɔlədʒist] s. radiologo m.

radiophone ['reidioufoun] s. radiotelefono m.

radioscopy [,reidi'ɔskəpi] s. radioscopia f.

radish ['rædiʃ] s. rafano m., ravanello m.

radium ['reidjəm] s. radio m. (chim.)

radius ['reidjəs] s. radio m. (anat.); raggio m. (geom.)

raft [ra:ft] s. zattera f.

rag [ræg] s. straccio m., brandello m.; – **doll** pupazzo di stoffa

rage [reidʒ] s. furia f., rabbia f.

to rage [reidʒ] v. intr. imperversare, infierire

raging ['reidʒiŋ] agg. furente

ragged ['rægid] agg. cencioso

raid [reid] s. incursione f., irruzione f.

to raid [reid] v. tr. e intr. assalire, fare un'incursione

rail [reil] s. parapetto m., battagliola f. (naut.); rotaia f., sbarra f., steccato m.

railing ['reiliŋ] s. cancellata f.

railroad ['reilroud] s. ferrovia f. (USA)

railway ['reilwei] agg. ferroviario • s. ferrovia f.; – **bridge** cavalcavia; – **track** binario

railwayman ['reilweimən] s. ferroviere m.

rain [rein] s. pioggia f. • agg. pluviale; – **pipe** grondaia

to rain [rein] v. intr. impers. piovere

rainbow ['reinbou] s. arcobaleno m.

raincoat ['rein,kout] s. impermeabile m.

rainfall ['rein,fɔ:l] s. quantità f. di pioggia

raininess ['reininis] s. piovosità f.

rainproof ['reinpru:f] agg. impermeabile

rainy ['reini] agg. piovoso

to raise [reiz] v. tr. alzare, issare; aumentare, elevare; erigere; allevare

raisin ['reizn] s. uva f. passa

raising ['reiziŋ] s. rilancio m.; sopralzo m.

rake [reik] s. rastrello m.

ram [ræm] s. montone m., ariete m.

to ram [ræm] v. tr. speronare

ramification [,ræmifi'keiʃən] s. diramazione f.

rampant ['ræmpənt] agg. dilagante, rampante

rampart ['ræmpa:t] s. terrapieno m., bastione m. (mil.)

rancid ['rænsid] agg. rancido

range [reindʒ] s. escursione f.; portata f.; intervallo m.

rank [ræŋk] s. fila f.; rango m.; grado m. (mil.)

to ransack ['rænsæk] v. tr. svaligiare • intr. frugare

ransom ['rænsəm] s. riscatto m.

to ransom ['rænsəm] v. tr. riscattare

ranunculus [rə'nʌŋkjuləs] s. ranuncolo m.

rap [ræp] s. colpetto m.

to rap [ræp] v. tr. e intr. colpire; bussare

rapacious [rə'peiʃəs] agg. rapace

rape [reip] s. ratto m.; stupro m.

to rape [reip] v. tr. violentare

rapid ['ræpid] agg. rapido • s. pl. rapide f. (di fiume)

rapidity [rə'piditi] s. rapidità f.

rapist ['reipist] s. stupratore m.

rapture ['ræptʃə*] s. rapimento m.

rare [rɛə*] agg. raro, singolare; al sangue; **rarely** raramente

rareness ['reanis] s. rarità f.
rarity ['reariti] s. rarità f.
rascal [ra:skal] s. mascalzone m.
rash [ræʃ] agg. imprudente, precipitoso • s. eruzione f. (med.)
rashness ['ræʃnis] s. imprudenza f.
raspberry ['ra:zbəri] s. lampone m.
rat [ræt] s. ratto m., topo m.; – **poison** topicida
rate [reit] s. tariffa f., prezzo m.; aliquota f., tasso m.; **exchange** – tasso di cambio
rather ['ra:ðə*] avv. abbastanza, piuttosto; **or** – ovvero
ratification [,rætifi'keiʃən] s. ratifica f.
rating ['reitiŋ] s. qualifica f., categoria f.
ratio ['reiʃiəu] s. proporzione f., rapporto m. (mat.)
ration ['ræʃən] s. razione f.
rational ['ræʃənl] agg. razionale
rationalism ['ræʃnəlizm] s. razionalismo m.
rationalistic [,ræʃnə'listik] agg. razionalista
rattle ['rætl] s. sonaglio m.; rumore m. secco
raucous ['rɔ:kəs] agg. rauco
to ravage ['rævidʒ] v. tr. devastare
rave [reiv] v. intr. delirare, farneticare; scatenarsi
raven ['reivn] s. corvo m.
ravine [rə'vi:n] s. burrone m.
raving ['reiviŋ] s. delirio m.
raw [rɔ:] agg. crudo, greggio; novellino
ray [rei] s. raggio m.
to raze [reiz] v. tr. radere al suolo, abbattere
razor ['reizə*] s. rasoio m.; – **blade** lametta
reach [ri:tʃ] s. tratto m. di fiume, braccio m. di mare
to reach [ri:tʃ] v. tr. ottenere, raggiungere • intr. arrivare, giungere, pervenire
to react [ri(:)'ækt] v. intr. rispondere, reagire
reaction [ri(:)'ækʃən] s. reazione f.
reactivity [,ri:æk'tiviti] s. reattività f.
to read [ri:d] v. tr. leggere; segnare (strumento)
readable ['ri:dəbl] agg. leggibile
reader ['ri:də*] s. lettore m.
reading ['ri:diŋ] s. lettura f.
ready ['redi] agg. pronto; **readily** prontamente; facilmente; **to get** – prepararsi; **to make** – preparare
to reaffirm [ri:ə'fə:m] v. tr. riaffermare
reagent [ri:'eidʒənt] s. reagente m.
real [riəl] agg. effettivo, reale, vero
realism ['riəlizəm] s. realismo m.
realist ['riəlist] s. realista
realistic [riə'listik] agg. realistico
reality [ri:'æliti] s. realtà f.

realization [,riəlai'zeiʃən] s. realizzo m.
to realize ['riəlaiz] v. tr. realizzare, accorgersi
really ['riəli] avv. davvero, effettivamente, veramente, proprio
realm [relm] s. regno m.
realtor [ri'əltɔ:*] s. agente m. e f. immobiliare (USA)
ream [ri:m] s. risma f.
to reap [ri:p] v. tr. mietere
reappointment [ri:ə'pɔintmənt] s. reincarico m., rielezione f.
to reappraise [ri:ə'preiz] v. tr. ridimensionare
rear [riə*] agg. posteriore
to rear [riə*] v. tr. crescere; allevare, aducare
rearrangement [ri:ə'reindʒmənt] s. riordinamento m.
reason ['ri:zən] s. motivo m., ragione f.
to reason ['ri:zn] v. intr. ragionare
reasonable ['ri:znəbl] agg. modico, ragionevole
reasoning ['ri:zniŋ] s. ragionamento m.
to reassume [ri:ə'sju:m] v. tr. riassumere
to reassure [,ri:ə'ʃuə*] v. tr. rassicurare
rebel ['rebl] agg. e s. ribelle m.
rebound [ri'baund] s. contraccolpo m., rimbalzo m.
to rebuild [ri:'bild] v. tr. ricostruire
rebuke [ri'bju:k] s. rimprovero m.
to rebuke [ri'bju:k] v. tr. rimproverare, sgridare
to recall [ri'kɔ:l] v. tr. rievocare, richiamare; ricordare
to recapitulate [,ri:kə'pitjuleit] v. tr. e intr. riepilogare
recapitulation [ri:kə,pitju'leiʃən] s. ricapitolazione f., riepilogo m.
to recede [ri:'si:d] v. intr. ritirarsi
receipt [ri'si:t] s. quietanza f., ricevuta f.
to receive [ri'si:v] v. tr. ricevere, accogliere; incassare (pugilato)
receiver [ri'si:və*] s. destinatario m.
recent ['ri:snt] agg. recente
reception [ri'sepʃən] s. ricevimento m.; ricezione f.
recess [ri'ses] s. rientranza f.
recharge [ri:'tʃa:dʒ] s. ricarica f.
to recharge [ri:'tʃa:dʒ] v. tr. ricaricare (elettr.)
recidivism [ri'sidivizəm] s. recidiva f.
recipe ['resipi] s. ricetta f.
reciprocal [ri'siprəkəl] agg. mutuo, reciproco
recitation [,resi'teiʃən] s. recitazione f.
to recite [ri'sait] v. tr. recitare
reckless ['reklis] agg. spericolato

to reckon ['rekən] v. tr. e intr. calcolare, contabilizzare

to reclaim [ri'kleim] v. tr. bonificare

reclamation [ˌreklə'meiʃən] s. bonifica f.

to recline [ri'klain] v. tr. reclinare

recognition [ˌrekəg'niʃən] s. riconoscimento m.

recognizable ['rekəgnaizəbl] agg. riconoscibile

to recognize ['rekəgnaiz] v. tr. riconoscere

recoil [ri'kɔil] s. contraccolpo m.

to recollect [ˌrekə'lekt] v. tr. e intr. ricordare

recollection [ˌrekə'lekʃən] s. ricordo m.

to recommence [ˌrekə'mens] v. tr. ricominciare

to recommend [ˌrekə'mend] v. tr. raccomandare

recommendation [ˌrekəmen'deiʃən] s. raccomandazione f.

recompense ['rekəmpens] s. ricompensa f.; compenso m.

to recompense ['rekəmpens] v. tr. premiare, ricompensare

to reconcile ['rekənsail] v. tr. conciliare, riconciliare

reconciliation [ˌrekənsili'eiʃən] s. riconciliazione f.

reconnaissance [ri'kɔnisəns] s. perlustrazione f., ricognizione f.

to reconsider [ˈriːkən'sidə*] v. tr. riconsiderare • intr. ripensarci su

to reconstruct [ˌriːkəns'trʌkt] v. tr. ricostruire

record ['rekɔːd] s. disco m. (mus.); documento m.; registro m.; primato m. (sport); – **library** discoteca; – **player** giradischi

to record [ri'kɔːd] v. tr. verbalizzare, registrare

recorder [ri'kɔːdə*] s. registratore m.

recording [ri'kɔːdiŋ] s. registrazione f., incisione f.

recourse [ri'kɔːs] s. ricorso m.

to recover [riː'kʌvə*] v. tr. riacquistare, ricuperare; ritrovare (fig.) • intr. rinvenire; guarire

recovery [ri'kʌvəri] s. rinvenimento m., guarigione f.; rimonta f.

recreation [ˌrekri'eiʃən] s. diporto m., ricreazione f.

recreational [ˌrekri'eiʃənl] agg. ricreativo

recreative ['rekrietiv] agg. ricreativo

recruit [ri'kruːt] s. recluta f.

to recruit [ri'kruːt] v. tr. reclutare

rectangular [rek'tæŋgjulə*] agg. rettangolare

rectification [ˌrektifi'keiʃən] s. rettifica f. (fig.)

rectilinear [ˌrekti'liniə*] agg. rettilineo

rector ['rektə*] s. rettore m.

to recur [ri'kə:*] v. intr. riandare (col pensiero)

recurrence [ri'kʌrəns] s. ricorrenza f.

recurrent [ri'kʌrənt] agg. ricorrente

to recycle ['riː'saikl] v. tr. riciclare

red [red] agg. rosso; – **hot** rovente; **the – ensign** la bandiera della marina mercantile (UK); – **currant** ribes

to redeem [ri'diːm] v. tr. riscattare

redeemer [ri'diːmə*] s. redentore m.

to rediscover ['riːdis'kʌvə*] v. tr. riscoprire, ritrovare

to reduce [ri'djuːs] v. tr. ridurre, decurtare, ridimensionare

reduction [ri'dʌkʃən] s. riduzione f.

redwood ['redwud] s. sequoia f.

reed [riːd] s. canna f. (bot.)

reef [riːf] s. scogliera f., banco m. (di corallo) • terzaruolo m. (naut.)

to re-elect ['riːi'lekt] v. tr. rieleggere

re-election ['riːi'lekʃən] s. rielezione f.

to re-enter ['riː'entə*] v. intr. rientrare

refection [ri'fekʃən] s. refezione f.

refectory [ri'fektəri] s. refettorio m.

to refer [ri'fə:*] v. tr. indirizzare, ascrivere • intr. riferirsi, riguardare, fare riferimento, alludere

referee [ˌrefə'riː] s. arbitro m. (sport)

to referee [ˌrefə'riː] v. tr. arbitrare (sport)

reference ['refrəns] s. referenza f.

referendum [ˌrefə'rendəm] s. referendum m. inv.

refill ['riː'fil] s. ricambio m., ricarica f.

refined [ri'faind] agg. raffinato, fine

refinement [ri'fainmənt] s. raffinatezza f.

refinery [ri'fainəri] s. raffineria f.

to reflect [ri'flekt] v. tr. riflettere; **to be reflected** specchiarsi

reflection [ri'flekʃən] s. riflessione f.; riflesso m.; considerazione f.

reflex ['riː'fleks] s. riflesso m. (med.)

reforestation [ˌriːfɔri'teiʃən] s. rimboschimento m.

reform [ri'fɔːm] s. riforma f.

to reform [ri'fɔːm] v. tr. riformare

Reformation [ˌrefə'meiʃən] s. riforma f. (stor.)

reformatory [ri'fɔːmətəri] s. riformatorio m.

reforming [ri'fɔːmiŋ] agg. riformatore

refraction [ri'frækʃən] s. rifrazione f.

refrain [ri'frein] s. ritornello m.

to refrain [ri'frein] v. intr. astenersi

to refresh [ri'freʃ] v. tr. e intr. rifocillare; rifocillarsi, dissetarsi

refreshing [ri'freʃiŋ] *agg.* rinfrescante

refreshment [ri'freʃmant] *s.* refrigerio *m.*; consumazione *f.* (al bar)

to refrigerate [ri'fridʒareit] *v. tr.* refrigerare

to refuel [ri'fjual] *v. tr.* rifornire (di carburante) • *intr.* fare rifornimento

refuge ['refju:dʒ] *s.* rifugio *m.*; **to take** – rifugiarsi

refugee [,refju:'dʒi:] *s.* profugo *m.*

refund [ri:'fʌnd] *s.* rimborso *m.*

to refund [ri:'fʌnd] *v. tr.* rimborsare

refusal [ri'fju:zal] *s.* rifiuto *m.*

refuse [ri'fju:z] *s.* rifiuti *m. pl.*, immondizia *f.*

to refuse [ri'fju:z] *v. tr.* rifiutare, negare

to regain [ri'gein] *v. tr.* riguadagnare

regard [ri'ga:d] *s.* considerazione *f.*, stima *f.* • *pl.* saluti *m.* (nelle formule di cortesia)

regent ['ri:dʒant] *s.* reggente *m. f.*

regime [rei'ʒi:m] *s.* regime *m.*

region ['ri:dʒan] *s.* regione *f.*

regional ['ri:dʒanl] *agg.* regionale

register ['redʒista*] *s.* registro *m.*

to register ['redʒista*] *v. tr.* intestare, trascrivere (*leg.*)

registered ['redʒistad] *agg.* immatricolato; – **letter** raccomandata

registration [,redʒist'treiʃan] *s.* immatricolazione *f.*; iscrizione *f.*

regnant ['regnant] *agg. e s.* regnante *m. f.*

regress ['ri:gres] *s.* regresso *m.*

regression [ri'greʃan] *s.* regresso *m.*

regret [ri'gret] *s.* rimpianto *m.*; rincrescimento *m.*

to regret [ri'gret] *v. tr.* rimpiangere

regrettable [ri'gretabl] *agg.* spiacevole, lamentevole

regular ['regjula*] *agg.* regolare

regularly ['regjulali] *avv.* regolarmente

to regulate ['regjuleit] *v. tr.* regolare

regulation [,regju'leiʃan] *s.* ordinamento *m.*, regolamento *m.*

to rehabilitate [,ri:a'biliteit] *v. tr.* riabilitare

rehabilitation ['ri:a,bili'teiʃan] *s.* riabilitazione *f.*

rehearsal [ri'ha:sal] *s.* prova *f.* (*teatro*)

to rehearse [ri'ha:s] *v. tr.* provare, fare le prove (*teatro*)

reign [rein] *s.* regno *m.*

to reimburse [,ri:im'ba:s] *v. tr.* rimborsare

reimbursement [ri:im'ba:smant] *s.* rimborso *m.*, risarcimento *m.*

reincarnation ['ri:inka:'neiʃan] *s.* reincarnazione *f.*

reindeer ['reindia*] *s.* renna *f.*

to reinforce [,ri:in'fɔ:s] *v. tr.* rinforzare

to reinstate [ri:in'steit] *v. tr.* riabilitare (persone)

to reject [ri'dʒekt] *v. tr.* rifiutare, respingere; bocciare, scartare

rejection [ri'dʒekʃan] *s.* scarto *m.*

to rejoice [ri'dʒɔis] *v. intr.* rallegrarsi

relapse [ri'læps] *s.* ricaduta *f.* (*med.*)

to relapse [ri'læps] *v. intr.* avere una ricaduta

to relate [ri'leit] *v. tr.* riferire, raccontare; collegare • *intr.* riferirsi

relation [ri'leiʃan] *s.* parente *m. e f.*; rapporto *m.*, relazione *f.*

relationship [ri'leiʃanʃip] *s.* parentela *f.*, rapporto *m.*

relative [relativ] *agg.* relativo • *s.* parente *m. e f.*

relativism ['relativizam] *s.* relativismo *m.*

relativity [,rela'tiviti] *s.* relatività *f.*

to relax [ri'læks] *v. tr.* rilassare; distendere • *intr.* rilassarsi; riposarsi

relaxation [,ri:læk'seiʃan] *s.* rilassamento *m.*, svago *m.*

relay [ri'lei] *s.* ricambio *m.*; staffetta *f.* (*sport*); relè *m.* (*elettr.*)

release [ri'li:s] *s.* rilascio *m.*; scarcerazione *f.*; scatto *m.* (*mecc.*)

to release [ri'li:s] *v. tr.* liberare, sbloccare, scaricare; – **on bail** rilasciare su cauzione

relentless [ri'lentlis] *agg.* inarrestabile

relevant ['relivant] *agg.* pertinente

reliable [ri'laiabl] *agg.* affidabile, fidato

reliance [ri'laians] *s.* fiducia *f.*

relic ['relik] *s.* cimelio *m.*, reliquia *f.*

relief [ri'li:f] *s.* rilievo *m.*; refrigerio *m.*, sollievo *m.*

to relieve [ri'li:v] *v. tr.* alleggerire, soccorrere; **reliever** soccorritore

religion [ri'lidʒan] *s.* religione *f.*, culto *m.*

religious [ri'lidʒas] *agg.* religioso

reliquary ['relikwari] *s.* reliquario *m.*, teca *f.*

to reload ['ri:'loud] *v. tr.* ricaricare

reluctance [ri'lʌktans] *s.* riluttanza *f.*

reluctant [ri'lʌktant] *agg.* riluttante, restio

to rely [ri'lai] *v. intr.* fare affidamento, fidarsi

to remain [ri'mein] *v. intr.* stare, rimanere

remainder [ri'meinda*] *s.* rimanenza *f.*, resto *m.*, avanzo *m.*

remains [ri'meinz] *s. pl.* rovine *f.*, ruderi *m.*

remake ['ri:'meik] *s.* rifacimento *m.* (di spettacolo)

to remake ['ri:'meik] *v. tr.* rifare

remark [ri'ma:k] s. osservazione f., commento m., nota f.

remarkable [ri'ma:kəbl] agg. egregio, notevole

to remarry ['ri:'mæri] v. tr. e intr. risposare

remedy ['remidi] s. rimedio m.

to remedy ['remidi] v. intr. rimediare

to remember [ri'membə°] v. tr. e intr. ricordare

remembrance [ri'membrəns] s. ricordo m., rievocazione f., memoria f.

to remind [ri'maind] v. tr. ricordare (ad altri)

reminiscence [,remi'nisns] s. reminiscenza f.

to remit [ri'mit] v. tr. condonare; inviare (denaro)

remittance [ri'mitəns] s. invio m. (di denaro)

remnant ['remnənt] s. scampolo m.

to remonstrate [ri'mɔnstreit] v. intr. protestare, fare rimostranze

remorse [ri'mɔːs] s. rimorso m.

remote [ri'mout] agg. remoto

removal [ri'mu:vəl] s. rimozione f., distacco m.; trasloco m.

to remove [ri'mu:v] v. tr. rimuovere, togliere; levare; allontanare, trasferire

to remunerate [ri'mju:nəreit] v. tr. retribuire

remuneration [ri,mju:nə'reiʃən] s. compenso m., retribuzione f.

Renaissance [rə'neisəns] agg. rinascimentale • s. rinascimento m.

to rend [rend] v. tr. spaccare, strappare

to render ['rendə°] v. tr. rendere

to renew [ri'nju:] v. tr. rinnovare, ripristinare

renewal [ri'nju:əl] s. rinnovo m.

rennet ['renit] s. caglio m.

to renounce [ri'nauns] v. tr. rinunziare

to renovate ['renouveit] v. tr. ripristinare, rinnovare

renovation [,renou'veiʃən] s. ristrutturazione f. edilizia

renown [ri'naun] s. notorietà f., fama f.

renowned [ri'naund] agg. celebre, rinomato

rent [rent] s. strappo m.

to rent [rent] v. tr. affittare

rentable ['rentəbl] agg. affittabile

renunciation [ri,nʌnsi'eiʃən] s. rinunzia f., sacrificio m.

to repaint ['ri:'peint] v. tr. ridipingere, riverniciare

repair [ri'pɛə°] s. riparazione f.

to repair [ri'pɛə°] v. tr. riparare, aggiustare

repairable [ri'pɛərəbl] agg. aggiustabile

to repatriate [ri:'pætrieit] v. intr. rimpatriare

repatriation ['ri:pætri'eiʃən] s. rimpatrio m.

to repay [ri:'pei] v. tr. contraccambiare

repayable [ri:'peiəbl] agg. rimborsabile

repeal [ri'pi:l] s. revoca f.

to repeal [ri'pi:l] v. tr. abrogare, revocare

to repeat [ri'pi:t] v. tr. replicare, ripetere

to repel [ri'pel] v. tr. respingere

repellent [ri'pelənt] agg. repellente, ripugnante

to repent [ri'pent] v. tr. e intr. pentirsi

repentance [ri'pentəns] s. pentimento m.

repertory ['repətəri] s. repertorio m.

repetition [,repi'tiʃən] s. ripetizione f.

to replace [ri'pleis] v. tr. sostituire; riporre

replaceable [ri'pleisəbl] agg. sostituibile

replacement [ri'pleismənt] s. sostituzione f.

reply [ri'plei] s. risposta f.

to reply [ri'plei] v. tr. rispondere, replicare

to repopulate [ri:'pɔpjuleit] v. tr. ripopolare

report [ri'pɔːt] s. rapporto m., referto m.; rimbombo m.

to report [ri'pɔːt] v. tr. riferire, comunicare; verbalizzare • intr. presentarsi, riferire a

reporter [ri'pɔːtə°] s. cronista m. e f.

reprehensible [,repri'hensəbl] agg. riprovevole

to represent [,repri'zent] v. tr. rappresentare

representation [,reprizen'teiʃən] s. raffigurazione f., rappresentazione f.

to repress [ri'pres] v. tr. reprimere; rimuovere (psic.)

repression [ri'preʃən] s. repressione f.

reprint ['ri:'print] s. ristampa f.

to reprint ['ri:'print] v. tr. ristampare

reprisal [ri'praizəl] s. rappresaglia f.

reproach [ri'prouʧ] s. rimprovero m.

to reproach [ri'prouʧ] v. tr. rimproverare, rinfacciare

to reproduce [,ri:prə'dju:s] v. tr. riprodurre

reproducible [,ri:prə'dju:səbl] agg. riproducibile

reproduction [,ri:prə'dʌkʃən] s. riproduzione f., copia f.

to reprove [ri'pru:v] v. tr. rimproverare

reptile ['reptail] s. rettile m.

republic [ri'pʌblik] s. repubblica f.

republican [ri'pʌblikən] agg. repubblicano

reputation [,repju:'teiʃən] s. reputazione f., fama f.

repute [ri'pju:t] s. reputazione f., fama f.; **of ill – malfamato**

request [ri'kwest] s. domanda f., richiesta f., sollecito m.

to require [ri'kwaiə°] v. tr. richiedere, esigere

required [ri'kwaiəd] agg. necessario, occorrente, richiesto

requirement [ri'kwaiəmənt] s. requisito m. • pl. fabbisogno m. sing.

requisite ['rekwizit] s. requisito m.

to requisition [,rekwi'ziʃən] v. tr. requisire

resale ['ri:seil] s. rivendita f.

to rescind [ri'sind] v. tr. rescindere

rescue ['reskju:] s. salvataggio m.

to rescue ['reskju:] v. tr. salvare

rescued ['reskju:*] agg. scampato

research [ri'sə:tʃ] s. ricerca f., indagine f.

to resell [ri:'sel] v. tr. rivendere

resemblance [ri'zembləns] s. somiglianza f.

to resemble [ri'zembl] v. tr. e intr. somigliare

resentment [ri'zentmənt] s. risentimento m.

reservation [,rezə'veiʃən] s. prenotazione f.

reserve [ri'zə:v] s. riserbo m.; riserva f.

to reserve [ri'zə:v] v. tr. prenotare, riservare

reserved [ri'zə:vd] agg. riservato

reservoir ['rezəvwa:*] s. cisterna f., serbatoio m.; riserva f.

to reside [ri'zaid] v. intr. abitare, risiedere

residence ['rezidəns] s. abitazione f., residenza f.; soggiorno m.

resident ['rezidənt] s. residente m. e f.

residential [,rezi'denʃəl] agg. residenziale

to resign [ri'zain] v. tr. lasciare, cedere, abbandonare • intr. dimettersi

resignation [,rezig'neiʃən] s. dimissioni f. pl.

resin ['rezin] s. resina f.

to resist [ri'zist] v. intr. resistere; resisting resistente

resistance [ri'zistəns] s. resistenza f., opposizione f.

to resole [ri:'soul] v. tr. risuolare

resolution [,rezə'lu:ʃən] s. risoluzione f.; scomposizione f. (chim.)

to resolve [ri'zɔlv] v. tr. risolvere; scomporre (chim.)

resonance ['rezənəns] s. risonanza f.

resonant ['rezənənt] agg. sonoro

resort [ri'zɔ:t] s. ricorso m.; ritrovo m.; luogo m. di villeggiatura

to resort [ri'zɔ:t] v. intr. ricorrere

resounding [ri'zaudiŋ] agg. strepitoso

resource [ris:s] s. risorsa f.

respect [ris'pekt] s. rispetto m.

to respect [ris'pekt] v. tr. rispettare

respectability [ri,spektə'biliti] s. rispettabilità f., perbenismo m.

respectable [ris'pektəbl] agg. rispettabile

respectful [ris'pektful] agg. rispettoso

respiration [,respə'reiʃən] s. respirazione f.

respite ['respait] s. pausa m., tregua f.

response [ris'pɔns] s. responso m.

responsibility [ris,pɔnsə'biliti] s. responsabilità f.

responsible [ris'pɔnsəbl] agg. responsabile

rest [rest] s. riposo m., sosta f.; pausa f. (mus.); resto m.

to rest [rest] v. tr. riposare • intr. posarsi, riposare, riposarsi

to restart [ri:'sta:t] v. tr. ricominciare • intr. ripartire

restaurant ['restərɔ̃:ŋ] s. ristorante m.

restless ['restlis] agg. inquieto, irrequieto

to restock [ri:'stɔk] v. tr. rifornire

restoration [,restə'reiʃən] s. restauro m.

to restore [ris:'tɔ:*] v. tr. restaurare, rifare

restorer [ris'tɔ:rə*] s. restauratore m.

to restrain [ris'trein] v. tr. reprimere; trattenere

to restrict [ris'trikt] v. tr. limitare; restringere

restriction [ris'trikʃən] s. restrizione f.

restrictive [ris'triktiv] agg. restrittivo

to restructure ['ri:'strʌktʃə*] v. tr. ristrutturare

result [ri'zʌlt] s. risultato m., riuscita f. • pl. classifica f. sing.

to result [ri'zʌlt] v. intr. risultare, sfociare (fig.)

to resume [ri'zju:m] v. tr. riprendere, ricominciare

resumption [ri'zʌmpʃən] s. ripresa f.

resurgence [ri'sə:dʒəns] s. rinascita f.

retailer [ri:'teilə*] s. dettagliante m., rivenditore m.

retaliation [ri,tæli'eiʃən] s. rappresaglia f.

to retard [ri'ta:d] v. tr. e intr. ritardare

retardation [,ri:ta:'deiʃən] s. ritardo m. (psic.)

to retch [ri:tʃ] v. tr. vomitare • intr. avere conati di vomito

reticence ['retisəns] s. reticenza f.

retina ['retinə] s. retina f.

to retire [ri'taiə*] v. intr. ritirarsi

retirement [ri'taiəmənt] s. pensionamento m.

retractive [ri'træktiv] agg. retrattile

retreat [ri'tri:t] s. ritirata f.; luogo m. appartato

retrospective [retrou'spektiv] s. retrospettiva f.

return [ri'tə:n] s. ritorno m.; resa f.; – **match** rivincita (sport)

to return [ri'tə:n] v. tr. respingere; restituire, ridare; contraccambiare • intr. ritornare

reunion [ri:'ju:njən] s. ricongiunzione f.

to reunite ['ri:ju:'nait] v. tr. riunire

rev [rev] *s.* giro *m.* (*mecc.*); – **counter** contagiri

to revalorize [ri:'vælɔraiz] *v. tr.* rivalutare (*econ.*)

revaluation [,ri:,vælju'eiʃən] *s.* rivalutazione *f.*

to revalue ['ri:'vælju] *v. tr.* rivalutare

to reveal [ri'vi:l] *v. tr.* rivelare

to revel ['revl] *v. intr.* divertirsi, far festa

revelation [,revi'leiʃən] *s.* rivelazione *f.*

revenge [ri'vendʒ] *s.* rivincita *f.* (*sport*); vendetta *f.*

to revenge [ri'vendʒ] *v. tr.* vendicare

revenue ['revinju:] *s.* fisco *m.*; rendita *f.*

reverberation [ri,və:bə'reiʃən] *s.* riverbero *m.*

to revere [ri'viə*] *v. tr.* venerare

reverence ['revərəns] *s.* riverenza *f.*

reverend ['revərənd] *agg.* reverendo

reversal [ri'va:səl] *s.* inversione *f.*

reverse [ri'va:s] *agg.* inverso • *s.* rovescio *m.*; – **gear** retromarcia

to reverse [ri'va:s] *v. tr.* invertire

reversibility [ri,və:sə'biliti] *s.* reversibilità *f.*

reversible [ri'va:səbl] *agg.* reversibile

to revert [ri'va:t] *v. intr.* ritornare

review [ri'vju:] *s.* rivista *f.*; rassegna *f.*; recensione *f.*

to review [ri'vju:] *v. tr.* riesaminare; recensire

reviewer [ri'vju:ə*] *s.* recensore *m.*

revisal [ri'vaizəl] *s.* revisione *f.*

to revise [ri'vaiz] *v. tr.* aggiornare, controllare

reviser [ri'vaizə*] *s.* revisore *m.*

revision [ri'viʒən] *s.* revisione *f.*

revisionist [ri'viʒənist] *s.* revisionista *m. e f.*

to revisit ['ri:'vizit] *v. tr.* rivisitare

revival [ri'vaivəl] *s.* rinascita *f.*; ripresa *f.*

to revive [ri'vaiv] *v. tr.* riaccendere (*fig.*)

revocation [,revə'keiʃən] *s.* revoca *f.*

to revoke [ri'vouk] *v. tr.* revocare

revolt [ri'voult] *s.* rivolta *f.*, sommossa *f.*

revolution [,revə'lu:ʃən] *s.* rivoluzione *f.*

revolutionary [,revə'lu:ʃnəri] *agg.* rivoluzionario

to revolve [ri'vɔlv] *v. intr.* ruotare

revolver [ri'vɔlvə*] *s.* rivoltella *f.*

revolving [ri'vɔlviŋ] *agg.* girevole; orientabile (*mecc.*)

reward [ri'wɔ:d] *s.* premio *m.*, ricompensa *f.*; taglia *f.*

to reward [ri'wɔ:d] *v. tr.* ricompensare, premiare; **to be rewarding** gratificare

to rewind ['ri:'waind] *v. tr.* ricaricare (un orologio); riavvolgere (una cassetta)

rhapsodist ['ræpsədist] *s.* rapsodista *m. e f.*

rhetoric ['retərik] *s.* retorica *f.*

rheumatism ['ru:mətizəm] *s.* reumatismo *m.*

rhinoceros [rai'nɔsərəs] *s.* rinoceronte *m.*

rhododendron [,roudə'dendrən] *s.* rododendro *m.*

rhomboidal [rɔm'bɔidl] *agg.* romboidale

rhombus ['rɔmbəs] *s.* rombo *m.*

rhubarb ['ru:ba:b] *s.* rabarbaro *m.*

rhyme [raim] *s.* rima *f.*

rhythm ['riðəm] *s.* ritmo *m.*

rib [rib] *s.* costola *f.*; nervatura *f.*

ribbon ['ribən] *s.* nastro *m.*

rice [rais] *s.* riso *m.*; –**field** risaia *f.*

rich [ritʃ] *agg.* ricco

richness ['ritʃnis] *s.* ricchezza *f.*

rickety ['rikiti] *agg.* rachitico (*med.*); – **vehicle** trabiccolo

to rid [rid] *v. tr.* liberare; sbarazzare; **to get rid** sbarazzarsi

riddle ['ridl] *s.* indovinello *m.*, rompicapo *m.*

to ride [raid] *v. tr. e intr.* cavalcare; – **a bike** andare in bicicletta

rider ['raidə*] *s.* cavaliere *m.*

ridge [ridʒ] *s.* crinale *m.*, dorsale *f.*, catena *f.* di montagne

ridicule ['ridikju:l] *s.* ridicolo *m.*, derisione *f.*

ridiculous [ri'dikjuləs] *agg.* ridicolo, assurdo

riding ['raidiŋ] *s.* equitazione *f.* – **track** galoppatoio

rifle ['raifl] *s.* fucile *m.*, schioppo *m.*; – **range** poligono di tiro

rigging ['rigiŋ] *s.* sartiame *m.* (*naut.*)

right [rait] *agg.* adatto, corretto; legittimo; destro; retto (*geom.*) • *s.* destra *f.*; diritto *m.*; facoltà *f.*; **on the –**, **to the –** a destra; – **of way** precedenza (*autom.*); **to be –** avere ragione

rigid ['ridʒid] *agg.* rigido

rigidity [ri'dʒiditi] *s.* rigidità *f.*

rigmarole ['rigməroul] *s.* filastrocca *f.*

rigorous ['rigərəs] *agg.* rigido, rigoroso

rigour ['rigə*] *s.* rigore *m.*, severità *f.*

rim [rim] *s.* ciglio *m.*; cerchione *m.* (*autom.*)

rime [raim] *s.* brina *f.*

rind [raind] *s.* buccia *f.*, pelle *f.*

ring [riŋ] *s.* anello *m.*; fascia *f.* (*mecc.*); quadrato *m.*, ring *m.* (*sport*); squillo *m.*, telefonata *f.* • *pl.* occhiaie *f.*

to ring [riŋ] *v. tr.* suonare (il campanello) • *intr.* squillare, suonare; – **up** telefonare

ringing ['riŋiŋ] *s.* scampanellio *m.*

to rinse [rins] *v. tr.* sciacquare

riot [raiət] *s.* tumulto *m.*, sommossa *f.*

to rip [rip] *v. tr.* strappare

ripe [raip] *agg.* maturo (di frutto)

to ripen ['raipən] v. tr. maturare; **ripening** maturazione

ripeness ['raipnis] s. maturità f.

rise [raiz] s. aumento m., crescita f.; salita f., rialzo m.

to rise [raiz] v. intr. crescere (di volume); elevarsi; – **up** insorgere

rising ['raiziŋ] agg. nascente • s. ascendente m.; rivolta f., sommossa f.

risk [risk] s. rischio m.

to risk [risk] v. tr. e intr. osare, rischiare

risky ['riski] agg. rischioso

rissole ['risoul] s. polpetta f.

rite [rait] s. rito m.

ritual ['ritjuəl] s. cerimonia f., rituale m.

rival ['raivəl] agg. e s. rivale m. e f.

rivalry ['raivəlri] s. rivalità f.

river ['rivə*] s. fiume m.

rivet ['rivit] s. rivetto m.

road [roud] s. strada f., via f.; – **bed** massicciata; – **slip** raccordo; **uneven** – strada dissestata; **one-way** – senso unico; – **hog** pirata della strada

roadway ['roudwei] s. carreggiata f.

to roam [roum] v. intr. vagare

roar [rɔ:*] s. ruggito m.

to roast [roust] v. tr. arrostire, tostare

roast [roust] agg. e s. arrosto m.

to rob [rɔb] v. tr. derubare, rapinare

robber ['rɔbə*] s. ladro m., rapinatore m.

robbery ['rɔbəri] s. rapina f.

robe [roub] s. toga f.

rock [rɔk] s. roccia f., macigno m., rupe f., scoglio m.; – **climber** rocciatore; – **goat** stambecco

to rock [rɔk] v. intr. ondeggiare

rocket ['rɔkit] s. razzo m.

rocky ['rɔki] agg. roccioso; rupestre

rococo [rə'koukou] s. cocò f.

rod [rɔd] s. barra f., stecca f.; **fishing** – canna da pesca

rodent ['roudənt] s. roditore m.

rodeo [rou'deiou] s. rodeo m. inv.

roe deer [rou diə*] s. capriolo m.

rogue [roug] s. furfante m., imbroglione m.

role [roul] s. ruolo m.

roll [roul] s. rotolo m., rullo m.; panino m.; – **up shutter** tapparella

to roll [roul] v. tr. rotolare, ruotare • intr. ondeggiare, rollare

rolled ['rould] agg. laminato

roller ['roulə*] s. rullo m., cilindro m.; onda f.,

frangente m.; – **coaster** montagne russe; – **skates** schettini

rolling ['rouliŋ] s. rollio m.

Roman ['roumən] agg. e s. romano m.

romance [rə'mæns] s. romanza f.; romanzo m.

Romanesque [,roumə'nesk] agg. romanico

romantic [rə'mæntik] agg. romantico

Romanticism [rə'mæntisizəm] s. romanticismo m.

roof [ru:f] s. tetto m.; tuga f. (naut.); – **rack** portabagagli

rook [ruk] s. torre f. (scacchi) • corvo m.

room [ru:m] s. camera f., stanza f., locale m.; ambiente m., spazio m.; **living** – soggiorno

roomy ['ru:mi] agg. spazioso

root [ru:t] s. radice f.

rope [roup] s. corda f., cima f.

rose [rouz] s. rosa f.

rosemary ['rouzməri] s. rosmarino m.

rostrum ['rɔstrəm] s. rostro m.

rot [rɔt] s. marciume m.

to rot [rɔt] v. intr. imputridire, marcire; decomporsi

rotary ['routəri] agg. rotante, rotatorio

to rotate [rou'teit] v. tr. e intr. ruotare

rotor ['routə*] s. girante f., rotore m.

rotten ['rɔtn] agg. marcio

rotula ['rɔtjulə] s. rotula f.

rotundity [rou'tʌnditi] s. rotondità f.

rough [rʌf] agg. grossolano, rozzo; ruvido; villano; impervio; turbolento; **roughly** approssimativamente, suppergiù; duramente

round [raund] agg. circolare, rotondo • avv. intorno • s. tondo m.

to round (off) [raund] v. tr. arrotondare

roundabout ['raundəbaut] s. rotatoria f.; giostra f. • agg. tortuoso

roundness ['raundnis] s. rotondità f.

to rouse [rauz] v. tr. svegliare

route [ru:t] s. itinerario m.; percorso m.

routine [ru:'ti:n] s. prassi f., procedura f., routine f.

to rove [rouv] v. intr. vagabondare

row [rou] s. fila f., riga f.; filare m.; baccano m.; vogata f.

to row [rou] v. intr. remare, vogare; litigare

rower ['rouə*] s. vogatore m.

royal ['rɔiəl] agg. reale; – **palace** reggia

to rub [rʌb] v. tr. e intr. sfregare, strpicciare; – **out**, – **away** cancellare

rubber ['rʌbə*] s. gomma f.; – **band** elastico; – **dinghy**, – **boat** gommone, canotto

rubbing ['rʌbiŋ] s. frizione f.

rubbish ['rʌbiʃ] s. immondizia f., spazzatura f.

rubble ['rʌbl] s. detrito m.

ruby ['ru:bi] s. rubino m.

rudder ['rʌdə*] s. timone m.

rude [ru:d] agg. e s. maleducato m., villano m.

rudeness ['ru:dnis] s. maleducazione f.

rudiment ['ru:dimənt] s. rudimento m.

rudimentary [,ru:di'mentəri] agg. rudimentale

ruffian ['rʌfjən] s. furfante m.

rug [rʌg] s. coperta f., tappeto m.

rugged ['rʌgid] agg. aspro, duro; irregolare; robusto

rugosity [ru'gɔsiti] s. rugosità f. (bot.)

ruin [ruin] s. rovina f., rudere m.

to ruin [ruin] v. tr. guastare, rovinare

ruinous ['ruinəs] agg. disastroso, fallimentare

rule [ru:l] s. regola f., regolamento m., norma f.; governo m., dominazione f. • pl. ordinamento m. sing.

to rule [ru:l] v. tr. e intr. governare, dominare

ruler ['ru:lə*] s. riga f. (da disegno); governante m.

rumble ['rʌmbl] s. rimbombo m.; rombo m.

ruminant ['ru:minənt] s. ruminante m.

to rummage ['rʌmidʒ] v. tr. e intr. frugare, perquisire

rummy ['rʌmi] s. ramino m.

rumour ['ru:mə*] s. diceria f.

run [rʌn] s. corsa f., percorso m.; – **down** rallentamento

to run [rʌn] v. intr. correre; circolare; funzionare • tr. amministrare, gestire; – **along** percorrere; – **away** fuggire, scappare; – **into** imbattersi, incontrare; – **over** investire; scorrere; – **short** esaurire; – **through** percorrere, attraversare

runner ['rʌnə*] s. corridore m.

running ['rʌniŋ] agg. corrente • avv. consecutivo • s. corsa f., podismo m.; – **in** rodaggio

rupture ['rʌptʃə*] s. rottura f.; ernia f.

rural ['ruərəl] agg. campestre, rurale

rush [rʌʃ] s. furia f., fretta f.; giunco m.

to rush [rʌʃ] v. tr. precipitare • intr. affrettarsi, precipitarsi

Russian ['rʌʃən] agg. russo

rust [rʌst] s. ruggine f.

to rust [rʌst] v. intr. arrugginire

rustic ['rʌstik] agg. rustico

rustle ['rʌsl] s. fruscio m.

rustproof ['rʌstpru:f] agg. antiruggine; inossidabile

rusty ['rʌsti] agg. rugginoso

rut [rʌt] s. solco m., carreggiata f.

rye [rai] s. segale f.

S

sabbatical [sə'bætikəl] *agg.* sabbatico
sable ['seibl] *s.* zibellino *m.*
sabotage ['sæbətɑ:ʒ] *s.* sabotaggio *m.*
sabre ['seibə*] *s.* sciabola *f.*
saccharin(e) ['sækərin] *s.* saccarina *f.*
saccharose ['sækərous] *s.* saccarosio *m.*
sack [sæk] *s.* sacco *m.*; saccheggio *m.*
to sack [sæk] *v. tr.* saccheggiare; licenziare
sacker ['sækə*] *s.* saccheggiatore *m.*
sacrament ['sækrəmənt] *s.* sacramento *m.*
sacrarium [sæ'kreəriəm] *s.* sacrario *m.*
sacred ['seikrid] *agg.* sacro
sacrifice ['sækrifais] *s.* sacrificio *m.*
to sacrifice ['sækrifais] *v. tr.* sacrificare; –
    oneself sacrificarsi
sacrilege ['sækrilidʒ] *s.* sacrilegio *m.*
sad [sæd] *agg.* triste; addolorato
saddle ['sædl] *s.* sella *f.*
to saddle ['sædl] *v. tr.* sellare
sadist ['sædist] *s.* sadico *m.*
sadistic [sæ'distik] *agg.* sadico
sadness ['sædnis] *s.* tristezza *f.*
sadomasochism [,seidou'mæsəkizəm] *s.* sa-
    domasochismo *m.*
safari [sə'fɑ:ri] *s.* safari *m. inv.*
safe [seif] *agg.* salvo; sicuro • *s.* cassaforte *f.*;
    – and sound incolume
safety ['seifti] *s.* salvezza *f.*; sicurezza *f.*
saffron ['sæfrən] *s.* zafferano *m.*
to sag [sæg] *v. tr. e intr.* incurvarsi, incurvare
saga ['sɑ:gə] *s.* saga *f.*
sage [seidʒ] *s.* salvia *f.*
sail [seil] *s.* vela *f.*
to sail [seil] *v. intr.* navigare (a vela)
sailer ['seilə*] *s.* veliero *m.*
sailing ['seiliŋ] *s.* navigazione *f.*; vela *f.*
sailor ['seilə*] *s.* marinaio *m.*; navigante *m.*
saint [seint] *s.* santo *m.*
salad ['sæləd] *s.* insalata *f.*
salami [sə'lɑ:mi] *s.* salame *m.*
salary ['sæləri] *s.* stipendio *m.*
sale [seil] *s.* vendita *f.*; liquidazione *f.*; saldo *m.*;
    for –, – on – in vendita; **sales** saldi
saleable ['seiləbl] *agg.* vendibile
salesman ['seilzmən] *s.* commesso *m.*

saliva [sə'laivə] *s.* saliva *f.*
salmi ['sælmi(:)] *s.* salmì *m.*
salmon ['sæmən] *s.* salmone *m.*; **smoked –** sal-
    mone affumicato
salmonellosis [,sælmənə'lousis] *s.* salmonel-
    losi *f.*
saloon [sə'lu:n] *s.* salone *m.*
salt [sɔ:lt] *s.* sale *m.* • *agg.* salato
to salt [sɔ:lt] *v. tr.* salare
salted ['sɔ:ltid] *agg.* salato
saltless ['sɔ:ltlis] *agg.* insipido
saltness ['sɔ:ltnis] *s.* salsedine *f.*
salty ['sɔ:lti] *agg.* salato
salubrious [sə'lu:briəs] *agg.* salubre, sano
salubrity [sə'lu:briti] *s.* salubrità *f.*
salutary ['sæljutəri] *agg.* salutare
salutation [,sælju:(')'teifən] *s.* saluto *m.*
salute [sə'lu:t] *s.* saluto *m.*
to salute [sə'lu:t] *v. tr.* salutare; rendere gli
    onori
salvage ['sælvidʒ] *s.* salvataggio *m.*, recupero
    m. (*naut.*)
salvation [sæl'veifən] *s.* salvezza *f.*
same [seim] *agg.* stesso, medesimo • *pron.* lo
    stesso; la stessa cosa • *avv.* allo stesso modo
sample ['sɑ:mpl] *s.* campione *m.* (*comm.*);
    esemplare *m.*
to sample ['sɑ:mpl] *v. tr.* assaggiare; campio-
    nare
sampling ['sɑ:mpliŋ] *s.* degustazione *f.*
sanatorium [,sænə'tɔ:riəm] *s.* sanatorio *m.*
sanction ['sæŋkʃən] *s.* sanzione *f.*
sanctity ['sæŋktiti] *s.* santità *f.*
sanctuary ['sæŋktjuəri] *s.* santuario *m.*
sand [sænd] *s.* sabbia *f.*; **– glass** clessidra; **– bath**
    sabbiatura
sandal ['sændl] *s.* sandalo *m.*
sandwich ['sænwidʒ] *s.* tramezzino *m.*
sandy ['sændi] *agg.* sabbioso
sane [sein] *agg.* sano (di mente)
sanitary ['sænitəri] *agg.* sanitario; igienico; **–**
    towel assorbente
sanity ['sæniti] *s.* salute *f.* mentale
sap [sæp] *s.* linfa *f.* (*bot.*)
sapid ['sæpid] *agg.* sapido

sapphire ['sæfaiə*] s. zaffiro m.

sarcasm ['sɑ:kæzəm] s. sarcasmo m.

sarcastic [sɑ:'kæstik] agg. sarcastico

sarcophagus [sɑ:'kɔfəgəs] s. sarcofago m.

sardine [sɑ:'di:n] s. sardina f.

Sardinian [sɑ:'dinjən] agg. sardo

sash [sæʃ] s. intelaiatura f.; fascia f.

satchel ['sætʃəl] s. cartella f.

satellite ['sætəlait] s. satellite m.

satiate(d) ['seiʃieit(id)] agg. sazio

satin ['sætin] s. raso m.

satire ['sætaiə*] s. satira f.

satiric(al) [sə'tirik(əl)] agg. satirico

satisfaction [,sætis'fækʃən] s. soddisfazione f.

satisfactory [,sætis'fæktəri] agg. soddisfacente, esauriente

to satisfy ['sætisfai] v. tr. soddisfare; contentare • intr. dar soddisfazione

to saturate ['sætʃəreit] v. tr. saturare

saturation [,sætʃə'reiʃən] s. saturazione f.

Saturday ['sætədi] s. sabato m.

sauce [sɔ:s] s. salsa f.; – **boat** salsiera

saucer ['sɔ:sə*] s. piattino m.

sausage ['sɔsidʒ] s. salsiccia f. • pl. salumi m.

savage ['sævidʒ] agg. selvaggio

savannah(h) [sə'vænə] s. savana f.

save [seiv] prep. tranne

to save [seiv] v. tr. salvare; conservare; risparmiare

saver ['seivə*] s. salvatore m.; risparmiatore m.

saving ['seiviŋ] s. salvezza f.; economia f. • pl. risparmi m.

savoury ['seivəri] agg. saporito

saw [sɔ:] s. sega f.

to saw [sɔ:] v. tr. segare

sawdust ['sɔ:dʌst] s. segatura f.

sawmill ['sɔ:mil] s. segheria f.

sax [sæks] s. sassofono m.

saxophone ['sæksəfoun] s. sassofono m.

saxophonist [sæk'sɔfənist] s. sassofonista m.

to say [sei] v. tr. e intr. dire

saying ['seiiŋ] s. detto m., proverbio m.

scab [skæb] s. crosta f. (med.)

scabrous ['skeibrəs] agg. scabroso

scaffold ['skæfəld] s. impalcatura f.; patibolo m.

to scald [skɔ:ld] v. tr. scottare, ustionare

scalding ['skɔ:ldiŋ] s. scottatura f., ustione f. • agg. bollente, che scotta

scale [skeil] s. scala f.; gradazione f. • squama f.; **the Scales** Bilancia (astr.)

to scale [skeil] v. tr. scalare • intr. arrampicarsi

scallop ['skɔləp] s. scaloppina f.; smerlo m.

scalpel ['skælpəl] s. scalpello m.

to scan [skæn] v. tr. esaminare, scrutare, scandire

scandal ['skændl] s. scandalo m.

to scandalize ['skændəlaiz] v. tr. scandalizzare, dare scandalo

scandalmongering ['skændl,mʌŋgəriŋ] agg. scandalistico

scandalous ['skændələs] agg. scandaloso

scanty ['skænti] agg. scarso

scapula ['skæpjulə] s. scapola f.

scar [skɑ:*] s. cicatrice f.

scarce [skɛəs] agg. scarso

scarcely ['skɛəsli] avv. appena, a malapena

scarcity ['skɛəsiti] s. scarsità f., penuria f.

scare [skɛə*] s. spavento m.

to scare [skɛə*] v. tr. spaventare; **to be scared** impressionarsi, spaventarsi

scarecrow ['skɛə-krou] s. spaventapasseri m.

scarf [skɑ:f] s. sciarpa f.

to scarify ['skɛərifai] v. tr. scarificare

scarlet ['skɑ:lit] agg. scarlatto; – **fever** scarlattina

to scatter ['skætə*] v. tr. cospargere • intr. disperdersi

scatterbrain ['skætə,brein] s. sbadato m.

scenario [si'nɑ:riou] s. sceneggiatura f.

scene [si:n] s. scena f.; scenata f.

scenery ['si:nəri] s. scenario m.

scenographer [si'nɔgrəfə*] s. scenografo m.

scenographic [,si:nou'græfik] agg. scenografico

scenography [si'nɔgrəfi] s. scenografia f.

scent [sent] s. odore m.; profumo m.

scented ['sentid] agg. profumato

sceptical ['skeptikəl] agg. e s. scettico m.

sceptre ['septə*] s. scettro m.

schedule ['ʃedju:l] s. tabella f.

schematic [ski'mætik] agg. schematico

scheme [ski:m] s. schema m.; piano m.; intrigo m.

to scheme [ski:m] v. tr. e intr. pianificare; complottare

schizophrenia [,skitsou'fri:njə] s. schizofrenia f.

schizophrenic [,skitsou'frenik] agg. schizofrenico

scholar ['skɔlə*] s. studioso m., erudito m.

scholarship ['skɔləʃip] s. borsa f. di studio

scholastic [skə'læstik] agg. scolastico

school [sku:l] s. scuola f. • agg. scolastico

schoolboy ['sku:lbɔi] s. scolaro m.

schooner ['sku:nə•] s. goletta f.
sciatica [saɪ'ætɪkə] s. sciatica f.
science ['saɪəns] s. scienza f.; – **fiction** fanta-
scienza
scientific [,saɪən'tɪfɪk] agg. scientifico
scientist ['saɪəntɪst] s. scienziato m.
scissors ['sɪzəz] s. pl. forbici f.
to scold [skould] v. tr. rimproverare, sgridare
scolding ['skouldɪŋ] s. rimprovero m.
scoliosis [,skɒlɪ'ousɪs] s. scoliosi f.
scope [skoup] s. portata f., ambito m.
scorch [skɔ:tʃ] s. scottatura f.
to scorch [skɔ:tʃ] v. tr. scottare
score [skɔ:•] s. tratto m.; punto m.; punteggio
m.; spartito m.; – **board** tabellone
to score [skɔ:•] v. tr. segnare; marcare, fare
punti (sport)
scorekeeper ['skɔ:,ki:pə•] s. segnapunti m. inv.
scoria ['skɔ:rɪə] s. scoria f.
scorn [skɔ:n] s. disprezzo m.
Scorpio ['skɔ:pɪou] s. Scorpione m. (astr.)
scorpion ['skɔ:pjən] s. scorpione m.
Scot [skɒt] agg. scozzese (di persone)
Scotch [skɒtʃ] agg. scozzese
Scotsman ['skɒtsmən] s. scozzese m.
Scottish ['skɒtɪʃ] agg. scozzese (di cose)
scoundrel ['skaundrəl] s. mascalzone m.
to scour ['skauə•] v. tr. strofinare; lucidare •
percorrere
scourge [skə:dʒ] s. frusta f.; flagello m.
scourging ['skə:dʒɪŋ] s. flagellazione f.
scowl [skaul] s. cipiglio m.; sguardo m. minaccioso
to scowl [skaul] v. intr. acigliarsi
to scramble ['skræmbl] v. intr. arrampicarsi;
mescolare; **scrambled eggs** uova strapazzate
scrap [skræp] s. avanzo m.; rottame m.; scarto
m.; frammento m.
scrape [skreip] s. scorticatura f.; guaio m.; impaccio m.
to scrape [skreip] v. tr. grattare; raschiare
scraper ['skreipə•] s. raschietto m.
scraping ['skreipɪŋ] s. scrostatura f.
scratch [skrætʃ] s. graffio m.
to scratch [skrætʃ] v. tr. graffiare; grattare
scrawl [skrɔ:l] s. scarabocchio m.
to scrawl [skrɔ:l] v. tr. e intr. scarabocchiare
scream [skri:m] s. grido m.
to scream [skri:m] v. tr. e intr. gridare
screen [skri:n] s. schermo m.; **wide** – schermo
panoramico
to screen [skri:n] v. tr. schermare
screening ['skri:nɪŋ] s. schermatura f.

screenplay ['skri:n,pleɪ] s. sceneggiatura f.
screenwriter ['skri:n,raɪtə•] s. sceneggiatore m.
screw [skru:] s. vite f. (mecc.)
to screw [skru:] v. tr. avvitare
screwdriver ['skru:,draɪvə•] s. cacciavite m.
inv.
scribble ['skribl] s. scarabocchio m.
to scribble ['skribl] v. tr. scarabocchiare
script [skript] s. testo m.; scaletta f.; sceneggiatura f.; – **writer** sceneggiatore
scrub [skrʌb] s. boscaglia f.
scruple ['skru:pl] s. scrupolo m.
scrupulous ['skru:pjuləs] agg. scrupoloso
scuba ['skju:bə] s. autorespiratore m.
scuffle ['skʌfl] s. mischia f., tafferuglio m.
sculptor ['skʌlptə•] s. scultore m.
sculptural ['skʌlptʃərəl] agg. scultoreo
sculpture ['skʌlptʃə•] s. scultura f.
scum [skʌm] s. feccia f.
scurry ['skʌrɪ] s. scorbuto m.
sea [si:] s. mare m.; – **gull** gabbiano; – **quake**
maremoto; – **storm** mareggiata; – **urchin** riccio di mare
seal [si:l] s. bollo m.; sigillo m. • foca f.
seam [si:m] s. cucitura f.
seaman ['si:mən] s. marinaio m.
seaplane ['si:-pleɪn] s. idrovolante m.
search [sə:tʃ] s. ricerca f.; perquisizione f.
to search [sə:tʃ] v. tr. e intr. ricercare, frugare
searchlight ['sə:tʃ-laɪt] s. proiettore m.; riflet-
tore m.
season ['si:zn] s. stagione f.; tempo m.; – **ticket** abbonamento; **off** – fuori stagione
to season ['si:zn] v. tr. stagionare; condire
seasonal ['si:zənl] agg. stagionale
seasoned ['si:zənd] agg. stagionato; condito
seasoning ['si:znɪŋ] s. stagionatura f.; condimento m.
seat [si:t] s. posto m. (a sedere); sedia f.; seggio
m.; sede f.
seaweed ['si:-wi:d] s. alga f.
sebaceous [sɪ'beɪʃəs] agg. sebaceo
secession [sɪ'seʃən] s. secessione f.
secessionist [sɪ'seʃnɪst] s. secessionista m. e f.
to seclude [sɪ'klu:d] v. tr. isolare; – **oneself**
isolarsi
secluded [sɪ'klu:dɪd] agg. appartato, isolato
seclusion [sɪ'kju:ʒən] s. isolamento m.; clausura f.
second ['sekənd] agg. e s. secondo m.; – **born**
secondogenito; – **hand** usato, di seconda
mano
secondary ['sekəndərɪ] agg. secondario

secondly ['sekəndli] *avv.* in secondo luogo
secrecy ['si:krisi] *s.* segretezza *f.*
secret ['si:krit] *agg. e s.* segreto *m.*
secretariat [,sekrə'teəriət] *s.* segretariato *m.*; segreteria *f.*
secretary ['sekrətri] *s.* segretario *m.*, segretaria *f.*
to secrete [si'kri:t] *v. tr.* secernere
secretion [si'kri:ʃən] *s.* secrezione *f.*
sect [sekt] *s.* setta *f.*; fazione *f.*
sectarian [sek'teəriən] *s.* settario *m.*
section ['sekʃən] *s.* sezione *f.*; scomparto *m.*; rubrica *f.*
sector ['sektə*] *s.* settore *m.*
secular ['sekjulə*] *agg.* secolare
secure [si'kju:ə*] *agg.* sicuro
to secure [si'kjuə*] *v. tr.* difendere; ottenere, procurarsi
security [si'kjuəriti] *s.* sicurezza *f.*; **social** - previdenza sociale
sedan [si'dæn] *s.* berlina *f.*; portantina *f.*
sedative ['sedətiv] *agg. e s.* sedativo *m.*
sedentary ['sedntəri] *agg.* sedentario
to seduce [si'dju:s] *v. tr.* sedurre; corrompere
seducer [si'dju:sə*] *s.* seduttore *m.*
seduction [si'dʌkʃən] *s.* seduzione *f.*
seductive [si'dʌktiv] *agg.* seducente
to see [si:] *v. tr. e intr.* vedere; capire; visitare; **see you (later)** ci vediamo (più tardi)
seed [si:d] *s.* seme *m.*; semenza *f.*
to seek [si:k] *v. tr. e intr.* cercare; ricercare
to seem [si:m] *v. intr.* parere, sembrare
seer [si:ə*] *s.* veggente *m. e f.*
segment ['segmənt] *s.* segmento *m.*
segregation [,segri'geiʃən] *s.* segregazione *f.*
seismic(al) ['saizmik(əl)] *agg.* sismico
seismologist [saiz'mɔlədʒist] *s.* sismologo *m.*
to seize [si:z] *v. tr.* afferrare, catturare; impadronirsi • *intr.* grippare
seizure ['si:ʒə*] *s.* presa *f.*; cattura *f.*
seldom ['seldəm] *avv.* raramente
to select [si'lekt] *v. tr.* scegliere, selezionare
selection [si'lekʃən] *s.* scelta *f.*, selezione *f.*
selective [si'lektiv] *agg.* selettivo
self [self] *s.* sé; di sé; automatico (nei composti); **-centred** egocentrico; **-defence** autodifesa; **-portrait** autoritratto; **-sticking** autoadesivo; **-timer** autoscatto
to sell [sel] *v. tr.* vendere; **- off** svendere
seller ['selə*] *s.* venditore *m.*
selling ['seliŋ] *s.* vendita *f.*; **- off** svendita
semaphore ['seməfɔ:*] *s.* semaforo *m.* (*ferr.*)

semblance ['sembləns] *s.* apparenza *f.*; somiglianza *f.*
semester [si'mestə*] *s.* semestre *m.*
semiaxis [,semi'æksis] *s.* semiasse *m.*
semicircle ['semi,sə:kəl] *s.* semicerchio *m.*
semicircular ['semi'sə:kjulə*] *agg.* semicircolare
semiconductor [,semikən'dʌktə*] *s.* semiconduttore *m.*
semifinal ['semi'fainl] *s.* semifinale *f.*
seminar ['semina:*] *s.* seminario *m.*
seminarist ['seminarist] *s.* seminarista *m.*
seminary ['seminəri] *s.* seminario *m.*
semolina [,semə'li:nə] *s.* semolino *f.*
senate ['senit] *s.* senato *m.*
senator ['senətə*] *s.* senatore *m.*
to send [send] *v. tr.* mandare, inviare, spedire; **- for** mandare a chiamare
sender ['sendə*] *s.* mittente *m. e f.*
senile ['si:nail] *agg.* senile
senility [si'niliti] *s.* senilità *f.*
senior ['si:niə*] *agg.* maggiore; più anziano
sensation [sen'seiʃən] *s.* sensazione *f.*
sensational [sen'seiʃənl] *agg.* sensazionale
sense [sens] *s.* senso *m.*, sensazione *f.*; buonsenso *m.*
sensibility [,sensi'biliti] *s.* sensibilità *f.*
sensible ['sensəbl] *agg.* sensibile
sensitive ['sensitiv] *agg.* sensibile; delicato
sensual ['sensjuəl] *agg.* sensuale
sensuality [,sensju'æliti] *s.* sensualità *f.*
sentence ['sentəns] *s.* sentenza *f.*; condanna *f.*; frase *f.*
to sentence ['sentəns] *v. tr.* condannare
sentiment ['sentimənt] *s.* sentimento *m.*
sentimental [,senti'mentl] *agg.* sentimentale
sentry ['sentri] *s.* sentinella *f.*; **- box** garitta *f.*
separate ['seprit] *agg.* separato; distinto
to separate ['sepəreit] *v. tr.* separare • *intr.* separarsi
separation [,sepə'reiʃən] *s.* separazione *f.*, distacco *m.*
separator ['sepəreitə*] *s.* separatore *m.*
sepia ['si:pjə] *s.* nero *m.* di seppia
September [səp'tembə*] *s.* settembre *m.*
septic ['septik] *agg.* settico; **to go** – infettarsi
septum ['septəm] *s.* setto *m.*
sepulchral [si'pʌlkrəl] *agg.* sepolcrale
sepulchre ['sepəlkə*] *s.* sepolcro *m.*
sepulture ['sepəltʃə*] *s.* sepoltura *f.*
sequel ['si:kwəl] *s.* seguito *m.*; effetto *m.*
sequence ['si:kwəns] *s.* sequenza *f.*, successione *f.*; serie *f.*

to sequestrate [si'kwestreit] v. tr. sequestrare

sequestration [ˌsi:kwes'treiʃən] s. sequestro m.

serene [si'ri:n] agg. sereno

serenity [si'reniti] s. serenità f.

sergeant ['sa:dʒənt] s. sergente m. (mil.); brigadiere m. (polizia)

serial ['siəriəl] agg. seriale; di serie • s. sceneggiato m.

series ['siəri:z] s. serie f. inv.

serious ['siəriəs] agg. serio; grave

seriousness ['siəriəsnis] s. serietà f.; gravità f.

sermon ['sə:mən] s. sermone m.

to sermonize ['sə:mənaiz] v. intr. predicare

serotherapy [ˌsiərou'θerəpi] s. sieroterapia f.

serpent ['sə:pənt] s. serpente m.

serpentine ['sə:pəntain] s. serpentina f.

serum ['siərəm] s. siero m.

servant ['sə:vənt] s. cameriere m.

to serve [sə:v] v. tr. e intr. servire

service ['sə:vis] s. servizio m.; prestazione f.

serviette [ˌsə:vi'et] s. salvietta f.

servile ['sə:vail] agg. servile

servo-brake ['sə:və'breik] s. servofreno m.

servo-control ['sə:vəkən'troul] s. servocomando m.

servo-mechanism ['sə:və'mekənizəm] s. servomeccanismo m.

servomotor ['sə:və'moutə*] s. servomotore m.

session ['seʃən] s. sessione f., seduta f.

set [set] s. complesso m., insieme m.

to set [set] v. tr. mettere, porre; prestabilire; regolare; – up installare

setting ['setiŋ] s. sistemazione f.; incastonatura f.; messa f. in scena; – up installazione

settle ['setl] s. cassapanca f.

to settle ['setl] v. tr. decidere; fissare; definire; saldare • intr. stabilirsi

settlement ['setlmənt] s. sistemazione f.; insediamento m.; saldo m.

several ['sevrəl] agg. e pron. parecchi; alcuni

severe [si'viə*] agg. severo

severity [si'veriti] s. severità f.

to sew [sou] v. tr. cucire

sewage ['sju:idʒ] s. fognatura f.

sewer ['sjuə*] s. fogna f.

sex [seks] s. sesso m. • agg. sessuale

sexist ['seksist] agg. maschilista

sextant ['sekstənt] s. sestante m.

sexual ['seksjuəl] agg. sessuale

sexuality [ˌseksju'æliti] s. sessualità f.

shabby ['ʃæbi] agg. malmesso; trasandato

shade [ʃeid] s. ombra f.; sfumatura f.

to shade [ʃeid] v. tr. ombreggiare

shading ['ʃeidiŋ] s. ombreggiatura f.

shadow ['ʃædou] s. ombra f.

to shadow ['ʃædou] v. tr. ombreggiare

shadowy ['ʃædoui] agg. ombroso

shady ['ʃeidi] agg. ombroso; ambiguo

shaft [ʃa:ft] s. asta f.; albero m. (mecc.)

shake [ʃeik] s. scossone m.; frullato m.

to shake [ʃeik] v. tr. agitare, scuotere • intr. traballare

shaken ['ʃeikən] agg. agitato

shaking ['ʃeikiŋ] agg. tremante • s. tremore m.; scossa f.

shaky ['ʃeiki] agg. malfermo

shallop ['ʃæləp] s. scialuppa f.

shallow ['ʃælou] agg. basso, poco profondo

shame [ʃeim] s. pudore m.; vergogna f.

shameful ['ʃeimful] agg. vergognoso

shameless ['ʃeimlis] agg. spudorato

shammy ['ʃæmi] agg. scamosciato (fam.)

shampoo [ʃæm'pu:] s. shampoo m. inv.

shank [ʃæŋk] s. stinco m.

shape [ʃeip] s. foggia f.; forma f.

to shape [ʃeip] v. tr. formare; plasmare

shapely ['ʃeipli] agg. armonioso, ben fatto (di persona)

share [ʃeə*] s. quota f.; azione f. (fin.)

to share [ʃeə*] v. tr. condividere; partecipare

sharecropping ['ʃeə'krɔpiŋ] s. mezzadria f.

sharing ['ʃeəriŋ] s. partecipazione f.

shark [ʃa:k] s. squalo m.

sharp [ʃa:p] agg. acuto; affilato; netto; tagliente; energico

to sharpen ['ʃa:pən] v. tr. affilare

to shatter ['ʃætə*] v. tr. infrangere

shave [ʃeiv] s. rasatura f.

to shave [ʃeiv] v. tr. radere • intr. radersi

shawl [ʃɔ:l] s. scialle m.

to shear [ʃiə*] v. tr. tosare

sheath [ʃi:θ] s. guaina f.

shed [ʃed] s. capannone m.

sheep [ʃi:p] s. pecora f.; – fold ovile; – farming pastorizia

sheer [ʃiə*] agg. puro

sheet [ʃi:t] s. lenzuolo m.; foglio m.; lastra f.; scotta f. (naut.)

sheik(h) [ʃeik] s. sceicco m.

shelf [ʃelf] s. mensola f., scaffale m.

shell [ʃel] s. guscio m.; conchiglia f.

shellfish ['ʃel-fiʃ] s. mollusco m.

shelter ['ʃeltə*] s. rifugio m.; riparo m.

to shelter ['ʃeltə*] v. tr. proteggere • intr. rifugiarsi

shepherd ['ʃepəd] s. pastore m.

sheriff ['ʃerif] *s.* sceriffo *m.*

shield [ʃi:ld] *s.* scudo *m.*; protezione *f.*

to shield [ʃi:ld] *v. tr.* proteggere; schermare

shift [ʃift] *s.* spostamento *m.*; turno *m.*

to shift [ʃift] *v. tr.* spostare; trasferire

shilling ['ʃiliŋ] *s.* scellino *m.*

to shine [ʃain] *v. intr.* brillare

shingle ['ʃiŋgl] *s.* ciottoli *m. pl.*

shining ['ʃainiŋ] *agg.* fulgido, lucente

ship [ʃip] *s.* nave *f.*

to ship [ʃip] *v. tr.* spedire; imbarcare

shipment ['ʃipmənt] *s.* imbarco *m.*; invio *m.*

shipping ['ʃipiŋ] *s.* spedizione *f.*; navigazione *f.*; – **agent** spedizioniere

shipyard ['ʃip-ja:d] *s.* cantiere *m.*

shirt [ʃɜ:t] *s.* camicia *f.*, camicetta *f.*

shiver ['ʃivə*] *s.* brivido *m.*

to shiver ['ʃivə*] *v. intr.* rabbrividire

shivering ['ʃivəriŋ] *s.* tremore *m.*

shoal [ʃoul] *s.* bassofondo *m.*

shock [ʃɔk] *s.* scossa *f.*; colpo *m.*; – **absorber** ammortizzatore

shocking ['ʃɔkiŋ] *agg.* scandaloso; sciocccante

shoe [ʃu:] *s.* scarpa *f.*; – **lace** stringa; – **rack** scarpiera; – **repairer** calzolaio

shoehorn ['ʃu:hɔ:n] *s.* calzascarpe *m. inv.*

shoemaker ['ʃu:meikə*] *s.* calzolaio *m.*

shoeshine ['ʃu:ʃain] *s.* lustrascarpe *m. e f. inv.*

shoot [ʃu:t] *s.* germoglio *m.*

to shoot [ʃu:t] *v. tr.* gettare; sparare; filmare

shooting ['ʃu:tiŋ] *s.* caccia *f.*; **trap** – tiro al piattello

shop [ʃɔp] *s.* bottega *f.*, negozio *m.*; – **assistant** commesso, commessa; – **lifter** taccheggiatore; – **window** vetrina

shopper ['ʃɔpə*] *s.* acquirente *m. e f.*

shopping ['ʃɔpiŋ] *s.* commissioni *f. pl.*; spesa *f.*

shore [ʃɔ:*] *s.* lido *m.*; riva *f.*, sponda *f.*; **off** – al largo

short [ʃɔ:t] *agg.* basso; corto; – **cut** scorciatoia; – **lived** momentaneo; – **sighted** miope; **in** – in breve

short-circuit ['ʃɔ:t'sə:kit] *s.* cortocircuito *m.*

to shorten ['ʃɔ:tn] *v. tr.* accorciare

shot [ʃɔt] *s.* sparo *m.*; ripresa *f.* (cin.)

shotgun ['ʃɔtgʌn] *s.* schioppo *m.*

shoulder ['ʃouldə*] *s.* spalla *f.*; corsia *f.*; **hard** – corsia d'emergenza

shout [ʃaut] *s.* grido *m.*

to shout [ʃaut] *v. intr.* gridare, urlare

shove [ʃʌv] *s.* spinta *f.*

to shove [ʃʌv] *v. tr.* spingere

shovel ['ʃʌvl] *s.* pala *f.*, paletta *f.*

to shovel ['ʃʌvl] *v. tr.* spalare

show [ʃou] *s.* mostra *f.*; dimostrazione *f.*; spettacolo *m.*

to show [ʃou] *v. tr.* mostrare, esibire; indicare; manifestare; **in** introdurre; – **off** ostentare; – **oneself** mostrarsi

shower ['ʃauə*] *s.* doccia *f.*; scroscio *m.*; **to take a** – fare la doccia

to shower ['ʃauə*] *v. intr.* diluviare; fare la doccia

showy ['ʃoui] *agg.* appariscente, vistoso

shrewd [ʃru:d] *agg.* furbo

shrill [ʃril] *agg.* squillante

shrimp [ʃrimp] *s.* gamberetto *m.*

shrine [ʃrain] *s.* reliquiario *m.*; santuario *m.*

to shrink [ʃriŋk] *v. intr.* ritirarsi

shroud [ʃraud] *s.* sartia *f.*

shrub [ʃrʌb] *s.* arbusto *m.*

to shrug [ʃrʌg] *v. intr.* scrollare le spalle; – **off** passare sopra a

shudder ['ʃʌdə*] *s.* brivido *m.*

to shudder ['ʃʌdə*] *v. intr.* rabbrividire

to shuffle ['ʃʌfl] *v. tr.* rimescolare

to shunt [ʃʌnt] *v. tr.* deviare; smistare

shunting ['ʃʌntiŋ] *s.* smistamento *m.*

shut [ʃʌt] *agg.* chiuso

to shut [ʃʌt] *v. tr.* chiudere • *intr.* chiudersi; **shut up!** piantala!

shutter ['ʃʌtə*] *s.* persiana *f.*; otturatore *m.*

shuttle ['ʃʌtl] *s.* navetta *f.*

shy [ʃai] *agg.* timido; pauroso

shyness ['ʃainis] *s.* timidezza *f.*

sick [sik] *agg.* ammalato; **to feel** – avere la nausea

to sicken ['sikn] *v. tr.* nauseare • *intr.* aver la nausea

sickening ['sikniŋ] *agg.* nauseabondo

sickle ['sikl] *s.* falce *f.*

side [said] *s.* lato *m.*; fiancata *f.* • *agg.* laterale; – **slip** sbandamento

to side [said] *v. intr.* parteggiare

siege [si:dʒ] *s.* assedio *m.*

sieve [siv] *s.* setaccio *m.*

to sigh [sai] *v. intr.* sospirare

sight [sait] *s.* vista *f.*; veduta *f.*

to sight [sait] *v. tr.* avvistare

sign [sain] *s.* cenno *m.*; indizio *m.*; insegna *f.*; segnale *m.*

to sign [sain] *v. tr.* firmare

signal ['signl] *s.* segnale *m.*; **warning** – segnale d'allarme

to signal ['signl] *v. tr.* segnalare

signalling ['signaliŋ] s. segnalazione f.
signature ['signitʃə*] s. firma f.
signboard ['sainbɔ:d] s. cartello m.; insegna f.
significant [sig'nifikənt] agg. significativo
to signify ['signifai] v. tr. significare, implicare
silence ['sailəns] s. silenzio m.
silencer ['sailənsə*] s. marmitta f.; silenziatore m.
silent ['sailənt] agg. silenzioso
silk [silk] s. seta f.
sill [sil] s. soglia f.; davanzale m.
silly ['sili] agg. scemo, sciocco
silvan ['silvən] agg. silvestre
silver ['silvə*] s. argento m.
silverware ['silvəweə*] s. argenteria f.
similar ['similə*] agg. simile
similarity [,simi'læriti] s. somiglianza f.; similitudine f.
similitude [si'militju:d] s. similitudine f.
simple ['simpl] agg. semplice
simplicity [sim'plisiti] s. semplicità f.
to simplify ['simplifai] v. tr. semplificare
simply ['simpli] avv. semplicemente
simulation [,simju'leiʃən] s. simulazione f.
simultaneous [,siməl'teinjəs] agg. simultaneo
sin [sin] s. peccato m.; colpa f.
to sin [sin] v. intr. peccare
since [sins] prep. da; da quando • cong. poiché, giacché
sincere [sin'siə*] agg. sincero
sincerity [sin'seriti] s. sincerità f.
sine [sain] s. seno m. (mat.)
sinew ['sinju:] s. tendine m.
sinewy ['sinju:i] agg. muscoloso
sinful ['sinful] agg. peccaminoso
to sing [siŋ] v. tr. e intr. cantare
singer ['siŋə*] s. cantante m. e f.
singing ['siŋiŋ] s. canto m.
single ['siŋgl] agg. singolo, semplice; scapolo
singly ['siŋgli] avv. singolarmente
singsong ['siŋ-sɔŋ] s. nenia f.
singular ['siŋgjulə*] agg. singolare
sinister ['sinistə*] agg. sinistro, infame, minaccioso
sink [siŋk] s. lavandino m.
to sink [siŋk] v. intr. affondare
sinner ['sinə*] s. peccatore m.
sinusitis [,sainə'saitis] s. sinusite f.
sip [sip] s. sorso m.
to sip [sip] v. tr. e intr. sorseggiare
siphon ['saifən] s. sifone m.
sir [sə:*] s. signore m.
siren ['saiərin] s. sirena f.

sister ['sistə*] s. sorella f.; **sister-in-law** cognata; **half** - sorellastra
to sit [sit] v. intr. sedere; - **down** accomodarsi
site [sait] s. ubicazione f.
sitting ['sitiŋ] s. seduta f.; - **room** salotto
situation [,sitju'eiʃən] s. situazione f.; posizione f.
size [saiz] s. dimensione f.; misura f., taglia f.; formato m.
skate [skeit] s. pattino m.
to skate [skeit] v. intr. pattinare
skating ['skeitiŋ] s. pattinaggio m.; **roller** - pattinaggio a rotelle; **figure** - pattinaggio artistico; **ice** - pattinaggio su ghiaccio
skein [skein] s. matassa f.
skeleton ['skelitn] s. scheletro m.; ossatura f.
sketch [sketʃ] s. schizzo m.; bozzetto m.
skewer ['skju:ə*] s. spiedino m.
ski [ski:] s. sci m.; - **rack** portasci; - **stick** racchetta; **water** - sci d'acqua
to ski [ski:] v. intr. sciare
skid [skid] s. slittata f.
to skid [skid] v. intr. scivolare; sbandare; slittare
skier ['ski:ə*] s. sciatore m.
skiing ['ski:iŋ] s. sci m.
skilful ['skilful] agg. abile, destro
skill [skil] s. destrezza f., maestria f.
to skim [skim] v. tr. scorrere, sfogliare
to skimp [skimp] v. tr. e intr. lesinare
skin [skin] s. pelle f.; epidermide f.; buccia f.; - **diver** subacqueo
to skin [skin] v. tr. spellare; sbucciare
skip [skip] s. salto m.
to skip [skip] v. tr. e intr. saltare
skipper ['skipə*] s. comandante m. (naut.)
skirmish ['skə:miʃ] s. scaramuccia f.
skirt [skə:t] s. gonna f.; **pleated** - gonna a pieghe
skittish ['skitiʃ] agg. vivace, volubile
skittle ['skitl] s. birillo m.
skull [skʌl] s. cranio m.; teschio m.
sky [skai] s. cielo m.; - **diving** paracadutismo
skylark ['skaila:k] s. allodola f.
skylight ['skailait] s. lucernario m.
skyscraper ['skai,skreipə*] s. grattacielo m.
slab [slæb] s. lastra f.; piastra f.; fetta f.
slack [slæk] agg. fiacco; lento, allentato
to slacken ['slækən] v. tr. mollare
slag [slæg] s. scoria f.
to slam [slæm] v. tr. sbattere
slander ['sla:ndə*] s. calunnia f.; diffamazione f.

slang [slæŋ] s. gergo m.

slant [sla:nt] s. pendio m.

to slant [sla:nt] v. intr. pendere

slap [slæp] s. ceffone m., sberla f., schiaffo m.

to slap [slæp] v. tr. schiaffeggiare

slash [slæʃ] s. taglio m.; sfregio m.; barra f.

to slash [slæʃ] v. tr. sfregiare; stroncare (fig.)

slate [sleit] s. ardesia f.; tegola f. d'ardesia

to slate [sleit] v. tr. criticare (fam.)

slating ['sleitiŋ] s. stroncatura f.

slaughter ['slɔ:tə°] s. massacro m.; strage f.; - house mattatoio

slave [sleiv] agg. e s. schiavo m.

slavery ['sleivəri] s. schiavitù f.

to slay [slei] v. tr. ammazzare

sled [sledʒ] s. slitta f.

sledge [sledʒ] s. slitta f.

sleep [sli:p] s. sonno m.; dormita f.; **sound** - sonno profondo

to sleep [sli:p] v. intr. dormire

sleepiness ['sli:pinis] s. sonnolenza f.

sleeping ['sli:piŋ] agg. addormentato; - **draught** sonnifero

sleeplessness ['sli:plisnis] s. insonnia f.

sleepy ['sli:pi] agg. assonnato; - **head** dormiglione

sleet [sli:t] s. nevischio m.

sleeve [sli:v] s. manica f.; custodia f.

sleigh [slei] s. slitta f.

slender ['slendə°] agg. esile, snello; tenue

slice [slais] s. fetta f., trancio m.

to slice [slais] v. tr. affettare

slick [slik] agg. sdrucciolevole; astuto

slide [slaid] s. scivolata f.; diapositiva f.

to slide [slaid] v. intr. scivolare

sliding ['slaidiŋ] agg. scorrevole

slight [slait] agg. leggero, lieve; piccolo; scarso; sottile; insignificante • s. affronto m.

slim [slim] agg. magro, snello

to slim [slim] v. intr. dimagrire

slime [slaim] s. limo m., melma f.

slimming ['slimiŋ] agg. dimagrante

slimy ['slaimi] agg. viscido

sling [sliŋ] s. fionda f.; fascia f., benda f. (med.)

slip [slip] s. scivolone m.; errore m.; svista f.; tagliando m.; sottoveste f.

to slip [slip] v. intr. scivolare; slittare (mecc.); - **up** sbagliare

slipper ['slipə°] s. pantofola f.

slippery ['slipəri] agg. scivoloso, sdrucciolevole, viscido

slipshod ['slipʃɔd] agg. trasandato

slipway ['slipwei] s. scivolo m.

slit [slit] s. fenditura f., fessura f., spacco m.

slope [sloup] s. pendio m., inclinazione f.

slot [slɔt] s. apertura f.; fessura f.

slow [slou] agg. lento • avv. lentamente, piano; **slowly** adagio

to slow [slou] v. tr. rallentare

slowness ['slou-nis] s. lentezza f.

slug [slʌg] s. lumaca f.; gettone m. (USA); proiettile m. (fam.)

sluggish ['slʌgiʃ] agg. indolente

slum [slʌm] s. catapecchia f.; bassifondi m. pl.

to slump [slʌmp] v. intr. crollare; piombare

slush [slʌʃ] s. poltiglia f.

sly [slai] agg. furbo, scaltro

smack [smæk] s. aroma m., gusto m.; schiaffo m.; bacio m.

to smack [smæk] v. tr. schiaffeggiare; baciare; - **of** sapere di

small [smɔ:l] agg. piccolo; **smaller** minore; **smallest** minimo

smart [sma:t] agg. elegante; intelligente; svelto

to smash [smæʃ] v. tr. fracassare, schiantare • intr. frantumarsi

smattering ['smætəriŋ] s. infarinatura f. (fig.)

smell [smel] s. odore m.

to smell [smel] v. tr. e intr. odorare, annusare; avere odore

smile [smail] s. sorriso m.

to smile [smail] v. intr. sorridere

smiling ['smailiŋ] agg. sorridente

smith [smiθ] s. fabbro m.

smoke [smouk] s. fumo m.

to smoke [smouk] v. tr. e intr. fumare; **smoked** affumicato

smoker ['smoukə°] s. fumatore m.

smoky ['smouki] agg. fumoso

smooth [smu:ð] agg. liscio, levigato; facile

to smooth [smu:ð] v. tr. lisciare, levigare

smoothness ['smu:ðnis] s. levigatezza f.

to smother ['smʌðə°] v. tr. soffocare

to smoulder ['smouldə°] v. intr. covare sotto la cenere

smuggler ['smʌglə°] s. contrabbandiere m.

smut [smʌt] s. oscenità f.

snack [snæk] s. spuntino m.

snail [sneil] s. lumaca f., chiocciola f.

snake [sneik] s. serpente m.

snap [snæp] s. scatto m.; schiocco m.

to snap [snæp] v. tr. e intr. azzannare; spezzare; scattare una foto (fam.)

snare [snɛə°] s. tranello m., trappola f.

to snarl [sna:l] v. intr. ringhiare

snarling ['sna:liŋ] agg. ringhioso

143

to snatch [snætʃ] *v. tr.* strappare; scippare

sneer [sniə*] *s.* ghigno *m.*; sogghigno *m.*

sneeze [sni:z] *s.* starnuto *m.*

to sneeze [sni:z] *v. intr.* starnutare

to sniff [snif] *v. tr. e intr.* annusare, fiutare

snobbery [snɔbəri] *s.* snobismo *m.*

to snoop [snu:p] *v. intr.* curiosare

to snore [snɔ:*] *v. intr.* russare

snout [snaut] *s.* muso *m.*, grugno *m.*

snow [snou] *s.* neve *f.*; – **field** nevaio *m.*; – **plough** spazzaneve; – **slide** slavina

to snow [snou] *v. intr.* nevicare

snowfall [snoufɔ:l] *s.* nevicata *f.*

snowy [snoui] *agg.* nevoso

snuff [snʌf] *s.* tabacco *m.* (da fiuto)

so [sou] *avv.* così, tanto, talmente, molto • *cong.* perciò, quindi, affinché; – **much** tanto, tanta; – **many** tanti, tante; – **far** finora; – **long** a presto!; – **what**? e allora?

to soak [souk] *v. tr.* immergere, mettere a bagno

soap [soup] *s.* sapone *m.*; – **dish** portasapone

to soap [soup] *v. tr.* insaponare

to soar [sɔ:*] *v. intr.* alzarsi in volo; veleggiare; aumentare vertiginosamente

to sob [sɔb] *v. intr.* singhiozzare, piangere

sober [soubə*] *agg.* sobrio; – **minded** morigerato

soccer [sɔkə*] *s.* calcio *m.* (*sport*); – **player** calciatore

sociable [soufəbl] *agg.* socievole

social [soufəl] *agg.* sociale; socievole; – **scientist** sociologo

socialism [soufəlizəm] *s.* socialismo *m.*

socialist [soufəlist] *agg.* socialista

society [sə'saiəti] *s.* società *f.*

sociology [,sousi'ɔlədʒi] *s.* sociologia *f.*

sock [sɔk] *s.* calza *f.* (da uomo); calzino *m.*

socket [sɔkit] *s.* cavità *f.*; presa *f.* di corrente; connettore *m.*

sod [sɔd] *s.* zolla *f.*; canaglia *f.*

sodium [soudjəm] *s.* sodio *m.*

sofa [soufə] *s.* divano *m.*

soft [sɔft] *agg.* molle, morbido; tenero; – **drink** bevanda non alcolica

to soften [sɔfn] *v. tr.* ammorbidire

soil [sɔil] *s.* suolo *m.*, terreno *m.*

to soil [sɔil] *v. tr.* imbrattare, sporcare

solar [soulə*] *agg.* solare

to solder [sɔldə*] *v. tr.* saldare

soldier [souldʒə*] *s.* soldato *m.*

soldierly [souldʒəli] *agg.* militaresco

sole [soul] *agg.* unico, singolo • *s.* suola *f.* • sogliola *f.*

to sole [soul] *v. tr.* risuolare

solely [soulli] *avv.* unicamente

solemn [sɔləm] *agg.* solenne

solemnity [sə'lemniti] *s.* solennità *f.*

solfeggio [sɔl'fedʒiou] *s.* solfeggio *m.*

solicitation [sə,lisi'teiʃən] *s.* sollecitazione *f.*

solicitor [sə'lisitə*] *s.* procuratore *m.* legale

solicitous [sə'lisitəs] *agg.* premuroso

solid [sɔlid] *agg.* solido

solidarity [,sɔli'dæriti] *s.* solidarietà *f.*

solidity [sə'liditi] *s.* solidità *f.*

soliloquy [sə'liləkwi] *s.* monologo *m.*

solitary [sɔlitəri] *agg.* solitario

solitude [sɔlitju:d] *s.* solitudine *f.*

soloist [soulouist] *s.* solista *m. e f.*

soluble [sɔljubl] *agg.* solubile

solution [sə'lu:ʃən] *s.* soluzione *f.*

to solve [sɔlv] *v. tr.* risolvere

solvent [sɔlvənt] *s.* solvente *m.*

sombre [sɔmbə*] *agg.* scuro; malinconico

some [sʌm, səm] *agg. e pron.* qualche; alcuni, alcune; un certo, una certa • *avv.* circa

somebody [sʌmbədi] *pron.* qualcuno

someday [sʌmdei] *avv.* un giorno o l'altro

somehow [sʌmhau] *avv.* in qualche modo, in un modo o nell'altro

someone [sʌmwʌn] *pron.* qualcuno

something [sʌmθiŋ] *pron.* qualcosa

sometimes [sʌmtaimz] *avv.* talvolta

somewhat [sʌmwɔt] *avv.* piuttosto, un po'

somewhere [sʌmweə*] *avv.* in qualche parte, altrove

son [sʌn] *s.* figlio *m.*; – **son-in-law** genero

song [sɔŋ] *s.* canto *m.*, canzone *f.*

sonnet [sɔnit] *s.* sonetto *m.*

sonneteer [,sɔni'tiə*] *s.* sonettista *m. e f.*

sonority [sə'nɔriti] *s.* sonorità *f.*

sonorous [sə'nɔ:rəs] *agg.* sonoro

soon [su:n] *avv.* presto, fra breve, fra poco; **as – as** appena; **sooner** prima

soot [sut] *s.* fuliggine *f.*

to soothe [su:ð] *v. tr.* consolare, calmare

soprano [sə'prɑ:nou] *s.* soprano *m. e f.*

sorbet [sɔ:bət] *s.* sorbetto *m.*

sorcery [sɔ:səri] *s.* stregoneria *f.*

sore [sɔ:*] *s.* piaga *f.*, infiammazione *f.* • *agg.* irritato, doloroso

sorrow [sɔrou] *s.* dolore *m.*, pena *f.*

sorrowful [sɔrəful] *agg.* addolorato, doloroso, malinconico

sorry [sɔri] *agg.* spiacente; **to be –** dispiacere

sort [sɔːt] s. genere m.; qualità f., categoria f.; ordinamento m.

to sort [sɔːt] v. tr. classificare; selezionare; smistare

soul [soul] s. anima f.

sound [saund] s. suono m.; audio m. inv. • agg. sano

to sound [saund] v. tr. e intr. suonare, risuonare • sondare (naut.)

sounding ['saundiŋ] s. scandaglio m.; fondale m.

soundness ['saundnis] s. sanità f.

soup [suːp] s. minestra f., zuppa f.; - **plate** piatto fondo; **vegetable** - zuppa di verdura

sour ['sauə*] agg. acidulo, aspro

to sour ['sauə*] v. tr. inacidire

source [sɔːs] s. sorgente f., fonte f.

soutane [suː'taːn] s. tonaca f.

south [sauθ] s. sud m., meridione m.

southern ['sʌðən] agg. meridionale

souvenir ['suː'vəniə*] s. ricordo m.

sovereign ['sɔvrin] s. sovrano m., sovrana f.

soviet ['souviet] agg. sovietico

sow [sou] s. scrofa f.

to sow [sou] v. tr. seminare

sowing ['souiŋ] s. semina f.

sown [soun] agg. seminato

soya-bean ['sɔi-biːn] s. soia f.

spa [spaː] s. terme f. pl.

space [speis] s. spazio m.

to space [speis] v. tr. distanziare

spaceship ['speisʃip] s. astronave f.

spacious ['speiʃəs] agg. spazioso

spade [speid] s. vanga f.; **spades** picche (carte da gioco)

to spade [speid] v. tr. vangare

span [spæn] s. spanna f., palmo m.

Spaniard ['spænjəd] s. spagnolo m.

Spanish ['spæniʃ] agg. spagnolo

to spank [spæŋk] v. tr. sculacciare

spanking ['spæŋkiŋ] agg. magnifico, ottimo (fam.)

spanner ['spænə*] s. chiave f. (mecc.)

spare [spɛə*] s. ricambio m. • agg. di scorta; - **time** tempo libero

to spare [spɛə*] v. tr. risparmiare

spark [spaːk] s. scintilla f.

sparking plug ['spaːkiŋ plʌg] s. candela f. (mecc.)

sparkling ['spaːkliŋ] agg. scintillante; effervescente; - **wine** spumante

sparrow ['spærou] s. passero m.

spasm ['spæzəm] s. spasmo m., accesso m. (med.)

spastic ['spæstik] agg. spastico

spate [speit] s. piena f.; grande quantità f.

spatter ['spætə*] s. schizzo m.

to spatter ['spætə*] v. tr. schizzare

to speak [spiːk] v. tr. e intr. dire, parlare

spear [spiə*] s. lancia f.

special ['speʃəl] agg. speciale; particolare

specialist ['speʃəlist] s. specialista

speciality [,speʃi'æliti] s. specialità f.

specialization [,speʃəlai'zeiʃən] s. specializzazione f.

to specialize ['speʃəlaiz] v. intr. specializzarsi

specialized ['speʃəlaizd] agg. specializzato

species ['spiːʃiːz] s. specie f. inv.

specific [spi'sifik] agg. specifico m.

to specify ['spesifai] v. tr. specificare

specimen ['spesimin] s. esemplare m.

speck [spek] s. granello m.

spectacle ['spektəkl] s. spettacolo m.

spectacular [spek'tækjulə*] agg. spettacolare

specular ['spekjulə*] agg. speculare

to speculate ['spekjuleit] v. intr. meditare, fare congetture; speculare

speculation [,spekju'leiʃən] s. speculazione f.

speech [spiːtʃ] s. linguaggio m.; parola f.; discorso m.

speed [spiːd] s. velocità f.; marcia f. (autom.)

speeding ['spiːdiŋ] s. eccesso m. di velocità

speedometer [spi'dɔmitə*] s. tachimetro m.

speedway ['spiːd-wei] s. autostrada f. (USA); pista f. (USA)

spelaeologist [,spiːli'ɔlədʒist] s. speleologo m.

spelaeology [,spiːli'ɔlədʒi] s. speleologia f.

spell [spel] s. incantesimo m.

to spend [spend] v. tr. e intr. trascorrere, passare; spendere

sphere [sfiə*] s. sfera f.

sphinx [sfiŋks] s. sfinge f.

spice [spais] s. spezie f. pl.; droga f.

spicy ['spaisi] agg. piccante, aromatico

spider ['spaidə*] s. ragno m.

spike [spaik] s. arpione m.; punta f.

to spill [spil] v. tr. e intr. versare, rovesciare; versarsi

to spin [spin] v. tr. filare; girare

spinach ['spinidʒ] s. spinacio m.

spindle ['spindl] s. mandrino m. (mecc.)

spine [spain] s. spina f.; spina f. dorsale; dorso m. (di libro)

spinet [spi'net] s. spinetta f.

spinning ['spiniŋ] agg. girevole; - **top** trottola

145

spinster ['spinstə*] s. zitella f.

spiral ['spaiərəl] s. spirale f.

spire ['spaiə*] s. guglia f.

spirit ['spirit] s. spirito m. • pl. liquori m.

spiritualism ['spiritjuəlizəm] s. spiritualismo m.; spiritismo m.

spit [spit] s. sputo m. • spiedo m.

to spit [spit] v. tr. sputare

spite [spait] s. ripicca f.; **in** – of nonostante

spittle ['spitl] s. saliva f.

splash [splæʃ] s. spruzzo m.; tonfo m.

to splash [splæʃ] v. tr. e intr. spruzzare

spleen [spli:n] s. milza f.

splendid ['splendid] agg. splendido

splendour ['splendə*] s. splendore m.

spline [splain] s. linguetta f.

splinter ['splintə*] s. scheggia f.

split [split] s. scissione f.

to split [split] v. tr. dividere; scindere; – **up** suddividere

splitting ['splitiŋ] s. suddivisione f.

to spoil [spoil] v. tr. guastare; viziare

spokesman ['spouksmən] s. portavoce m. inv.

spokeswoman ['spouks,wumən] s. portavoce f. inv.

sponge [spʌndʒ] s. spugna f.; – **cloth** tessuto di spugna

to sponsor ['spɔnsə*] v. tr. sponsorizzare

sponsorship ['spɔnsəʃip] s. patrocinio m.

spontaneity [,spɔntə'ni:ti] s. spontaneità f.

spontaneous [spɔn'teinjəs] agg. spontaneo

spool [spu:l] s. bobina f.

spoon [spu:n] s. cucchiaio m.

spoonful ['spu:nful] s. cucchiaiata f.

sporadic [spə'rædik] agg. sporadico

sporting ['spɔ:tiŋ] agg. sportivo

sportswear ['spɔ:tswɛə*] s. abbigliamento m. sportivo

spot [spɔt] s. macchia f.; punto m.

to spot [spɔt] v. tr. macchiare, individuare

sprain [sprein] s. distorsione f., slogatura f.; sosta f.

to sprain [sprein] v. tr. slogarsi

spray [sprei] s. spruzzo m.

to spread [spred] v. tr. diffondere, disseminare; spalmare

spring [spriŋ] s. salto m.; fonte f.; molla f. • primavera f.; – **board** trampolino, pedana

to spring [spriŋ] v. intr. saltare; – **from** derivare

sprinkle ['spriŋkl] s. spruzzo m.

to sprinkle ['spriŋkl] v. tr. spruzzare

sprint [sprint] s. scatto m., volata f.

sprinter ['sprintə*] s. scattista m. e f., velocista m. e f.

sprout [spraut] s. germoglio m.; getto m.; **Brussels sprouts** cavolini di Bruxelles

to sprout [spraut] v. intr. germogliare, spuntare

spur [spə:*] s. sperone m.

spurt [spə:t] s. getto m., zampillo m.

to spurt [spə:t] v. tr. schizzare

spy [spai] s. spia f.

squabble ['skwɔbl] s. diverbio m., litigio m.

squad [skwɔd] s. nucleo m.; squadra f.

squalid ['skwɔlid] agg. squallido

squall [skwɔ:l] s. grido m.; groppo m. di vento

squalor ['skwɔlə*] s. squallore m.

to squander ['skwɔndə*] v. tr. dilapidare; dissipare

square [skwɛə*] s. quadrato f.; riquadro m.; piazza f.

squash [skwɔʃ] s. spremuta f.

to squash [skwɔʃ] v. tr. schiacciare

squat [skwɔt] agg. tozzo; accovacciato

to squat [skwɔt] v. intr. accovacciarsi; occupare abusivamente

to squeak [skwi:k] v. intr. squittire; stridere

to squeeze [skwi:z] v. tr. spremere; strizzare

squid [skwid] s. calamaro m.

squint [skwint] s. strabismo m.

squirrel ['skwirəl] s. scoiattolo m.

squirt [skwə:t] s. schizzo m.

to squirt [skwə:t] v. tr. schizzare

to stab [stæb] v. tr. pugnalare

stability [stə'biliti] s. stabilità f.

stable ['steibl] s. stalla f.; – **man** stalliere

stack [stæk] s. catasta f.

to stack [stæk] v. tr. accatastare, ammucchiare, ammassare

stadium ['steidjəm] s. stadio m.

staff [sta:f] s. personale m.

stage [steidʒ] s. palcoscenico m.; stadio m., fase f.; tappa f.

to stagger ['stægə*] v. intr. barcollare

stagnant ['stægnənt] agg. stagnante

stagy ['steidʒi] agg. teatrale

stain [stein] s. macchia f.; – **remover** smacchiatore m.

to stain [stein] v. tr. macchiare, sporcare

stainless ['steinlis] agg. inossidabile

stair [stɛə*] s. scalino m. • pl. scala f. sing.

staircase ['stɛəkeis] s. scala f.

stake [steik] s. palo m.; puntata f.

stalactite ['stæləktait] s. stalattite f.

stalagmite ['stæləgmait] s. stalagmite f.

stale [steil] *agg.* raffermo

stall [stɔ:l] *s.* chiosco *m.*, edicola *f.*; bancarella *f.*; poltrona *f.* (*teatro*)

to stall [stɔ:l] *v. tr. e intr.* spegnersi (*mecc.*); far spegnere; tirare per le lunghe (*fam.*)

to stammer ['stæmə*] *v. intr.* balbettare

stamp [stæmp] *s.* bollo *m.*; stampo *m.*; francobollo *m.*

to stamp [stæmp] *v. tr.* timbrare; affrancare

stamping ['stæmpiŋ] *s.* affrancatura *f.*

stand [stænd] *s.* posto *m.*; palco *m.*; supporto *m.*; fermata *f.*

to stand [stænd] *v. intr.* stare in piedi; stare, trovarsi; resistere • *tr.* tollerare; – **up** alzarsi; – **out** distinguersi

standard ['stændəd] *s.* stendardo *m.*; criterio *m.*; norma *f.* • *agg.* standard; comune

standardization [ˌstændədai'zeiʃən] *s.* standardizzazione *f.*; massificazione *f.*

to standardize ['stændədaiz] *v. tr.* standardizzare; normalizzare; unificare

standing ['stændiŋ] *s.* posizione *f.* • *agg.* stabile

standstill ['stændstil] *s.* arresto *m.*, stasi *f.*, punto *m.* morto

staple ['steipl] *s.* forcella *f.*; graffetta *f.*; prodotto *m.* principale, alimento *m.* principale • *agg.* di base, di prima necessità

star [sta:*] *s.* stella *f.*, astro *m.*

starboard ['sta:bəd] *s.* dritta *f.*, destra *f.* (*naut.*)

starch [sta:tʃ] *s.* amido *m.*

to starch [sta:tʃ] *v. tr.* inamidare

to stare [steə*] *v. tr.* fissare, guardare fisso

starry ['sta:ri] *agg.* stellato

start [sta:t] *s.* inizio *m.*, avvio *m.*; partenza *f.*

to start [sta:t] *v. tr.* cominciare • *intr.* sobbalzare, trasalire; cominciare

starter ['sta:tə*] *s.* antipasto *m.*; motorino *m.* d'avviamento

starting ['sta:tiŋ] *s.* inizio *m.*; avviamento *m.*

starvation [sta:'veiʃən] *s.* inedia *f.*; fame *f.*

state [steit] *s.* stato *m.*, condizione *f.*, situazione *f.*; nazione *f.*

to state [steit] *v. tr.* dichiarare, affermare, stabilire

stately ['steitli] *agg.* grandioso

statement ['steitmənt] *s.* dichiarazione *f.*

statesman ['steitsmən] *s.* statista *m.* e *f.*

station ['steiʃən] *s.* stazione *f.*

stationary ['steiʃnəri] *agg.* stazionario, fermo

stationer ['steiʃnə*] *s.* cartolaio *m.*

stationery ['steiʃnəri] *s.* cartoleria *f.*

statistics [stə'tistiks] *s. pl.* statistica *f.* sing.

statue ['stætju:] *s.* statua *f.*

statute ['stætju:t] *s.* statuto *m.*

stave [steiv] *s.* pentagramma *m.*; strofa *f.*

to stave [steiv] *v. tr. e intr.* sfondare; – **off** sfuggire a

stay [stei] *s.* soggiorno *m.*; strallo *m.*; – **sail** fiocco (*naut.*)

to stay [stei] *v. intr.* rimanere; sostare

steady ['stedi] *agg.* fermo, fisso

steak [steik] *s.* bistecca *f.*; **grilled** – bistecca ai ferri; **rare** – al sangue; **well-done** – ben cotta

to steal [sti:l] *v. tr.* rubare

steam [sti:m] *s.* vapore *m.*

steel [sti:l] *s.* acciaio *m.*; **stainless** – acciaio inossidabile

steep [sti:p] *agg.* ripido, scosceso

steeple ['sti:pl] *s.* campanile *m.*; guglia *f.*

to steer [stiə*] *v. tr. e intr.* guidare; sterzare; timonare, manovrare

steering ['stiəriŋ] *s.* sterzo *m.*; – **wheel** volante; – **look** bloccasterzo; – **gear** sterzo

steersman ['stiəzmən] *s.* timoniere *m.*

stele ['sti:li(:)] *s.* stele *f.*

stem [stem] *s.* gambo *m.*, stelo *m.*

stench [stentʃ] *s.* puzza *f.*

step [step] *s.* passo *m.*; gradino *m.*

stepfather ['step,fa:ðə*] *s.* patrigno *m.*

stepladder ['step,lædə*] *s.* scaletta *f.*

stepmother ['step,mʌðə*] *s.* matrigna *f.*

stepsister ['step,sistə*] *s.* sorellastra *f.*

sterility [ste'riliti] *s.* sterilità *f.*

sterilization [ˌsterilai'zeiʃən] *s.* sterilizzazione *f.*

to sterilize ['sterilaiz] *v. tr.* sterilizzare

sterilizer ['sterilaizə*] *s.* sterilizzatore *m.*

stern [stə:n] *s.* poppa *f.*

stew [stju:] *s.* stufato *m.*

stick [stik] *s.* bastone *m.*; bacchetta *f.*

to stick [stik] *v. tr.* conficcare; attaccare • *intr.* attaccarsi; incepparsi

sticky ['stiki] *agg.* appiccicoso

stiff [stif] *agg.* duro, rigido; – **neck** torcicollo

stiffening ['stifniŋ] *s.* indolenzimento *m.*

stifling ['staifliŋ] *agg.* soffocante

still [stil] *agg.* immobile; calmo • *avv.* ancora • *cong.* pure, tuttavia

stillness ['stilnis] *s.* tranquillità *f.*

stilt [stilt] *s.* trampolo *m.*

to stimulate ['stimjuleit] *v. tr.* incentivare; stimolare

stimulus ['stimjuləs] *s.* stimolo *m.*

sting [stiŋ] *s.* pungiglione *f.*; puntura *f.*; stimolo *m.*

to sting [stiŋ] v. tr. pungere
stingy ['stindʒi] agg. avaro, taccagno
stink [stiŋk] s. puzza f.
to stink [stiŋk] v. intr. puzzare
stinking ['stiŋkiŋ] agg. maleodorante
to stipulate ['stipjuleit] v. tr. stipulare; pattuire, convenire
to stir [stɜː*] v. tr. agitare; rimestare
stirrup ['stirəp] s. staffa f.
stitch [stitʃ] s. maglia f.; punto m.
to stitch [stitʃ] v. tr. e intr. cucire
stock [stɔk] s. ceppo m.; assortimento m.; scorta f.; – **exchange** borsa valori; – **farm** allevamento
stocking ['stɔkiŋ] s. calza f.
stomach ['stʌmək] s. stomaco m., pancia f.
stone [stoun] s. pietra f., masso m.; nocciolo m.
stool [stuːl] s. sgabello m.
to stoop [stuːp] v. intr. chinarsi
stop [stɔp] s. fermata f., sosta f.
to stop [stɔp] v. tr. arrestare; fermare; interrompere • intr. fermarsi; smettere; – **up** intasare, ostruire
stopover ['stɔp,ouvə*] s. fermata f.
stoppage ['stɔpidʒ] s. intasamento m.
stopper ['stɔpə*] s. tappo m., turacciolo m.
store [stɔː*] s. scorta f.; negozio m.; magazzino m.; – **room** dispensa, ripostiglio; **department** – grande magazzino
to store [stɔː*] v. tr. immagazzinare
storey ['stɔːri] s. piano m. (di casa)
stork [stɔːk] s. cicogna f.
storm [stɔːm] s. tempesta f., burrasca f.; uragano m.
to storm [stɔːm] v. tr. assalire; tempestare • intr. infuriare
stormy ['stɔːmi] agg. tempestoso
story ['stɔːri] s. storia f.; racconto m., narrazione f.; – **teller** narratore
stout [staut] agg. robusto; corpulento
stove [stouv] s. stufa f.
to stow [stou] v. tr. mettere via, stivare
strabismus [strə'bizməs] s. strabismo m.
straight [streit] agg. diritto; retto • avv. direttamente, diritto; – **on** sempre dritto
to straighten ['streitn] v. tr. raddrizzare
strain [strein] s. sforzo m.; tensione f.; slogatura f.
to strain [strein] v. tr. tendere; sforzare; distorcere
strained [streind] agg. sforzato
strainer ['streinə*] s. colino m., filtro m.
strait [streit] s. stretto m.

strand [strænd] s. ciocca f. (di capelli); filo m.; fune f.; trefolo m.
to strand [strænd] v. tr. e intr. arenarsi, incagliarsi
strange [streindʒ] agg. strano; estraneo
stranger ['streindʒə*] s. sconosciuto m.
to strangle ['stræŋgl] v. tr. strangolare, strozzare
strap [stræp] s. cinghia f.; cinturino m.
strategist ['strætidʒist] s. stratega m. e f.
stratosphere ['strætousfiə*] s. stratosfera f.
stratum ['straːtəm] s. strato m., falda f.
straw [strɔː] s. paglia f.; cannuccia f.
strawberry ['strɔːbəri] s. fragola f.
stray [strei] agg. randagio
to stray [streit] v. intr. deviare; divagare
stream [striːm] s. corrente f.; fiumana f.; torrente m.
street [striːt] s. strada f., via f.
streetcar ['striːtkaː*] s. tram m.
strength [streŋθ] s. forza f.; potenza f.
to strengthen ['streŋθən] v. tr. fortificare; potenziare; rinforzare
strenuous ['strenjuəs] agg. attivo, faticoso
stress [stres] s. sforzo m.; sollecitazione f. (mecc.); accento m.
stretch [stretʃ] s. stiramento m.; allungamento m.; distesa f.
to stretch [stretʃ] v. tr. tendere, distendere; allungarsi, stendersi
stretcher ['stretʃə*] s. barella f.
stretching ['stretʃiŋ] s. stiramento m.; allungamento m.
strict [strikt] agg. severo; rigoroso; preciso
strictness ['striknis] s. severità f.; rigore m.
strife [straif] s. conflitto m.
strike [straik] s. sciopero m.
to strike [straik] v. tr. battere, colpire; impressionare • intr. scioperare
striking ['straikiŋ] agg. impressionante
string [striŋ] s. stringa f.; legaccio m.; sfilza f.; corda f. (mus.); – **bean** fagiolino
strip [strip] s. striscia f.; pista f. (aer.)
to strip [strip] v. tr. strappare, togliere • intr. denudarsi
stripe [straip] s. striscia f.
stroke [strouk] s. colpo m.; bracciata f. (nuoto); tocco m.
to stroke [strouk] v. tr. lisciare; accarezzare
stroll [stroul] s. passeggiata f.
to stroll [stroul] v. intr. passeggiare
strong [strɔŋ] agg. forte, robusto; – **box** cassaforte

stronghold ['strɔŋhould] s. roccaforte f.

strongly ['strɔŋli] avv. forte; vivamente

strophe ['stroufi] s. strofa f.

structuralism ['strʌktʃərəlizəm] s. strutturalismo m.

structure ['strʌktʃə•] s. struttura f.

struggle ['strʌgl] s. lotta f.

to struggle ['strʌgl] v. intr. lottare

stub [stʌb] s. mozzicone m.

stubborn ['stʌbən] agg. ostinato, testardo

stubborness ['stʌbənnis] s. ostinazione f.; puntiglio m.

stucco ['stʌkou] s. stucco m. (arch.)

stud [stʌd] s. bottoncino m., borchia f.; chiodo m. • stallone m.

student ['stju:dənt] s. studente

studious ['stju:djəs] agg. studioso

study ['stʌdi] s. studio m.

to study ['stʌdi] v. tr. studiare; esaminare

stuff [stʌf] s. materiale m.; sostanza f.

to stuff [stʌf] v. tr. riempire; imbottire; farcire

stuffing ['stʌfiŋ] s. imbottitura f., ripieno m.; - box premistoppa

stuffy ['stʌfi] agg. soffocante

stump [stʌmp] s. moncone m.

to stun [stʌn] v. tr. stordire

stunted ['stʌntid] agg. stentato; rachitico

stupendous [stju:'pendəs] agg. stupendo

stupid ['stju:pid] agg. stupido, cretino

stupidity [stju:'piditi] s. stupidità f.

sturdy ['stə:di] agg. robusto

to stutter ['stʌtə•] v. intr. tartagliare

sty [stai] s. porcile m.; orzaiolo m.

style [stail] s. stile m.; modo m.

stylist ['stailist] s. stilista m. e f.

stylobate ['stailəbeit] s. stilobate m.

subaqueous ['sʌb'eikwiəs] agg. subacqueo

subcutaneous ['sʌbkju:'teinjəs] agg. sottocutaneo

to subdivide [sʌbdi'vaid] v. tr. e intr. suddividere

subdue [səb'dju:] v. tr. sottomettere, dominare; attenuare

subject ['sʌbdʒikt] s. argomento m.; materia f.

subjective [sʌb'dʒektiv] agg. soggettivo

to sublet [sʌb'let] v. tr. subaffittare

sublime [sə'blaim] agg. sublime, eccelso

submarine ['sʌbməri:n] agg. subacqueo

submersion [səb'mə:ʃən] s. immersione f.

submission [səb'miʃən] s. presentazione f.; sottomissione f.

to submit [səb'mit] v. tr. e intr. sottoporre; presentare; sottomettersi

subordinate [sə'bɔ:dinit] agg. subordinato; dipendente

to subordinate [sə'bɔ:dineit] v. tr. subordinare, assoggettare

subscriber [səb'skraibə•] agg. e s. abbonato m.

subscription [səb'skripʃən] s. abbonamento m.; sottoscrizione f.; **to take out a** – abbonarsi; **to discontinue a** – disdire un abbonamento

subsequent ['sʌbsikwənt] agg. successivo

subsidence [səb'saidəns] s. avvallamento m.

subsidy ['sʌbsidi] s. sussidio m.

subsistence [səb'sistəns] s. sussistenza f.

substance ['sʌbstəns] s. sostanza f.

substantial [səb'stænʃəl] agg. sostanzioso

substantive ['sʌbstəntiv] s. sostantivo m.

substitute ['sʌbstitju:t] s. sostituto m.; surrogato m.

substitution [ˌsʌbsti'tju:ʃən] s. sostituzione f.

to subtilize ['sʌti,laiz] v. tr. sottilizzare

to subtract [səb'trækt] v. tr. sottrarre

subtraction [səb'trækʃən] s. sottrazione f.

suburb ['sʌbə:b] s. sobborgo m., periferia f.

suburban [sə'bə:bən] agg. periferico

subvention [səb'venʃən] s. sovvenzione f.

subversive [sʌb'və:siv] agg. sovversivo

subway ['sʌbwei] s. sottopassaggio m.; metropolitana f. (USA)

to succeed [sək'si:d] v. intr. riuscire; succedere, subentrare

success [sək'ses] s. successo m.

successful [sək'sesful] agg. vittorioso; riuscito, di successo

succession [sək'seʃən] s. successione f.

successive [sək'sesiv] agg. successivo

successor [sək'sesə•] s. successore m.

such [sʌtʃ, sətʃ] agg. tale; simile; tanto; – **as** come; – **that** tale che

to suck [sʌk] v. tr. succhiare

sucker ['sʌkə•] s. ventosa f.

to suckle ['sʌkl] v. tr. allattare

sudden ['sʌdn] agg. improvviso; **suddenly** improvvisamente

to sue [sju:] v. tr. querelare, citare in giudizio

to suffer ['sʌfə•] v. tr. e intr. patire, soffrire

sufferer ['sʌfərə•] s. sofferente m. e f.

suffering ['sʌfəriŋ] s. sofferenza f. • agg. sofferente

to suffice [sə'fais] v. intr. bastare

sufficient [sə'fiʃənt] agg. sufficiente, bastante

to suffocate ['sʌfəkeit] v. tr. e intr. soffocare

suffocation [ˌsʌfə'keiʃən] s. soffocamento m.

sugar ['ʃugə•] s. zucchero m.; – **bowl** zuccheriera; **lump** – zucchero in zollette

to sugar ['ʃugə*] v. tr. zuccherare

sugared ['ʃugəd] agg. zuccherato

sugary ['ʃugəri] agg. mellifluo

to suggest [sə'dʒest] v. tr. suggerire; proporre

suggestible [sə'dʒestəbl] agg. suggestionabile

suggestion [sə'dʒestʃən] s. suggerimento m.

suicide ['sjuisaid] s. suicida m. e f.; suicidio m.

suit [sju:t] s. abito m. (da uomo); lite f.; seme m. (gioco)

to suit [sju:t] v. tr. adattarsi, soddisfare • intr. convenire; andare bene

suitable ['sju:təbl] agg. adatto, appropriato

suitcase ['sju:tkeis] s. valigia f.

suite [swi:t] s. appartamento m.

suitor ['sju:tə*] s. pretendente m. e f.

sulky ['sʌlki] agg. imbronciato

sullen ['sʌlən] agg. scontroso

to sully ['sʌli] v. tr. deturpare

sulphate ['sʌlfeit] s. solfato m.

sulphur ['sʌlfə*] s. zolfo m.

sultan ['sʌltən] s. sultano m.

sultanate ['sʌltənit] s. sultanato m.

sultriness ['sʌltrinis] s. afa f.

sultry ['sʌltri] agg. afoso, soffocante; passionale

sum [sʌm] s. somma f., addizione f.

to sum [sʌm] v. tr. sommare

summary ['sʌməri] s. compendio m., riassunto m.

summer ['sʌmə*] s. estate f. • agg. estivo

summertime ['sʌmətaim] s. estate f.

summit ['sʌmit] s. sommità f., vertice m.

summons ['sʌmənz] s. citazione f.

sumptuous ['sʌmptjuəs] agg. sontuoso

sun [sʌn] s. sole m.

sunburn ['sʌnbə:n] s. scottatura f.

Sunday ['sʌndi] s. domenica f.

sundial ['sʌndaiəl] s. meridiana f.

sunny ['sʌni] agg. soleggiato

sunset ['sʌnset] s. tramonto m.

sunshade ['sʌn-ʃeid] agg. parasole inv.

sunshine ['sʌnʃain] s. sole m. (luce)

sunstroke ['sʌn-strouk] s. insolazione f.

super ['sju:pə*] agg. eccellente, di prim'ordine

superb [sju:'pə:b] agg. superbo

superconductivity ['sju:pə,kəndʌk'tiviti] s. superconduttività f.

superficial [,sju:pə'fiʃəl] agg. superficiale

superfluous [sju(:)'pə:fluə] agg. superfluo

superior [sju:'piəriə*] agg. superiore

supermarket ['sju:pə,ma:kti] s. supermercato m.

superstition [,sju:pə'stiʃən] s. superstizione f.

superstitious [,sju:pə'stiʃəs] agg. superstizioso

to supervene [,sju:pə'vi:n] v. intr. sopraggiungere

to supervise ['sju:pəvaiz] v. tr. sovrintendere, seguire

supervision [,sju:pə'viʒən] s. supervisione f.

supervisor ['sju:pəvaizə*] s. supervisore m. e f.

supper ['sʌpə*] s. cena f.

to supplant [sə'pla:nt] v. tr. soppiantare; scavalcare

supple ['sʌpl] agg. flessibile

supplement ['sʌplimənt] s. supplemento m.

supplementary [,sʌpli'mentəri] agg. supplementare

supplier [sə'plaiə*] s. fornitore m.

supply [sə'plai] s. provvista f.; offerta f. (econ.)

to supply [sə'plai] v. tr. fornire, provvedere

support [sə'pɔ:t] s. supporto m., appoggio m.

to support [sə'pɔ:t] v. tr. sostenere, fiancheggiare

supporter [sə'pɔ:tə*] s. sostenitore m., tifoso m.; fautore m.

to suppose [sə'pouz] v. tr. supporre

supposition [,sʌpə'ziʃən] s. supposizione f.

suppository [sə'pɔzitəri] s. supposta f.

to suppress [sə'pres] v. tr. reprimere

supremacy [sə'preməsi] s. supremazia f.; primato m.

surcharge ['sə:tʃa:dʒ] s. sovraccarico m.; maggiorazione f., sovrapprezzo m.

to surcharge [sə:'tʃa:dʒ] v. tr. sovraccaricare; applicare un sovrapprezzo

sure [ʃuə*] agg. certo, sicuro • avv. naturalmente

surface ['sə:fis] s. superficie f. • agg. superficiale

surgeon ['sə:dʒən] s. chirurgo m.

surgery ['sə:dʒəri] s. chirurgia f.

surgical ['sə:dʒikəl] agg. chirurgico

surname ['sə:neim] s. cognome m.

to surpass [sə:'pa:s] v. tr. superare

surplus ['sə:pləs] s. eccesso m. • agg. eccedente; ~ value plusvalore

surprise [sə'praiz] s. sorpresa f.

to surprise [sə'praiz] v. tr. meravigliare, sorprendere

surprising [sə'praiziŋ] agg. sorprendente

surrealism [sə'riəlizəm] s. surrealismo m.

surrealist [sə'riəlist] s. surrealista m. e f.

to surrender [sə'rendə*] s. resa f.

to surround [sə'raund] v. tr. circondare

surrounding [sə'raundiŋ] agg. circostante

surveillance [sə:'veiləns] s. sorveglianza f.

survey ['sə:vei] *s.* rassegna *f.*; verifica *f.*; inchiesta *f.*; rilevamento *m.*

to survey [sə:'vei] *v. tr.* esaminare; sondare

surveyor [sə:'veiə*] *s.* ispettore *m.*

survival [sə'vaivəl] *s.* sopravvivenza *f.*

to survive [sə'vaiv] *v. intr.* sopravvivere, scampare a

survivor [sə'vaivə*] *s.* superstite *m.* e *f.*

susceptible [sə'septəbl] *agg.* suscettibile

to suspect [səs'pekt] *v. tr. e intr.* sospettare

to suspend [səs'pend] *v. tr.* sospendere; appendere

suspended [səs'pendid] *agg.* sospeso, pensile

suspension [səs'penʃən] *s.* sospensione *f.*

suspicion [səs'piʃən] *s.* sospetto *m.*

to sustain [səs'tein] *v. tr.* sostenere, sopportare, reggere

sustenance ['sʌstinəns] *s.* sostentamento *m.*

sutler ['sʌtlə*] *s.* vivandiere *m.*

suture ['su:tʃə*] *s.* sutura *f.*

to suture ['su:tʃə*] *v. tr.* suturare

swallow ['swɔlou] *s.* rondine *f.*; boccone *m.*; sorso *m.*

to swallow ['swɔlou] *v. tr. e intr.* deglutire, inghiottire

swamp ['swɔmp] *s.* palude *f.*

swampy ['swɔmpi] *agg.* paludoso

swan [swɔn] *s.* cigno *m.*

to swap [swɔp] *v. tr.* barattare, scambiare

swarm [swɔ:m] *s.* sciame *m.*; folla *f.*

to sway [swei] *v. tr. e intr.* distogliere; ondeggiare, vacillare, influenzare

swear [swɛə*] *s.* parolaccia *f.*

to swear [swɛə*] *v. tr. e intr.* giurare; bestemmiare

sweat [swet] *s.* sudore *m.*; faticata *f.*

to sweat [swet] *v. tr. e intr.* sudare; sgobbare

sweater ['swetə*] *s.* maglione *m.*

sweaty ['sweti] *agg.* sudato

Swede [swi:d] *s.* svedese *m.* e *f.*

Swedish ['swi:diʃ] *agg.* svedese

to sweep [swi:p] *v. tr. e intr.* scopare, spazzare

sweet [swi:t] *agg.* dolce; piacevole • *s.* caramella *f.*; dolce *m.*

to sweeten ['swi:tn] *v. tr.* addolcire; zuccherare

sweetener ['swi:tənə*] *s.* dolcificante *m.*

sweetish ['swi:tiʃ] *agg.* dolciastro

to swell [swel] *v. intr.* dilatarsi, gonfiarsi

swelling ['sweliŋ] *s.* gonfiore *m.*; rigonfiamento *m.*

swift [swift] *agg.* rapido, veloce

swim [swim] *s.* nuoto *m.*; nuotata *f.*

to swim [swim] *v. intr.* nuotare; fare il bagno

swimming ['swimiŋ] *s.* nuoto *m.*; – **pool** piscina; – **belt** salvagente

swindle ['swindl] *s.* truffa *f.*, imbroglio *m.*

to swindle ['swindl] *v. tr.* ingannare, raggirare

swine [swain] *s.* suino *m.*, porco *m.*

to swing [swiŋ] *v. intr.* dondolare; oscillare

swinging ['swiŋiŋ] *s.* oscillazione *f.* • *agg.* orientabile

Swiss [swis] *agg.* e *s.* svizzero *m.*

switch [switʃ] *s.* interruttore *m.*

to switch [switʃ] *v. tr.* scambiare; – **on** accendere; – **off** spegnere

switchboard ['switʃbɔ:d] *s.* centralino *m.*

swollen ['swoulən] *agg.* gonfio

sword [sɔ:d] *s.* spada *f.*

syllable ['siləbl] *s.* sillaba *f.*

symbiosis [,simbi'ousis] *s.* simbiosi *f.*

symbol ['simbəl] *s.* simbolo *m.*

symbolical [sim'bɔlikəl] *agg.* simbolico

symbolist ['simbəlist] *s.* simbolista *m.* e *f.*

symmetrical [si'metrikəl] *agg.* simmetrico

symmetry ['simitri] *s.* simmetria *f.*

sympathetic [,simpə'θetik] *agg.* comprensivo; simpatico (*anat.*)

sympathizer ['simpəθaizə*] *s.* simpatizzante

sympathy ['simpəθi] *s.* simpatia *f.*

symphonic [sim'fɔnik] *agg.* sinfonico

symphony ['simfəni] *s.* sinfonia *f.*

symptom ['simptəm] *s.* sintomo *m.*

symptomatology [,simptəmə'tɔlədʒi] *s.* sintomatologia *f.*

synagogue [,sinəgɔg] *s.* sinagoga *f.*

synchrony ['siŋkrəni] *s.* sincronia *f.*

syndicalist ['sindikəlist] *s.* sindacalista *m.* e *f.*

syndicate ['sindikit] *s.* sindacato *m.*

syndrome ['sindroum] *s.* sindrome *f.*

synonym ['sinənim] *s.* sinonimo *m.*

synonimous [si'nɔniməs] *agg.* sinonimo

syntax ['sintæks] *s.* sintassi *f.*

synthesis ['sinθisis] *s.* sintesi *f.*

synthetic(al) [sin'θetik(əl)] *agg.* sintetico

syringe ['sirindʒ] *s.* siringa *f.*

syrup ['sirəp] *s.* sciroppo *m.*

system ['sistim] *s.* impianto *m.*; sistema *m.*, apparato *m.*; rete *f.*

T

tabernacle ['tæbə(:)nækl] s. tabernacolo m.

table ['teibl] s. tavola f., tavolata f., mensa f.; tabella f.; – **companion** commensale; –**cloth** tovaglia

tablet ['tæblit] s. compressa f., pastiglia f.; tavoletta f.

tachycardia [,tæki'ka:diə] s. tachicardia f.

taciturn ['tæsitə:n] agg. taciturno

to tack [tæk] v. tr. imbastire • intr. bordeggiare (naut.)

to tackle [tækl] v. tr. affrontare; afferrare; esaminare

tact [tækt] s. tatto m. (fig.)

tactics ['tæktiks] s. pl. tattica f. sing.

taenia ['ti:njə] s. tenia f.

tag [tæg] s. cartellino m.

to tag [tæg] v. tr. contrassegnare; – **after**, – **behind** pedinare

tail [teil] v. s. coda f.; – **lamp** fanalino

to tail [teil] v. tr. pedinare

tailor ['teilə*] s. sarto m.; –'s **workshop** sartoria

to take [teik] v. tr. prendere; tenere; portare; accompagnare • intr. far presa (mecc.); – **away** allontanare, levare; togliere; – **back** riaccompagnare; riprendere; – **off** decollare; staccare; togliere; – **over** insediare; riprendere; – **part (in)** presenziare; **take it easy!** calma!; **taken up** occupato (di posto)

take-away ['teikəwei] agg. da asporto

take-off ['teikɔ:f] s. decollo m.

taking ['teikiŋ] agg. affascinante (fam.) • s. presa f.; prelievo m. (med.) • pl. incasso m. sing.

talc [tælk] s. talco m.

talcum ['tælkəm] s. borotalco m.

tale [teil] s. racconto m., novella f.

talent ['tælənt] s. talento m.

talisman ['tælizmən] s. talismano m.

talk [tɔ:k] s. colloquio m., discorso m.; negoziato m.

to talk [tɔ:k] v. intr. chiacchierare, conversare, dialogare

tall [tɔ:l] agg. alto (di statura)

tamarind ['tæmərind] s. tamarindo m.

tambour ['tæmbuə*] s. tamburo m. (arch.)

tambourine [,tæmbə'ri:n] s. tamburello m.

tame [teim] agg. addomesticato

tamer ['teimə*] s. domatore m. (di animali)

to tamper ['tæmpə*] v. intr. manomettere (leg.)

tampon ['tæmpən] s. tampone m. (med.)

to tampon ['tæmpən] v. tr. tamponare (med.)

tamponage ['tæmpənidʒ] s. tamponamento m. (med.)

tan [tæn] s. tintarella f.

to tan [tæn] v. tr. e intr. conciare; abbronzare; abbronzarsi

tangent ['tændʒənt] agg. e s. tangente f.

tangerine ['tændʒə'ri:n] s. mandarino m.

tangle ['tæŋgl] s. imbroglio m., groviglio m.; matassa f.

to tangle ['tæŋgl] v. tr. imbrogliare; arruffare

tango ['tæŋgou] s. tango m.

tank [tæŋk] s. bidone m., serbatoio m., tanica f.

tanker ['tæŋkə*] s. autobotte f.; petroliera f.

tanning ['tæniŋ] s. abbronzatura f.; – **cream** abbronzante

tap [tæp] s. rubinetto m.; spina f.; tappo m.; **on** – alla spina

to tap [tæp] v. tr. e intr. picchiettare, bussare

tape [teip] s. nastro m.; – **player** mangianastri

taper ['teipə*] s. rastremazione f.

tapestry ['tæpistri] s. arazzo m.; tappezzeria f.

tapeworm ['teip-wə:m] s. tenia f.

tar [ta:*] s. catrame m.

target ['ta:git] s. bersaglio m., obiettivo m.

tariff ['tærif] s. tariffa f.

tarot ['tærou] s. tarocco m.

tarpaulin [ta:'pɔ:lin] s. telone m.

tarsia ['ta:siə] s. tarsia f.

tart [ta:t] s. torta f.

task [ta:sk] s. compito m., mansione f.

to taste [teist] v. tr. sentire (col gusto), assaggiare, gustare

taste [teist] s. gusto m., sapore m.; assaggio m.

tasteless ['teistlis] agg. insapore, insipido

tasting ['teistiŋ] s. assaggio m., degustazione f.

tasty ['teisti] agg. gustoso

tattoo [tə'tu:] s. tatuaggio m.

to tattoo [tə'tu:] v. tr. tatuare

152

tauromachy [tɔ:'rɔməki] *s.* tauromachia *f.*

Taurus ['tɔ:rəs] *s.* toro *m.* (*astr.*)

tavern ['tævən] *s.* osteria *f.*, taverna *f.*

tax [tæks] *agg.* fiscale • *s.* tassa *f.*; – **office** fisco; – **stamp** bollo; – **allowance** detrazione fiscale; **inheritance** – tassa di successione

taxable ['tæksəbl] *agg.* tassabile

taxation [tæk'seiʃən] *s.* tassazione *f.*

taxi ['tæksi] *n.* taxi *m.*; – **driver** tassista; – **rank** (UK), – **stand** (USA) posteggio di taxi

tea [ti:] *s.* tè *m. inv.*

to teach [ti:tʃ] *v. tr. e intr.* insegnare

teacher ['ti:tʃə*] *s.* insegnante *m. e f.*, docente *m. e f.*, maestro *m.*

teaching ['ti:tʃiŋ] *s.* insegnamento *m.*

team [ti:m] *s.* squadra *f.* (*sport*)

teapot ['ti:pɔt] *s.* teiera *f.*

tear [teə*] *s.* lacerazione *f.*; lacrima *f.*

to tear [teə*] *v. tr. e intr.* lacerare, strappare; – **off** staccare

tearful ['tiəful] *agg.* lacrimoso

to tease [ti:z] *v. tr.* canzonare, molestare, fare dispetti

teaspoon ['ti:spu:n] *s.* cucchiaino *m.*

technical ['teknikəl] *agg.* tecnico; **technically** tecnicamente

technician [tek'niʃən] *s.* tecnico *m.*

technique [tek'ni:k] *s.* tecnica *f.*

technology [tek'nɔlədʒi] *s.* tecnologia *f.*

tedious ['ti:djəs] *agg.* noioso

teen-ager ['ti:n,eidʒə*] *s.* adolescente *m. e f.*

teens [ti:nz] *s pl.* adolescenza *f. sing.*

teetotal [ti:'toutl] *agg. e s.* astemio *m.*

telecamera [,teli'kæmərə] *s.* telecamera *f.*

telecontrol ['telikən'troul] *s.* telecomando *m.*

telegram ['teligræm] *s.* telegramma *m.*

telegraph ['teligra:f] *s.* telegrafo *m.*

telematics [,teli'mætiks] *s. pl.* (*v. al sing.*) telematica *f. sing.*

telepathy [ti'lepəθi] *s.* telepatia *f.*

telephone ['telifoun] *s.* telefono *m.*; – **exchange** centralino

to telephone ['telifoun] *v. tr. e intr.* telefonare

telescope ['teliskoup] *s.* cannocchiale *m.*, telescopio *m.*

television [teli,viʒən] *agg.* televisivo • *s.* televisione *f.*; – **set** televisore

to tell [tel] *v. tr.* dire, raccontare; insegnare;

temper ['tempə*] *s.* umore *m.*; collera *f.*

tempera ['tempərə] *s.* tempera *f.*

temperament ['tempərəmənt] *s.* temperamento *m.*

temperate ['tempərit] *agg.* temperato

temperature ['tempritʃə*] *s.* temperatura *f.*; febbre *f.*

tempest ['tempist] *s.* tempesta *f.*

Templar ['templə*] *s.* templare *m.*

temple ['templ] *s.* tempio *m.*; tempia *f.*

temporary ['tempərəri] *agg.* supplente, temporaneo

to tempt [tempt] *v. tr.* invogliare; tentare (indurre in tentazione)

tempting ['temptiŋ] *agg.* invitante, lusinghiero

tenacious [ti'neiʃəs] *agg.* tenace

tenant ['tenənt] *s.* inquilino *m.*

tench [tenʃ] *s.* tinca *f.*

tendency ['tendənsi] *s.* tendenza *f.*

tendentious [ten'denʃəs] *agg.* tendenzioso

tender ['tendə*] *agg.* tenero, molle, morbido

tenderness ['tendənis] *s.* tenerezza *f.*

tendon ['tendən] *s.* tendine *m.*

tenor ['tenə*] *s.* tenore *m.* (*mus.*)

tense [tens] *s.* tempo *m.* (*gramm.*)

tension ['tenʃən] *s.* tensione *f.*

tent [tent] *s.* tenda *f.*; tendone *m.* (di circo)

to tent [tent] *v. intr.* attendarsi

tenuous ['tenjuəs] *agg.* tenue

tepid ['tepid] *agg.* tiepido

term [tə:m] *s.* condizione *f.*; termine *m.*; vocabolo *m.*

terminal ['tə:minl] *s.* terminale *m.*; morsetto *m.* (*elettr.*)

to terminate [tə:mineit] *v. tr.* terminare

terminology [,tə:mi'nɔlədʒi] *s.* terminologia *f.*

terminus ['tə:minəs] *s.* capolinea *m. inv.*

termite ['tə:mait] *s.* termite *f.*

terrace ['terəs] *s.* terrazza *f.*

terracotta ['terə'kɔtə] *s.* terracotta *f.*

terrestrial [ti'restriəl] *agg.* terrestre

terrible ['terəbl] *agg.* terribile, tremendo

terrific [tə'rifik] *agg.* fantastico, straordinario

to terrify ['terifai] *v. tr.* spaventare, terrorizzare

territorial [,teri'tɔ:riəl] *agg.* territoriale

territory ['teritəri] *s.* territorio *m.*

terror ['terə*] *s.* terrore *m.*; birichino *m.*, peste *f.* (*fam.*)

terrorism ['terərizəm] *s.* terrorismo *m.*

terrorist ['terərist] *s.* terrorista *m. e f.*

tertiary ['tə:ʃəri] *s.* terziario *m.*

test [test] *s.* esame *m.*, analisi *f.*, collaudo *m.*, prova *f.*

to test [test] *v. tr.* analizzare, collaudare, sperimentare

testament ['testəmənt] *s.* testamento *m.*

testator [tes'teitə*] *s.* testatore *m.*

testicle ['testikl] s. testicolo m.
to testify ['testifai] v. tr. e intr. testimoniare
testimony ['testiməni] s. testimonianza f.
testis ['testis] s. testicolo m.
tetanus ['tetənəs] s. tetano m.
text [tekst] s. testo m.
textile ['tekstail] agg. tessile
texture ['tekstʃə*] s. trama f.; struttura f.
than [ðæn] cong. che; di, di quello che; di quanto (non)
to thank [θæŋk] v. tr. ringraziare; thank you grazie!
thankful ['θæŋkful] agg. riconoscente
thankfulness ['θæŋkfulnis] s. riconoscenza f.
thanks [θæŋks] s. pl. ringraziamenti m.
that [ðæt] pron. rel. che, quale • agg. e pron. dimostr. quello, codesto; ciò • cong. che; - is cioè
thaw [θɔ:] s. disgelo m.
to thaw [θɔ:] v. tr. e intr. sgelare
the [ði:] art. il, lo, la, i, gli, le
theatre ['θiətə*] s. teatro m.
theatrical [θi'ætrikəl] agg. teatrale
theft [θeft] s. furto m.
them [ðem, ðəm] pron. li, le, loro, essi, esse; - selves se stessi
theme [θi:m] s. tema m.
then [ðen] cong. così • avv. dopo, poi, quindi, allora
theologian [θiə'loudʒjən] s. teologo m.
theology [θi'ɔlədʒi] s. teologia f.
theorem ['θiərəm] s. teorema m.
theory ['θiəri] s. teoria f.
therapeutic [,θerə'pju:tik] agg. terapeutico
therapy ['θerəpi] s. terapia f.
there [ðeə*] avv. là; lì; ci; vi; -after in seguito
therefore ['ðeəfɔ:*] cong. e avv. dunque, perciò, quindi
thermae ['θə:mi] s. pl. terme f. (archeol.)
thermal ['θə:məl] agg. termale
thermic ['θə:mik] agg. termico
thermodynamics ['θə:moudai'næmiks] s. pl. (v. al sing.) termodinamica f. sing.
thermometer [θə'mɔmitə*] s. termometro m.
thermostat ['θə:moustæt] s. termostato m.
these [ði:z] agg. e pron. dimostr. questi, queste
thick [θik] agg. denso, folto; ristretto
to thicken ['θikən] v. tr. e intr. ingrossare, ispessire; ingrossarsi; addensarsi; complicarsi
thicket ['θikit] s. boscaglia f.
thickness ['θiknis] s. densità f., spessore m.
thief [θi:f] s. ladro m.; - proof device antifurto
thigh [θai] s. coscia f.; - bone femore

thimble ['θimbl] s. ditale m.
thin [θin] agg. sottile; magro
to thin [θin] v. tr. sfoltire
thing [θiŋ] s. cosa f.
to think [θiŋk] v. tr. pensare
thinker ['θiŋkə*] s. pensatore m.
thinness ['θinnis] s. magrezza f.
thirst [θə:st] s. sete f.
thirsty ['θə:sti] agg. assetato
this [ðis] agg. e pron. dimostr. questo, costui; - evening stasera; - morning stamattina; - night stanotte; - time stavolta
thong [θɔŋ] s. cinghia f. (di cuoio)
thorn [θɔ:n] s. spina f.; - bush rovi
thorough ['θʌrə] agg. completo, minuzioso, profondo
thoroughbred ['θʌrə-bred] s. purosangue m.
those [ðouz] agg. e pron. dimostr. quelli, quelle
though [ðou] cong. benché, malgrado
thought [θɔ:t] s. pensiero m.
thoughtful ['θɔ:tful] agg. pensieroso; pieno di attenzioni
thoughtless ['θɔ:tlis] agg. sconsiderato, non-curante
thousand ['θauzənd] s. migliaio m. • agg. num. inv. mille; - millions miliardo
thread [θred] s. filo m.
threat [θret] s. minaccia f.
to threaten ['θretn] v. tr. e intr. minacciare
threatening ['θretniŋ] agg. minaccioso
threshing ['θreʃiŋ] s. trebbiatura f.; - floor aia
threshold ['θreʃhould] s. soglia f.
to thrill [θril] v. tr. esaltare, eccitare • intr. entusiasmarsi, eccitarsi
thrilling ['θriliŋ] agg. elettrizzante, eccitante; sensazionale
to thrive [θraiv] v. intr. prosperare
throat [θrout] s. gola f.; - specialist laringoiatra
to throb [θrɔb] v. intr. fremere, vibrare; battere, pulsare
thrombosis [θrɔm'bousis] s. trombosi f.
throne [θroun] s. trono m.
throng [θrɔŋ] s. folla f., ressa f.
through [θru:] prep. attraverso; mediante; per, tra; durante
throw [θrou] s. lancio m.; - in rimessa laterale (calcio)
to throw [θrou] v. tr. e intr. buttare, lanciare; - up vomitare
thrush [θrʌʃ] s. tordo m.
thrust [θrʌst] s. spinta f.

to thrust [θrʌst] v. tr. e intr. piantare, spingere con forza; spingersi

thud [θʌd] s. tonfo m.

thumb [θʌmb] s. pollice m.

thunder ['θʌndə*] s. tuono m.

to thunder ['θʌndə*] v. intr. tuonare

thunderbolt ['θʌndəboult] s. fulmine m.

thundering ['θʌndəriŋ] agg. scrosciante (di applauso)

Thursday ['θə:zdi] s. giovedì m.

thus [ðʌs] avv. e cong. così, pertanto, quindi

thyme [taim] s. timo m. (bot.)

thymus ['θaiməs] s. timo m. (anat.)

thyroid ['θairoid] s. tiroide f.

tibia ['tibiə] s. tibia f.

tick [tik] s. zecca f. (zool.)

ticket ['tikit] s. biglietto m., scontrino m.; **return** – biglietto di andata e ritorno; **one-way** – biglietto di sola andata; – **clerk** bigliettaio (in stazione); – **collector** bigliettaio (in treno), controllore (sui mezzi pubblici); – **window** sportello della biglietteria; – **office** biglietteria

to tickle ['tikl] v. tr. solleticare

tide [taid] s. marea f.

to tidy (up) ['taidi] v. tr. riordinare

tie [tai] s. legame m., vincolo m.; cravatta f.; spareggio m.; – **beam** tirante

to tie [tai] v. tr. legare, annodare; spareggiare; – **up** immobilizzare

tier [tiə*] s. fila f. di posti; strato m.

tiger ['taigə*] s. tigre f.

tight [tait] agg. stretto (di abito); sbronzo (fam.) • pl. calzamaglia f. sing., collant m. sing.

to tighten ['taitn] v. tr. stringere

tile [tail] s. piastrella f., tegola f.

till [til] cong. finché • prep. fino a (temporale); – **now** finora

to till [til] v. tr. coltivare, dissodare

tiller ['tilə*] s. barra f. del timone (naut.)

to tilt [tilt] v. intr. piegare

timbal ['tæm'ba:l] s. timballo m.; timpano m. (mus.)

timber ['timbə*] s. legname m.

timbre [tɛ̃:mbr] s. timbro m. (mus.)

time [taim] s. tempo m.; momento m.; volta f.; **at the same** – contemporaneamente; **at times** talvolta; – **table** orario m.; **on** – puntuale; **opening** – ora d'apertura

timeliness ['taimlinis] s. tempestività f.

timely ['taimli] agg. tempestivo

timid ['timid] agg. timoroso

tin [tin] s. stagno m. (chim.); latta f., lattina f.,

barattolo m.; **tinned food** scatolame; – **opener** apriscatole

tinning ['tiniŋ] s. stagnatura f.

tiny ['taini] agg. minuscolo, piccino

tip [tip] s. mancia f.; punta f.

to tire [taiə*] v. tr. stancare

tired ['taiəd] agg. stanco; **to get** – affaticarsi

tiredness ['taiədnis] s. stanchezza f.

tiresome ['taiəsəm] agg. noioso

tiring ['taiəriŋ] agg. faticoso

tissue ['tisju:] s. tessuto m.; trama f.; – **paper** carta velina

titbit ['titbit] s. golosità f., leccornia f.

title ['taitl] s. titolo m.; – **page** frontespizio

to [tu:, tu, tə] prep. a, in, da (moto a luogo); a (compl. di termine)

toad [toud] s. rospo m.

toast [toust] s. pane m. tostato; brindisi m.

to toast [toust] v. tr. e intr. abbrustolire, tostare; brindare

toaster ['toustə^] s. tostapane m. inv.

tobacco [tə'bækou] s. tabacco m.

tobacconist [tə'bækənist] s. tabaccaio m.

today [tə'dei] avv. oggi

toe [tou] s. dito m. (del piede); **big** – alluce; **little** – mignolo del piede

toffee ['tɔfi] s. caramella f.

together [tə'geðə*] avv. insieme

toilet ['tɔilit] s. gabinetto m.; – **case** necessaire

token ['toukən] s. gettone m.

tolerance ['tɔlərəns] s. tolleranza f. (med.)

tolerant ['tɔlərənt] agg. tollerante

to tolerate ['tɔləreit] v. tr. tollerare

toll [toul] s. pedaggio m.; rintocco m.

tomato [tə'ma:tou] s. pomodoro m.

tomb [tu:m] s. tomba f., tumulo m.; arca f. (archeol.)

tombola ['tɔmbələ] s. tombola f.

tombstone ['tu:m-stoun] s. lapide f.

tome [toum] s. tomo m.

tomfoolery [tɔm'fu:ləri] s. buffonata f.

tomorrow [tə'mɔrou] avv. domani; **the day after** – dopodomani

ton [tʌn] s. tonnellata f.

tonality [tou'næliti] s. tonalità f.

tone [toun] s. tono m.; tonalità f.

tongs [tɔŋz] s. pl. pinza f. sing.

tongue [tʌŋ] s. lingua f.; – **twister** scioglilingua

tonic ['tɔnik] s. ricostituente m.; tonificante m.

tonight [tə'nait] avv. stasera, stanotte (la prossima)

tonsil ['tɔnsl] s. tonsilla f.

tonsillitis [,tɔnsi'laitis] s. tonsillite f.

too [tu:] *avv.* anche, pure; troppo (con agg. e avv.); – **bad** che peccato!; – **many** troppi; – **much** troppo; **none** – ... per niente ...

tool [tu:l] *s.* attrezzo *m.*, strumento *m.*, utensile *m.*

tooth [tu:θ] *s.* dente *m.*; – **brush** spazzolino da denti; – **paste** dentifricio

toothpick ['tu:θpik] *s.* stuzzicadenti *m.*

top [tɔp] *s.* cima *f.*, punta *f.*, cucuzzolo *m.*

topaz ['toupæz] *s.* topazio *m.*

topic ['tɔpik] *s.* argomento *m.*, tema *m.*

toponym ['tɔpənim] *s.* toponimo *m.*

torch [tɔ:tʃ] *s.* fiaccola *f.*; lampadina *f.* tascabile

tornado [tɔ:'neidou] *s.* tornado *m. inv.*

torpor ['tɔ:pə*] *s.* torpore *m.*

torrent ['tɔrənt] *s.* torrente *m.*

torrential [tə'renʃəl] *agg.* torrenziale

torsion ['tɔ:ʃən] *s.* torsione *f.*

tortoise ['tɔ:təs] *s.* testuggine *f.*

tortuous ['tɔ:tjuəs] *agg.* tortuoso (*fig.*)

torture ['tɔ:tʃə*] *s.* tortura *f.*

to toss [tɔs] *v. tr.* sballottare, scuotere; lanciare, scagliare

total ['toutl] *agg.* globale, totale

tottery ['tɔtəri] *agg.* pericolante; traballante

touch [tʌtʃ] *s.* tatto *m.*, tocco *m.*; pizzico *m.*; – **up** ritocco

to touch [tʌtʃ] *v. tr. e intr.* toccare; arrivare a

touching ['tʌtʃiŋ] *agg.* toccante

touchy ['tʌtʃi] *agg.* permaloso

tough [tʌf] *agg.* coriaceo; **toughly** duramente

toughness ['tʌfnis] *s.* durezza *f.*

tour [tuə*] *s.* giro *m.*, viaggio *m.*; **package** – viaggio tutto compreso

touring ['tuəriŋ] *s.* escursionismo *m.*

tourist ['tuərist] *s.* turista *m. e f.*

tow [tou] *s.* rimorchio *m.*

to tow [tou] *v. tr.* trainare; **towing** traino; – **away** rimozione (di automobili)

toward(s) [tə'wɔ:dz] *prep.* incontro, verso

towel ['tauəl] *s.* asciugamano *m.*

tower ['tauə*] *s.* torre *f.*, pilone *m.*

town [taun] *agg.* cittadino; comunale • *s.* città *f.*; – **hall** municipio

toxic ['tɔksik] *agg.* tossico

toxin ['tɔksin] *s.* tossina *f.*

toy [tɔi] *s.* giocattolo *m.*

trace [treis] *s.* traccia *f.*, orma *f.*

to trace [treis] *v. tr.* tracciare

trachea [trə'ki(:)ə] *s.* trachea *f.*

tracing ['treisiŋ] *s.* tracciato *m.*

track [træk] *s.* pista *f.*, sentiero *m.*; traccia *f.*; battistrada *m. inv.*

to track [træk] *v. tr.* rintracciare

tractable ['træktəbl] *agg.* trattabile

traction ['trækʃən] *s.* trazione *f.*

tractor ['træktə*] *s.* trattore *m.*

trade [treid] *s.* commercio *m.*, mestiere *m.* • *agg.* commerciale; – **winds** alisei; – **union** sindacato; – **mark** marchio registrato

to trade [treid] *v. intr.* trafficare, commerciare

trader ['treidə*] *s.* commerciante *m. e f.*, mercante *m.*

tradition [trə'diʃən] *s.* tradizione *f.*

traditional [trə'diʃənl] *agg.* tradizionale

traffic ['træfik] *s.* traffico *m.*, circolazione *f.*; – **divider** spartitraffico; – **light** semaforo

tragedy ['trædʒidi] *s.* dramma *m.*, tragedia *f.*

tragic ['trædʒik] *agg.* tragico

tragicomic(al) [trædʒi'kɔmik(əl)] *agg.* tragicomico

trail [treil] *s.* scia *f.*, traccia *f.*

trailer ['treilə*] *s.* rimorchio *m.*, roulotte *f. inv.*; presentazione *f.* (di un film)

train [trein] *s.* treno *m.*; **slow** – accelerato; **through** – diretto; **fast** – direttissimo; **express** – rapido

to train [trein] *v. tr.* allenare, addestrare

trainer ['treinə*] *s.* allenatore *m.*, istruttore *m.*

training ['treiniŋ] *s.* allenamento *m.*, preparazione *f.*

traitor ['treitə*] *s.* traditore *m.*

trajectory ['trædʒiktəri] *s.* traiettoria *f.*

tram [træm] *s.* tram *m.*

tramp [træmp] *s.* vagabondo *m.*; scarpinata *f.*

to tramp [træmp] *v. intr.* scarpinare

to trample ['træmpl] *v. tr.* calpestare

tranquillity [træŋ'kwiliti] *s.* tranquillità *f.* (di spirito)

tranquillizer ['træŋkwilaizə*] *s.* tranquillante *m.*, calmante *m.*

transaction [træn'zækʃən] *s.* transazione *f.*

to transcribe [træns'kraib] *v. tr.* trascrivere

transcript ['trænskript] *s.* trascrizione *f.*

transcription [træns'kripʃən] *s.* trascrizione *f.*

transept ['trænsept] *s.* transetto *m.*

transfer [træns'fə:*] *s.* trasbordo *m.*, trasferimento *m.*; trasferta *f.*

to transfer [træns'fə(:)*] *v. tr.* trasferire

to transform [træns'fɔ:m] *v. tr. e intr.* trasformare, trasformarsi

transformer [træns'fɔ:mə*] *s.* trasformatore *m.*

transfusion [træns'fju:ʒən] *s.* trasfusione *f.*

transgression [træns'greʃən] s. trasgressione f., infrazione f.

transiency ['trænziənsi] s. caducità f.

transit ['trænsit] s. transito m., passaggio m.

transitory ['trænsitəri] agg. passeggero

to translate [træns'leit] v. tr. tradurre

translation [træns'leiʃən] s. traduzione f.

translator [træns'leitə*] s. traduttore m.

transliteration ['trænzlitə'reiʃən] s. traslitterazione f.

transmission [trænz'miʃən] s. trasmissione f.

to transmit [trænz'mit] v. tr. trasmettere

transparency [træns'pɛərənsi] s. trasparenza f.

transparent [træns'pɛərənt] agg. trasparente

transpiration [,trænspi'reiʃən] s. traspirazione f.

transplant ['trænsplɑ:nt] s. trapianto m.

transplantation [,trænspla:n'teiʃən] s. trapianto m.

transport [træns'pɔ:t] s. trasporto m.

to transport ['trænspɔ:t] v. tr. trasportare

transportable [træns,pɔ:təbl] agg. trasportabile

transporter [træns'pɔ:tə*] s. trasportatore m.

transsexual [træn'sekʃual] s. transessuale m. e f.

transversal [trænz'və:səl] agg. trasversale

trap [træp] s. trappola f., tranello m.; tagliola f.

trap-door [træp dɔ:*] s. botola f.

trapeze [trə'pi:z] s. trapezio m. (sport)

trapezium [trə'pi:zjəm] s. trapezio m. (geom.)

trash [træʃ] s. immondizia f., scarto m.

trauma ['trɔ:mə] s. trauma m.

to travel ['trævl] v. intr. viaggiare

traveller ['trævlə*] s. viaggiatore m., viandante m. e f.

travertine ['trævə(:)tin] s. travertino m.

tray [trei] s. vassoio m.

treacherous ['tretʃərəs] agg. sleale, infido, pericoloso

treachery ['tretʃəri] s. tradimento m., slealtà f.

tread [tred] s. battistrada m. inv.

to tread [tred] v. tr. calpestare

treason ['tri:zn] s. tradimento m. (leg.)

treasure ['treʒə*] s. tesoro m.

to treat [tri:t] v. tr. e intr. trattare; curare, medicare; offrire; - **a dinner** offrire a ... una cena

treatable ['tri:təbl] agg. trattabile (chim.)

treatise ['tri:tiz] s. trattato m.

treatment ['tri:tmənt] s. trattamento m., cura f.

treaty ['tri:ti] s. trattato m., accordo m.

tree [tri:] s. albero m., pianta f.

to trek [trek] v. intr. scarpinare

tremble ['trembl] s. tremito m.

to tremble ['trembl] v. intr. tremare

trembling ['trembliŋ] s. tremore m.

tremendous [tri'mendəs] agg. formidabile, immane; mostruoso

tremor ['tremə*] s. tremore m. (med.)

trend [trend] s. tendenza f., andamento m., orientamento m.

trestle ['tresl] s. traliccio m. (di un ponte)

trial ['traiəl] s. esperimento m., prova f.; fastidio m.; processo m. (leg.)

triangular [trai'æŋgjulə*] agg. triangolare

triangulation [trai,æŋgju'leiʃən] s. triangolazione f.

tribe [traib] s. tribù f.

tribunal [trai'bju:nl] s. tribunale m.

tribune ['tribju:n] s. tribuna f.

tributary ['tribjutəri] s. affluente m., immissario m.

trichologist [tri'kɔlədʒist] s. tricologo m.

trick [trik] s. scherzo m., trucco m., raggiro m., inganno m.

to trick [trik] v. tr. ingannare, raggirare

tricolour ['trikələ*] agg. tricolore

tricycle ['traisikl] s. triciclo m.

tridimensional [,traidi'menʃənl] agg. tridimensionale

trifle ['traifl] s. inezia f., minuzia f., sciocchezza f.; scherzo m.

trifling ['traifliŋ] agg. irrilevante

triglyph ['traiglif] s. triglifo m.

to trill [tril] v. intr. gorgheggiare

to trim [trim] v. tr. regolare (naut. e aer.); potare (bot.); guarnire

trinity ['triniti] s. trinità f.

trinkets ['triŋkitz] s. pl. bigiotteria f. sing.

trio ['tri:ou] s. trio m.

trip [trip] s. gita f., viaggio m.

tripe [traip] s. trippa f.

tripod ['traipɔd] s. cavalletto m.

triptych ['triptik] s. trittico m.

triumph ['traiəmf] s. trionfo m.

to triumph ['traiəmf] v. intr. trionfare

triumphal [trai'ʌmfəl] agg. trionfale

trivial ['triviəl] agg. banale

troglodyte ['trɔglədait] s. troglodita m. e f.

trolley ['trɔli] s. carrello m.

trophy ['troufi] s. trofeo m., cimelio m.

tropical ['trɔpikəl] agg. tropicale

trot [trɔt] s. trotto m.

trotter ['trɔtə*] s. trottatore m.

trouble ['trʌbl] s. guaio m., disturbo m., seccatura f.; disgrazia f., pena f.; **to get out of** – tirarsi fuori dai guai

to trouble ['trʌbl] v. tr. e intr. disturbare; preoccupare

troublesome ['trʌblsəm] agg. fastidioso

trousers ['trauzəz] s. pl. calzoni m.

trout [traut] s. trota f.

trowel ['trauəl] s. paletta f.

truce [tru:s] s. tregua f.

truck [trʌk] s. camion m. inv.; – **driver** camionista

true [tru:] agg. sincero, vero

truffle ['trʌfl] s. tartufo m.

truly ['tru:li] avv. veramente

trumpet ['trʌmpit] s. tromba f.

truncheon ['trʌnʃən] s. sfollagente m. inv.

trunk [trʌŋk] s. baule m.; bagagliaio m. (USA); tronco m.

trust [trʌst] s. confidenza f., fiducia f.

to trust [trʌst] v. tr. fidarsi di

trustworthy ['trʌst,wə:ði] agg. fidato

truth [tru:θ] s. verità f.

try [trai] s. tentativo m.

to try [trai] v. tr. e intr. provare, sperimentare, tentare; processare; – **out** collaudare; – **on** provare (un abito)

tub [tʌb] s. tinozza f.

tube [tju:b] s. tubo m.; **inner** – camera d'aria

Tuesday ['tju:zdi] s. martedì m.; **Shrove** – martedì grasso

tufa ['tju:fə] s. tufo m.

tuft [tʌft] s. ciuffo m.

tug [tʌg] s. rimorchiatore m.; tirata f. (di capelli)

tuition [tju(:)'iʃən] s. istruzione f.; tassa f. scolastica

tulip ['tju:lip] s. tulipano m.

tumble ['tʌmbl] s. capitombolo m.

to tumble ['tʌmbl] v. intr. cascare

tumbler ['tʌmblə*] s. bicchiere m.; saltimbanco m.

tumefaction [,tju:mi'fækʃən] s. tumefazione f.

tummy ['tʌmi] s. pancia f. (fam.)

tumour ['tju:mə*] s. tumore m.

tumulus ['tju:mjuləs] s. tumulo m. (archeol.)

tun [tʌn] s. tino m.

tuna ['tju:nə] s. tonno m.

tundra ['tʌndrə] s. tundra f.

tune [tju:n] s. tono m. (mus.); **out of** – stonato

tunic ['tju:nik] s. tunica f.

tunnel ['tʌnl] s. cunicolo m., galleria f.

tunny ['tʌni] s. tonno m.

turban ['tə:bən] s. turbante m.

turbine ['tə:bin] s. turbina f.

turbulent ['tə:bjulənt] agg. turbolento, agitato

turf [tə:f] s. zolla f., tappeto m. erboso

Turk [tə:k] s. turco m.

turkey ['tə:ki] s. tacchino m.

Turkish ['tə:kiʃ] agg. turco

turn [tə:n] s. svolta f.; giro m.; turno m.; – **off** svincolo; – **up** risvolto (dei pantaloni); **up** – inversione

to turn [tə:n] v. tr. girare, curvare; indirizzare ● intr. diventare; girare; diventare; – **over** rivoltare; – **off** spegnere; disinteressarsi; – **on** accendere; eccitare; – **out** riuscire, scacciare; – **over** cappottare; – **up** sopraggiungere; – **upside down** capovolgere; – **against** rivoltarsi contro

turning ['tə:niŋ] agg. girevole

turnip ['tə:nip] s. rapa f.; – **tops** cime di rapa

turnover ['tə:n,ouvə*] s. rovesciamento m.; ricambio m.

turtle ['tə:tl] s. tartaruga f.

tusk [tʌsk] s. zanna f.

TV [ti:'vi:] s. televisore m. (fam.)

twice [twais] avv. due volte

twig [twig] s. ramoscello m.

twilight ['twailait] s. crepuscolo m.

twin [twin] agg. gemello

twine [twain] s. spago m.

to twinkle ['twiŋkl] v. intr. brillare

twinkling ['twiŋkliŋ] s. scintillio m.

twinning ['twiniŋ] s. gemellaggio m.

twirl [twə:l] s. giravolta f.

to twist [twist] v. tr. distorcere, intrecciare, attorcigliare

twisted ['twistid] agg. contorto

twofold ['tu:-fould] agg. duplice

twosome ['tu:səm] agg. per due ● s. duo m.; paio m.

tycoon [tai'ku:n] s. magnate m.

tying ['taiiŋ] s. legatura f.

tympanum ['timpənəm] s. timpano m.

type [taip] s. tipo m., specie f.; carattere m. (tipografico)

to type [taip] v. tr. battere (a macchina)

typewriter ['taip,raitə*] s. macchina f. per scrivere

typhoon [tai'fu:n] s. tifone m.

typhus ['taifəs] s. tifo m. (med.)

typical ['tipikəl] agg. tipico

typist ['taipist] s. dattilografo m.

typographer [tai'pɔgrəfə*] s. tipografo m.

typography [tai'pɔgrəfi] s. tipografia f.
typology [tai'pɔlədʒi] s. tipologia f.
tyrant ['taiərənt] s. tiranno m.

tyre [taiə°] s. pneumatico m., gomma f.; – **re-pairer** gommista; – **rim** cerchione; – **tread** battistrada

U

ubiquitous [ju(:)'bikwitəs] *agg.* onnipresente

ugly ['ʌgli] *agg.* cattivo, brutto

ulcer ['ʌlsə*] *s.* ulcera *f.*

ulna ['ʌlnə] *s.* ulna *f.*

ultimate ['ʌltimit] *agg.* ultimo, definitivo

ultrasound ['ʌltrə'saund] *s.* ultrasuono *m.*

ultraviolet ['ʌltrə'vaiəlit] *agg.* ultravioletto

umbrella [ʌm'brelə] *s.* ombrello *m.*; – **stand** portaombrelli

umpire ['ʌmpaiə*] *s.* arbitro *m.* (*sport*)

to umpire ['ʌmpaiə*] *v. tr. e intr.* arbitrare (*sport*)

unable [ʌn'eibl] *agg.* incapace, impossibilitato, inadatto

unabridged ['ʌnə'bridʒd] *agg.* integrale (edizione)

unacceptable [ʌnək'septəbl] *agg.* inaccettabile

unaccountable [ʌnə'kauntəbl] *agg.* inesplicabile; irresponsabile

unacquainted [ʌnə'kweintid] *agg.* non pratico, non abituato

unaffected [ʌnə'fektid] *agg.* spontaneo, sincero; non soggetto

unaided [ʌn'eidid] *agg.* da solo, senza aiuto

unalterable [ʌn'ɔ:ltərəbl] *agg.* inalterabile

unanimity [ju:nə'nimiti] *s.* unanimità *f.*

unanimous [ju:'næniməs] *agg.* unanime

unanswerable [ʌn'ɑ:nsərəbl] *agg.* incontestabile, irrefutabile

unapproachable [ˌʌnə'prəutʃəbl] *agg.* inavvicinabile

unattainable [ʌnə'teinəbl] *agg.* irraggiungibile

unattended [ʌnə'tendid] *agg.* incustodito

unavoidable [ˌʌnə'vɔidəbl] *agg.* inevitabile

unaware [ˌʌnə'weə*] *agg.* ignaro

unbalanced [ʌn'bælənst] *agg.* squilibrato

unbearable [ʌn'bɛərəbl] *agg.* insopportabile

unbeatable [ʌn'bi:təbl] *agg.* imbattibile

unbelievable [ʌnbi'li:vəbl] *agg.* incredibile

unbreakable [ʌn'breikəbl] *agg.* infrangibile

to unbutton [ʌn'bʌtn] *v. tr.* sbottonare

unceasing [ʌn'si:siŋ] *agg.* incessante

uncertain [ʌn'sə:tn] *agg.* incerto

uncertainty [ʌn'sə:tnti] *s.* incertezza *f.*

to unchain [ʌn'tʃein] *v. tr.* sciogliere

unchanging [ʌn'tʃeindʒiŋ] *agg.* immutabile

uncivil [ʌn'sivl] *agg.* incivile

uncle ['ʌŋkl] *s.* zio *m.*

uncomfortable [ʌn'kʌmfətəbl] *agg.* disagevole, scomodo

uncommon [ʌn'kɔmən] *agg.* raro, insolito

unconditional ['ʌn-kən'diʃənl] *agg.* incondizionato

unconscious [ʌn'kɔnʃəs] *agg. e s.* inconscio *m.*, incosciente *m. e f.*

unconstitutional ['ʌn,kɔnsti'tju:ʃənl] *agg.* anticostituzionale

to uncover [ʌn'kʌvə*] *v. tr.* scoprire

undamaged ['ʌn'dæmidʒd] *agg.* indenne (di cose)

undaunted [ʌn'dɔ:ntid] *agg.* imperterrito

undecided ['ʌndi'saidid] *agg.* non deciso, incerto

undeniable [ʌndi'naiəbl] *agg.* innegabile

under ['ʌndə*] *avv. e prep.* sotto, giù; – **age** minorenne; – **clothing** biancheria intima

underdevelopment ['ʌndədi'veləpmənt] *s.* sottosviluppo *m.*

underdone ['ʌndə'dʌn] *agg.* poco cotto

underfed ['ʌndə'fed] *agg.* denutrito

to undergo [ʌndə'gou] *v. tr.* patire, subire

undergraduate ['ʌndə'grædjuit] *s.* studente *m.* universitario

underground ['ʌndə'graund] *agg.* sotterraneo • *s.* metropolitana *f.*

to underline [ˌʌndə'lain] *v. tr.* sottolineare, evidenziare

underlying [ˌʌndə'laiiŋ] *agg.* sottostante

underneath [ˌʌndə'ni:θ] *avv. e prep.* sotto, disotto

underpass ['ʌndəpɑ:s] *s.* sottopassaggio *m.*

to understand [ˌʌndə'stænd] *v. tr. e intr.* capire, intendere

to undertake [ˌʌndə'teik] *v. tr.* intraprendere; – **oneself** impegnarsi

undertaking [ˌʌndə'teikiŋ] *s.* impresa *f.*

underwater ['ʌndə'wɔ:tə*] *agg.* subacqueo

underwear ['ʌndəweə*] *s.* biancheria *f.* intima

underwood ['ʌndəwud] *s.* sottobosco *m.*

underworld ['ʌndəwəːld] *s.* malavita *f.*
undeserved ['ʌndi'zəːvd] *agg.* immeritato
undesirable ['ʌndi'zaiərəbl] *agg.* indesiderabile, sgradito
undifferentiated ['ʌn,difə'renʃieitid] *agg.* indifferenziato
undisturbed ['ʌndis'təːbd] *agg.* indisturbato
to undo ['ʌn'duː] *v. tr.* disfare, sbrogliare
undoubted [ʌn'dautid] *agg.* indubbio
to undress ['ʌn'dres] *v. intr.* denudarsi, spogliarsi
undulation [,ʌndju'leiʃən] *s.* ondulazione *f.*
undulatory ['ʌndjulətəri] *agg.* ondulato
uneasiness [ʌn'iːzinis] *s.* disagio *m.*, inquietudine *f.*
uneasy [ʌn'iːzi] *agg.* inquieto, preoccupato
uneatable ['ʌn'iːtəbl] *agg.* immangiabile
uneducated ['ʌn'edjukeitid] *agg.* ignorante, illetterato
unemployed ['ʌnim'plɔid] *s.* disoccupato *m.*
unemployment ['ʌnim'plɔimənt] *s.* disoccupazione *f.*
unequal ['ʌn'iːkwəl] *agg.* disuguale
unequalled ['ʌn'iːkwəld] *agg.* incomparabile
uneven ['ʌn'iːvən] *agg.* dispari
unevenness ['ʌn'iːvənis] *s.* disuguaglianza *f.*
unexceptionable [ˌʌnik'sepʃnəbl] *agg.* ineccepibile
unexpected ['ʌniks'pektid] *agg.* imprevisto, improvviso, inatteso
unexplored ['ʌniks'plɔːd] *agg.* inesplorato
unfailing [ʌn'feiliŋ] *agg.* immancabile
unfair [ʌn'fɛə*] *agg.* ingiusto, sleale
unfaithful ['ʌn'feiθful] *agg.* infedele
to unfasten ['ʌn'fɑːsn] *v. tr.* slegare
unfavourable ['ʌn'feivərəbl] *agg.* sfavorevole
unfinished ['ʌn'finiʃt] *agg.* incompiuto
unfit ['ʌn'fit] *agg.* inadatto
to unfold [ʌn'fould] *v. tr.* stendere, spiegare
unforeseeable ['ʌn-fɔː'siːəbl] *agg.* imprevedibile
unforeseen ['ʌn-fɔː'siːn] *agg.* imprevisto
unforgettable ['ʌn-fə'getəbl] *agg.* indimenticabile
unforgivable ['ʌn-fə'givəbl] *agg.* imperdonabile
unfounded ['ʌn'faundid] *agg.* inattendibile
unfruitful ['ʌ'fruːtful] *agg.* infruttuoso
unfulfilled ['ʌn-ful'fild] *agg.* incompiuto; inappagato, insoddisfatto
ungrateful [ʌn'greitful] *agg.* ingrato
ungratefulness [ʌn'greitfulnis] *s.* ingratitudine *f.*

unhappy [ʌn'hæpi] *agg.* infelice
unharmed [ʌn'haːmd] *agg.* illeso, incolume
unhealthy [ʌn'helθi] *agg.* malsano
unheard [ʌn'həːd] *agg.* inascoltato; – **off** inaudito, incredibile
to unhinge [ʌn'hindʒ] *v. tr.* scardinare
to unhook [ʌn'huk] *v. tr.* sganciare
unification [,juːnifi'keiʃən] *s.* unificazione *f.*
uniform ['juːnifɔːm] *s.* divisa *f.* • *agg.* uniforme
uniformity [,juːni'fɔːmiti] *s.* uniformità *f.*
to unify ['juːnifai] *v. tr.* unificare
unimaginable [ʌni'mædʒinəbl] *agg.* inimmaginabile
uninhabitable ['ʌnin'hæbitəbl] *agg.* inabitabile
uninhabited ['ʌnin'hæbitid] *agg.* disabitato
uninjured [ʌn'indʒəd] *agg.* illeso
unintelligible ['ʌnin'telidʒəbl] *agg.* incomprensibile
unintentional ['ʌnin'tenʃənl] *agg.* involontario
uninterrupted ['ʌn,intə'rʌptid] *agg.* ininterrotto, incessante
union ['juːnjən] *s.* unione *f.*; consorzio *m.*; sindacato *m.*
unique [juː'niːk] *agg.* unico
unit ['juːnit] *s.* unità *f.*; gruppo *m.* (*fis.*); scatto *m.* (telefonico); reparto *m.* (*mil.*); **family** – nucleo familiare
to unite [juː'nait] *v. tr.* unire
unity ['juːniti] *s.* unità *f.*; accordo *m.*
universal [juː'nivəːsəl] *agg.* universale
universe ['juːnivəːs] *s.* universo *m.*
university [juː'nivəːsiti] *s.* università *f.*
univocal ['juː'nivoukəl] *agg.* univoco
unkind [ʌn'kaind] *agg.* scortese; crudele
unkindness [ʌn'kaindnis] *s.* scortesia *f.*
unknown [ʌn'noun] *agg. e s.* sconosciuto *m.*
to unlace [ʌn'leis] *v. tr.* slacciare
unlawful [ʌn'lɔːful] *agg.* abusivo, illegale
unless [ən'les] *cong.* eccetto che; a meno che
unlike [ʌn'laik] *agg.* diverso
unlikely [ʌn'laikli] *avv.* improbabile
unlimited [ʌn'limitid] *agg.* illimitato
unlined [ʌn'laind] *agg.* sfoderato
to unload [ʌn'loud] *v. tr.* scaricare
unloaded [ʌn'loudid] *agg.* scarico
unloading [ʌn'loudiŋ] *s.* scarico *m.*
unlucky [ʌn'lʌki] *agg.* sfortunato
to unmake [ʌn'meik] *v. tr.* disfare
unmarried [ʌn'mærid] *agg.* nubile
unmatched ['ʌn'mætʃt] *agg.* scompagnato

161

unmistakable ['ʌnmis'teikəbl] *agg.* inconfondibile

to unnail [ʌn'neil] *v. tr.* schiodare

unnecessary [ʌn'nesisəri] *agg.* non necessario, superfluo

unnoticed [ʌn'noutist] *agg.* inosservato

to unpack [ʌn'pæk] *v. tr.* disfare (le valigie)

unpleasant [ʌn'plɛznt] *agg.* antipatico, sgradevole

unpopular ['ʌn'pɔpjulə*] *agg.* impopolare, malvisto

unprecedented [ʌn'presidəntid] *agg.* inaudito

unprepared ['ʌn-pri'pɛəd] *agg.* impreparato

unprotected ['ʌn-prə'tektid] *agg.* indifeso

unprovided ['ʌn-prə'vaidid] *agg.* sprovvisto

unpublished ['ʌn'pʌbliʃt] *agg.* inedito

unquestionable [ʌn'kwestʃənəbl] *agg.* indiscutibile

to unravel [ʌn'rævəl] *v. tr.* sbrogliare

unreal [ʌn'riəl] *agg.* irreale

unreality [ʌnri'æliliti] *s.* irrealtà *f.*

unrelated (to) [ʌnri'leitid] *agg.* estraneo

unreliable [ʌnri'laiəbl] *agg.* inaffidabile, inattendibile

unrest [ʌn'rest] *s.* agitazione *f.*

unrestricted [ʌnris'triktid] *agg.* illimitato, senza limiti

unripe [ʌn'raip] *agg.* acerbo

to unrivet [ʌn'rivit] *v. tr.* schiodare

to unroll [ʌn'roul] *v. tr.* srotolare

unsafe [ʌn'seif] *agg.* pericolante; pericoloso

unsaleable [ʌn'seiləbl] *agg.* invendibile

to unscrew [ʌn'skru:] *v. tr.* svitare

unseasoned [ʌn'si:znd] *agg.* scondito

unseizable [ʌn'si:zəbl] *agg.* inafferrabile

unselfishness [ʌn'selfiʃnis] *s.* altruismo *m.*; disinteresse *m.*

unshakable [ʌn'ʃeikəbl] *agg.* irremovibile

to unsheathe [ʌn'ʃi:ð] *v. tr.* sfoderare

unskilfulness [ʌn'skilfulnis] *s.* imperizia *f.*

unsound [ʌn'saund] *agg.* malsano

unstable [ʌn'steibl] *agg.* instabile

unsteady [ʌn'stedi] *agg.* malfermo

to unstick [ʌn'stik] *v. tr.* scollare

to unstitch [ʌn'stitʃ] *v. tr.* scucire

unsuitable [ʌn'sju:təbl] *agg.* inadatto

untenable [ʌn'tenəbl] *agg.* insostenibile

unthinkable [ʌn'θiŋkəbl] *agg.* impensabile

untidiness [ʌn'taidinis] *s.* disordine *m.*

untidy [ʌn'taidi] *agg.* disordinato

to untie [ʌn'tai] *v. tr.* slegare

until [ən'til] *cong.* finché

untimely [ʌn'taimli] *agg.* inopportuno

untiring [ʌn'taiəriŋ] *agg.* instancabile

untranslatable ['ʌntræns'leitəbl] *agg.* intraducibile

unusable [ʌn'ju:zəbl] *agg.* inutilizzabile

unusual [ʌn'ju:ʒuəl] *agg.* inconsueto, insolito

unwelcome [ʌn'welkəm] *agg.* sgradito

unworthy [ʌn'wɔ:ði] *agg.* immeritevole, indegno

to unwrap [ʌn'ræp] *v. tr.* scartare

up [ʌp] *avv.* su; – **there** lassù; – **to** fino a (temporale); – **to date** aggiornato; – **to now** finora; – **here** quassù

upbringing ['ʌp,briŋiŋ] *s.* allevamento *m.* (di bambini)

to update [ʌp'deit] *v. tr.* aggiornare

upkeep ['ʌpki:p] *s.* manutenzione *f.*

upon [ə'pɔn] *prep.* sopra, su

upper ['ʌpə*] *agg.* superiore, più alto

upright ['ʌp-rait] *agg.* dritto, eretto

uproar ['ʌp,rɔ:*] *s.* pandemonio *m.*, tumulto *m.*

upset [ʌp'set] *agg.* agitato, sconvolto • *s.* turbamento *m.*

to upset [ʌp'set] *v. tr.* agitare, sconvolgere

upsetting [ʌp'setiŋ] *agg.* sconvolgente

upside ['ʌpsaid] *avv.* di sopra; – **down** sottosopra, alla rovescia

upstairs ['ʌp'stɛəz] *avv.* al piano superiore

to upvalue [ʌp'vælju:] *v. tr.* sopravvalutare (*fig.*)

uranium [juə'reinjəm] *s.* uranio *m.*

urban ['ə:bən] *agg.* urbano

urbanism ['ə:bənizəm] *s.* urbanistica *f.*

urbanist ['ə:benist] *s.* urbanista *m. e f.*

urbanization [,ə:bənai'zeiʃən] *s.* urbanizzazione *f.*

urea ['juəriə] *s.* urea *f.*

urethra [juə'ri:θrə] *s.* uretra *f.*

to urge [ə:dʒ] *v. tr.* sollecitare • *intr.* essere urgente

urgency ['ə:dʒənsi] *s.* urgenza *f.*

urgent ['ə:dʒənt] *agg.* urgente

urine ['juərin] *s.* urina *f.*

urn [ə:n] *s.* urna *f.*

urologist [juə'rɔlədʒst] *s.* urologo *m.*

urticaria [,ə:ti'kɛəriə] *s.* orticaria *f.*

use [ju:s] *s.* uso *m.*, utilizzo *m.*, impiego *m.*

to use [ju:z] *v. tr.* usare, adoperare; fruire; – **up** esaurire

useful ['ju:sful] *agg.* utile

usefulness ['ju:sfulnis] *s.* utilità *f.*

useless ['ju:slis] *agg.* inservibile, inutile

user ['ju:zə*] *s.* utente *m. e f.*

usher ['ʌʃə*] *s.* usciere *m.*

usual ['ju:ʒŭəl] *agg.* consueto, usuale
usually ['ju:ʒŭəli] *avv.* abitualmente, solita-
  mente
usufruct ['ju:sju:frʌkt] *s.* usufrutto *m.*
utensil [ju:'tensl] *s.* utensile *m.*
uterus ['ju:tərəs] *s.* utero *m.*
utility [ju:'tiliti] *s.* utilità *f.*
utilization [ˌju:tilai'zeiʃən] *s.* utilizzo *m.*
to utilize ['ju:tilaiz] *v. tr.* utilizzare

utmost ['ʌtmoust] *agg.* estremo, massimo; **to
  the –** ad oltranza; **at the –** al più, tutt'al più;
  to try one's – fare del proprio meglio
utopia [ju:'toupjə] *s.* utopia *f.*
utopian [ju:'toupjən] *s.* utopista *m. e f.*
utter ['ʌtə*] *agg.* totale
to utter ['ʌtə*] *v. tr.* pronunciare; emettere (un
  suono)
uxoricide [ʌk'sɔ:risaid] *s.* uxoricida *m. e f.*

V

vacancy ['veikənsi] s. disponibilità f. (di spazio); vacanza f.
vacant ['veikənt] agg. libero, disponibile
to vacate [və'keit] v. tr. sgombrare
vacation [və'keiʃən] s. vacanza f., villeggiatura f.
to vaccinate ['væksineit] v. tr. vaccinare
vaccination [,væksi'neiʃən] s. vaccinazione f.
vaccine ['væksi:n] s. vaccino m.
vacuum ['vækjuəm] s. vuoto m.; – cleaner aspirapolvere; in a – sottovuoto
vagina [və'dʒainə] s. vagina f.
vaginitis [,vædʒi'naitis] s. vaginite f.
vagrant ['veigrənt] agg. e s. girovago m.
vague [veig] agg. vago
valerian [və'liəriən] s. valeriana f.
valiant ['væljənt] agg. valoroso
valid ['vælid] agg. valido
to validate ['vælideit] v. tr. omologare, invalidare
validity [və'liditi] s. validità f.
valley ['væli] s. vallata f., valle f.
valuable ['væljuəbl] agg. pregevole
valuation [,vælju'eiʃən] s. stima f.
value ['vælju:] s. pregio m.
to value ['vælju:] v. tr. valutare, stimare
valve [vælv] s. valvola f.
vampire ['væmpaiə*] s. vampiro m.
van [væn] s. furgone m.
vandal ['vændəl] s. vandalo m.
vandalic [væn'dælik] agg. vandalico
vane [vein] s. banderuola f.
vanguard ['vænga:d] s. avanguardia f.
vanilla [və'nilə] s. vaniglia f.
to vanish ['væniʃ] v. intr. sparire
to vanquish ['væŋkwiʃ] v. tr. debellare
vaporizer ['veipəraizə*] s. vaporizzatore m.
variable ['veəriəbl] agg. mutevole
variation [,veəri'eiʃən] s. variazione f.
varicella [,væri'selə] s. varicella f.
varie ['veərid] agg. variato
variegated ['veərigeitid] agg. variegato
variety [və'raiəti] s. varietà f.
various ['veəriəs] agg. molteplice
varix ['veəriks] s. varice f.

varnish ['va:niʃ] s. vernice f. (trasparente)
to vary ['veəri] v. tr. variare; **varying** variabile
vase [va:z] s. vaso m.
vaseline ['væsili:n] s. vasellina f.
vast [va:st] agg. vasto
vaudeville ['voudəvil] s. varietà m. (teatro)
vault [vɔ:lt] s. volteggio m.; volta f. (arch.); sotterraneo m.; **barrel** – volta a botte
vaulting ['vɔ:ltiŋ] s. volteggio m.
veal [vi:l] s. vitello m. (alim.)
vector ['vektə*] s. vettore m. (mat.)
veer [viə*] s. virata f.
to veer [viə*] v. tr. e intr. virare
vegetable ['vedʒitəbl] agg. vegetale • s. ortaggio m. • pl. verdure f.
vegetarian [,vedʒi'teəriən] agg. e s. vegetariano m.
vegetation [,vedʒi'teiʃən] s. vegetazione f.
vehemence ['vi:iməns] s. impetuosità f.
vehicle ['vi:ikl] s. veicolo m.
veil [veil] s. velo m.
vein [vein] s. vena f., venatura f.
velocity [vi'lɔsiti] s. velocità f.
velvet ['velvit] s. velluto m.
vendor ['vendɔ:*] s. venditore m.
to venerate ['venəreit] v. tr. venerare
vengeance ['vendʒəns] s. vendetta f.
venom ['venəm] s. veleno m.
venomous ['venəməs] agg. velenoso
vent [vent] s. sfogo m.; foro m.
to ventilate ['ventileit] v. tr. ventilare
ventilation [,venti'leiʃən] s. aerazione f.
to venture ['ventʃə*] v. tr. rischiare
veranda(h) [və'rændə] s. portico m., veranda f.
verb [və:b] s. verbo m.
verbena [və'bi:nə] s. verbena f.
verdant ['və:dənt] agg. verdeggiante
verdict ['və:dikt] s. verdetto m.
verifiable ['verifaiəbl] agg. verificabile
to verify ['verifai] v. tr. verificare
verism ['viərizəm] s. verismo m.
verist ['viərist] s. verista m. f.
vermilion [və'miljən] agg. vermiglio
vernacular [və'nækjulə*] s. vernacolo m.

164

verruca [ve'ru:kə] s. verruca f.

versant ['və:sənt] s. versante m.

versatile ['və:sətail] agg. versatile

verse [və:s] s. verso m., versetto m.

to versify ['və:sifai] v. intr. verseggiare

version ['və:ʃən] s. versione f.

versus ['və:səs] prep. contro

vertebra ['və:tibrə] s. vertebra f.

vertebral ['və:tibrəl] agg. vertebrale

vertebrate ['və:tibrit] s. vertebrato m.

vertical ['və:tikəl] agg. verticale

vervain [və:vein] s. verbena f.

very ['veri] avv. molto, proprio

vesper ['vespə*] s. vespro m.

vessel ['vesl] s. nave f., vascello m.; recipiente m.

vest [vest] s. canottiera f., maglia f.; **life** – giubbotto di salvataggio

vestibule ['vestibju:l] s. vestibolo m.

veterinary ['vetərinəri] s. veterinario m.

veto ['vi:tou] s. veto m.

vexation [vek'seiʃən] s. dispetto m.

viaduct ['vaiədʌkt] s. viadotto m.

to vibrate [vai'breit] v. tr. e intr. vibrare; fremere

vibration [vai'breiʃən] s. vibrazione f.

vicar ['vikə*] s. vicario m.

vicarage ['vikəridʒ] s. canonica f.

vice [vais] s. vizio m. • morsa f. (mecc.)

vice-president ['vais'prezidənt] s. vicepresidente m.

viceroy ['vais-rɔi] s. viceré m.

vicious ['viʃəs] agg. vizioso

vicissitude [vi'sisitju:d] s. peripezia f., vicenda f.

victim ['viktim] s. vittima f.

victorious [vik'tɔ:riəs] agg. vittorioso

victory ['viktəri] s. vittoria f.

victual [vitl] s. vettovaglie f. pl.

vicugna [vi'kju:nə] s. vigogna f.

video ['vidiou] s. schermo m., video m. inv. (nei composti)

view [vju:] s. veduta f.; paesaggio m., panorama m.

vigil ['vidʒil] s. veglia f.

vigilance ['vidʒiləns] s. vigilanza f.

vigilant ['vidʒilənt] agg. vigile

vigorous ['vigərəs] agg. vigoroso

vigour ['vigə*] s. vigore m.

vignette [vi'njet] s. vignetta f.

vile [vail] agg. meschino

villa ['vilə] s. villa f.

village ['vilidʒ] s. villaggio m., paese m., borgo m.

to vindicate ['vindikeit] v. tr. rivendicare

vine [vain] s. vite f. (bot.), vitigno m.

vinegar ['vinigə*] s. aceto m.

vineyard ['vinjəd] s. vigneto m.

vintage ['vintidʒ] s. vendemmia f.

viola ['vai,lə] s. viola f. (mus.)

to violate ['vaiəleit] v. tr. violare; stuprare

violence ['vaiələns] s. violenza f.

violent ['vaiələnt] agg. violento

violet ['vaiəlit] s. viola f. (bot.)

violin [,vaiə'lin] s. violino m.

violinist ['vaiəlinist] s. violinista m. e f.

violoncellist [,vaiələn'tʃelist] s. violoncellista m. e f.

violoncello [,vaiələn'tʃelou] s. violoncello m.

viper ['vaipə*] s. vipera f.

viral ['vairəl] agg. virale

virgin ['və:dʒin] s. vergine f.

virginity [və:'dʒniti] s. verginità f.

Virgo ['və:gou] s. vergine f. (astr.)

virility [vi'riliti] s. virilità f.

virtue ['və:tju:] s. vanto m., merito m.

virtuoso [,və:tju'ouzou] agg. virtuoso (mus.)

virtuous ['və:tjuəs] agg. virtuoso

virus ['vaiərəs] s. virus m.

visa ['vi:zə] s. visto m.; **entry** – visto d'ingresso

to visa ['vi:zə] v. tr. vistare, mettere il visto

viscount ['vaikaunt] s. visconte m.

viscountess ['vaikauntis] s. viscontessa f.

visibility [,vizi'biliti] s. visibilità f.; **poor** – visibilità scarsa

visible ['vizəbl] agg. osservabile, visibile

vision ['viʒən] s. visione f.

visionary ['viʒnəri] agg. e s. visionario m.

visit ['vizit] s. visita f.

to visit ['vizit] v. tr. visitare

visitor ['vizitə*] s. visitatore m.

vitality [vai'tæliti] s. vitalità f.

vitamin ['vitəmin] s. vitamina f.

vivarium [vai'veəriəm] s. vivaio m. (di pesci)

vivisection [,vivi'sekʃən] s. vivisezione f.

vocabulary [və'kæbjuləri] s. vocabolario m.

vocalization [,voukalai'zeiʃən] s. vocalizzo m.

vocation [vou'keiʃən] s. vocazione f.

voice [vɔis] s. voce f.; **in a low** – a bassa voce

volcano [vɔl'keinou] s. vulcano m.

volley ['vɔli] s. raffica f. (di armi)

volleyball ['vɔlibɔ:l] s. pallavolo f.

voltage ['voultidʒ] s. voltaggio m.

volume ['vɔljum] s. volume m.

voluminous [vəˈljuːmɪnəs] *agg.* voluminoso
volute [vəˈljuːt] *s.* voluta *f.* (*arch.*)
vomit [ˈvɔmɪt] *s.* vomito *m.*
to vomit [ˈvɔmɪt] *v. tr. e intr.* vomitare
vortex [ˈvɔːteks] *s.* vortice *m.*
vote [vout] *s.* voto *m.*
to vote [vout] *v. tr. e intr.* votare
voter [ˈvoutə*] *s.* elettore *m.*

voting [ˈvoutɪŋ] *agg.* votante • *s.* votazione *f.*
votive [ˈvoutiv] *agg.* votivo
voucher [ˈvautʃə*] *s.* scontrino *m.*, buono *m.*
vowel [ˈvauəl] *s.* vocale *f.*
voyage [ˈvɔidʒ] *s.* viaggio *m.*, traversata *f.*
vulgar [ˈvʌlgə*] *agg.* volgare
vulnerable [ˈvʌlnərəbl] *agg.* vulnerabile
vulture [ˈvʌltʃə*] *s.* avvoltoio *m.*

W

wad [wɔd] *s.* batuffolo *m.* (di cotone)

to wade [weid] *v. tr. e intr.* guadare; sguazzare

wader ['weidə*] *s.* trampoliere *m.*

wage [weidʒ] *s.* paga *f.*, salario *m.*

wagon ['wægən] *s.* vagone *m.*

waist [weist] *s.* vita *f.* (*anat.*)

wait [weit] *s.* attesa *f.*

to wait [weit] *v. tr. e intr.* aspettare

waiter ['weitə*] *s.* cameriere *m.*

waitress ['weitris] *s.* cameriera *f.*

to waive [weiv] *v. tr.* rinunciare

wake [weik] *s.* scia *f.*

to wake (up) [weik] *v. tr. e intr.* svegliare

walk [wɔːk] *s.* camminata *f.*, passeggiata *f.*; **- on** comparsa (*cin.*)

to walk [wɔːk] *v. intr.* camminare, passeggiare

wall [wɔːl] *s.* muro *m.*, parete *f.*; mura *f. pl.*

wallet ['wɔlit] *s.* portafoglio *m.*

wallpaper ['wɔːl,peipə*] *s.* tappezzeria *f.*

walnut ['wɔːlnʌt] *s.* noce *m.*

to wander (about) ['wɔndə*] *v. intr.* vagare, girovagare

wandering ['wɔndəriŋ] *s.* peregrinazione *f.*

want [wɔnt] *s.* mancanza *f.*, bisogno *m.*

to want [wɔnt] *v. tr.* volere, aver bisogno di

war [wɔː*] *s.* guerra *f.* • *agg.* bellico

ward [wɔːd] *s.* reparto *m.*, corsia *f.* (di ospedale)

warden ['wɔːdn] *s.* guardiano *m.*

warder ['wɔːdə*] *s.* carceriere *m.*

wardrobe ['wɔːdroub] *s.* armadio *m.*, guardaroba *m. inv.*

warehouse ['weəhaus] *s.* magazzino *m.*

warm [wɔːm] *agg.* caldo, caloroso; **warmly** caldamente, calorosamente

to warm [wɔːm] *v. tr.* scaldare, riscaldare • *intr.* scaldarsi, riscaldarsi

warmth [wɔːmθ] *s.* tepore *m.*

to warn [wɔːn] *v. tr.* avvertire; diffidare (*leg.*)

warning ['wɔːniŋ] *s.* avviso *m.*, allarme *m.*

warp [wɔːp] *s.* ordito *m.*

to warp [wɔːp] *v. tr. e intr.* distorcere

warrant ['wɔrənt] *s.* garanzia *f.*; **search -** mandato di perquisizione

to warrant ['wɔrənt] *v. tr.* garantire

warrior ['wɔriə*] *s.* guerriero *m.*

warship ['wɔː,ʃip] *s.* nave *f.* da guerra

wart [wɔːt] *s.* verruca *f.*

wary ['weəri] *agg.* cauto, diffidente

wash [wɔʃ] *s.* bucato *m.*

to wash [wɔʃ] *v. tr.* lavare

washable ['wɔʃəbl] *agg.* lavabile

washer ['wɔʃə*] *s.* rondella *f.*

washing ['wɔʃiŋ] *s.* bucato *m.*, lavaggio *m.*; **- machine** lavabiancheria

wasp [wɔsp] *s.* vespa *f.*

waste [weist] *s.* perdita *f.*, spreco *m.*, scarto *m.*; **radioactive -** scorie radioattive

to waste [weist] *v. tr.* dissipare, sciupare; perdere

watch [wɔtʃ] *s.* guardia *f.*, ronda *f.*, sorveglianza *f.*; orologio *m.* da polso

to watch [wɔtʃ] *v. tr.* sorvegliare, osservare; **- over** vigilare

watchful ['wɔtʃful] *agg.* vigile

watchmaker ['wɔtʃ,meikə*] *s.* orologiaio *m.*

watchman ['wɔtʃmən] *s.* sorvegliante *m. e f.*, guardiano *m.*

water ['wɔːtə*] *s.* acqua *f.*; **drinking -** acqua potabile; **mineral -** acqua minerale; **plane -** acqua naturale (USA); **running -** acqua corrente; **high, low -** alta, bassa marea; **shallow -** bassofondo; **- line** bagnasciuga; **- melon** cocomero; **- lily** ninfea; **- polo** pallanuoto;

to water ['wɔːtə*] *v. tr.* annaffiare • *intr.* lacrimare

watercolour ['wɔːtə,kʌlə*] *s.* acquerello *m.*

watercolourist ['wɔːtə,kʌlərist] *s.* acquerellista *m. e f.*

waterfall ['wɔːtəfɔːl] *s.* cascata *f.*

waterproof ['wɔːtəpruːf] *agg.* impermeabile

watershed ['wɔːtəʃed] *s.* spartiacque *m. inv.*

waterway ['wɔːtəwei] *s.* canale *m.*, via *f.* d'acqua

waterworks ['wɔːtəwəːks] *s. pl.* acquedotto *m. sing.*, impianto *m.* idrico

watery ['wɔːtəri] *agg.* acquoso, brodoso

wave [weiv] *s.* onda *f.*

to wave [weiv] *v. tr. e intr.* ondeggiare

to waver ['weivə*] v. intr. oscillare, essere dubbioso

wavy ['weivi] agg. ondulato

wax [wæks] s. cera f.

to wax [wæks] v. tr. lucidare

way [wei] s. maniera f., modo m.; direzione f., percorso m.; – **in** entrata; – **out** uscita, scappatoia

wayfarer ['wei,fɛərə*] s. viandante m. e f.

wc [,dʌbəlju:'si] s. gabinetto m.

weak [wi:k] agg. debole; diluito; molle

to weaken ['wi:kən] v. tr. e intr. indebolire

weakly ['wi:kli] agg. delicato (di salute)

weakness ['wi:knis] s. debolezza f.

wealth [welθ] s. ricchezza f.

wealthy ['welθi] agg. agiato

weaning ['wi:niŋ] s. svezzamento m.

weapon ['wepən] s. arma f.

wear [wɛə*] s. uso m., consumo m.; resistenza f. all'uso

to wear [wɛə*] v. tr. indossare, portare; – **out** logorare

weariness ['wiərinis] s. fiacca f.

weary ['wiəri] agg. estenuante, fiacco

weather ['weðə*] s. tempo m. (atmosferico); **bad, fine** – tempo cattivo, buono; – **forecast** previsioni del tempo

weathercock ['weðəkɔk] s. banderuola f.

weaver ['wi:və*] s. tessitore m.

weaving ['wi:viŋ] s. tessitura f.

web [web] s. trama f., ragnatela f.

wedding ['wediŋ] agg. nuziale • s. matrimonio m., nozze f. pl.; – **ring** fede

wedge [wedʒ] s. zeppa f.

Wednesday ['wenzdi] s. mercoledì m.

week [wi:k] s. settimana f. • agg. settimanale, feriale; **next** – la settimana prossima; **last** – la settimana scorsa

weekly ['wi:kli] agg. e s. settimanale m.

to weep [wi:p] v. tr. e intr. piangere

weeping ['wi:piŋ] s. pianto m.

weft [weft] s. trama f. (del tessuto)

to weigh [wei] v. tr. e intr. pesare, incidere

weight [weit] s. peso m.; **to put on** – ingrassare

weird [wiəd] agg. strano

welcome ['welkəm] agg. gradito • s. accoglienza f.; **you're** – ! benvenuto!, prego!

to welcome ['welkəm] v. tr. accogliere, dare il benvenuto

to weld [weld] v. tr saldare

welder ['weldə*] s. saldatrice f.

welding ['weldiŋ] s. saldatura f.

well [wel] avv. bene • cong. ebbene; allora?

west [west] s. ovest m., ponente m. • agg. occidentale

western ['westən] agg. occidentale

wet [wet] agg. bagnato; – **suit** muta (da sub); – **through** fradicio

to wet [wet] v. tr. bagnare

whale [weil] s. balena f.

whaler ['weilə*] s. baleniera f.

wharf [wɔ:f] s. pontile m., scalo m.

what [wɔt] agg. e pron. rel. e interr. quale, quanto; – **for?** perché?; – **a lot (of)** ... quanti ... !; – **is more** peraltro

whatever [wɔt'evə*] agg. e pron. indef. qualunque, qualsiasi cosa

wheat [wi:t] s. frumento m., grano m.

wheel [wi:l] s. ruota f.; volante m. (autom.); – **chair** carrozzella; **spare** – ruota di scorta

when [wen] avv. e cong. quando, mentre

whenever [wen'evə*] avv. e cong. ogniqualvolta, quando

where [wɛə*] avv. dove

whereas [wɛər'æz] cong. mentre (avversativo)

whereby [wɛə'bai] avv. con cui, per cui

wherever [wɛər'evə*] avv. dovunque

whether ['weðə*] cong. se (dubitativo); – ... **or** sia... sia

whey [wei] s. siero m.

which [witʃ] agg. e pron. rel. e interr. che cosa, quale

whichever [witʃ'evə*] agg. e pron. chiunque, qualunque

whiff [wif] s. zaffata f.

while [wail] cong. mentre

whim [wim] s. capriccio m.

to whimper ['wimpə*] v. intr. mugolare, piagnucolare

whimsical ['wimzikəl] agg. capriccioso

to whine [wain] v. intr. piagnucolare

whinny ['wini] s. nitrito m.

whip [wip] s. frusta f.

to whip [wip] v. tr. frustare; – **up** frullare

whirl [wə:l] s. vortice m.; – **pool** mulinello d'acqua; – **wind** tromba d'aria

to whisk [wisk] v. tr. mantecare

whisker ['wiskə*] s. basetta f.

to whisper ['wispə*] v. tr. bisbigliare, sussurrare

whispering ['wispəriŋ] s. sussurrio m.

whistle ['wisl] s. fischio m.

to whistle ['wisl] v. tr. e intr. fischiare

white [wait] *agg.* bianco; – **coffee** caffellatte; – **hot** incandescente; – **washer** imbianchino
Whitsunday ['wit'sandi] *s.* pentecoste *f.*
who [hu:,hu] *pron. rel., indef. e interr.* chi, che (soggetto, rif. a persone); – **knows** chissà
whoever [hu:'eva°] *pron. rel. indef.* chiunque
whole [houl] *agg.* intero, tutto • *s.* insieme *m.*
wholesale ['houl-seil] *avv.* all'ingrosso
wholesome ['houlsəm] *agg.* salubre, salutare
wholly ['houlli] *avv.* interamente
whom [hu:m] *pron. rel., indef. e interr.* che, chi, quale (complemento, rif. a persone)
whore [hɔ:°] *s.* prostituta *f.*
whose [hu:z] *pron. rel.* del quale (possessivo)
why [wai] *avv.* perché
wick [wik] *s.* stoppino *m.*
wicked ['wikid] *agg.* cattivo; peccaminoso • *s.* cattiveria *f.*
wickedness ['wikidnis] *s.* cattiveria *f.*
wide [waid] *agg.* ampio, largo; – **angle** grandangolo
to widen ['waidn] *v. tr.* allargare
widespread ['waidspred] *agg.* diffuso
widow ['widou] *s.* vedova *f.*
widower ['widouə°] *s.* vedovo *m.*
width [widθ] *s.* ampiezza *f.*, larghezza *f.*
wife [waif] *s.* moglie *f.*
wig [wig] *s.* parrucca *f.*
wild [waild] *agg.* feroce, selvaggio
wilfulness ['wilfulnis] *s.* premeditazione *f.* (*leg.*); testardaggine *f.*
will [wil] *s.* arbitrio *m.*, volontà *f.*; testamento *m.*
willing ['wilin] *agg.* volenteroso
willingly ['wilinli] *avv.* volentieri
willow ['wilou] *s.* salice *m.*; **weeping** – salice piangente
win [win] *s.* vincita *f.*, vittoria *f.* (*sport*)
to win [win] *v. tr.* vincere, ottenere
winch [wintʃ] *s.* verricello *m.*
wind [wind] *s.* vento *m.*
to wind [waind] *v. tr.* avvolgere
winding ['waindiŋ] *s.* meandro *m.* • *agg.* tortuoso
windmill ['winmil] *s.* girandola *f.*
window ['windou] *s.* finestra *f.*, sportello *m.*
windowsill ['windousil] *s.* davanzale *m.*
windpipe ['windpaip] *s.* trachea *f.*
windscreen ['wind,skri:n] *s.* parabrezza *m. inv.*; – **wiper** tergicristallo
windshield ['wind,ʃi:ld] *s.* parabrezza *m. inv.* (USA)
windy ['windi] *agg.* ventoso

wine [wain] *s.* vino *m.*; **sparkling** – spumante
wing [wiŋ] *s.* ala *f.*; padiglione *m.*; quinta *f.* (*teatro*)
winner ['winə°] *agg.* vincitore
winning ['winiŋ] *agg. e s.* vincente *m.*
winter ['wintə°] *s.* inverno *m.* • *agg.* invernale
to winter ['wintə°] *v. intr.* svernare
to wipe [waip] *v. tr.* strofinare, asciugare; colpire; – **off** cancellare
wire ['waiə°] *s.* filo *m.* (metallico); telegramma *m.* (*fam.*)
wireless ['waiəlis] *s.* radio *f.*
wisdom ['wizdəm] *s.* saggezza *f.*
wise [waiz] *agg.* previdente, saggio
wish [wiʃ] *s.* augurio *m.*, desiderio *m.*
to wish [wiʃ] *v. tr. e intr.* augurare; desiderare
wistaria [wis'tɛəriə] *s.* glicine *m.*
wit [wit] *s.* brio *m.*, spirito *m.*
witch [witʃ] *s.* strega *f.*
witchcraft ['witʃkra:ft] *s.* sortilegio *m.*
with [wið] *prep.* con; insieme a
to withdraw [wið'drɔ:] *v. tr.* prelevare, ritirare • *intr.* allontanarsi, indietreggiare
withdrawal [wið'drɔ:əl] *s.* prelievo *m.* (*med.*); ritiro *m.*
to wither ['wiðə°] *v. tr.* folgorare • *intr.* sfiorire
within [wi'ðin] *prep.* entro, all'interno di; tra (temporale)
without [wi'ðaut] *prep. e cong.* senza
witness ['witnis] *s.* testimone *m. e f.*
to witness ['witnis] *v. tr. e intr.* testimoniare
witticism ['witisizəm] *s.* spiritosaggine *f.*
witty ['witi] *agg.* spiritoso
wizard ['wizəd] *s.* mago *m.*
wolf [wulf] *s.* lupo *m.*
woman ['wumən] *s.* donna *f.*
womanly ['wumənli] *agg.* femminile
wonder ['wandə°] *s.* fenomeno *m.*, meraviglia *f.*, prodigio *m.*
to wonder ['wandə°] *v. tr. e intr.* meravigliare, meravigliarsi; chiedersi
wonderful ['wandəful] *agg.* meraviglioso
wood [wud] *s.* bosco *m.*, legna *f.*, legno *m.*
woodcock ['wudkɔk] *s.* beccaccia *f.*
woodcut ['wudkʌt] *s.* incisione *f.* (nel legno)
wooded ['wudid] *agg.* boscoso
woodman ['wudmən] *s.* boscaiolo *m.*
woodpecker ['wud,pekə°] *s.* picchio *m.*
woodworm ['wudwɔ:m] *s.* tarlo *m.*
woody ['wudi] *agg.* boscoso
wool [wul] *s.* lana *f.*

word [wɔːd] *s.* parola *f.*, vocabolo *m.*

work [wɔːk] *s.* lavoro *m.*, opera *f.* • *pl.* meccanica *f. sing.*; meccanismo *m. sing.*; **out of** – disoccupato

to work [wɔːk] *v. tr.* lavorare • *intr.* operare, funzionare; – **out** elaborare

worker ['wɔːkə*] *s.* lavoratore *m.*, operaio *m.*

working ['wɔːkiŋ] *s.* funzionamento *m.*, lavorazione *f.* • *agg.* lavorativo, feriale

workman ['wɔːkmən] *s.* operaio *m.*

workshop ['wɔːkʃɔp] *s.* laboratorio *m.*, officina *f.*

world [wɔːld] *s.* mondo *m.* • *agg.* mondiale, universale

worldly [wɔːldli] *agg.* mondano, terreno

worm [wɔːm] *s.* serpentina *f.*; verme *m.*; –**eaten** bacato

worn [wɔːn] *agg.* logoro; – **out** esausto

worried ['wʌrid] *agg.* preoccupato

worry ['wʌri] *s.* preoccupazione *f.*

to worry ['wʌri] *v. tr. e intr.* preoccupare

worrying ['wʌriiŋ] *agg.* inquietante, preoccupante

worse [wɔːs] *agg.* peggiore • *avv. e s.* peggio *m.*; **to get** – peggiorare

to worsen ['wɔːsn] *v. tr. e intr.* peggiorare; **worsening** peggioramento

worship ['wɔːʃip] *s.* culto *m.*

to worship ['wɔːʃip] *v. tr.* adorare

(the) worst [wɔːst] *agg.* il peggiore • *s.* il peggio *m.*; **at** – al peggio

worth [wɔːθ] *s.* valore *m.*; **to be** – meritare, valere

worthwhile ['wɔːθ'wail] *agg.* meritevole, che vale la pena

worthy ['wɔːði] *agg.* meritevole

to wound [wuːnd] *v. tr.* ferire; **wounding** ferimento

wound [wuːnd] *s.* ferita *f.*

to wrap [ræp] *v. tr.* fasciare; – **up** impacchettare, avvolgere

wrapping ['ræpiŋ] *s.* confezione *f.*, involucro *m.*

wreath [riːθ] *s.* ghirlanda *f.*

wreck [rek] *s.* disastro *m.*; naufragio *m.*; relitto *m.*

to wreck [rek] *v. intr.* naufragare, distruggere

wrench [rentʃ] *s.* chiave (USA, *mecc.*)

to wrestle ['resl] *v. intr.* lottare (*sport*)

wrestling ['resliŋ] *s.* lotta *f.* (*sport*)

wretched ['retʃid] *agg.* miserabile

to wring [riŋ] *v. tr.* strizzare, torcere

wrinkle ['riŋkl] *s.* ruga *f.*

wrist [rist] *s.* polso *m.*

to write [rait] *v. tr.* scrivere, redigere; – **down** prendere nota

writer ['raitə*] *s.* scrittore *m.*

writing ['raitiŋ] *s.* scritta *f.*, scrittura *f.*

written ['ritn] *agg.* scritto

wrong [rɔŋ] *avv.* male • *s.* male *m.*; torto *m.*, offesa *f.*; **to be** – ingannarsi, sbagliarsi

X

xenophobia [,zenə'foubjə] s. xenofobia f.
xerography [zi'rɔgrəfi] s. xerografia f.
Xmas ['eksməs] s. Natale m.

X-ray ['eks'rei] s. radiografia f.; – **therapy** röntgenterapia f.
xylography [zai'lɔgrəfi] s. xilografia f.

Y

yard [ja:d] s. cantiere m.; cortile m.; iarda f. (unità di misura)
yawn [jɔ:n] s. sbadiglio m.
to yawn [jɔ:n] v. intr. sbadigliare
year [ja:*, jiə*] s. annata f., anno m.; **leap –** anno bisestile; – **end bonus** tredicesima; – **book** annuario
yearly ['jə:li] agg. annuale, annuo • avv. annualmente
yeast [ji:st] s. lievito m.
yellow ['jelou] agg. giallo
yelp [jelp] s. guaito m.
to yelp [jelp] v. intr. guaire
yes [jes] avv. sì

yesterday ['jestədi] avv. ieri; **the day before –** ieri l'altro
yet [jet] cong. ma, però, tuttavia • avv. finora; ancora (in frasi neg.) • s. tasso m. (bot.)
yield [ji:ld] s. gettito m., produzione f.
to yield [ji:ld] v. tr. rendere • intr. cedere, piegare
yoghurt ['jɔgət] s. yogurt m. inv.
yolk [jouk] s. tuorlo m.
young [jʌŋ] agg. giovane; – **child** bimbo; – **lady** signorina; – **looking** giovanile; – **people** i giovani
youth [jo:θ] s. gioventù f., giovinezza f.

Z

zeal [zi:l] s. zelo m.
zebra ['zi:brə] s. zebra f.; – **crossing** passaggio pedonale
zero ['ziərou] s. zero m.
zinc [ziŋk] s. zinco m.
Zionist ['zaiənist] s. sionista m. e f.
zip [zip] s. cerniera f.

zircon ['zə:kɔn] s. zircone m.
zodiac ['zoudiæk] s. zodiaco m.
zone [zoun] s. zona f.
zoo [zu:] s. zoo m. inv.
zoologist [zou'ɔlədʒist] s. zoologo m.
zoology [zou'ɔlədʒi] s. zoologia f.
zygomatic [,zaigou'mæytik] s. zigomo m.

171

ITALIAN PRONUNCIATION

Accent Marks

Italian spelling provides most of the information needed to pronounce Italian correctly. This dictionary uses additional accents, both grave and acute, to indicate the stressed syllable in each multi-syllabic word. Accents are also used to distinguish "open" and "closed" vowels. In this dictionary, é = IPA [e] (closed and stressed, è = IPA [ɛ] (open and stressed), ó = IPA [o] (closed and stressed), and ò = IPA [ɔ] (open and stressed). Unstressed vowels do not have accents. Outside of dictionaries, the only accents written or printed are grave accents used (1) to mark a final stressed vowel, and (2) to distinguish otherwise identical single-syllable words.

Vowels

The five Italian vowels have a clear-cut sound; they are never drawn out or slurred as in English. Italian vowels correspond approximately to the following English sounds.

a	as "a" in "father": **casa, ama, lana**
e *(closed)*	as "a" in "make": **sera, mele, vedere**
e *(open)*	as "e" in "let": **sedia, festa, bene**
i *(closed)*	as "ee" in "feet": **liti, tini, piccolo**
o *(closed)*	as "o" in "note": **coda, molto, conto**
o *(open)*	as "o" in "law": **cosa, toro, donna**
u	as "oo" in "mood": **luna, uno, lupo**

Consonants

b	like English *b* in "boy": **bello, bianco, abete**
c	before *a, o* and *u,* like English *k* in "kind": **cura, come, casa**
c	before *e* and *i,* like English *ch* in English "cherry": **cento, celeste, baci**
cc	before *e* and *i,* like a double ch: **accento, accidenti**
ch	(used only before *e* or *i*) like English *k* in "kick": **perchè, chiaro, bianchi**
ci	before *a, o,* u, like English *ch* in "cherry": , **ciao, cioccolata, ciuffo**
d	like English *d* in "dance": **dedalo, davanti, dove**
g	before *a, o,* and *u,* like English *g* in "go": **gara, lago, gufo**
g	before *e* and *i,* like English *g* in "gem": **gelo, giro, vagito.** If the *i* is unstressed and followed by another vowel, its sound is unheard, as in English "joke": **giovane, giacca, giocare, giugno**
gh	(used only before *e* and *i*) like English *g* in "go": **ghirlanda, fughe, laghi**

gli	sounds somewhat like -*lli*- in "million": **egli, migliore, figlia.** However *gli* is pronounced hard like English "negligence" 1) when it is initial (except in the article *gli*) as in *glioma*, 2) when it is preceded by a consonant as in *ganglio*, and 3) when it is followed by a consonant as in *negligenza*.
gn	sounds approximately like *ni* in "onion": **lavagna, signore, legno.**
gu	sounds like English *gw* in "Gwen": **guerra, guida, guasto.**
h	is always silent: *ho, hai, ha, ah.*
l	like English *l* in "lamb": **lana, lavoro, levare**
m	like English *m* in "money": **male, merito, moto**
n	like English *n* in "net": **nano, nebbia, nido**
p	like English *p* in "pot", but without the aspiration that sometimes accompanies the English sound: **porta, ape, lupa**
qu	like English *qu* in "quart": **questo, quasi, quinto**
r	is well trilled and pronounced with the tip of the tongue against the upper front teeth: **rosa, mare, ora.**
s	has two sounds: 1) when it is followed by a vowel, it is called "pure" and sounds like English hard *s* in "some": **sale, falso**; 2) when it is followed by a consonant (except *p*), especially at the beginning of a word, it is called "impure" and sounds like English *z* in "rose" or *z* in "zero": **sbaglio, svenire, snello.**
sc	before *a, o,* and *u*, like English *sk* in "skip": **scatola, scopo, scusa**
sc	before *e* or *i*, like English *sh* in "ship": **scena, scelta, scivolare**
sch	has the sound of English *sc* in "scope" or English *sch* in "school": **schiavo, dischi, mosche, schema, maschio.**
t	like English *t* in "table": **tale, tutto, patire**
z	sometimes sounds like English *ts* in "nuts": **grazia, forza, zucchero**; sometimes like English *dz* in "adze": **zero, mezzo, zelo.**

Double Consonants

In Italian, double consonants are longer and more emphatic than single consonants, it takes much more time and force to pronounce them: **mamma fratello battaglia cappello atto pello bocca tetto.**

Stress

Generally, Italian words are stressed on the last syllable but one, that is, the penultimate syllable: cu*ci*na vo*ta*na col*la*na ma*ti*ta.

Sometimes the words are stressed on the last syllable but two, that is antepenultimate syllable: *ma*gico *lo*gico *al*bero dif*fi*cile.

In certain cases the words are stressed on the last syllable but three: *collo-cano* *portatemelo* *eccotelo* and *andandosene.*

In certain cases the words are stressed on the last syllable: *città* *volontà.*

Rhythm and Intonation

Intonation in Italian is dictated by the speaker's feeling. However, as a general rule, intonation can be:

a. rising at the end of a "yes"/"no" question: **Sei stato promosso?**

b. falling at the end of an affirmative or a negative sentence, or interrogative sentence introduced by an interrogative word:

   Carlo legge sempre i giornali.

c. unchanged in the everyday expressions: **Mi lasci passare** or **Grazie tante.**

ITALIANO
INGLESE

a *prep.* at, in (stato in luogo), to (moto a luogo e compl. di termine), at (tempo determinato), in (tempo indeterminato)

àbaco *s. m.* abacus (*arch.*)

abàte *s. m.* abbot

abbagliànte *s. m.* high-beam headlight • *pl.* brights

abbaìno *s. m.* attic

abbandonàre *v. tr.* to abandon, to desert, to leave

abbassàre *v. tr.* to lower

abbastànza *avv.* enough; quite, rather (alquanto)

abbazìa *s. f.* abbey

abbigliaménto *s. m.* clothing, clothes *pl.*; dress, style (modo di vestire); sportswear (sportivo)

abbinàre *v. tr.* to couple, to combine

abbonaménto *s. m.* season ticket; subscription (giornale)

abbonàrsi *v. rifl.* to take out a subscription

abbonàto *agg. e s. m.* season ticket holder; subscriber (giornale)

abbondànte *agg.* abundant, plentiful

abbondànza *s. f.* abundance, plenty

abbreviàre *v. tr.* to shorten, to cut short, to abbreviate

abbreviazióne *s. f.* abbreviation

abbronzànte *s. m.* sun-tan lotion; tanning cream

abbronzatùra *s. f.* sun-tan

abbrustolìre *v. tr.* to toast

abdicàre *v. intr.* to abdicate

abète *s. m.* fir

abìsso *s. m.* abyss

abitàcolo *s. m.* cockpit (*aer.*); driver's cab (*autom.*)

abitànte *agg. e s. m. e f.* inhabitant

abitàre *v. intr.* to live, to reside • *tr.* to inhabit

abitazióne *s. f.* residence, house

àbito *s. m.* suit (da uomo); dress (da donna)

abitualménte *avv.* usually, regularly

abituàto *agg.* accustomed (to), used (to)

abitùdine *s. f.* habit, custom

abolìre *v. tr.* to abolish, to suppress

abolizionìsmo *s. m.* abolitionism

aborìgeno *s. m.* aboriginal

abortìre *v. intr.* to abort, to miscarry

abòrto *s. m.* abortion, miscarriage

abrasióne *s. f.* abrasion

abrogàre *v. tr.* to abrogate, to repeal

àbside *s. f.* apse

abusàre *v. intr.* to abuse; to misuse; to take advantage (approfittarsi)

abusivaménte *avv.* illegally, unlawfully

abusìvo *agg.* illegal, unlawful, unauthorized

acàcia *s. f.* acacia

acànto *s. m.* acanthus

accadèmia *s. f.* academy

accadèmico *agg.* academic; **corpo –** faculty

accadére *v. intr.* to happen, to occur, to take place

accalappiacàni *s. m.* dog-catcher

accampaménto *s. m.* camp

accampàrsi *v. rifl.* to camp

accànto *avv.* nearby, next door

accappatóio *s. m.* bathrobe

accarezzàre *v. tr.* to caress, to stroke

accattóne *s. m.* beggar

acceleratóre *s. m.* accelerator

accèndere *v. tr.* to light; to switch on, to turn on (luce, radio, TV, ecc.)

accendìno *s. m.* lighter

accennàre *v. intr.* to nod (col capo); to hint (alludere)

accensióne *s. f.* switching on, lighting; ignition (*autom.*)

accènto *s. m.* accent, stress

accentràre *v. tr.* to centralize

accèsso *s. m.* access, admittance, entry

accessòrio *s. m.* accessory; attachment

accettàre *v. tr.* to accept, to admit

acciàio *s. m.* steel; **– inossidàbile** stainless steel

accidènti *inter.* my goodness!, damn!

acciottolàto *s. m.* cobbled paving

acciùga *s. f.* anchovy

acclùdere *v. tr.* to enclose

acclùso *agg.* enclosed

accogliénte *agg.* comfortable, cosy, cozy (USA), welcoming

accògliere *v. tr.* to receive, to welcome

accomodàrsi *v. rifl.* to come in (entrare); to sit down (sedersi); to make oneself comfortable

accompagnàre *v. tr.* to accompany, to take

accompagnatóre *s. m.* guide, escort

acconciatùra *s. f.* hairstyle

accónto *s. m.* advance, account; **in** – in advance, on account

accorciàre *v. tr.* to shorten, to contract, to abridge

accordàre *v. tr.* to grant (concedere); to match (armonizzare) • *intr. pron.* to agree

accòrgersi *v. intr. pron.* to notice (notare); to realize (rendersi conto)

accumulatóre *s. m.* accumulator

accùsa *s. f.* accusation, charge

accusàre *v. tr.* to accuse, to charge

acéfalo *agg.* acephalous

acèrbo *agg.* unripe, green; sour (aspro); sharp (*fig.*)

àcero *s. m.* maple

acéto *s. m.* vinegar

àcido *s. m.* acid

acìdulo *agg.* acidulous, sour

àcino *s. m.* grape, berry

aconfessionàle *agg.* non-denominational

àcqua *s. f.* water; – **minerale** mineral water; – **potabile** drinking water

acquafòrte *s. f.* etching

acquamarina *s. f.* aquamarine

acquàrio *s. m.* aquarium; Aquarius (*astr.*)

acquasantièra *s. f.* stoup

acquavite *s. f.* brandy

acquazzóne *s. m.* downpour

acquedótto *s. m.* aqueduct; waterworks (impianto idrico)

acquerellista *s. m. e f.* watercolourist

acquerèllo *s. m.* watercolour

acquirènte *s. m. e f.* purchaser, buyer; shopper (in un negozio)

acquisto *s. m.* purchase

acquitrino *s. m.* bog, marsh, swamp (palude)

acquóso *agg.* watery

acrìlico *agg.* acrylic

acrìtico *agg.* dogmatic

acròbata *s. m. e f.* acrobat

acrobazìa *s. f.* acrobatics *pl.*

acròpoli *s. f.* acropolis

acrotèrio *s. m.* acroterium

acùleo *s. m.* aculeus

acùme *s. m.* acumen (perspicacia); sharpness (acutezza)

acùstica *s. f.* acoustics *pl.* (v. *al sing.*)

acùto *agg.* sharp; acute (angolo, accento)

adàgio *avv.* slowly

adattàre *v. tr.* to fit, to adapt • *rifl.* to adapt oneself, to fit in

adàtto *agg.* suitable, right, fit (for)

addebitàre *v. tr.* to debit, to charge

addèbito *s. m.* debit, charge

addétto *s. m.* employee, agent

addìo *inter.* goodbye

addirittùra *avv.* absolutely; even (persino); really (veramente)

additìvo *s. m.* additive

addizióne *s. f.* addition, sum

addòbbo *s. m.* decoration, ornament

addòme *s. m.* abdomen

addomesticàto *agg.* tame

addominàle *agg.* abdominal

addormentàrsi *v. intr. pron.* to fall asleep

addormentàto *agg.* sleeping; asleep (*pred.*)

addòsso *avv.* on, on one's back

adeguàrsi *v. rifl.* to conform

adèpto *s. m.* follower

aderènte *agg.* adherent; close-fitting (di vestito)

adescaménto *s. m.* enticement, allurement

adesìvo *agg.* adhesive, self-sticking

adèsso *avv.* now; nowadays (ai giorni nostri); just, just now (proprio ora; poco fa); any moment now (fra poco)

adiacènte *agg.* adjacent, adjoining

adiràrsi *v. intr. pron.* to get angry

adolescènte *s. m. e f.* adolescent, teenager

adolescènza *s. f.* adolescence, teens

adoperàre *v. tr.* to use, to employ

adoràre *v. tr.* to adore, to worship

adottàre *v. tr.* to adopt

adottìvo *agg.* adoptive

adozióne *s. f.* adoption

adultèrio *s. m.* adultery

adùlto *s. m.* adult; grown-up; mature

adunàta *s. f.* assembly; gathering

aerazióne *s. f.* ventilation, aeration

aèreo *s. m.* airplane, plane

aeròbico *agg.* aerobic

aerodinàmico *agg.* aerodynamic

aerofotografìa *s. f.* aerial photography

aeronàutico *agg.* aeronautic

aeroplàno *s. m.* airplane, plane

aeropòrto *s. m.* airport

aerosól *s. m.* aerosol

àfa s. f. sultriness

affamàto agg. hungry

affàre s. m. business; bargain (occasione); matter (argomento); affair (faccenda); thing, gadget (fam.) (aggeggio)

affascinànte agg. charming, fascinating

affaticàrsi v. rifl. to tire oneself, to get tired

affermàre v. tr. to assert, to affirm, to state

affermativo agg. affirmative, affirmatory

afferràre v. tr. to seize, to grasp, to catch

affettàre v. tr. to slice

affettivo agg. affective

affettuosaménte avv. affectionately, lovingly; with love (lettera)

affettuóso agg. affectionate, fond, loving

affezionàto agg. affectionate, fond

affidàbile agg. reliable

affidàre v. tr. to entrust

affìggere v. tr. to stick up; to post up (manifesto)

affilàre v. tr. to sharpen

affilàto agg. sharp

affinità s. f. affinity

affittàbile agg. rentable

affittacàmere s. m. e f. inv. landlord m.; landlady f.

affittàre v. tr. to let, to lease (dare in affitto); to rent (prendere in affitto)

affitto s. m. lease

affluènte s. m. tributary

affluènza s. f. flow

affogàre v. tr. e intr. to drown

affogàto agg. drowned; poached (uovo)

affollaménto s. m. crowding

affollàto agg. crowded

affondàre v. intr. to sink

affrancàre v. tr. to free; to stamp (lettera)

affrancatùra s. f. stamping; postage (tassa di spedizione)

affrescàre v. tr. to fresco

affrésco s. m. fresco

affrettàrsi v. rifl. to hurry (up), to hasten

affumicàto agg. smoked

afóso agg. sultry

africàno agg. e s. m. African

afrodisìaco s. m. aphrodisiac

àgave s. f. agave

agènda s. f. diary, agenda

agènte s. m. agent; – di polizia police officer; – di cambio stockbroker; – immobiliare realtor, land broker

agenzìa s. f. agency

agevolazióne s. f. facilitation; concession; reduction

aggettìvo s. m. adjective

aggiornàre v. tr. to update; to revise (rivedere); to adjourn (rinviare) • rifl. to bring oneself up to date

aggiràre v. tr. to circle

aggiùngere v. tr. to add • intr. pron. to join

aggiustàbile agg. mendable, repairable

aggiustàre v. tr. to mend, to repair, to fix up

agglomeràto s. m. agglomerate; – urbano built up area

aggredìre v. tr. to attack, to assault

aggressività s. f. aggressiveness

aggressóre s. m. aggressor

agiàto agg. wealthy, well-to-do

àgile agg. agile, nimble

agilità s. f. agility, nimbleness

agiografìa s. f. hagiography

agitàre v. tr. to shake; to upset (turbare) • rifl. to toss about; to become upset (turbarsi)

agitàto agg. shaken; upset (turbato)

agitazióne s. f. agitation, unrest

àglio s. m. garlic

agnèllo s. m. lamb; – arrosto roast lamb

agnòstico agg. agnostic

àgo s. m. needle

agopuntùra s. f. acupuncture

agósto s. m. August

agrìcolo agg. agrarian, agricultural

agricoltóre s. m. farmer

agricoltùra s. f. agriculture, farming

agrifòglio s. m. holly

agriturìsmo s. m. farm holidays

agrodólce agg. bitter-sweet

agrùme s. m. citrus fruit; citrus tree (pianta)

aguzzo agg. sharp

àia s. f. threshingfloor

airóne s. m. heron

aiuòla s. f. flowerbed

aiutàre v. tr. to help, to assist, to aid • rifl. rec. to help each other

alabàstro s. m. alabaster

àlba s. f. dawn

albergatóre s. m. hotel keeper

albèrgo s. m. hotel

àlbero s. m. tree (bot.); mast (naut.); shaft (mecc.)

albicòcca s. f. apricot

albùme s. m. albumen, white

àlce s. m. elk

àlcol s. m. alcohol

179

alcólico *agg.* alcoholic; **bevande** – spirits
alcolismo *s. m.* alcoholism
alcolizzato *agg.* alcoholic
alesàggio *s. m.* bore
alessandrino *agg.* Alexandrian
alettóne *s. m.* aileron
alfabèto *s. m.* alphabet
àlga *s. f.* alga, seaweed
aliànte *s. m.* glider
alice *s. f.* anchovy
alienazióne *s. f.* alienation
alimentàre *agg.* alimentary; food (*attr.*); **ge-neri alimentàri** foodstuffs
aliquota *s. f.* share, quota; rate (*fin.*)
aliscàfo *s. m.* hydrofoil
alisèo *s. m.* trade; **gli alisei** trades winds
allacciàre *v. tr.* to lace up; to button up (abbottonare)
allagaménto *s. m.* flooding
allargàre *v. tr.* to widen, to enlarge
allàrme *s. m.* alarm
allarmismo *s. m.* alarmism
allattàre *v. tr.* to nurse, to suckle
alleànza *s. f.* alliance
alleàto *agg. e s. m.* allied
allegàre *v. tr.* to enclose, to append
alleggerìre *v. tr.* to lighten, to relieve
allegorìa *s. f.* allegory
allegrìa *s. f.* mirth, cheerfulness
allègro *agg.* cheerful, happy, merry
allenaménto *s. m.* training
allenàrsi *v. rifl.* to train
allenatóre *s. m.* trainer, coach
allergìa *s. f.* allergy
allèrgico *agg.* allergic
allettàre *v. tr.* to attract
allevaménto *s. m.* upbringing (bambini); breeding (animali); stockfarm (luogo di –)
allevàre *v. tr.* to raise, to bring up (bambini); to breed (animali)
allibratóre *s. m.* bookmaker
allièvo *s. m.* pupil
alligatóre *s. m.* alligator
allòdola *s. f.* skylark
alloggiàre *v. intr.* to lodge
allòggio *s. m.* accomodation, lodging, house; **vitto e** – board and lodging
allontanàre *v. tr.* to remove, to take away • *rifl. e intr. pron.* to go away, to go off
allòro *s. m.* laurel
allucinazióne *s. f.* hallucination
allùdere *v. intr.* to allude to
allungàre *v. tr.* to lengthen, to prolong

allusióne *s. f.* allusion
alluvionàle *agg.* alluvial
alluvióne *s. f.* flood, alluvion
alméno *avv.* at least
alpinismo *s. m.* alpinism, mountaineering
alpinista *s. m. e f.* alpinist, mountain-climber
alt *inter.* halt, stop
altàre *s. m.* altar
alternatìva *s. f.* alternative, alternation
alternatóre *s. m.* alternator
altézza *s. f.* height
altitùdine *s. f.* altitude
àlto *agg.* high; tall (di statura); upper (*geog.*)
altoparlànte *s. m.* loudspeaker
altopiàno *s. m.* plateau, highland
altorilièvo *s. m.* alto rilievo, high relief
altrettànto *agg. e pron.* as much...as; as many...as *pl.*; the same (la stessa cosa) • *avv.* as...as (con agg. e avv.); as much... as (con verbi); likewise (nello stesso modo)
àltro *agg.* other, another (un altro), more (in aggiunta), else • *pron.* (the) other; another (one), more (in aggiunta)
altróve *avv.* somewhere else, elsewhere
altrùi *agg.* other's; other people's
altruismo *s. m.* altruism, unselfishness
altùra *s. f.* high ground; high sea (*naut.*)
alùnno *s. m.* pupil
alveàre *s. m.* hive
alzàre *v. tr.* to lift up, to raise • *intr. pron.* to get up (dal letto); to stand up (in piedi)
amàca *s. f.* hammock
amànte *agg.* fond of, keen on • *s. m. e f.* lover
amàre *v. tr.* to love; to be fond of
amarèna *s. f.* sour cherry
amàro *agg.* bitter • *s. m.* bitters *pl.*
ambasciàta *s. f.* embassy
ambasciatóre *s. m.* ambassador
ambientàle *agg.* environmental
ambientàre *v. tr.* to acclimatize; to set (*lett.*, *cin.*) • *rifl.* to get acclimatized
ambiènte *s. m.* environment; background (sociale, culturale); room (stanza)
ambiguità *s. f.* ambiguity
ambìguo *agg.* ambiguous
ambizióso *agg.* ambitious
àmbra *s. f.* amber; ambergris (grigia); jet (nera)
ambulànte *agg.* itinerant; **venditore** – pedlar
ambulànza *s. f.* ambulance
ambulatòrio *s. m.* consulting room; first-aid station (pronto soccorso)
améno *agg.* pleasant; funny (bizzarro)

amenorrèa *s. f.* amenorrhea

americàno *agg. e s. m.* American

ametista *s. f.* amethyst

amiànto *s. m.* amiantus

amichévole *agg.* friendly; amicable (di accordo)

amicizia *s. f.* friendship

amico *agg.* friendly • *s. m.* friend

àmido *s. m.* starch

ammaccatùra *s. f.* bruise (*med.*); dent (di metallo)

ammainàre *v. tr.* to furl

ammalàrsi *v. intr. pron.* to fall ill

ammalàto *agg.* ill, sick

ammaràggio *s. m.* water landing

ammazzàre *v. tr.* to murder, to kill • *rifl.* to kill oneself

ammènda *s. f.* amends *pl.*; fine (multa)

amměsso *agg.* admitted, accepted

amměttere *v. tr.* to admit

ammezzàto *s. m.* mezzanine

amministràre *v. tr.* to administer, to run, to manage

amministrazióne *s. f.* administration, management

ammiràglio *s. m.* admiral

ammiràre *v. tr.* to admire

ammiratóre *s. m.* admirer, fan

ammissibile *agg.* admissible

ammoniàca *s. f.* ammonia

ammontàre *v. intr.* to amount, to come to

ammorbidire *v. tr.* to soften

ammortizzàre *v. tr.* to dampen (*mecc.*); to amortize (*fin.*)

ammortizzatóre *s. m.* shock absorber (*mecc.*); damper (*autom.*)

ammuffito *agg.* mouldy

amnesia *s. f.* amnesia

amnistia *s. f.* amnesty

àmo *s. m.* fish-hook

amoràle *agg.* amoral

amóre *s. m.* love

amperòmetro *s. m.* amperometer

ampiézza *s. f.* width

àmpio *agg.* wide

amplèsso *s. m.* embrace

amplificatóre *s. m.* amplifier

amputàre *v. tr.* to amputate

amulèto *s. m.* amulet

anabbagliànte *s. m.* low-beam headlight

anacronístico *agg.* anachronistic

anagràmma *s. m.* anagram

analcòlico *agg.* nonalcoholic • *s. m.* soft drink

analfabèta *agg. e s. m. e f.* illiterate

analgèsico *s. m.* analgesic

analisi *s. f.* analysis, test

analista *s. m. e f.* analyst

analizzàre *v. tr.* to analyse, to test

analogia *s. f.* analogy

analogo *agg.* analogous

ananas *s. m.* pineapple

anarchia *s. f.* anarchy; anarchism (dottrina)

anatomia *s. f.* anatomy

ànatra *s. f.* duck

ànca *s. f.* hip

ancèlla *s. f.* maid

ànche *avv.* too, also; as well (in aggiunta); so (allo stesso modo); – se even if

àncora *s. f.* anchor

ancóra *avv.* still; yet (in frasi neg.); again (di nuovo); somemore (di più)

ancoràggio *s. m.* anchorage; mooring

ancoràre *v. tr.* to anchor • *rifl.* to moor; to drop anchor

andàre *v. intr.* to go; – in macchina to go by car

andatùra *s. f.* gait

andróne *s. m.* entrance-hall

anèddoto *s. m.* anecdote

anèllo *s. m.* ring

anemia *s. f.* anemia

anèmico *agg. s. m.* anemic

anemòmetro *s. m.* anemometer

anestesia *s. f.* anaesthesia

anestètico *s. m.* anaesthetic

anestetizzàre *v. tr.* to anaesthetize

aneurisma *s. m.* aneurism

anfetamina *s. f.* amphetamine

anfibio *agg.* amphibian

anfiteatro *s. m.* amphitheatre

ànfora *s. f.* amphora

àngelo *s. m.* angel

anglicàno *agg. e s. m.* Anglican

anglosàssone *agg. e s. m. e f.* Anglo-Saxon

angolàre *agg.* angular

àngolo *s. m.* angle, corner

àngora *s. f.* angora

anguilla *s. f.* eel

angùria *s. f.* watermelon

ànice *s. m.* anise

ànima *s. f.* soul

animàle *s. m.* animal

animàto *agg.* animate, living, animated; lively (vivace); cartoni animati cartoons

animatóre *s. m.* animator; **– di gruppo** team leader

annaffiàre *v. tr.* to water

annàta *s. f.* year

annegàre *v. tr. e intr.* to drown

annèsso *agg.* attached, annexed

annidàrsi *v. rifl.* to nest

anniversàrio *s. m.* anniversary

ànno *s. m.* year

annodàre *v. tr.* to knot; to tie (legare)

annoiàrsi *v. intr. pron.* to be bored, to get bored

annotazióne *s. f.* annotation, note

annuàle *agg.* annual, yearly

annualménte *avv.* annually, yearly

annuire *v. intr.* to nod

annullaménto *s. m.* annulment, cancellation

annullàre *v. tr.* to annul, to cancel

annunciàre *v. tr.* to announce

annuvolàrsi *v. intr. pron.* to cloud over

àno *s. m.* anus

anòmalo *agg.* anomalous

anònimo *agg.* anonymous

anoressìa *s. f.* anorexia

anormàle *agg.* abnormal

ànsa *s. f.* loop

ànsia *s. f.* anxiety

ansiolìtico *s. m.* tranquillizer

ansióso *agg.* anxious

antagonìsta *agg. e s. m. e f.* antagonistic, antagonist

antàrtico *agg.* antarctic

antenàto *s. m.* ancestor, forefather

antènna *s. f.* aerial

antepríma *s. f.* preview

anterióre *agg.* front (luogo); former, previous (tempo)

antiallèrgico *s. m.* anti-allergic

antiatòmico *agg.* anti-atomic

antibiòtico *s. m.* antibiotic

anticaménte *avv.* in ancient times; formerly (in precedenza)

anticàmera *s. f.* anteroom, antechamber

antichità *s. f.* antiquity; antique (oggetto)

anticiclóne *s. m.* anticyclone

anticipàre *v. tr.* to move up, to anticipate; **– una somma** to advance a sum

anticipàto *agg.* early (tempo); in advance (denaro)

anticìpo *s. m.* anticipation (tempo); advance (denaro)

anticlericàle *agg. e s. m. e f.* anticlerical

antìco *agg.* ancient

anticoncezionàle *agg. e s. m.* contraceptive

anticonformìsmo *s. m.* nonconformism

anticostituzionàle *agg.* anticonstitutional, unconstitutional

anticrittogàmico *s. m.* fungicide

antidolorìfico *s. m.* analgesic, pain-killer

antiemorràgico *agg.* haemostatic

antifascìsta *agg.* antifascist

antifecondatìvo *s. m.* contraceptive

antifùrto *s. m. inv.* anti-theft device

antigèlo *agg. e s. m.* antifreeze, antifreezing

antìlope *s. f.* antelope

antinevràlgico *agg.* antineuralgic

antinfluenzàle *s. m.* anti-influenza

antioràrio *agg.* counterclockwise, anticlockwise

antipàsto *s. m.* hors d'oeuvre, appetizer, starter

antipàtico *agg.* unpleasant, disagreeable

antiquariàto *s. m.* antique trade (*comm.*); **mobili d'–** antique furniture

antiquàrio *s. m.* antiquarian

antiràbbico *agg.* antirabic

antireumàtico *agg.* antirheumatic

antirùggine *agg. inv.* antirust, rustproof

antisìsmico *agg.* antiseismic

antitetànico *agg.* antitetanic

antologìa *s. f.* anthology

antonomàsia *s. f.* antonomasia

antropologìa *s. f.* anthropology

antropològico *agg.* anthropological

antropòlogo *s. m.* anthropologist

antropomòrfo *agg.* anthropomorphous

ànzi *cong.* on the contrary

anziàno *s. m.* elderly person; **gli – the elderly**

àpe *s. f.* bee

aperitìvo *s. m.* aperitif

apèrto *agg.* open; **all'aria –** in the open air

apertùra *s. f.* opening; **orario d'–** opening time

apicoltùra *s. f.* apiculture

apnèa *s. f.* apnea

apòcrifo *agg.* apocryphal

apòstolo *s. m.* apostle

apòstrofo *s. m.* apostrophe

apparecchiàre *v. tr.* to lay the table

apparenteménte *avv.* apparently

apparìre *v. intr.* to appear

appartaménto *s. m.* flat

appartenère *v. intr.* to belong

appassionàto *agg.* impassioned, passionate

appéna *avv.* hardly, scarcely; just (tempo) • *cong.* as soon as

appèndere *v. tr.* to hang

appendice *s. f.* appendix; **romanzo d'**– serial

appendicite *s. f.* appendicitis

appesantire *v. tr.* to make heavy

appéso *agg.* hanging

appetito *s. m.* appetite

appetitóso *agg.* appetizing

appiccicóso *agg.* sticky; clinging (di persona)

appiglio *s. m.* support, hold

appisolársi *v. intr. pron.* to doze off

applaudire *v. tr. e intr.* to clap, to applaud

applàuso *s. m.* applause, cheering

applicàre *v. tr.* to apply; to enforce (*leg.*)

appoggiàre *v. tr.* to lean, to lay • *rifl.* to lean

appoggiatésta *s. m. inv.* headrest

appòggio *s. m.* support

appositaménte *avv.* expressly, on purpose

apprèndere *v. tr.* to learn; to hear (venire a sapere)

apprendista *s. m. e f.* apprentice

apprensivo *agg.* apprehensive, uptight, anxious

apprezzàre *v. tr.* to appreciate

approdàre *v. intr.* to land

appròdo *s. m.* landing

approfittàre *v. intr.* to take advantage of

appropriàto *agg.* appropriate, suitable

approssimativo *agg.* approximate

approvàre *v. tr.* to approve

appuntaménto *s. m.* appointment, date

appuràre *v. tr.* to ascertain

apribile *agg.* opening

apribottiglie *s. m. inv.* bottle-opener

aprile *s. m.* April

apripista *s. m.* bulldozer

aprire *v. tr. e intr.* to open

apriscàtole *s. m. inv.* tin-opener, can-opener

àptero *agg.* apterous

àquila *s. f.* eagle

aquilóne *s. m.* kite

àra *s. f.* are (misura); altar (*relig.*)

arabésco *s. m.* arabesque

aràbico *agg.* Arabic, Arabian

àrabo *agg. e s. m.* Arab, Arabian

aràchide *s. f.* peanut

aragósta *s. f.* lobster

aràldico *agg.* heraldic

arància *s. f.* orange

aranciàta *s. f.* orangeade

arancióne *agg.* orange

aràtro *s. m.* plough

aràzzo *s. m.* tapestry

arbitràre *v. tr.* to arbitrate; to referee, to umpire (*sport*)

arbitràrio *agg.* arbitrary

arbitrio *s. m.* will; liberty (abuso)

àrbitro *s. m.* arbiter; referee, umpire (*sport*)

arbòreo *agg.* arboreal

arboricoltùra *s. f.* arboriculture

arbùsto *s. m.* shrub

arcàdico *agg.* Arcadian

arcàico *agg.* archaic

arcàngelo *s. m.* archangel

arcàno *agg.* arcane, mysterious

arcàta *s. f.* arch; arcade (portico)

archeologia *s. f.* archaeology

archeológico *agg.* archaeologic

archeòlogo *s. m.* archaeologist

archètipo *s. m.* archetype

archibùgio *s. m.* harquebus

architétto *s. m.* architect

architettònico *agg.* architectonic

architettùra *s. f.* architecture

architràve *s. f.* lintel, architrave (*arch.*)

archiviàre *v. tr.* to archive, to file; – **un proces**-so to dismiss a case

archìvio *s. m.* archives *pl.*; file (*comm.*)

archivòlto *s. m.* archivolt

arcière *s. m.* archer, bowman

arcipèlago *s. m.* archipelago

arcivéscovo *s. m.* archbishop

àrco *s. m.* arch; bow (*mil.*, *mus.*); arc (*fis.*, *geom.*)

arcobaléno *s. m.* rainbow

ardèsia *s. f.* slate

aréna *s. f.* arena (*arch.*); sand (sabbia)

arenìle *s. m.* beach

argentería *s. f.* silverware

argènto *s. m.* silver

argìlla *s. f.* clay, argil

àrgine *s. m.* bank, embankment, dyke

argoménto *s. m.* subject, matter, topic

ària *s. f.* air; – **condizionata** air conditioned; **camera d'**– inner tube

àrido *agg.* dry, arid

arieggiàre *v. tr.* to air

arióso *agg.* airy

arìnga *s. f.* herring

aristocràtico *agg.* aristocratic, upper-class • *s. m.* aristocrat

aristocrazìa *s. f.* aristocracy

aritmètica *s. f.* arithmetic

àrma *s. f.* arm, weapon

armàdio *s. m.* cupboard, wardrobe

armàto *agg.* armed

armatùra *s. f.* armour; framework (telaio)

armería *s. f.* armoury

armistizio s. m. armistice

armonia s. f. harmony

armonióso agg. harmonious

arnése s. m. tool, implement

aromàtico agg. aromatic

àrpa s. f. harp

arpióne s. m. harpoon

arrabbiàrsi v. intr. pron. to get angry

arrabbiàto agg. angry

arrampicàrsi v. intr. pron. to scramble up, to climb up

arrampicàta s. f. climb

arrangiàrsi v. intr. pron. to manage; to settle; to come to an agreement

arredaménto s. m. furnishing, fitting; furniture (mobili)

arrestàre v. tr. to arrest; to halt, to stop (fermare)

arricchìre v. tr. to enrich

arrivàre v. intr. to arrive (at, in), to get (to), to reach

arrivàto agg. successful

arrivedérci inter. see you soon, see you later

arrìvo s. m. arrival

arrossaménto s. m. reddening

arrostìre v. tr. to roast

arròsto agg. e s. m. roast

arrotolàre v. tr. to roll up

arrotondàre v. tr. to round (off)

arrugginìre v. intr. e intr. pron. to rust

arsenàle s. m. shipyard, dockyard (naut.); arsenal (mil.)

àrte s. f. art

artèria s. f. artery

arterioscleròsi s. f. arteriosclerosis

arterióso agg. arterial

àrtico agg. arctic

artìcolo s. m. item; article (gramm.)

artificiàle agg. artificial

artigianàto s. m. handicraft; **mostra dell'** - arts and crafts exhibition

artigiàno s. m. artisan, craftsman

artiglierìa s. f. artillery

artìglio s. m. claw

artìsta s. m. e f. artist

artìstico agg. artistic

artrìte s. f. arthritis

ascèlla s. f. armpit

ascendènte agg. e s. m. ascending, rising

ascensóre s. m. lift, elevator (USA)

ascèsso s. m. abscess

ascetìsmo s. m. asceticism

asciugacapèlli s. m. inv. hairdryer

asciugamàno s. m. towel

asciugàre v. tr. to dry • rifl. to dry oneself

asciugatùra s. f. drying

asciùtto agg. dry

ascoltàre v. tr. to listen to

ascoltatóre s. m. listener; **gli ascoltatori** audience

ascoltazióne s. f. listening

asfaltàre v. tr. to asphalt

asfàlto s. m. asphalt

asfissiàre v. intr. to asphyxiate

asiàtico agg. e s. m. Asiatic, Asian

asìlo s. m. kindergarten, nursery school; shelter, asylum (rifugio)

asimmètrico agg. asymmetric

àsino s. m. ass, donkey

àsma s. f. o m. asthma

asmàtico agg. e s. m. asthmatic

àsola s. f. buttonhole

aspàrago s. m. asparagus

aspettàre v. tr. to wait for, to await; to expect (prevedere)

aspirapólvere s. m. inv. vacuum cleaner

asportàre v. tr. to remove, to carry away

àspro agg. sour

assaggiàre v. tr. to taste

assàggio s. m. tasting; taste (piccola quantità)

assài avv. much (molto); enough (a sufficienza); more then enough (fin troppo)

assalìre v. tr. to assail, to storm

assassìnio s. m. murder, assassination

assassìno s. m. murderer, assassin

àsse s. m. axis • s. f. board; - **da stiro** ironing board

assediàre v. tr. to besiege

assèdio s. m. siege

assegnàre v. tr. to assign, to allot

assegnàto agg. assigned

assègno s. m. cheque; - **in bianco** blank cheque; - **a vuoto** uncovered cheque

assemblèa s. f. assembly meeting

assentàrsi v. intr. pron. to absent oneself

assènte agg. absent

assènza s. f. absence; lack (mancanza)

assetàto agg. thirsty

assicuràre v. tr. to assure, to ensure; to insure (fare un'assicurazione)

assicurazióne s. f. insurance, assurance; - **sulla vita** life insurance; - **contro l'incendio** fire insurance

assìduo agg. assiduous

assillàre v. tr. to pester, to bother

assistènte *s. m. e f.* assistant

assistènza *s. f.* help, assistance; attendance (presenza)

assistere *v. tr.* to help, to assist; to treat (curare) • *intr.* to be present, to attend

àsso *s. m.* ace

associàre *v. tr.* to associate, to combine

assomigliàre *v. intr.* to resemble, to be like

assorbènte *agg.* absorbent; – igienico sanitary towel

assorbìre *v. tr.* to absorb

assordàre *v. tr.* to deafen

assuefazióne *s. f.* habit, inurement; tolerance (med.)

assùnto *agg.* engaged hired, employer

assùrdo *agg.* absurd

àsta *s. f.* pole; rod (mecc.); auction (comm.)

astèmio *agg.* teetotal • *s. m.* teetotaller

astenérsi *v. rifl.* to abstain, to refrain

àstice *s. m.* lobster

asticèlla *s. f.* crossbar

astinènza *s. f.* abstinence

astigmàtico *agg.* astigmatic

astràgalo *s. m.* astragalus (bot.); astragal (arch.)

astrattìsmo *s. m.* abstractionism

astrattìsta *s. m. e f.* abstractionist, abstract artist

astràtto *agg.* abstract

astringènte *agg.* astringent

àstro *s. m.* star, planet

astrolàbio *s. m.* astrolabe

astrologìa *s. f.* astrology

astrològico *agg.* astrologic

astròlogo *s. m.* astrologer

astronàuta *s. m. e f.* astronaut

astronàutico *agg.* astronautical

astronàve *s. f.* spaceship

astronomìa *s. f.* astronomy

astronòmico *agg.* astronomical

astrònomo *s. m.* astronomer

astùccio *s. m.* case, box

astùto *agg.* astute, crafty, cunning

atàvico *agg.* atavic

ateìsmo *s. m.* atheism

àteo *agg.* atheist

atìpico *agg.* atypical

atlànte *s. m.* atlas

atlàntico *agg.* Atlantic

atlèta *s. m. e f.* athlete

atlètica *s. f.* athletics pl. (v. al sing.)

atlètico *agg.* athletic

atmosfèra *s. f.* atmosphere

atmosfèrico *agg.* atmospheric

atòllo *s. m.* atoll

atòmico *agg.* atomic

àtomo *s. m.* atom

àtrio *s. m.* entrance, hall, lobby

atròce *agg.* atrocious

attaccànte *s. m.* attacker, forward (sport)

attaccapànni *s. m.* clothes-peg

attaccàre *v. tr.* to attach, to fasten, to tie (unire); to stick, to glue (appiccicare); to attack, to assail (assalire)

attàcco *s. m.* attack, assault

attempàto *agg.* elderly

attendàrsi *v. intr. pron.* to camp

attèndere *v. tr.* to wait for, to await; to expect (prevedere)

attentaménte *avv.* attentively, carefully

attentàto *s. m.* attempt

attènto *agg.* attentive, alert

attenzióne *s. f.* attention; care (cura)

atterràggio *s. m.* landing; pista d'– landing strip

atterràre *v. intr.* to land

attésa *s. f.* wait; expectation (aspettativa)

attéso *agg.* waited for; longed for (desiderato)

àttico *s. m.* attic

attìguo *agg.* adjacent, next (to)

attillàto *agg.* close-fitting

attiràre *v. tr.* to attract

attività *s. f.* activity

attìvo *agg.* busy, active

àtto *s. m.* act, action, deed

attóre *s. m.* actor

attraccàre *v. tr. e intr.* to berth, to dock

attràcco *s. m.* berthing, docking

attrattìva *s. f.* attraction

attraversaménto *s. m.* crossing

attraversàre *v. tr.* to cross, to go through

attravèrso *avv.* crosswise, askew • *prep.* through, across; over (di tempo)

attrezzatùra *s. f.* equipment, outfit

attrèzzo *s. m.* tool, implement

attribuìbile *agg.* attributable, ascribable

attribuìre *v. tr.* to attribute, to ascribe; to award (assegnare)

attrìto *s. m.* friction, attrition; disagreement (disaccordo)

attuàle *agg.* present, current

attualità *s. f.* up-to-dateness

attualménte *avv.* at present

àudio *s. m. inv.* sound, audio

audiovisìvo *agg.* audiovisual

auguràre *v. tr.* to wish

augùrio s. m. wish; omen (presagio); i migliori auguri best wishes

àula s. f. hall; courtroom (di tribunale); classroom (di scuola)

àulico agg. stately

aumentàre v. tr. to increase, to raise, to augment

auménto s. m. increase, rise

àureo agg. gold

auréola s. f. halo

auricolàre s. m. earphone

auriga s. m. charioteer

auròra s. f. dawn; – boreale aurora borealis

auspicàbile agg. desirable

austerità s. f. austerity

austèro agg. austere

australe agg. southern, austral

australiàno agg. e s. m. Australian

austriaco agg. e s. m. Austrian

autenticità s. f. authenticity

autèntico agg. authentic, genuine, original

autista s. m. e f. driver; – privato chauffeur

autoadesivo agg. self-sticking

autobiogràfico agg. autobiographic(al)

autobótte s. f. tanker, tank lorry

autobus s. m. bus; – a due piani double-decker

autocàrro s. m. lorry, truck (USA)

autodidàtta s. m. e f. self-taught person, autodidact

autodifésa s. f. self-defence

autódromo s. m. autodrome

autofilettànte agg. self-threading

autogòl s. m. inv. own-goal

autógrafo agg. autographed • s. m. autograph

autogrù s. f. break-down lorry, tow truck (USA)

autolinea s. f. bus-line

automàtico agg. automatic

automòbile s. f. car

automobilista s. m. e f. (car) driver

automobilistico agg. motor (attr.), auto (attr.)

autonoléggio s. m. car hire, car rental

autonomia s. f. autonomy

autònomo agg. autonomous

autorádio s. f. inv. car radio

autóre s. m. author

autorespiratóre s. m. aqualung, scuba

autorévole agg. authoritative

autoriméssa s. f. garage

autorità s. f. authority

autoritràtto s. m. self-portrait

autorizzàre v. tr. to authorize

autorizzazióne s. f. authorization

autoscàtto s. m. self-timer

autoscuòla s. f. driving school

autostóp s. m. inv. hitchhiking

autostoppista s. m. e f. hitchhiker

autostràda s. f. motorway, speedway

autostradàle agg. motorway (attr.)

autosufficiènte agg. self-sufficient

autotrèno s. m. lorry with trailer, trailer truck (USA)

autunnàle agg. autumnal

autùnno s. m. autumn, fall (USA)

avambràccio s. m. forearm

avampósto s. m. outpost

avanguàrdia s. f. vanguard; avant-garde (arte)

avanti avv. forward, head, on (luogo); before, on (tempo) • inter. come in!

avantrèno s. m. forecarriage

avanzàre v. intr. to advance, to go forward; to be left (restare) • tr. to advance, to put forward

avànzo s. m. remainder, scrap; gli avanzi di un pasto leftovers

avaria s. f. breakdown (mecc.); average (naut.)

avàro agg. greedy, miserly, stingy (fam.)

avéna s. f. oats pl.; farina d'– oatmeal

avére v. tr. to have; to possess, to own (possedere)

aviazióne s. f. aviation; Air Force (mil.)

avicoltura s. f. aviculture

avifàuna s. f. avifauna

àvo s. m. forefather

avocàdo s. m. inv. avocado

avòrio s. m. ivory

avvallaménto s. m. subsidence

avvelenaménto s. m. poisoning

avvelenàre v. tr. to poison

avveniménto s. m. event

avveniristico agg. futuristic

avventùra s. f. adventure; – sentimentale affair

avventuriéro s. m. adventurer

avventuróso agg. adventurous, eventful

avversàrio s. m. opponent, adversary

avversità s. f. adversity

avvertènza s. f. care, caution; avvertenze directions

avvertire v. tr. to point out, to inform; to warn (ammonire); to feel (sentire)

avviaménto s. m. start, starting

avvicinàre v. tr. to move near, to bring near • intr. pron. to come near, to approach

avvincènte agg. charming

avvisàre v. tr. to inform, to advise

avviso *s. m.* announcement, notice
avvistàre *v. tr.* to sight
avvitàre *v. tr.* to screw
avvocàto *s. m.* lawyer
avvòlgere *v. tr.* to wrap up, to wind
avvoltòio *s. m.* vulture

azalèa *s. f.* azalea
aziènda *s. f.* firm, business, establishment
azióne *s. f.* deed, action; share (*fin.*)
azòto *s. m.* azote
azzeccàre *v. tr.* to guess, to get it, to guess right
azzùrro *agg.* blue

B

bàbbo *s. m.* father, dad, daddy, pa

bacàto *agg.* worm-eaten, maggoty

bàcca *s. f.* berry

baccalà *s. m.* dried salted cod

baccàno *s. m.* racket

baccèllo *s. m.* pod

baciàre *v. tr.* to kiss • *rifl. rec.* to kiss each other

bàcio *s. m.* kiss

bàffo *s. m.* moustache; whiskers *pl.* (animali)

bagagliàio *s. m.* luggage van (*ferr.*); boot, trunk (USA) (*autom.*)

bagàglio *s. m.* luggage; baggage (USA); – **a mano** hand-luggage; **deposito bagagli** left-luggage office, checkroom

bagnànte *s. m. e f.* bather

bagnàre *v. tr.* to bathe, to wet; to water (annaffiare) • *rifl.* to bathe

bagnasciùga *s. m. inv.* water line

bagnàto *agg.* wet

bagnìno *s. m.* bathing-attendant

bàgno *s. m.* bath (nella vasca); bathe, swim (in mare); **stanza da** – bathroom

bagnomarìa *s. m.* bain-marie

bagnoschiùma *s. m.* bath bubble

bàia *s. f.* bay

balaùstra *s. f.* banisters *pl.*, balustrade

balconàta *s. f.* balcony; gallery (*teatro*)

balcóne *s. m.* balcony

baldacchìno *s. m.* baldachin, canopy

balèna *s. f.* whale

baleniéra *s. f.* whaling ship, whaler

baléno *s. m.* flash

balèstra *s. f.* crossbow; leaf spring (*mecc.*)

ballàre *v. tr. e intr.* to dance

ballerìna *s. f.* dancer; ballerina, ballet-dancer (professionista)

ballerìno *s. m.* dancer

ballétto *s. m.* dance, ballet

bàllo *s. m.* dance, ball, dancing

balneàre *agg.* bathing

balórdo *agg.* foolish

balsàmico *agg.* balsamic, balmy

bàlsamo *s. m.* balm, balsam

baluàrdo *s. m.* bulwark

bàlza *s. f.* crag; frill (di vestito)

bambìna *s. f.* little girl, child

bambìno *s. m.* little boy, child, kid

bàmbola *s. f.* doll

banàle *agg.* banal, commonplace, trivial

banàna *s. f.* banana

bànca *s. f.* bank

bancarèlla *s. f.* stall

bancàrio *agg.* banking, bank (*attr.*)

bancaròtta *s. f.* bankruptcy; **fare** – to go bankrupt

banchétto *s. m.* banquet

banchière *s. m.* banker

banchìna *s. f.* quay, wharf, pier

banchìsa *s. f.* ice pack

bànco *s. m.* bench (panca); counter (*comm.*), desk (per scrivere); bank (*geog.*)

bàncomat *s. m. inv.* cash dispenser

banconòta *s. f.* bank note, bill

bànda *s. f.* band; gang (di uomini armati); band (*mus.*); stripe (di stoffa)

banderuòla *s. f.* weathercock, vane

bandièra *s. f.* flag, banner

bandìto *s. m.* bandit, outlaw

baràcca *s. f.* hovel

bàratro *s. m.* chasm

barattàre *v. tr.* to barter, to swap

baràttolo *s. m.* jar, pot; tin, can (di latta)

bàrba *s. f.* beard; – **e capelli** shave and haircut

barbabiètola *s. f.* beet; – **da zucchero** sugar beet

barbacàne *s. m.* barbican

barbàrico *agg.* barbaric, barbarian

bàrbaro *agg.* barbarous, barbaric

barbière *s. m.* barber; barbershop (negozio)

barbitùrico *s. m.* barbiturate

barbóne *s. m.* long beard; tramp (vagabondo); poodle (cane)

barbóso *agg.* boring

barbùto *agg.* bearded

bàrca *s. f.* boat; – **a motore** motor boat; – **a remi** row boat; – **a vela** sailing boat

barcaiòlo *s. m.* boatman

barèlla *s. f.* stretcher

barìle *s. m.* barrel, cask

barista *s. m. e f.* barman *m.*; barmaid *f.*

baritono *agg.* baritone

baròcco *agg. e s. m.* Baroque

baròmetro *s. m.* barometer

baróne *s. m.* baron

bàrra *s. f.* bar, rod; helm, tiller *(naut.)*

barricàta *s. f.* barricade

barrièra *s. f.* barrier

barzellétta *s. f.* joke

bàse *s. f.* base; basis *(fig.)*

basétta *s. f.* whisker

basìlica *s. f.* basilica

basìlico *s. m.* basil

bàsso *agg.* low; short (di statura); **bassa stagione** off season • *avv.* low

bassofóndo *s. m.* shallow, shoal

bassopiàno *s. m.* lowland

bassorilièvo *s. m.* bas-relief, basso-rilievo

bàsta *inter.* enough!, that will do!

bastànte *agg.* sufficient, enough

bastàrdo *agg.* bastard, hybrid; crossbred
(*zool., bot.*)

bastàre *v. intr.* to be sufficient, to be enough,
to suffice; to last (durare)

bastióne *s. m.* bastion, rampart

bastóne *s. m.* stick

batòsta *s. f.* blow

battàglia *s. f.* battle

battèllo *s. m.* boat; - **da pesca** fishing boat

bàttere *v. tr.* to beat, to strike, to hit, to knock;
to beat (vincere); to type (scrivere a macchina) • *intr. pron.* to fight

battesimàle *agg.* baptismal

battésimo *s. m.* baptism; **nome di** – Christian
name

battezzàre *v. tr.* to baptize, to christen

battistèro *s. m.* baptistery

battistràda *s. m. inv.* tread, track; – **lìscio**
smooth tread

battùto *agg.* beaten

batùffolo *s. m.* flock (di lana); wad (di cotone)

baùle *s. m.* trunk

bavaglìno *s. m.* bib

beccàccia *s. f.* woodcock

bécco *s. m.* beak

befàna *s. f.* epiphany, Befana

begònia *s. f.* begonia

bèlga *agg. e s. m. e f.* Belgian

bellézza *s. f.* beauty

bèllico *agg.* war (*attr.*)

bèllo *agg.* fine, beautiful, lovely, handsome,
nice, pretty, good-looking; **bel tempo** fine
weather

benché *cong.* although, though

bènda *s. f.* bandage

bendàggio *s. m.* bandaging, bandages *pl.*

bendàre *v. tr.* to bandage

bène *s. m.* good; goods *pl.*, property (i beni) •
avv. well; very, really, quite (rafforzativo) •
inter. well, all right, okay

benedettìno *agg.* Benedictine

benedétto *agg.* blessed

benedizióne *s. f.* blessing, benediction

benefattóre *s. m.* benefactor

beneficénza *s. f.* charity, beneficence; **istituto
di** – charitable institution

beneficiàre *v. intr.* to profit, to benefit (by)

benefìcio *s. m.* benefit, profit

benvenùto *agg.* welcome

benzìna *s. f.* petrol, gas, gasoline

benzinàio *s. m.* service-station keeper

bére *v. tr.* to drink

berlìna *s. f.* sedan, limousine, limo

berrétto *s. m.* cap, beret

bersàglio *s. m.* target

bestemmiàre *v. intr.* to curse, to swear

bestiàme *s. m.* livestock, cattle

bestiàrio *s. m.* bestiary

betùlla *s. f.* birch

bevànda *s. f.* drink, beverage

bevìbile *agg.* drinkable, potable

bevitóre *s. m.* drinker, boozer

biancherìa *s. f.* linen; – **ìntima** underwear

biànco *agg.* white; blank (non scritto)

bìbbia *s. f.* Bible

biberón *s. m. inv.* feeding bottle, (baby's) bottle

bìbita *s. f.* drink

bìblico *agg.* biblical

bibliòfilo *s. m.* bibliophile

bibliografìa *s. f.* bibliography

bibliotèca *s. f.* library

bibliotecàrio *s. m.* librarian

bicarbonàto *s. m.* bicarbonate

bicchière *s. m.* glass; – **di carta** paper cup

biciclétta *s. f.* bicycle, cycle, bike; **andare in** –
to ride one's bike

bicolóre *agg.* two-coloured, bicoloured

bidóne *s. m.* tank, drum, bin; swindle (imbroglio)

biennàle *agg.* two-year (che dura due anni);
biennial (ogni due anni)

bifocàle *agg.* bifocal

bigamìa *s. f.* bigamy

bìgamo *s. m.* bigamist

bighellonàre *v. intr.* to lounge about, to loaf

bigiotteria *s. f.* trinkets *pl.*, costume jewelry

bigliettaio *s. m.* ticket clerk (in stazione); ticket collector (in treno); conductor

biglietteria *s. f.* ticket office; box office (*cin.*, *teatro*)

biglietto *s. m.* ticket; **– d'andata e ritorno** return ticket; **– di sola andata** one-way ticket; **– da visita** visiting card

bignè *s. m. inv.* cream puff

bigodino *s. m.* curler

bilància *s. f.* balance, scales *pl.*; the Scales *pl.* (*astr.*)

biliardo *s. m.* billiards *pl.* (*v. al sing.*)

bilingue *agg.* bilingual

bilinguismo *s. m.* bilingualism

bimbo *s. m.* young child; baby, kid (*fam.*)

bimensile *agg.* fortnightly

bimestrale *agg.* bimonthly

bimotóre *agg.* twin-engined, bimotored

binàrio *s. m.* railway track, line; platform (marciapiede)

binòcolo *s. m.* binoculars *pl.*

biodegradàbile *agg.* biodegradable

biografia *s. f.* biography, life

biogràfico *agg.* biographical

biologia *s. f.* biology

biológico *agg.* biological

biondo *agg.* fair, blond, golden

birillo *s. m.* skittle

biro *s. f. inv.* biro, ballpoint pen

birra *s. f.* beer, ale; **– scura** stout; **– alla spina** draught beer

birreria *s. f.* beer house

bisbigliare *v. tr.* to whisper

biscòtto *s. m.* biscuit, cookie (USA)

bisessuale *agg.* bisexual

bisestile *agg.* bissextile; **anno** – leap year

bisettimanale *agg.* twice-weekly, biweekly

bisnònno *s. m.* great-grandfather

bisognare *v. intr. impers.* to be necessary, to have to, must

bisógno *s. m.* need; **aver** – to need

bistécca *s. f.* steak; **– ai ferri** grilled steak; **– al pepe** pepper steak; **– al sangue** rare steak; **– ben cotta** well-done steak

bistecchiera *s. f.* grill

bisticciare *v. intr.* to quarrel

bisturi *s. m.* bistoury

bitta *s. f.* bollard, bit

bivio *s. m.* fork; crossroads (*fig.*)

bizantino *agg.* Byzantine

bizzarro *agg.* odd, quaint, bizarre

blasfèmo *agg.* blasphemous

blindàto *agg.* armoured

bloccàre *v. tr.* to block • *intr. pron.* to jam, to stall (*mecc.*)

bloccastèrzo *s. m.* steering lock

blòcco *s. m.* block; **posto di** – road block

bloc-notes *s. m. inv.* writing pad, notebook

blu *agg.* blue

bòa *s. f.* buoy

bócca *s. f.* mouth

boccàglio *s. m.* nosepipe

boccale *s. m.* jug, mug

boccapòrto *s. m.* hatch

boccétta *s. f.* small bottle

boccheggiàre *v. intr.* to gasp

bocchettóne *s. m.* pipe union

bocchino *s. m.* cigarette holder; mouthpiece (pipa e strumenti musicali)

bòccia *s. f.* bowl

bocciàre *v. tr.* to reject

boccino *s. m.* jack, kitty

bocciòdromo *s. m.* bowling green

bocciòlo *s. m.* bud

boccóne *s. m.* mouthful, morsel, bite

bòga *s. f.* boce

boicottàre *v. tr.* to boycott

bolina *s. f.* close-hauling; **navigare di** – to sail close-hauled

bólla *s. f.* bubble; bill, note (*comm.*)

bollènte *agg.* boiling, hot

bollétta *s. f.* bill, note; **essere in** – to be broke (*fam.*)

bollire *v. tr. e intr.* to boil

bollito *agg.* boiled

bóllo *s. m.* stamp; seal (sigillo); tax stamp (*autom.*)

bóma *s. m.* boom

bómba *s. f.* bomb

bombardaménto *s. m.* bombing, bombardment

bómbola *s. f.* bottle, bomb, cylinder

bomboniéra *s. f.* bonbonnière

bomprèsso *s. m.* bowsprit

bonifica *s. f.* reclamation, drainage

bonificàre *v. tr.* to reclaim

bonìfico *s. m.* allowance; **– bancario** money transfer

bontà *s. f.* goodness

borbottàre *v. tr.* to mumble, to mutter

bòrdo *s. m.* hem, border, hedge; board (*naut.*); **a** – aboard, on board

borgàta *s. f.* village

borghése *agg.* middle-class (*attr.*)

borghesia *s. f.* bourgeoisie, middle classes *pl.*

bórgo *s. m.* hamlet, village

borotàlco *s. m.* talcum powder

bórsa *s. f.* bag; stock exchange (*fin.*); – **della spesa** shopping bag; – **di studio** scholarship; – **da viaggio** travelling bag

borseggiatóre *s. m.* pickpocket

borsellino *s. m.* purse

borsétta *s. f.* handbag

boscàglia *s. f.* thicket, brush, scrub

boscaiòlo *s. m.* woodman

boschivo *agg.* wooded, woody

bòsco *s. m.* wood

boscóso *agg.* woody, wooded

botànico *agg.* botanic; **orto** – botanic garden

bòtola *s. f.* trapdoor

bòtte *s. f.* barrel, cask, butt; **volta a** – barrel-vault

bottéga *s. f.* shop

botteghino *s. m.* box office

bottiglia *s. f.* bottle; **vino in** – bottled wine

bottóne *s. m.* button; – **automatico** press stud; **bottoni gemelli** cuff links

bovino *agg.* bovine

bozzétto *s. m.* sketch

braccialétto *s. m.* bracelet

bracciànte *s. m.* day-labourer, farmer

bracciàta *s. f.* armful; stroke (nuoto)

bràccio *s. m.* arm; fathom (misura); – **di fiume** branch; – **di mare** strait

bràce *s. f.* embers *pl.*

bradisismo *s. m.* bradyseism

branzino *s. m.* bass

brasàto *agg.* braise

bràvo *agg.* good, clever • *inter.* bravo!, well done!

bretèlle *s. f. pl.* braces

bréve *agg.* short, brief

brevettàre *v. tr.* to patent

briciola *s. f.* crumb

brillànte *agg.* bright, brilliant

brillàre *v. intr.* to shine, to glitter, to twinkle, to sparkle

brina *s. f.* frost, rime

brindisi *s. m.* toast; **fare un** – to give a toast

britànnico *agg.* British

brìvido *s. m.* shiver, shudder

brizzolàto *agg.* grizzled

bròcca *s. f.* pitcher, jug

broccàto *s. m.* brocade

bróccolo *s. m.* broccoli

bròdo *s. m.* broth

brodóso *agg.* watery, thin

bronchite *s. f.* bronchitis

bróncio *s. m.* pout; **tenere il** – to sulk

broncopolmonite *s. f.* bronchopneumonia

bronzina *s. f.* bushing; bearing

brónzo *s. m.* bronze

bruciàre *v. tr.* to burn, to set fire to

bruciàto *agg.* burned, burnt

bruciatùra *s. f.* burn

brucióre *s. m.* burning; – **di stomaco** heartburn

brùco *s. m.* caterpillar

brughièra *s. f.* moor, heath

brùno *agg.* brown, dark

brùsco *agg.* brusque, abrupt

brùto *agg.* brute

brùtto *agg.* ugly; bad (cattivo); nasty; – **tempo** bad weather; **brutta copia** rough copy; **alle brutte** at (the) worst; **fare una brutta figura** to cut a poor figure

bùca *s. f.* hole; – **delle lettere** letter box, mailbox (USA)

bucàre *v. tr.* to hole

bucàto *s. m.* wash, washing; **fare il** – to do the washing

bùccia *s. f.* peel, rind, skin; pod (di legumi), husk shuck (USA)

bùco *s. m.* hole

bucòlico *agg.* bucolic

buddismo *s. m.* Buddhism

budino *s. m.* pudding

bùe *s. m.* ox; **carne di** – beef

bùfalo *s. m.* buffalo

bufèra *s. f.* storm, tempest; – **di neve** blizzard; – **di vento** windstorm

bùffo *agg.* funny, droll; **opera** – comic opera

buffonàta *s. f.* tomfoolery

buggeràre *v. tr.* to trick, to cheat

bugìa *s. f.* lie, fib; candlestick (candela)

bugiàrdo *agg.* lying

bugigàttolo *s. m.* storeroom, closet

bugnàto *s. m.* ashlar; **rustico** – rusticated ashlar

bùio *agg.* dark • *s. m.* darkness, dark

bùlbo *s. m.* bulb (*bot.*); – **oculare** eyeball

bùlgaro *agg. e s. m.* Bulgarian

bullóne *s. m.* bolt

buonanòtte *inter.* goodnight

buonaséra *inter.* good evening

buongiórno *inter.* good morning

buongustàio *s. m.* gourmet

buòno *agg.* good • *s. m.* good; voucher, coupon (tagliando)

burattinàio *s. m.* puppeteer

burattino *s. m.* puppet

burlésco *agg.* burlesque

burocràtico *agg.* bureaucratic
burocrazia *s. f.* bureaucracy
bùrro *s. m.* butter; **un panetto di** – a roll of butter; – **di cacao** cacao butter
burróne *s. m.* ravine

bussàre *v. intr.* to knock (at), to tap
bùssola *s. f.* compass
bùsta *s. f.* envelope; portfolio (per documenti), briefcase (USA)
bùsto *s. m.* bust; corset (indumento)
buttàre *v. tr.* to throw

cabalistico *agg.* cabalistic

cabina *s. f.* cabin; bathing hut (al mare); – **telefonica** telephone booth, phone box; – **di pilotaggio** cockpit

cabinato *s. m.* cabin cruiser

cabinovia *s. f.* carway, cableway

cabotàggio *s. m.* coasting trade

cacào *s. m.* cocoa; cacao (*bot.*)

càccia *s. f.* hunting, smooting, chase; **licenza di** – game licence

cacciagióne *s. f.* game

cacciàre *v. tr.* to hunt, to go hunting, to go shooting; – **via** to send away, to turn out

cacciatóre *s. m.* hunter

cacciavite *s. m. inv.* screwdriver

cadàvere *s. m.* (dead) body, corpse

cadènte *agg.* falling

cadènza *s. f.* cadence, rhythm; intonation (voce)

cadére *v. intr.* to fall, to drop

cadétto *agg.* younger; cadet (*attr.*)

cadùta *s. f.* fall, falling, drop; downfall (*fig.*); – **massi** falling rocks

cadùto *agg.* fallen

caffè *s. m.* coffee; – **ristretto** strong coffee; – **lungo** weak coffee

caffeina *s. f.* caffeine

caffellàtte *s. m. inv.* white coffee

cafóne *agg.* boorish

cagionévole *agg.* weak

càglio *s. m.* rennet

càgna *s. f.* bitch

càla *s. f.* inlet, hold

calabróne *s. m.* hornet

calamàro *s. m.* squid

calamìta *s. f.* magnet

calamità *s. f.* calamity, disaster

calànco *s. m.* gully

calàre *v. tr.* to lower • *intr.* to sink, to drop, to lower

càlca *s. f.* throng, crowd

calcàgno *s. m.* heel

calcàreo *agg.* calcareous

calcestrùzzo *s. m.* concrete

calciatóre *s. m.* footballer, soccer player

càlcio *s. m.* calcium (*chim.*); kick; football, soccer (*sport*); stock (di arma); – **d'angolo** corner(-kick); – **di rigore** penalty (kick); – **di punizione** free kick

càlco *s. m.* mould

calcolàre *v. tr.* to reckon; to compute, to calculate (*mat.*)

calcolatrice *s. f.* calculator

càlcolo *s. m.* calculation; calculus (*mat.*)

caldàia *s. f.* boiler

caldaménte *avv.* warmly, heartily

caldarròsta *s. f.* roast chestnut

càldo *agg.* warm, hot • *s. m.* heat, hot weather

caleidoscòpio *s. m.* kaleidoscope

calendàrio *s. m.* calendar

càlibro *s. m.* gauge, caliber

càlice *s. m.* goblet; calice (*relig.*)

caligine *s. f.* haze

calligràfico *agg.* calligraphic

callista *s. m. e f.* chiropodist

càllo *s. m.* corn, callus

càlma *s. f.* calm • *inter.* easy!, take it easy!, cool it!

calmànte *agg.* calming • *s. m.* sedative

calmàre *v. tr.* to calm (down) • *intr. pron.* to calm down, to cool it

calmière *s. m.* ceiling price

càlmo *agg.* calm

càlo *s. m.* fall, drop

calóre *s. m.* heat

caloria *s. f.* calorie

calòrico *agg.* caloric

calorìfero *s. m.* radiator

calorosaménte *avv.* warmly, enthusiastically

caloróso *agg.* warm, hearty

calpestàre *v. tr.* to trample down, to tread upon

calpestio *s. m.* stamping

calùnnia *s. f.* slander

calùra *s. f.* great heat

calvinismo *s. m.* Calvinism

calvinista *agg.* Calvinist

calvizie *s. f. inv.* baldness

càlvo *agg.* bald

cálza s. f. stocking (da donna); sock (da uomo)

calzamáglia s. f. tights pl., leotards pl.

calzáre v. intr. to fit

calzascárpe s. m. inv. shoehorn

calzatúra s. f. footwear; **negozio di calzature** shoe shop

calzaturifício s. m. shoe factory

calzettóne s. m. knee sock

calzino s. m. sock

calzolàio s. m. shoemaker, shoe repairer

calzoleria s. f. shoe shop

calzóni s. m. pl. trousers, pants

cambiále s. f. bill

cambiaménto s. m. change

cambiàre v. tr. e intr. to change • rifl. to change one's clothes

cambiavalúte s. m. e f. inv. money-changer

càmbio s. m. change, exchange (fin.); gear (autom.)

cambúsa s. f. storeroom, galley

camèlia s. f. camelia

càmera s. f. room; – **ammobiliata** furnished room; – **a due letti** double bedroom; **si affittano camere** rooms to let

cameráta s. f. dormitory

cameratésco agg. comradely

camerière s. m. waiter

camerièra s. f. waitress, maid

camerino s. m. dressing room

càmice s. m. white coat

camicétta s. f. blouse, shirt

camicia s. f. shirt; – **da notte** nightgown

caminétto s. m. fireplace

camino s. m. chimney

càmion s. m. inv. lorry, truck (USA); – **con rimorchio** lorry with trailer, trailer truck (USA)

camioncino s. m. light lorry, van (chiuso), pick-up (aperto)

camionista s. m. e f. lorry driver, truck driver (USA)

cammèllo s. m. camel

cammèo s. m. cameo

camminàre v. intr. to walk, to go on foot

camminàta s. f. walk; gait (andatura)

camomilla s. f. camomile

camóscio s. m. chamois; **pelle di –** shammy leather

campágna s. f. country, farmland, countryside; campaign (pubblicità e mil.)

campagnòlo agg. country (attr.)

campále agg. openfield

campána s. f. bell

campanário agg. bell (attr.)

campanèllo s. m. bell

campanile s. m. bell tower, church tower, belfry

campàta s. f. span, bay

campeggiàre v. intr. to camp

campeggiatóre s. m. camper

campéggio s. m. camping

campéstre agg. rural; country (attr.)

campionário s. m. sample; – **di tessuti** pattern book

campionàto s. m. championship

campióne s. m. champion; sample (comm.) • agg. champion; model (esemplare)

càmpo s. m. field; camp (mil.); ground (sport)

camposànto s. m. cemetery

canále s. m. channel; canal (artificiale)

canalizzazióne s. f. canalization

cànapa s. f. hemp

canàsta s. f. canasta

cancellàre v. tr. to cancel; – **con la gomma** to rub out

cancellàta s. f. railing, iron fence

cancellazióne s. f. cancellation, annulment

cancelleria s. f. chancellery (politica); stationery (cartoleria)

cancellière s. m. clerk; chancellor (politica)

cancéllo s. m. gate

cancerógeno agg. carcinogenic

candéggio s. m. bleaching

candéla s. f. candle; sparking plug (autom.)

candelàbro s. m. candelabrum

candelière s. m. candlestick

candidàto s. m. candidate; applicant (aspirante)

candidatúra s. f. candidature

candito s. m. candied fruit

càne s. m. dog

canèstro s. m. basket

cangùro s. m. kangaroo

canile s. m. kennel

canino agg. e s. m. canine

cànna s. f. reed, canna (bot.); stick (bastoncino); pipe (organo); – **da zucchero** sugar cane; – **da pesca** fishing rod

cannèlla s. f. cinnamon

cannéto s. m. cane thicket

cannibalismo s. m. cannibalism

cannocchiàle s. m. telescope, binoculars pl.

cannóne s. m. gun

cannúccia s. f. straw

canòa s. f. canoe

canònica s. f. vicarage

canònico agg. canonical; canon (attr.)

canòro *agg.* singing

canottàggio *s. m.* boat racing

canottièra *s. f.* vest

canòtto *s. m.* rubber boat

cantànte *s. m. e f.* singer

cantàre *v. tr. e intr.* to sing

cantàta *s. f.* cantata

cantautóre *s. m.* singer-song writer

canticchiàre *v. tr. e intr.* to hum

cantière *s. m.* yard, building site; shipyard (*naut.*)

cantìna *s. f.* cellar

cànto *s. m.* song, singing; – liturgico chant

cantonàle *agg.* cantonal

cantonàta *s. f.* corner; blunder (*fig.*)

cantóne *s. m.* corner; canton (*geog.*)

canzonàre *v. tr.* to tease

canzóne *s. f.* song

càos *s. m.* chaos

caòtico *agg.* chaotic

capàce *agg.* able, capable; capacious (ampio)

capànna *s. f.* hut, cabin

capannèllo *s. m.* knot (of people)

capannóne *s. m.* shed

capàrra *s. f.* deposit

capéllo *s. m.* hair

capiènza *s. f.* capacity

capillàre *agg.* capillary (*anat.*); detailed (*fig.*)

capìre *v. tr.* to understand, to see

capitàle *s. f.* capital city • *s. m.* capital; – azionario share capital

capitalìsmo *s. m.* capitalism

capitalìsta *s. m. e f.* capitalist

capitaneria *s. f.* harbour office

capitàno *s. m.* captain

capitàre *v. intr. impers.* to happen

capitéllo *s. m.* capital

capitolàre *v. intr.* to capitulate

capìtolo *s. m.* chapter

capitómbolo *s. m.* tumble

càpo *s. m.* head (testa); chief, leader (persona); cape (*geog.*)

capodànno *s. m.* New Year's Day

capofamìglia *s. m. e f.* head of the family

capogìro *s. m.* giddiness

capolavóro *s. m.* masterpiece

capolìnea *s. m.* terminus

capoluògo *s. m.* chief town

caposcuòla *s. m. e f.* leader of a movement

capostazióne *s. m. e f.* stationmaster

capostìpite *s. m. e f.* founder of a family

capotréno *s. m.* guard, conductor

cappèlla *s. f.* chapel; cap (*bot.*)

cappèllo *s. m.* hat; – a cilindro top hat

cappottàre *v. intr.* to turn over

cappòtto *s. m.* (over) coat

cappuccìno *s. m.* cappuccino; capuchin (*relig.*)

cappùccio *s. m.* hood

càpra *s. f.* goat

caprétto *s. m.* kid

capriccióso *agg.* whimsical, naughty

caprìno *agg.* caprine; goat (*attr.*)

capriòlo *s. m.* roedeer

càpsula *s. f.* capsule; crown (di dente)

caramélla *s. f.* sweet, toffee, candy

caràttere *s. m.* character, temper; type (tipografico)

caratterìstica *s. f.* characteristic

caratterìstico *agg.* characteristic

caratterizzàre *v. tr.* to characterize

carboidràto *s. m.* carbohydrate

carbóne *s. m.* coal

carbonizzàrsi *v. intr. pron.* to carbonize

carburatóre *s. m.* carburettor; carburetor (USA); – ingolfato floodied carburettor

carceràrio *agg.* prison (*attr.*)

carceràto *s. m.* prisoner

càrcere *s. m.* jail

carcerière *s. m.* jailor, warder

carciòfo *s. m.* artichoke

cardìaco *agg.* cardiac; heart (*attr.*); attacco – heart attack; trapianto – heart transplant

cardinàle *agg. e s. m.* cardinal; punti cardinali cardinal points

cardinalìzio *agg.* cardinal (*attr.*)

càrdine *s. m.* hinge, pivot

cardiocircolatòrio *agg.* cardiocirculatory

cardiòlogo *s. m.* cardiologist

cardiopàtico *agg. e s. m.* cardiopath

carèna *s. f.* bottom

carènte *agg.* lacking

carestìa *s. f.* famine

carézza *s. f.* caress

cariàtide *s. f.* caryatid

caricàre *v. tr.* to load up; to charge (*mil.*)

caricatùra *s. f.* caricature

càrico *agg.* loaded, laden • *s. m.* load

càrie *s. f. inv.* caries *pl.*

carìno *agg.* cute, pretty, nice

carismàtico *agg.* charismatic

carità *s. f.* charity; alms *pl.* (elemosina)

carlìnga *s. f.* nacelle

càrne *s. f.* flesh; meat (*alim.*)

carnéfice *s. m.* executioner

carnevàle *s. m.* Carnival

carnívoro agg. carnivorous

carnóso agg. plump

cáro agg. dear; expensive (costoso)

caròta s. f. carrot

carovàna s. f. caravan, convoy

carovíta s. m. high cost of living

carpóni avv. on all fours

carràio agg. carriage (attr.)

carreggiàta s. f. roadway, rut, track

carrellàta s. f. tracking shot, dolly shot

carrèllo s. m. trolley

carrétto s. m. handcart

carrièra s. f. career

carròzza s. f. carriage, coach

carrozzèlla s. f. wheel chair

carrozzería s. f. bodywork; car repairer's (officina)

carrozzière s. m. car-body repairer

carrozzína s. f. pram

carrúcola s. f. pulley

cárta s. f. paper; – **da lettere** writing paper; – **geografica** map, chart, plan; – **da gioco** playing card; – **d'identità** identity card

cartáceo agg. paper (attr.)

cartapésta s. f. papier-mâché

cartéggio s. m. correspondence

cartèlla s. f. folder (di cartone); file (pratica); portfolio (per disegni); satchel (di scolaro)

cartellíno s. m. label, tag

cartèllo s. m. signboard; – **stradale** road sign, guidepost

cartellóne s. m. poster, board

càrter s. m. inv. chainguard; oil sump (autom.)

cartilàgine s. f. cartilage

cartína s. f. map

cartòccio s. m. paper bag, cornet

cartográfico agg. cartographic

cartolàio s. m. stationer

cartolería s. f. stationery shop

cartolibrería s. f. stationery and book shop

cartolína s. f. postcard

cartomànte s. m. e f. fortune-teller

cartóne s. m. cardboard; **imballaggio di** – carton; **cartoni animati** cartoons

cartúccia s. f. cartridge

càsa s. f. house, building; home (propria abitazione)

casalínga s. f. housewife

casalíngo agg. home (attr.)

casàto s. m. stock, birth

cascàre v. intr. to fall, to tumble

cascàta s. f. waterfall, cascade

cascína s. f. farmhouse

càsco s. m. helmet; – **per capelli** hair dryer

caseggiàto s. m. block of flats

caseifício s. m. dairy, cheese factory

casellànte s. m. e f. signalman m., signalwoman f.; trackman m., trackwoman f.

casèllo s. m. trackman's lodging (ferr.); tollbooth (autom.)

casèrma s. f. barracks pl.

càso s. m. chance, case

casolàre s. m. homestead

càspita inter. good heavens!, good Lord!

càssa s. f. case, chest, box; cash desk (comm.); counter (sportello); – **continua** night safe

cassafòrte s. f. safe, strongbox

cassapànca s. f. chest, settle

cassétta s. f. box; cassette (mus.); – **delle lettere** letter box

cassétto s. m. drawer

cassière s. m. cashier

castàgna s. f. chestnut

castàgno s. m. chestnut

castàno agg. brown

castellàno s. m. lord of a castle

castèllo s. m. castle

castigàto agg. chaste, decent, restrained

castígo s. m. punishment

castità s. f. chastity

castòro s. m. beaver

castràre v. tr. to castrate

castrénse agg. castrensian

casuàle agg. casual, fortuitous; chance (attr.)

casualménte avv. by chance, accidentally

cataclìsma s. m. cataclysm

catacómba s. f. catacomb

catalogàre v. tr. to catalogue

catàlogo s. m. catalogue

catamaràno s. m. catamaran

catapécchia s. f. hovel, slum

catàrro s. m. catarrh

catàstrofe s. f. catastrophe

catastròfico agg. catastrophic

catechìsmo s. m. catechism

categoría s. f. category

caténa s. f. chain

cateràtta s. f. cataract

catràme s. m. tar

càttedra s. f. desk; – **universitaria** chair

cattedràle s. f. cathedral

cattedràtico s. m. professor

cattivèria s. f. wickedness, naughtiness; wicked action (atto)

cattìvo agg. bad, wicked, evil; naughty (di bambino)

cattolicésimo *s. m.* Catholicism
cattòlico *agg.* Catholic
cattùra *s. f.* arrest, capture
catturàre *v. tr.* to capture, to seize, to arrest
càusa *s. f.* cause
causàle *agg.* causal
causàre *v. tr.* to cause, to bring about
càustico *agg.* caustic
cautéla *s. f.* caution
cautelàrsi *v. rifl.* to take precautions
cauzióne *s. f.* caution; **essere liberato su –** to be released on bail
càva *s. f.* quarry
cavalcàre *v. tr. e intr.* to ride
cavalcavia *s. m. inv.* overpass
cavalière *s. m.* rider; knight (*stor.*)
cavalerésco *agg.* chivalrous
cavalleria *s. f.* cavalry; chivalry (*stor.*)
cavallerizzo *s. m.* skilled horseman
cavallétto *s. m.* easel (*arte*); tripod (per fotografare)`
cavàllo *s. m.* horse
cavatàppi *s. m.* corkscrew
càvea *s. f.* cavea
cavèrna *s. f.* cave, cavern
càvia *s. f.* guinea pig (anche *fig.*)
caviàle *s. m.* caviar
caviglia *s. f.* ankle; belayng pin (*naut.*)
cavillo *s. m.* cavil
cavità *s. f.* cavity, hollow
càvo *agg.* hollow • *s. m.* cable, rope
cavolfióre *s. m.* cauliflower
càvolo *s. m.* cabbage; **– di Bruxelles** Brussels sprout
cazzòtto *s. m.* punch
cèdere *v. intr.* to yield, to give up, to give in; to sink (sprofondare)
cédro *s. m.* citron; cedar (albero)
céduo *agg.* coppice (*attr.*)
cefaléa *s. f.* cephalalgy, headache
ceffóne *s. m.* slap, cuff
celebèrrimo *agg.* very famous
celebrànte *s. m.* celebrant
celebràre *v. tr.* to celebrate
celebrazióne *s. f.* celebration
cèlebre *agg.* celebrated, famous, renowned
celebrità *s. f.* celebrity
celèste *agg.* heavenly, celestial • *s. m.* light blue
cèlibe *agg.* single, unmarried
cèlla *s. f.* cell; cella (*archeol.*)
cèllula *s. f.* cell
cellulàre *agg.* cellular

cellulite *s. f.* cellulitis
cèltico *agg.* Celtic
cemènto *s. m.* cement
céna *s. f.* dinner, supper
cenàcolo *s. m.* cenaculum; coterie (*fig.*)
cencióso *agg.* ragged
cénere *s. f.* ash(es)
cénno *s. m.* sign, nod
censiménto *s. m.* census
censùra *s. f.* censorship
centàuro *s. m.* centaur (*mitol.*); motorcycle racer
centenàrio *agg.* centenary, centennial • *s. m.* centenary; centenarian (di persona)
centèsimo *agg.* hundredth
centimetro *s. m.* centimetre
cénto *agg. num.* a hundred
centràggio *s. m.* cent(e)ring
centràle *agg.* central
centralinista *s. m. e f.* operator
centralino *s. m.* telephone exchange; switchboard (di albergo)
centralizzàre *v. tr.* to centralize
centràre *v. tr.* to hit the centre; to centre (*mecc.*)
centravànti *s. m. inv.* centre forward
centrifugàto *agg.* centrifugated
centrifugo *agg.* centrifugal
centripeto *agg.* centripetal
céntro *s. m.* centre
centrocàmpo *s. m.* centre field
céra *s. f.* wax, polish; look (aspetto)
ceràmica *s. f.* ceramics *pl.* (*v. al sing.*); pottery
ceramista *s. m. e f.* ceramist
cercàre *v. tr.* to look for, to seek
cérchio *s. m.* circle; rim (di ruota)
cereàli *s. m. pl.* cereals
cerimònia *s. f.* ceremony, ritual
cèrnia *s. f.* grouper
cernièra *s. f.* zip; hinge (*mecc.*)
ceròtto *s. m.* plaster
certaménte *avv.* certainly; of course! sure!
certézza *s. f.* certainty; conviction (convinzione)
certificàto *s. m.* certificate
cèrto *agg.* certain, sure • *agg. indef.* certain; some (qualche)
certòsa *s. f.* Chartreuse
cervellétto *s. m.* cerebellum
cervèllo *s. m.* brain
cervicàle *agg.* cervical
cèrvo *s. m.* deer; **carne di –** venison
cesellàre *v. tr.* to chisel; to polish (*fig.*)

cespúglio *s. m.* bush

cessáre *v. intr.* to stop, to cease

cestino *s. m.* basket; – **per i rifiuti** litterbin, wastebasket

cetriólo *s. m.* cucumber

che *pron. rel.* who, that (sogg. rif. a persona); which, that (sogg. rif. a cose o animali); whom, that (ogg. rif. a persona); which, that (ogg. rif. a cose o animali); when, in which, that (in cui, quando) • *pron. interr.* what • *cong.* that

chi *pron. rel. e indef.* who (sogg.); whom (ogg.) • *pron. interr.* who (sogg.); whom, who (ogg. e compl. indir.)

chiacchieráre *v. intr.* to chat, to talk

chiamáre *v. tr.* to call; to name (dar nome) • *intr. pron.* to be called

chiaraménte *avv.* clearly

chiariménto *s. m.* explanation

chiaríre *v. tr.* to clear up, to explain

chiáro *agg.* clear; light (di colore)

chiaroscúro *s. m.* chiaroscuro

chiáve *s. f.* key; spanner, wrench (*mecc.*)

chiédere *v. tr.* to ask; to ask for (per avere) • *intr. pron.* to wonder

chiérico *s. m.* cleric

chiésa *s. f.* church

chilográmmo *s. m.* kilogram

chilométrico *agg.* kilometric

chilómetro *s. m.* kilometre

chímico *agg.* chemical

chinársi *v. rifl.* to stoop, to bow

chincaglieria *s. f.* trinkets *pl.*, fancy goods *pl.*

chiòdo *s. m.* nail; – **di garofano** clover

chiòsco *s. m.* kiosk, stall, stand

chiòstro *s. m.* cloister

chirománte *s. m. e f.* chiromancer

chirurgía *s. f.* surgery

chirúrgo *s. m.* surgeon

chissà *avv.* who knows; possibly (forse)

chitárra *s. f.* guitar

chitarrísta *s. m. e f.* guitarist

chiúdere *v. tr. e intr.* to shut, to close

chiúnque *pron. indef.* anyone, anybody • *pron. rel. indef.* whoever; who(m)ever (ogg. e compl.)

chiúsa *s. f.* lock

chiúso *agg.* closed, shut

chiusúra *s. f.* fastening, lock

ciambélla *s. f.* bun; life ring (salvagente)

cianfruságlia *s. f.* knick-knacks *pl.*, junk

ciào *inter.* hullo, hi (USA); bye-bye, so long, cheerio (commiato)

ciarlatáno *s. m.* charlatan, quack

ciascúno *agg. indef.* every (ogni); each (distributivo) • *pron. indef.* everybody, everyone (ognuno); each (distributivo)

cibársi *v. rifl.* to feed

cibo *s. m.* food

cicála *s. f.* cicada

cicalíno *s. m.* buzzer

cicatríce *s. f.* scar

ciceróne *s. m.* guide, cicerone

cíclico *agg.* cyclic

ciclísmo *s. m.* cycling

ciclísta *s. m. e f.* cyclist; bicycle repairer (chi ripara)

ciclomotóre *s. m.* motor-bicycle, moped

ciclópico *agg.* cyclopean

cicógna *s. f.* stork

ciéco *agg.* blind

ciélo *s. m.* sky; heaven (*lett.*)

cifra *s. f.* figure, digit, numeral; sum, amount (importo)

cíglio *s. m.* eyelashes *pl.*; edge, brink, rim (orlo); **senza batter** – without flinching

cígno *s. m.* swan

cigolío *s. m.* squeaking

ciliégia *s. f.* cherry

cilindráta *s. f.* swept volume, displacement; **auto di grossa** – high-powered car

cilíndrico *agg.* cylindrical

cilíndro *s. m.* cylinder

címa *s. f.* top, peak; line, rope (*naut.*)

cimélio *s. m.* relic; trophy (trofeo)

ciminiéra *s. f.* chimney; funnel (*naut.*)

cimiteriále *agg.* cemeterial

cimitéro *s. m.* graveyard, churchyard

cinábro *s. m.* cinnabar

cineamatóre *s. m.* amateur film-maker

cínema *s. m. inv.* cinema

cinematográfico *agg.* cinematographic; movie (*attr.*)

cineprésa *s. f.* cine camera, movie camera

cinerário *agg.* cinerary

cinése *agg. e s. m. e f.* Chinese

cinético *agg.* kinetic

cíngere *v. tr.* to gird, to encircle; to enclose (circondare)

cínghia *s. f.* strap; thong (di cuoio)

cinghiále *s. m.* (wild) boar; **pelle di** – pigskin

cinguettío *s. m.* chirping

cínico *agg.* cynical

cinísmo *s. m.* cynism

cinófilo *s. m.* cynophilist

cinquecentésco *agg.* sixteenth-century (*attr.*)

cintùra s. f. belt; waist (vita); – di sicurezza safety belt, seat belt

cinturino s. m. strap

cioccolàta s. f. chocolate; – con panna chocolate and whipped cream; – al latte milk chocolate

cioè avv. thàt is, i.e. (id est), namely

ciòndolo s. m. pendant

ciononostànte avv. in spite of this

ciòtola s. f. bowl

ciòttolo s. m. pebble, cobble

cipiglio s. m. scowl

cipòlla s. f. onion

cippo s. m. cippus; – funerario memorial stone

ciprèsso s. m. cypress

cipria s. f. (face) powder

circa prep. with regard to, about • avv. about, approximately

circo s. m. circus

circolànte agg. circulating; biblioteca – lending library

circolàre v. intr. to move on, to keep moving; to run (autom.); to spread (di notizie) • agg. circular, round

circolazióne f. s. circulation; traffic (traffico)

circolo s. m. circle; club (associazione)

circoncisióne s. f. circumcision

circondàre v. tr. to surround, to encircle

circonferènza s. f. circumference

circonvallazióne s. f. ring road

circoscrìvere v. tr. to circumscribe

circostànte agg. surrounding

circostànza s. f. circumstance

circuìto s. m. circuit; circular track (sport)

cistercènse agg. Cistercian

cistèrna s. f. reservoir; nave – tanker

citàre v. tr. to quote; – come esempio to cite; – in tribunale to sue

citazióne s. f. quotation, citation; summons (leg.)

citòfono s. m. interphone, buzzer

città s. f. city, town

cittadèlla s. f. citadel

cittadinànza s. f. citizens pl. (popolazione); citizenship

cittadino agg. town (attr.), city (attr.) • s. m. citizen

ciùffo s. m. tuft

civico agg. civic

civile agg. civil

civilizzazióne s. f. civilization

civiltà s. f. civilization; civility (cortesia)

clàcson s. m. inv. horn

clamoróso agg. clamorous

clandestino s. m. clandestine

clarinétto s. m. clarinet

clàsse s. f. class; prima – first class

classicismo s. m. classicism

classicista s. m. e f. classicist

classicità s. f. classical antiquity

clàssico agg. classic(al)

classifica s. f. classification; results pl. (sport)

classificàre v. tr. to classify

classista agg. class (attr.)

clàusola s. f. clause

claustrofobìa s. f. claustrophobia

clausùra s. f. seclusion; suora di – cloistered nun

clavicémbalo s. m. harpsichord

clavìcola s. f. clavicle

cleptòmane s. m. kleptomaniac

clericale agg. clerical

clèro s. m. clergy

clessidra s. f. sandglass, clepsydra

cliènte s. m. e f. client; customer (comm.)

clima s. m. climate

climàtico agg. climatic; stazione climàtica health resort

clinica s. f. clinic

clinico agg. clinical

clòro s. m. chlorine

clorofilla s. f. chlorophyl

coabitazióne s. f. cohabitation

coagulànte s. m. coagulant

coalizióne s. f. coalition, alliance

coautóre s. m. coauthor

còcco s. m. coconut

coccodrillo s. m. crocodile

cocòmero s. m. watermelon

còda s. f. tail; queue; line (fila); fare la – to queue up

codèsto agg. e pron. that

còdice s. m. code

codifica s. f. codification

coefficiènte s. m. coefficient, factor

coerènte agg. coherent; consistent (fig.)

coesistènte agg. coexistent

coetàneo agg. e s. m. contemporary

coèvo agg. coeval, contemporary (with)

còfano s. m. chest, coffer; bonnet (autom.) • s. m. citizen

cògliere v. tr. to pick, to gather

cognàta s. f. sister-in-law

cognàto s. m. brother-in-law

cognóme s. m. surname, family name

coincidènza s. f. coincidence; connection (trasporti)

coincidere v. *intr.* to coincide
coinvòlgere v. *tr.* to involve
colazióne s. *f.* breakfast; lunch (pranzo)
colesteròlo s. *m.* cholesterol
còlica s. *f.* colic
còlla s. *f.* glue
collaboràre v. *intr.* to cooperate, to collaborate
collaborazióne s. *f.* cooperation, collaboration; contribution (a un giornale)
collàna s. *f.* necklace; string, collection (raccolta)
collàsso s. *m.* collapse, breakdown
collaudàre v. *tr.* to test, to try out
collàudo s. *m.* test
còlle s. *m.* hill
collèga s. *m.* e *f.* colleague
collegaménto s. *m.* connection
collegàre v. *tr.* to connect, to joint, to link • *rifl. rec.* to join
collegiàta s. *f.* collegiate church
collègio s. *m.* boarding school, public school, college; constituency (politico)
còllera s. *f.* anger, fury
collètta s. *f.* collection
collettivaménte *avv.* collectively
collettività s. *f.* collectivity, community
collettìvo *agg.* collective
collétto s. *m.* collar
collezionàre v. *tr.* to collect
collezióne s. *f.* collection
collezionìsta s. *m.* e *f.* collector
collìna s. *f.* hill
collinóso *agg.* hilly
collìrio s. *m.* eye drops *pl.*
còllo s. *m.* neck; item (bagaglio)
collocàre v. *tr.* to place
collòquio s: *m.* talk, interview
collutòrio s. *m.* mouthwash
còlon s. *m.* colon
colònia s. *f.* colony, settlement
coloniàle *agg.* colonial; **generi coloniali** groceries
colonialìsta s. *m.* colonialist
colonizzàre v. *tr.* to colonize
colónna s. *f.* column; pillar (anche *fig.*); – **vertebrale** backbone
colonnàto s. *m.* colonnade
colorànte s. *m.* dye
coloràto *agg.* coloured, colored (USA)
colóre s. *m.* colour, color (USA)
cólpa s. *f.* fault; sin (peccato); guilt (*leg.*)
colpévole s. *m.* e *f.* culprit; offender (*leg.*)

colpìre v. *tr.* to hit, to strike
cólpo s. *m.* blow, stroke; bang (rimbombo); – **di sole** sunstroke
coltèllo s. *m.* knife
coltivàbile *agg.* cultivable
coltivàre v. *tr.* to till, to farm, to grow; to cultivate (*fig.*)
coltivàto *agg.* cultivated
cólto *agg.* learned, well-educated
coltùra s. *f.* cultivation
còma s. *m. inv.* coma
comandànte s. *m.* commander, captain
comandàre v. *intr.* to order, to command
combaciàre v. *intr.* to meet, to join
combàttere v. *tr.* e *intr.* to fight
combattiménto s. *m.* fight, combat
combinàre v. *tr.* to combine, to match • *intr.* to agree, to fit in
combinazióne s. *f.* chance, coincidence
combustìbile s. *m.* fuel
come *avv.* e *cong.* as, like
comèta s. *f.* comet
comicità s. *f.* comicality
còmico *agg.* comic • s. *m.* comic, comedian
comignolo s. *m.* chimney
cominciàre v. *tr.* e *intr.* to begin, to start
comitàto s. *m.* committee; board (*leg.*)
comitìva s. *f.* party, group
comìzio s. *m.* meeting
commèdia s. *f.* comedy, play
commediògrafo s. *m.* playwright
commemoràre v. *tr.* to commemorate
commemorazióne s. *f.* commemoration
commensàle s. *m.* e *f.* table companion
commentatóre s. *m.* commentator
comménto s. *m.* comment; commentary (radio, televisione)
commerciàle *agg.* commercial; trade (*attr.*); business (*attr.*)
commercialìsta s. *m.* e *f.* business consultant
commerciànte s. *m.* e *f.* trader
commèrcio s. *m.* trade
commèssa s. *f.* shop assistant; order (*econ.*)
commèsso s. *m.* shop assistant; – **viaggiatore** salesman
commestìbile *agg.* eatable, edible
commiseràre v. *tr.* to commiserate
commissariàto s. *m.* police station
commissióne s. *f.* errand; shopping (compere); commission (*comm.*); committee (gruppo di persone)
committènte s. *m.* e *f.* client
commòsso *agg.* moved

commovènte *agg.* moving

commuòversi *v. intr. pron.* to be moved, to break down

comodino *s. m.* bedside table

comodità *s. f.* convenience, comfort

compaesàno *s. m.* fellow countryman

compagnìa *s. f.* company; corporation (*fin.*)

compàgno *s. m.* companion, mate, chum

comparàbile *agg.* comparable

compàrsa *s. f.* appearance; walk-on (*teatro, cin.*)

compàrso *agg.* appeared

compartimènto *s. m.* section

compassàto *agg.* measured, cool

compàsso *s. m.* compass

compatìbile *agg.* compatible; forgivable (da compatire)

compatibilmènte *avv.* compatibly, in line with

compatto *agg.* compact

compèndio *s. m.* outline, summary

compensàre *v. tr.* to compensate

compènso *s. m.* remuneration

competènte *agg.* competent

competènza *s. f.* competence

competitività *s. f.* competitiveness

competitivo *agg.* competitive

competizióne *s. f.* competition; contest (gara)

compiàngere *v. tr.* to pity

cómpiere *v. tr.* to accomplish, to achieve, to be (età) • *intr. e intr. pron.* to end, to come true (avverarsi)

compilazióne *s. f.* compilation; filling in (modulo)

cómpito *s. m.* task, duty, job; homework (di scuola)

compleànno *s. m.* birthday

complementàre *agg.* complementary

complessàto *agg.* neurotic, full of complexes

complessità *s. f.* complexity

complessivo *agg.* overall (*attr.*); comprehensive

complèsso *agg.* complex • *s. m.* combination, set; ensemble (*mus.*); plant (industriale); complex (*psic.*)

complèto *agg.* complete; full up (pieno)

complicàre *v. tr.* to complicate • *intr. pron.* to thicken

complicàto *agg.* complicated

cómplice *s. m. e f.* accomplice

compliménto *s. m.* compliment

complòtto *s. m.* conspiracy

componènte *s. m. e f.* component

componìbile *agg.* modular

componimènto *s. m.* essay, composition

compórre *v. tr.* to compose

comportaménto *s. m.* behaviour

compòsito *agg.* composite

compositóre *s. m.* composer

compràre *v. tr.* to buy, to purchase

compratóre *s. m.* buyer, purchaser

comprèndere *v. tr.* to comprise, to include; to understand, to see (capire)

comprensìbile *agg.* understandable

comprensivo *agg.* inclusive; sympathetic (di persona)

comprèssa *s. f.* tablet

compressóre *s. m.* compressor

comprìmere *v. tr.* to press, to compress

compromésso *s. m.* to compromise

comprométtere *v. tr.* to compromise; to implicate (coinvolgere)

comproprietà *s. f.* joint ownership

comproprietàrio *s. m.* joint owner

comunàle *agg.* municipal; town (*attr.*)

comùne *agg.* common • *s. m.* municipality, town council; town hall (palazzo)

comunemènte *avv.* commonly, generally

comunicàre *v. tr. e intr.* to communicate

comunicazióne *s. f.* communication

comunismo *s. m.* Communism

comunità *s. f.* community

comùnque *avv.* however, anyhow, in any case • *cong.* however, whatever

con *prep.* with; by (mezzo, strumento)

conàto *s. m.* retching

concatenazióne *s. f.* concatenation

còncavo *agg.* concave

concèdere *v. tr.* to grant, to allow

concentràre *v. tr.* to concentrate

concentrazióne *s. f.* concentration

concèntrico *agg.* concentric

concepìbile *agg.* conceivable

concepìre *v. tr.* to conceive; to contrive (escogitare)

concertìsta *s. m. e f.* concert player

concèrto *s. m.* concert

concessionàrio *s. m.* concessionaire, agent; - d'auto car distributor

concessióne *s. f.* concession; franchise (*leg.*)

concètto *s. m.* concept, conception

concettuàle *agg.* conceptual

conchìglia *s. f.* shell, conch

conciàre *v. tr.* to tan • *rifl.* to dirty oneself; to mess oneself up

conciliàre *v. tr.* to reconcile, to conciliate •

intr. pron. to be compatible; – **una multa** to
settle a fine

concilio *s. m.* council

concime *s. m.* manure, dung

conciso *agg.* concise

concittadino *s. m.* fellow citizen

conclùdere *v. tr.* to conclude • *intr. pron.* to
end up, to conclude

concomitante *agg.* concomitant

concordàre *v. tr.* to arrange • *intr.* to agree

concorrènte *s. m. e f.* competitor

concorrènza *s. f.* competition

concórrere *v. intr.* to compete; to concur (contribuire)

concórso *s. m.* competition, contest

concretézza *s. f.* concreteness

concrèto *agg.* concrete

condànna *s. f.* condemnation; sentence (sentenza)

condannàre *v. tr.* to convict, to sentence, to
condemn

condannàto *agg. e s. m.* condemned, convict

condènsa *s. f.* condensation

condensàre *v. tr.* to condense

condensàto *agg.* condensed

condensazióne *s. f.* condensation, conden-
sing

condiménto *s. m.* flavouring; condiment (spezie); – **per insalata** salad dressing

condire *v. tr.* to flavour, to season; to dress (insalata)

condiscendènza *s. f.* condescension; compliance (remissività)

condividere *v. tr.* to share

condizionaménto *s. m.* conditioning

condizionatóre *s. m.* conditioner

condizióne *s. f.* condition

condoglìànze *s. f. pl.* condolences

condominio *s. m.* apartment building, condominium

condonàre *v. tr.* to remit, to condone, to forgive (perdonare)

condótta *s. f.* conduct; piping (tubazione)

condottièro *s. m.* leader

conducènte *s. m.* driver

condùrre *v. tr.* to lead; to drive (guidare)

conduttùra *s. f.* plumbing; – **dell'acqua** water
mains; – **del gas** gas mains

confederazióne *s. f.* confederation

conferènza *s. f.* lecture; conference (riunione)

conferenzière *s. m.* lecturer

conferire *v. tr.* to confer, to give

confèrma *s. f.* confirmation

confermàre *v. tr.* to confirm, to attest

confessàre *v. tr.* to confess

confessionàle *agg. e s. m.* confessional

confettería *s. f.* confectionery

confètto *s. m.* sugared almond

confettùra *s. f.* jam

confezióne *s. f.* wrapping; clothing industry
(abbigliamento)

confidàre *v. tr.* to confide • *intr. pron.* to
confide in

confidènza *s. f.* confidence, trust; intimacy
(familiarità)

confidenziàle *agg.* confidential

confinànte *agg.* neighbouring

confine *s. m.* boundary; border (tra nazioni)

confisca *s. f.* confiscation

conflitto *s. m.* conflict

confluènza *s. f.* confluence

confóndere *v. tr.* to confuse, to mix up •
intr. pron. to get confused

conformismo *s. m.* conformism

confortévole *agg.* comforting, comfortable

confrontàre *v. tr.* to compare • *rifl.* to confront

confusionàrio *agg.* muddling • *s. m.* muddler

confusióne *s. f.* muddle, confusion, mess

confutàre *v. tr.* to confute

congèdo *s. m.* leave; discharge (*mil.*)

congégno *s. m.* device

congelàre *v. tr. e intr. pron.* to freeze

congelatóre *s. m.* freezer

congestióne *s. f.* congestion

congettùra *s. f.* conjecture

congiuntivite *s. f.* conjunctivitis

congiùra *s. f.* conspiracy

conglobàre *v. tr.* to conglobate; to lump together; to incorporate (*fin.*)

conglomeràto *s. m.* conglomerate

congratulàrsi *v. intr. pron.* to congratulate

congratulazióni *s. f. pl.* congratulation *sing.*

congregazióne *s. f.* congregation

congrèsso *s. m.* congress

congruènza *s. f.* congruency

conguàglio *s. m.* balance, adjustment

coniàre *v. tr.* to coin, to mint

cònico *agg.* conical

conifere *s. f. pl.* conifers

coniglio *s. m.* rabbit

coniugàre *v. tr.* to conjugate

coniugàto *agg.* married; conjugate (*gramm.*)

còniuge *s. m.* consort

connazionále s. m. e f. fellow countryman m., fellow countrywoman f.

connésso agg. connected

còno s. m. cone; **- gelato** ice-cream cone

conoscénte s. m. e f. acquaintance

conoscénza s. f. knowledge

conóscere v. tr. to know • rifl. rec. to meet (fare conoscenza)

conoscitóre s. m. connoisseur

conquísta s. f. conquest

conquistáre v. tr. to conquer

consacráre v. tr. to consecrate

consanguíneo agg. akin • s. m. kinsman

consapévole agg. aware

consecutívo agg. consecutive

conségna s. f. delivery; **- a domicilio** home delivery; **pagamento alla -** cash on delivery

consegnáre v. tr. to deliver, to hand over, to consign

conseguénte agg. consequent

conseguénza s. f. consequence

consénso s. m. consent

consérva s. f. preserve

conservánte s. m. preservative

conserváre v. tr. to keep, to preserve • intr. pron. to keep

conservatóre agg. conservative

conservatório s. m. conservatory

consideráre v. tr. to consider • rifl. to consider oneself

consigliábile agg. advisable

consigliáre v. tr. to advise, to counsel • intr. pron. to consult

consigliére s. m. adviser, counsellor

consíglio s. m. advice (solo sing.); counsel, opinion; council, board (politica)

consístere v. intr. to consist (of), to be composed (of); to consist in (avere fondamento in)

consociáto agg. e s. m. associated, associate

consoláre v. tr. to console, to soothe, to comfort • intr. pron. to take comfort; to cheer up (rallegrarsi)

cònsole s. m. consul

consolidáre v. tr. e intr. pron. to consolidate

consonánte s. f. consonant

consòrte s. m. e f. consort

consortería s. f. clique

consòrzio s. m. union

constáre v. intr. to consist(of), to be made (of)

constatáre v. tr. to ascertain; to note (notare)

consuèto agg. usual, customary

consuetúdine s. f. custom

consulénte agg. e s. m. e f. consultant

consulénza s. f. advice, consultation

consultáre v. tr. to consult • intr. pron. to confer (with); to consult

consultívo agg. advisory

consumáre v. tr. to consume; to use up (esaurire)

consumazióne s. f. consummation, refreshment (al bar)

consuntívo s. m. final balance, survey (fig.)

contábile s. m. e f. book-keeper, accountant

contabilizzáre v. tr. to reckon

contachilómetri s. m. mileometer, odometer (USA)

contadíno s. m. farmer • agg. country (attr.)

contagiáre v. tr. to infect • intr. pron. to be infected

contágio s. m. contagion, infection

contagióso agg. contagious, infectious

contagíri s. m. inv. rev counter

contagócce s. m. inv. dropper

contamináre v. tr. to contaminate

contaminazióne s. f. contamination

contánte s. m. cash

contáre v. tr. e intr. to count

contatóre s. m. meter; **- del gas** gas meter

contátto s. m. contact

cónte s. m. count

contéa s. f. county

contéggio s. m. count

contempláre v. tr. to contemplate

contemplatívo agg. contemplative

contemporaneaménte avv. at the same time

contemporáneo agg. contemporary

contendénte s. m. e f. contender

contenére v. tr. to contain

contenitóre s. m. container

contentáre v. tr. to satisfy • intr. pron. to be content

contentézza s. f. cheerfulness, satisfaction

conténto agg. pleased, cheerful, happy

contenúto s. m. contents pl.; content, subject (argomento)

contésa s. f. argument, contention

contéssa s. f. countess

contestáre v. tr. to contest, to protest (against), to dispute

contíguo agg. adjoining

continentále agg. continental

continénte s. m. continent

continuaménte avv. continuously; continually (frequentemente)

continuáre v. tr. e intr. to go on, to continue, to keep on

continuo *agg.* continuous; continual (frequente)

cónto *s. m.* account; bill (ristorante); – **corrente** current account

contorcimento *s. m.* contortion

contórno *s. m.* contour; vegetables *pl.* (menù)

contòrto *agg.* twisted; warped (*fig.*)

contrabbandière *s. m.* smuggler

contraccambiàre *v. tr.* to return, to repay

contraccettivo *agg. e s. m.* contraceptive

contraccòlpo *s. m.* rebound, recoil

contraddire *v. tr. e intr.* to contradict • *rifl.* to contradict oneself

contraddistinguere *v. tr.* to check, to mark

contraddizióne *s. f.* contradiction

contraffazióne *s. f.* counterfeit

contrappórre *v. tr. e rifl.* to oppose

contrapposizióne *s. f.* contrast, opposition; contraposition

contrariaménte *avv.* contrarily; otherwise; – **a** contrary to

contrarietà *s. f.* setback

contràrio *agg. e s. m.* contrary, opposite

contrasségno *loc. avv.* on delivery

contrasto *s. m.* contrast

contrattàre *v. tr.* to bargain over, to negotiate over

contrattèmpo *s. m.* mishap, hitch

contràtto *s. m.* agreement, contract

contravvenzióne *s. f.* infringment, violation; fine (multa)

contrazióne *s. f.* contraction; fall-off (*econ.*)

contribuire *v. intr.* to contribute

contribùto *s. m.* contribution

cóntro *prep.* against; versus (*sport, leg.*) • *avv.* against

controbàttere *v. tr.* to answer back

controcorrènte *avv.* countercurrent

controfigùra *s. f.* double

controindicazióne *s. f.* contraindication

controllàre *v. tr.* to check, to control • *rifl.* to control oneself

contròllo *s. m.* control

controllóre *s. m.* controller; ticket collector (mezzi pubblici)

controlùce *avv.* against the light

contromàno *avv.* in the wrong direction

controproducènte *agg.* counter productive

contrordine *s. m.* counterorder, countermand

controrifórma *s. f.* Counter-Reformation

controsènso *s. m.* nonsense

controspionàggio *s. m.* counter-espionage

controvalóre *s. m.* exchange value

controvèrsia *s. f.* controversy

controvòglia *avv.* unwillingly

contumàcia *s. f.* absence, contumacy

contusióne *s. f.* bruise

contùso *agg.* bruised

convalescènte *agg. e s. m. e f.* convalescent

convalidàre *v. tr.* to bear out, to corroborate

convègno *s. m.* meeting, congress

conveniènte *agg.* convenient; cheap (a basso prezzo)

conveniènza *s. f.* convenience

convenire *v. intr.* to agree • *intr. impers.* to be necessary, to be better; to suit (confarsi)

convènto *s. m.* convent

convenzionàle *agg.* conventional

convenzióne *s. f.* convention

convergènza *s. f.* convergence

convèrgere *v. intr.* to converge

conversàre *v. intr.* to talk

conversazióne *s. f.* conversation

conversióne *s. f.* conversion

convertìre *v. tr.* to convert • *rifl.* to be converted; **convertirsi al buddhismo** to become a Buddhist

convèsso *agg.* convex

convezióne *s. f.* convection

convincere *v. tr.* to convince • *rifl.* to convince oneself

convinzióne *s. f.* conviction

convivènte *s. m. e f.* cohabitant

convivere *v. intr.* to cohabit

convocazióne *s. f.* convocation

convulsióne *s. f.* fit, convulsion

cooperativa *s. f.* cooperative

coordinaménto *s. m.* coordination

coordinatóre *s. m.* coordinator

copèrchio *s. m.* cover; lid (di pentola)

copèrta *s. f.* blanket, rug; deck (*naut.*)

copertìna *s. f.* binding, cover

copèrto *s. m.* cover; cover charge (nel conto del ristorante) • *agg.* covered; hidden (nascosto); clothed (di vestiti)

copertóne *s. m.* tyre

copertùra *s. f.* cover

cópia *s. f.* copy

copiàre *v. tr.* to copy

copistería *s. f.* copying office

còppia *s. f.* couple, pair

coprifuòco *s. m.* curfew

coprilètto *s. m. inv.* bedcover

coprìre *v. tr.* to cover • *rifl.* to cover oneself, to wrap up

coràggio *s. m.* courage • *inter.* cheer up!

coraggióso *agg.* courageous, brave

coràle *agg.* choral

corallino *agg.* coral

corállo *s. m.* coral; **banco di –** coral reef

córda *s. f.* rope; string (*mus.*); **– vocale** vocal cord

cordàta *s. f.* roped party

cordialità *s. f.* cordiality

cordialménte *avv.* cordially

coreografìa *s. f.* choreography

coriàceo *agg.* tough, coriaceous

corìnzio *agg.* Corinthian

corista *s. m. e f.* chorister

cormoràno *s. m.* cormorant

córnea *s. f.* cornea

cornice *s. f.* frame; moulding (modanatura)

cornicióne *s. m.* cornice

córno *s. m.* horn

cornucòpia *s. f.* cornucopia

còro *s. m.* chorus, choir

coròlla *s. f.* corolla

coróna *s. f.* crown

córpo *s. m.* body

corporatùra *s. f.* build

corporazióne *s. f.* guild

corpulènto *agg.* stout

corpùscolo *s. m.* corpuscle

corrèggere *v. tr.* to correct

correlazióne *s. f.* correlation

corrènte *s. f.* stream, current • *agg.* running, flowing; current (attuale); **acqua –** running water

córrere *v. tr. e intr.* to run

corrètto *agg.* correct; right (giusto)

correzióne *s. f.* correction

corridóio *s. m.* passage, corridor

corridóre *s. m.* runner

corrièra *s. f.* coach

corrière *s. m.* carrier

corrimàno *s. m.* handrail

corrispettivo *agg.* corresponding • *s. m.* equivalent; compensation (compenso)

corrispondènte *agg.* corresponding

corródere *v. tr.* to corrode

corrómpere *v. tr.* to corrupt • *intr. pron.* to rot

corrosìvo *agg.* corrosive

corruzióne *s. f.* corruption

córsa *s. f.* run, race (gara)

corsìa *s. f.* ward (d'ospedale); lane (di strada); **– d'emergenza** hard shoulder

córte *s. f.* court

cortéccia *s. f.* bark

corteggiàre *v. tr.* to court

cortèo *s. m.* procession

cortése *agg.* polite, courteous

cortesìa *s. f.* courtesy, politeness; favour (favore)

cortigiàno *agg.* court (*attr.*)

cortìle *s. m.* courtyard

cortisóne *s. m.* cortisone

córto *agg.* short

cortocircùito *s. m.* short circuit

corvè *s. f. inv.* corvée

córvo *s. m.* crow, raven

còsa *s. f.* thing

còscia *s. f.* thigh

cosciènte *agg.* conscious

cosciènza *s. f.* conscience

cosciòtto *s. m.* leg

così *avv.* so, thus • *cong.* so, then

cosicché *cong.* so that

cosiddétto *agg.* so-called

cosmètico *s. m.* cosmetic

còsmico *agg.* cosmic

còsmo *s. m.* cosmos

cosmopolìta *agg.* cosmopolitan

cospàrgere *v. tr.* to scatter

cospìcuo *agg.* conspicuous

cospiratóre *s. m.* conspirator

cósta *s. f.* coast

costànte *agg.* constant

costàre *v. intr.* to cost

costàta *s. f.* chop; **– d'agnello** lamb chop

costellazióne *s. f.* constellation

costièro *agg.* coastal

costipazióne *s. f.* constipation

costituìre *v. tr.* to constitute • *intr. pron.* to become

costituzionàle *agg.* constitutional

costituzióne *s. f.* constitution

còsto *s. m.* cost

còstola *s. f.* rib

costolétta *s. f.* cutlet; **– di vitello** veal cutlet

costóso *agg.* dear, expensive

costrìngere *v. tr.* to force, to compel

costruìre *v. tr.* to build

costruzióne *s. f.* construction, building

costùi *pron. dimostr.* he (sogg.); him (compl.); this, that man

costùme *s. m.* custom, habit; behaviour (comportamento); costume (abito); **– da bagno** bathing costume, bathing suit

cotógna *s. f.* quince

cotóne *s. m.* cotton

còtto agg. cooked, done; – **al forno** baked; – **ai ferri** grilled

cottùra s. f. cooking

còzza s. f. mussel

cràmpo s. m. cramp

crànico agg. cranial

crànio s. m. skull, cranium

cratère s. m. crater

cravàtta s. f. tie, necktie

creàre v. tr. to create

creativìtà s. f. creativity

creazióne s. f. creation

credènte s. m. e f. believer

crédere v. tr. e intr. to believe • rifl. to consider oneself

credìbile agg. believable

crédito s. m. credit; esteem (stima)

creditóre s. m. creditor

cremazióne s. f. cremation

cremóso agg. creamy

crèn s. m. horseradish

crèpa s. f. crack, crevice

crepàccio s. m. cleft

crepuscolàre agg. crepuscular

crepùscolo s. m. twilight

crescèndo s. m. crescendo

créscere v. intr. to grow; to rise (di volume) • tr. to rear, to bring up

créscita s. f. growth, increase; rise (aumento)

crèsta s. f. crest; ridge (crinale)

créta s. f. clay

cretinàta s. f. silly thing

cretino agg. e s. m. stupid

cric s. m. jack

criminàle s. m. e f. criminal

crinàle s. m. crest, ridge

crinièra s. f. mane

cripta s. f. crypt

criptico agg. cryptic

crisi s. f. crisis

cristalleria s. f. glassware

cristallìno agg. crystalline

cristallizzàre v. intr. e intr. pron. to crystallize

cristàllo s. m. crystal

cristianésimo s. m. Christianity

cristianità s. f. Christendom

cristiàno agg. Christian

critèrio s. m. criterion, standard

critica s. f. criticism; review (recensione); critics pl. (insieme dei critici)

criticàbile agg. criticizable

criticàre v. tr. to criticize

critico agg. critical; crucial (crisi) • s. m. critic; reviewer (recensore)

croccànte agg. crisp

crocchètta s. f. croquette

cróce s. f. cross

crocevìa s. m. inv. crossroads

crociàta s. f. crusade

crocìcchio s. m. crossroads

crocièra s. f. cruise; cross vault (arch.); **nave da** – cruise ship

crocifissióne s. f. crucifixion

crocifìsso s. m. crucifix

crogiolàrsi v. intr. pron. to bask

crollàre v. intr. to collapse

cròllo s. m. collapse

cromàtico agg. chromatic

cromatùra s. f. chromium-plating

crònaca s. f. chronicle; news (di giornale); – **nera** crime news; – **mondana** society news

crònico agg. chronic

cronista s. m. e f. chronicler; reporter (giornalista)

cronistòria s. f. chronicle

cronològico agg. chronologic

cronòmetro s. m. chronometer

cròsta s. f. crust; scab (med.); – **di formaggio** cheese rind

crostàcei s. m. pl. crustaceans

crostàta s. f. jam tart

crostìno s. m. crouton

crucifórme agg. cruciform; cruciate (bot.)

crucivèrba s. m. inv. crossword puzzle

crudeltà s. f. cruelty

crùdo agg. raw; underdone (poco cotto)

crùsca s. f. bran

cruscòtto s. m. dashboard

cubìsmo s. m. cubism

cùbo s. m. cube

cucchiaiàta s. f. spoonful

cucchiaìno s. m. teaspoon

cucchiàio s. m. spoon

cùccia s. f. bed

cùcciolo s. m. puppy; kitten (di gatto)

cucìna s. f. kitchen; cooking (il cucinare); – **casalinga** homecooking; – **vegetariana** vegetarian food

cucinàre v. tr. to cook

cucìre v. tr. to sew, to stitch

cucitùra s. f. seam

cucùzzolo s. m. top

cùffia s. f. cap, bonnet; headphones pl. (auricolari)

cugìno s. m. cousin

culinàrio *agg.* culinary

cùlla *s. f.* cradle

culminàre *v. intr.* to culminate

cùlto *s. m.* worship, religion, adoration, cult; creed (credo)

cultùra *s. f.* culture

culturàle *agg.* cultural

cùmulo *s. m.* heap; cumulus (nube)

cuneifórme *agg.* cuneiform

cunicolo *s. m.* tunnel

cuòcere *v. tr. e intr.* to cook

cuòco *s. m.* cook

cuòio *s. m.* leather; – **conciato** dressed leather; **articoli di** – leather goods

cuòre *s. m.* heart

cùpo *agg.* dark, gloomy

cùpola *s. f.* dome

cùra *s. f.* care; treatment (*med.*); **casa di** – nursing home

curàbile *agg.* curable

curàre *v. tr.* to take care of; to treat (*med.*); to cure (guarire) • *rifl.* to take care of oneself, to follow a treatment (*med.*)

cùria *s. f.* curia

curiosàre *v. intr.* to pry, to snoop

curiosità *s. f.* curiosity

curióso *agg.* curious

curtènse *agg.* court (*attr.*)

cùrva *s. f.* bend, curve

curvàre *v. tr.* to bend, to curve • *intr.* to corner, to turn

curvilineo *agg.* curvilinear

cuscinétto *s. m.* pad; bearing (*mecc.*); – **a sfera** ball bearing

cuscino *s. m.* cushion; pillow (guanciale)

cùspide *s. f.* spire

custòde *s. m. e f.* caretaker; janitor, porter (portiere)

custòdia *s. f.* care, custody; case, holder (astuccio); sleeve, jacket (*mus.*)

custodire *v. tr.* to keep, to preserve

cutàneo *agg.* cutaneous; skin (*attr.*)

cùte *s. f.* cutis, skin

D

da *prep.* from (provenienza); by (agente); for, since (tempo continuato); to (moto a luogo); at (stato in luogo)

daccàpo *avv.* over again, from the beginning

dadaìsmo *s. m.* Dadaism

dàdo *s. m.* die; nut (*mecc.*); **– da brodo** stock cube

dàino *s. m.* fallow deer

daltònico *agg.* colour-blind

dàma *s. f.* draughts *pl.* (*v. al sing.*) (gioco)

damàsco *s. m.* damask

danneggiàre *v. tr.* to damage; to harm (nuocere)

dànno *s. m.* damage, harm; injury (a persona)

dànza *s. f.* dance

danzàre *v. intr.* to dance

danzatóre *s. m.* dancer

dapprìma *avv.* at first

dàre *v. tr.* to give

dàrsena *s. f.* wet dock

dàta *s. f.* date

datàre *v. tr. e intr.* to date

dàttero *s. m.* date

dattilògrafo *s. m.* typist

davànti *avv.* in front; **– a** in front of, opposite

davanzàle *s. m.* windowsill

davvéro *avv.* really, indeed

dàzio *s. m.* duty; **esente da –** duty free

dèa *s. f.* goddess

deambulatòrio *s. m.* (de)ambulatory

debellàre *v. tr.* to vanquish, to eliminate

debilitàrsi *v. intr. pron.* to weaken

dèbito *s. m.* debt

debitóre *s. m.* debtor

dèbole *agg.* weak; dim (di luce)

debolézza *s. f.* weakness

debuttàre *v. intr.* to make one's debut

debùtto *s. m.* debut

dècade *s. f.* decade (dieci anni); ten days (dieci giorni)

decadènte *agg.* decadent

decadentìsmo *s. m.* decadentism

decadènza *s. f.* decadence, decline

decadùto *agg.* impoverished

decaffeinàto *agg.* decaffeinated

decàno *s. m.* dean

decapitàre *v. tr.* to behead, to decapitate

decelerazióne *s. f.* deceleration

decènnio *s. m.* decade, decennium

decènte *agg.* decent

decentramènto *s. m.* decentralization

decìdere *v. tr. e intr.* to decide • *intr. pron.* to decide, to make up one's mind

decìduo *agg.* deciduous

decifràre *v. tr.* to decipher, to decode

decimàle *agg.* decimal; **sistema metrico –** metric system

decimàre *v. tr.* to decimate

decisióne *s. f.* decision

decisìvo *agg.* decisive; crucial (critico)

declamàre *v. tr.* to declaim

declassàre *v. tr.* to declass, to degrade

declìno *s. m.* decline

decollàre *v. intr.* to take off

decòllo *s. m.* take-off

decolorazióne *s. f.* decolo(u)rization

decompórsi *v. intr. pron.* to decompose, to rot, to decay

decongestionàre *v. tr.* to decongest

decoràre *v. tr.* to decorate

decoratìvo *agg.* decorative

decoratóre *s. m.* decorator

decorazióne *s. f.* decoration

decòtto *s. m.* decoction

decrèpito *agg.* decrepit

decretàre *v. tr.* to decree

decrèto *s. m.* decree

decurtàre *v. tr.* to curtail, to reduce

dèdalo *s. m.* maze

dèdica *s. f.* dedication

dedicàre *v. tr.* to dedicate • *rifl.* to devote oneself

deducìbile *agg.* deducible, deductible

deduzióne *s. f.* deduction

defezióne *s. f.* defection, desertion

deficiènte *agg.* deficient; stupid (stupido)

deficitàrio *agg.* showing a deficit

definìre *v. tr.* to define

definitivaménte *avv.* definitively, once and for all

definitìvo *agg.* definitive, final

definizióne *s. f.* definition

deflagrazióne *s. f.* deflagration

deflettóre *s. m.* quarter light

defluire *v. intr.* to flow

deformàbile *agg.* deformable

deformazióne *s. f.* deformation; deformity (*med.*)

defórme *agg.* deformed

defunto *s. m.* deceased; late (*attr.*)

degeneràre *v. intr.* to degenerate

degenerazióne *s. f.* degeneration

degènte *agg. • s. m. e f.* in-patient

deglutire *v. tr.* to swallow

degradànte *agg.* degrading

degràdo *s. m.* decay

degustàre *v. tr.* to taste, to sample

degustazióne *s. f.* tasting, sampling

delazióne *s. f.* delation

dèlega *s. f.* proxy

delegàre *v. tr.* to delegate

delegazióne *s. f.* delegation

deletèrio *agg.* deleterious

delfìno *s. m.* dolphin

deliberàre *v. tr.* to deliberate

deliberataménte *avv.* deliberately

delicàto *agg.* delicate; sensitive (sensibile); weakly (di salute)

delimitàre *v. tr.* to delimit

delimitazióne *s. f.* delimitation

delineàre *v. tr.* to outline • *intr. pron.* to take shape

delinquènte *s. m. e f.* criminal, delinquent

deliràre *v. intr.* to rave

delìrio *s. m.* delirium, raving

delìtto *s. m.* crime

delìzia *s. f.* delight

delizióso *agg.* delightful; delicious (di sapore)

dèlta *s. m. inv.* delta

deltaplàno *s. m.* hang-glider

delucidazióne *s. f.* elucidation

delùdere *v. tr.* to disappoint

delusióne *s. f.* disappointment

demagogìa *s. f.* demagogy

demaniàle *agg.* state (*attr.*)

demènte *agg.* insane • *s. m. e f.* lunatic

demenziàle *agg.* crazy, demential (*med.*)

demistificazióne *s. f.* demystification

democràtico *agg.* democratic

democrazìa *s. f.* democracy

demogràfico *agg.* demographic

demolire *v. tr.* to demolish

demolizióne *s. f.* demolition

dèmone *s. m.* demon

demònio *s. m.* demon, fiend

demoralizzàre *v. tr.* to demoralize • *intr. pron.* to lose heart

denàro *s. m.* money

denigràre *v. tr.* to denigrate

denominàre *v. tr.* to name

denotàre *v. tr.* to denote; to imply (implicare)

densità *s. f.* density, thickness

dènso *agg.* dense, thick

dènte *s. m.* tooth; **spazzolìno da dènti** toothbrush; **– cariàto** decayed tooth

dentellàto *agg.* indented

dentièra *s. f.* denture, false teeth *pl.*

dentifrìcio *s. m.* tooth-paste

dentìsta *s. m. e f.* dentist

déntro *avv.* in, inside • *prep.* inside, in; within (entro)

denudàrsi *v. rifl.* to strip, to undress

denùncia *s. f.* denunciation, accusation; complaint (*leg.*)

denunciàre *v. tr.* to declare; to denounce (*leg.*)

denutrito *agg.* underfed

deodorànte *agg. e s. m.* deodorant

deperìbile *agg.* perishable

deperìre *v. intr.* to decline, to perish; to decay (di cose)

depilatòrio *agg.* depilatory

depilazióne *s. f.* depilation

deploràvole *agg.* deplorable

deportàre *v. tr.* to deport

depositàre *v. tr.* to leave; to deposit (in banca)

depòsito *s. m.* deposit; **– bagàgli** left-luggage office, checkroom

depravazióne *s. f.* depravity

deprecàbile *agg.* deprecable; disgraceful

depressióne *s. f.* depression

deprèsso *agg.* depressed

deprezzaménto *s. m.* depreciation

depuràre *v. tr.* to depurate

depuratóre *s. m.* depurator

deputàto *s. m.* deputy

deragliaménto *s. m.* derailment

derattizzazióne *s. f.* deratization

deridere *v. tr.* to deride, to mock

derìva *s. f.* drift; keel (*naut.*)

derivàre *v. intr.* to derive; to originate from

derivazióne *s. f.* derivation; shunt (*elettr.*)

dermatìte *s. f.* dermatitis

dermatòlogo *s. m.* dermatologist

déroga s. f. derogation

derubáre v. tr. to steal, to rob

descrittivo agg. descriptive

descrívere v. tr. to describe

descrizióne s. f. description

desértico agg. desert (attr.)

desérto agg. deserted; desert (attr.) • s. m. desert

desideráre v. tr. to desire, to wish, to want; **che cosa desìdera?** what can I do for you?

desidério s. m. desire, wish

designáre v. tr. to designate, to appoint

desinénza s. f. ending, desinence

desìstere v. intr. to desist

desolazióne s. f. desolation

dessert s. m. inv. dessert, pudding

destinatário s. m. receiver; addressee (di lettera, ecc.)

destinazióne s. f. destination

destìno s. m. destiny

destituíto agg. devoid, destitute

déstra s. f. right; **a –** on the right, to the right of

déstro agg. right

desùmere v. tr. to infer, to guess

detenúto agg. imprisoned • s. m. convict

detergénte agg. cleansing, detergent

deterioràbile agg. perishable

determináre v. tr. to determine

detersìvo agg. detersive, detergent

detestáre v. tr. to detest • rifl. rec. to detest each other

detràrre v. tr. e intr. to deduct, to detract

detrazióne s. f. deduction, detraction; **– fiscale** tax allowance

detrìto s. m. debris, rubble

dettagliánte s. m. e f. retailer

dettagliataménte avv. in detail

détto s. m. saying

deturpáre v. tr. to disfigure, to sully

devastáre v. tr. to devastate, to ravage

deviáre v. intr. to divert

deviazióne s. f. deviation; detour (stradale)

devozióne s. f. devotion

di prep. of; in, by (tempo); **– mattina** in the morning; **– giorno** by day

diabéte s. m. diabetes

diabético agg. diabetic

diadéma s. m. diadem

diàgnosi s. f. diagnosis

diagnosticáre v. tr. to diagnose

diagonále agg. diagonal

dialettále agg. dialectal

dialèttico agg. dialectic

dialétto s. m. dialect

diàlisi s. f. dialysis

dialogáre v. intr. to talk

diàlogo s. m. dialogue

diamánte s. m. diamond

diametralménte avv. diametrically

diàmetro s. m. diameter

diapositíva s. f. slide; **– a colori** colour slide

diàrio s. m. diary, journal; **– scolastico** notebook

diarréa s. f. diarr(ho)ea

diàvolo s. m. devil

dibàttito s. m. debate, teach-in

dicèmbre s. m. December

dicerìa s. f. rumour, gossip

dichiaráre v. tr. to declare, to state

dichiarazióne s. f. declaration, statement

didascàlico agg. didactic

didàttica s. f. didactics

diéta s. f. diet; **essere a –** to be on a diet

dietético agg. dietetic

dietòlogo s. m. dietician, nutritionist

diétro avv. behind, at the back • prep. behind, at the back of, after

difèndere v. tr. to defend, to protect • rifl. to defend oneself

difensìvo agg. defensive

difésa s. f. defence

difétto s. m. defect, fault; deficiency, lack (mancanza)

difettóso agg. defective, faulty

diffamazióne s. f. defamation, slander

differenteménte avv. differently

differénza s. f. difference

differenziále s. m. differential

difficile agg. difficult, hard

difficilménte avv. with difficulty, unlikely

difficoltà s. f. difficulty

diffidáre v. intr. to distrust, to beware (of); to warn (leg.)

diffidénza s. f. distrust

diffóndere v. tr. to spread, to diffuse

difformità s. f. difference, dissimilarity

diffusaménte avv. diffusely, at length

diffusióne s. f. diffusion; circulation (di un giornale)

diffúso agg. widespread; diffused (di luce)

díga s. f. dike, dam

digerìbile agg. digestible

digerìre v. tr. to digest

digestióne s. f. digestion

digestivo *agg.* digestive • *s. m.* digestive, digester

digiunàre *v. intr.* to fast

digiùno *s. m.* fast

dignitóso *agg.* dignified; decent (di aspetto)

digressióne *s. f.* digression

dilagànte *agg.* rampant

dilapidàre *v. tr.* to squander, to waste

dilatàre *v. tr.* to dilate, to expand • *intr. pron.* to swell, to expand

dilatazióne *s. f.* dilatation, expansion

dilazionàre *v. tr.* to delay

dileguàre *v. intr. e intr. pron.* to vanish, to disappear, to fade away

dilèmma *s. m.* dilemma

dilettànte *agg. e s. m. e f.* amateur

dilettantésco *agg.* amateurish

dilètto *s. m.* pleasure, delight

diligènte *agg.* diligent; careful (accurato)

diluire *v. tr.* to dilute; to dissolve (sciogliere)

diluviàre *v. intr.* to pour, to shower

dilùvio *s. m.* deluge, flood

dimagrànte *agg.* slimming

dimagrìre *v. intr.* to grow thin, to slim, to lose weight

dimensióne *s. f.* dimension; size (grandezza)

dimenticànza *s. f.* forgetfulness, oversight

dimenticàre *v. tr. e intr. pron.* to forget

dimezzàre *v. tr.* to halve

diminuìre *v. tr.* to diminish, to lessen • *intr.* to diminish, to grow less

diminutìvo *s. m.* diminutive

dimissióni *s. f. pl.* resignation *sing.*

dimòra *s. f.* abode, home, residence

dimostràbile *agg.* demonstrable

dimostràre *v. tr.* to demonstrate, to show; to prove (provare) • *rifl.* to show oneself, to prove (to be)

dimostrazióne *s. f.* demonstration, show; proof, evidence (prova)

dinàmica *s. f.* dynamics *pl.* (v. al sing.); **la – dell'incidente** the mechanism of the accident

dinàmico *agg.* dynamic

dinamìsmo *s. m.* dynamism

dìnamo *s. f. inv.* dynamo, generator

dinànzi a *loc. prep.* in front of, opposite, before

dinastìa *s. f.* dynasty

dinosàuro *s. m.* dinosaur

Dìo *s. m.* God

diòcesi *s. f.* diocese

diottrìa *s. f.* diopter

dipartiménto *s. m.* department

dipendènte *agg.* dependent, subordinate • *s. m. e f.* employee, subordinate

dipéndere *v. intr.* to depend (on), to come from (derivare); to be under the authority (of) (essere alle dipendenze)

dipìngere *v. tr.* to paint • *rifl.* to make up

dipìnto *s. m.* painting

diplòma *s. m.* diploma, certificate

diplomàtico *agg.* diplomatic

diplomazìa *s. f.* diplomacy

dipòrto *s. m.* recreation

diramazióne *s. f.* branch, ramification

dìre *v. tr.* to say; to tell (raccontare); to talk, to speak (parlare)

direttaménte *avv.* directly, straight

dirètto *agg.* direct, straight; addressed (indirizzato); bound (for) (di veicolo)

direttóre *s. m.* director, manager; editor (di un giornale); conductor (d'orchestra)

direzionàle *agg.* directional

direzióne *s. f.* direction, management (il dirigere)

dirigènte *s. m. e f.* manager, executive

dirìgere *v. tr.* to direct, to manage, to run • *rifl.* to turn (to)

diritto *s. m.* right; law (leg.) • *agg.* straight, upright • *avv.* straight, directly; **vada sempre** – go straight on

diroccàto *agg.* ruined

dirottaménto *s. m.* hijacking, diversion

dirùpo *s. m.* crag

disabitàto *agg.* uninhabited; deserted (abbandonato)

disabituàrsi *v. intr. pron.* to lose the habit (of)

disaccòrdo *s. m.* disagreement

disagévole *agg.* uncomfortable

disàgio *s. m.* uneasiness, inconvenience; trouble (disturbo)

disapprovàre *v. tr.* to disapprove (of), to object (to)

disarmàre *v. tr.* to disarm

disarmònico *agg.* discordant, ill-matched

disastràto *agg.* badly-hit

disàstro *s. m.* disaster; wreck (incidente)

disastróso *agg.* disastrous

disattènto *agg.* inattentive, careless

disattenzióne *s. f.* carelessness; oversight (svista)

disavventùra *s. f.* mishap

disboscàre *v. tr.* to deforest

discàrica *s. f.* dump

discendènte *s. m. e f.* descendant

discéndere *v. intr.* to descend

discépolo *s. m.* disciple

discésa *s. f.* descent; slope (declivio); fall (di barometro, prezzi, ecc.)

discesista *s. m. e f.* downhiller

disciplina *s. f.* discipline

disco *s. m.* disk; record (*mus.*); discus (*sport*)

discolpáre *v. tr.* to clear, to justify

discontìnuo *agg.* discontinuous

discordánte *agg.* discordant

discòrdia *s. f.* discord, disagreement

discorsìvo *agg.* conversational

discórso *s. m.* speech; talk, conversation (conversazione)

discotèca *s. f.* record library; disco(thèque) (locale)

discrepánza *s. f.* discrepancy

discretaménte *avv.* discreetly; fairly well (benino)

discrezióne *s. f.* discretion; moderation (moderazione)

discriminàre *v. tr.* to discriminate

discussióne *s. f.* discussion

discùtere *v. tr. e intr.* to discuss

disdìre *v. tr.* to cancel, to call off; – **un abbonamento** to discontinue a subscription

diseducatìvo *agg.* miseducating

disegnáre *v. tr.* to draw, to outline

disegnatóre *s. m.* draftsman; designer (progettista)

diségno *s. m.* drawing; design (progetto); pattern (motivo decorativo)

diserbánte *s. m.* herbicide

disertóre *s. m.* deserter

disfaciménto *s. m.* decay, break-up

disfáre *v. tr.* to undo, to unmake • *rifl.* to come undone; to melt; – **le valige** to unpack

disfátta *s. f.* defeat, overthrow

disgèlo *s. m.* thaw

disgràzia *s. f.* accident; misfortune (sventura); trouble (guaio); **che –!** what bad luck!

disgraziataménte *avv.* unfortunately

disguìdo *s. m.* miscarriage; hitch (contrattempo); – **postale** wrong delivery

disgustáre *v. tr.* to disgust, to sicken • *intr. pron.* to become disgusted (at)

disgústo *s. m.* disgust, distaste; dislike (avversione)

disgustóso *agg.* disgusting

disidratáre *v. tr.* to dehydrate

disidratazióne *s. f.* dehydration

disincagliáre *v. tr.* to get (a ship) afloat

disinfestáre *v. tr.* to disinfest

disinfettánte *s. m.* disinfectant

disinfettáre *v. tr.* to disinfect

disinibìto *agg.* disinhibited

disintegráre *v. tr. e intr. pron.* to disintegrate

disinteressársi *v. intr. pron.* to lose one's interest (in), to turn off

disinterèsse *s. m.* unselfishness; lack of interest, indifference

disintossicazióne *s. f.* detoxication

disinvòlto *agg.* easy; fresh (sfacciato)

dislivèllo *s. m.* difference in level

dislocaménto *s. m.* displacement (*naut.*); dislocation

dismisùra *s. f.* excess

disoccupáto *s. m.* unemployed; out of work (*pred.*)

disoccupazióne *s. f.* unemployment

disonèsto *agg.* dishonest

disópra *avv.* upstairs

disordináto *agg.* untidy, muddled

disórdine *s. m.* disorder, untidiness

disorganizzazióne *s. f.* disorganization

disorientaménto *s. m.* disorientation; bewilderment (*fig.*)

disorientáto *agg.* bewildered; at a loss (*pred.*)

disótto *avv.* downstairs

disparáto *agg.* different, disparate

dìspari *agg.* odd, uneven; unequal (inferiore)

dispendióso *agg.* expensive, costly

disperáre *v. intr.* to give up hope, to despair • *intr. pron.* to give oneself up to despair

disperáto *agg.* desperate; in despair (*pred.*)

dispèrdersi *v. intr. pron.* to disperse, to scatter; to be lost (andare perduto)

dispersióne *s. f.* dispersion; – **di calore** loss of heat

dispètto *s. m.* vexation, annoyance; **fare dispetti** to tease

dispiacére *v. intr. pron.* to be sorry for

displùvio *s. m.* ridge; hip (*arch.*)

disponìbile *agg.* available; vacant (libero); **una camera** – a vacant room

dispórre *v. tr.* to place, to arrange; to dispose (sistemare); to order (ordinare) • *intr.* to dispose (of) (*leg.*); to have (avere a disposizione)

disposizióne *s. f.* disposal, disposition; arrangement (collocamento); order (ordine)

dispòtico *agg.* despotic

dispregiatìvo *agg.* disparaging; contemptuous; pejorative (*gramm.*)

disprezzáre *v. tr.* to despise

dispùta *s. f.* dispute; quarrel (lite)

dissalatóre *s. m.* desalter

dissanguaménto *s. m.* bleeding

disseminàre *v. tr.* to disseminate, to spread

dissentería *s. f.* dysentery

dissentíre *v. intr.* to dissent (from)

dissèsto *s. m.* impairment; failure (*fin.*)

dissetàrsi *v. rifl.* to quench one's thirst, to refresh oneself

dissidènte *agg.* dissident

dissímile *agg.* unlike, dissimilar

dissimulàre *v. tr.* to dissimulate; to feign (fingere)

dissipàre *v. tr.* to dissipate, to waste; to squander (scialacquare)

dissociàre *v. tr. e rifl.* to dissociate

dissodàre *v. tr.* to plough, to till

dissolùto *agg.* dissolute, debauched

dissolvènza *s. f.* fading

dissonànte *agg.* dissonant

dissuadére *v. tr.* to dissuade

distaccàre *v. tr.* to detach • *intr. pron.* to be detached; to stand out (distinguersi); to withdraw (allontanarsi)

distàcco *s. m.* removal; parting (partenza); detachment (indifferenza)

distànte *agg.* distant, far-away

distànza *s. f.* distance

distanziàre *v. tr.* to space out; to leave behind (sport)

distàre *v. intr.* to be distant, to be ... away

distèndere *v. tr.* to spread; to stretch (out) (parti del corpo); to relax (rilassare) • *rifl.* to lie down, to relax

distensióne *s. f.* stretching out; relaxation (rilassamento)

distésa *s. f.* expanse, stretch

distillàre *v. tr.* to distill

distillàto *s. m.* distillate

distillería *s. f.* distillery

distìnguere *v. tr.* to distinguish; to mark (contrassegnare) • *intr. pron.* to distinguish oneself

distintìvo *agg.* distinctive • *s. m.* badge

distògliere *v. tr.* to dissuade; to sway (distrarre)

distòrcere *v. tr.* to distort, to twist

distorsióne *s. f.* distortion; sprain (*med.*)

distràrre *v. tr.* to distract; to entertain (divertire) • *intr. pron.* to amuse oneself

distrattaménte *avv.* absent-mindedly

distràtto *agg.* absent-minded

distrazióne *s. f.* absent-mindedness; distraction (divertimento)

distribuíre *v. tr.* to distribute

distributóre *s. m.* dispenser; – **di benzina** petrol pump, gasoline pump

districàrsi *v. rifl.* to disentangle oneself; to manage (cavarsela)

distrùggere *v. tr.* to destroy

distruzióne *s. f.* destruction

disturbàre *v. tr.* to bother, to disturb, to trouble • *rifl.* to bother, to trouble

distùrbo *s. m.* bother, trouble, inconvenience

disubbidíre *v. intr.* to disobey; to break (trasgredire)

disuguagliànza *s. f.* inequality, uneveness

disumàno *agg.* inhuman

ditàle *s. m.* thimble

ditàta *s. f.* finger-print

díto *s. m.* finger; toe (del piede)

dittatóre *s. m.* dictator

dittatùra *s. f.* dictatorship

diurètico *agg.* diuretic

diùrno *agg.* day-time (*attr.*)

divagàre *v. intr.* to stray, to digress

divàno *s. m.* sofa, divan

divàrio *s. m.* discrepancy, gap

diventàre *v. intr.* to become; to turn (con *agg.*); to grow (con *agg.*); to get (con *agg.*)

divèrbio *s. m.* altercation, squabble

divèrgere *v. intr.* to diverge

diversaménte *avv.* differently, otherwise

diversità *s. f.* diversity, difference

diversìvo *s. m.* diversion, distraction

divèrso *agg.* unlike, different

divertènte *agg.* amusing, funny

divertiménto *s. m.* fun, amusement

divertíre *v. tr.* to amuse, to entertain • *rifl.* to amuse oneself, to have fun, to enjoy oneself

divìdere *v. tr.* to divide; to split (scindere); to share (condividere); to part (separare) • *rifl.* to separate, to divide

divièto *s. m.* prohibition; – **d'accesso** no entry; – **di parcheggio** no parking

divinità *s. f.* divinity

divíno *agg.* divine

divìsa *s. f.* uniform

divisìbile *agg.* divisible

divisióne *s. f.* division; sharing out (spartizione)

divisionìsmo *s. m.* pointillism

divìsmo *s. m.* star system; showing off (esibizionismo)

divìso *agg.* divided

dìvo *s. m.* star

divoràre *v. tr.* to devour, to eat up

divorziàre *v. intr.* to divorce

divorziáto *agg.* divorced

divòrzio *s. m.* divorce

divulgàre *v. tr.* to divulge, to spread

divulgativo *agg.* popular

dizionàrio *s. m.* dictionary

dizióne *s. f.* diction

dòccia *s. f.* shower; **fare la** – to take a shower

docènte *agg.* teaching • *s. m. e f.* teacher

docènza *s. f.* teaching

dòcile *agg.* docile, meek

documentàbile *agg.* documentable

documentàre *v. tr.* to document • *rifl.* to gather information

documentàrio *s. m.* documentary

documénto *s. m.* document, record; **– di identità** papers

dogàna *s. f.* customs; **dichiarazione per la** – customs declaration; **pagare la** – to pay duty

doganière *s. m.* customs officer

dògma *s. m.* dogma

dogmàtico *agg.* dogmatic

dólce *agg.* sweet; soft (di materia); fresh (di acqua) • *s. m.* sweets *pl.*; cake (torta)

dolciàstro *agg.* sweetish

dolcificànte *s. m.* sweetener

dòllaro *s. m.* dollar; buck (*fam.*)

doloránte *agg.* aching

dolóre *s. m.* pain, ache; sorrow (morale)

doloróso *agg.* painful; sorrowful; sad

dolóso *agg.* fraudulent; **incendio** – arson

domànda *s. f.* question, query; request (richiesta)

domandàre *v. tr.* to ask for (per ottenere q. c.); to demand (esigere)

domàni *avv.* tomorrow • *s. m.* tomorrow, (the) next day, (the) following day

domatóre *s. m.* tamer

doménica *s. f.* Sunday

domèstico *agg.* domestic; home (*attr.*)

domicìlio *s. m.* domicile; **consegna a** – home delivery

dominànte *agg.* dominant, prevailing

dominàre *v. tr.* to dominate • *intr.* to overlook (sovrastare)

dominatóre *s. m.* dominator, ruler

dominazióne *s. f.* domination, rule

donàre *v. tr.* to give (as a present)

donatóre *s. m.* donor, giver; **– di sangue** blood donor

dondolàre *v. intr. e rifl.* to swing

dònna *s. f.* woman

dóno *s. m.* gift, present

dópo *avv.* after, afterwards, then; later (più tardi) • *prep.* after, beyond, past; since (a partire da) • *cong.* after, when

dopobàrba *s. m. inv.* aftershave (lotion)

dopodomàni *avv.* the day after tomorrow

dopoguèrra *s. m. inv.* post-war period

dopoprànzo *avv.* after lunch

doposci *s. m.* après-ski shoes

doppiàggio *s. m.* dubbing

doppiatóre *s. m.* dubber

dóppio *agg.* double; twofold (*pred.*) • *s. m.* double; doubles (*sport*); twice (*mat.*) • *avv.* double

doppióne *s. m.* doublet

doppiopètto *s. m.* double-breasted jacket

doràto *agg.* gilt; golden (color d'oro)

dòrico *agg.* Doric

dormiglióne *s. m.* sleepy-head

dormire *v. intr.* to sleep, to be asleep

dormitòrio *s. m.* dormitory; **– pubblico** doss house (*fam.*)

dorsàle *s. f.* ridge • *agg.* dorsal; **spina** – backbone

dòrso *s. m.* back; spine (di libro)

dosàggio *s. m.* dosage

dosàre *v. tr.* to dose, to measure out

dòse *s. f.* dose; amount (di un ingrediente)

dòsso *s. m.* hump

dotazióne *s. f.* endowment; outfit (attrezzatura)

dòte *s. f.* dowry, endowment; gift (pregio)

dòtto *agg.* learned

dottóre *s. m.* doctor, physician

dottrìna *s. f.* doctrine

dóve *avv.* where

dovére *v. intr.* must; to have to, to be to; shall, should, ought to (al condizionale) • *s. m.* duty

dovùnque *avv.* everywhere, anywhere, wherever

dozzìna *s. f.* dozen

dozzinàle *agg.* cheapish

dràgo *s. m.* dragon

dràmma *s. m.* play, drama; tragedy (*fig.*)

drammàtico *agg.* dramatic

drammaturgo *s. m.* playwright, dramatist

drappéggio *s. m.* drapery

dritto *agg.* straight, upright; cunning (astuto)

drizza *s. f.* halyard

dròga *s. f.* drug, dope (*fam.*); spice (spezie)

drogàto *s. m.* drug addict

droghería *s. f.* grocery

dromedàrio *s. m.* dromedary

dualismo *s. m.* dualism

dùbbio *agg.* doubtful, dubious, questionable
  • *s. m.* doubt; **senza** – no doubt, without
  doubt
dubitàre *v. intr.* to doubt; to suspect (temere);
  to distrust (diffidare)
dùca *s. m.* duke
ducàto *s. m.* dukedom, duchy
duchéssa *s. f.* duchess
duecentésco *agg.* thirteenth-century (*attr.*)
duèllo *s. m.* duel
dùna *s. f.* dune §
dùnque *cong. e avv.* so, therefore, then
dùo *s. m. inv.* duo, duet
duòmo *s. m.* cathedral
duplicazióne *s. f.* duplication

dùplice *agg.* double, twofold
duraménte *avv.* roughly, toughly; hard (in
  modo duro)
durànte *prep.* during, in; throughout (per un
  intero periodo)
duràre *v. intr.* to last; to last out (resistere); to
  keep (conservarsi)
duràta *s. f.* duration, length; wear (di stoffa,
  ecc.)
duratùro *agg.* lasting, sound; fast (di colore)
durévole *agg.* lasting, durable; **articoli dure-
  voli** durables
durézza *s. f.* hardness, toughness
dùro *agg.* hard, tough; stiff (di meccanismo)
dùttile *agg.* ductile, pliable

215

E

e *cong.* and

èbano *s. m.* ebony

ebbène *cong.* well

ebbrézza *s. f.* intoxication, drunkenness

ebollizióne *s. f.* boiling

ebràico *agg.* Hebrew, Hebraic, Jewish • *s. m.* Hebrew

ebúrneo *agg.* ivory (*attr.*)

ecatómbe *s. f.* hecatomb; mass slaughter (*fig.*)

eccedènte *agg.* excess (*attr.*) • *s. m.* excess, surplus

eccellènte *agg.* excellent, first-rate

eccèllere *v. intr.* to excel

eccèlso *agg.* sublime

eccèntrico *agg.* eccentric

eccepire *v. tr.* to object

eccessivo *agg.* excessive

eccèsso *s. m.* excess, surplus

eccètera *loc.* et cetera, etc., and so on

eccètto *prep.* except (for), but; – **che** unless

eccezionàle *agg.* exceptional

eccezionalménte *avv.* exceptionally

ecchimosi *s. f.* ecchymosis, bruise

eccidio *s. m.* slaughter

eccitàbile *agg.* excitable

eccitànte *agg.* exciting

eccitàre *v. tr.* to excite, to turn on (*fam.*) • *intr. pron.* to get excited, to be turned on

ecclesiàstico *agg.* ecclesiastic, clerical

ècco *avv.* here (qui); there (là)

eccóme *avv.* indeed!, sure!

echeggiàre *v. intr.* to echo (with)

eclèttico *agg.* eclectic

eclettismo *s. m.* eclecticism

eclissàre *v. tr.* to eclipse

eclissi *s. f.* eclipse

eclittico *agg.* ecliptic

èco *s. m. e f.* echo

ecologia *s. f.* ecology

ecològico *agg.* ecological

economia *s. f.* economy, saving; economics *pl.* (*v. al sing.*) (scienza)

económico *agg.* economical, cheap; economic (che riguarda l'economia)

economista *s. m. e f.* economist

economizzàre *v. intr.* to economize

ecosistèma *s. m.* ecosystem

ecuménico *agg.* (o)ecumenical

eczéma *s. m.* eczema

edèma *s. m.* (o)edema

édera *s. f.* ivy

edicola *s. f.* news-stand, kiosk, bookstall; niche (*arch.*)

edificàbile *agg.* building (*attr.*)

edificàre *v. tr.* to build

edificio *s. m.* building

edilizio *agg.* building (*attr.*)

editóre *s. m.* publisher

editoriàle *s. m.* editorial

editto *s. m.* edict

edizióne *s. f.* edition

edonismo *s. m.* hedonism

educàre *v. tr.* to educate; to bring up (allevare)

educativo *agg.* educational

educazióne *s. f.* education; manners *pl.*, politeness (buone maniere)

efèbico *agg.* ephebic

effeméride *s. f.* ephemeris, almanac

effeminàto *agg.* effeminate, campy (*fam.*)

efferàto *agg.* ferocious, savage

effervescènte *agg.* sparkling, fizzy

effettivaménte *avv.* really, actually

effettivo *agg.* real, actual

effètto *s. m.* effect; **effetti personali** personal belongings

effettuàbile *agg.* practicable

effettuàre *v. tr.* to effect, to carry out

efficàce *agg.* effective

efficàcia *s. f.* effectiveness, efficacy

efficiènte *agg.* efficient

efficiènza *s. f.* efficiency

effigie *s. f.* effigy

effimero *agg.* ephemeral

efflùvio *s. m.* scent, effluvium

effrazióne *s. f.* effraction, burglary

effusióne *s. f.* effusion

egemonia *s. f.* hegemony

egittologia *s. f.* Egyptology

egizio *agg.* Egyptian

egocèntrico *agg.* egocentric, self-centred

egoismo *s. m.* selfishness

egoista *s. m. e f.* egoist

egrègio *agg.* remarkable; – **signore** dear sir

elaboràre *v. tr.* to work out, to elaborate; to process (dati)

elargizióne *s. f.* donation

elasticità *s. f.* elasticity, flexibility

elàstico *agg.* elastic • *s. m.* rubber band

elefànte *s. m.* elephant

elegànte *agg.* smart, elegant, dressy

elèggere *v. tr.* to elect; to appoint (nominare)

elegìaco *agg.* elegiac

elementàre *agg.* elementary

eleménto *s. m.* element; constituent (componente)

elemòsina *s. f.* alms

elencàre *v. tr.* to list

elènco *s. m.* list; – **telefonico** telephone directory

elettoràle *agg.* electoral

elettóre *s. m.* elector, voter

elettràuto *s. m. inv.* car electrician; car electrical repairs (officina)

elettricìsta *s. m.* electrician

elettricità *s. f.* electricity

elèttrico *agg.* electric; **centrale elettrica** power station

elettrizzànte *agg.* electrifying, thrilling

elettrocardiogràmma *s. m.* electrocardiogram

elettrodomèstico *s. m.* appliance, household

elettroencefalogràmma *s. m.* electroencephalogram

elettromagnètico *agg.* electromagnetic

elettrònico *agg.* electronic

elettrotècnico *s. m.* electrotechnician

elevàre *v. tr. e intr. pron.* to raise

elezióne *s. f.* election

èlica *s. f.* propeller

elicòttero *s. m.* helicopter

eliminàre *v. tr.* to eliminate

elioterapìa *s. f.* heliotherapy

elipòrto *s. m.* heliport

elisabettiàno *agg.* Elizabethan

elitàrio *agg.* elitist

ellènico *agg.* Hellenic

ellenìstico *agg.* Hellenistic

ellìttico *agg.* elliptic

élmo *s. m.* helmet

elògio *s. m.* praise

eloquènte *agg.* eloquent

elucubrazióne *s. f.* elucubration

elusìvo *agg.* elusive

emaciàto *agg.* emaciated

emanàre *v. tr.* to exhale; to issue (emettere) • *intr.* to emanate, to issue (from)

emancipazióne *s. f.* emancipation

emarginàre *v. tr.* to marginalize

ematòlogo *s. m.* haematologist

emblemàtico *agg.* emblematic

embolìa *s. f.* embolism

embrióne *s. m.* embryo

emergènte *agg.* emergent

emergènza *s. f.* emergency

emèrgere *v. intr.* to emerge

emersióne *s. f.* emersion

eméttere *v. tr.* to utter (voce); to give out (calore, ecc.); to issue (fin., leg.)

emettitóre *s. m.* emitter

emicrània *s. f.* migraine

emigrànte *s. m. e f.* emigrant

emigràre *v. intr.* to emigrate

emigrazióne *s. f.* emigration

eminènte *agg.* eminent

emiràto *s. m.* emirate

emisfèro *s. m.* hemisphere

emissióne *s. f.* issue; emission (di calore, ecc.)

emorragìa *s. f.* haemorrhage

emorròidi *s. f. pl.* piles

emostàtico *agg.* haemostatic

emotìvo *agg.* emotional

emottìsi *s. f.* haemoptysis

emozionànte *agg.* exciting

empìrico *agg.* empiric

empòrio *s. m.* general shop, stores *pl.*

emulàre *v. tr.* to emulate

èmulo *s. m.* emulator

emulsióne *s. f.* emulsion

enciclopedìa *s. f.* encyclop(a)edia

encomiàbile *agg.* praiseworthy

endèmico *agg.* endemic

endocrinòlogo *s. m.* endocrinologist

endovenósa *s. f.* intravenous injection

energètico *agg.* energetic; energy (*attr.*)

energìa *s. f.* energy; power (elettrica, idraulica)

ènfasi *s. f.* emphasis, stress

enfàtico *agg.* emphatic

enfisèma *s. m.* emphysema

enìgma *s. m.* enigma; riddle (indovinello)

enigmàtico *agg.* enigmatic

enigmìstica *s. f.* puzzles *pl.*

ennèsimo *agg.* nth

enològico *agg.* oenological

enórme *agg.* enormous, huge

ènte *s. m.* corporation, body, agency

entràmbi *agg. e pron.* both

entràre v. intr. to go in, to come in, to enter

entràta s. f. entrance, way in; entry (ingresso); income (reddito)

entrotèrra s. m. inv. inland

entusiasmàre v. tr. to thrill, to delight, to stir • intr. pron. to enthuse over

entusiàsmo s. m. enthusiasm

entusiàsta agg. enthusiastic

enumeràre v. tr. to enumerate

enunciàre v. tr. to enounce

enurèsi s. f. enuresis

eòlico agg. aeolian

epàtico agg. hepatic; liver (attr.); **colica epatica** liver attack

epatite s. f. hepatitis

epicèntro s. m. epicentre

èpico agg. epic

epicureìsmo s. m. Epicureanism; epicurism (modo di vivere)

epidemìa s. f. epidemic

epidèmico agg. epidemic(al)

epidèrmico agg. epidermic

epìgono s. m. imitator, follower

epìgrafe s. f. epigraph

epilessìa s. f. epilepsy

epìlogo s. m. epilogue

episcopàle agg. episcopal

episòdio s. m. episode

epistàssi s. f. epistaxis

epitàffio s. m. epitaph

epìteto s. m. epithet

època s. f. epoch, age

epònimo agg. eponymous • s. m. eponym

epopèa s. f. epic (poem), epos

eppùre cong. and yet, nevertheless

epurazióne s. f. expulsion; purge (politica)

equatóre s. m. equator

equatoriàle agg. equatorial

equèstre agg. equestrian; **circo** – circus

equidistànte agg. equidistant

equilibràto agg. balanced; level-headed (fig.)

equilibratùra s. f. balancing

equilìbrio s. m. balance

equìno agg. equine; horse (attr.); **carne equina** horse heat; **razza equina** breed of horses

equinòzio s. m. equinox

equipaggiaménto s. m. equipment, outfit

equipaggiàre v. tr. to equip • rifl. to equip oneself

equipàggio s. m. crew

equitazióne s. f. riding

equivalènte agg. equivalent

equivalére v. intr. to be equivalent (to), to be the same (as)

equivocàre v. intr. to misunderstand, to mistake

equìvoco agg. equivocal; dubious (sospetto) • s. m. misunderstanding

èra s. f. era, age

èrba s. f. grass; herb (medicinale)

erbàrio s. m. herbarium

erbìvoro agg. herbivorous

erède s. m. e f. heir m., heiress f.

eredità s. f. inheritance, heritage; heredity (biologica)

ereditàre v. tr. to inherit

ereditàrio agg. hereditary

eremìta s. m. hermit

èremo s. m. hermitage

eresìa s. f. heresy

erètico agg. heretical

erètto agg. erect, upright

ergàstolo s. m. life sentence

èrica s. f. heather

erìgere v. tr. to erect, to raise; to build (costruire)

eritèma s. m. erythema; – **solare** sun-rash

ermafrodito agg. hermaphrodite

èrnia s. f. hernia

eròe s. m. hero

erogatóre s. m. dispenser

eròico agg. heroic

erosióne s. f. erosion

eròtico agg. erotic

erotìsmo s. m. erotism

erróre s. m. mistake, error

erudìto s. m. scholar

eruzióne s. f. eruption; rash (med.)

esacerbàre v. tr. to exacerbate

esageràre v. tr. e intr. to exaggerate, to overdo

esagerazióne s. f. exaggeration

esagonàle agg. hexagonal

esalàre v. tr. to exhale

esalazióne s. f. exhalation

esaltàre v. tr. to exalt; to thrill (entusiasmare)

esàme s. m. examination, exam, test

esaminàre v. tr. to examine

esasperàre v. tr. to exasperate • intr. pron. to become exasperated

esàtto agg. exact; accurate (preciso)

esaudìre v. tr. to fulfil

esauriènte agg. exhaustive

esaurìre v. tr. to exhaust • rifl. to get exhausted; **esaurito** out of print (di libro)

esàusto *agg.* exhausted, worn out

esautoràre *v. tr.* to downgrade

esbórso *s. m.* disbursement

ésca *s. f.* bait

escatològico *agg.* eschatologic

esclamàre *v. tr. e intr.* to exclaim, to cry (out)

esclùdere *v. tr.* to exclude, to leave out • *rifl. rec.* to annul each other

esclusivaménte *avv.* exclusively

esclusivo *agg.* exclusive

escogitàre *v. tr.* to contrive, to devise

escoriazióne *s. f.* excoriation, graze

escursióne *s. f.* excursion; range (*meteor.*)

escursionismo *s. m.* touring; hiking (a piedi)

esecuzióne *s. f.* execution, performance

esèdra *s. f.* exedra

eseguìre *v. tr.* to execute, to carry out, to perform

esèmpio *s. m.* example, instance; **per** - for example, for instance

esemplàre *agg.* exemplary; model (*attr.*) • *s. m.* specimen; model (modello); sample (campione)

esemplificazióne *s. f.* exemplification

esènte *agg.* exempt, free

esercitàre *v. tr.* to practise; to train (allenare); to exercise (il potere, ecc.) • *rifl.* to practise

esèrcito *s. m.* army

esercìzio *s. m.* exercise; practice (di una professione); - **fìsico** physical training

esibìre *v. tr.* to exhibit, to show • *rifl.* to show off; to perform (teatro)

esigènte *agg.* exacting, demanding

esigènza *s. f.* demand, need

esigere *v. tr.* to demand, to require; to exact (pretendere)

esìguo *agg.* exiguous, scanty

esilarànte *agg.* exhilarating

esìle *agg.* slender; faint (debole)

esìlio *s. m.* exile

esistènte *agg.* existing

esistènza *s. f.* existence

esìstere *v. intr.* to exist, to be

esitàre *v. intr.* to hesitate

èsito *s. m.* outcome, issue

èsodo *s. m.* exodus

esoneràre *v. tr.* to exonerate, to free, to extempt

esorbitànte *agg.* exorbitant

esorcizzàre *v. tr.* to exorcize

esòrdio *s. m.* start, opening

esortazióne *s. f.* exhortation

esotèrico *agg.* esoteric

esòtico *agg.* exotic

espàndere *v. tr. e intr. pron.* to expand

espansióne *s. f.* expansion

espansivo *agg.* expansive

espatriàre *v. intr.* to expatriate

espediènte *s. m.* contrivance, device, trick

esperiènza *s. f.* experience

esperiménto *s. m.* experiment; trial (prova)

espèrto *agg.* expert

espiàre *v. tr.* to expiate

espiràre *v. tr. e intr.* to expire, to breathe out

espletàre *v. tr.* to dispatch

esplicativo *agg.* explanatory, explicative

esplicito *agg.* explicit

esplòdere *v. intr.* to explode, to burst

esploràre *v. tr.* to explore

esploratóre *s. m.* explorer

esplorazióne *s. f.* exploration

esplosióne *s. f.* explosion, burst

esplosivo *agg. e s. m.* explosive

esponènte *s. m. e f.* exponent

espórre *v. tr.* to expose, to explain; to express (spiegare) • *rifl.* to expose oneself

esportàre *v. tr.* to export

esportazióne *s. f.* export

esposìmetro *s. m.* exposure meter

esposizióne *s. f.* exposure; exhibition, exposition (mostra)

espressaménte *avv.* explicitly; on purpose (apposta)

espressióne *s. f.* expression

espressionismo *s. m.* expressionism

espressivo *agg.* expressive

esprèsso *agg.* express, explicit; fast (rapido); **caffè** - espresso; **lettera** - express letter

esprìmere *v. tr.* to express • *intr. pron.* to express oneself

espròprio *s. m.* expropriation

espulsióne *s. f.* expulsion

essènza *s. f.* essence

essenziàle *agg.* essential

essenzialménte *avv.* essentially

èssere *v. intr.* to be

essiccàre *v. tr.* to dry (up); to drain (prosciugare)

èst *s. m.* east

èstasi *s. f.* ecstasy

estàte *s. f.* summer; **in** - summertime

estemporàneo *agg.* extemporary

estèndere *v. tr.* to extend, to spread, to expand • *intr. pron.* to extend, to spread, to stretch

estensióne *s. f.* extension

estenuànte *agg.* weary, exhausting

esterióre *agg.* external, outer, outward

esternaménte *avv.* externally

èstero *agg.* foreign • *s. m.* foreign countries *pl.*; **all'** - abroad

esteròfilo *agg.* xenophilous • *s. m.* xenophile

estéso *agg.* broad, extensive

estètica *s. f.* aesthetics *pl.* (*v. al sing.*)

estètico *agg.* aesthetic

estetismo *s. m.* aestheticism

estetista *s. m. e f.* beautician

estimatóre *s. m.* estimator

estinto *agg.* extinct; paid off (debito)

estintóre *s. m.* extinguisher

estirpàre *v. tr.* to extirpate

estivo *agg.* summer (*attr.*)

estòrcere *v. tr.* to extort

estradòsso *s. m.* extrados

estraìbile *agg.* extractable

estràneo *agg.* extraneous, foreign, unrelated (to) • *s. m.* stranger; outsider (non membro); foreigner (straniero)

estràrre *v. tr.* to extract; to mine (miniera)

estrazióne *s. f.* extraction; mining (miniera)

estremaménte *avv.* extremely

estremista *s. m. e f.* extremist

estremità *s. f.* extremity; end (parte estrema)

estrèmo *agg.* extreme; l'- **Oriente** the Far East

estrinseco *agg.* extrinsic

estrovèrso *agg.* extroverted

estuàrio *s. m.* estuary

esuberànte *agg.* exuberant

esulàre *v. intr.* to lie outside

èsule *s. m. e f.* exile

esultàre *v. intr.* to exult

età *s. f.* age; **mezz'** - middle age

etèreo *agg.* ethereal

eternaménte *avv.* eternally

eternità *s. f.* eternity

etèrno *agg.* eternal

eterodòsso *agg.* heterodox

eterogèneo *agg.* heterogeneous

eterosessuàle *agg.* heterosexual

ètica *s. f.* ethics *pl.* (*v. al sing.*)

ètichétta *s. f.* label; etiquette (cerimoniale)

ètico *agg.* ethical

etilismo *s. m.* alcoholism

etimologìa *s. f.* etymology

ètnico *agg.* ethnic

etnologìa *s. f.* ethnology

etrùsco *agg.* Etruscan

èttaro *s. m.* hectare

eufemistico *agg.* euphemistic

euforìa *s. f.* euphoria

euristico *agg.* heuristic

europeìsmo *s. m.* Europeanism

europèo *agg.* European

eurovisióne *s. f.* Eurovision

eutanasìa *s. f.* euthanasia

evacuàre *v. tr.* to evacuate

evàdere *v. intr.* to escape, to get away • *tr.* to evade, to carry out (sbrigare)

evangèlico *agg.* gospel (*attr.*); evangelical

evaporàre *v. intr.* to evaporate

evasióne *s. f.* escape, get-away

eveniènza *s. f.* event, eventuality

evènto *s. m.* event

eventuàle *agg.* possible

eventualménte *avv.* in case

evidènte *agg.* evident, plain

evitàre *v. tr.* to avoid; to escape (sfuggire a)

èvo *s. m.* epoch, ages *pl.*; **il Medio** - the Middle Ages

evolutìvo *agg.* evolutive

evoluzióne *s. f.* evolution

evvìva *inter.* long live!, hurrah!

extraeuropèo *agg.* non-European

extraterrèstre *agg.* extraterrestrial

F

fabbisógno *s. m.* needs *pl.*, requirements *pl.*

fàbbrica *s. f.* factory, works, mill

fabbricáre *v. tr.* to manufacture, to produce; to build (costruire)

fàbbro *s. m.* smith

facchino *s. m.* porter

fàccia *s. f.* face

facciàta *s. f.* front, façade, face; page (pagina)

facèzia *s. f.* witty remark, joke

fachiro *s. m.* fakir

fàcile *agg.* easy, simple; likely (probabile)

facilitàre *v. tr.* to make (st.) easy

facilitazióne *s. f.* facilitation; facility (agevolazione)

facoltà *s. f.* faculty; power, right (potere); department, faculty (di università)

facoltativo *agg.* optional; **fermata facoltativa** request stop

facoltóso *agg.* well-off, well-to-do

facsimile *s. m. inv.* facsimile

fàggio *s. m.* beech

fagiàno *s. m.* pheasant

fagiolino *s. m.* string bean

fagiòlo *s. m.* bean

fagocitàre *v. tr.* to phagocytize, to absorb, to engulf, to swallow

falànge *s. f.* phalanx

falanstério *s. m.* phalanstery

fàlce *s. f.* sickle

fàlco *s. m.* hawk

fàlda *s. f.* stratum, layer; tail (di abito); brim (di cappello)

falegnàme *s. m.* carpenter

falésia *s. f.* cliff

fàlla *s. f.* leak

fallimentàre *agg.* bankruptcy (*attr.*); ruinous (disastroso)

falliménto *s. m.* bankruptcy; failure (*fig.*)

fallíre *v. intr.* to go bankrupt; to fail (*fig.*)

falò *s. m.* bonfire

falsàrio *s. m.* forger, falsifier

falsificàre *v. tr.* to falsify, to fake; to forge (firma, ecc.)

falsificazióne *s. f.* falsification; forgery (di firma, ecc.)

fàlso *agg.* false

fàma *s. f.* fame, renown; repute (reputazione)

fàme *s. f.* hunger; **avere –** to be hungry

famiglia *s. f.* family

familiàre *agg.* family (*attr.*); domestic

familiarizzàre *v. intr. e intr. pron.* to become friendly, to familiarize oneself

famóso *agg.* famous

fanalino *s. m.* tail-lamp

fanàtico *agg.* fanatic

fàngo *s. m.* mud

fannullóne *s. m.* lounger

fantascientifico *agg.* science-fiction (*attr.*)

fantasciènza *s. f.* science-fiction

fantasia *s. f.* fantasy

fantàsma *s. m.* ghost, phantom

fantàstico *agg.* fantastic, immaginary; terrific (straordinario)

fanteria *s. f.* infantry

faraónico *agg.* pharaonic

farcíre *v. tr.* to stuff, to farce

fàre *v. tr.* to do, to make; to act (agire, recitare)

farètra *s. f.* quiver

farfàlla *s. f.* butterfly

farina *s. f.* flour, meal

farinàceo *agg.* farinaceous

faringite *s. f.* pharyngitis

farmacia *s. f.* pharmacy; chemist's, drugstore (USA)

farmacista *s. m. e f.* chemist

farneticàre *v. intr.* to rave

fàro *s. m.* light (*autom.*); lighthouse (*naut.*); beacon (*aer.*)

fàrsa *s. f.* farce

fàscia *s. f.* band; bandage (*med.*)

fasciàre *v. tr.* to bandage; to wrap (avvolgere)

fasciatùra *s. f.* bandaging

fàscino *s. m.* fascination, charm

fascismo *s. m.* Fascism

fàse *s. f.* stage, phase

fastidióso *agg.* troublesome

fastóso *agg.* gorgeous

fàta *s. f.* fairy

fatalista *s. m. e f.* fatalist

fatalità *s. f.* fate, destiny, fatality

fatica s. f. labour, hard work; fatigue (stanchezza)

faticàta s. f. exertion, effort; sweat (lavoro ingrato)

faticóso agg. tiring; difficult (difficile)

fatìdico agg. fatal

fàto s. m. fate

fattìbile agg. feasible

fàtto s. m. fact, event

fattorìa s. f. farm

fattorìno s. m. page, bell hop (USA) (d'albergo); floor boy, office boy (di un ufficio)

fattùra s. f. make (fabbricazione); cut (confezione); invoice, bill (comm.)

fàuna s. f. fauna

fàuno s. m. faun

fàva s. f. broad bean

fàvola s. f. fable, story

favolóso agg. fabulous

favóre s. m. favour; **per** – please

favorévole agg. favourable

favorìtismo s. m. favouritism

fazióso agg. factious

fazzolétto s. m. handkerchief; – **di carta** paper tissue

febbràio s. m. February

fébbre s. f. temperature, fever; – **da fieno** hay-fever

febbricitànte agg. feverish

fèci s. f. pl. faeces

fécola s. f. flour; – **di patate** potato flour

fecondàre v. tr. to fecundate

fecóndo agg. fertile, fruitful, prolific

féde s. f. faith; wedding ring (anello)

fedéle agg. faithful, loyal

fedeltà s. f. faithfulness; fidelity (mus.)

fédera s. f. pillow-case

federazióne s. f. federation

fégato s. m. liver

félce s. f. fern

felìce agg. happy, pleased, glad

felicitazióni s. f. pl. congratulations

felìno agg. feline, catlike

félpa s. f. plush

fémmina s. f. female

femminìle agg. female, feminine; womanly (femmineo)

fèmore s. m. femur, thigh-bone

fenìcio agg. Phoenician

fenomenàle agg. phenomenal

fenòmeno s. m. phenomenon; wonder, case (caso)

feriàle agg. week (attr.), work (attr.), working (attr.)

ferìmento s. m. wounding

ferìre v. tr. to wound, to injure, to hurt • rifl. to hurt oneself, to wound oneself

ferìta s. f. wound, injury

feritóia s. f. loop-hole

fermàglio s. m. clasp, clip

fermàre v. tr. e intr. pron. to stop, to halt

fermàta s. f. stop, halt, stop-over; – **obbligatoria** regular stop; **divieto di** – no stopping

fermentazióne s. f. fermentation

férmo agg. firm, still; steady (stabile); stationary (di veicolo)

férmo pòsta loc. avv. poste restante, general delivery (USA)

feróce agg. ferocious, fierce, wild

ferragósto s. m. mid-August holiday(s)

ferraménta s. f. hardware; **negozio di** – hardware store

férro s. m. iron; knitting-needle (da calza)

ferrovìa s. f. railway, railroad

ferroviàrio agg. railway (attr.)

ferrovière s. m. railwayman, trainman

fèrtile agg. fertile, fruitful

fertilizzànte agg. fertilizing • s. m. fertilizer

fesserìa s. f. nonsense; foolishness (comportamento)

fessùra s. f. fissure; slot (per gettone)

fèsta s. f. feast; holiday (vacanza); party (ricevimento)

festeggiaménto s. m. celebration

festeggiàre v. tr. to celebrate

festività s. f. festivity; – **civile** public holiday

festìvo agg. holiday (attr.)

feticismo s. m. fetishism

fétta s. f. slice; – **di torta** piece of cake

feudàle agg. feudal

feudalésimo s. m. feudalism

fèudo s. m. fief, feud

fiàba s. f. fairy-tale

fiabésco agg. fairy; fairy-tale (attr.)

fiàcca s. f. weariness

fiàcco agg. weary, slack

fiàccola s. f. torch

fiàmma s. f. flame

fiammàta s. f. blaze, flare

fiammìfero s. m. match

fiammìngo agg. Flemish • s. m. Fleming

fiancàta s. f. side, flank

fiancheggiàre v. tr. to flank, to line; to support (spalleggiare)

fiànco s. m. side, flank

fiàto s. m. breath

fibbia s. f. buckle

fibra s. f. fibre; staple (tessile)

fico s. m. fig

fidanzaménto s. m. engagement

fidanzàto agg. engaged • s. m. fiancé

fidàrsi v. intr. pron. to trust

fidàto agg. trustworthy, reliable

fidùcia s. f. confidence, reliance, trust

fienìle s. m. barn

fièno s. m. hay

fièra s. f. fair; wild beast (zool.); – **campionaria** trade fair

fierìstico agg. fair (attr.)

figlia s. f. daughter

figlio s. m. son

figùra s. f. figure; picture (illustrazione); **che –!** what a disgrace!

figuràccia s. f. sorry figure

figurativo agg. figurative

fila s. f. line, file, row, queue; **fare la –** to queue (up)

filàntropo s. m. philanthropist

filàre v. tr. to spin

filarmònica s. f. philharmonic society

filastròcca s. f. rigmarole

filatelìa s. f. philately

filifórme agg. filiform

filigràna s. f. filigree; watermark (della carta)

film s. m. inv. movie, film, picture

filmàre v. tr. to film, to shoot

filo s. m. thread; wire (di metallo)

filologìa s. f. philology

filosofìa s. f. philosophy

filosòfico agg. philosophic

filòsofo s. m. philosopher

filtràre v. tr. to filter, to strain

filtro s. m. filter

finàle agg. final • s. m. end • s. f. ending, finals pl.

finalìsta s. m. e f. finalist

finalità s. f. aim, purpose, end

finalménte avv. at last, in the end

finànza s. f. finance

finanziaménto s. m. financing, funds pl.

finanziàrio agg. financial

finché cong. until, till; as long as (per tutto il tempo che)

fine s. f. end • agg. fine; refined (raffinato)

finèstra s. f. window

finestrino s. m. window

fìngere v. intr. to pretend, to feign

finìre v. tr. to finish, to end • intr. to end, to end up; to stop (smettere); to finish up (esaurirsi)

finitùra s. f. finish

fìno prep. until, till, up to (di tempo); as far as (di luogo) • avv. even

finòcchio s. m. fennel

finóra avv. till now, up to now, yet

finzióne s. f. pretence, make-believe

fiòcco s. m. bow; flake (di neve); jib (naut.)

fiòcina s. f. harpoon

fioràio s. m. florist

fiòrdo s. m. fiord

fióre s. m. flower; blossom (di albero da frutto); clubs pl. (carte da gioco); **un mazzo di fiori** a bunch of flowers

fiorènte agg. blooming

fiorièra s. f. flower box

fiorìre v. intr. to flower, to blossom, to bloom

fioritùra s. f. flowering, blooming

firma s. f. signature

firmaménto s. m. firmament

firmàre v. tr. to sign

fiscàle agg. fiscal; tax (attr.)

fischiàre v. intr. to whistle • tr. to whistle; to boo (per disapprovazione)

fischio s. m. whistle; hiss, hoot (di disapprovazione)

fisco s. m. revenue; tax office (ufficio delle imposte)

fìsica s. f. physics pl. (v. al sing.)

fìsico agg. physical

fisiològico agg. physiologic

fisionomìsta s. m. e f. physiognomist

fisioterapìa s. f. physiotherapy

fisioterapìsta s. m. e f. physiotherapist

fissàre v. tr. to fix; to fasten (fermare); to book (prenotare); to stare at (guardare) • intr. pron. to settle (stabilirsi); to insist (ostinarsi)

fissazióne s. f. fixing; obsession (idea ossessiva)

fisso agg. fixed, steady

fittìzio agg. fictitious

fiumàna s. f. stream, flood

fiùme s. m. river

fiutàre v. tr. to smell, to sniff

flagellazióne s. f. flagellation, scourging

flagèllo s. m. scourge

flanèlla s. f. flannel

flàuto s. m. flute

flèbo s. m. phleboclysis

flemmàtico agg. phlegmatic; cool (fam.)

flessìbile agg. flexible, supple

flessuóso agg. flexuous

flèttere *v. tr. e rifl.* to bend
flogòsi *s. f.* phlogosis
flòra *s. f.* flora
floreàle *agg.* floral; **stile** – liberty style
floricoltùra *s. f.* floriculture
flòrido *agg.* healthy, florid
florilègio *s. m.* anthology
flòtta *s. f.* fleet
flottìglia *s. f.* flotilla
flùido *agg.* fluid, flowing
fluorescènte *agg.* fluorescent
fluòro *s. m.* fluorine
flùsso *s. m.* flow; flux (*fis.*)
fluttuànte *agg.* fluctuating, floating
fluttuàre *v. intr.* to fluctuate, to float
fluviàle *agg.* river (*attr.*)
fobìa *s. f.* phobia
fòca *s. f.* seal
focàccia *s. f.* cake, bun
focalizzàre *v. tr.* to focus
fòce *s. f.* mouth
focolàre *s. m.* hearth; fireplace (camino)
fòdera *s. f.* lining, cover
foderàre *v. tr.* to line (internamente); to cover (esternamente)
fòggia *s. f.* manner, fashion; shape (forma)
fòglia *s. f.* leaf
fogliàme *s. m.* foliage
fogliètto *s. m.* slip of paper
fòglio *s. m.* sheet
fògna *s. f.* sewer, drain
fognatùra *s. f.* sewage; sewers *pl.*
folclóre *s. m.* folklore
folclorìstico *agg.* folk (*attr.*)
folgoràre *v. intr.* to wither; to electrocute (*elettr.*)
folgorazióne *s. f.* electrocution (*med.*)
fòlla *s. f.* crowd, swarm, throng
fòlle *agg.* mad, insane
folleggiàre *v. intr.* to frolic
follemènte *avv.* madly
follìa *s. f.* madness
fòlto *agg.* thick
fomentàre *v. tr.* to encourage; to foment; to foster
fóndaco *s. m.* warehouse
fondàle *s. m.* back-drop (*teatro*); sounding (*naut.*)
fondamentàle *agg.* fundamental, basic
fondàre *v. tr.* to found; to establish (formare) • *rifl.* to base oneself; to rely (fare affidamento)
fondatóre *s. m.* founder • *agg.* founding
fondazióne *s. f.* foundation

fondènte *agg.* melting; **caramella** – fondant; **cioccolato** – plain chocolate
fóndere *v. tr. e intr. pron.* to melt, to fuse; to blend (mescolare) • *rifl. rec.* to merge, to incorporate
fondiàrio *agg.* land (*attr.*); landed
fondìsta *s. m. e f.* long-distance runner, langlaufer (sciatore)
fóndo *s. m.* bottom; end (estremità); long distance race (*sport*) • *agg.* deep; **piatto** – soupplate
fondovàlle *s. m.* valley bottom
fonètico *agg.* phonetic
fontàna *s. f.* fountain
fónte *s. f.* source, spring; – **di energia** source of power; – **battesimale** font
foràggio *s. m.* forage, fodder
foràre *v. tr.* to pierce, to punch; – **una gomma** to get a flat tyre, to get a puncture
foratùra *s. f.* piercing; puncture (di una gomma)
fòrbice *s. f.* scissors *pl.*
fórca *s. f.* fork; gallows *pl.* (patibolo)
forchétta *s. f.* fork
forènse *agg.* forensic
forèsta *s. f.* forest
forestièro *agg.* foreign, alien • *s. m.* foreigner
forgiàre *v. tr.* to forge, to mould
fórma *s. f.* shape, form
formàggio *s. m.* cheese; – **magro** skimmed cheese; – **piccante** strong cheese
formàle *agg.* formal
formalìsmo *s. m.* formalism
formalità *s. f.* formality; **senza** – informally
formalizzàrsi *v. intr. pron.* to be too formal
formàre *v. tr.* to form, to shape, to make • *intr. pron.* to form
formazióne *s. f.* formation, forming; training (addestramento)
formìca *s. f.* ant
formicolìo *s. m.* swarming; pins and needles (intorpidimento)
formidàbile *agg.* formidable, tremendous
formóso *agg.* shapely, buxom
fòrmula *s. f.* formula
formulàrio *s. m.* formulary, form
fornàce *s. f.* furnace; kiln (laterizi)
fornàio *s. m.* baker
fornèllo *s. m.* gas ring
fórnice *s. f.* barrel-vault
fornìre *v. tr.* to supply, to provide, to furnish

• *rifl.* to provide oneself; to deal (with) (*comm.*)

fornitóre *s. m.* supplier

fórno *s. m.* oven; bakery (*negozio*)

fóro *s. m.* hole • forum, court of justice (*leg.*)

fórse *avv.* perhaps, maybe

fórte *agg.* strong; heavy (*gravoso*); hard (*duro*); deep (*di sentimenti*); loud (*di suono*) • *avv.* strongly, hard (*duramente*); loudly, loud (*di suono*); fast (*velocemente*)

fortificàre *v. tr.* to strengthen; to fortify (*mil.*)

fortificazióne *s. f.* fortification

fortíno *s. m.* blockhouse

fortùito *agg.* chance (*attr.*)

fortùna *s. f.* luck, fortune

fortunataménte *avv.* luckily

fortunàto *agg.* lucky

fòrza *s. f.* strength; force

forzàre *v. tr.* to force, to compel; to break open (*aprire con la forza*) • *intr.* to be too tight

forzataménte *avv.* forcedly, of necessity

forzatùra *s. f.* forcing

forzière *s. m.* coffer

fóschia *s. f.* haze, mist

fosforescènte *agg.* phosphorescent

fòssa *s. f.* pit, hollow

fossàto *s. m.* ditch, moat

fòssile *agg.* fossil (*attr.*); fossilized

fossilizzàrsi *v. intr. pron.* to fossilize

fotocòpia *s. f.* photocopy

fotogènico *agg.* photogenic

fotografàre *v. tr.* to photograph, to take a picture

fotografìa *s. f.* photo(graph)

fotogràfico *agg.* photographic; **macchina fotografica** camera

fotògrafo *s. m.* photographer

fotomodèlla *s. f.* model, cover-girl

fotorepòrter *s. m. inv.* press-photographer

fra *prep.* between, among (*fra più di due*); amid, in the middle of (*in mezzo a*); within, in (*tempo*); of (*partitivo*)

fracàsso *s. m.* din, racket

fràdicio *agg.* wet through, soaked; **ubriaco –** dead drunk

fràgile *agg.* fragile; frail (*fig.*)

fràgola *s. f.* strawberry

fraintèndere *v. tr.* to misunderstand

frammentàrio *agg.* fragmentary

frammènto *s. m.* fragment; splinter (*scheggia*)

frammezzàre *v. tr.* to interpolate

fràna *s. f.* landslide

franàre *v. intr.* to slide down; to collapse (*di edificio*)

francaménte *avv.* frankly, openly

francése *agg.* French • *s. m. e f.* Frenchman *m.*; Frenchwoman *f.*; French (*lingua*)

franchìgia *s. f.* immunity, franchise

francobòllo *s. m.* stamp

francòfono *agg.* Francophone

frangènte *s. m.* breaker (*onda*); predicament (*situazione difficile*)

fràngia *s. f.* fringe

frangiflùtti *s. m.* breakwater

franóso *agg.* subject to landslides

frantóio *s. m.* oil press

frappé *s. m.* milk-shake

frappórre *v. tr. e rifl.* to interpose

fràse *s. f.* sentence, phrase

fraseològico *agg.* phraseologic

fràssino *s. m.* ash

frastagliàto *agg.* indented; fretted (*di roccia*)

frastornàto *agg.* bewildered

fràte *s. m.* friar, monk

fratèllo *s. m.* brother

fraternizzàre *v. intr.* to fraternize

frattàglie *s. f. pl.* chitterlings

frattànto *avv.* meanwhile

frattùra *s. f.* break, fracture

frazionàre *v. tr. e intr. pron.* to split up

fraziόne *s. f.* fraction; hamlet (*di un comune*)

fréccia *s. f.* arrow, dart

freddaménte *avv.* coldly

fréddo *agg.* cold, cool • *s. m.* cold, chill

fregatùra *s. f.* cheat, swindle

frégio *s. m.* frieze (*arch.*); decoration (*ornamento*)

frèmere *v. intr.* to tremble, to quiver; to throb (*palpitare*)

frenàre *v. tr.* to brake; to check (*fig.*) • *intr.* to brake • *rifl.* to control oneself

frenàta *s. f.* braking

frenètico *agg.* frantic, frenzied

frequentàre *v. tr.* to attend

frequènte *agg.* frequent

frequenteménte *avv.* frequently, often

frequènza *s. f.* frequency, frequence; attend-'ance (*assiduità*)

freschézza *s. f.* freshness

frésco *agg.* fresh; cool, chilly (*di temperatura*) • *s. m.* coolness

frétta *s. f.* hurry, haste

frettolóso *agg.* hasty, hurried

friàbile *agg.* friable

friggere *v. tr.* to fry

frigorifero *s. m.* fridge
frittata *s. f.* omelette
fritto *agg.* fried
frittùra *s. f.* fry
frivolo *agg.* frivolous
frizióne *s. f.* rubbing, friction; friction (*fis.*); clutch (*mecc.*)
frizzànte *agg.* fizzy, sparkling
fróde *s. f.* fraud; – **fiscale** tax-evasion
frontàle *agg.* frontal
frónte *s. f.* front
frontespizio *s. m.* frontispiece; title-page (di libro)
frontièra *s. f.* frontier, boundary
frontóne *s. m.* pediment, fronton
frónzoli *s. m. pl.* frippery *sing.*
frugàle *agg.* frugal
frugàre *v. intr.* to rummage, to ransack
fruire *v. intr.* to use, to enjoy
frullàre *v. tr.* to whip up, to whisk
frullàto *s. m.* shake
fruménto *s. m.* wheat
fruscìo *s. m.* rustle
frùsta *s. f.* whip
frustàre *v. tr.* to whip, to flog
frustrazióne *s. f.* frustration
frùtta *s. f.* fruit
fruttéto *s. m.* orchard
fruttivéndolo *s. m.* greengrocer
fucìle *s. m.* gun, rifle
fùga *s. f.* escape, flight; leak (di gas, ecc.)
fugacità *s. f.* transiency
fuggìre *v. intr.* to flee, to run away, to escape • *tr.* to avoid
fùlcro *s. m.* fulcrum (*mecc.*); heart (*fig.*)
fùlgido *agg.* shining
fulìggine *s. f.* soot
fulminànte *agg.* fulminant
fùlmine *s. m.* thunderbolt; lightning (lampo)
fulmìneo *agg.* instantaneous
fumaiòlo *s. m.* chimney
fumàre *v. intr.* to smoke
fumatóre *s. m.* smoker
fumétti *s. m. pl.* comics, cartoons
fùmo *s. m.* smoke

fumóso *agg.* smoky; obscure (*fig.*)
fùne *s. f.* rope
fùnebre *agg.* funeral (*attr.*); funereal, mournful (lugubre)
funeràle *s. m.* funeral
funeràrio *agg.* funeral (*attr.*); funerary
fùngo *s. m.* mushroom; fungus (*bot.*, *med.*); – **velenoso** toadstool
funicolàre *s. f.* funicular, cable car
funivìa *s. f.* cableway
funzionàle *agg.* functional
funzionalìsmo *s. m.* functionalism
funzionalità *s. f.* functionality
funzionaménto *s. m.* working, operation
funzionàre *v. intr.* to work, to operate; to run (*autom.*); **non –** to be out of order
funzionàrio *s. m.* official, functionary
funzióne *s. f.* function; office (carica); service (*relig.*)
fuòco *s. m.* fire
fuorché *prep.* except
fuòri *avv.* out, outside • *prep.* out, out of
fuoribórdo *s. m. inv.* outboard motor
fuoristràda *s. m. inv.* cross-country vehicle
fuoriuscìta *s. f.* discharge, emission
furbo *agg.* shrewd, sly
furènte *agg.* raging, furious
furgóne *s. m.* van
fùria *s. f.* fury, rage, haste; rush (gran fretta)
furibóndo *agg.* enraged, wrathful
furióso *agg.* furious
furóre *s. m.* fury, rage
furto *s. m.* theft
fuscèllo *s. m.* twig
fusìbile *agg.* fusible • *s. m.* fuse (*elettr.*)
fusióne *s. f.* fusion
fùso *agg.* fused
fusolièra *s. f.* fuselage
fustàgno *s. m.* fustian
fustigazióne *s. f.* flogging
fùsto *s. m.* stem; trunk (tronco); shaft (*arch.*); drum (recipiente)
futilità *s. f.* futility
futurìsmo *s. m.* futurism
futùro *agg. e s. m.* future

G

gabbia *s. f.* cage

gabbiàno *s. m.* sea-gull

gabinétto *s. m.* toilet, lavatory, wc; loo (*fam.*); cabinet (*politica*)

gagliardétto *s. m.* pennant

gàla *s. f.* pomp; gala; frill (trina)

galànte *agg.* gallant; love (*attr.*)

galàssia *s. f.* galaxy

galatèo *s. m.* manners *pl.*; etiquette

galeóne *s. m.* galleon

galeòtto *s. m.* convict

galèra *s. f.* galley; jail (prigione)

galleggiàre *v. intr.* to float

gallerìa *s. f.* gallery; tunnel (traforo); circle (*teatro*); balcony (*cin.*)

gallicìsmo *s. m.* Gallicism

gallìna *s. f.* hen

gàllo *s. m.* cock

galoppàre *v. intr.* to gallop

galoppatòio *s. m.* riding-track

galòppo *s. m.* gallop

gàmba *s. f.* leg

gàmbero *s. m.* crayfish

gàmbo *s. m.* stem

garage *s. m. inv.* garage

garagista *s. m. e f.* garage-hand

garantìre *v. tr.* to guarantee, to warrant • *intr. pron.* to secure oneself

garanzìa *s. f.* guaranty (*leg.*); guarantee, warrant, security (pegno)

garbàto *agg.* polite

gardènia *s. f.* gardenia

gareggiàre *v. intr.* to compete

garìtta *s. f.* sentry-box

garòfano *s. m.* carnation; **chiodi di –** cloves

gàrza *s. f.* gauze

garzóne *s. m.* boy

gas *s. m.* gas

gasòlio *s. m.* gas-oil, diesel oil

gastrìte *s. f.* gastritis

gastrointestinàle *agg.* gastroenteric

gastronomìa *s. f.* gastronomy

gastronòmico *agg.* gastronomic

gàtto *s. m.* cat

gavitéllo *s. m.* buoy

gelàre *v. tr. e intr.* to freeze, to congeal

gelatàio *s. m.* ice-cream man

gelatìna *s. f.* jelly, gel; gelatin (*chim.*)

gelàto *agg.* icy, frozen • *s. m.* ice-cream

gèlido *agg.* icy

gèlo *s. m.* cold; frost (brina)

gelosaménte *avv.* jealously

gelosìa *s. f.* jealousy

gelóso *agg.* jealous

gèlso *s. m.* mulberry

gelsomìno *s. m.* jasmin

gemellàggio *s. m.* twinning

gemèllo *agg.* twin

gèmere *v. intr.* to moan, to groan

gemìto *s. m.* moan, groan

gèmma *s. f.* gem, jewel; bud (*bot.*)

genealogìa *s. f.* genealogy

generàle *agg.* general, common • *s. m.* general

generalità *s. f.* generality

generalizzàre *v. tr.* to generalize

generalménte *avv.* generally, as a rule

generàre *v. tr.* to procreate; to produce (produrre); to beget (causare)

generatóre *s. m.* generator

generazionàle *agg.* generational

generazióne *s. f.* generation

gènere *s. m.* kind, sort; gender (*gramm.*)

genèrico *agg.* generic, general

gènero *s. m.* son-in-law

generóso *agg.* generous, liberal

gènesi *s. f.* genesis, origin

genètico *agg.* genetic

gengìva *s. f.* gum

geniàle *agg.* ingenious

genialità *s. f.* ingeniousness

gènio *s. m.* genius; genie (folletto)

genitàli *s. m. pl.* genitals, genitalia

genitóre *s. m.* father, parent; **i genitori** parents

gennàio *s. m.* January

gènte *s. f.* people, folk (*v. al pl.*)

gentìle *agg.* kind, polite; gentle (dolce)

gentilézza *s. f.* kindness; politeness (cortesia)

gentilìzio *agg.* aristocratic

genuinità *s. f.* genuineness

genuino agg. genuine, authentic
geocentrismo s. m. geocentrism
geografia s. f. geography
geográfico agg. geographic; **carta geografica** map
geologia s. f. geology
geometria s. f. geometry
geométrico agg. geometric
geórgico agg. georgic
geotérmico agg. geothermal
gerànio s. m. geranium
gerarchia s. f. hierarchy
gerárchico agg. hierarchic
gérgo s. m. slang, jargon
gérme s. m. germ
germogliare v. intr. to bud, to sprout, to germinate
germóglio s. m. bud, sprout
geroglifico s. m. hieroglyph
gèsso s. m. chalk; plaster (med., arte)
gèsta s. f. pl. deeds
gestante s. f. pregnant woman
gestazione s. f. pregnancy, gestation
gestione s. f. management
gestire v. tr. to run, to manage
gèsto s. m. gesture; deed (azione)
gestóre s. m. manager
gesuita s. m. Jesuit
gettare v. tr. to throw • rifl. to throw oneself, to flow (sfociare)
géttito s. m. yield; – **fiscale** tax revenue
gètto s. m. jet, spurt, shoot; sprout (bot.)
gettóne s. m. token, counter; – **telefonico** telephone counter
ghètto s. m. ghetto
ghiacciàio s. m. glacier
ghiacciare v. intr. e intr. pron. to freeze
ghiacciato agg. frozen
ghiàccio s. m. ice
ghiàia s. f. gravel
ghiaióso agg. gravelly
ghiànda s. f. acorn
ghiàndola s. f. gland
ghigliottina s. f. guillotine
ghiótto agg. gluttonous; appetizing (di cibo)
ghirigóro s. m. scribble
ghirlanda s. f. wreath
già avv. already; formerly (un tempo)
giàcca s. f. coat, jacket; – **a vento** wind-cheater, anorak
giacché cong. as, since
giacére v. intr. to lie
giacimento s. m. layer, body, deposit

giacobino s. m. Jacobin
giallo agg. yellow; **un libro** – a thriller
giapponése agg. e s. m. e f. Japanese
giardinàggio s. m. gardening
giardinière s. m. gardener
giardino s. m. garden; **giardini pubblici** public gardens; – **d'infanzia** kindergarten
giavellòtto s. m. javelin
gigànte s. m. giant • agg. gigantic; giant (attr.)
gigantésco agg. gigantic, huge
gigantismo s. m. gigantism
gigionismo s. m. hamming
giglio s. m. lily
ginecólogo s. m. gynaecologist
ginepràio s. m. fix, hole
ginèstra s. f. broom
gingillarsi v. intr. pron. to dawdle, to fiddle
ginnàsio s. m. gymnasium (stor.); high school
ginnàstica s. f. gymnastics pl. (v. al sing.), gym
ginòcchio s. m. knee
giocare v. tr. e intr. to play; – **d'azzardo** to gamble
giocatóre s. m. player; – **d'azzardo** gambler
giocattolo s. m. toy
gioco s. m. game, play; – **di prestigio** conjuring tricks
giocolière s. m. juggler
giocóso agg. playful, merry
gioia s. f. joy
gioiellerìa s. f. jeweller's shop, jewellery
gioièllo s. m. jewel
gioire v. intr. to rejoice (at)
giornalàio s. m. news-agent
giornale s. m. newspaper; – **radio** news; – **di bordo** log
giornalièro agg. daily; everyday (attr.)
giornalismo s. m. journalism
giornalista s. m. e f. journalist
giornalmente avv. daily
giornata s. f. day
giorno s. m. day; **buon** –! good morning!
giòstra s. f. merry-go-round, roundabout
giovamento s. m. benefit; improvement (miglioramento)
gióvane agg. young • s. m. e f. young man m., young woman f.; **i giovani** young people, the young
giovanile agg. young-looking
giovare v. intr. to be useful; to be good (for) (far bene)
giovedì s. m. Thursday
gioventù s. f. youth; young people (i giovani)

gioviàle *agg.* jovial, jolly

giovinézza *s. f.* youth

giradischi *s. m.* record-player

giràffa *s. f.* giraffe; boom (*cin., tel.*)

giramóndo *s. m. e f. inv.* globe trotter, rolling stone

giràndola *s. f.* Catherine-wheel, windmill

girànte *s. f.* impeller, rotor

giràre *v. tr.* to turn • *intr.* to turn, to spin; to wander (vagare); to circulate (circolare)

girarròsto *s. m.* spit

giravòlta *s. f.* twirl

girévole *agg.* turning, revolving; **ponte** – swing-bridge

giro *s. m.* turn, circle; circuit (circuito); tour (viaggio, percorso)

gironzolàre *v. intr.* to stroll about

girotóndo *s. m.* ring-a-ring of roses

girovagàre *v. intr.* to wander about

giróvago *s. m.* vagrant

gita *s. f.* trip, excursion

gitàno *s. m.* gipsy

gitànte *s. m. e f.* excursionist

giù *avv.* down, under; below (sotto)

giubbòtto *s. m.* jacket; – **di salvataggio** life jacket

giubiléo *s. m.* jubilee

giudicàre *v. tr. e intr.* to judge

giùdice *s. m. e f.* judge

giudiziàrio *agg.* judicial, judiciary

giudìzio *s. m.* judgment

giùgno *s. m.* June

giullàre *s. m.* jester

giùnco *s. m.* rush

giùngere *v. intr.* to arrive (at, in), to reach, to get to

giunònico *agg.* Junoesque

giùnto *s. m.* joint

giunzióne *s. f.* junction

giuraménto *s. m.* oath

giuràre *v. tr. e intr.* to swear

giurìa *s. f.* jury

giuridicaménte *avv.* juridically

giurisdizionàle *agg.* jurisdictional

giurisprudènza *s. f.* jurisprudence, law

giurìsta *s. m. e f.* jurist

giustapposizióne *s. f.* juxtaposition

giustézza *s. f.* exactness

giustificàbile *agg.* justifiable

giustificàre *v. tr.* to justify; to excuse (scusare) • *rifl.* to justify oneself; to excuse oneself (scusarsi)

giustificazióne *s. f.* justification, excuse

giustìzia *s. f.* justice

giustiziàre *v. tr.* to execute

giùsto *agg.* just; fair (equo); correct (senza errori) • *avv.* correctly (esattamente); just (proprio)

glaciàle *agg.* glacial

glàssa *s. f.* icing

glicemìa *s. f.* glycemia

glicerìna *s. f.* glycerin

glìcine *s. m.* wistaria

globàle *agg.* global, total

glòbo *s. m.* globe

glòria *s. f.* glory

glorióso *agg.* glorious

glossàrio *s. m.* glossary

glottologìa *s. f.* glottology

glucòsio *s. m.* glucose

glùteo *s. m.* gluteus

gnòmo *s. m.* gnome, goblin

goal *s. m. inv.* goal

gòbba *s. f.* hump

góccia *s. f.* drop

gocciolàre *v. intr.* to drip

godére *v. tr. e intr.* to enjoy; to be delighted

godiménto *s. m.* enjoyment, pleasure

góffo *agg.* awkward, clumsy

góla *s. f.* throat; gorge (geog.)

golétta *s. f.* schooner

golf *s. m. inv.* golf (sport); jumper, sweater

gólfo *s. m.* gulf

goliàrdico *agg.* student (attr.)

golosità *s. f.* greediness; titbit (boccone prelibato)

golóso *agg.* greedy, gluttonous

gómito *s. m.* elbow; crank (mecc.)

gomìtolo *s. m.* ball

gómma *s. f.* rubber, eraser (per cancellare); gum (resina); tyre (pneumatico)

gommapiùma *s. f.* foam-rubber

gommìsta *s. m.* tyre repairer

gommóne *s. m.* rubber dinghy

gonfiàre *v. tr.* to blow(up), to inflate

gónfio *agg.* swollen; inflated (riempito d'aria)

gonfióre *s. m.* swelling

gónna *s. f.* skirt; – **a pieghe** pleated skirt

gorgheggiàre *v. intr.* to trill

gorgogliàre *v. intr.* to gurgle

gòtico *agg.* Gothic

governànte *s. m.* governor (politica); housekeeper, nurse (di bambini)

governàre *v. tr.* to govern, to rule; to run (dirigere)

governativo agg. government (attr.), State (attr.)

govèrno s. m. government; rule (dominio)

gràcile agg. frail

gradàsso s. m. boaster

gradazióne s. f. gradation; shade (di colori)

gradévole agg. pleasant, agreeable

gradiménto s. m. liking

gradinàta s. f. steps pl.; tiers pl. (di teatro, stadio)

gradino s. m. step

gradìre v. tr. to appreciate, to like

gradito agg. pleasant; welcome (bene accetto)

gràdo s. m. degree; grade (in una graduatoria); ratio (proporzione)

graduàle agg. gradual

gradualménte avv. gradually

graduatòria s. f. classification; list (in un concorso)

graffétta s. f. staple

graffiànte agg. biting

graffiàre v. tr. to scratch

gràffio s. m. scratch

graffito s. m. graffito

grafìa s. f. handwriting

gràfica s. f. graphics pl. (v. al sing.)

graficaménte avv. graphically

gràfico agg. graphic

grammàtica s. f. grammar

gràmmo s. m. gram

gràna s. f. trouble (problema); dough (soldi)

granàio s. m. barn, granary

grànchio s. m. crab

grandàngolo s. m. wide-angle lens

grànde agg. great, big

grandézza s. f. greatness; width (ampiezza); height (altezza)

grandinàre v. intr. impers. to hail

grandinàta s. f. hail-storm

gràndine s. f. hail

grandiosità s. f. grandeur, magnificence

grandióso agg. grand, magnificent

granducàto s. m. Grand Duchy

granèllo s. m. grain; speck (di polvere)

granito s. m. granite

gràno s. m. wheat; corn, grain (cereale)

grantùrco s. m. maize; corn (USA); **pannocchia di –** corn-cob

granulóso agg. granular; granulation (attr.)

gràppolo s. m. cluster, bunch; **un – d'uva** a bunch of grapes

gràsso agg. fat; plump (paffuto) • s. m. fat, grease

gràta s. f. grill, lattice

gratificàre v. tr. to be rewarding

gratin s. m. inv. gratin

gratis avv. free, gratis

gràto agg. grateful; pleasant (gradito)

grattacièlo s. m. skyscraper

grattàre v. tr. to scratch; to scrape (raschiare) • rifl. to scratch oneself

grattugiàre v. tr. to grate

gratùito agg. free; **ingresso –** admission free

gràve agg. grave, serious; heavy (pesante); deep, low (di suono)

gravidànza s. f. pregnancy; **analisi di –** pregnancy test

gravità s. f. gravity; seriousness (importanza)

gravóso agg. burdensome; demanding (di un lavoro)

gràzia s. f. grace; favour (favore)

graziàre v. tr. to pardon (leg.)

gràzie inter. thank you!, thanks!

grazióso agg. pretty

grecìsmo s. m. Grecism

grèco agg. e s. m. Greek

gregàrio s. m. follower

grègge s. m. flock

gréggio agg. raw

grembiùle s. m. apron; smock; pinafore (da bambino)

gréto s. m. pebbly shore

grétto agg. mean, narrow-minded

gridàre v. tr. e intr. to shout, to cry, to scream

grido s. m. cry, shout, scream

grifóne s. m. griffin

grigio agg. grey

griglia s. f. grill, grate; **pesce alla –** grilled fish

grigliàta s. f. grill; **– mista** mixed grill

grillo s. m. cricket; whim (fig.)

grinta s. f. grit

grinzóso agg. wrinkled

grippàre v. intr. e intr. pron. to seize, to bind

grissino s. m. bread-stick

grondàia s. f. gutter, rain-pipe

gròsso agg. big, large, great

grossolàno agg. coarse, rough

gròtta s. f. cave

grottésco agg. grotesque

grovìglio s. m. tangle

gru s. f. crane

grùccia s. f. crutch; coat-hanger (per abiti)

grùmo s. m. clot

grùppo s. m. group; unit (mecc.)

grùzzolo s. m. hoard

guadagnàre v. tr. to earn, to gain

guadàgno s. m. gain; profits pl. (di un'azienda); earnings pl. (salario)

guadàre v. tr. to ford, to wade

guàdo s. m. ford

guaìna s. f. sheath

guàio s. m. trouble, fix

guaìto s. m. yelp

guància s. f. cheek

guanciàle s. m. pillow

guànto s. m. glove

guardacàccia s. m. inv. gamekeeper

guardàre v. tr. to look at; – **fissamente** to watch

guardaròba s. m. inv. linen-room (stanza); wardrobe (armadio); cloak-room (di un locale pubblico)

guàrdia s. f. guard; watch (azione del vigilare); policeman (poliziotto); warder (carceraria)

guardiàno s. m. keeper, warden; – **notturno** night-watchman

guardiòla s. f. porter's lodge; guard-room (mil.)

guaribile agg. curable

guarigióne s. f. recovery, cure; healing (di ferita)

guarìre v. intr. to recover; to heal (di ferita)

guarnigióne s. f. garrison

guarnìre v. tr. to trim (ornare); to garnish (cucina)

guastàre v. tr. to spoil; to ruin (rovinare)

guàsto agg. spoilt, ruined; damaged (rovinato); rotten (marcio) (mecc.); • s. m. breakdown (mecc.); damage (danno)

guazzabùglio s. m. hotch-potch

guàzzo s. m. puddle; gouache (arte)

guerreggiàre v. intr. to wage war, to fight

guerrièro s. m. warrior

guerrìglia s. f. guerrilla

gùglia s. f. spire; steeple (di campanile)

guìda s. f. guide; guide-book (libro); direction, leadership (direzione); steering (autom.)

guidàre v. tr. to drive (autom.); to guide (fare da guida); to lead (comandare)

guidatóre s. m. driver

guinzàglio s. m. lead, leash

gùscio s. m. shell

gustàre v. tr. to taste; to enjoy (apprezzare)

gùsto s. m. taste; flavour (aroma)

gustóso agg. tasty

gutturàle agg. guttural

H

hall s. f. hall, foyer, lobby (USA)

handicappàto agg. handicapped

hascisc s. m. hashish, hash (pop.)

hobbista s. m. e. f. hobbyst

hostess s. f. air-hostess, stewardess

hurrà inter. hurrah

I

iàto s. m. hiatus
ibrido agg. hybrid
icàstico agg. figurative
icòna s. f. icon
iconoclàsta agg. iconoclast
iconografìa s. f. iconography
iconogràfico agg. iconographic
idèa s. f. idea; intention (intenzione)
ideàle agg. e s. m. ideal
idealìsmo s. m. idealism
idealizzàre v. tr. to idealize
idealménte avv. ideally
ideàre v. tr. to conceive; to invent (inventare)
ideazióne s. f. ideation, invention, plan
ìdem avv. the same, idem
idèntico agg. identical
identificàbile agg. identifiable
identificàre v. tr. to identify
identità s. f. identity; carta d'– identity card
ideogràmma s. m. ideogram
ideologìa s. f. ideology
ideològico agg. ideological
idillìaco agg. idyllic
idiòma s. m. idiom
idiosincrasìa s. f. idiosyncrasy
idiozìa s. f. idiocy; nonsense (stupidaggine)
idolatrìa s. f. idolatry
ìdolo s. m. idol
idoneità s. f. fitness, capacity
idòneo agg. fit, suitable
idrànte s. m. hydrant
idratànte agg. moisturizing • s. m. moisturizer
idràulica s. f. hydraulics pl. (v. al sing.)
idràulico agg. hydraulic • s. m. plumber
idrobiologìa s. f. hydrobiology
idrocarbùro s. m. hydrocarbon
idrocoltùra s. f. hydroponics pl. (v. al sing.)
idrofobìa s. f. hydrophobia
idrògeno s. m. hydrogen
idrografìa s. f. hydrography
idrostàtico agg. hydrostatic
idrotermàle agg. hydrothermal
idrovolànte s. m. seaplane
ieràtico agg. hieratic, solemn

ièri avv. yesterday; – mattina yesterday morning; – l'altro the day before yesterday
iettatùra s. f. evil eye; bad luck (sfortuna)
igiène s. f. hygiene; ufficio d'– public-health office
igiènico agg. hygienic, sanitary; carta igienica toilet paper
ignàro agg. unaware
ignìfugo agg. fireproof
ignòbile agg. ignoble, base
ignorànte agg. ignorant, uneducated
ignorànza s. f. ignorance
ignoràre v. tr. not to know; to ignore (trascurare)
ignòto agg. unknown • s. m. (the) unknown
igròmetro s. m. hygrometer
ilarità s. f. hilarity
illazióne s. f. illation, inference
illécito agg. illicit
illegàle agg. illegal, unlawful
illegalità s. f. illegality
illegìttimo agg. illegitimate
illéso agg. unharmed; undamaged (di cose)
illetteràto agg. illiterate
illimitàto agg. boundless, unlimited
illògico agg. illogical
illùdere v. tr. to delude, to beguile • rifl. to delude oneself
illuminàre v. tr. to light up; to enlighten (fig.)
illuminazióne s. f. lighting, illumination
illusióne s. f. delusion, illusion
illùso agg. deluded • s. m. dupe
illustràre v. tr. to illustrate
illustràto agg. illustrated; cartolina illustrata picture-postcard
illustrazióne s. f. illustration, picture
illùstre agg. distinguished
imbaccuccàto agg. wrapped up
imballàggio s. m. packing
imballàre v. tr. to pack
imbàllo s. m. packing
imbalsamàre v. tr. to embalm; to stuff (impagliare)
imbandieràre v. tr. to deck with flags
imbarazzànte agg. embarrassing

232

imbarazzàre v. tr. to embarrass

imbaràzzo s. m. embarrassment

imbarbariménto s. m. barbarization

imbarcadéro s. m. landing-stage, jetty

imbarcàre v. tr. to embark, to ship • rifl. to go aboard, to board a ship • intr. pron. to warp

imbarcazióne s. f. boat, craft

imbàrco s. m. shipping, embarkation

imbastíre v. tr. to tack, to baste

imbàttersi v. intr. pron. to run into

imbattíbile agg. unbeatable

imbecíllе agg. stupid, imbecile

imbellíre v. tr. to embellish, to adorn

imbestialíre v. intr. e intr. pron. to become furious, to fly into a rage

imbianchíno s. m. whitewasher, house-painter

imboccàre v. tr. to feed; to come on to, to enter (una strada)

imboccatúra s. f. mouth

imbonitóre s. m. barker

imboscàre v. tr. to corner

imboscàta s. f. ambush

imboschíre v. tr. to afforest

imbottigliàre v. tr. to bottle; to blockade (bloccare)

imbottíre v. tr. to stuff, to pad; to fill (riempire)

imbottitúra s. f. stuffing, padding

imbrattàre v. tr. to dirty, to soil

imbroccàre v. tr. to hit

imbrogliàre v. tr. to cheat; to mix up (confondere) • intr. pron. to get mixed up (confondersi); to thicken (complicarsi)

imbròglio s. m. cheat, swindle; scrape (impiccio); tangle (intrico)

imbronciàto agg. sulky

imbruttíre v. tr. to make ugly

imbucàre v. tr. to post, to mail

imbúto s. m. funnel

imitàre v. tr. to imitate, to copy

imitatóre s. m. imitator

imitazióne s. f. imitation; fake (falsificazione)

immagazzinàre v. tr. to store (up)

immaginàre v. tr. to imagine, to fancy

immaginàrio agg. imaginary, fictitious

immàgine s. f. image, picture

immancàbile agg. unfailing

immancabilménte avv. without fail

immàne agg. appalling, tremendous

immanénte agg. immanent

immangiàbile agg. uneatable

immatricolazióne s. f. admission (di uno studente); registration (di un veicolo)

immatúro agg. immature

immedesimàrsi v. rifl. to identify oneself (with)

immediataménte avv. immediately

immediàto agg. immediate; consegna immediata prompt delivery

immemoràbile agg. immemorial

immensità s. f. immensity

immènso agg. immense, huge

immèrgere v. tr. to soak, to plunge • rifl. to plunge, to bathe; to immerse (fig.)

immeritàto agg. undeserved

immeritévole agg. unworthy

immersióne s. f. immersion, plunge; submersion (di sottomarino)

immèttere v. tr. to introduce, to put in (o on)

immigràto agg. e s. m. immigrant

immigrazióne s. f. immigration

imminénte agg. imminent; impending (minaccioso)

immischiàrsi v. intr. pron. to meddle in

immissàrio s. m. tributary

immissióne s. f. immission; inlet (tecn.)

immòbile agg. still; beni immòbili real estate

immobiliàre agg. immovable; agenzia – real estate agency

immobilizzàre v. tr. to immobilize; to tie up (fin.)

immondìzia s. f. garbage, rubbish, trash; vietato depositare – no dumping

immoràle agg. immoral

immortalàre v. tr. to immortalize

immortàle agg. immortal

immortalità s. f. immortality

immúne agg. immune (from) (med., leg.); exempt (from)

immunizzàre v. tr. to immunize

immutàbile agg. immutable, unchanging

impacchettàre v. tr. to wrap (st.) up

impàccio s. m. hindrance; scrape (situazione difficile)

impàcco s. m. compress

impadronírsi v. intr. pron. to appropriate; to seize (con la violenza); to master (fig.)

impagàbile agg. priceless

impalcatúra s. f. scaffolding

impallidíre v. intr. to turn pale

impalpàbile agg. impalpable

impanàre v. tr. to crumb, to bread

impantanàrsi v. intr. pron. to stick in the mud; to get bogged down (fig.)

impappinàrsi *v. intr. pron.* to falter

imparàre *v. tr.* to learn

impareggiàbile *agg.* peerless, incomparable

imparentàrsi *v. intr. pron.* to become related to; to marry (into a family)

imparzialità *s. f.* impartiality

impasse *s. f. inv.* impasse

impassìbile *agg.* impassive

impastàre *v. tr.* to knead; to pug (argilla)

impasto *s. m.* dough; mixture (miscuglio)

impatto *s. m.* impact

impaurìre *v. tr.* to frighten, to scare • *intr. e intr. pron.* to get frightened

impaziènte *agg.* impatient

impazzìre *v. intr.* to go mad

impeccàbile *agg.* impeccable

impediménto *s. m.* impediment

impedìre *v. tr.* to prevent; to forbid (proibire)

impegnàre *v. tr.* to engage; to pawn (al monte di pietà); to bind (vincolare) • *rifl.* to undertake, to engage, to commit oneself

impegnativo *agg.* binding, exacting

impégno *s. m.* engagement; obligation (*comm.*); care (cura); commitment (interessamento)

impellènte *agg.* impelling

impenetràbile *agg.* impenetrable

impensàbile *agg.* unthinkable

imperatóre *s. m.* emperor

impercettìbile *agg.* imperceptible

imperdonàbile *agg.* unforgivable

imperfezióne *s. f.* imperfection, flaw

imperiàle *agg.* imperial

imperialismo *s. m.* imperialism

imperìzia *s. f.* unskilfulness

impermeàbile *agg.* waterproof, rainproof • *s. m.* mackintosh, raincoat

impèro *s. m.* empire

impersonàle *agg.* impersonal

impersonàre *v. tr.* to impersonate; to play (interpretare)

impertèrrito *agg.* undaunted, cool

impertinènte *agg.* impertinent, cheeky

imperturbàbile *agg.* imperturbable

imperversàre *v. intr.* to rage

impeto *s. m.* impetuosity; fit (impulso); force (violenza)

impetuóso *agg.* impetuous

impiànto *s. m.* plant, system; installation (l'impiantare)

impiastricciàre *v. tr.* to daub

impiccagióne *s. f.* hanging

impicciàrsi *v. intr. pron.* to interfere

impiegàto *s. m.* employee

impiègo *s. m.* job (posto di lavoro); employment (occupazione); use (uso)

impietóso *agg.* pitiless

impietrìre *v. intr. e intr. pron.* to petrify

impigliàre *v. tr.* to entangle

implacàbile *agg.* implacable

implicazióne *s. f.* implication

implicito *agg.* implicit

implùvio *s. m.* impluvium

impollinazióne *s. f.* pollination

imponènte *agg.* imposing, grand

impopolàre *agg.* unpopular

impórre *v. tr.* to impose, to order; to force (costringere) • *rifl.* to impose oneself

importànte *agg.* important

importànza *s. f.* importance

importàre *v. tr.* to import • *intr.* to matter; to care

importazióne *s. f.* importation, import

impòrto *s. m.* amount, price

importunàre *v. tr.* to importune, to pester

impossessàrsi *v. intr. pron.* to embezzle

impossìbile *agg.* impossible

impossibilità *s. f.* impossibility

impossibilitàto *agg.* unable

impostàre *v. tr.* to post, to mail; to set out, to plan (progettare)

impostazióne *s. f.* setting out

impostùra *s. f.* imposture

impotènte *agg.* impotent, powerless

impratichìrsi *v. intr. pron.* to practise, to get practice

imprecazióne *s. f.* course, imprecation

imprecisàto *agg.* indeterminate

impregnàre *v. tr.* to impregnate • *intr. pron.* to become impregnated

imprenditóre *s. m.* entrepreneur

impreparàto *agg.* unprepared

imprésa *s. f.* enterprise, undertaking

impressionàbile *agg.* sensitive

impressionànte *agg.* impressive, striking; shocking (che spaventa)

impressionàre *v. tr.* to impress, to affect, to strike • *intr. pron.* to be struck; to be scared (impaurirsi)

impressióne *s. f.* impression; feeling (sensazione); imprint (impronta)

impressionismo *s. m.* impressionism

imprestàre *v. tr.* to lend; to loan (*fin.*)

imprevedìbile *agg.* unforeseeable

imprevisto *agg.* unforeseen, unexpected • *s. m.* unexpected event, contingency

Impreziosire v. tr. to make precious

Imprigionare v. tr. to put in prison, to jail; to confine (rinchiudere)

improbabile agg. improbable, unlikely

impronta s. f. imprint, impression, mark; **l'- di un piede** footprint; **- digitale** fingerprint

improperio s. m. abuse

improprio agg. improper

improrogabile agg. not to be extended, unalterable

improvvisamente avv. suddenly

improvvisare v. tr. to improvise

improvvisata s. f. surprise

improvviso agg. sudden, unexpected

imprudente agg. imprudent, rash

imprudenza s. f. imprudence, rashness; imprudent act (atto)

impudente agg. shameless, impudent

impudico agg. immodest

impugnare v. tr. to seize, to grasp; to contest (contestare)

impulsivo agg. impulsive

impulso s. m. impulse; boost (incremento)

impunemente avv. with impunity

impuntarsi v. intr. pron. to jib

impuntura s. f. back-stitch

impurità s. f. impurity

impuro agg. impure

imputare v. tr. to accuse, to blame

imputato s. m. defendant

imputridire v. tr. to rot, to putrefy

in prep. in, at (stato in luogo); to (moto a luogo); into (in luogo chiuso); by (mezzo)

inabissarsi v. intr. pron. to sink

inabitabile agg. uninhabitable

inaccessibile agg. inaccessible

inaccettabile agg. unacceptable

inacidire v. tr. to sour • intr. pron. to turn sour

inadatto agg. unsuitable, unfit; unable (incapace)

inadeguato agg. inadequate

inadempienza s. f. default

inafferrabile agg. uncatchable; slippery, elusive, incomprehensible

inaffidabile agg. unreliable

inalare v. tr. to inhale

inalienabile agg. inalienable

inalterabile agg. unalterable

inamidare v. tr. to starch

inammissibile agg. inadmissible

inanimato agg. inanimate

inappuntabile agg. faultless

inaridire v. tr. e intr. pron. to dry up

inarrestabile agg. relentless

inarrivabile agg. unattainable; unequalled (incomparabile)

inascoltato agg. unheard

inaspettato agg. unexpected

inattendibile agg. unreliable, unfounded

inatteso agg. unexpected

inaudito agg. unprecedented

inaugurale agg. inaugural, opening

inaugurare v. tr. to inaugurate, to open

inaugurazione s. f. inauguration, opening

inavvertitamente avv. inadvertently

inavvicinabile agg. unapproachable (inaccessibile)

incagliare v. intr. e intr. pron. to ground, to strand

incalcolabile agg. incalculable

incamminarsi v. intr. pron. to set off, to start

incanalare v. tr. to canalize • intr. pron. to direct

incandescente agg. white-hot

incantare v. tr. to charm, to bewitch • intr. pron. to stick

incantesimo s. m. spell, charm

incantevole agg. enchanting, charming

incanto s. m. spell, enchantment

incapace agg. unable (to) • s. m. e f. incompetent

incappare v. intr. to run into

incaricare v. tr. to charge (sb. with st.); to ask (pregare)

incaricato s. m. appointee

incarico s. m. charge, appointment (nomina), nomination (politica)

incarnare v. tr. to incarnate, to embody

incartare v. tr. to wrap up

incassare v. tr. to cash; to embed (edil.); to receive (pugilato)

incasso s. m. collection; proceeds pl. (somma incassata)

incastonatura s. f. setting

incastrare v. tr. to insert, to fit in; to involve (impegolare) • intr. pron. to stick

incastro s. m. joint

incatenare v. tr. to chain

incavato agg. hollow

incendiare v. tr. to set fire to (st.)

incendio s. m. fire; **- doloso** arson

incenso s. m. incense

incentivare v. tr. to stimulate

incentivo s. m. incentive

incentràre v. tr. e intr. pron. to centre

inceppàre v. tr. to clog (up); to hinder (fig.) • intr. pron. to jam, to stick

incertézza s. f. uncertainty

incèrto agg. uncertain

incessànte agg. never-ending, unceasing

incèsto s. m. incest

inchièsta s. f. inquiry, survey

inchìno s. m. bow

inchiodàre v. tr. to nail • intr. pron. to pull up short

inchiòstro s. m. ink

incidentàle agg. incidental

incidentalménte avv. incidentally

incidènte s. m. incident; accident (disgrazia)

incidènza s. f. influence, effect

incìdere v. intr. to weigh (on); to affect (influire) • tr. to engrave, to carve

incìnta agg. pregnant

incisióne s. f. engraving; etching (acquaforte); woodcut (xilografia); recording (registrazione)

incisìvo agg. incisive • s. m. incisor

incisóre agg. engraver

incitàre v. tr. to incite

incivìle agg. uncivil

inciviltà s. f. incivility

inclinàbile agg. inclinable

inclinàre v. tr. to incline, to tilt • intr. to tend

inclinazióne s. f. inclination

inclùdere v. tr. to include

inclusìvo agg. inclusive

incoerènte agg. incoherent, inconsistent

incògnito agg. unknown

incollàre v. tr. to stick, to glue

incolonnaménto s. m. column formation

incolpàre v. tr. to blame

incòlume agg. unharmed, safe and sound

incombènte agg. impending

incominciàre v. tr. e intr. to begin, to start

incomparàbile agg. incomparable

incompetènte agg. incompetent

incomplùto agg. unfinished, unfulfilled

incomplèto agg. incomplete

incomprensìbile agg. incomprehensible

inconcepìbile agg. unconceivable

inconfondìbile agg. unmistakable

incongruènte agg. incongruous, inconsequent

inconsapévole agg. unaware

inconscio agg. e s. m. unconscious

inconsistènte agg. insubstantial

inconsuèto agg. unusual

incontenìbile agg. uncontainable

incontràre v. tr. to meet • intr. pron. to run into (sb.) (imbattersi); to coincide (coincidere) • rifl. rec. to meet

incóntro s. m. meeting; match (sport) • avv. toward(s), to

inconveniènte s. m. drawback

incoraggiaménto s. m. encouragement

incorniciàre v. tr. to frame

incoronàre v. tr. to crown

incoronazióne s. f. coronation

incorporàre v. tr. to incorporate; to annex (un territorio); to merge (fin.)

incórrere v. intr. to incur

incorruttìbile agg. incorruptible

incosciènte agg. unconscious; irresponsible (irresponsabile)

incostànte agg. inconstant

incredìbile agg. unbelievable

incrèdulo agg. incredulous

increménto s. m. increase

incriminàre v. tr. to incriminate

incrinàre v. tr. to crack • intr. pron. to crack; to deteriorate (fig.)

incrociàre v. tr. e rifl. rec. to cross

incrócio s. m. crossing; cross-fertilization (bot.)

incrostazióne s. f. encrustation

inculcàre v. tr. to inculcate, to instil

incunàbolo s. m. incunabulum

incuràbile agg. incurable

incurànte agg. careless, thoughtless

incùria s. f. carelessness

incuriosìre v. tr. to excite (sb's) curiosity • intr. pron. to become curious

incustodìto agg. unattended

indaffaràto agg. busy

indagàre v. tr. to investigate, to inquire (into)

indàgine s. f. investigation, inquiry; research (ricerca)

indebitàrsi v. rifl. to run into debt

indebolìre v. tr. e intr. pron. to weaken

indecènte agg. indecent

indecifràbile agg. indecipherable; unintelligible (incomprensibile)

indecìso agg. undecided

indecisióne s. f. indecision

indefinìbile agg. indefinable

indeformàbile agg. undeformable

indégno agg. unworthy

indelèbile agg. indelible

indennìzzo s. m. indemnification; **domanda d'**– claim for damages

inderogàbile agg. unbreakable

indesideràbile agg. undesirable

indeterminatézza s. f. indeterminateness
indeterminàto agg. indeterminate; **a tempo –** indefinitely
indicàre v. tr. to point (to, at, out); to show (mostrare); to mean (significare)
indicazióne s. f. indication, sign; direction (istruzioni)
indice s. m. index; forefinger (dito); contents pl. (di un libro); sign (indizio)
indietreggiàre v. intr. to draw back, to withdraw
indiètro avv. back, behind; **all' –** backwards
indifferènte agg. indifferent
indifferenziàto agg. undifferentiated
indigeno agg. native
indigestióne s. f. indigestion
indigèsto agg. indigestible; **cibi –** heavy food
indimenticàbile agg. unforgettable
indipendènte agg. independent
indipendenteménte avv. independently
indipendènza s. f. independent
indirètto agg. indirect
indirizzàre v. tr. to address; to turn; to send • rifl. to apply, to turn; to address (rivolgere la parola)
indirizzo s. m. address
indiscréto agg. indiscreet, pushing
indiscutibile agg. unquestionable
indispensàbile agg. indispensable
indisposizióne s. f. indisposition
indissolùbile agg. indissoluble
indistruttibile agg. indestructible
indisturbàto agg. undisturbed
individuàle agg. individual
individualismo s. m. individualism
individualménte avv. individually
individuàre v. tr. to individualize; to locate (localizzare); to identify (distinguere)
individuo s. m. individual, fellow; guy (tipo)
indivisibile agg. indivisible
indizio s. m. sign, clue
indoeuropèo agg. Indo-european
indolènte agg. sluggish
indolenziménto s. m. stiffening
indolóre agg. painless
indossàre v. tr. to wear, to put on
indovinàre v. tr. to guess
indovinèllo s. m. riddle
indùbbio agg. undoubted
indùgio s. m. delay
induménto s. m. garment
indùstria s. f. industry
industriàle agg. industrial

industrializzazióne s. f. industrialization
ineccepibile agg. unexceptionable
inèdito agg. unpublished
inefficàce agg. ineffective
inefficiènza s. f. inefficiency
ineluttàbile agg. ineluctable
inerènte agg. inherent (in)
inerpicàrsi v. intr. pron. to climb
inèrzia s. f. inertia (fis.); inertness, inactivity
inesàttezza s. f. inexactitude; slip (svista)
inesauribile agg. inexhaustible
inesistènte agg. inexistent
inespèrto agg. inexpert, inexperienced
inesploràto agg. unexplored
inespugnàbile agg. inpregnable, inexpugnable; incorruptible (fig.)
inestimàbile agg. invaluable, priceless
inevitàbile agg. unavoidable, inevitable
inèzia s. f. trifle
infallibile agg. infallible, sure
infantile agg. infantile
infànzia s. f. infancy, childhood
infarinatùra s. f. sprinkling of flour; smattering (fig.)
infàrto s. m. infarct
infastidire v. tr. to annoy • intr. pron. to get annoyed
infàtti cong. infact, as a matter of fact
infedéle agg. unfaithful
infelice agg. unhappy
inferióre agg. inferior; lower (più in basso)
inferiorità s. f. inferiority
infermière s. m. male nurse
infèrmo agg. invalid
infèrno s. m. hell
inferriàta s. f. iron bars pl.
infestàre v. tr. to infest
infettivo agg. infectious, catching
infètto agg. infected
infezióne s. f. infection
infiammàbile agg. inflammable
infiammazióne s. f. inflammation
inferire v. intr. to rage
infiltràrsi v. intr. pron. to infiltrate
infine avv. in the end, finally
infinità s. f. infinity
infinitesimàle agg. infinitesimal
infinito agg. infinite, endless • s. m. infinity
infischiàrsi v. intr. pron. not to care a rap, to care nothing
inflazionàre v. tr. to inflate
inflazióne s. f. inflation
inflessibile agg. inflexible

237

influènte *agg.* influential

influènza *s. f.* influence; influenza, flu (*med.*)

influenzàbile *agg.* influenceable

influenzàto *agg.* influenced; sick with flu (malato)

influìre *v. intr.* to influence, to bear on

inflùsso *s. m.* influence

infondàto *agg.* groundless

infóndere *v. tr.* to infuse

informàle *agg.* informal

informàre *v. tr.* to inform • *intr. pron.* to inform oneself

informàtica *s. f.* informatics *pl.* (*v. al sing.*)

informàtico *agg.* computer (*attr.*)

informazióne *s. f.* information

infortunàrsi *v. intr. pron.* to get injured

infortùnio *s. m.* accident

infràngere *v. tr.* to break, to shatter • *intr. pron.* to break down

infrasettimanàle *agg.* midweek

infreddatùra *s. f.* cold

infruttuóso *agg.* fruitless

infuriàre *v. intr.* to rage

infusióne *s. f.* infusion

ingaggiàre *v. tr.* to engage

ingannàre *v. tr.* to swindle, to deceive • *intr. pron.* to be mistaken, to be wrong

ingannévole *agg.* deceptive

ingegnàrsi *v. intr. pron.* to contrive, to manage

ingegnère *s. m.* engineer

ingegnerìa *s. f.* engineering

ingégno *s. m.* brains *pl.*; ingenuity (abilità)

ingegnosità *s. f.* cleverness, ingenuity

ingènte *agg.* huge

ingenuità *s. f.* ingenuousness, naïvety

ingènuo *agg.* ingenuous, naïve

ingerìre *v. tr.* to ingest

ingessàre *v. tr.* to plaster

inghiottìre *v. tr.* to swallow

inginocchiàrsi *v. intr. pron.* to kneel

ingiùria *s. f.* insult; offence (*leg.*)

ingiuriàre *v. tr.* to insult, to abuse • *rifl. rec.* to insult each other

ingiustificàto *agg.* unjustified

ingiustìzia *s. f.* injustice

ingiùsto *agg.* unjust

inglése *agg.* English • *s. m. e f.* Englishman *m.*, Englishwoman *f.*; English (lingua)

inglesìsmo *s. m.* Anglicism

ingoiàre *v. tr.* to swallow up

ingolfàre *v. tr.* to choke • *intr. pron.* to plunge (into); to get flooded (*autom.*)

ingombrànte *agg.* cumbersome

ingórdo *agg.* greedy

ingorgàre *v. tr.* to choke up, to clog • *intr. pron.* to choke up, to block

ingórgo *s. m.* block; jam, bottleneck (del traffico)

ingranàggio *s. m.* gear

ingrandiménto *s. m.* enlargement; lènte d'– magnifying glass

ingrandìre *v. tr.* to enlarge • *intr. pron.* to expand; to spread (*comm.*)

ingrassàggio *s. m.* greasing

ingrassàre *v. tr.* to grease, to fatten • *intr.* to put on weight; to thrive (*fig.*)

ingratitùdine *s. f.* ungratefulness

ingràto *agg.* ingrato

ingrediènte *s. m.* ingredient

ingrèsso *s. m.* entrance; hall (atrio)

ingrossaménto *s. m.* swelling; increase (aumento)

all'ingròsso *avv.* wholesale

inguaribile *agg.* incurable

inibìre *v. tr.* to inhibit

inibizióne *s. f.* inhibition

iniettóre *s. m.* injector

iniezióne *s. f.* injection

inimitàbile *agg.* inimitable

inimmaginàbile *agg.* unimaginable

ininterròtto *agg.* uninterrupted; non-stop (*attr.*)

iniziàle *agg.* initial, beginning

inizialménte *avv.* initially

iniziàre *v. tr. e intr.* to begin, to start

iniziatìva *s. f.* initiative

iniziàto *s. m.* initiate

iniziatóre *agg.* initiator

inìzio *s. m.* beginning, start

innamoràre *v. tr.* to charm • *intr. pron.* to fall in love

innamoràto *agg.* in love (*pred.*)

innàto *agg.* innate, inborn

innegàbile *agg.* undeniable

innervosìre *v. tr.* to get on (sb's) nerves • *intr. pron.* to get nervous

innestàre *v. tr.* to graft (*agr.*); to plug in (*elettr.*); to engage (*autom.*) • *intr. pron.* to be inserted

innèsto *s. m.* graft (*agr.*); connection (*elettr.*)

ìnno *s. m.* hymn; l'– nazionàle the national anthem

innocènte *agg.* innocent; not guilty (*leg.*)

innocènza *s. f.* innocence

innòcuo *agg.* innocuous, harmless

innovatóre s. m. e agg. innovator
innumerévole agg. innumerable, countless
inoffensìvo agg. harmless, inoffensive
inoltràre v. tr. to forward • intr. pron. to advance
inóltre avv. besides, moreover
inondàre v. tr. to flood
inondazióne s. f. flooding, flood; inundation (effetto)
inopportùno agg. inopportune, untimely
inorgànico agg. inorganic
inorridìre v. intr. to be horrified
inospitàle agg. inhospitable
inossidàbile agg. stainless; **acciaio** – stainless steel
inquadràre v. tr. to organize; to frame (in fotografia) • intr. pron. to fit (into)
inqualificàbile agg. disgraceful
inquietànte agg. worrying, alarming
inquièto agg. restless, uneasy (preoccupato)
inquilìno s. m. tenant
inquinaménto s. m. pollution
inquinàre v. tr. to pollute
inquisizióne s. f. inquisition
insaccàti s. m. pl. sausages
insalàta s. f. salad
insaponàre v. tr. to soap
insapóre agg. flavourless, tasteless
insaziàbile agg. insatiable
inscatolàre v. tr. to box; to tin, to can (in lattine)
insediaménto s. m. installation; settlement (lo stabilirsi)
insediàre v. tr. to install • intr. pron. to take over; to settle (stabilirsi)
inségna s. f. sign, sign-board
insegnaménto s. m. teaching
insegnànte s. m. e f. teacher
insegnàre v. tr. to teach; to train (addestrare); to tell (indicare) • intr. tr. to teach
inseguìre v. tr. to pursue
insenatùra s. f. inlet, creek
insensìbile agg. insensitive
inseparàbile agg. inseparable
inseriménto s. m. fitting in; connection (elettr.)
inserìre v. tr. to insert, to fit in; to include (includere); to connect (elettr.); to put in (infilare)
inservìbile agg. useless
inserzióne s. f. insertion
insetticìda s. m. insecticide
insètto s. m. insect, bug
insicurézza s. f. insecurity

insidióso agg. insidious
insième s. m. whole, set • avv. together; at the same time (contemporaneamente) – **a** together with
insìgne agg. great
insignificànte agg. insignificant, negligible
insinuàre v. tr. to insinuate • intr. pron. to squeeze oneself in (fam.)
insìpido agg. tasteless, insipid
insistènte agg. insistent; nagging (noioso)
insìstere v. intr. to persevere, to insist
insoddisfazióne s. f. dissatisfaction
insolazióne s. f. insolation; sunstroke (colpo di sole)
insolènza s. f. insolence
insòlito agg. unusual
insolùbile agg. insoluble
insolvènte agg. insolvent
insómma avv. in short • inter. well!
insònnia s. f. insomnia (med.); sleeplessness
insopportàbile agg. unbearable
insórgere v. intr. to rise (up); to arise (manifestarsi all'improvviso)
insospettàbile agg. beyond suspicion
insostenìbile agg. untenable, unbearable
insostituìbile agg. irreplaceable
inspiegàbile agg. inexplicable
instàbile agg. unstable; changeable (di tempo)
installàre v. tr. to install
instancàbile agg. indefatigable, untiring
instauràre v. tr. to set up, to establish • intr. pron. to be established; to begin (avere inizio)
insuccèsso s. m. failure, flop
insufficiènte agg. insufficient
insulàre agg. insular
insùlso agg. insipid, dull
insultàre v. tr. to insult, to abuse
insùlto s. m. insult, abuse
insurrezióne s. f. insurrection
intagliàre v. tr. to carve
intànto avv. meanwhile; – **che** while, as
intàrsio s. m. inlay
intasaménto s. m. stoppage, block
intasàre v. tr. to stop up, to choke; to jam (traffico) • intr. pron. to get stopped up
intascàre v. tr. to pocket
intàtto agg. intact; uninjured (illeso)
integràle agg. integral; unabridged (di edizione); **pane** – wholemeal bread
integralménte avv. in full
integrànte agg. integrant
intelaiatùra s. f. framework; sash (di finestra)
intellettuále agg. intellectual

239

intellettualismo *s. m.* intellectualism
intelligénte *agg.* intelligent
intelligénza *s. f.* intelligence
intelligíbile *agg.* intelligible
intempérie *s. f. pl.* bad weather *sing.*
inténdere *v. tr.* to mean, to intend, to understand (capire)
intenditóre *s. m.* connoisseur
intensificáre *v. tr.* to intensify
intensità *s. f.* intensity
inténso *agg.* intense
intenzionále *agg.* intentional
intenzióne *s. f.* intention
interaménte *avv.* wholly
interazióne *s. f.* interaction
intercaláre *s. m.* stock phrase
intercapédine *s. f.* hollow space
intercessióne *s. f.* intercession
intercolúnnio *s. m.* intercolumn
intercomunicánte *agg.* communicating
intercontinentále *agg.* intercontinental
interdisciplináre *agg.* interdisciplinary
interessaménto *s. m.* interest
interessánte *agg.* interesting
interessáre *v. tr.* to interest; to concern (riguardare) • *intr.* to be in the interest of, to matter • *intr. pron.* to be interested in, to care (curarsi)
interésse *s. m.* interest
interferènza *s. f.* interference
interfóno *s. m.* intercom
interióre *agg.* interior
interlocutóre *s. m.* interlocutor
intermédio *agg.* intermediate
intermèzzo *s. m.* intermezzo
interminábile *agg.* interminable
intermittènte *agg.* intermittent
internaménte *avv.* internally, inside
internazionále *agg.* international
intèrno *agg.* internal, inside • *s. m.* inside, interior; **commercio** - home trade
intéro *agg.* whole, entire
interpretáre *v. tr.* to interpret
interpretazióne *s. f.* interpretation
intèrprete *s. m. e f.* interpreter
interrogáre *v. tr.* to ask, to question; to examine (uno studente)
interrómpere *v. tr.* to interrupt • *intr. pron.* to stop, to break off
interruttóre *s. m.* switch
intersezióne *s. f.* intersection
interstízio *s. m.* interstice, space, crack

interurbáno *agg.* interurban; **telefonata interurbana** trunk-call
intervállo *s. m.* interval; break (pausa)
interveníre *v. intr.* to intervene, to be present; to attend (assistere)
intervènto *s. m.* intervention; operation (*med.*)
intervista *s. f.* interview
intervistáre *v. tr.* to interview
intestáre *v. tr.* to register (una proprietà); to open (un conto); to make out (un assegno)
intestinále *agg.* intestinal
intestino *s. m.* intestine, bowels *pl.*
intimista *agg.* intimist
intimità *s. f.* intimacy
íntimo *agg.* intimate, close
intitoláre *v. tr.* to entitle • *intr. pron.* to be entitled
intolleràbile *agg.* intolerable
intollerànte *agg.* intolerant
intònaco *s. m.* plaster
intórno *avv.* round, around, about
intossicazióne *s. f.* intoxication; – **alimentare** food poisoning
intradòsso *s. m.* intrados
intraducíbile *agg.* untranslatable
intransigènte *agg.* intransigent
intrapréndere *v. tr.* to undertake
intrattenére *v. tr.* to entertain • *intr. pron.* to dwell (upon st.)
intrecciáre *v. tr.* to twist, to intertwine
intréccio *s. m.* intertwinement; plot (trama)
intrico *s. m.* tangle
introdúrre *v. tr.* to introduce; to put in (inserire); to show in (far entrare) • *intr. pron.* to get in
introduzióne *s. f.* introduction; foreword (*lett.*)
intromèttere *v. tr.* to interpose • *rifl.* to interfere, to intrude upon
introspettivo *agg.* introspective
introvàbile *agg.* not to be found
introvèrso *agg.* introverted
intrusióne *s. f.* intrusion
intruso *s. m.* intruder
intuíre *v. tr.* to know, to guess
intuitivo *agg.* intuitive
intuizióne *s. f.* intuition
inumidíre *v. tr.* to dampen, to moisten
inútile *agg.* useless
inutilizzàbile *agg.* unusable
inutilménte *avv.* uselessly
invadènte *agg.* intrusive
invádere *v. tr.* to invade, to overcome

invalidità *s. f.* infirmity; disability (al lavoro); invalidity (*leg.*)

invàlido *agg.* invalid

invàno *avv.* in vain, to no purpose

invasióne *s. f.* invasion

invasóre *s. m.* invader

invecchiaménto *s. m.* ageing

invecchiàre *v. intr.* to age, to grow old; to go out of date (passare di moda) • *tr.* to age

invéce *avv.* instead, on the contrary, but; **– di** instead of

invendìbile *agg.* unsaleable

inventàre *v. tr.* to invent

inventàrio *s. m.* inventory

inventìva *s. f.* inventiveness

inventóre *s. m.* inventor

invenzióne *s. f.* invention

invernàle *agg.* winter (*attr.*)

invèrno *s. m.* winter

inverosìmile *agg.* improbable

inversióne *s. f.* inversion, reversal; **– di marcia** U-turn

invertebràto *agg.* invertebrate

invertìre *v. tr.* to reverse, to invert

investigàre *v. tr.* to investigate, to inquire into

investiménto *s. m.* investment

investìre *v. tr.* to invest; to run over (*autom.*); to assail (assalire)

investitóre *s. m.* investor (*fin.*)

inviàre *v. tr.* to forward, to send; to remit (denaro)

invìdia *s. f.* envy

invidióso *agg.* envious

invincìbile *agg.* invincible

invìo *s. m.* dispatch, forwarding; shipment (di merce); remittance (di denaro)

invisìbile *agg.* invisible

invitànte *agg.* tempting

invitàre *v. tr.* to invite, to ask

invitàto *agg. e s. m.* guest

invìto *s. m.* invitation

invogliàre *v. tr.* to induce, to tempt

involontàrio *agg.* unintentional, involuntary

involtìno *s. m.* roulade

invòlucro *s. m.* wrapping

involuzióne *s. f.* involution

iònico *agg.* Ionic (*arch.*); ionic (*chim.*)

ipercrìtico *agg.* hypercritical

ipermercàto *s. m.* hypermarket

ipermetropìa *s. f.* hypermetropia

iperrealìsmo *s. m.* hyperealism

ipertensióne *s. f.* hypertension

ipòcrita *agg.* hypocrite

ipogèo *s. m.* hypogeum

ipotèca *s. f.* mortgage

ipòtesi *s. f.* hypothesis

ìppica *s. f.* horse-racing

ìppico *agg.* horse (*attr.*)

ippocàmpo *s. m.* sea-horse

ippòdromo *s. m.* race-course

ippopòtamo *s. m.* hippopotamus, hippo (*fam.*)

irascìbile *agg.* irascible, quick-tempered

irlandése *agg.* Irish • *s. m. e f.* Irishman *m.*, Irishwoman *f.*; Irish (lingua)

ironìa *s. f.* irony

irònico *agg.* ironical

irraggiungìbile *agg.* unattainable

irrazionàle *agg.* irrational

irreàle *agg.* unreal

irrealtà *s. f.* unreality

irredentìsmo *s. m.* irredentism

irregolàre *agg.* irregular

irremovìbile *agg.* unshakable

irreparàbile *agg.* irreparable

irrequièto *agg.* restless

irresistìbile *agg.* irresistible

irrespiràbile *agg.* unbreathable

irresponsàbile *agg.* irresponsible

irrigazióne *s. f.* irrigation

irrìguo *agg.* irrigation (*attr.*); (well-)watered (irrigato)

irrilevànte *agg.* trifling

irrimediàbile *agg.* irremediable

irripetìbile *agg.* unrepeatable

irrisòrio *agg.* ridiculous

irritàbile *agg.* irritable

irritànte *agg.* irritating

irritàre *v. tr.* to irritate • *intr. pron.* to become irritated, to get annoyed

irritazióne *s. f.* irritation

irruènza *s. f.* vehemence

iscrìvere *v. tr.* to enroll, to enter; to inscribe (*geom.*) • *rifl.* to enrol, to enter; to matriculate (all'università)

iscrizióne *s. f.* enrolment; registration (registrazione); entry (a una gara); inscription (su una lapide)

islàmico *agg.* Islamic

islamìsmo *s. m.* Islamism

isòbara *s. f.* isobar

isòbata *s. f.* isobath

ìsola *s. f.* island, isle

isolaménto *s. m.* isolation; insulation (*elettr.*)

isolàno *agg.* island (*attr.*)

isolànte *s. m.* insulating

isolare *v. tr.* to isolate; to insulate (*elettr.*) • *intr. pron.* to seclude oneself
isolato *agg.* isolated; insulated (*elettr.*)
ispanico *agg.* Hispanic
ispettóre *s. m.* inspector, surveyor
ispezióne *s. f.* inspection; check (controllo)
ispirare *v. tr.* to inspire • *intr. pron.* to draw inspiration
ispiratóre *s. m.* inspirer
ispirazióne *s. f.* inspiration
israelitico *agg.* Israelite
istantaneaménte *avv.* instantly
istante *s. m.* instant
isterico *agg.* hysteric
isterismo *s. m.* hysteria
istintivo *agg.* instinctive
istinto *s. m.* instinct
istituire *v. tr.* to found, to institute
istituto *s. m.* institute; institution (istituzione); – **di bellezza** beauty parlour

istituzionale *agg.* institutional
istituzióne *s. f.* institution
istmo *s. m.* isthmus
istrióne *s. m.* histrion; mountbank (ciarlatano)
istruire *v. tr.* to educate, to instruct; to direct (dare istruzioni)
istruttivo *agg.* instructive
istruttóre *s. m.* instructor; trainer (*sport*)
istruzióne *s. f.* education, learning; instruction, direction (norma); – **obbligatoria** compulsory education
italianista *s. m. e f.* Italianist
italiano *agg. e s. m.* Italian
italico *agg.* Italic
iterativo *agg.* iterative
itineránte *agg.* itinerant
itinerário *s. m.* itinerary, route
ittico *agg.* fish (*attr.*); **mercato** – fish market
ittiologìa *s. f.* ichthyology
ittita *agg.* Hittite

J

jazz *s. m.* jazz; **orchestra** – jazz band
jazzista *s. m.* jazzman

jazzistico *agg.* jazz (*attr.*)
jolly *s. m. inv.* joker

K

keniòta *agg. e s. m. e f.* Kenyan
kermesse *s. f.* kermess

kivi *s. m.* kiwi
k-way *s. f. inv.* K-Way (marchio), wind jacket

L

là avv. there
làbbro s. m. lip
labirinto s. m. labyrinth, maze
laboratòrio s. m. laboratory, lab, workshop
laburista agg. Labour (attr.)
làcca s. f. lacquer; – **per capelli** hair spray
làccio s. m. noose; shoelace (da scarpe)
laceràre v. tr. e intr. pron. to tear
lacerazióne s. f. tear; laceration (med.)
lacònico agg. laconic
làcrima s. f. tear
lacrimàre v. intr. to water; to drip (stillare)
lacrimóso agg. tearful
lacuàle agg. lake (attr.)
lacùna s. f. gap, blank
lacùstre agg. lake (attr.)
làdro s. m. thief, robber; **al –!** stop thief!
laggiù avv. down there, over there
lagnànza s. f. complaint
lagnàrsi v. intr. pron. to moan, to complain
làgo s. m. lake
lagùna s. f. lagoon
lagunàre agg. lagoon (attr.)
laicìsmo s. m. laicism
làico agg. lay
làma s. f. blade • s. m. lama (zool.)
lamentàre v. tr. to mourn, to lament • intr. pron. to complain, to moan
lamentèla s. f. complaint
laménto s. m. moan; complaint (reclamo)
lamétta s. f. razor-blade
lamièra s. f. plate, sheet
làmina s. f. lamina; – **d'oro** gold leaf
laminàto agg. rolled
làmpada s. f. lamp
lampadàrio s. m. chandelier
lampadina s. f. bulb
lampànte agg. clear, evident
lampeggiàre v. intr. to flash; to blink (di segnalazione) • intr. impers. to lighten
lampeggiatóre s. m. blinker
lampióne s. m. lamp-post
làmpo s. m. lightning; flash (guizzo di luce); **chiusura** – zip
lampóne s. m. raspberry

làna s. f. wool; **pura** – pure wool; **gomitolo di –** ball of wool
lancétta s. f. hand
lància s. f. lance, spear
lanciàre v. tr. to throw, to toss • rifl. to throw oneself, to dash; to jump (col paracadute)
lancinànte agg. stabbing, piercing
làncio s. m. throw; launching (pubblicitario)
languóre s. m. faintness, weakness
lantèrna s. f. lantern
lapalissiàno agg. self-evident
lapidàre v. tr. to stone
lapidàrio agg. lapidary • s. m. epigraphic museum
làpide s. f. tombstone; memorial tablet (commemorativa)
làpis s. m. inv. pencil
làpsus s. m. inv. lapse, slip
làrdo s. m. bacon fat, lard
larghézza s. f. broadness, width; largeness (abbondanza)
làrgo agg. broad, wide; loose (di vestito) • s. m. open sea; **al –** offshore
larìnge s. f. larynx
laringìte s. f. laryngitis
laringoiàtra s. m. e f. throat-specialist
larvàle agg. larval
lasciapassàre s. m. inv. pass
lasciàre v. tr. e intr. to leave; to let (permettere) • rifl. rec. to separate
lassatìvo agg. laxative
lassù avv. up there
làstra s. f. slab; plate (di metallo); x-ray (radiografia); sheet (di vetro)
lastricàto agg. paved
lastróne s. m. large slab
latènte agg. latent
lateràle agg. lateral; side (attr.)
lateralménte avv. laterally
latifòglio agg. broad-leaved
latifondista s. m. e f. big landowner
latinìsmo s. m. Latinism
latinista s. m. e f. Latinist
latinità s. f. Latinity

243

latino *agg.* Latin
latinonamericáno *s. m.* Latin American
latitánte *s. m. e f.* absconder
latitúdine *s. f.* latitude
láto *s. m.* side; standpoint (punto di vista)
látta *s. f.* tin-plate, can, tin
lattánte *s. m.* breast-fed
látte *s. m.* milk; **– scremato** skimmed milk; **– in polvere** powdered milk; **– cagliato** curdled milk
lattína *s. f.* tin, can
lattúga *s. f.* lettuce
láurea *s. f.* degree; **conseguimento della –** graduation
laureársi *v. intr. pron.* to graduate
laureáto *s. m.* graduate
láuro *s. m.* laurel, bay-tree
láva *s. f.* lava
lavábile *agg.* washable
lavággio *s. m.* washing
lavágna *s. f.* blackboard
lavánda *s. f.* lavender; **– gastrica** gastric lavage
lavandería *s. f.* laundry, launderette
lavandíno *s. m.* sink
laváre *v. tr.* to wash • *rifl.* to wash oneself
lavastovíglie *s. f. inv.* dish-washer
lavatríce *s. f.* washing-machine
làvico *agg.* lavic
lavoráre *v. tr. e intr.* to work
lavoratívo *agg.* working
lavoratóre *s. m.* worker
lavorazióne *s. f.* working; **metodo di –** processing
lavóro *s. m.* work; job (fam.)
lazzarétto *s. m.* lazaretto
lealtà *s. f.* loyalty
lebbrosário *s. m.* leper hospital
leccáre *v. tr.* to lick
léccio *s. m.* ilex, holm-oak
leccornía *s. f.* titbit
lécito *agg.* right, permitted; licit, lawful (leg.)
léga *s. f.* league; alloy (metallo)
legáccio *s. m.* string
legále *agg.* legal; lawful (legittimo)
legalizzáre *v. tr.* to legalize
legáme *s. m.* tie, bond, link
legáre *v. tr.* to tie, to fasten • *intr.* to join up; to connect (essere collegato)
legatória *s. f.* bookbinders, bookbindery (USA)
legatúra *s. f.* tying, binding
légge *s. f.* law
leggénda *s. f.* legend

leggendário *agg.* legendary
léggere *v. tr.* to read
leggerézza *s. f.* lightness
leggéro *agg.* light
leggiádro *agg.* fair, graceful
leggíbile *agg.* readable
léggio *s. m.* book-reset; music-stand (mus.)
legióne *s. f.* legion
legislatívo *agg.* legislative
legislazióne *s. f.* legislation
legittimáre *v. tr.* to legitimize
legíttimo *agg.* legitimate; right (giusto)
légna *s. f.* wood
legnáme *s. m.* timber
légno *s. m.* wood
legúme *s. m.* legume
lémbo *s. m.* edge
leninísmo *s. m.* Leninism
lenitívo *agg.* lenitive, soothing
lénte *s. f.* lens; **lenti a contatto** contact lenses
lentézza *s. f.* slowness
lentícchia *s. f.* lentil
lentíggine *s. f.* freckle
lénto *agg.* slow
lénza *s. f.* fishing-line
lenzuòlo *s. m.* sheet
leóne *s. m.* lion; the Lion (astr.)
leonéssa *s. f.* lioness
leopárdo *s. m.* leopard
lépre *s. f.* hare
leséna *s. f.* pilaster strip
lesináre *v. tr. e intr.* to skimp
lesionáre *v. tr.* to damage
lesióne *s. f.* lesion (med.); injury (leg.)
lessáre *v. tr.* to boil
léssico *s. m.* lexicon, vocabulary
lésso *agg.* boiled • *s. m.* boiled beef, boiled meat
letále *agg.* lethal
letáme *s. m.* manure, dung
letárgo *s. m.* lethargy
léttera *s. f.* letter
letterále *agg.* literal
letteralménte *avv.* literally
letterário *agg.* literary, bookish
letteráto *agg.* lettered
letteratúra *s. f.* literature
lètto *s. m.* bed; **– a una piazza** single bed; **– matrimoniale** double bed; **vagone –** sleeping car; **– a castello** brunk bed
lettóre *s. m.* reader
lettúra *s. f.* reading
leucemía *s. f.* leukaemia

lèva *s. f.* lever; levy (chiamata alle armi)

levànte *s. m.* east

levàre *v. tr.* to take away, to remove, to take from, to take off • *rifl.* to get up (alzarsi da letto); to stand up (alzarsi in piedi) • *intr. pron.* to rise

levatrice *s. f.* midwife

levigàre *v. tr.* to smooth, to polish

levigatézza *s. f.* smoothness

levrièro *s. m.* greyhound

lezióne *s. f.* lesson

lezióso *agg.* affected

libagióne *s. f.* libation

libbra *s. f.* pound

liberàle *agg.* liberal

liberalismo *s. m.* liberalism

liberalizzazióne *s. f.* liberalization; deregulation

liberaménte *avv.* freely

liberàre *v. tr.* to free, to liberate, to release • *rifl.* to free oneself; to get rid (sbarazzarsi)

libero *agg.* free, available, vacant

libertà *s. f.* freedom, liberty

libertino *agg.* libertine

liberty *s. m. inv.* art nouveau

libidine *s. f.* lust

libràio *s. m.* bookseller

librerìa *s. f.* bookshop; bookcase (mobile)

librettista *s. m. e f.* librettist

librétto *s. m.* booklet; bank-book (di banca); libretto (*mus.*)

libro *s. m.* book

licéale *agg.* high-school (*attr.*)

licènza *s. f.* licence

licenziàre *v. tr.* to dismiss

licenzióso *agg.* dissolute, licentious

licèo *s. m.* lycée, high school

lido *s. m.* shore, beach

lièto *agg.* glad

lìeve *agg.* light

lièvito *s. m.* yeast

lìgneo *agg.* wood (*attr.*)

lilla *agg. inv.* lilac

limaccióso *agg.* muddy

limàre *v. tr.* to file

limétta *s. f.* nail-file

limitàre *v. tr.* to limit • *rifl.* to limit oneself

limitazióne *s. f.* limitation

lìmite *s. m.* limit

limìtrofo *agg.* neighbouring

limonàta *s. f.* lemon juice

limóne *s. m.* lemon

limpidézza *s. f.* clearness

lìmpido *agg.* clear, limpid

linciàggio *s. m.* lynching

lindo *agg.* neat

lìnea *s. f.* line

lineàre *agg.* linear; coherent (*fig.*)

linearità *s. f.* linearity

linfa *s. f.* sap (*bot.*); lymph (*biol.*)

lìngua *s. f.* tongue; language (linguaggio)

linguàggio *s. m.* language, speech; slang (di un gruppo)

linguétta *s. f.* spline

linguistico *agg.* linguistic

lino *s. m.* flax (*bot.*); linen (tessuto)

lìpide *s. m.* lipid

liquefàre *v. tr. e intr. pron.* to liquefy, to melt

liquidàre *v. tr.* to liquidate (*leg.*, *fin.*); to pay off (saldare)

liquidazióne *s. f.* liquidation (*leg.*, *fin.*); sale (di merce)

liquidità *s. f.* liquidity

lìquido *agg.* liquid, fluid • *s. m.* liquid; denaro – cash

liquirizia *s. f.* licorice

liquóre *s. m.* liquor; spirits *pl.*

lìrica *s. f.* opera (*mus.*); lyrical poem (componimento lirico)

lìrico *agg.* lyric(al)

lirismo *s. m.* lyricism

lisca *s. f.* fish-bone

lisciàre *v. tr.* to smooth; to stroke (accarezzare)

lìscio *agg.* smooth

lista *s. f.* list

listino *s. m.* list; – prezzi price-list

litanìa *s. f.* litany; string (sfilza)

lìte *s. f.* quarrel; lawsuit (*leg.*)

litigàre *v. intr.* to quarrel • *rifl. rec.* to contend for

litìgio *s. m.* quarrel

litigióso *agg.* quarrelsome

litografìa *s. f.* lithography (procedimento); lithograph (riproduzione)

litoràle *s. m.* coast

litoràneo *agg.* coast (*attr.*)

litro *s. m.* litre; **mezzo** – half a litre

liturgìa *s. f.* liturgy

litùrgico *agg.* liturgical

liutàio *s. m.* lutist

liùto *s. m.* lute

livellàre *v. tr.* to level, to even up

livèllo *s. m.* level; **passaggio a** – level crossing

lìvido *agg.* livid • *s. m.* bruise

livrèa *s. f.* livery
locàle *s. m.* room • *agg.* local; **treno** – slow train
località *s. f.* place; – **di villeggiatura** resort
localizzàre *v. tr.* to localize
locànda *s. f.* inn
locandina *s. f.* playbill
locomotìva *s. f.* locomotive
lodàre *v. tr.* to praise
lòde *s. f.* praise
lòggia *s. f.* loggia; lodge (massonica)
loggiàto *s. m.* portico, gallery
loggióne *s. m.* gallery
lògica *s. f.* logic
logicaménte *avv.* logically; obviously (naturalmente)
lògico *agg.* logical; obvious (ovvio)
logoràre *v. tr.* to wear out
lógoro *agg.* worn
logorròico *agg.* logorrheic, verbose
lombàggine *s. f.* lumbago
londinése *agg.* London (*attr.*) • *s. m. e f.* Londoner
longèvo *agg.* long-lived
longilìneo *agg.* long-limbed, slender
longitudinàle *agg.* longitudinal
longitùdine *s. f.* longitude
lontanànza *s. f.* distance
lontàno *agg.* far, distant • *avv.* far away, far off; – **da** far from
loquàce *agg.* loquacious
lordùra *s. f.* filth
losànga *s. f.* lozenge
lósco *agg.* shady
lòtta *s. f.* struggle, fight; wrestling (*sport*)
lottàre *v. intr.* to struggle, to fight; to wrestle (*sport*)
lotterìa *s. f.* lottery
lozióne *s. f.* lotion
lubrificànte *agg.* lubricating • *s. m.* lubricant
lubrificàre *v. tr.* to lubricate, to oil
lubrificazióne *s. f.* lubrication
lucchétto *s. m.* padlock
lùce *s. f.* light
lucènte *agg.* shining

lucernàrio *s. m.* skylight
lucèrtola *s. f.* lizard
lucidàre *v. tr.* to polish; to wax (a cera)
lucidatrìce *s. f.* floor-polisher
lucidità *s. f.* lucidity
lùcido *agg.* polished; shining (che risplende); lucid (*fig.*) • *s. m.* polish
lucràre *v. tr.* to make money
lùcro *s. m.* lucre, profit
lùdico *agg.* ludic
lùglio *s. m.* July
lùgubre *agg.* gloomy, dismal
lumàca *s. f.* snail
lùme *s. m.* lamp, light
luminosità *s. f.* brightness, luminosity
luminóso *agg.* bright, luminous
lùna *s. f.* moon; – **di miele** honeymoon
lùna park *loc. sost. m. inv.* fun-fair
lunàre *agg.* lunar; moon (*attr.*)
lunàtico *agg.* moody
lunedì *s. m.* Monday
lunétta *s. f.* lunette
lunghézza *s. f.* length
lungimirànte *agg.* far-sighted
lùngo *agg.* long, weak; watered (diluito) • *prep.* along, by
lungolàgo *s. m.* lake-front
lungomàre *s. m.* sea-front, promenade
lunòtto *s. m.* back window
luògo *s. m.* place
lùpo *s. m.* wolf
lùppolo *s. m.* hop
lùrido *agg.* filthy
lusingàre *v. tr.* to flatter
lusinghièro *agg.* flattering, tempting
lussazióne *s. f.* dislocation
lùsso *s. m.* luxury
lussuóso *agg.* luxurious
lussureggiànte *agg.* luxuriant
lussurióso *agg.* lustful
lustràre *v. tr.* to polish
lustrascàrpe *s. m. e f. inv.* shoe-shine
lùstro *s. m.* lustre
luteranésimo *s. m.* Lutheranism
lùtto *s. m.* mourning
luttuóso *agg.* sad, mournful

ma *cong.* but, yet; still (eppure)

màcabro *agg.* macabre

macché *inter.* of course not!

màcchia *s. f.* stain spot, bush; copse (boscaglia)

macchiàre *v. tr.* to stain, to spot

macchiàto *agg.* stained

macchiétta *s. f.* speck, character; odd fish (tipo originale)

màcchina *s. f.* engine, machine; car (*autom.*); – **per scrivere** typewriter

macchinàrio *s. m.* machinery

macchinazióne *s. f.* machination, plot

macchinista *s. m.* engineer, machine operator (industria)

macchinóso *agg.* intricate, complex

macedònia *s. f.* fruit-salad

macellàio *s. m.* butcher

macellería *s. f.* butcher's shop

maceràre *v. tr.* to macerate, to steep

macigno *s. m.* rock

màcina *s. f.* millstone

macinapépe *s. m. inv.* pepper-mill

macinàre *v. tr.* to grind, to mill

macrobiòtico *agg.* macrobiotic

macroscòpico *agg.* macroscopic; gross (*fig.*)

maculàto *agg.* spotted

màdia *s. f.* kneading-trough

madornàle *agg.* enormous, gross

màdre *s. f.* mother

madrelingua *s. f.* mother tongue

madrepàtria *s. f.* motherland, mother country

madrepèrla *s. f.* mother-of-pearl

madrigàle *s. m.* madrigal

maestà *s. f.* majesty

maestóso *agg.* majestic, grand; maestoso (*mus.*)

maestrànze *s. f. pl.* hands

maèstro *s. m.* master; teacher (di scuola); – **di sci** ski instructor

màga *s. f.* magician

magàgna *s. f.* flaw; infirmity (acciacco)

magàri *inter.* if only! • *cong.* even if

magazzino *s. m.* store, warehouse; **grande –** department store

màggio *s. m.* May

maggioràsco *s. m.* majorat

maggiorazióne *s. f.* increase; surcharge (di prezzo)

maggióre *agg.* major; greater (più grande); bigger (più grosso); older (di età); elder (fra consanguinei)

maggiorènne *s. m. e f.* major, adult

maggioritàrio *agg.* majority (*attr.*)

maggiorménte *avv.* mostly

magìa *s. f.* magic

màgico *agg.* magic

magistràle *agg.* masterly

magistràto *s. m.* magistrate

màglia *s. f.* stitch; knitting (lavoro a –); vest (indumento); cardigan (giacca di lana); mesh (di rete); link (di catena)

magliétta *s. f.* jersey, t-shirt

magnànimo *agg.* magnanimous, noble

magnàte *s. m.* magnate, tycoon

magnète *s. m.* magnet

magnètico *agg.* magnetic

magnetismo *s. m.* magnetism

magnificaménte *avv.* magnificently

magnìfico *agg.* magnificent

magnòlia *s. f.* magnolia

màgo *s. m.* magician, wizard

magrézza *s. f.* thinness, leanness

màgro *agg.* thin, lean, slim

mài *avv.* never

maiàle *s. m.* pig; pork (*alim.*); **braciole di –** pork chops

maiòlica *s. f.* majolica

maionése *s. f.* mayonnaise

maiuscòlo *agg.* capital

malaféde *s. f.* bad faith

malaménte *avv.* badly

malandàto *agg.* in bad condition; shabbily dressed (malvestito)

malànno *s. m.* illness, infirmity; misfortune (disgrazia)

malària *s. f.* malaria

malàto *agg.* sick (*attr.*); ill (*pred.*)

malattìa *s. f.* illness, disease

malauguratamènte *avv.* unfortunately

malaugùrio s. m. ill omen

malavita s. f. (the) underworld

malcóncio agg. bedraggled, battered

maldéstro agg. clumsy

maldicènza s. f. slander

màle avv. badly, wrong • s. m. evil, ill, wrong; pain (dolore)

maledétto agg. cursed, damned; dreadful (insopportabile)

maledizióne s. f. curse, malediction

maleducáto agg. rude, ill-bred, impolite

maleducazióne s. f. rudeness

maleodoránte agg. stinking

malèssere s. m. malaise; uneasiness (inquietudine)

malfamáto agg. of ill repute

malfátto agg. ill-one, misshapen, awkward

malférmo agg. unsteady, shaky, wobbly; weak (debole)

malformazióne s. f. malformation; deformity (med.)

malgrádo prep. notwithstanding, in spite of • cong. although, though

malignità s. f. malignity

maligno agg. malignant, malicious, malevolent

malinconìa s. f. melancholy

malincònico agg. melancholy, melancholic, gloomy

a malincuòre loc. avv. unwillingly

malintenzionáto agg. ill-intentioned

malintéso s. m. misunderstanding

malizióso agg. malicious

malleábile agg. malleable

malleòlo s. m. malleolus

malmenàre v. tr. to knock about

malmésso agg. shabby

malnutrito agg. ill-fed

malóre s. m. indisposition

malsáno agg. unhealthy; unsound (fig.)

maltèmpo s. m. bad weather

màlto s. m. malt

maltrattaménto s. m. abuse

malumóre s. m. ill temper, bad mood; **essere di** – to feel blue

màlva s. f. mallow; mauve (colore)

malvisto agg. disliked, unpopular

malvolentièri avv. unwillingly

màmma s. f. mother, mummy, mum, ma, mom

mammífero agg. mammalian • s. m. mammal; **i mammíferi** The Mammalia

mancaménto s. m. faint

mancànza s. f. want, lack; absence (assenza); fault (fallo); defect (difetto)

mancàre v. intr. to lack; to be absent (non esserci); to fail (venire meno) • tr. to miss

mància s. f. tip

manciàta s. f. handful

mancino agg. left-handed; dirty (fig.)

mandàre v. tr. to send, to forward, to dispatch; – **a chiamare** to send for

mandarino s. m. tangerine

mandìbola s. f. jaw, mandible

mandolino s. m. mandolin(e)

màndorla s. f. almond; **pasta di** – marzipan

mandrino s. m. mandrel, spindle, chuck

maneggévole agg. handy

maneggiàre v. tr. to handle

manéggio s. m. manége; intrigue (fig.); handing (manipolazione)

mangiàbile agg. eatable

mangianàstri s. m. tape-player

mangiàre v. tr. to eat

mangiàta s. f. square meal, bellyful

mangime s. m. fodder

manìa s. f. mania, craze; – **di persecuzione** persecution complex

maniaco agg. maniac, insane; mad, crazy (fig.)

mànica s. f. sleeve; **senza maniche** sleeveless; – **a vento** wind-cone

manicarétto s. m. dainty, delicacy

mànico s. m. handle

manicòmio s. m. mental hospital, madhouse (fam.)

manicùre s. f. manicure

manièra s. f. manner, way

manierismo s. m. mannerism

manifattùra s. f. manufacture; factory (fabbrica)

manifestaménte avv. openly

manifestàre v. tr. to manifest, to show, to display, to express • intr. to demonstrate • rifl. to manifest oneself, to reveal oneself, to prove oneself

manifestazióne s. f. manifestation, display; demonstration (dimostrazione)

manifèsto s. m. placard, poster, bill; notice (avviso)

manìglia s. f. handle, knob; pull (da tirare); strap, handhold (di sostegno)

manipolàre v. tr. to manipulate, to handle

manipolazióne s. f. manipulation; plotting (fig.)

maniscálco s. m. farrier

mànna s. f. manna

màno s. f. hand; side (lato); **contro** – on the wrong side of the road; **di seconda** – second-hand

manòmetro s. m. manometer, gauge

manométtere v. tr. to tamper (with); to open unduly, to rummage; to falsify (falsificare)

manòpola s. f. hand grip (mecc.); knob (pomello)

manoscritto s. m. manuscript

manovàle s. m. labourer

manovèlla s. f. crank, winch

manòvra s. f. manoeuvre

manovràre v. tr. to manoeuvre; to steer (naut.); to handle (guidare) • intr. to manoeuvre

mansàrda s. f. mansard, garret, attic

mansióne s. f. function, task

mantecàre v. tr. to whisk

mantèlla s. f. mantle, cloak

mantèllo s. m. mantle, cloak, coat; hair, fur (di animale)

mantenére v. tr. to maintain, to keep, to preserve (conservare) • rifl. to earn one's living, to keep • intr. pron. to keep, to remain

mantenimènto s. m. maintenance; support (sostentamento); preservation (conservazione)

mànto s. m. mantle

manuàle agg. manual • s. m. manual, handbook

manualità s. f. manual dexterity

manualménte avv. manually

manùbrio s. m. handle; handle bar (di bicicletta); dumb-bell (attrezzo ginnico)

manufàtto s. m. handwork

manutenzióne s. f. maintenance, upkeep

mànzo s. m. steer; beef (alim.)

maomettàno agg. Mohammedan

màppa s. f. map; plan (di una zona)

mappamóndo s. m. globe

màrca s. f. brand, mark

marcàre v. tr. to mark, to check, to brand; to score (sport)

marchése s. m. marquis, marquess

màrchio s. m. brand, mark; – **di fabbrica** trademark

màrcia s. f. march, gear; speed (autom.); march (mus.)

marciapiède s. m. pavement; platform (ferr.)

marciàre v. intr. to march

màrcio agg. rotten

marcìre v. intr. to rot, to go bad

marcìume s. m. rot; corruption (fig.)

màre s. m. sea; **frutti di** – seafood

maréa s. f. tide

mareggiàta s. f. sea-storm

maremòto s. m. sea-quake

margarìna s. f. margarine

margherìta s. f. daisy

marginàle agg. marginal

màrgine s. m. margin

mariàno agg. Marian

marìna s. f. navy; marine (arte)

marinàio s. m. seaman, sailor, mariner; blue jacket (soldato di marina)

marinarésco agg. sea (attr.), sailor (attr.)

marìno agg. marine; sea (attr.)

marionétta s. f. puppet

marìto s. m. husband

marìttimo agg. maritime; sea (attr.)

marmellàta s. f. jam; – **di agrumi** marmalade

màrmo s. m. marble

marmìtta s. f. silencer (autom.)

marmòreo agg. marble (attr.)

marmòtta s. f. marmot; drone (fig.)

marróne s. m. brown; chestnut, marron (castagna)

martedì s. m. Tuesday

martellamènto s. m. hammering

martèllo s. m. hammer

màrtire s. m. e f. martyr

marxìsmo s. m. Marxism

marzapàne s. m. marzipan

marziàle agg. martial

marziàno s. m. Martian

màrzo s. m. March

mascalzóne s. m. rascal, scoundrel

mascàra s. m. inv. mascara

mascèlla s. f. jaw

màschera s. f. mask; – **di bellezza** face-mask; **un ballo in** – a masked ball

mascheràre v. tr. to mask; to disguise (travestire) • rifl. to mask, to disguise oneself, to masquerade

maschìle agg. masculine, male; manly (virile)

maschilìsta agg. sexist, male chauvinist

màschio s. m. boy, man; male (di animale); keep, donjon (di castello)

mascòtte s. f. inv. mascot

masochìsmo s. m. masochism

màssa s. f. mass; earth, ground (elettr.)

massacrànte agg. exhausting

massàcro s. m. massacre, slaughter

massaggiàre v. tr. to massage

massàggio s. m. massage

massàia s. f. housewife, housekeeper

massicciàta s. f. road-bed; ballast (ferr.)

249

massiccio *agg.* massive; bulky (grosso); square-built (tozzo)
massificazióne *s. f.* standardization
massimalismo *s. m.* maximalism
màssimo *agg.* maximum, greatest • *s. m.* maximum
màsso *s. m.* stone, block, rock; **caduta massi** falling rocks!
massonerìa *s. f.* Masonry
masticàre *v. tr.* to chew, to masticate
màstice *s. m.* mastic, adhesive, putty
mastodòntico *agg.* colossal, enormous
matàssa *s. f.* skein, hank; tangle (*fig.*)
matemàtica *s. f.* mathematics, maths *pl.* (*v. al sing.*)
matemàtico *agg.* mathematical
materassino *s. m.* mattress; – **gonfiàbile** inflatable mattress
materàsso *s. m.* mattress
matèria *s. f.* matter; material (materiale); substance (sostanza); subject (disciplina); **materie prime** raw materials
materiàle *agg.* material • *s. m.* material, stuff
materialismo *s. m.* materialism
materialménte *avv.* materially; really, quite (effettivamente)
maternità *s. f.* maternity, motherhood; maternity hospital (ospedale); **congèdo per** – maternity leave
matèrno *agg.* maternal, mother, motherly; mother (*attr.*)
matita *s. f.* pencil; crayon (pastello)
matriarcàle *agg.* matriarchal
matrìce *s. f.* matrix; counterfoil (*comm.*)
matrìcola *s. f.* roll (registro); number (numero); fresher (studente)
matrigna *s. f.* stepmother
matrimoniàle *agg.* matrimonial; marriage (*attr.*); wedding (*attr.*); **càmera** – double room; **lètto** – double bed
matrimònio *s. m.* marriage; wedding (cerimonia)
matronèo *s. m.* women's gallery
matronìmico *agg.* matronymic
mattatóio *s. m.* slaughter-house
mattinàta *s. f.* morning
mattinièro *agg.* early-rising
mattìno *s. m.* morning
màtto *agg.* mad, insane, crazy; **scàcco** – checkmate
mattóne *s. m.* brick
mattonèlla *s. f.* tile

mattutìno *agg.* morning (*attr.*)
maturàre *v. tr.* to mature, to bring, to ripeness • *intr. e intr. pron.* to mature, to ripen
maturazióne *s. f.* maturation, ripening
maturità *s. f.* maturity, ripeness
matùro *agg.* mature, mellow; ripe (frutta)
mausolèo *s. m.* mausoleum
màzza *s. f.* staff, club
mazzétto *s. m.* little bunch, bouquet, bundle
màzzo *s. m.* bunch, bundle; – **di càrte** pack of cards
meàndro *s. m.* meander, winding
meccànica *s. f.* mechanics *pl.* (*v. al sing.*); mechanism, works *pl.* (meccanismo)
meccanicaménte *avv.* mechanically
meccànico *agg.* mechanical
meccanìsmo *s. m.* mechanism, machinery, gear; works *pl.*
meccanizzazióne *s. f.* mechanization
mecenàte *s. m. e f.* Maecenas, patron
mecenatìsmo *s. m.* Maecenatism, patronage
mèda *s. f.* seamark, beacon
medàglia *s. f.* medal
medaglióne *s. m.* locket; medallion (*arch.*)
medèsimo *agg.* same • *pron.* the same
mèdia *s. f.* average; mean (*mat.*)
mediaménte *avv.* on the average
mediànte *prep.* by, by means of, through
mediatóre *s. m.* mediator; middleman; broker (*comm.*)
medicaménto *s. m.* medicament
medicàre *v. tr.* to medicate, to treat; to dress (una ferita) • *rifl.* to medicate oneself
medicazióne *s. f.* dressing, medicament
medicìna *s. f.* medicine
medicinàle *agg.* medicinal, healing
mèdico *s. m.* doctor, physician
medievàle *agg.* medi(o)eval
mèdio *agg.* middle, medium
mediòcre *agg.* mediocre, second-rate, ordinary
mediocrità *s. f.* mediocrity, mean
meditàre *v. tr.* to meditate, to ponder • *intr.* to meditate (on), to brood, to muse (over)
meditazióne *s. f.* meditation
mediterràneo *agg.* Mediterranean
medùsa *s. f.* jelly-fish, medusa
megàfono *s. m.* megaphone
megalìtico *agg.* megalithic
megàlomane *s. m.* megalomaniac
megalòpoli *s. f.* megalopolis
mèglio *avv.* better • *s. m. e f. inv.* (the) best (thing)

méla s. f. apple; **torta di – apple pie; – cotogna** quince

melagràna s. f. pomegranate

melanzàna s. f. egg-plant; aubergine (frutto)

melènso agg. doltish

mellìfluo agg. honeyed, sugary

mélma s. f. mud, mire

melmóso agg. muddy, miry

melodìa s. f. melody

melodìoso agg. melodious, musical

melodrammàtico agg. operatic (mus.); melodramatic (fig.)

melóne s. m. melon

membràna s. f. membrane

mèmbro s. m. member; limb (arto)

memoràbile agg. memorable

memòria s. f. memory, remembrance; recollection (ricordo)

mendicànte s. m. e f. beggar

menefreghìsmo s. m. indifference

meningìte s. f. meningitis

menìsco s. m. meniscus

méno avv. less • agg. less, not so much • s. m. inv. less; minus (mat.); **a – che** unless

menomazióne s. f. disability

menopàusa s. f. menopause

mènsa s. f. table, board; canteen, cafeteria (locale)

mensìle agg. monthly

mensilménte avv. monthly

mènsola s. f. shelf; console (arch.)

ménta s. f. peppermint

mentalità s. f. mentality, outlook

mentalménte avv. mentally

ménte s. f. mind; memory (memoria)

mentìre v. intr. to lie

ménto s. m. chin

méntre cong. while, as • s. m. inv. meantime, meanwhile

menu s. m. inv. menù

menzógna s. f. lie

meravìglia s. f. wonder; marvel (cosa meravigliosa)

meravigliàre v. tr. to surprise, to astonish, to amaze • intr. pron. to wonder

meraviglióso agg. wonderful, marvellous

mercànte s. m. merchant, trader, dealer

mercantìle agg. merchant (attr.); mercantile

mercantilìsmo s. m. mercantilism

mercatìno s. m. flea market

mercàto s. m. market; market-place (luogo)

mèrce s. f. goods pl.

mercenàrio agg. mercenary

mercerìa s. f. haberdashery

mercoledì s. m. Wednesday

mercùrio s. m. mercury, quicksilver

merènda s. f. snack

meretrìce s. f. meretrix, prostitute

meridiàna s. f. sundial

meridionàle agg. southern; south (attr.)

meridióne s. m. south

merìnga s. f. meringue

meritàre v. tr. to deserve, to merit • intr. to be worth

meritévole agg. deserving; worthy (degno)

mèrito s. m. merit

merlétto s. m. lace

mèrlo s. m. ouzel, blackbird; merlon (arch.)

merlùzzo s. m. cod

meschìno agg. mean, petty

mescolànza s. f. mixing, blending; mixture, blend, medley (miscuglio)

mescolàre v. tr. to mix, to blend, to mingle

mése s. m. month

méssa s. f. Mass

messaggèro s. m. messenger

messàggio s. m. message

messàle s. m. missal, Mass-book

messiànico agg. Messianic

messinscèna s. f. staging (teatro); act (fig.)

mestàre v. tr. to stir (up) • intr. to meddle

mestière s. m. trade, craft; job, work (lavoro)

méstolo s. m. ladle

mestruazióni s. f. pl. menstruation sing., menses, courses

méta s. f. destination; goal (traguardo); aim, end (fine)

metà s. f. half

metafìsico agg. metaphysical

metàfora s. f. metaphor

metafòrico agg. metaphoric(al)

metàllico agg. metallic; metal (attr.)

metàllo s. m. metal

metallùrgico agg. metallurgic(al)

metamorfìsmo s. m. metamorphism

metamòrfosi s. f. metamorphosis

metàno s. m. methane

metèora s. f. meteor

meteorologìa s. f. meteorology

meteorològico agg. meteorologic(al)

meticolóso agg. meticulous, scrupulous; fussy (pignolo)

metòdico agg. methodic(al)

metodìsta s. m. e f. Methodist

mètodo s. m. method

metodològico agg. methodological

métopa *s. f.* metope

métrico *agg.* metric

métro *s. m.* metre, meter (USA); ruler (strumento); – **quadro** square metre; – **cubo** cubic metre

metropolita *s. m.* metropolitan

metropolitáno *agg.* metropolitan

méttere *v. tr.* to put, to set; to place (collocare); to arrange (disporre) • *rifl.* to put on • *intr. pron.* to start, to begin, to set to

mezzadría *s. f.* métayage, share-cropping

mezzalúna *s. f.* half-moon, crescent

mezzanótte *s. f.* midnight

mézzo *agg.* half, semi-; middle (medio) • *s. m.* half (metà); middle, centre (parte centrale); means (espediente)

mezzogiórno *s. m.* midday, noon, twelve o'clock; **a** – at noon

mezz'óra *s. f.* half an hour

miagolàre *v. intr.* to mew, to miaow

micenèo *agg.* Mycenaean

micidiàle *agg.* deadly, fatal

micio *s. m.* cat, pussycat

micròbo *s. m.* microbe

microcòsmo *s. m.* microcosm

microfilm *s. m. inv.* microfilm

micròfono *s. m.* microphone, mike

microrganismo *s. m.* micro-organism

microscópio *s. m.* microscope

midóllo *s. m.* marrow; – **spinale** spinal marrow

miéle *s. m.* honey; **luna di** – honeymoon

miètere *v. tr.* to reap

mietitúra *s. f.* harvest

migliàio *s. m.* thousand

miglio *s. m.* millet (*bot.*); mile (misura); – **marino** nautical mile

miglioraménto *s. m.* improvement

miglioràre *v. tr.* to improve, to better • *intr.* to improve, to get better

migliore *agg.* better (comparat.); (the) best (superl. relat.)

migliorìa *s. f.* improvement

mìgnolo *s. m.* little finger (mano), little toe (piede)

migràre *v. intr.* to migrate

migratòrio *agg.* migratory, migrant

miliardàrio *agg.* multi-millionaire, billionaire (USA)

miliàrdo *s. m.* milliard; billion (USA)

milionàrio *agg.* millionaire

milióne *s. m.* million

militànte *agg.* militant

militàre *s. m.* military • *v. intr.* to militate

militarésco *agg.* soldierly

mille *agg. num. inv.* thousand

millenàrio *agg.* millenary

millènnio *s. m.* millennium

millèsimo *agg. num. ord.* thousandth, millesimal

millimetro *s. m.* millimetre

milza *s. f.* spleen

mimético *agg.* mimetic, imitative

mimetizzàre *v. tr. e rifl.* to camouflage

mimo *s. m.* mime

minàccia *s. f.* menace, threat

minacciàre *v. tr.* to threaten, to menace

minaccióso *agg.* threatening, menacing

minaréto *s. m.* minaret

minerále *agg. e s. m.* mineral; **acqua** – mineral water

mineralogìa *s. f.* mineralogy

minerário *agg.* mining, mineral; ore (*attr.*)

minèstra *s. f.* soup; – **di verdura** vegetable soup

miniatúra *s. f.* miniature

miniaturista *s. m. e f.* miniaturist

minièra *s. f.* mine

minigólf *s. m. inv.* minigolf

minigònna *s. f.* miniskirt

minimizzàre *v. tr.* minimize

mìnimo *agg.* (the) least, smallest, slightest (il più piccolo); (the) lowest (il più basso); very small (piccolissimo) • *s. m.* minimum, least; lowest gear (di motore)

ministèro *s. m.* ministry

ministro *s. m.* minister

minóre *agg.* smaller, less, lesser (comparat.); (the) smaller (tra due); minor (meno importante); younger, youngest (più giovane)

minorènne *s. m. e f.* minor, under age person

minuétto *s. m.* minuet

minúscolo *agg.* small, tiny; lower case (carattere tipografico)

minúto *agg. e s. m.* minute; **la lancetta dei minuti** the minute hand

minùzia *s. f.* trifle

mìope *agg.* myopic, short-sighted

mìra *s. f.* aim, sight, end; design (scopo)

miràcolo *s. m.* miracle

miracolóso *agg.* miraculous

miràggio *s. m.* mirage

mirìade *s. f.* myriad

mirtìllo *s. m.* bilberry

misàntropo *agg.* misanthropic • *s. m.* misanthrope

miscéla *s. f.* mixture, blend

miscelatóre *s. m.* mixer

miscellánea s. f. miscellany

mischia s. f. scuffle, fray; scrummage (sport)

miscredénte agg. misbelieving • s. m. e f. misbeliever

miscúglio s. m. mixture, huddle; jumble (fig.)

miserábile agg. miserable, wretched; poor (povero); mean (meschino)

miséria s. f. poverty; misery (infelicità); trifle (inezia)

misericòrdia s. f. mercy

misero agg. miserable, wretched; poor (povero)

misfatto s. m. misdeed; crime (delitto)

misógino agg. misogynic • s. m. misogynist

missile s. m. missile

missionário s. m. missionary

missióne s. f. mission

misterióso agg. mysterious

mistéro s. m. mystery

mistica s. f. mystical theology

misticismo s. m. mysticism, mystical theology

mistico agg. mystic(al)

mistificatóre s. m. mystifier

misto agg. mixed, mingled

misúra s. f. measure; size (taglia); measure (provvedimento)

misurábile agg. measurable

misuráre v. tr. to measure, to estimate (valutare) • rifl. to measure oneself; to try on (indumenti)

misuratóre s. m. meter, gauge

misurino s. m. (small) measure

mite agg. mild; meek (mansueto); moderate (moderato)

mitico agg. mythical

mitigáre v. tr. to mitigate • intr. pron. to calm down; to become mild (del clima)

mítilo s. m. mussel

mitizzáre v. tr. to mythicize

mito s. m. myth

mitología s. f. mythology

mitológico agg. mythologic(al)

mitòmane agg. mythomaniac

mitra s. f. mitre

mitténte s. m. e f. sender

mnemónico agg. mnemonic

móbile agg. movable • s. m. furniture

mobilità s. f. mobility

mobilitazióne s. f. mobilization

mocassino s. m. moccasin

móda s. f. fashion, style; alla - fashionable

modalità s. f. formality, modality

modanatúra s. f. moulding

modèlla s. f. model

modelláre v. tr. to model, to mould

modellismo s. m. modelling

modèllo s. m. model, pattern

moderáre v. tr. to moderate, to reduce (ridurre) • rifl. to moderate oneself

moderáto agg. moderate

moderatóre s. m. moderating

moderazióne s. f. moderation

modernismo s. m. modernism

modernità s. f. modernity

modernizzáre v. tr. to modernize • rifl. to bring oneself up-to-date

modèrno agg. modern, up-to-date

modèsto agg. modest

módico agg. moderate, reasonable

modifica s. f. modification

modificábile agg. modifiable

modificáre v. tr. to modify, to correct (correggere) • intr. pron. to change

moduláre agg. modular

módulo s. m. form; module (arch.)

mògano s. m. mahogany

móglie s. f. wife

móle s. f. bulk, mass

molécola s. f. molecule

molestáre v. tr. to molest, to bother, to tease

molèsto agg. troublesome, annoying, bothering

mólla s. f. spring

molláre v. tr. to slacken • intr. to give in

mòlle agg. soft, tender, weak; flabby (debole)

mollétta s. f. clothes-peg, clothes-ping (per panni); hair-grip (per capelli)

mollica s. f. crumb

mollusco s. m. shellfish

mòlo s. m. mole, pier

moltéplice agg. manifold, various

moltiplicáre v. tr. e intr. pron. to multiply

moltiplicazióne s. f. multiplication

moltitúdine s. f. multitude; crowd (folla)

mólto avv. very, much • agg. indef. much sing., many pl. • pron. indef. much, a lot, many • s. m. the lot of things

momentaneaménte avv. at the moment, at present

momentáneo agg. momentary; short-lived (di breve durata)

momènto s. m. moment; time (tempo)

monacále agg. monastic

monachésimo s. m. monachism

mónaco s. m. monk

monarchia *s. f.* monarchy
monàrchico *agg.* monarchic(al)
monastèro *s. m.* monastery
monàstico *agg.* monastic
moncóne *s. m.* stump
mondanità *s. f.* wordlyness
mondàno *agg.* wordly, earthly, mundane
mondiàle *agg.* world (*attr.*); world-wide
móndo *s. m.* world
monéta *s. f.* coin, piece
monetàrio *agg.* monetary
mongolfièra *s. f.* hot-hair balloon
monocoltùra *s. f.* single-crop system
monocòrde *agg.* monotonous
monocromàtico *agg.* monochrome
monogamia *s. f.* monogamy
monografia *s. f.* monograph
monolitico *agg.* monolithic
monolocàle *s. m.* bedsitter
monòlogo *s. m.* monologue, soliloquy (soliloquio)
monomaniaco *agg.* monomaniac
monopòlio *s. m.* monopoly
monopósto *agg. inv.* single-seater
monosillabo *s. m.* monosyllable
monoteismo *s. m.* monotheism
monotonia *s. f.* monotony
monòtono *agg.* monotonous
monsóne *s. m.* monsoon
montacàrichi *s. m. inv.* goods-lift
montàggio *s. m.* assembly; cutting (*cin.*)
montàgna *s. f.* mountain
montagnóso *agg.* mountainous
montàre *v. tr.* to mount, to climb; to ride (cavalcare), to assemble (*mecc.*) • *intr.* to mount, to climb
mónte *s. m.* mountain; mount (davanti a nome proprio)
montóne *s. m.* tup, ram; **carne di** – mutton; **pelle di** – sheepskin
montuóso *agg.* mountainous
monumentàle *agg.* monumental
monuménto *s. m.* monument
moquette *s. f. inv.* moquette, carpet
mòra *s. f.* blackberry (*bot.*); delay (*leg.*)
moràle *agg.* moral • *s. f.* moral; morals *pl.* (moralità) • *s. m.* morale
moralismo *s. m.* moralism
moralizzàre *v. tr.* to moralize
moralmente *avv.* morally
mòrbido *agg.* soft, tender, smooth
morbillo *s. m.* measles *pl.* (*v. al sing.*)

morbóso *agg.* morbid; pathological (patologico)
mòrdere *v. tr.* to bite
morèna *s. f.* moraine
morènte *agg.* dying
morfologia *s. f.* morphology
morfològico *agg.* morphologic(al)
moribóndo *agg.* dying
morigeràto *agg.* sober-minded
morire *v. intr.* to die
mormoràre *v. tr. e intr.* to murmur
morosità *s. f.* arrearage
mòrsa *s. f.* vice
morsètto *s. m.* clamp; terminal (*elettr.*)
morsicàre *v. tr.* to gnaw; to bite (mordere)
mòrso *s. m.* bite; sting (puntura); morsel, bit (boccone)
mortàio *s. m.* mortar
mortàle *agg.* mortal
mortalità *s. f.* mortality
mòrte *s. f.* death
mortificàre *v. tr.* to mortify
mortificazióne *s. f.* mortification
mòrto *s. m.* dead person; the dead *pl.*
mosàico *s. m.* mosaic
mósca *s. f.* fly
moscerino *s. m.* midge
moschèa *s. f.* mosque
mòssa *s. f.* movement; move (nel gioco)
móstra *s. f.* show, exhibition
mostràre *v. tr.* to show, to display; to show off (ostentare) • *rifl.* to show oneself; to appear (apparire)
móstro *s. m.* monster
mostruóso *agg.* monstrous; tremendous (straordinario)
motivo *s. m.* reason, ground, motif; motive (*mus.*), pattern (elemento decorativo)
mòto *s. m.* motion
motocicletta *s. f.* motorbike, motorcycle
motociclista *s. m. e f.* motor-cyclist
motóre *s. m.* engine, motor
motorino *s. m.* moped; – **d'avviamento** starter
motoscàfo *s. m.* motorboat
motoslitta *s. f.* motorsled
movènte *s. m.* motive
moviménto *s. m.* movement; motion (moto); gesture (gesto)
mozzicóne *s. m.* stub, end
mùcca *s. f.* cow
mùcchio *s. m.* heap; **un** – **di gente** a lot of people; **a mucchi** plenty
mucósa *s. f.* mucosa, mucous membrane

mùffa *s. f.* mould
muggito *s. m.* bellow
mughétto *s. m.* lily of the valley; thrush (*med.*)
mugolàre *v. intr.* to howl, to whimper
mulattièra *s. f.* mule-track
mulino *s. m.* mill; – **a vento** windmill
mùlo *s. m.* mule
mùlta *s. f.* fine
multàre *v. tr.* to fine
multicolóre *agg.* multicoloured
multifórme *agg.* multiform, many-sided
multinazionàle *agg.* multinational
mùltiplo *agg.* multiple
mùmmia *s. f.* mummy
mùngere *v. tr.* to milk
municipàle *agg.* municipal; town (*attr.*)
municipalità *s. f.* municipality
municipio *s. m.* municipality, town council; town hall (sede)
munificènza *s. f.* munificence, liberality
munizióni *s. f. pl.* ammunitions
muòvere *v. tr.* to move, to drive • *intr.* to move, to go • *rifl.* to move, to stir, to go; to hurry (sbrigarsi)
mùra *s. f. pl.* walls
muràle *s. m.* mural
muràre *v. tr.* to wall up

muratóre *s. m.* bricklayer
murèna *s. f.* moray
mùro *s. m.* wall
mùschio *s. m.* musk; moss (*bot.*)
muscolàre *agg.* muscular
mùscolo *s. m.* muscle
muscolóso *agg.* muscular, sinewy
muséo *s. m.* museum
museruòla *s. f.* muzzle
mùsica *s. f.* music
musicàle *agg.* musical
musicassétta *s. f.* musicassette
musicista *s. m. e f.* musician
mussulmàno *agg.* Muslim, Moslen
mùta *s. f.* moult (di animali); wet suit (subacquea)
mutaménto *s. m.* change
mutànde *s. f. pl.* pants (da uomo); panties (da donna)
mutévole *agg.* hangeable, variable
mutilàto *s. m.* cripple
mutilazióne *s. f.* mutilation
mutismo *s. m.* mutism, silence
mùto *agg.* dumb; **film** – silent film
mùtua *s. f.* health insurance schema, medical insurance plan
mùtuo *agg.* mutual, reciprocal

N

nabàbbo s. m. nabob

nàfta s. f. diesel oil, naphta

nàiade s. f. naiad

naif agg. inv. naive

narcisista s. m. e f. narcissist

narcòtico s. m. narcotic

narice s. f. nostril

narràre v. tr. to tell, to narrate

narrativa s. f. fiction

narratòre s. m. narrator, story-teller

narrazióne s. f. narration, telling; tale, story (racconto)

nartéce s. m. narthex

nasàle agg. nasal

nascènte agg. rising

nàscere v. intr. to be born; to come (trarre origine); to arise (sorgere); to grow (di piante)

nàscita s. f. birth; origin (origine); **luogo di –** birth-place

nascitùro agg. future

nascóndere v. tr. to hide, to conceal • rifl. to hide (oneself)

nascondíglio s. m. hiding-place

nascósto agg. hidden

nasèllo s. m. hake

nàso s. m. nose

nàstro s. m. ribbon; tape (tecn.)

natàle agg. native • s. m. Christmas; **buon –** Merry Christmas

natalità s. f. natality, birth-rate

natalízio agg. Christmas (attr.)

nàtica s. f. buttock

nativià s. f. nativity

nàto agg. born

natùra s. f. nature; **– mòrta** still-life

naturàle agg. natural

naturalismo s. m. naturalism

naturalista s. m. e f. naturalist

naturalizzàre v. tr. to naturalize • rifl. to become naturalized

naturalménte avv. naturally; of course, sure (certo)

naturismo s. m. naturism

naturista s. m. e f. naturist

naufragàre v. intr. to wreck

naufràgio s. m. wreck

naumachia s. f. naumachia

nàusea s. f. nausea; **sentire –** to feel sick

nauseabóndo agg. nauseating, sickening

nauseàre v. tr. e intr. to nauseate, to sicken

nàutico agg. nautical, naval

navàle agg. naval

navàta s. f. nave (centrale); aisle (laterale)

nàve s. f. ship, vessel, boat

navétta s. f. shuttle

navigàbile agg. navigable

navigabilità s. f. navigability

navigàre v. intr. to sail, to be at sea, to navigate

navigatóre agg. seafaring

navigazióne s. f. navigation; **compagnia di –** shipping line

nazionàle agg. national

nazionalismo s. m. nationalism

nazionalità s. f. nationality

nazióne s. f. nation

nazismo s. m. Nazism

neànche avv. not... even • cong. nor, neither, not... either

nébbia s. f. fog; mist (leggera)

nebbióso agg. foggy, misty

nebulósa s. f. nebula

nebulóso agg. nebulous; hazy, vague (fig.)

nécessaire s. m. inv. toilet-case; **– per barba** shaving set

necessariaménte avv. necessarily, of necessity

necessàrio agg. necessary, indispensable; required (richiesto)

necessità s. f. necessity; need (bisogno)

necrològio s. m. obituary

necròpoli s. f. necropolis

nefàsto agg. inauspicious

negàre v. tr. to deny; to refuse (non concedere)

negativaménte avv. in the negative, negatively

negativo agg. negative

negazióne s. f. negation, denial; negative (gramm.)

negligènza s. f. negligence
negoziànte s. m. e f. shop-keeper, dealer, trader
negoziàto s. m. negotiation, talk
negòzio s. m. shop, store
négro agg. black, colo(u)red
nemico s. m. enemy
nemméno avv. e cong. not... even
nènia s. f. sing-song
neoclassicismo s. m. neoclassicism
neoclàssico agg. neoclassic(al)
neòfita s. m. e f. neophyte
neolatino agg. neo-Latin
neolìtico s. m. Neolithic Age
neologismo s. m. neologism
neonàto s. m. baby
neorealismo s. m. neorealism
nepotismo s. m. nepotism
neppùre avv. e cong. not... even
nerétto s. m. boldface
néro agg. black
nervatùra s. f. rib(s) (arch., mecc.); nervation (bot.)
nèrvo s. m. nerve
nervosismo s. m. nervousness
nervóso agg. nervous
néspola s. f. medlar
nèsso s. m. connection, nexus
nessùno agg. indef. no, not... any • pron. indef. nobody, no one; not... anybody, not... anyone; none, none... any (con partitivo)
nèttare s. m. nectar
nétto agg. clean; sharp (chiaro); flat (reciso); net (comm.); prezzo – net price
netturbino s. m. dustman, street-sweeper
neuròlogo s. m. neurologist
neutràle agg. neutral
neutralità s. f. neutrality
neutralizzàre v. tr. to neutralize
nèutro agg. neutral; neuter (gramm.)
nevàio s. m. snow-field
néve s. f. snow; fiocco di – snow-flake
nevicàre v. intr. impers. to snow
nevicàta s. f. snowfall
nevischio s. m. sleet
nevóso agg. snowy; snow-clad (coperto di neve)
nevralgìa s. f. neuralgia
nevròsi s. f. neurosis
nevròtico agg. neurotic
nicchia s. f. niche
nichilismo s. m. nihilism
nicotìna s. f. nicotine
nidiàta s. f. litter; brood (uccelli)

nidificàre v. intr. to nest
nìdo s. m. nest; – d'infanzia crèche, nursery
niènte pron. indef. nothing, not... anything • agg. indef. no, not... any • s. m. nothing
ninfa s. f. nymph
ninfèa s. f. water-lily
ninfèo s. m. nymphaeum
ninnanànna s. f. lullaby, cradle-song
nipóte s. m. e f. nephew m., niece f. (di zii); grandson m., grand-daughter f. (di nonni)
nirvàna s. m. inv. nirvana
nìtido agg. clear
nitrìto s. m. neigh, whinny; nitrite (chim.)
no avv. no, not
nòbile agg. e s. m. e f. noble
nobiliàre agg. nobiliary
nobiltà s. f. nobility
nocciòla s. f. hazel • agg. light brown, hazel
nocciòlo s. m. hazel
nóce s. m. walnut
nocìvo agg. harmful, noxious
nòdo s. m. knot; junction (ferr.)
nodóso agg. knotty; nodose (bot.)
nolóso agg. boring, tiresome
noleggiàre v. tr. to hire; to charter (naut., aer.)
noleggiatóre s. m. hirer, charterer
noléggio s. m. hire, charter, freightage
nòmade s. m. e f. nomad
nóme s. m. name; noun (gramm.)
nomìgnolo s. m. nickname
nominàre v. tr. to mention, to designate; to appoint (eleggere)
nominatìvo agg. nominative (gramm.); registered (comm.)
non avv. not; non (davanti a sost. o agg.)
nonché cong. as well as
noncuranza s. f. nonchalance, care
nònna s. f. grandmother; granny, grandma (fam.)
nònno s. m. grandfather; grandpa, grand-dad (fam.)
nonnùlla s. m. inv. trifle
nonostànte prep. in spite of, notwithstanding • cong. (even) though, although
nòrd s. m. north
nòrdico agg. Nordic
nòrma s. f. rule, norm, standard
normàle agg. normal
normalità s. f. normality
normànno agg. Norman
normatìva s. f. set of rules
nosocòmio s. m. hospital
nostalgìa s. f. homesickness

257

nostàlgico *agg.* nostalgic; homesick (*persona*)
nostràno *agg.* local, home-made
notàble *s. m.* notable
notàio *s. m.* notary (public)
notévole *agg.* remarkable, notable
notizia *s. f.* piece of news; news
notiziàrio *s. m.* (the) news
nòto *agg.* well-known, known
notorietà *s. f.* notoriety, renown
nòtte *s. f.* night; **buona** – good night; **questa** –
tonight; **la** – **scorsa** last night; **di** – by night
nottùrno *agg.* nocturnal; night (*attr.*)
novecentésco *agg.* twentieth-century (*attr.*)
novecènto *s. m. inv.* the twentieth century
novèlla *s. f.* tale, story
novellino *agg.* raw, green
novèmbre *s. m.* November
novità *s. f.* novelty; change (*innovazione*)
nòzze *s. f. pl.* wedding *sing.*
nùbe *s. f.* cloud
nubifràgio *s. m.* cloudburst, storm
nùbile *agg.* unmarried
nùca *s. f.* nape
nucleàre *agg.* nuclear
nùcleo *s. m.* nucleus; squad (*gruppo*); unit
(*unità*); – **familiare** family unit
nudismo *s. m.* nudism
nudista *s. m. e f.* nudist

nùdo *agg.* bare; naked (*svestito*)
nùlla *pron. indef. e avv.* nothing, not... anything • *s. m. inv.* nothing; **per** – not at all
nullaòsta *s. m. inv.* permit, authorization
numeràre *v. tr.* to number; to count (*calcolare*)
numeràto *agg.* numbered; **posti numerati**
numbered seats
numerazióne *s. f.* numbering, numeration;
notation (*mat.*)
numericaménte *avv.* numerically
nùmero *s. m.* number; size (*misura*; *taglia*)
numeróso *agg.* numerous
numismàtica *s. f.* numismatics *pl.* (*v. al sing.*)
nuòcere *v. intr.* to do harm (to), to harm
nuòra *s. f.* daughter-in-law
nuotàre *v. intr.* to swim
nuotàta *s. f.* swim
nuòto *s. m.* swimming
nuovaménte *avv.* again (*di nuovo*)
nuòvo *agg.* new
nutriènte *agg.* nourishing
nutriménto *s. m.* nourishment, food
nutrire *v. tr.* to feed, to nourish; to foster (*fig.*)
• *rifl.* to feed
nùvola *s. f.* cloud
nuvolóso *agg.* cloudy, overcast
nuziàle *agg.* wedding (*attr.*); nuptial

O

o *cong.* or

òasi *s. f.* oasis

obbediènza *s. f.* obedience

obbligàre *v. tr.* to oblige, to compel • *rifl.* to bind oneself, to engage (oneself)

obbligatòrio *agg.* compulsory

òbbligo *s. m.* obligation

obelisco *s. m.* obelisk

oberàto *agg.* overburdened

obesità *s. f.* obesity

obèso *agg.* obese

obiettàre *v. tr.* to object

obiettività *s. f.* objectivity

obiettivo *agg.* objective

oblìo *s. m.* oblivion

oblìquo *agg.* oblique

oblò *s. m.* bull's eye

oblùngo *agg.* oblong

òbolo *s. m.* mite

obsolèto *agg.* obsolete

òca *s. f.* goose

occasionàle *agg.* occasional; chance (*attr.*)

occasionalménte *avv.* on occasion, occasionally

occasióne *s. f.* opportunity, chance, occasion

òcchiaie *s. f. pl.* shadows, rings (under the eyes)

occhialàio *s. m.* optician

occhiàli *s. m. pl.* glasses; – da sole sun-glasses; – da sci goggles

occhiàta *s. f.* look, glance; saddled bream (*zool.*)

occhieggiàre *v. intr.* to peep

occhièllo *s. m.* buttonhole

òcchio *s. m.* eye

occidentàle *agg.* west (*attr.*); western

occidènte *s. m.* west

occlusióne *s. f.* occlusion

occorrènte *agg.* necessary, required

occultàre *v. tr.* to occult, to hide; to conceal (nascondere)

occupàre *v. tr.* to occupy, to hold • *intr. pron.* to occupy oneself, to be interested (in)

occupàto *agg.* occupied, busy, engaged; taken (non libero); questo posto è – this seat is taken; sono – I have an engagement

occupazióne *s. f.* occupation; qual è la tua – ? what is your job?

oceànico *agg.* oceanic

oceàno *s. m.* ocean

oceanografìa *s. f.* oceanography

òcra *agg. inv.* ochre

oculàre *agg.* ocular; eye (*attr.*); testimone – eyewitness

oculàto *agg.* cautious

oculìsta *s. m. e f.* oculist

odiàre *v. tr.* to hate • *rifl. rec.* to hate each other

odièrno *agg.* today's (*attr.*)

òdio *s. m.* hatred, hate

odióso *agg.* hateful, hideous, detestable

odissèa *s. f.* odyssey

odontoiàtra *s. m. e f.* dental surgeon, dentist

odontotècnico *s. m.* dental mechanic

odoràre *v. tr. e intr.* to smell

odóre *s. m.* smell; odour, scent (piacevole)

odoróso *agg.* sweet-smelling, fragrant

offèndere *v. tr.* to offend, to insult (insultare) • *rifl. rec.* to insult each other • *intr. pron.* to take offence

offensìva *s. f.* offensive

offensìvo *agg.* offensive, insulting

offèrta *s. f.* offer

offésa *s. f.* offence; wrong (torto)

officiàre *v. tr.* to serve

officìna *s. f.* workshop; – meccanica machineshop

offrìre *v. tr.* to offer • *rifl.* to offer oneself; offrirsi volontàrio to volunteer

offuscàre *v. tr.* to darken; to dim (fig.) • *intr. pron.* to darken, to get dark; to become obscured (fig.)

oftalmologìa *s. f.* ophthalmology

oggettivàre *v. tr.* to objectify

oggettìvo *agg.* objective

oggètto *s. m.* object, subject; subject-matter (argomento); oggetti preziósi valuables; oggetti personàli personal belongings

òggi *avv.* today

oggigiórno *avv.* nowadays

ogiva *s. f.* ogive

ógni *agg. indef.* every, each

ognúno *pron. indef.* everybody, everyone

olandése *agg.* Dutch • *s. m. e f.* Dutchman *m.*; Dutchwoman *f.*; Dutch (lingua)

oleóso *agg.* oily

olfàtto *s. m.* olfaction, smelling

oliàre *v. tr.* to oil

oliatóre *s. m.* oiler

oligarchìa *s. f.* oligarchy

olìmpiade *s. f.* Olympiad; Olympic games *pl.*; Olympics *pl.*

olìmpico *agg.* Olympic, Olympian

olimpiònico *s. m.* Olympic

òlio *s. m.* oil; – **d'oliva** olive oil; **sott'**– in oil; **quadro a** – oil-painting

olìva *s. f.* olive

olìvo *s. m.* olive tree

ólmo *s. m.* elm

oltràggio *s. m.* outrage

óltre *avv.* farther, further, far (di luogo); longer, more (di tempo) • *prep.* beyond, over; more than, over (più di); besides (in aggiunta); – **tutto** and besides

oltremàre *avv.* beyond the sea, overseas

oltrepassàre *v. tr.* to overstep, to exceed, to pass

omàggio *s. m.* homage; present (offerta); free sample (articolo dato in –); compliments *pl.* • *agg. inv.* free, complimentary; **un biglietto in** – a complimentary ticket; **una copia in** – a presentation copy

ómbra *s. f.* shade, shadow

ombreggiàre *v. tr.* to shade, to shadow

ombreggiatùra *s. f.* shading

ombrellàio *s. m.* umbrella-maker; umbrella-seller (venditore)

ombréllo *s. m.* umbrella; – **da sole** sunshade, parasol

ombrellóne *s. m.* beach-umbrella

ombrétto *s. m.* eyeshadow

ombrìna *s. f.* umbrina

ombróso *agg.* shady, shadowy; skittish (che si adombra)

omelette *s. f. inv.* omelette

omeopatìa *s. f.* hom(o)eopathy

omeopàtico *agg.* hom(o)eopathic

ómero *s. m.* humerus

ométtere *v. tr.* to omit, to leave out

omicìda *s. m. e f.* homicide, murder

omicìdio *s. m.* homicide

omissióne *s. f.* omission; neglect (*leg.*)

omogeneità *s. f.* homogeneity

omogeneizzàto *s. m.* homogenized food

omogèneo *agg.* homogeneous

omologàre *v. tr.* to homologate; to validate (ratificare), to recognize

omologìa *s. f.* homology

omònimo *agg.* homonymous • *s. m.* homonym

omosessuàle *agg.* homosexual, gay

ónda *s. f.* wave

ondàta *s. f.* wave; – **di caldo** heat-wave

ondeggiàre *v. intr.* to rock, to roll; to wave (oscillare)

ondulàto *agg.* undulatory, wavy; corrugated (di lamiera; cartone)

ondulazióne *s. f.* undulation

ònere *s. m.* burden, charge

oneróso *agg.* onerous, burdensome, hard

onestà *s. f.* honesty

onèsto *agg.* honest

ónice *s. f.* onyx

onìrico *agg.* oneiric

onnipotènte *agg.* omnipotent, almighty

onnipresènte *agg.* omnipresent, ubiquitous

onnìvoro *agg.* omnivorous

onomàstico *s. m.* name-day

onoràrio *agg.* honorary

onóre *s. m.* honour

onorificènza *s. f.* honour, dignity

opàco *agg.* opaque

opàle *s. f.* opal

opalescènte *agg.* opalescent

òpera *s. f.* work; opera (*mus.*); institution (ente); **mano d'** – labour

operàio *s. m.* workman, worker, hand

operàre *v. tr.* to work, to perform, to carry out • *intr.* to operate, to work, to act; to operate (*med.*)

operazióne *s. f.* operation; transaction (*comm.*)

operétta *s. f.* operetta, light opera

operóso *agg.* industrious, active

opinàbile *agg.* debatable

opinióne *s. f.* opinion

oppórre *v. tr. e rifl.* to oppose, to object (obiettare)

opportunaménte *avv.* opportunely, suitably, conveniently

opportunìsmo *s. m.* opportunism

opportunità *s. f.* expediency, opportunity, occasion; chance (circostanza opportuna)

opportùno *agg.* opportune, expedient, appropriate

opposizióne *s. f.* opposition; resistance (resistenza); objection (obiezione)

oppósto *s. m.* opposite; opposed (contrapposto); contrary (contrario); **l'uno – all'altro** facing each other

oppressióne *s. f.* oppression

oppressóre *s. m.* oppressor

opprimènte *agg.* oppressive

oppùre *cong.* or

optáre *v. intr.* to opt (for), to decide (for)

opulènza *s. f.* wealth (ricchezza); opulence

opùscolo *s. m.* pamphlet; booklet (libretto)

opzionále *agg.* optional

óra *s. f.* hour • *avv.* now; just (poco fa); **un'– e mezza** an hour and a half; **ore di punta** peak hours; **– di chiusura** closing time; **che – è?** what time is it?; **– legale** summer time; **prima d'–** before; **or –** just now

oràcolo *s. m.* oracle

òrafo *s. m.* goldsmith

oràle *agg.* oral

orário *s. m.* time-table, time

oráta *s. f.* gilthead

oratóre *s. m.* orator, speaker

oratòrio *s. m.* oratory

òrbita *s. f.* orbit; eye-socket (*anat.*); orbit (*astr.*, *fis.*)

orchèstra *s. f.* orchestra (*mus.*); band (da ballo); **direttore d'–** conductor

orchidèa *s. f.* orchid

òrda *s. f.* horde

ordígno *s. m.* implement

ordinále *agg.* ordinal

ordinaménto *s. m.* order, arrangement, organization; regulations *pl.*, rules *pl.* (complesso di leggi)

ordinánza *s. f.* ordinance, order, injunction

ordináre *v. tr.* to order, to command, to direct; to arrange (disporre in un certo ordine) • *rifl.* to arrange oneself, to draw up (disporsi)

ordinário *agg.* ordinary

ordináto *agg.* tidy, neat

ordinazióne *s. f.* order; ordination (*relig.*)

órdine *s. m.* order

ordíto *s. m.* warp

orecchiàbile *agg.* catchy

orecchíno *s. m.* ear-ring

orécchio *s. m.* ear

oréfice *s. m.* jeweller (gioielliere)

oreficería *s. f.* gold-work (*arte*); jeweller's (shop) (negozio)

órfano *s. m.* orphan

organicità *s. f.* organicity

orgànico *agg.* organic

organismo *s. m.* organism

organizzáre *v. tr. e rifl.* to organize

organizzazióne *s. f.* organization·

órgano *s. m.* organ

órgia *s. f.* orgy

orgóglio *s. m.* pride

orientàbile *agg.* rotary, swinging; revolving (*mecc.*)

orientàle *agg.* oriental, eastern

orientaménto *s. m.* orientation; trend (tendenza); direction; **senso dell'–** sense of direction

orientáre *v. tr.* to orient, to orientate • *rifl.* to orientate oneself, to take up (indirizzarsi)

orientatívo *agg.* indicative

oriènte *s. m.* east, orient

originále *agg.* original; queer (bizzarro) • *s. m.* original

originalità *s. f.* originality

originário *agg.* original (primitivo); primary (che dà origine); native (nativo)

orígine *s. f.* origin

orizzontále *agg.* horizontal

orizzontalménte *avv.* horizontally

orizzontàrsi *v. rifl.* to orientate oneself; to get one's bearings; to find one's way (*fig.*)

orizzónte *s. m.* horizon

orláre *v. tr.* to hem; to border (bordare)

órlo *s. m.* border, edge, brink, brim; hem (di vestito)

órma *s. f.* footprint; trace (*fig.*)

ormái *avv.* by now; by then (rif. al passato)

ormeggiáre *v. tr. e intr. pron.* to moor

orméggio *s. m.* mooring

ormóne *s. m.* hormone

ornamentále *agg.* ornamental

ornaménto *s. m.* ornament

ornáre *v. tr.* to adorn • *rifl.* to adorn oneself

ornáto *s. m.* ornamental design

ornitología *s. f.* ornithology

óro *s. m.* gold; **– zecchino** fine gold; **placcato in – ** gold plated

orografía *s. f.* orography

orologiáio *s. m.* watch-maker; watch-seller (venditore)

orològio *s. m.* watch (da polso); clock (da muro); alarm clock (sveglia)

oròscopo *s. m.* horoscope

orrèndo *agg.* horrid, horrible

orribile *agg.* horrible, dreadful

orripilànte *agg.* horrifying

orróre *s. m.* horror, dread; **film dell'–** horror film

órso s. m. bear; – **bruno** brown bear; – **grigio** grizzly; – **polare** sea bear

ortàggio s. m. vegetable

ortica s. f. nettle

orticària s. f. urticaria, nettle-rash

orticoltùra s. f. horticulture

òrto s. m. garden

ortodossìa s. f. orthodoxy

ortodòsso agg. orthodox

ortogonàle agg. orthogonal

ortografìa s. f. orthography

ortopédico s. m. orthopaedist

orzaiòlo s. m. sty(e)

òrzo s. m. barley

osàre v. tr. e intr. to dare, to risk; to attempt (arrischiare)

oscèno agg. obscene

oscillàre v. intr. to swing; to fluctuate (di prezzi); to waver (essere dubbioso); to oscillate (elettr.)

oscillazione s. f. oscillation; fluctuation (di prezzi, ecc.)

oscurantìsmo s. m. obscurantism

oscurità s. f. darkness; obscurity (fig.)

oscùro agg. dark, gloomy, sombre

ospedàle s. m. hospital

ospedaliéro agg. hospital (attr.)

ospitàle agg. hospitable, friendly

ospitalità s. f. hospitality

ospitàre v. tr. to lodge

òspite s. m. e f. host m., hostess f. (persona che ospita); guest (persona ospitata); – **pagante** paying guest; **camera degli ospiti** guest-room; – **d'onore** special guest

ospìzio s. m. hospice, home

ossatùra s. f. skeleton, bones

òsseo agg. bony, osseous

ossequióso agg. deferential, respectful

osservàbile agg. noticeable, visible

osservàre v. tr. to observe

osservatóre s. m. observer

osservatòrio s. m. observatory

osservazione s. f. observation; remark (commento)

ossessióne s. f. obsession

ossessìvo agg. obsessive

ossìa cong. or; that is, namely (cioè)

ossidàrsi v. intr. pron. to oxidize

òssido s. m. oxide

ossìgeno s. m. oxygen

òsso s. m. bone; stone, pit (nocciolo)

ostacolàre v. tr. to hinder, to hamper

ostàcolo s. m. obstacle, hindrance, handicap

ostàggio s. m. hostage

óste s. m. host, innkeeper

osteggiàre v. tr. to oppose, to be against

ostèllo s. m. hostel

ostensòrio s. m. ostensory

ostentàre v. tr. to show off, to parade

ostentazione s. f. ostentation, showing off

osterìa s. f. inn, tavern, pub

ostètrica s. f. obstetrician; midwife (levatrice)

òstico agg. harsh, hard, unpleasant

ostìle agg. hostile

ostilità s. f. hostility

ostinàto agg. obstinate, stubborn

ostinazione s. f. obstinacy, stubborness

òstrica s. f. oyster

ostruìre v. tr. to obstruct, to occlude, to block

ostruzióne s. f. obstruction

ostruzionìsmo s. m. obstructionism, filibustering

otìte s. f. otitis

otorinolaringoiàtra s. m. e f. otorhinolaryngologist; ear, nose and throat specialist

ottagonàle agg. octagonal

ottenére v. tr. to obtain, to get, to reach

òttica s. f. optics pl. (v. al sing.); point of view (punto di vista)

òttico agg. optic, optical

ottimàle agg. optimal; optimum (attr.)

ottimaménte avv. very well

ottimìsmo s. m. optimism

ottimìsta agg. optimist

ottimizzàre v. tr. to optimize

òttimo agg. very good, quite good, excellent, first-rate

ottóbre s. m. October

ottocentésco agg. nineteenth-century (attr.)

ottomàno agg. Ottoman

ottóne s. m. brass

otturàre v. tr. to stop, to fill; to clog (intasare); to stop up (ostruire) • intr. pron. to close up, to clog

otturatóre s. m. obturator; shutter (fotografia)

otturazione s. f. filling

ottùso agg. blunt, obtuse; dull (lento nel comprendere)

ovàle agg. oval

óvest s. m. west

ovìle s. m. sheepfold, sheep-pen

ovìno agg. ovine

ovìparo agg. oviparous animal

ovoidàle agg. ovoidal, ovoid

ovùnque avv. wherever, anywhere; every-where (dappertutto)

ovvéro *cong.* or, or rather
ovviaménte *avv.* obviously
ovviàre *v. intr.* to obviate
òvvio *agg.* obvious, evident

oziàre *v. intr.* to idle about, to laze
òzio *s. m.* idleness
ozióso *agg.* idle
ozòno *s. m.* ozone

P

pacchétto *s. m.* packet

pacchiàno *agg.* garish, showy

pàcco *s. m.* parcel, package

pàce *s. f.* peace

pacificazióne *s. f.* pacification

pacìfico *agg.* peaceful, pacific

pacifìsmo *s. m.* pacifism

padèlla *s. f.* frying-pan

padiglióne *s. m.* pavilion; block, wing (ospedale); auricle (*anat.*)

pàdre *s. m.* father

padronàle *agg.* master's; main (principale)

padronànza *s. f.* mastery, command, control

padróne *s. m.* master, boss; owner (proprietario); landlord (padrone di casa)

padroneggiàre *v. tr.* to master, to command, to rule; to sway (dominare)

paesàggio *s. m.* landscape, view, panorama

paesaggìsta *s. m. e f.* landscape-painter

paesàno *agg.* country (*attr.*)

paése *s. m.* country; land (nazione, terra); village (villaggio)

pàga *s. f.* pay, wage

pagàbile *agg.* payable

pagàia *s. f.* paddle

pagaménto *s. m.* payment; **condizioni di –** terms of payment; **– alla consegna** cash on delivery

paganésimo *s. m.* paganism, heathenism

pagàre *v. tr.* to pay; to settle (saldare)

pagèllo *s. m.* sea-bream

pàgina *s. f.* page

pàglia *s. f.* straw; **un cappello di –** a straw hat

pagliàccio *s. m.* clown, buffoon

pagliàio *s. m.* strawstack

pagnòtta *s. f.* loaf

pagòda *s. f.* pagoda

pàio *s. m.* pair; couple (due o tre)

pàla *s. f.* shovel; blade, form; vane (remo, elica); ancona, altar-piece (d'altare)

paladìno *s. m.* paladin, champion

palafìtta *s. f.* piles *pl.*; palafitte (*archeol.*)

palàmito *s. m.* boulter

palàto *s. m.* palate

palàzzo *s. m.* palace (reggia); mansion (casa signorile); building (edificio)

pàlco *s. m.* platform; stand (tribuna); box (*teatro*)

palcoscènico *s. m.* stage

paleocristiàno *agg.* early Christian

paleografìa *s. f.* palaeography

paleolìtico *agg.* Palaeolithic

palése *agg.* manifest, clear

palèstra *s. f.* gymnasium

palétta *s. f.* shovel; dustpan (per la spazzatura); trowel (da giardiniere)

palétto *s. m.* stake, pole, post; bolt (chiavistello)

pàlio *s. m.* contest, competition; prize (premio)

palizzàta *s. f.* fence

pàlla *s. f.* ball

pallacanèstro *s. f.* basket-ball

pallamàno *s. f.* handball

pallanuòto *s. f.* water polo

pallavólo *s. f.* volley-ball

palliatìvo *s. m.* palliative

pàllido *agg.* pale

pallóne *s. m.* ball; football (gioco); balloon (*aer.*)

pallottolière *s. m.* abacus

pàlma *s. f.* palm; **– da datteri** date-palm; **– da cocco** coconut-palm

palmìpede *s. m.* palmiped, web-footed bird

palmìzio *s. m.* palm-grove

pàlmo *s. m.* span (spanna); palm (della mano)

pàlo *s. m.* pole, post, stake

palombàro *s. m.* diver

palómbo *s. m.* smooth hound

palpàre *v. tr.* to palpate, to feel, to finger

palpèbra *s. f.* eyelid

palpitazióne *s. f.* palpitation

paludàto *agg.* overdressed

palùde *s. f.* marsh, bog, swamp, fen

paludóso *agg.* marshy, boggy, swampy, fenny

pànca *s. f.* bench, form; pew (di chiesa)

pancétta *s. f.* paunch, belly; bacon (*alim.*)

panchìna *s. f.* bench

pància *s. f.* belly, paunch, tummy; **mal di –** belly-ache

pànda s. m. inv. panda
pandemònio s. m. pandemonium, uproar
pàne s. m. bread; – **fresco** fresh bread; – **integrale** wholemeal bread
panegìrico s. m. panegyric
panellenismo s. m. Panhellenism
panetteria s. f. bakery (forno); baker's (shop) (negozio)
pànico s. m. panic, alarm; **farsi prendere dal** – to panic
panière s. m. basket; hamper (con coperchio)
panifìcio s. m. bakery
panino s. m. roll; **un** – **al prosciutto** a ham sandwich
pànna s. f. cream; – **montata** whipped cream; **caffè con** – coffee with cream
pannéggio s. m. draping
pannéllo s. m. panel
pannòcchia s. f. cob (mais)
pannolino s. m. napkin, nappy, diaper
panoràma s. m. panorama; view (veduta)
panoràmica s. f. panning
panoràmico agg. panoramic; **schermo** – wide screen; **strada panoramica** panoramic drive
pantagruèlico agg. pantagruelian, huge
pantalóni s. m. pl. trousers, pants; **un paio di** – a pair of trousers; – **corti** shorts
pantàno s. m. quagmire
panteismo s. m. pantheism
pantòfola s. f. slipper
pantomìma s. f. pantomime
paonàzzo agg. purple, blue, livid
pàpa s. m. pope
papà s. m. daddy, dad, papa, pa
papàle agg. papal
papàto s. m. papacy
papàvero s. m. poppy; **semi di** – poppy-seed
papiro s. m. papyrus
papismo s. m. papism
pappagàllo s. m. parrot
paràbola s. f. parable; parabola (geom.)
parabrézza s. m. inv. windscreen; windshield (USA)
paracadùte s. m. inv. parachute
paracadutismo s. m. parachuting; – **acrobatico** skydiving
paracàrro s. m. kerbstone
paradìso s. m. paradise, heaven
paradossàle agg. paradoxical
paradòsso s. m. paradox
paràfrasi s. f. paraphrase
parafùlmine s. m. lightning-rod
paragonàbile agg. comparable

paragonàre v. tr. to compare, to confront • rifl. to compare oneself
paragóne s. m. comparison
paràlisi s. f. paralysis
paralizzàre v. tr. to paralyse
parallelepìpedo s. m. parallelepiped
parallelismo s. m. parallelism
parallèlo agg. e s. m. parallel
paralùme s. m. lamp-shade
paràmetro s. m. parameter
paranòia s. f. paranoia
paranormàle agg. paranormal
parapètto s. m. parapect; rail (naut.)
parapsicologìa s. f. parapsychology
parasóle s. m. inv. parasol, sunshade
parassita s. m. parasite
paràta s. f. parade
paratìa s. f. bulkhead
paraùrti s. m. bumper
paravènto s. m. screen
parcèlla s. f. bill
parcheggiàre v. tr. to park
parchéggio s. m. parking; **divieto di** – no parking
parchìmetro s. m. parking-meter
pàrco s. m. park
parécchio agg. e pron. indef. quite a lot of (quantità); quite a long (tempo); several pl. • avv. quite a bit
pareggiàre v. tr. to equalize, to match, to level • intr. to draw, to tie
paréggio s. m. draw, tie; balance (comm.)
parentàdo s. m. relatives pl.
parènte s. m. e f. relative, relation
parentèla s. f. kinship, relationship
parèntesi s. f. parenthesis; brackets pl. (segno grafico)
parére v. intr. to seem, to appear, to look (like) • s. m. opinion, advice
paréte s. f. wall
pàri agg. equal, same, like, similar; even (numero)
parigino agg. Parisian
parità s. f. parity; equality (uguaglianza)
parlamentàre agg. parliamentary
parlaménto s. m. Parliament
parlàre v. intr. to speak, to talk • tr. to speak • rifl. rec. to speak to each other
parlàta s. f. dialect, accent
parlatòrio s. m. parlour
parodìa s. f. parody
paròla s. f. word; speech (il parlare)
paroláccia s. f. swear-word, curse

parossistico *agg.* paroxysmal, violent

parròcchia *s. f.* parish

parrocchiàle *agg.* parish (*attr.*); parochial

pàrroco *s. m.* parish priest (cattolico); parson (anglicano)

parrùcca *s. f.* wig

parrucchière *s. m.* hairdresser

parsimonióso *agg.* parsimonious

pàrte *s. f.* part, share; portion (quota)

partecipàre *v. intr.* to participate (in); to share (condividere); to attend (essere presente)

partecipazióne *s. f.* participation; presence (presenza)

parteggiàre *v. intr.* to side (with)

partènza *s. f.* departure, leaving; start (*sport*)

particèlla *s. f.* particle

particolàre *agg.* particular, special, peculiar (singolare) • *s. m.* particular, detail

particolarità *s. f.* particularity, peculiarity (peculiarità)

partigiàno *agg.* partisan

partìre *v. intr.* to leave; to sail (salpare); to take off (decollare); to start (mettersi in moto)

partìta *s. f.* lot; parcel (*comm.*); game (gioco), match (*sport*)

partìto *s. m.* party

partizióne *s. f.* partition, division

pàrto *s. m.* childbirth, labour, delivery; **sala – ** delivery room

partorìre *v. tr.* to bear, to give birth; to bring forth (di animali)

parvènza *s. f.* shadow; trace (ombra)

parziàle *agg.* partial

pascolàre *v. intr.* to graze

pàscolo *s. m.* pasture, grazing-land; pasturage (il pascolare)

pàsqua *s. f.* Easter

pasquàle *agg.* Easter (*attr.*)

pasquétta *s. f.* Easter Monday

passàbile *agg.* fairly good

passàggio *s. m.* passage, passing; crossing (il passare); transit (transito); **vietato il – ** no transit

passapòrto *s. m.* passport; **mettere il visto su un – ** to visa a passport

passàre *v. intr.* to pass (by), to go along; to stop, to end (cessare) • *tr.* to pass, to cross; to spend (trascorrere), to go through (sopportare)

passatèmpo *s. m.* pastime, hobby

passàto *s. m.* past

passeggèro *agg.* passing, transitory • *s. m.* passenger

passeggiàre *v. intr.* to walk, to stroll

passeggiàta *s. f.* walk, stroll; promenade (luogo)

passeggìno *s. m.* push-cart

passéggio *s. m.* walk, stroll; public walk, promenade (luogo)

pàssero *s. m.* sparrow

passionàle *agg.* passional; passionate (temperamento)

passióne *s. f.* passion

passìvo *agg.* passive

pàsso *s. m.* step; pace (andatura); passage (brano); pass (*geog.*)

pàsta *s. f.* dough (per pane); pastry (per dolci); cake, pastry (pasticcino); paste (sostanza cremosa)

pastasciùtta *s. f.* pasta

pastìcca *s. f.* tablet, lozenge

pasticcerìa *s. f.* confectionery; pastry-shop (negozio)

pasticciàre *v. tr.* to mess up

pasticcìno *s. m.* pastry

pastìglia *s. f.* pastil(le), tablet, lozenge, drop; lining (*autom.*)

pàsto *s. m.* meal

pastoràle *agg.* pastoral

pastóre *s. m.* shepherd; pastor (*relig.*)

pastorìzia *s. f.* sheep-farming

pastóso *agg.* pasty, mellow

patàta *s. f.* potato; **patate fritte** fried potatoes, French fries

paté *s. m. inv.* paté

patènte *s. f.* licence, permit; **– di guida** driving licence; bill (*naut.*); patent (brevetto)

paternalismo *s. m.* paternalism

paternità *s. f.* paternity, fatherhood

patèrno *agg.* paternal, fatherly

patètico *agg.* pathetic

pàthos *s. m.* pathos

patìbolo *s. m.* gallows, block

pàtina *s. f.* patina

pàtio *s. m.* patio

patìre *v. tr.* to suffer, to undergo

patologìa *s. f.* pathology

patològico *agg.* pathologic(al)

pàtria *s. f.* country, native land, home

patriàrca *s. m.* patriarch

patriarcàto *s. m.* patriarchate, patriarchy

patrìcida *s. m.* parricide

patrìgno *s. m.* stepfather

patrimoniàle *agg.* patrimonial

patrimònio *s. m.* patrimony, estate, property

patriòta *s. m. e f.* patriot

patrocìnio s. m. patronage, sponsorship
patronìmico s. m. patronymic
patróno s. m. patron
pàtta s. f. flap, fly, lap
pattinàggio s. m. skating; – **artistico** figure-skating; – **su ghiaccio** ice-skating; – **a rotelle** roller-skating; **pista di** – skating-rink
pattinàre v. intr. to skate
pàttino s. m. skate
pàtto s. m. agreement, pact
pattùglia s. f. patrol
pattuìre v. tr. to stipulate
pattumièra s. f. dustbin, garbage-can (USA)
paùra s. f. fear, dread, fright, scare
pauróso agg. fearful, frightful; dreadful (che mette paura)
pàusa s. f. pause; rest (mus.)
pavimentàre v. tr. to floor (casa), to pave (strada)
pavimentazióne s. f. flooring (casa), paving (strada)
paviménto s. m. floor
pavóne s. m. peacock
pazientàre v. intr. to be patient
paziènte agg. patient
paziènza s. f. patience
pazzésco agg. crazy, foolish; incredible (straordinario)
pazzìa s. f. madness
pàzzo agg. mad, crazy, insane, lunatic • s. m. madman, lunatic
peccaminóso agg. sinful, wicked
peccàre v. intr. to sin; to be faulty (essere difettoso)
peccàto s. m. sin; **che** –! what a pity!
peccatóre s. m. sinner
pècora s. f. sheep
peculiarità s. f. peculiarity
pedàggio s. m. toll; **autostrada a** – toll motorway
pedagogìa s. f. pedagogy
pedalàre v. intr. to pedal, to cycle
pedàle s. m. pedal
pedàna s. f. footboard; spring-board (sport)
pedànte agg. pedantic • s. m. e f. pedant, hair-splitter
pedanterìa s. f. pedantry
pedèstre agg. pedestrian, dull
pediàtra s. m. e f. p(a)ediatrician
pedicùre s. m. e f. inv. pedicure, chiropodist
pedìna s. f. man (dama); pawn (scacchi e fig.)
pedinàre v. tr. to tag after, to tail
pedonàle agg. pedestrian (attr.)

pedonalizzàre v. tr. to pedestrianize
pedóne s. m. pedestrian
pèggio agg. inv. worse • avv. worse (compar.); (the) worst (superl. relat.) • s. m. e f. inv. the worst (thing)
peggioraménto s. m. worsening
peggioràre v. tr. to worsen – intr. to get worse
peggióre agg. worse (compar.); (the) worst (superl. relat.)
pégno s. m. pawn, pledge
pelàre v. tr. to peel, to skin
pelàto agg. bald; hairless (senza capelli); peeled (sbucciato)
pèlle s. f. skin; complexion (carnagione); hide, leather (cuoio); peel, skin, rind (buccia)
pellegrinàggio s. m. pilgrimage
pellegrìno s. m. pilgrim
pelletterìa s. f. leatherwear (oggetti); leather goods shop (negozio)
pelliccerìa s. f. furrier's
pellìccia s. f. fur
pellìcola s. f. film
pélo s. m. hair (sing. collett.); coat hair (pel-lame)
pelóso agg. hairy
péltro s. m. pewter
pèna s. f. punishment, penalty; pain, suffering, sorrow (dolore); trouble (disturbo); sentence (leg.)
penàle agg. criminal, penal; **il codice** – the criminal code
penalità s. f. penalty
penalizzàre v. tr. to penalize
pendènte agg. hanging; leaning (inclinato); pending (leg.)
pendènza s. f. slope, incline; gradient (grado d'inclinazione)
pèndere v. intr. to hang; to lean (inclinare); to slant (essere in pendenza)
pendìo s. m. slope, slant
pendolàre agg. pendular • s. m. e f. commuter
pèndolo s. m. pendulum; **orologio a** – pendulum-clock
pène s. m. penis
penetràre v. intr. to penetrate into, to enter; to steal into (introdursi); to touch (fig.)
penetrazióne s. f. penetration
penicillìna s. f. penicillin
peninsulàre agg. peninsular
penìsola s. f. peninsula
penitènte s. m. e f. penitent

penitènza *s. f.* penance, penitence; forfeit (nei giochi)

penitenziàrio *agg.* penitentiary

pénna *s. f.* pen; feather (di uccello); **– a sfera** ballpoint pen; **– stilografica** fountain-pen

pennellàta *s. f.* brush stroke, brush work

pennèllo *s. m.* brush; **– da barba** shaving-brush

pennino *s. m.* nib

penómbra *s. f.* half-light

penóso *agg.* painful

pensàre *v. tr.* to think • *intr.* to think (of), to mind; to see to (badare)

pensatóre *s. m.* thinker

pensièro *s. m.* thought; mind (opinione)

pensieróso *agg.* thoughtful, pensive

pensile *agg.* pensile, hanging, suspended

pensilina *s. f.* platform-roof (ferr.); bus-shelter (mezzi pubblici); cantilever roof (arch.)

pensionaménto *s. m.* retirement

pensionàto *s. m.* pensioner, retired person (persona); boarding-house (istituto)

pensióne *s. f.* pension, annuity; bed and board (vitto e alloggio); boarding-house, pension (luogo)

pensóso *agg.* thoughtful, pensive

pentagonàle *agg.* pentagonal

pentagràmma *s. m.* stave

pentecòste *s. f.* Whitsunday

pentiménto *s. m.* regret; repentance

pentirsi *v. intr. pron.* to regret; to repent

pèntola *s. f.* pot, pan; **– a pressione** pressure cooker

penùltimo *agg.* last but one, penultimate

penùria *s. f.* scarcity, lack; penury (povertà)

penzolàre *v. intr.* to dangle, to hang down

pepàto *agg.* peppery; pepper (attr.)

pépe *s. m.* pepper

peperoncino *s. m.* hot pepper, paprika, Cayenne pepper

peperóne *s. m.* pepper (bot.); **– sott'aceto** pickled peppers

péplo *s. m.* peplum, peplos

pér *prep.* for (direzione, tempo, vantaggio, fine, causa); through (moto per luogo, mezzo); by (mezzo, tempo, misura)

péra *s. f.* pear

peràltro *avv.* moreover, what is more

perbàcco *inter.* by Jove!

perbenismo *s. m.* respectability

percènto *s. m. inv.* percentage

percentuàle *agg.* percent

percepìre *v. tr.* to perceive, to feel, to cash, to receive (ricevere)

percezióne *s. f.* perception

perché *avv.* why • *cong.* because, for, since, as • *s. m.* reason, motive

perciò *cong.* for this (o that) reason, therefore, so, consequently

percórrere *v. tr.* to run along, to scour; to run through (attraversare)

percórso *s. m.* route; way (tratto percorso); journey, run (viaggio)

percòssa *s. f.* blow, stroke

percuòtere *v. tr.* to strike, to hit, to beat, to knock

pèrdere *v. tr.* to lose, to miss (lasciarsi sfuggire); to waste (sprecare) • *intr.* to lose, to leak (fare acqua) • *intr. pron.* to get lost

pèrdita *s. f.* loss; waste (spreco); leak (falla, fuga); **subire una –** to make a loss

perdonàbile *agg.* forgivable

perdonàre *v. tr.* to forgive, to pardon, to excuse (scusare) • *intr.* to forgive, to pardon • *rifl. rec.* to forgive each other

perdóno *s. m.* forgiveness, pardon

peregrinazióne *s. f.* peregrination, wandering

perènne *agg.* perennial, perpetual, everlasting

perentòrio *agg.* peremptory; final (decisivo)

perfettaménte *avv.* perfectly

perfètto *agg.* perfect

perfezionaménto *s. m.* improvement; completion (completamento); specialization (specializzazione)

perfezionàre *v. tr.* to perfect; to improve (migliorare) • *intr. pron.* to perfect oneself, to specialize

perfezióne *s. f.* perfection

perfezionìsta *s. m. e f.* perfectionist

pèrfido *agg.* perfidious, treacherous

perfìno *avv.* even, just

perforàre *v. tr.* to pierce, to punch

perforazióne *s. f.* perforation

pergamèna *s. f.* parchment

pergolàto *s. m.* pergola, bower

pericolànte *agg.* precarious, tottery

perìcolo *s. m.* danger, peril

pericolosità *s. f.* danger, dangerousness

pericolóso *agg.* dangerous, unsafe

periferìa *s. f.* outskirts pl.; suburbs pl.

perifèrico *agg.* suburban

perifrasi *s. f.* periphrasis

perimetràle *agg.* perimetric(al); external; outer; **i muri perimetrali** the external walls

perìmetro *s. m.* boundary; perimeter (geom.)

periodicaménte *avv.* periodically

periodicità *s. f.* periodicity

periòdico *agg.* periodic(al); recurring (*mat.*)
　• *s. m.* periodical, magazine
periodo *s. m.* period
peripezìa *s. f.* vicissitude
periscòpio *s. m.* periscope
perito *s. m.* expert
peritonìte *s. f.* peritonitis
perìzia *s. f.* skill, mastery (abilità); appraisal,
　survey (stima); experts' report (relazione di un
　perito)
pèrla *s. f.* pearl; bead (di collana)
perlàceo *agg.* pearly
perloméno *avv.* at least
perlopiù *avv.* mainly
perlustrazióne *s. f.* patrol; reconnaissance
　(l'esplorare)
permalóso *agg.* touchy, peevish
permanènte *agg.* permanent, standing　• *s. f.*
　permanent; permanent exhibition (mostra)
permeàre *v. tr.* to permeate
permésso *s. m.* permission, leave, licence, per-
　mit (autorizzazione)
perméttere *v. tr.* to allow, to permit, to let
permissivo *agg.* permissive
pérmuta *s. f.* exchange (*comm.*); permutation,
　barter (*leg.*)
pernice *s. f.* partridge
pernicióso *agg.* pernicious; harmful; inju-
　rious; malignant
pernottaménto *s. m.* overnight stay
pernottàre *v. intr.* to stay overnight
péro *s. m.* pear
però *cong.* but, however, yet
peróne *s. m.* perone, fibula
perpendicolàre *agg.* perpendicular
perpètuo *agg.* perpetual
perplessità *s. f.* perplexity
perplèsso *agg.* perplexed, puzzled
perquisizióne *s. f.* perquisition, search; **man-
　dato di -** search-warrant
persecuzióne *s. f.* persecution
perseguire *v. tr.* to pursue; to prosecute (*leg.*)
perseverànza *s. f.* perseverance
perseveràre *v. intr.* to persevere
persiàna *s. f.* shutter, blind
pèrsico *s. m.* perch, bass
persino *avv.* even, just
persistere *v. intr.* to persist
persóna *s. f.* person; somebody (un tale)　• *pl.*
　people, persons
personàggio *s. m.* personage, character (di un
　romanzo, ecc.); **il - principale** the main char-
　acter

personàle *agg.* personal
personalità *s. f.* personality
personalizzàre *v. tr.* to personalize
personalménte *avv.* personally, in person
personificazióne *s. f.* personification
perspicàcia *s. f.* sharpness; perspicacity
persuadére *v. tr.* to persuade　• *rifl.* to per-
　suade oneself
persuasióne *s. f.* persuasion
persuasivo *agg.* persuasive
pertànto *cong.* therefore, thus, so
pertinènte *agg.* pertinent
pertòsse *s. f.* whooping-cough
pertùgio *s. m.* hole, opening
perturbazióne *s. f.* perturbation, disturbance
pervàdere *v. tr.* to pervade
pervenire *v. intr.* to reach, to attain, to achieve;
　to arrive at (giungere)
perversióne *s. f.* perversion
pesànte *agg.* heavy; close, stuffy (di aria)
pesantézza *s. f.* heaviness
pesàre *v. tr.* to weigh　• *intr.* to weigh; to be
　heavy (essere pesante)　• *rifl.* to weigh one-
　self
pèsca *s. f.* peach
pèsca *s. f.* fishing; catch (pesci pescati)
pescàre *v. tr.* to fish; to fish out (riuscire a tro-
　vare); to pick up (estrarre a caso)　• *intr.* to
　draw (*naut.*)
pescatóre *s. m.* fisherman
pésce *s. m.* fish
pescheréccio *agg.* fishing
pescheria *s. f.* fishmonger's, fish-shop
pèsco *s. m.* peach; **fiori di -** peach-blossom
péso *s. m.* weight; load (carico); burden (one-
　re); importance (fig.)
pessimismo *s. m.* pessimism
pessimista *s. m. e f.* pessimist
pèssimo *agg.* very bad
pestàre *v. tr.* to crush, to pound; to grind (ri-
　durre in polvere); to tread on, to trample on
　(calpestare); to beat (picchiare)
pèste *s. f.* plague
pestifero *agg.* pestiferous; stinking (di odore);
　pest (di bambino)
pestilènza *s. f.* pestilence, plague
pètalo *s. m.* petal
petàrdo *s. m.* petard, fire-cracker
petrolifero *agg.* oil (*attr.*); **pozzo -** oil-well; **in-
　dustria petrolifera** oil industry
petròlio *s. m.* petroleum, oil
pettegolézzo *s. m.* gossip
pettégolo *agg.* gossipy　• *s. m.* gossip

269

pettinàre v. tr. to comb • rifl. to comb one's hair

pettinàta s. f. combing of the hair

pettinatùra s. f. hair-style, hair-do

pèttine s. m. comb

pètto s. m. chest, breast

petulànza s. f. insolence, cheek

pèzzo s. m. piece, bit

phòn s. m. inv. hair dryer

placère v. intr. to like • s. m. pleasure; favour (servigio); **per –** please

placévole agg. pleasing, pleasant

piàga s. f. sore, wound, scourge; plague (flagello)

piagnistèo s. m. whining

piagnucolàre v. intr. to whine, to whimper

piàlla s. f. plane

piàna s. f. plain

pianeggiànte agg. level, flat

pianeròttolo s. m. landing

pianèta s. m. planet

piàngere v. tr. to weep; to mourn (lamentare) • intr. to weep, to cry, to sob

pianificàre v. tr. to plan, to scheme

pianista s. m. e f. pianist

piàno avv. in a low voice (a bassa voce); slowly (lentamente); softly • agg. flat, level • s. m. plan, scheme, project (progetto); plain, level ground; plane (geom.); floor, storey (di casa)

pianofòrte s. m. piano

pianotèrra s. m. inv. ground floor, first floor (USA)

piànta s. f. plant, tree (albero); plan (disegno di edificio, città)

piantagióne s. f. plantation

piantàre v. tr. to plant; to thrust, to drive (conficcare); to leave, to quit (abbandonare) • intr. pron. to plant oneself, to place oneself; to part (abbandonarsi)

pianterréno s. m. ground floor, first floor (USA)

piànto s. m. weeping, crying

pianùra s. f. plain, flatland, lowland

piàstra s. f. plate; slab (di pietra)

piastrèlla s. f. tile

piattafórma s. f. platform

piattèllo s. m. disk; **tiro al –** trap-shooting, clay-pidgeon shooting

piattìno s. m. saucer

piàtto agg. flat • s. m. plate; dish (da portata e vivande); **lavare i –** to wash up

piàzza s. f. square

piazzaménto s. m. placement

piccànte agg. spicy, hot

picchiàre v. tr. to beat, to hit; to strike (battere); to tap (battere leggermente) • intr. to beat; to knock (bussare) • rifl. rec. to fight; to come to blows (venire alle mani)

picchiettàre v. tr. to tap, to drum

picchio s. m. woodpecker

piccìno agg. tiny, very small, little

picción s. m. pigeon; **– viaggiatore** carrier-pigeon

picco s. m. peak

piccolo agg. small, little

piccóne s. m. pick

piccòzza s. f. axe

pidòcchio s. m. louse

piède s. m. foot

piedistàllo s. m. pedestal

pièga s. f. fold, folding, ply

piegàre v. tr. to fold; to bend (flettere) • intr. to tilt, to bend; to turn (voltare)

pieghévole agg. pliable, pliant, folding

pièna s. f. flood, spate; **un fiume in –** a river in flood

pièno agg. full; solid (massiccio); full up (sazio)

pienóne s. m. big crowd

pietà s. f. pity, compassion, mercy

pietànza s. f. dish; course (portata)

piètra s. f. stone

pietrificàrsi v. intr. pron. to be petrified

pigiàma s. m. pyjamas pl.

pigiàre v. tr. to press, to push

pigmentazióne s. f. pigmentation

pigna s. f. pine-cone

pignoleria s. f. pedantry, fussiness

pignolo agg. pedantic, fussy • s. m. pedant

pignoràre v. tr. to distrain, to attach

pigrìzia s. f. laziness

pigro agg. lazy

pila s. f. pile, stack (di oggetti); cell, battery (elettr.); torch (lampadina tascabile); **a –** battery operated

pilàstro s. m. pillar

pillola s. f. pill

pilóne s. m. pier (di ponte); tower, pylon (elettr.)

pilòta s. m. e f. pilot

pilotàre v. tr. to pilot

pinacotèca s. f. picture-gallery

pinéta s. f. pine-wood

pinguìno s. m. penguin

pinna s. f. fin, flipper

pinnàcolo s. m. pinnacle

pino s. m. pine

pinòlo s. m. pine-seed

pinza s. f. pliers pl.; pincers pl.; tongs pl.

piòggia s. f. rain

piombàre v. intr. to plump, to fall, to slump, to plunge; to rush (arrivare all'improvviso)

piómbo s. m. lead

pionière s. m. pioneer

piòppo s. m. poplar

piovàno agg. rain (attr.)

piòvere v. intr. impers. to rain; to pour (fig.)

piovigginàre v. intr. impers. to drizzle

piovosità s. f. raininess; rainfall (quantità di pioggia)

piovóso agg. rainy

piòvra s. f. octopus

pipa s. f. pipe

pipì s. f. pee; **fare –** to pee

pipistrèllo s. m. bat

piramidàle agg. pyramidal

piràmide s. f. pyramid

piràta s. m. pirate; **– della strada** road-hog

piraterìa s. f. piracy

piròmane s. m. e f. pyromaniac

pirotècnico agg. pyrotechnic(al); **fuochi pirotecnici** fireworks

piscicoltùra s. f. fish breeding

piscina s. f. swimming-pool

pisèllo s. m. pea

pisolino s. m. nap, doze; **fare un –** to take a nap

pista s. f. track; lane, track (corsia, sentiero); strip (aer.); **– da ballo** dance floor; **– da sci** ski sloper

pistàcchio s. m. pistachio

pistòla s. f. pistol, gun

pistóne s. m. piston; ram (idraulica)

pitóne s. m. python

pittóre s. m. painter

pittorésco agg. picturesque

pittòrico agg. pictorial

pittùra s. f. painting; picture (dipinto); paint (vernice); **– fresca** wet paint

pitturàre v. tr. to paint

più agg. e avv. more (comparat.); (the) most (superl. relat.) • prep. plus

piùma s. f. feather, down

piuttòsto avv. rather, somewhat; **– di** rather, sooner, better... than

pizzicàre v. tr. to pinch, to burn (sapore); to catch (cogliere di sorpresa) • intr. to itch, to be hot (sapore)

pìzzico s. m. pinch, nip, touch; bit (piccola quantità)

pizzicòtto s. m. pinch

pizzo s. m. lace; pointed beard (barba)

placàre v. tr. to placate, to calm (down) • intr. pron. to abate, to calm down

plàcido agg. placid, calm

plagiàre v. tr. to plagiarize

plàgio s. m. plagiarism

planàre v. intr. to glide, to plane

planàta s. f. glide, plane

planimetrìa s. f. planimetry

planisfèro s. m. planisphere

plasmàre v. tr. to mould, to shape

plàstica s. f. plastic

plasticità s. f. plasticity

plàstico agg. plastic

plastificàre v. tr. to plasticize

plàtano s. m. plane

plateàle agg. blatant

platonicaménte avv. platonically

platònico agg. platonic

plausìbile agg. plausible

plenilùnio s. m. full moon

pleonàstico agg. pleonastic

plèttro s. m. plectrum

pleurite s. f. pleurisy

plinto s. m. plinth

plùmbeo agg. leaden

pluràle agg. plural

pluralismo s. m. pluralism

pluralità s. f. plurality

plusvalóre s. m. surplus-value

plutocrazìa s. f. plutocracy

pluviàle agg. pluvial; rain (attr.)

pneumàtico s. m. tyre

pòco avv. not very, little, not much; rather (un po') • agg. indef. little, not much; short (tempo); few, not many, a few (alcuni) • pron. indef. little, not much, a little (un po'); some, few, not many, a few (alcuni)

podére s. m. farm; estate (proprietà terriera)

poderóso agg. strong, powerful, mighty

pòdio s. m. podium; stand (palco rialzato)

podismo s. m. walking (marcia); running (corsa); **fare del –** to be a walker

poèma s. m. poem

poesìa s. f. poetry; poem (componimento)

poèta s. m. poet

poètica s. f. poetics pl. (v. al sing.)

poètico agg. poetic

poggiàre v. tr. to lean, to rest; to lay (posare) • intr. to rest, to stand

poggiatèsta s. m. inv. headrest

pòggio s. m. knoll, hillock

pòi avv. then, after; afterwards (dopo); later on (più tardi)

poiché cong. as, since, because

polàre agg. polar; pole (attr.); **la stella** – the North star

polarizzàre v. tr. to polarize

polèmica s. f. polemic, controversy

polèmico agg. polemic

policlìnico s. m. polyclinic, general hospital

policromàtico agg. polychromatic

polièdrico agg. polyhedric

poliennàle agg. multiannual

polifònico agg. polyphonic

polìgamo agg. polygamous • s. m. polygamist

poliglòtta agg. polyglot

poligonàle agg. polygonal

polìgono s. m. polygon; – **di tiro** rifle-range

polimòrfo agg. polymorphous

polìpo s. m. polyp (zool.); polypus (med.)

politècnico s. m. polytechnic

politeìsmo s. m. polytheism

polìtica s. f. politics pl. (v. al sing.); policy (indirizzo politico); – **interna** home politics, home affairs; – **estera** foreign politics, foreign policy

politicaménte avv. politically

polìtico agg. political

polìttico s. m. polyptych

polivalènte agg. polyvalent

polizìa s. f. police; **commissariato di** – police station; **agente di** – policeman; – **stradale** traffic police

poliziésco agg. police (attr.); **racconto** – detective story, thriller

poliziòtto s. m. policeman

pólizza s. f. policy; – **di assicurazione** insurance policy

pollàio s. m. poultry-pen, hen-house

pollàme s. m. poultry

pòllice s. m. thumb; inch (misura)

pòlline s. m. pollen

póllo s. m. chicken; – **arrosto** roast chicken

polmonàre agg. pulmonary

polmonìte s. f. pneumonia

pòlo s. m. pole

pólpa s. f. pulp; lean (meat) (carne)

polpàccio s. m. calf

polpastrèllo s. m. pulp

polpétta s. f. rissole; meat-ball (di carne); croquette (patate)

pólpo s. m. octopus

polsìno s. m. cuff

pólso s. m. wrist; pulse (med.); nerve (fig.)

poltìglia s. f. mash, slush

poltróna s. f. armchair; stall (teatro)

pólvere s. f. dust, powder

polverizzàre v. tr. e intr. pron. to pulverize

polveróso agg. dusty

pomàta s. f. pomade, cream; ointment (farmacia)

pomèllo s. m. knob

pomeridiàno agg. afternoon (attr.)

pomerìggio s. m. afternoon

pomodòro s. m. tomato; **salsa di** – tomato sauce; **succo di** – tomato juice

pómpa s. f. pump

pompàre v. tr. to pump, to draw up

pompèlmo s. m. grape-fruit

pompière s. m. fireman

pompóso agg. pompous

ponderàre v. tr. e intr. to ponder, to weigh

ponderazióne s. f. careful consideration

ponènte s. m. west

pónte s. m. bridge; deck (naut.)

pontéfice s. m. pontifex, pope

pontificàto s. m. pontificate

pontifìcio agg. pontifical, papal

pontìle s. m. wharf

popolàre v. tr. to populate, to people • intr. pron. to become populated • agg. popular

popolarità s. f. popularity

popolazióne s. f. population

pòpolo s. m. people

popolóso agg. populous, densely populated

póppa s. f. stern

populìsmo s. m. populism

porcellàna s. f. china, porcelain, chinaware

porcellìno s. m. little pig; – **d'India** guinea pig; – **di latte** sucking-pig

porcherìa s. f. filth, muck; obscenity, smut (indecenza)

porcìle s. m. pigsty

pòrco s. m. pig, swine; pork (carne)

pòrfido s. m. porphyry

pòrgere v. tr. to hand, to pass, to give

pornogràfico agg. pornographic

pòro s. m. pore

pórpora s. f. purple; purpura (med.)

pórre v. tr. to lay, to put, to place; to suppose (supporre); to set (stabilire) • rifl. to put oneself, to place oneself, to set to (accingersi)

pòrro s. m. leek

pòrta s. f. door; gate (di città)
portabagàgli s. m. porter (facchino); roof rack (autom.), trunk (autom., USA)
portàbile agg. portable
portacénere s. m. inv. ash-tray
portachiàvi s. m. inv. key-chain
portaérei s. m. inv. aircraft-carrier
portafinèstra s. f. French-window
portafòglio s. m. wallet
portafortùna s. m. inv. amulet, mascot(te)
portàle s. m. portal
portànte agg. load-bearing
portantina s. f. sedan (chair); litter (lettiga)
portaombrèlli s. m. inv. umbrella-stand
portapàcchi s. m. inv. carrier
portàre v. tr. to bring (verso chi parla); to fetch (andare a prendere); to take (lontano da chi parla, accompagnare); to carry (trasportare); to wear (indossare)
portasapóne s. m. inv. soap-dish, soap-box
portasci s. m. inv. ski-rack
portasciugamàno s. m. towel-rack
portàta s. f. course (piatto); capacity (di automezzo); range, reach (occhio, strumento ottico); importance (significato)
portavóce s. m. inv. spokesman m., spokeswoman f.
portènto s. m. portent, wonder; prodigy (fig.)
pòrticato s. m. arcade, colonnade
pòrtico s. m. portico, arcade, veranda
portièra s. m. goal-keeper (sport); doorkeeper (portinaio)
portinàia s. f. doorkeeper
portinàio s. m. doorkeeper, porter
portineria s. f. porter's lodge
pòrto s. m. port, harbour
portolàno s. m. pilot-book
portóne s. m. main entrance
portuàle agg. port (attr.); harbour (attr.); diritti portuali harbour duties
porzióne s. f. portion, share; helping (quantità di cibo)
posacénere s. m. inv. ash-tray
posàre v. tr. to put (down), to lay (down) • intr. to rest, to stand; to pose (restare in posa) • intr. pron. to alight; to settle (di uccello, di cosa); to land (aer.)
posàta s. f. cutlery
positivìsmo s. m. positivism
positìvo agg. positive; definite (certo); affirmative (affermativo)
posizionàre v. tr. to position

posizióne s. f. position; posture; situation (ubicazione); luci di – parking lights
posologìa s. f. posology, dosage
pospórre v. tr. to postpone, to subordinate
possedére v. tr. to possess, to own, to have
possessìvo agg. possessive
possèsso s. m. possession
possìbile agg. possible
possibilìsmo s. m. possibilism
possibilità s. f. possibility, opportunity
possibilménte avv. if possible
pòsta s. f. post, mail; post office (ufficio postale); per – by mail; – aèrea air mail
postàle agg. postal; post (attr.); mail (attr.); cartolina – postcard; cassetta – letter box; pacco – parcel
postazióne s. f. posting
postbèllico agg. post-war (attr.)
postdatàre v. tr. to post-date
posteggiàre v. tr. e intr. to park
posteggiatóre s. m. car-park attendant
postéggio s. m. parking
poster s. m. inv. poster
posterióre agg. posterior, back, hinder, rear; later (che viene dopo)
posterità s. f. posterity
postìccio agg. artificial, false
posticipàre v. tr. to put off, to postpone
postilla s. f. marginal note; gloss (chiosa)
postìno s. m. postman, mailman
postmodèrno agg. post-modern
pòsto s. m. place, seat (a sedere); post, job (lavoro)
postrìbolo s. m. brothel
postulàto s. m. postulate
pòstumo agg. posthumous
potàbile agg. drinkable
potàre v. tr. to prune, to trim
potènte agg. powerful, potent
potènza s. f. power, might; strength (forza); potency (efficacia)
potenziàle agg. potential
potenziàre v. tr. to potentiate, to strengthen, to develop
potére v. intr. can, to be able (essere in grado); may, to be allowed (avere il permesso); may, to be likely (essere probabile) • s. m. power, influence; sway (dominio)
pòvero agg. poor • s. m. poor man; poor people pl.; the poor pl.
pozzànghera s. f. puddle
pòzzo s. m. well
pragmàtico agg. pragmatic

273

pranzàre v. intr. to dine, to have dinner, to lunch, to have lunch; – **fuori** to dine out

prànzo s. m. dinner, lunch

pràssi s. f. praxis, practice, routine, procedure

prateria s. f. prairie, grass-land

praticàbile agg. practicable

praticaménte avv. practically

praticànte agg. practising

praticàre v. tr. to practise • intr. to frequent, to associate with

praticità s. f. practicality

pràtico agg. practical; experienced (esperto)

pràto s. m. meadow, lawn

preallàrme s. m. warning signal

preàmbolo s. m. preamble

preavvisàre v. tr. to forewarn

preavviso s. m. notice, warning

prebèllico agg. pre-war (attr.)

precarietà s. f. precariousness

precàrio agg. precarious; temporary (temporaneo)

precauzióne s. f. precaution; caution, core (cautela)

precedènte agg. preceding, previous

precedènza s. f. precedence, priority; right of way (autom.)

precèdere v. tr. e intr. to precede; to head (essere alla testa di); to anticipate (prevenire); to come first

precètto s. m. precept

precipitàre v. tr. to precipitate, to hurl down; to rush (affrettare) • intr. to fall headlong; to crash (aer.) • intr. pron. to rush, to dash; to hasten (affrettarsi)

precipitazióne s. f. precipitation

precipitóso agg. precipitous, headlong; rash (avventato)

precisaménte avv. precisely; exactly (proprio)

precisàre v. tr. to state, to specify, to tell precisely

precisazióne s. f. precise statement, precise information

precisióne s. f. precision

preciso agg. precise

preclusióne s. f. bar; barring (il precludere)

precòce agg. precocious; early (anticipato)

precocità s. f. precocity

precolombiàno agg. pre-Columbian

preconcètto s. m. preconception

precórrere v. tr. to anticipate

precursóre s. m. precursor, forerunner

prèda s. f. prey; quarry (animale); booty (bottino)

predatóre agg. predatory

predèlla s. f. platform, dais; predella (di altare)

predellino s. m. foot-board

predestinàre v. tr. to destine, to predestinate

predestinazióne s. f. predestination

predeterminàre v. tr. to predetermine

predétto agg. mentioned above, aforesaid

prèdica s. f. sermon, lecture

predicàre v. tr. e intr. to preach

predicatóre s. m. preacher

predicazióne s. f. preaching

predilètto agg. e s. m. favourite

prediligere v. tr. to prefer

predispórre v. tr. to predispose, to arrange in advance • rifl. to prepare oneself

predominànte agg. predominant, prevailing

predominàre v. intr. to predominate, to dominate, to prevail

predominio s. m. predominance, supremacy

preesistènte agg. pre-existent

preesistere v. intr. to pre-exist

prefabbricàto agg. prefabricated; **una casa prefabbricata** a prefab

prefazióne s. f. preface, foreword

preferènza s. f. preference

preferibile agg. preferable

preferibilménte avv. preferably; sooner (piuttosto)

preferire v. tr. to prefer

prefettùra s. f. prefecture

prefiggere v. tr. to fix; to establish (in advance)

prefiguràre v. tr. to prefigure, to foreshadow

prefisso s. m. prefix; area code (tel.); – **interurbano** dialling code

pregàre v. tr. e intr. to pray; to ask, to beg (chiedere)

pregévole agg. valuable

preghièra s. f. prayer; request (richiesta)

prègio s. m. quality; merit (qualità); value (valore)

pregiudizio s. m. prejudice

pregnànte agg. pregnant

prègo inter. don't mention it!, you're welcome; pardon? (per invitare a ripetere); please (in formule di cortesia)

pregustàre v. tr. to foretaste, to anticipate

preistòria s. f. prehistory

preistòrico agg. prehistoric

prelàto s. m. prelate

prelevàre v. tr. to withdraw; to collect (passare a prendere)

prelibatézza s. f. daintiness; tit-bit (cosa prelibata)

prelibàto agg. dainty

prelièvo s. m. withdrawal; taking (med.)

preliminàre s. m. preliminary matter; preliminaries pl.

prelùdio s. m. prelude

prematrimoniàle agg. premarital; pre-marriage (attr.)

prematùro agg. premature

premeditazióne s. f. premeditation; wilfulness (leg.)

prémere v. tr. to press • intr. to urge; to matter (importare)

preméssa s. f. introduction, premise

preméttere v. tr. to premise, to prefix, to state beforehand; to put (to place) before (mettere prima)

premiàre v. tr. to give (to award) a prize to (sb.); to reward, to recompense (ricompensare)

premiazióne s. f. prize-giving

preminènte agg. pre-eminent, prominent

prèmio s. m. prize, award; reward (ricompensa); – **Nobel** Nobel prize

premistóppa s. m. inv. stuffing box

premorire v. intr. to die before, to pre-decease

premunirsi v. rifl. to take precautions; to provide oneself (with) (provvedersi)

premùra s. f. care (sollecitudine); kindness (cortesia); hurry, haste (urgenza)

premuróso agg. solicitous, considerate

prèndere v. tr. to take, to catch, to seize; to get (ottenere)

prenotàre v. tr. to book, to reserve; – **una stanza in un albergo** to book a room at a hotel; – **un posto in treno** to book a seat on a train

prenotazióne s. f. booking, reservation; **ufficio** – booking-office; **annullare una** – to cancel a booking

preoccupànte agg. worrying

preoccupàre v. tr. to worry, to trouble • intr. pron. to worry, to be troubled

preoccupàto agg. worried, troubled

preoccupazióne s. f. worry, care

preparàre v. tr. to prepare, to make (st.) ready; to arrange (predisporre) • rifl. to prepare oneself, to get ready; to be about to (accingersi)

preparatìvo s. m. preparation, arrangement

preparazióne s. f. preparation; training (addestramento)

preponderànte agg. preponderant, predominant

prepórre v. tr. to place before, to prefer; to set above (preferire)

prepotènte agg. arrogant, bossy

prepotènza s. f. excessive power

prerogativa s. f. prerogative

présa s. f. taking; seizure, capture (cattura); hold (stretta); intake (d'acqua, d'aria); tap, socket (elettr.)

presàgio s. m. presage, omen

presagire v. tr. to presage, to foresee, to forebode

présbite agg. long-sighted

presbiteriàno agg. Presbyterian

presbitèrio s. m. presbytery

prescégliere v. tr. to select, to choose out

prescìndere v. intr. to leave aside, to prescind

prescrìvere v. tr. to prescribe

prescrizióne s. f. prescription

presentàbile agg. presentable

presentàre v. tr. to present, to show, to produce; to propose (proporre); to introduce, to present (far conoscere) • rifl. to present oneself; to appear (comparire); to introduce oneself (farsi conoscere) • intr. pron. to occur, to arise; to seem, to appear (sembrare)

presentatóre s. m. announcer; talk-showman (varietà)

presentazióne s. f. presentation; introduction (far conoscere una persona a un'altra)

presènte agg. present • s. m. (the) present; present (tense) (gramm.); gift (dono)

presentiménto s. m. presentiment

presènza s. f. presence; attendance (il frequentare)

presenziàre v. tr. e intr. to be present (at), to attend, to take part (in)

presèpe s. m. crib

preservàre v. tr. to preserve

preservatìvo s. m. prophylactic, condom

presidènte s. m. president

presidènza s. f. presidency, chairmanship

presidenziàle agg. presidential

presièdere v. tr. to preside • intr. to take the chair, to act as chairman

pressapochìsmo s. m. inaccuracy

pressappòco avv. about, more or less

pressióne s. f. pressure; – **del sangue** blood pressure; **pentola a** – pressure-cooker

prèsso prep. nearby, near, close • avv. near, beside, next to, by (accanto a)

pressoché avv. almost, all but

275

prestabilire *v. tr.* to arrange beforehand; to fix, to set (fissare)

prestànte *agg.* good-looking, handsome

prestàre *v. tr.* to lend • *rifl. e intr. pron.* to lend oneself; to consent (acconsentire); to help (rendersi utile); to be fit (essere idoneo)

prestigiatóre *s. m.* conjurer

prestìgio *s. m.* glamour (fascino); prestige (autorità); **giochi di** – conjuring tricks

prestigióso *agg.* prestigious

prèstito *s. m.* loan

prèsto *avv.* soon, in a short time, before long; early (di buon'ora); quickly (in fretta)

presùmere *v. tr.* to presume

presuntuóso *agg.* presumptuous, conceited

presuppórre *v. tr.* to suppose, to assume

presuppósto *s. m.* presupposition, conjecture

prète *s. m.* priest, clergyman (anglicano); parson (protestante)

pretendènte *s. m. e f.* pretender; suitor (corteggiatore)

pretèndere *v. tr.* to claim, to pretend, to exact; to expect (esigere) • *intr.* to pretend (to), to claim (to)

pretésa *s. f.* pretension, claim

pretèsto *s. m.* pretext, pretence; occasion (occasione)

prevalènza *s. f.* prevalence; majority (maggioranza)

prevalére *v. intr.* to prevail

prevaricàre *v. intr.* to abuse one's office

prevedére *v. tr.* to foresee, to foretell; to provide for (disciplinare)

prevedìbile *agg.* predictable

prevenìre *v. tr.* to precede, to arrive before (precedere); to anticipate, to forestall (anticipare); to forewarn (avvertire); to prevent (cercare di evitare)

preventìvo *s. m.* estimate, budget

prevenùto *agg.* prejudiced

prevenzióne *s. f.* prevention

previdènte *agg.* provident, wise

previdènza *s. f.* providence; – **sociale** social security

previsióne *s. f.* prevision; expectation (aspettativa); – **del tempo** weather forecast

preziosìsmo *s. m.* preciosity

prezióso *agg.* precious

prezzémolo *s. m.* parsley

prèzzo *s. m.* price; rate, fee (tariffa)

prigióne *s. f.* prison, jail

prigionìa *s. f.* imprisonment, confinement

prigioniéro *agg.* imprisoned, confined • *s. m.* prisoner

prìma *avv.* before, beforehand; in advance (in anticipo); once, formerly (un tempo); earlier, sooner (più presto); – **di** before

primàrio *agg.* primary

primàto *s. m.* supremacy; record (sport)

primavèra *s. f.* spring

primaverìle *agg.* spring (attr.)

primitivìsmo *s. m.* primitivism

primitìvo *agg.* primitive

primìzie *s. f. pl.* first fruits, first vegetables; hot news (notizie)

prìmo *agg. num. ord.* first

primogènito *agg.* first-born

primordiàle *agg.* primordial

prìmula *s. f.* primrose, cowslip

principàle *agg.* principal, chief, main

principalménte *avv.* principally, chiefly, mainly

principàto *s. m.* princedom; principality (stato); principate (stor.)

prìncipe *s. m.* prince

principéssa *s. f.* princess

principiànte *s. m. e f.* beginner

princìpio *s. m.* beginning, start; principle (massima); origin (origine)

prióre *s. m.* prior

priorità *s. f.* priority

prìsma *s. m.* prism

privàre *v. tr.* to deprive • *rifl.* to deprive oneself; to deny oneself (negarsi)

privataménte *avv.* in private

privàto *agg.* private

privilegiàre *v. tr.* to privilege

privilègio *s. m.* privilege

prìvo *agg.* deprived (of); devoid (of); lacking (in) (mancante)

probàbile *agg.* probable; likely (verosimile)

probabilità *s. f.* probability, chance

probabilménte *avv.* probably, likely; possibly (forse)

problèma *s. m.* problem

problemàtica *s. f.* problems *pl.*

problemàtico *agg.* problematic

procacciàre *v. tr.* to procure, to get, to provide, to obtain

procèdere *v. intr.* to proceed, to go on; to start (iniziare)

procedimènto *s. m.* conduct; proceedings *pl.* (leg.); process (tecn.)

procedùra *s. f.* procedure, proceedings *pl.*

processàre *v. tr.* to try

processióne s. f. procession

procésso s. m. trial, course, process (procedimento); process (tecn.)

procióne s. m. racoon

proclamáre v. tr. to proclaim, to declare

proclamazióne s. f. proclamation, declaration

procreáre v. tr. to procreate, to beget

procuráre v. tr. to procure, to get, to provide; to cause, to bring about (causare)

prodézza s. f. deed, feat, exploit

prodigalità s. f. prodigality, extravagance

prodigio s. m. prodigy, marvel, wonder

prodigióso agg. prodigious, portentous, wonderful

prodótto s. m. product, produce

prodúrre v. tr. to produce; to cause (causare)

produttività s. f. productivity

produzióne s. f. production

profanatóre agg. profaning • s. m. profaner

profáno agg. profane; ignorant (inesperto)

professionále agg. professional

professióne s. f. profession

professionismo s. m. professionalism

professionista s. m. e f. professional

professóre s. m. teacher (scuola); professor (università)

proféta s. m. prophet

profético agg. prophetic

profezía s. f. prophecy

proficuo agg. profitable

profilássi s. f. prophylaxis

profilo s. m. profile (volto); outline (contorno)

profitto s. m. profit, advantage

profondimetro s. m. depth-gauge

profondità s. f. depth

profóndo agg. deep

prófugo s. m. refugee

profumáre v. intr. to smell sweet • rifl. to perfume oneself

profumataménte avv. dearly

profumáto agg. perfumed, scented

profumería s. f. perfumer's (shop)

profúmo s. m. perfume

progenitóre s. m. progenitor, forefather

progettáre v. tr. to plan

progettazióne s. f. planning

progettista s. m. e f. planner, designer

progétto s. m. plan, project, design

prógnosi s. f. prognosis

prográmma s. m. programme, program

programmáre v. tr. to program, to plan

programmazióne s. f. programming

progredíre v. intr. to progress; to improve (fare progressi)

progressióne s. f. progression

progressivaménte avv. progressively

progressivo agg. progressive

progrésso s. m. progress; development (sviluppo)

proibíre v. tr. to forbid; to prohibit (impedire)

proibizióne s. f. prohibition

proiettáre v. tr. to project

proiéttile s. m. bullet

proiettóre s. m. projector (film e diapositive); searchlight (sorgente luminosa)

proiezióne s. f. projection

proliferáre v. intr. to proliferate

prolifico agg. prolific

prolisso agg. prolix

prólogo s. m. prologue

prolungaménto s. m. prolongation; extension (proroga)

prolungáre v. tr. to prolong, to protract, to extend • intr. pron. to grow longer (tempo); to stretch (spazio)

promemória s. m. inv. memorandum, memo

proméssa s. f. promise

prométtere v. tr. to promise

promiscuità s. f. promiscuity

promontório s. m. headland

promotóre s. m. promoter

promozióne s. f. promotion

promuóvere v. tr. to promote; to pass (uno studente)

prònao s. m. pronaos

pronipóte s. m. e f. grand-nephew m., grand-niece f.

pronóme s. m. pronoun

pronóstico s. m. prognostic

prontaménte avv. readily, quickly

prónto agg. ready; prompt (rapido); – **soccorso** first aid

pronúnzia s. f. pronunciation

pronunziáre v. tr. to pronounce; to say, to utter (dire); to deliver (recitare) • intr. pron. to pronounce, to declare oneself

propagánda s. f. propaganda

propagandístico agg. propaganda (attr.)

propagáre v. tr. to propagate • intr. pron. to spread

propàggine s. f. offshoot

propéndere v. intr. to incline, to be inclined, to tend

propiléo s. m. propylaeum

propiziáre v. tr. to propitiate, to soothe

propizio *agg.* propitious

proponibile *agg.* proposable

proporre *v. tr.* to propose, to suggest; to set (sottoporre)

proporzionale *agg.* proportional

proporzione *s. f.* proportion, ratio

proposito *s. m.* purpose, intention, design

proposta *s. f.* proposal

proprietario *s. m.* owner

proprio *agg.* own; peculiar (particolare); suitable (appropriato) • *agg. poss.* his *m.*, her *f.*, their *pl.* • *avv.* really, quite; just, exactly (precisamente)

propulsione *s. f.* propulsion

proroga *s. f.* extension, delay

prorogare *v. tr.* to extend, to delay

prosa *s. f.* prose

prosciutto *s. m.* ham; – **affumicato** smoked han

prosecuzione *s. f.* prosecution, continuation

proseguimento *s. m.* prosecution, pursuance, continuation

proseguire *v. tr.* to prosecute, to carry on, to continue • *intr.* to continue, to go on, to pursue

prosperare *v. intr.* to prosper, to flourish, to boom

prosperoso *agg.* prosperous, flourishing

prospettico *agg.* perspective (*attr.*)

prospettiva *s. f.* perspective, prospect (*fig.*)

prospiciente *agg.* facing, overlooking

prossimamente *avv.* before long

prossimità *s. f.* proximity

prossimo *agg.* near, close, at hand; next (successivo)

prostilo *s. m.* prostyle

prostituta *s. f.* prostitute, whore

protagonista *s. m. e f.* protagonist (anche *fig.*); star (*cin.*)

proteggere *v. tr.* to protect, to shield, to shelter, to take care of

proteina *s. f.* protein

protesi *s. f.* prothesis; – **dentaria** dental prothesis

protesta *s. f.* protest, complaint

protestante *agg.* Protestant

protestantesimo *s. m.* Protestantism

protestare *v. intr.* to protest, to remonstrate

protezione *s. f.* protection, patronage

protezionismo *s. m.* protectionism

protocollo *s. m.* protocol; record (registro)

protomartire *s. m.* protomartyr

prototipo *s. m.* prototype

protuberanza *s. f.* protuberance

prova *s. f.* trial, test; experiment (esperimento); proof (dimostrazione); evidence (testimonianza); exam (esame); rehearsal (*teatro*)

provare *v. tr.* to try; to prove (dimostrare); to feel (sentire); to try on (indumenti) • *intr. pron.* to try, to attempt

provenienza *s. f.* place of origin, provenance; source (fonte)

provenire *v. intr.* to derive, to proceed, to originate

provenzale *agg.* Provençal

proverbiale *s. m.* proverbial

proverbio *s. m.* proverb, saying

provincia *s. f.* province

provinciale *agg.* provincial

provincialismo *s. m.* provincialism

provocante *agg.* provoking, provocative

provocare *v. tr.* to provoke; to arouse (suscitare)

provocazione *s. f.* provocation

provvedere *v. intr.* to provide (for); to arrange for (disporre)

provvedimento *s. m.* measure, action

provvidenza *s. f.* providence

provvidenziale *agg.* providential

provvisorio *agg.* provisional

provvista *s. f.* provision, supply

prua *s. f.* bow

prudente *agg.* prudent, cautious

prudenza *s. f.* prudence, caution

prudere *v. intr.* to itch

prugna *s. f.* plum; – **secca** prune

pruno *s. m.* blackthorn

prurito *s. m.* itch

pseudonimo *s. m.* pseudonym

psichiatra *s. m. e f.* psychiatrist

psichico *agg.* psychic(al), mental

psicoanalisi *s. f.* psychoanalysis

psicofarmaco *s. m.* psychotropic drug

psicologia *s. f.* psychology

psicologicamente *avv.* psychologically

psicologico *agg.* psychological

psicosi *s. f.* psychosis

pubblicare *v. tr.* to publish; to issue (di editore)

pubblicazione *s. f.* publication, issue; – **trimestrale** quarterly

pubblicità *s. f.* publicity; advertising (comm.); commercials *pl.* (radio, televisione)

pubblicizzare *v. tr.* to publicize

pubblico *agg.* e *s. m.* public

pubertà *s. f.* puberty

pudóre *s. m.* modesty, decency; shame (vergogna)

puericultúra *s. f.* puericulture

puerìle *agg.* childish

pugilàto *s. m.* boxing

pùgile *s. m.* boxer

pugnalàre *v. tr.* to stab

pugnàle *s. m.* dagger

pùgno *s. m.* fist; punch, blow (colpo); fistful (manciata)

pùlce *s. f.* flea

pulcìno *s. m.* chick

pulédro *s. m.* colt

pulìre *v. tr.* to clean

pulìto *agg.* clean

pulizìa *s. f.* cleaning

pùllman *s. m. inv.* coach

pullóver *s. m. inv.* pullover

pùlpito *s. m.* pulpit

pulsànte *s. m.* push-button

pulsazióne *s. f.* pulsation, throbbing

pulvìno *s. m.* dosseret, pulvino

pulvìscolo *s. m.* fine dust; – **atmosferico** motes

pùngere *v. tr.* to prick, to sting, to pierce; to pinch (pizzicare)

pungiglióne *s. f.* sting

punìre *s. f.* to punish

punizióne *s. f.* punishment; penalty (*sport*)

pùnta *s. f.* point, tip; end (parte terminale); top, peak (cima); cape (promontorio)

puntàle *s. m.* ferrule, shoe, cap

puntàre *v. tr.* to point, to direct; to aim (mirare); to bet (scommettere) • *intr.* to head for (dirigersi); to aim at (mirare); to count (on) (fare assegnamento)

puntàta *s. f.* bet, stake (somma scommessa);

flying visit (breve visita); instalment (di romanzo)

puntellàre *v. tr.* to prop

puntìglio *s. m.* stubbornness

pùnto *s. m.* point; stitch (cucito e maglia); score (punteggio); fullstop (*gramm.*)

puntuàle *agg.* punctual, on time

puntualità *s. f.* punctuality

puntùra *s. f.* puncture, sting; bite (d'insetto); injection, shot (iniezione)

pupàzzo *s. m.* puppet; rag doll (di stoffa)

pupìlla *s. f.* pupil

purché *cong.* provided (that), on condition that

pùre *cong.* even if (anche se); but, still (tuttavia) • *avv.* also, too, as well (anche); certainly, if you like (concessione)

purè *s. m.* mash, purée; – **di patate** mashed potatoes

pùrga *s. f.* purge

purgànte *s. m.* purge, purgative, laxative

purgatìvo *agg.* purgative, purging

purgatòrio *s. m.* purgatory

purìsmo *s. m.* purism

puritanésimo *s. m.* Puritanism

pùro *agg.* pure; sheer, mere (semplice)

purtròppo *avv.* unfortunately

pus *s. m. inv.* pus

putrefazióne *s. f.* putrefaction, corruption, decay

puttàna *s. f.* whore, bitch

pùtto *s. m.* putto

pùzza *s. f.* stench, stink, nasty smell

puzzàre *v. intr.* to stink, to smell (bad); to smack of, to smell (*fig.*)

pùzzola *s. f.* polecat

puzzolénte *agg.* stinking, ill-smelling

Q

qua *avv.* here; **- fuori** out here; **- giù** down here; **- su** up here

quácchero *s. m.* Quaker

quadèrno *s. m.* exercise-book, copy-book

quadrangoláre *agg.* quadrangular

quadránte *s. m.* quadrant; dial (di orologio)

quadráto *s. m.* square, ring (box)

quadriennále *agg.* quadriennial; four-year (*attr.*)

quadrifóglio *s. m.* four-leaved clover; quatre-foil (*arch.*)

quadrimestrále *agg.* four-monthly

quadrimotóre *s. m.* four-engined aircraft

quádro *s. m.* picture, painting; description (*fig.*); board, panel (*cin.*)

quádri *s. m. pl.* cadres (*mil.*); diamonds (nelle carte)

quadrúpede *agg.* quadruped

quádruplo *agg.* quadruple

quáglia *s. f.* quail

quálche *agg. indef.* some (frasi afferm.); any (frasi interr. e neg.)

qualcòsa *pron. indef.* something (frasi afferm.); anything (frasi interr. e neg.)

qualcúno *pron. indef.* somebody, someone, some (frasi afferm.); anybody, anyone, any (frasi interr. e neg.)

quále *agg. interr.* which • *pron. interr.* which; what (indeterminato) • *agg. escl.* what • *pron. rel.* Rif. a persone: who, that (sogg.) whom, that (ogg.); whom (indir.); whose (poss.) - Rif. a cose: which, that (sogg., ogg. e indir.); of which, whose (poss.) • *avv.* as

qualífica *s. f.* qualification, rating (giudizio)

qualità *s. f.* quality, property (proprietà); kind, sort (genere, varietà)

qualóra *cong.* in case, if

qualsíasi *agg. indef.* any

qualúnque *agg. indef.* any, whatever

quándo *avv.* e *cong.* when

quantità *s. f.* quantity

quantitativo *s. m.* quantity, amount

quánto *agg.* e *pron. interr.* how much *sing.*, how many *pl.*; how long (tempo) • *agg.*

escl. what a lot (of); how much *sing.*; how many *pl.* • *agg. rel.* as much *sing.*, as many *pl.*; so much *sing.*, so many *pl.* (in frasi neg.) • *pron. rel.* whoever, all that (tutto quello che); what (quello che); all those who *pl.* • *avv.* how (con agg. e avv.); how much, what a lot (rif. a verbi); **in -** since, as

quarantèna *s. f.* quarantine

quarésima *s. f.* Lent

quartétto *s. m.* quartet; **- d'archi** string quartet

quartière *s. m.* district, neighbourhood

quartina *s. f.* quatrain (*lett.*)

quàrzo *s. m.* quartz; **un orologio al -** a quartz watch

quàsi *avv.* almost, nearly; hardly (a malapena)

quassù *avv.* up here

quattrini *s. m. pl.* money *sing.*, dough *sing.*

quattrocentésco *agg.* fifteenth-century (*attr.*)

quattrocènto *s. m. inv.* four hundred

quéllo *agg. dimostr.* that *sing.*, those *pl.* • *pron. dimostr.* that (one) *sing.*, those *pl.*

quèrcia *s. f.* oak

querèla *s. f.* action (*leg.*)

quereláre *v. tr.* to sue

quesíto *s. m.* question

questionário *s. m.* questionnaire

questióne *s. f.* question, issue

quésto *agg. dimostr.* this *sing.*, these *pl.* • *pron. dimostr.* this (one) *sing.*, these *pl.*

qui *avv.* here; now (temporale); **- dentro** in here

quietánza *s. f.* receipt

quiète *s. f.* quiet

quièto *agg.* quiet, calm

quindi *avv.* then, afterwards • *cong.* so, therefore

quindicinále *agg.* fortnightly

quinta *s. f.* wing, side-scene

quintále *s. m.* quintal, hundred kilograms

quintétto *s. m.* quintet(te)

quotazióne *s. f.* quotation

quotidianaménte *avv.* daily

quotidiáno *agg.* e *s. m.* daily

quoziènte *s. m.* quotient

R

rabárbaro *s. m.* rhubarb

rábbia *s. f.* anger, rage, wrath; rabies, hydrophobia (*med.*)

rabbino *s. m.* rabbin, rabbi

rabbióso *agg.* hot-tempered; angry (adirato); rabid (d'animale)

rabbrividíre *v. intr.* to shudder, to shiver

racchétta *s. f.* racket, bat; ski-stick (sci)

racchiúdere *v. tr.* to contain

raccógliere *v. tr.* to pick (up); to reap (mietere); to gather, to collect (riunire)

raccólto *s. m.* crop, harvest

raccomandáre *v. tr.* to entrust, to recommend

raccomandáta *s. f.* registered letter

raccomandáto *agg.* recommended

raccomandazióne *s. f.* recommendation, advice

raccontáre *v. tr.* to tell

raccónto *s. m.* story, tale

raccórdo *s. m.* joint, connection; side-track (*ferr.*); – **autostradale** slip road, access road

rachítico *agg.* rickety (*med.*); stunted

raddoppiáre *v. tr.* to double, to duplicate

raddóppio *s. m.* doubling, duplication

raddrizzáre *v. tr.* to straighten

radénte *agg.* grazing

rádere *v. tr.* to shave; to raze (abbattere) • *rifl.* to shave

radiánte *agg.* radiant

radiatóre *s. m.* radiator

rádica *s. f.* briar

radicále *s. m. e f.* radical

radícchio *s. m.* chicory

radíce *s. f.* root

rádio *s. m.* radius (*anat.*); radium (*chim.*) • *s. f.* radio, wireless

radioamatóre *s. m.* radio-amateur; ham (*fam.*)

radioattività *s. f.* radio-activity

radioattivo *agg.* radio-active

radiocrónaca *s. f.* running commentary

radiocronista *s. m. e f.* radio commentator

radiofáro *s. m.* (radio) beacon

radiografia *s. f.* radiography; x-ray (lastra)

radiologo *s. m.* radiologist

radioscopia *s. f.* radioscopy

radiosegnále *s. m.* radio signal

radiosvéglia *s. f.* clock radio

radiotaxi *s. m.* radiotaxi

radiotécnico *s. m.* radio engineer

radioteléfono *s. m.* radiophone

radiotrasmissióne *s. f.* broadcast

radúno *s. m.* gathering

radúra *s. f.* clearing, glade

ráfano *s. m.* radish

rafférmo *agg.* stale

ráffica *s. f.* gust, blast

raffigurazióne *s. f.* representation

raffinatézza *s. f.* refinement, elegance

raffináto *agg.* refined, elegant

raffinería *s. f.* refinery

raffreddáre *v. tr.* to cool, to chill • *intr. pron.* to cool down, to catch a cold

raffreddóre *s. m.* cold

ragázza *s. f.* girl

ragázzo *s. m.* boy

rággio *s. m.* ray, beam; radius (*geom.*)

raggiráre *v. tr.* to deceive, to cheat, to swindle

raggiro *s. m.* cheat, swindle, trick

raggiúngere *v. tr.* to reach, to join

raggiungibile *agg.* attainable, achievable

raggruppáre *v. tr.* to group, to assemble

ragguáglio *s. m.* (piece of) information

ragionaménto *s. m.* reasoning

ragionáre *v. intr.* to reason; to argue (discutere)

ragióne *s. f.* reason; **avere** – to be right

ragionévole *agg.* reasonable, sensible

ragioniere *s. m.* accountant

ráglio *s. m.* braying

ragnatéla *s. f.* (spider's) web

rágno *s. m.* spider

rallegráre *v. tr.* to cheer up • *intr. pron.* to cheer up, to rejoice; to congratulate (congratularsi)

rallentaménto *s. m.* slowing down

rallentáre *v. tr.* to slow, to slow down

ramárro *s. m.* green lizard

ramázza *s. f.* broom

ráme *s. m.* copper

ramíno *s. m.* rummy

rammàrico *s. m.* regret
rammendàre *v. tr.* to darn, to mend
rammèndo *s. m.* darning, mending
ràmo *s. m.* branch
ramoscèllo *s. m.* twig
ràmpa *s. f.* ramp, slope; flight (scale); pad (missile); slip-road (autostrada)
rampànte *agg.* rampant
rampicànte *agg.* climbing, creeping • *s. m.* climber, creeper
rampino *s. m.* hook
rampòllo *s. m.* offspring
ràna *s. f.* frog
ràncido *agg.* rancid
ràncio *s. m.* mess
rancóre *s. m.* grudge
rànda *s. f.* mainsail
randàgio *agg.* stray
randèllo *s. m.* cudgel, club
ràngo *s. m.* rank
ranòcchio *s. m.* frog
ranùncolo *s. m.* ranunculus, buttercup
ràpa *s. f.* turnip
rapàce *agg.* rapacious • *s. m.* bird of prey
rapidità *s. f.* rapidity
ràpido *agg.* rapid, swift • *s. m.* express
rapiménto *s. m.* kidnapping; rapture (*fig.*)
rapina *s. f.* robbery
rapinàre *v. tr.* to rob
rapinatóre *s. m.* robber
rapire *v. tr.* to carry off; to abduct (una donna); to kidnap (un bambino)
rapitóre *s. m.* abductor (di donna); kidnapper (di bambino)
rappòrto *s. m.* report; connection, relation (correlazione); ratio (*mat.*)
rappresàglia *s. f.* retaliation, reprisal
rappresentàre *v. tr.* to represent, to perform; to stage (una commedia)
rappresentazióne *s. f.* representation; performance (recita)
rapsodista *s. m. e f.* rhapsodist
raraménte *avv.* seldom, rarely
rarità *s. f.* rarity, rareness
ràro *agg.* rare
rasàre *v. tr. e rifl.* to shave
rasatùra *s. f.* shave
raschiàre *v. tr.* to scrape
rasènte *prep.* close to
ràso *s. m.* satin
rasóio *s. m.* razor; – **elèttrico** electric razor
rassègna *s. f.* review
rassettàre *v. tr.* to tidy up

rassicuràre *v. tr.* to reassure
rassomigliànte *agg.* similar, like
rassomiglianza *s. f.* resemblance
rastrèllo *s. m.* rake
rastremazióne *s. f.* taper
ràta *s. f.* instalment; **comprare a** – to buy by instalments
rateàle *agg.* instalment (*attr.*)
rateazióne *s. f.* division into instalments
ratifica *s. f.* ratification
ràtto *s. m.* abduction; rat (*zool.*)
rattoppàre *v. tr.* to patch, to mend
raucèdine *s. f.* hoarseness
ràuco *agg.* hoarse, raucous
ravanèllo *s. m.* radish
razionàle *agg.* rational
razionalismo *s. m.* rationalism
razionalista *agg.* rationalistic
razióne *s. f.* ration
ràzza *s. f.* race; breed (di animali)
razzismo *s. m.* racism
razzista *agg.* racist
ràzzo *s. m.* rocket
re *s. m. inv.* king
reagènte *s. m.* reagent
reagire *v. intr.* to react
reàle *agg.* real; actual (effettivo)
realismo *s. m.* realism
realista *agg.* realist
realistico *agg.* realistic
realizzàre *v. tr.* to accomplish, to carry out; to score (*sport*); to realize (rendersi conto)
realizzo *s. m.* realization
realménte *avv.* really; actually (effettivamente)
realtà *s. f.* reality
reàto *s. m.* offence, crime
reattività *s. f.* reactivity
reazióne *s. f.* reaction
recapitàre *v. tr.* to deliver
recàpito *s. m.* address; delivery (consegna)
recensióne *s. f.* review
recensire *v. tr.* to review
recensóre *s. m.* reviewer
recènte *agg.* recent, late
recenteménte *avv.* recently, lately, of late
recidere *v. tr.* to cut off, to chop off
recidiva *s. f.* recidivism; relapse (*med.*)
recinto *s. m.* pen (per animali); play-pen (per bambini); fence (staccionata)
recipiènte *s. m.* container, vessel
reciproco *agg.* reciprocal, mutual
rècita *s. f.* performance

recitàre *v. tr.* to recite; to say (dire); to perform, to act, to play • *intr.* to act, to play

recitazióne *s. f.* recitation, acting; **scuola di** – dramatic school

reclamàre *v. tr.* to claim, to ask for • *intr.* to protest, to make a complaint

reclàmo *s. m.* claim, complaint

reclinàre *v. tr.* to recline, to bend down

rècluta *s. f.* recruit

recriminazióne *s. f.* complaint

redattóre *s. m.* editor; drawer (compilatore); reporter (di un giornale)

redazionàle *agg.* editorial

redazióne *s. f.* editing; editorial staff (il personale)

redditività *s. f.* profitability

redditízio *agg.* profitable

rèddito *s. m.* income

redentóre *s. m.* redeemer

redìgere *v. tr.* to draw up, to write, to compile

referèndum *s. m. inv.* referendum

referènza *s. f.* reference

refèrto *s. m.* report

refettòrio *s. m.* refectory

refezióne *s. f.* refection, meal

refrigeràre *v. tr.* to refrigerate, to cool

refrigèrio *s. m.* refreshment, relief

refurtìva *s. f.* stolen goods *pl.*, loot

refùso *s. m.* misprint

regalàre *v. tr.* to give, to present

regàlo *s. m.* present, gift

regàta *s. f.* race

reggènte *s. m. e f.* regent

règgia *s. f.* royal palace

reggicàlze *s. m. inv.* garter belt

reggisèno *s. m.* brassière, bra

regìa *s. f.* production (teatro); direction (cin.)

regìme *s. m.* regime

regìna *s. f.* queen

regionàle *agg.* regional

regióne *s. f.* region, district

regìsta *s. m. e f.* producer (teatro); director (cin.)

registratóre *s. m.* recorder

registrazióne *s. f.* recording, entry

regìstro *s. m.* register

regnànte *agg.* regnant, reigning, ruling

régno *s. m.* kingdom; reign (durata)

règola *s. f.* rule

regolàbile *agg.* adjustable

regolaménto *s. m.* rule, regulations *pl.*; settlement (fig., comm.)

regolàre *agg.* regular • *v. tr.* to regulate; to control (disciplinare); to set (mecc.)

regolarménte *avv.* regularly, duly

regrèsso *s. m.* regress, regression

reincàrico *s. m.* re-appointment

reincarnazióne *s. f.* reincarnation

reinserìre *v. tr.* to reinstate (persone); to reinsert (cose)

relativìsmo *s. m.* relativism

relatività *s. f.* relativity

relatìvo *agg.* relevant; pertinent (che ha relazione); relative (gramm.)

relatóre *s. m.* chairman

relazionàre *v. tr.* to report to (so.), to inform

relazióne *s. f.* report, account; connection, relation (collegamento)

religióne *s. f.* religion

religióso *agg.* religious

relìquia *s. f.* relic

reliquiàrio *s. m.* reliquary, shrine

relìtto *s. m.* wreck; outcast (fig.)

remàre *v. intr.* to row

rematóre *s. m.* oar

reminiscènza *s. f.* reminiscence

rèmo *s. m.* oar; paddle (pagaia)

remòto *agg.* distant, remote

rèndere *v. tr.* to give back; to return (contraccambiare); to render (dare, fare); to yield (fruttare)

rendiménto *s. m.* yield; output (produzione); efficiency (fis., mecc.); progress (scol.)

rèndita *s. f.* revenue; annuity (leg., comm.)

rène *s. m.* kidney

rèni *s. f. pl.* loins

rènna *s. f.* reindeer; **pelle di** – buckskin

repàrto *s. m.* department; ward (di ospedale); unit (mil.)

repèrto *s. m.* find

repertòrio *s. m.* repertory

rèplica *s. f.* repeat performance (teatro); replica (d'opera d'arte); reply (risposta)

replicàre *v. tr.* to repeat; to answer back (controbattere); to reply (rispondere)

repressióne *s. f.* repression

reprìmere *v. tr.* to repress, to restrain

repùbblica *s. f.* republic

repubblicàno *agg.* republican

reputazióne *s. f.* reputation

requisìre *v. tr.* to requisition

requisìto *s. m.* requisite, requirement

rèsa *s. f.* surrender; return (restituzione)

rescìndere *v. tr.* to cancel

residènza *s. f.* residence

residenziále *agg.* residential

rèsina *s. f.* resin

resistènte *agg.* resisting; –proof (nei composti); – **al calore** heat-proof; – **al fuoco** fireproof

resistènza *s. f.* resistance

resistere *v. intr.* to resist; to endure (sopportare)

respingènte *s. m.* buffer, bumper

respingere *v. tr.* to repel; to reject (non accettare); to return (rimandare al mittente)

respirare *v. intr.* to breathe

respiratóre *s. m.* aqualung

respirazióne *s. f.* respiration, breathing

respiro *s. m.* breath; respite (pausa)

responsábile *agg.* responsible

responsabilità *s. f.* responsibility

respònso *s. m.* response, answer

rèssa *s. f.* throng, crowd

restaurare *v. tr.* to restore

restauratóre *s. m.* restorer

restáuro *s. m.* restoration

restituíre *v. tr.* to return, to give back

rèsto *s. m.* remainder, rest; change (denaro)

restringere *v. tr.* to tighten; to restrict (ridurre)

restrittívo *agg.* restrictive

réte *s. f.* net, network; – **da pesca** fishing-net

reticènza *s. f.* reticence

reticolo *s. m.* network, grid

rètina *s. f.* retina

retòrica *s. f.* rhetoric

retráttile *agg.* retractive

retribuíre *v. tr.* to remunerate

rètro *s. m. inv.* back

retromárcia *s. f.* reverse gear

retroscèna *s. f.* back-stage (teatro)

retrospettíva *s. f.* retrospective

retrotèrra *s. m. inv.* hinterland; background (fig.)

rètta *s. f.* straight line

rettangolàre *agg.* rectangular

rettángolo *s. m.* rectangle

rettífica *s. f.* rectification (fig.); grinding (mecc.)

rèttile *s. m.* reptile

rettilíneo *agg.* rectilinear, straight

rètto *agg.* straight, right; upright (fig.)

rettóre *s. m.* rector; chancellor (univ. UK); president (univ. USA)

reumatismo *s. m.* rheumatism

reverèndo *agg.* reverend

reversíbile *agg.* reversible; reversionary (leg.)

reversibilità *s. f.* reversibility

revisióne *s. f.* revision, revisal; overhaul (mecc.)

revisionísta *s. m. e f.* revisionist

revisóre *s. m.* reviser

rèvoca *s. f.* revocation, repeal

revocáre *v. tr.* to revoke, to repeal

riabilitáre *v. tr.* to rehabilitate

riabilitazióne *s. f.* rehabilitation

riabituáre *v. tr.* to reaccustom

riaccèndere *v. tr.* to light again; to switch on again (luce); to revive (fig.)

riaccompagnáre *v. tr.* to take back

riacquistáre *v. tr.* to buy back; to recover (recuperare)

riadattáre *v. tr.* to readapt

riaddormentáre *v. tr.* to put to sleep again • *intr. pron.* to fall asleep again

riaffermáre *v. tr.* to reaffirm

rialzáre *v. tr.* to raise higher; to lift up (sollevare)

rialzo *s. m.* rise, increase; bull run (Borsa)

riannodáre *v. tr.* to knot again; to renew (fig.)

riassúmere *v. tr.* to reassume; to sum up (compendiare)

riassúnto *s. m.* summary

riavére *v. tr.* to get back (recuperare); to recover (riacquistare)

ribadíre *v. tr.* to confirm

ribálta *s. f.* flap (piano ribaltabile); apron (teatro); limelight (notorietà)

ribaltábile *agg.* tip-up (attr.)

ribaltaménto *s. m.* overturn

ribaltáre *v. tr. e intr. pron.* to overturn

ribásso *s. m.* fall, decline; discount (sconto); bear run (Borsa)

ribèlle *s. m. e f.* rebel

ríbes *s. m.* ribes, redcurrant

ricadére *v. intr.* to fall again; to relapse (avere una ricaduta); to fall (riversarsi)

ricaduta *s. f.* relapse

ricámbio *s. m.* refill (ricarica); spare (part) (mecc.)

ricámo *s. m.* embroidery

ricàrica *s. f.* recharge

ricaricáre *v. tr.* to reload; to refill (riempire); to rewind (di orologio); to recharge (elettr.)

ricattáre *v. tr.* to blackmail

ricattatóre *s. m.* blackmailer

ricátto *s. m.* blackmail

ricaváre *v. tr.* to get, to derive

ricávo *s. m.* proceeds pl.

ricchézza *s. f.* richness, wealth

riccio *s. m.* curl; hedgehog (*zool.*); – **di mare** sea-urchin

ricco *agg.* rich

ricérca *s. f.* search; research (scientifica)

ricercàre *v. tr.* to seek (for), to search

ricercatóre *s. m.* researcher

ricetrasmittènte *s. f.* transmitter-receiver

ricétta *s. f.* recipe (*alim.*); prescription (*med.*)

ricettàrio *s. m.* cook-book (*alim.*); book of prescriptions (*med.*)

ricévere *v. tr.* to receive

ricevimento *s. m.* welcome; reception (accoglienza); reception, party (trattenimento)

ricevitòria *s. f.* receiving office

ricevùta *s. f.* receipt

richiamàre *v. tr.* to call back; to attract (attirare)

richièdere *v. tr.* to ask back; to ask for (per avere); to demand (esigere); to require (necessitare)

richièsta *s. f.* request, demand

riciclàre *v. tr.* to recycle

ricognizióne *s. f.* reconnaissance

ricominciàre *v. tr.* to begin again, to start again; to resume (riprendere)

ricompènsa *s. f.* recompense, reward

ricompensàre *v. tr.* to recompense, to reward

ricompràre *v. tr.* to buy back

riconciliàre *v. tr.* to reconcile • *rifl. rec.* to make friends again, to make it up

riconciliazióne *s. f.* reconciliation

ricondùrre *v. tr.* to bring again, to bring back, to take back

riconférma *s. f.* reconfirmation

riconfermàre *v. tr.* to reconfirm, to confirm (again)

ricongiunzióne *s. f.* rejoining, reunion

riconoscènte *agg.* thankful, grateful

riconoscènza *s. f.* thankfulness, gratitude

riconóscere *v. tr.* to recognize, to acknowledge; to admit (ammettere) • *rifl.* to recognize each other

riconoscìbile *agg.* recognizable

riconoscimènto *s. m.* recognition, admission; avowal (ammissione); identification (identificazione)

riconsideràre *v. tr.* to reconsider

ricopiàre *v. tr.* to copy, to recopy

ricoprìre *v. tr.* to cover; to line (rivestire); to plate (placcare)

ricordàre *v. tr.* to remember; to recollect (cercare di –); to recall (richiamare alla memo-

ria); to remind (richiamare alla memoria altrui); to mention (menzionare)

ricòrdo *s. m.* memory, recollection, remembrance; souvenir (oggetto)

ricorrènte *agg.* recurrent

ricorrènza *s. f.* recurrence; anniversary (anniversario)

ricórso *s. m.* resort, recourse; petition (*leg.*)

ricostituènte *s. m.* tonic

ricostruìre *v. tr.* to reconstruct, to rebuild

ricoveràre *v. tr.* to shelter; – **all'ospedale** to hospitalize

ricòvero *s. m.* shelter; admission (ospedale); poor-house (per poveri); old people's home (per anziani)

ricreativo *agg.* recreative, recreational

ricreazióne *s. f.* recreation

ricucìre *v. tr.* to sew again, to stitch

ricuòcere *v. tr.* to recook

ridàre *v. tr.* to give back, to return

rìdere *v. intr.* to laugh (at)

rìdicolo *agg.* funny; paltry (esiguo) • *s. m.* ridicule

ridimensionàre *v. tr.* to reorganize; to reduce (ridurre); to reappraise (*fig.*)

ridipìngere *v. tr.* to repaint

ridìre *v. tr.* to tell again, to say again; to find fault with (criticare)

ridòsso *s. m.* shelter, lee; **a – di** under (the) lee of, at the back of, behind

ridùrre *v. tr.* to reduce, to cut down; to adapt (adattare)

riduttivo *agg.* reductive

riduzióne *s. f.* reduction, cut; discount (sconto); – **cinematogràfica** screen adaption

riedizióne *s. f.* new edition; remake (*cin.*)

rielaboràre *v. tr.* to work out again

rieléggere *v. tr.* to re-elect

rielezióne *s. f.* re-election

riempìre *v. tr.* to fill (up), to stuff

rientrànza *s. f.* recess

rientràre *v. intr.* to re-enter; to be included in (far parte)

riepilogàre *v. tr.* to recapitulate, to sum up

riepìlogo *s. m.* recapitulation, summing up

riesumàre *v. tr.* to exhume

rievocàre *v. tr.* to recall

rievocazióne *s. f.* memory, remembrance

rifacimènto *s. m.* remaking; remake (*cin.*)

rifàre *v. tr.* to do (o to make) again, to remake; to imitate (imitare); to restore (ripristinare); to repair (riparare)

rifasciàre *v. tr.* to wrap up again

riferire v. tr. to report; to attribute (a scrivere)

rifinire v. tr. to finish (up)

rifinitùra s. f. finishing up

rifiutàre v. tr. to refuse; to reject (respingere)

rifiùto s. m. refusal, waste; refuse (scarto)

rifiùti s. m. pl. rubbish sing., litter sing.

riflessióne s. f. reflection, consideration

riflèsso s. m. reflection; reflex (med.)

riflèttere v. tr. to reflect

rifocillàre v. tr. to refresh • rifl. to refresh oneself

rifórma s. f. reform; Reformation (stor.)

riformatóre agg. reforming • s. m. reformer, reformist

riformatòrio s. m. reformatory

rifornire v. tr. to furnish, to supply; to restock (fornire di nuovo); to refuel (di carburante)

rifrazióne s. f. refraction

rifugiàrsi v. intr. pron. to shelter, to take refuge

rifùgio s. m. refuge, shelter

riga s. f. line; row (fila); parting (scriminatura)

rigattière s. m. junk dealer

rigidità s. f. rigidity

rigido agg. rigid, stiff, hard, rigorous; harsh (di clima)

rigoglióso agg. luxuriant

rigonfiaménto s. m. swelling, bulge

rigóre s. m. rigour; calcio di – penalty kick

rigoróso agg. rigorous, strict

rigovernàre v. tr. to wash up

rilàncio s. m. raising; relaunching (fig.)

rilàscio s. m. release; grant (concessione)

rilassàre v. tr. e rifl. to relax

rilegàre v. tr. to bind

rilegatóre s. m. binder

rilegatùra s. f. binding

rilevaménto s. m. survey; bearing (naut.); prominence (sporgenza)

rilièvo s. m. relief; rise (parte rilevata); high ground (complesso di alture); importance (importanza); mettere in – to point out

rìloga s. f. curtain rod

riluttànza s. f. reluctance, aversion

rima s. f. rhyme

rimaneggiàre v. tr. to remash, to adapt

rimanènza s. f. remainder, surplus; rimanenze left-overs

rimanére v. intr. to remain, to stay; to be left (avanzare)

rimarchévole agg. remarkable, notable

rimbàlzo s. m. rebound; ricochet (di proiettile)

rimbómbo s. m. rumble

rimborsàbile agg. repayable

rimborsàre v. tr. to reimburse, to refund

rimbórso s. m. reimbursement, refund

rimboschiménto s. m. reforestation

rimediàre v. intr. to remedy, to make up for

rimèdio s. m. remedy, cure

rimescolàre v. tr. to mix up, to stir up; to shuffle (le carte)

rimèssa s. f. remittance (denaro); depot (autobus); throw-in (calcio)

rimónta s. f. recovery

rimorchiatóre s. m. tug

rimórchio s. m. tow

rimòrso s. m. regret

rimozióne s. f. removal; towing away (di automobili)

rimpatriàre v. intr. to repatriate

rimpàtrio s. m. repatriation

rimpiàngere v. tr. to regret

rimpiànto s. m. regret

rimpiazzàre v. tr. to replace

rimpinguàre v. tr. to fatten

rimproveràre v. tr. to scold, to rebuke, to reproach

rimpròvero s. m. reproach, scolding, rebuke

rimuneràre v. tr. to remunerate

rimuòvere v. tr. to remove

rinascimentàle agg. Renaissance (attr.)

rinasciménto s. m. Renaissance

rinàscita s. f. renascence, revival

rincaràre v. tr. to raise

rincominciàre v. tr. to begin again, to start again

rincórsa s. f. run

rincréscersi v. intr. pron. to be sorry, to mind

rincresciménto s. m. regret

rinfacciàre v. tr. to reproach

rinforzàre v. tr. to strengthen, to reinforce; to back (edil.)

rinfrescànte agg. refreshing

rinfrescàrsi v. rifl. to refresh oneself (ristorarsi); to freshen oneself up (lavarsi)

rinfrèsco s. m. refreshments pl.; party (ricevimento)

ringhiàre v. intr. to snarl

ringhièra s. f. railing(s); banisters pl. (di scala)

ringhióso agg. snarling

ringiovanìre v. tr. to make (sb.) look younger • intr. e intr. pron. to get younger

ringraziaménto s. m. thanks pl.

ringraziàre v. tr. to thank

rinnegàre v. tr. to deny

rinnovàre v. tr. to renew; to repeat (ripetere)

rinnòvo s. m. renewal
rinocerónte s. m. rhinoceros
rinomàto agg. renowned
rintòcco s. m. toll
rintracciàre v. tr. to trace, to track down
rinùnzia s. f. renunciation
rinunziàre v. intr. to renounce
rinvenim'ento s. m. recovery, finding
rinvenìre v. tr. to find, to recover; to discover • intr. to recover one's senses, to come to
rinviàre v. tr. to send back, to return; to put off (rimandare)
rinvìo s. m. return (il mandare indietro); putting off, postponement (differimento)
rionàle agg. district (attr.); local
rióne s. m. district, quarter
riordinàre v. tr. to put in order, to tidy up; to reform (dare un nuovo ordinamento)
riórdino s. m. rearrangement
riparàre v. tr. to repair (aggiustare); to shelter (proteggere) • rifl. to protect oneself
riparazióne s. f. repair, fixing
ripàro s. m. shelter, cover, protection
ripartizióne s. f. division
ripercórrere v. tr. to run through again; to go over again (fig.)
ripétere v. tr. to repeat
ripetizióne s. f. repetition
ripiàno s. m. shelf
ripicca s. f. spite, pique
ripido agg. steep
ripiegàre v. tr. to fold up, to refold
ripièno agg. stuffed, filled • s. m. stuffing
ripiègo s. m. expedient, makeshift
ripopolàre v. tr. to repopulate
ripórre v. tr. to put away
riportàre v. tr. to bring (verso chi parla); to take (lontano da chi parla); to report (riferire); to quote (citare); - **indietro** to bring back
riposàre v. tr. e rifl. to rest
ripòso s. m. rest
ripostìglio s. m. lumber-room, store-room, closet
riprèndere v. tr. to take again; to take back (riavere); to begin again (ricominciare)
riprésa s. f. restarting, resumption; revival (rinascita); shot (cin.)
ripristinàre v. tr. to restore; to revive (far rinascere)
riproducìbile agg. reproducible
riprodùrre v. tr. to reproduce
riproduzióne s. f. reproduction; reprint (ristampa)

riprovàre v. intr. to try again
riprovévole agg. reprehensible
ripulìre v. tr. to clean up • rifl. to tidy oneself
riquàdro s. m. square; panel (arch.)
risàcca s. f. backwash
risàia s. f. rice-field
risalìre v. tr. to climb up, to ascend
risalìta s. f. ascent, climb
risarciménto s. m. compensation; **richiesta di** - claim for damages
risarcìre v. tr. to make up for, to indemnify
risàta s. f. laughter, laugh
riscaldaménto s. m. heating; - **centrale** central heating; **impianto di** - heating system
riscaldàre v. tr. to warm (up), to heat (up) • rifl. to warm oneself, to warm up, to get excited (infervorarsi)
riscattàre v. tr. to ransom, to redeem
riscàtto s. m. ransom
rischiàre v. tr. to risk, to venture
rischio s. m. risk
rischióso agg. risky
risciacquàre v. tr. to rinse
riscontràre v. tr. to find out, to notice
riscoprìre v. tr. to rediscover
riscrìvere v. tr. to rewrite
riscuòtere v. tr. to collect, to draw, to cash
risentiménto s. m. resentment
risèrbo s. m. reserve, discretion
risèrva s. f. reserve; preserve (di caccia o pesca)
riservàre v. tr. to reserve, to keep; to book (prenotare)
riservatézza s. f. reserve
riservàto agg. reserved; confidential (segreto)
risguàrdo s. m. fly-leaf
risièdere v. intr. to reside, to live
risma s. f. ream
riso s. m. laughter; rice (bot.)
risoluzióne s. f. resolution; solution (mat.)
risòlvere v. tr. to solve, to resolve; to settle (definire)
risonanza s. f. resonance; renown (fig.)
risorgìva s. f. resurgence
risórsa s. f. resource
risparmiàre v. tr. to save, to put by, to spare
risparmiatóre s. m. saver
risparmio s. m. saving; **i risparmi** the savings
rispedìre v. tr. to send again (di nuovo); to send back (indietro)
rispettàbile agg. respectable
rispettabilità s. f. respectability
rispettàre v. tr. to respect
rispètto s. m. respect

rispettóso *agg.* respectful

rispóndere *v. tr. e intr.* to answer, to reply; – **al telefono** to answer the telephone

rispósta *s. f.* answer, reply

rissa *s. f.* brawl

rissóso *agg.* brawling, quarrelsome

ristampa *s. f.* reprint

ristampàre *v. tr.* to reprint

ristorànte *s. m.* restaurant

ristoratóre *s. m.* restaurateur

ristorazióne *s. f.* catering

ristrétto *agg.* narrow; thick (concentrato); strong (caffè)

ristrutturàre *v. tr.* to restructure

ristrutturazióne *s. f.* restructuration, renovation

risultàto *s. m.* result, outcome

risuolàre *v. tr.* to sole, to resole

risvéglio *s. m.* waking up; revival (*fig.*)

risvòlto *s. m.* lapel (giacca); turn-up (pantaloni); implication (*fig.*)

ritagliàre *v. tr.* to cut out

ritàglio *s. m.* cutting; scrap (stoffa); press-clipping (giornale); spare time (tempo)

ritardàre *v. intr.* to retard, to be delayed; to be late (essere in ritardo)

ritardatàrio *s. m.* late-comer

ritàrdo *s. m.* delay; retardation (*psic.*)

ritiràre *v. tr.* to withdraw, to draw back, to take back; to draw (riscuotere); to collect (farsi consegnare) • *rifl.* to retire; to shrink (tessuto)

ritiràta *s. f.* retreat; lavatory (servizi)

ritiro *s. m.* withdrawal; retreat (luogo appartato); **in** – retired

ritmo *s. m.* rhythm

rito *s. m.* rite

ritócco *s. m.* touch-up, finishing touch; revision (prezzi)

ritornàre *v. intr.* to return; to go back (andare indietro); to come back (venire indietro)

ritornèllo *s. m.* refrain

ritórno *s. m.* return

ritràtto *s. m.* portrait, image; picture (*fig.*)

ritrovaménto *s. m.* finding; recovery (recupero)

ritrovàre *v. tr.* to find again (di nuovo); to find; to recover (*fig.*); to meet (again) (incontrare di nuovo) • *rifl.* to find oneself

ritròvo *s. m.* meeting; meeting-place, resort (luogo)

rituale *s. m.* ritual

riunire *v. tr.* to reunite; to gather up (adunare)

riuscire *v. intr.* to succeed, to manage; to be able (essere capace); to come out, to turn out (avere un esito); to go out again (uscire di nuovo)

riuscita *s. f.* issue, result, outcome

riva *s. f.* bank (di fiume); shore (di lago, mare)

rivàle *agg. e s. m. e f.* rival

rivalità *s. f.* rivalry

rivalutàre *v. tr.* to revalue; to revaluate (*fin.*)

rivalutazióne *s. f.* revaluation

rivedére *v. tr.* to see again (vedere di nuovo); to meet again (incontrare di nuovo); to correct, to check (controllare); to inspect (ispezionare)

rivelàre *v. tr.* to reveal, to disclose; show (manifestare)

rivelazióne *s. f.* revelation

rivéndere *v. tr.* to resell

rivendicàre *v. tr.* to vindicate, to claim

rivéndita *s. f.* resale; (retail) shop (negozio)

rivenditóre *s. m.* retailer

rivèrbero *s. m.* reverberation, echo

riverènza *s. f.* reverence; bow (inchino)

riverniciàre *v. tr.* to repaint

riversàre *v. tr.* to pour again; to turn over (rovesciare); to throw (*fig.*)

rivestiménto *s. m.* covering, coating; lining (interno); facing (*arch.*)

rivestire *v. tr.* to dress again (vestire di nuovo); to cover; to coat (ricoprire); to line (foderare)

rivincita *s. f.* return match (*sport*); revenge (*fig.*)

rivisitàre *v. tr.* to revisit

rivista *s. f.* review; parade (*mil.*); magazine (giornale); show (*teatro*)

rivòlta *s. f.* revolt, rising

rivoltàre *v. tr.* to turn (over); to turn inside out (con l'interno verso l'esterno); to turn upside-down (capovolgere)

rivoltèlla *s. f.* revolver

rivoluzionàrio *agg.* revolutionary

rivoluzióne *s. f.* revolution

robùsto *agg.* strong, sturdy

ròcca *s. f.* fortress, stronghold

roccafòrte *s. f.* stronghold

ròccia *s. f.* rock

rocciatóre *s. m.* rock-climber

roccióso *agg.* rocky

rococò *s. m.* rococo

rodàggio *s. m.* running-in

ròdeo *s. m. inv.* rodeo

roditóre *s. m.* rodent

rododéndro *s. m.* rhododendron

rognóne s. m. kidney

rògo s. m. pyre; stake (supplizio); fire (incendio)

rollío s. m. rolling

románico agg. Romanesque

románo agg. e s. m. Roman

romanticísmo s. m. Romanticism

romántico agg. romantic

románza s. f. romance

romanzière s. m. novelist

románzo s. m. novel; romance (storia inverosimile)

rómbo s. m. rhombus (geom., zool.); rumble (rumore)

romboidále agg. rhomboid(al)

rómpere v. tr. to break

rompicápo s. m. riddle, puzzle

rompiscátole s. m. e f. inv. nuisance

rónda s. f. patrol; watch

rondèlla s. f. washer

róndine s. f. swallow

ròsa s. f. rose • agg. pink

rosmaríno s. m. rosemary

rosolía s. f. German measles; rubella

rosóne s. m. rose-window

róspo s. m. toad

rossétto s. m. lip-stick

rósso agg. red

rotàia s. f. rail

rotatíva s. f. rotary press

rotatória s. f. roundabout

rotèlla s. f. roller

rotolàre v. tr. to roll

rótolo s. m. roll; coil (corda)

rotónda s. f. rotunda (arch.); round terrace (terrazza)

rotondità s. f. rotundity, roundness

rotóndo agg. round

rótta s. f. course, route

rottáme s. m. scrap

rótto agg. broken

rótula s. f. rotula

roulotte s. f. inv. caravan, trailer

rovènte agg. red-hot, burning

róvere s. m. o f. oak

rovesciàre v. tr. to overthrow

rovìna s. f. ruin

rovìne s. f. pl. ruins, remains

róvo s. m. bramble, thorn bush

rubàre v. tr. to steal; to rob (sb. of st.)

rubinétto s. m. tap

rubíno s. m. ruby

rubrìca s. f. index-book; address-book (per indirizzi); phone-book (telefonica); column, section (di giornale)

rúdere s. m. ruin

rúderi s. m. pl. ruins, remains

rudimentále agg. rudimentary

rudiménto s. m. rudiment

rúga s. f. wrinkle

rúggine s. f. rust

rugginóso agg. rusty

ruggíto s. m. roar

rugiàda s. f. dew

rugosità s. f. roughness, wrinkledness; rugosity (bot.)

rúllo s. m. roll

ruminànti s. m. pl. ruminants

rumóre s. m. noise

rumoróso agg. noisy

ruòlo s. m. role

ruòta s. f. wheel; – di scorta spare wheel

ruotàre v. tr. to rotate, to roll • intr. to rotate, to revolve

rúpe s. f. cliff, rock

rupèstre agg. rocky

rurále agg. rural

ruscèllo s. m. brook

rúspa s. f. scraper, bulldozer

ruspànte agg. farmyard

russàre v. intr. to snore

rùsso agg. e s. m. Russian

rústico agg. rustic; country (attr.) • s. m. cottage

rúvido agg. rough

S

sàbato *s. m.* Saturday
sabbàtico *agg.* sabbatical
sàbbia *s. f.* sand
sabbiatùra *s. f.* sand-bath (*med.*); sand-blasting (*tecn.*); shot-blasting (*mecc.*)
sabbióso *agg.* sandy
sabotàggio *s. m.* sabotage
sàcca *s. f.* bag, knapsack; pocket (*fig.*)
saccarina *s. f.* saccharine
saccaròsio *s. m.* saccharose
saccheggiàre *v. tr.* to sack, to pillage, to plunder, to lot
saccheggiatóre *s. m.* sacker, pillager
sacchéggio *s. m.* sack, pillage, plunder
sacchétto *s. m.* (small) bag, shopping bag
sàcco *s. m.* sack, bag; **- a pelo** sleeping bag
sacerdóte *s. m.* priest
sacerdotéssa *s. f.* priestess
sacerdòzio *s. m.* priesthood
sacralgia *s. f.* sacralgia
sacralità *s. f.* sacral character
sacraménto *s. m.* sacrament
sacràrio *s. m.* sacrarium (*archeol.*); sanctuary (*santuario*)
sacrificàre *v. tr.* to sacrifice • *rifl.* to sacrifice oneself
sacrificio *s. m.* sacrifice
sacrilègio *s. m.* sacrilege
sàcro *agg.* sacred, holy
sàdico *agg.* sadistic • *s. m.* sadist
sadomasochismo *s. m.* sadomasochism
safàri *s. m. inv.* safari
sàga *s. f.* saga
saggézza *s. f.* wisdom
sàggio *agg.* wise
saggista *s. m. e f.* essayist
saggistica *s. f.* essay-writing
sàgola *s. f.* line
sàgra *s. f.* festival, feast
sagràto *s. m.* church-square
sàio *s. m.* frock, cowl
sàla *s. f.* hall, room
salàme *s. m.* salami
salamòia *s. f.* brine, pickle

salàre *v. tr.* to salt; to salt (down), to corn (per conservare)
salàrio *s. m.* wage, salary
salàsso *s. m.* bleeding; drain (*fig.*)
salatino *s. m.* cocktail snack
salàto *agg.* salt (*attr.*); salty, salted (conservato col sale)
saldàre *v. tr.* to bind, to solder, to weld; to settle (*comm.*)
saldatóre *s. m.* solderer
saldatrice *s. f.* welder
saldatùra *s. f.* soldering, welding
sàldo *s. m.* settlement, balance; sale (liquidazione); **saldi invernali** winter sales
sàle *s. m.* salt; **senza -** saltless
salesiàno *agg.* Salesian
sàlice *s. m.* willow; **- piangente** weeping willow
salire *v. tr.* to climb, to go up, to mount, to get on; to ascend
salita *s. f.* climb, slope; ascent (ascesa); rise (aumento)
saliva *s. f.* saliva, spittle
sàlma *s. f.* corpse
salmi *s. m.* salmi
sàlmo *s. m.* psalm
salmóne *s. m.* salmon; **- affumicato** smoked salmon
salmonellòsi *s. f.* salmonellosis
salóne *s. m.* saloon, hall, show; exhibition (mostra)
salòtto *s. m.* sitting-room
salpàre *v. tr.* to set sail, to weigh (anchor)
sàlsa *s. f.* sauce
salsédine *s. f.* saltness
salsiccia *s. f.* sausage
salsièra *s. f.* sauce-boat; gravy-boat
saltàre *v. tr.* to jump, to leap, to spring over; to skip over (tralasciare); to blow up (in aria)
saltatóre *s. m.* jumper
saltellàre *v. intr.* to dance about, to skip about, to hop, to caper
saltimbànco *s. m.* acrobat, tumbler
sàlto *s. m.* jump, leap, spring
saltuariaménte *avv.* discontinuously
saltuàrio *agg.* discontinuous, intermittent

salùbre *agg.* salubrious, wholesome, healthy

salubrità *s. f.* salubrity

salùmi *s. m. pl.* cold cuts

salumeria *s. f.* delicatessen (shop)

salumière *s. m.* delicatessen seller

salumifício *s. m.* sausage factory

salutàre *v. tr.* to greet, to say hullo, to say good-bye • *agg.* salutary, wholesome, healthy

salùte *s. f.* health; **buona – good** health; **– men-tale** sanity

salutista *s. m. e f.* health fiend

salùto *s. m.* greeting, salutation, regards *pl.*

salvacondótto *s. m.* safe-conduct

salvadanàio *s. m.* money-box

salvagènte *s. m.* life-belt

salvagócce *s. m. inv.* drip-catcher

salvàre *v. tr.* to save, to deliver, to rescue

salvatàggio *s. m.* rescue; **battello di –** lifeboat; **cintura di –** life-belt

sàlve *inter.* hullo! hello!

salvézza *s. f.* salvation; safety (sicurezza); es-cape (scampo)

sàlvia *s. f.* sage

salviétta *s. f.* serviette, (table) napkin

sàlvo *agg.* safe

sambùco *s. m.* elder

sanatòria *s. f.* deed of indemnity

sanatòrio *s. m.* sanatorium

sàndalo *s. m.* sandal, sandalwood (*bot.*); san-dal (calzatura)

sàngue *s. m.* blood; **al –** underdone, rare

sanità *s. f.* soundness; salubrity (salubrità)

sanitàrio *agg.* sanitary; health (*attr.*)

sàno *agg.* healthy; sane (di mente); salubrious (salubre)

santìno *s. m.* holy picture

santità *s. f.* holiness, sanctity

sànto *s. m.* holy; saint (seguito da nome pro-prio)

santóne *s. m.* santon; guru (*fig.*)

santuàrio *s. m.* sanctuary, shrine

sanzióne *s. f.* sanction; approval

sapére *v. tr.* to know, to know how; can (po-tere) • *s. m.* knowledge, learning

sàpido *agg.* sapid

sapiènte *s. m. e f.* scholar

sapiènza *s. f.* learning, knowledge; wisdom (saggezza)

sapóne *s. m.* soap; **– da barba** shaving soap

saponétta *s. f.* cake of soap

sapóre *s. m.* taste; **senza –** tasteless

saporìto *agg.* savoury

saracinésca *s. f.* roll-up shutter

sàrago *s. m.* white-bream

sarcàsmo *s. m.* sarcasm

sarcàstico *agg.* sarcastic

sarcòfago *s. m.* sarcophagus

sardìna *s. f.* sardine

sàrdo *agg.* Sardinian

sàrta *s. f.* dress-maker

sàrtia *s. f.* shroud

sartiàme *s. m.* shrouds *pl.*, rigging

sàrto *s. m.* tailor

sartoria *s. f.* tailor's workshop

sàsso *s. m.* stone; pebble (ciottolo)

sassofonìsta *s. m. e f.* saxophonist

sassòfono *s. m.* saxophone, sax

sàssola *s. f.* bailer

satèllite *s. m.* satellite

satinatùra *s. f.* glazing; glaze (effetto)

sàtira *s. f.* satire

satìrico *agg.* satiric, satirical

saturazióne *s. f.* saturation

sàturo *agg.* saturated; full (pieno)

savàna *s. f.* savanna(h)

sàzio *agg.* satiated, glutted; full up (*fam.*)

sbadàggine *s. f.* inadvertence

sbadàto *agg.* careless • *s. m.* scatter-brain

sbadigliàre *v. intr.* to yawn

sbadìglio *s. m.* yawn

sbagliàre *v. tr.* to mistake; to miss (fallire) • *intr. pron.* to make a mistake, to be wrong, to be mistaken

sbàglio *s. m.* mistake, error

sballottàre *v. tr.* to toss, to push about

sbalordìre *v. intr.* to be bewildered

sbalordìtivo *agg.* amazing, astonishing

sbalzàre *v. tr.* to hurl, to fling, to throw

sbàlzo *s. m.* jolt, jerk; bound (salto)

sbancàre *v. tr.* to break (the bank) (gioco d'az-zardo); to excavate (scavare)

sbandaménto *s. m.* disbandment; side-slip (*autom.*); heeling (*naut.*)

sbandàre *v. intr.* to skid (*autom.*); to heel (*naut.*); to lean (*fig.*)

sbarbàre *v. tr. e rifl.* to shave

sbarcàre *v. intr.* to land

sbàrco *s. m.* landing

sbàrra *s. f.* bar

sbarràto *agg.* barred; blocked (ostruito)

sbàttere *v. tr.* to bang, to slam; to knock (ur-tare); to shake (scuotere)

sbattùto *agg.* tossed (sballottato); beaten (montato); tired out (stanco)

sbèrla *s. f.* slap, cuff

sberléffo *s. m.* sneer; grimace (smorfia)

sbiadíto *agg.* faded; dull (scialbo)

sbloccàre *v. tr.* to release, to free

sbócco *s. m.* mouth; outlet (*comm.*); way out (via d'uscita)

sbórnia *s. f.* drunkenness

sbraitàre *v. intr.* to shout

sbrigàre *v. tr.* to dispatch, to settle, to arrange • *intr. pron.* to hurry up, to get on with it

sbrigatívo *agg.* hasty, expeditious; **modi sbrigativi** brusque ways

sbrinaménto *s. m.* defrosting

sbrinàre *v. tr.* to defrost

sbrinatóre *s. m.* defroster

sbrogliàre *v. tr.* to disentangle, to unravel, to undo • *rifl.* to disentangle (oneself), to manage by oneself

sbrónza *s. f.* drunkenness

sbronzàrsi *v. rifl.* to get drunk

sbrónzo *agg.* drunk; tight (*fam.*)

sbruffóne *s. m.* boaster

sbucciàre *v. tr.* to peel

scacchièra *s. f.* chess-board, draught-board

scacciacàni *s. m. e f. inv.* blank pistol

scacciàre *v. tr.* to drive away, to turn out, to expel

scaccomàtto *s. m.* checkmate; **dare – checkmate**

scadènte *agg.* poor, second-rate

scadènza *s. f.* expiration; deadline (ultima data utile)

scadenzàrio *s. m.* due register, bill-book

scadére *v. intr.* to expire; to decline (declinare); to be due, to mature (di obbligazioni)

scaffalatùra *s. f.* shelves *pl.*; rack

scaffàle *s. m.* shelf; bookcase (mobile)

scàfo *s. m.* hull

scagionàre *v. tr.* to exculpate

scàglia *s. f.* flake (di sapone); scale (*zool.*)

scàla *s. f.* staircase, stairs *pl.*; ladder (portatile); scale (*mus., geog., mat.*); **– mobile** escalator; **– di corda** rope-ladder

scalàre *v. tr.* to scale, to climb

scalàta *s. f.* climb, ascent

scalatóre *s. m.* climber

scaldabàgno *s. m.* water heater

scaldalètto *s. m.* warming pan

scaldàre *v. tr.* to warm (up), to heat • *rifl.* to warm oneself, to get warm, to warm up; to fuss (affannarsi)

scaldavivànde *s. m. inv.* chafing-dish

scalétta *s. f.* step-ladder; script, summary (*fig.*)

scalfittùra *s. f.* graze, scratch

scalinàta *s. f.* flight of steps

scalíno *s. m.* step, stair

scàlo *s. m.* port (of call), call; wharf (banchina); landing (*aer.*)

scalógna *s. f.* bad-luck, misfortune

scalóne *s. m.* grand staircase

scaloppína *s. f.* escalope

scalpèllo *s. m.* chisel; scalpel (*med.*)

scalpóre *s. m.* noise, sensation

scàltro *agg.* sly, cunning

scàlzo *agg.* barefoot

scambiàre *v. tr.* to change, to exchange; to mistake (confondere per errore)

scàmbio *s. m.* change, exchange

scamosciàto *agg.* chamois, suede; shammy (*fam.*); **guanti scamosciati** suede gloves

scampagnàta *s. f.* outing, picnic

scampanellío *s. m.* ringing

scampanío *s. m.* peal, pealing

scampàre *v. tr.* to escape, to avoid; to save (salvare)

scampàto *agg.* rescued

scàmpo *s. m.* escape; prawn (*zool.*), shrimp (*alim.*)

scàmpolo *s. m.* remnant

scanalatùra *s. f.* groove, flute; fluting (*arch.*)

scandalístico *agg.* scandalmongering, sensational

scandalizzàre *v. tr.* to scandalize

scàndalo *s. m.* scandal

scandalóso *agg.* scandalous, shocking

scandíre *v. tr.* to articulate; to stress (*mus.*)

scansàre *v. tr.* to avoid, to escape, to parry

scantinàto *s. m.* basement

scàpola *s. f.* scapula, shoulder-blade

scàpolo *agg.* unmarried, single • *s. m.* bachelor; **essere – to be single**

scappaménto *s. m.* exhaust; **tubo di – exhaust pipe**

scappàre *v. intr.* to flee, to run away, to get away, to escape

scappatèlla *s. f.* escapade, prank

scappatóia *s. f.* way out, shift; pretext, excuse (pretesto)

scarabèo *s. m.* beetle

scarabocchiàre *v. tr.* to scribble, to scrawl

scarabòcchio *s. m.* scribble, scrawl; daub (disegno malfatto)

scarafàggio *s. m.* cockroach

scaramanzía *s. f.* charm, spell

scaramùccia *s. f.* skirmish

scarceràre *v. tr.* to release, to set (sb.) free

scarcerazióne *s. f.* release

scardinàre *v. tr.* to unhinge

scàrica *s. f.* discharge; volley (di armi)

scaricàre *v. tr.* to unload, to discharge, to release

scàrico *agg.* unloaded, run-down; exhausted (di orologio e sim.); flat (*elettr.*) • *s. m.* unloading; exhaust (*mecc.*); waste (rifiuti); **scarichi industriali** industrial waste

scarlattina *s. f.* scarlatina, scarlet fever

scarlàtto *agg.* scarlet

scàrpa *s. f.* shoe; **scarpe basse** flat shoes; **scarpe da ginnastica** sneakers, gymshoes; **lucido da scarpe** shoe polish

scarpàta *s. f.* escarpment

scarplèra *s. f.* shoe-rack

scarpinàre *v. intr.* to tramp, to trek

scarpinàta *s. f.* long walk, tramp

scarpóne *s. m.* boot

scarsità *s. f.* scarcity; lack, want (mancanza)

scàrso *agg.* scarce, scanty; lacking (manchevole)

scartaménto *s. m.* gauge

scartàre *v. tr.* to unwrap, to discard; to reject (eliminare)

scàrto *s. m.* discard; trash, scrap, rejection (cosa scartata)

scartòffie *s. f. pl.* (heap of) papers

scassàre *v. tr.* to break up

scassinatóre *s. m.* burglar; bank-robber (di banche)

scàsso *s. m.* burglary

scàtola *s. f.* box; case; **in** – tinned, canned (USA)

scatoláme *s. m.* tins *pl.*, cans *pl.*; tinned food, canned food (USA) (generi alimentari in scatola)

scattista *s. m. e f.* sprinter

scàtto *s. m.* release; click (*mecc.*); self-timer (fotografico); unit (*tel.*); increase (di stipendio); sprint (*sport*)

scavalcàre *v. tr.* to pass over, to climb over, to supplant (*fig.*)

scavàre *v. tr.* to dig, to excavate

scavatrice *s. f.* excavator, digger

scàvo *s. m.* excavation; mining (*min.*)

scégliere *v. tr.* to choose, to pick out, to single out, to select

sceicco *s. m.* sheik(h)

scellìno *s. m.* shilling

scèlta *s. f.* choice, selection

scèlto *agg.* choice, selected

scémo *agg.* deficient, stupid, silly

scèna *s. f.* scene

scenàrio *s. m.* scenery; scenario, script (*cin.*)

scenàta *s. f.* scene, row

scéndere *v. intr.* to go down, to get down, to come down

scendilètto *s. m. inv.* bedside carpet

sceneggiàre *v. tr.* to dramatize

sceneggiàto *m.* dramatization, screen-play; serial

sceneggiatóre *s. m.* screenwriter, scriptwriter

sceneggiatùra *s. f.* script

scenétta *s. f.* sketch

scènico *agg.* stage (*attr.*)

scenografìa *s. f.* scenography (*teatro*); setting (*cin.*)

scenogràfico *agg.* scenographic, showy; stagy (*fig.*)

scenògrafo *s. m.* scenographer (*teatro*); art-director (*cin.*)

scèttico *agg.* sceptical

scèttro *s. m.* sceptre

schéda *s. f.* card

schedàre *v. tr.* to file, to index

schedàrio *s. m.* file, card-index; card-holder (mobile)

schedìna *s. f.* coupon

schéggia *s. f.* splinter

schéletro *s. m.* skeleton

schèma *s. m.* scheme, outline, draft, diagram; hook-up (di montaggio)

schemàtico *agg.* schematic

schèrma *s. f.* fencing

schermàglia *s. f.* skirmish

schermàre *v. tr.* to screen, to shield

schermatùra *s. f.* screening

schèrmo *s. m.* screen, shield

schermografìa *s. f.* x-ray

schèrno *s. m.* mockery, sneer

scherzàre *v. intr.* to joke, to jest

schèrzo *s. m.* joke, jest; trick (tiro); trifle (inezia); **per** – in joke

schettinàre *v. intr.* to roller-skate

schettìno *s. m.* roller-skate

schiaccianóci *s. m. inv.* nutcrackers *pl.*

schiacciàre *v. tr.* to crush, to squeeze, to squash, to mash; to crush, to overwhelm (annientare)

schiaffeggiàre *v. tr.* to slap, to smack, to cuff

schiàffo *s. m.* slap, smack, cuff

schiamazzàre *v. intr.* to make a din, to kick up a racket, to clamour

schiamàzzo *s. m.* noise, din, clamour

schiarìre *v. tr.* to clear • *intr.* to clear up, to brighten up, to fade

293

schiarita *s. f.* clearing up
schiavitù *s. f.* slavery
schiavo *s. m.* slave • *agg.* enslaved, subject
schiéna *s. f.* back; **mal di** – backache
schienále *s. m.* back
schieraménto *s. m.* array; formation (*mil.*); line-up (politica)
schifézza *s. f.* filth
schifo *s. m.* disgust
schifóso *agg.* nasty, foul, disgusting
schiodáre *v. tr.* to unrivet, to unnail
schióppo *s. m.* gun, rifle, shotgun
schiúma *s. f.* foam, froth; lather (di sapone)
schlumóso *agg.* foamy, frothy; lathery (di sapone)
schivo *agg.* loath; coy (ritroso)
schizofrenia *s. f.* schizophrenia
schizofrénico *agg.* schizophrenic
schizzáre *v. tr.* to squirt, to sprinkle, to spurt; to spatter (di fango)
schizzo *s. m.* squirt, spurt; spatter (di fango); sketch (disegno); draft (abbozzo)
sci *s. m.* ski; skiing (sport); – **d'acqua** water-ski; – **alpinismo** ski touring
scia *s. f.* wake; trail (traccia)
sciábola *s. f.* sabre
sciacquáre *v. tr.* to rinse
sciacquóne *s. m.* flushing device
sciagùra *s. f.* disaster, calamity
sciàlle *s. m.* shawl
scialùppa *s. f.* shallop; – **di salvataggio** lifeboat
sciàme *s. m.* swarm
sciaráda *s. f.* charade
sciàre *v. intr.* to ski
sciàrpa *s. f.* scarf
sciàtica *s. f.* sciatica
sciatóre *s. m.* skier
scientifico *agg.* scientific
sciènza *s. f.* science; knowledge (sapere)
scienziàto *s. m.* scientist
scimmia *s. f.* monkey, ape
scimpanzé *s. m.* chimpanzee
scintigrafia *s. f.* scintigraphy
scintilla *s. f.* spark
scintillio *s. m.* sparkling, twinkling
sciocchézza *s. f.* foolish, thing, nonsense; trifle (cosa da nulla)
sciòcco *agg.* silly, foolish • *s. m.* fool, silly
sciògliere *v. tr.* to loose, to untie (slegare); to dissolve (porre fine); to solve (risolvere)
scioglilíngua *s. m. inv.* tongue-twister
sciolina *s. f.* ski wax

scioltézza *s. f.* agility; fluency (facilità)
scioperáre *v. intr.* to strike, to go (o to be) on strike
sciòpero *s. m.* strike
sciovia *s. f.* ski-lift
scippáre *v. tr.* to snatch
scippatóre *s. m.* bag-snatcher
scippo *s. m.* bag-snatching
sciróppo *s. m.* syrup
scissióne *s. f.* split, splitting
sciupáre *v. tr.* to waste
scivoláre *v. intr.* to slide, to glide; to skid (*autom.*); to slip (involontariamente)
scivoláta *s. f.* slide; slip (involontaria); skid (*autom.*)
scivolo *s. m.* slide, slipway (*naut., aer.*); chute (industria)
scivolóne *s. m.* slip
scivolóso *agg.* slippery
scocciatóre *s. m.* bore, bother, nuisance
scocciatúra *s. f.* bore, bother, nuisance
scodèlla *s. f.* soup-plate; bowl (ciotola)
scoglièra *s. f.* reef, cliff
scòglio *s. m.* rock, cliff, crag
scoiáttolo *s. m.* squirrel
scolapásta *s. m. inv.* colander
scolapiátti *s. m. inv.* draining-board; plate-rack (a rastrelliera)
scoláre *agg.* school (*attr.*)
scolarésca *s. f.* pupils *pl.*
scoláro *s. m.* schoolboy, pupil
scolástico *agg.* scholastic; school (*attr.*); **tasse scolastiche** school fees
scollòsi *s. f.* scoliosis
scolláre *v. tr.* to unglue, to unstick
scollatúra *s. f.* neckline, neck-hole (di abiti); unsticking
scolorire *v. tr.* to discolour, to fade
scolpire *v. tr.* to engrave, to cut, to carve
scombussoláre *v. tr.* to upset
scomméssa *s. f.* bet; stake (somma scommessa); **fare una** – to make a bet
scomméttere *v. tr.* to bet; – **alle corse** to bet on horses
scommettitóre *s. m.* better, bettor
scomodáre *v. tr.* to be inconvenient
scomodità *s. f.* discomfort; bother (fastidio)
scòmodo *agg.* uncomfortable, uneasy; bothersome (fastidioso)
scompagnato *agg.* unmatched, odd
scomparire *v. intr.* to disappear
scompàrso *agg.* disappeared
scompartiménto *s. m.* compartment

scompàrto *s. m.* compartment, section

scompigliàre *v. tr.* to muddle, to upset; to dishevel (scarmigliare)

scompìglio *s. m.* muddle, mess, confusion

sccomponìbile *agg.* decomposable, dismountable

componibilità *s. f.* decomposability

scompórre *v. tr.* to decompose, to undo; to resolve (chim.); to factorize (mat.)

scomposizióne *s. f.* decomposition, splitting up; resolution (chim.); factorization (mat.)

scomùnica *s. f.* excommunication

scomunicàre *v. tr.* to excommunicate

sconcertànte *agg.* disconcerting, puzzling

scondìto *agg.* unseasoned

sconfiggere *v. tr.* to defeat

sconfìtta *s. f.* defeat

sconfortànte *agg.* discouraging

sconfòrto *s. m.* discouragement, dejection

scongelàre *v. tr.* to defreeze, to defrost

scongiùro *s. m.* (magic) charm, spell

sconnèsso *agg.* disconnected; incoherent

sconosciùto *agg.* unknown • *s. m.* stranger

sconsacràre *v. tr.* to desecrate

sconsolànte *agg.* disheartening, sad

sconsolàto *agg.* disconsolate, desolate, sad

scontàbile *agg.* discountable

scontàre *v. tr.* to discount (comm.); to deduct (detrarre); to expiate (espiare)

scontàto *agg.* discounted; foregone (previsto)

scontentàre *v. tr.* to displease; to disappoint (deludere)

scontentézza *s. f.* discontent, dissatisfaction

scónto *s. m.* discount, rebate

scontràrsi *v. intr. pron.* to collide (autom.); to run into (di persone); to clash (divergere)

scontrìno *s. m.* ticket; voucher (comm.)

scóntro *s. m.* collision, crash (tra veicoli); clash (contrasto d'opinioni)

scontróso *agg.* sullen, peevish

sconvolgènte *agg.* upsetting

scópa *s. f.* broom

scopàre *v. tr.* to sweep

scopèrta *s. f.* discovery, finding out

scopèrto *agg.* discovered, found out; bare (non coperto)

scòpo *s. m.* aim, end, object, purpose

scoppiàre *v. tr.* to burst, to explode, to split, to blow up

scòppio *s. m.* burst, explosion; bang (rumore)

scoprìre *v. tr.* to uncover, to bare; to disclose (rivelare); to discover, to find out (trovare)

scopritóre *s. m.* discoverer

scoraggiàre *v. tr.* to discourage

scorbùtico *agg.* cantankerous

scorciàre *v. tr.* to shorten

scorciatóia *s. f.* short cut

scórcio *s. m.* foreshortening (arte)

scordàre *v. tr. e intr. pron.* to forget

scòria *s. f.* scoria, slag; **scorie radioattive** radioactive waste

scorpacciàta *s. f.* bellyful

scorpióne *s. m.* scorpion; Scorpio (astr.)

scórrere *v. tr.* to run over, to skim (through)

scorrettézza *s. f.* incorrectness; error (errore)

scorrètto *agg.* incorrect; improper (non educato)

scorrévole *agg.* flowing, fluent; sliding (mecc.)

scorrevolézza *s. f.* fluency

scórso *agg.* last, past

scòrta *s. f.* escort (mil.); guard (guardia); store (provviste)

scortàre *v. tr.* to escort

scortése *agg.* rude, impolite

scortesìa *s. f.* unkindness

scorticàre *v. tr.* to skin

scòrza *s. f.* rind, peel, skin; – **d'arancia** orange-peel

scoscéso *agg.* steep

scòssa *s. f.* shake; shock (elettr.)

scossóne *s. m.* jolt, bump

scostànte *agg.* disagreeable

scostàre *v. tr.* to remove, to push aside

scòtta *s. f.* sheet

scottàre *v. tr.* to scorch, to scald, to burn • *rifl. e intr. pron.* to burn oneself, to burn, to be burning

scottatùra *s. f.* scorch, burn, scald; sunburn (da sole)

scovàre *v. tr.* to find out

scozzése *agg.* Scottish • *s. m. e f.* Scotsman *m.*, Scotswoman *f.*; Scotch (lingua); **gli scozzesi** the Scots

screpolàre *v. tr.* to chap

screpolatùra *s. f.* chap

scricchiolìo *s. m.* creaking

scrìgno *s. m.* casket, coffer

scriminatùra *s. f.* parting (of the hair)

scrìtta *s. f.* writing; notice (su cartelli)

scrìtto *agg.* written • *s. m.* writing

scrittóio *s. m.* writing-desk

scrittóre *s. m.* writer

scrittùra *s. f.* writing

scrivanìa *s. f.* writing-table, desk

scrìvere *v. tr.* to write

scroccóne *s. m.* sponge

scròfa *s. f.* sow

scrosciànte *agg.* pelting (di pioggia); roaring (di risa); thundering (di applausi)

scròscio *s. m.* pelting, shower; roar (di risa)

scrostàre *v. tr.* to scrape off

scrostatùra *s. f.* scraping

scrùpolo *s. m.* scruple

scrupolóso *agg.* scrupulous

scucìre *v. tr.* to unstitch

scucitùra *s. f.* seam-rent

scuderìa *s. f.* stable; racing stable (*autom.*)

scudétto *s. m.* badge; championship (*fig.*)

scùdo *s. m.* shield

sculacciàre *v. tr.* to spank

scultóre *s. m.* sculptor

scultóreo *agg.* sculptural

scultùra *s. f.* sculpture

scuòcere *v. intr.* to become overcooked

scuòla *s. f.* school

scuòtere *v. tr.* to shake, to toss

scùre *s. f.* axe

scurìre *v. tr.* to darken, to obscure

scùro *agg.* dark

scùsa *s. f.* excuse, apology

scusàre *v. tr.* to excuse; to pardon, to forgive (perdonare)

sdoganàre *v. tr.* to clear (through the custom)

sdoppiàre *v. tr.* to single

sdraiàrsi *v. rifl.* to lie down

sdràio *s. f.* deck-chair

sdrucciolévole *agg.* slippery

se *cong.* if; whether (dubit.)

sebàceo *agg.* sebaceous

sebbène *cong.* although

sécca *s. f.* shallows *pl.*

seccànte *agg.* boring, annoying

seccàre *v. tr.* to dry, to drain (prosciugare); to bore, to bother (importunare)

seccatóre *s. m.* bore, drag

seccatùra *s. f.* bother, annoyance, trouble

secchièllo *s. m.* bucket

sécchio *s. m.* pail

sécco *agg.* dry; dried (disseccato); withered (appassito)

secessióne *s. f.* secession

secessionìsta *s. m. e f.* secessionist

secolàre *agg.* secular

sécolo *s. m.* century

secondariaménte *avv.* secondly, secondarily

secondàrio *agg.* secondary

secondìno *s. m.* jailer

secóndo *agg. num. ord.* second • *s. m.* second; main course (piatto)

secondogènito *agg.* second-born, junior

secrezióne *s. f.* secretion

sédano *s. m.* celery

sedatìvo *s. m.* sedative

séde *s. f.* seat

sedentàrio *agg.* sedentary

sèdia *s. f.* chair

sedìle *s. m.* seat

seducènte *agg.* seductive

seduttóre *agg.* seductive • *s. m.* seducer

seduzióne *s. f.* seduction

séga *s. f.* saw

ségale *s. f.* rye

segàre *v. tr.* to saw

segatùra *s. f.* sawdust

sèggio *s. m.* seat, chair, stall; – **elettorale** polling station

seggiolìno *s. m.* baby's chair

seggiolóne *s. m.* high chair

seggiovìa *s. f.* chair-lift

segherìa *s. f.* saw-mill

segménto *s. m.* segment

segnalàre *v. tr.* to signal; to announce (rendere noto); to point out (far conoscere)

segnalàto *agg.* signal (*attr.*)

segnalazióne *s. f.* signalling

segnàle *s. m.* signal; – **d'allarme** warning signal; – **orario** time signal; – **stradale** road sign

segnalética *s. f.* signs *pl.*, signals *pl.*

segnalìbro *s. m.* book-mark

segnalìnee *s. m. inv.* linesman

segnapósto *s. m.* place card

segnapùnti *s. m. e f. inv.* scorekeeper; scoreboard (tabellone)

segnàre *v. tr.* to mark; to write down (prendere nota); to show, to read (indicare)

segnatùra *s. f.* signature

segregazióne *s. f.* segregation

segréta *s. f.* dungeon

segretariàto *s. m.* secretariat(e)

segretàrio *s. m.* secretary

segreterìa *s. f.* secretariat(e); – **telefonica** answering machine

segretézza *s. f.* secrecy

segréto *agg. e s. m.* secret

seguàce *s. m. e f.* follower

seguènte *agg.* following, next

segùgio *s. m.* bloodhound (*zool.*)

seguìre *v. tr.* to follow; to attend (frequentare); to supervise (sorvegliare); to continue (continuare)

seicentésco *agg.* seventeenth-century (*attr.*)

seicènto *s. m. inv.* six hundred

sélce *s. f.* flint

selciàto *s. m.* pavement

selettivo *agg.* selective

selezionàre *v. tr.* to select, to pick out, to sort

selezióne *s. f.* selection

sèlla *s. f.* saddle

sellàre *v. tr.* to saddle

sellino *s. m.* saddle

sélva *s. f.* wood

selvaggina *s. f.* game

selvàggio *agg.* wild, savage

semàforo *s. m.* traffic-lights; semaphore (*ferr.*); signal

sembiànza *s. f.* semblance; looks *pl.* (fattezze); features *pl.* (lineamenti)

séme *s. m.* seed; pip (di frutta); stone, pit (nocciolo); suit (delle carte da gioco)

semènza *s. f.* seed

semestràle *agg.* semestral, six-monthly

semèstre *s. m.* semester

semiàsse *s. m.* axle-shaft (*autom.*)

semiautomàtico *agg.* semi-automatic

semicérchio *s. m.* semicircle

semicircolàre *agg.* semicircular

semiconduttóre *s. m.* semiconductor

semifinàle *s. f.* semifinal

semilavoràto *agg.* semifinished

sémina *s. f.* sowing

seminàre *v. tr.* to sow; to scatter (spargere)

seminàrio *s. m.* seminary (*relig.*); seminar (università)

seminarista *s. m.* seminarist

seminàto *agg.* sown

seminfermità *s. f.* partial infirmity; partial insanity (mentale)

seminterràto *s. m.* basement

semioscurità *s. f.* half-dark, twilight

semolino *s. m.* semolina

sémplice *agg.* simple; single (costituito da un solo elemento); natural (schietto)

semplicemènte *avv.* simply

semplicità *s. f.* simplicity

semplificàre *v. tr.* to simplify

sèmpre *avv.* always, ever; – che provided (that)

semprevérde *agg.* evergreen

sènape *s. f.* mustard

senàto *s. m.* senate

senatóre *s. m.* senator

senilità *s. f.* senility

séno *s. m.* breast, bosom; sine (*mat.*)

sensazionàle *agg.* sensational, thrilling

sensazióne *s. f.* sensation, feeling

sensìbile *agg.* sensible, perceptible; sensitive (che ha sensibilità)

sensibilità *s. f.* sensibility

sensuàle *agg.* sensual

sensualità *s. f.* sensuality

sentènza *s. f.* sentence (*leg.*)

sentièro *s. m.* path, lane, track

sentimentàle *agg.* sentimental

sentimènto *s. m.* sentiment, feeling

sentìna *s. f.* bilge

sentinèlla *s. f.* sentry

sentìre *v. tr.* to feel; to taste (gusto); to hear (udire)

sènza *prep. e cong.* without

separàre *v. tr.* to separate, to part, to split

separàto *agg.* separate, separated; distinct (distinto)

separatóre *s. m.* separator

separazióne *s. f.* separation

sepolcràle *agg.* sepulchral; dismal (*fig.*)

sepólcro *s. m.* grave, sepulchre

sepólto *agg.* buried

sepoltùra *s. f.* burial

seppellìre *v. tr.* to bury

séppia *s. f.* cuttle-fish (*zool.*); nero di – sepia; osso di – cuttle-bone

sequènza *s. f.* sequence

sequestràbile *agg.* sequestrable, seizable

sequestràre *v. tr.* to sequestrate, to confiscate

sequèstro *s. m.* sequestration; kidnapping (a scopo di ricatto)

sequòia *s. f.* redwood, giant sequoia

seràta *s. f.* evening, night

serbàre *v. tr.* to lay aside (mettere da parte); to keep (conservare)

serbatóio *s. m.* tank, reservoir

serenità *s. f.* serenity

seréno *agg.* serene

sergènte *s. m.* sergeant

seriàle *agg.* serial

sèrie *s. f. inv.* series; set (assortimento); line (*comm.*)

serietà *s. f.* seriousness; gravity (gravità)

serigrafìa *s. f.* silk-screen printing; serigraph (il prodotto)

sèrio *agg.* serious, grave

sermóne *s. m.* sermon

serpènte *s. m.* snake

sèrra *s. f.* greenhouse

serramènto *s. m.* frame

serrànda *s. f.* roll-up

serràta *s. f.* lock-out

serratùra *s. f.* lock

servìle *agg.* servile; menial (di lavori umili)

servìre *v. tr. e intr.* to serve

servitù s. f. servants pl.

serviziévole agg. helpful

servizio s. m. service; article (giornalistico)

sèrvo s. m. (domestic) servant

servocomàndo s. m. servocontrol

servofréno s. m. servobrake

servomeccanismo s. m. servomechanism

servomotóre s. m. servomotor

servostèrzo s. m. power steering

sessióne s. f. session

sèsso s. m. sex

sessuàle agg. sexual; sex (attr.)

sessualità s. f. sexuality

sestànte s. m. sextant

séta s. f. silk

setàccio s. m. sieve

séte s. f. thirst; avere - to be thirsty

setifício s. m. silk mill

settàrio s. m. sectarian; party (attr.)

settecènto s. m. inv. seven hundred

settèmbre s. m. September

settentrionàle agg. northern; north (attr.)

settimàna s. f. week; la prossima - next week; la scorsa - last week

settimanàle agg. weekly; week (attr.) • s. m. weekly (newspaper)

settimanalménte avv. weekly, every week

sètto s. m. septum

settóre s. m. sector; field (fig.)

severità s. f. severity, strictness, rigour

sevèro agg. severe, strict

sezióne s. f. section, division; department (d'ufficio)

sfacciatàggine s. f. impudence; cheek (fam.)

sfacciàto agg. impudent, cheeky

sfàrzo s. m. pomp, magnificence

sfasaménto s. m. phase-displacement (elettr.); bewilderment, confusion

sfasciàre v. tr. to unbandage; to shatter (rompere)

sfavorévole agg. unfavourable

sfèra s. f. sphere; ball (mecc.); cuscinetto a - ball-bearing

sfidàre v. tr. to challenge, to defy; to face, to brave (affrontare)

sfidùcia s. f. mistrust, distrust; no-confidence (politica)

sfilàta s. f. parade

sfìnge s. f. sphinx

sfiorìre v. intr. to fade, to wither

sfociàre v. tr. to flow (into); to result (in) (fig.)

sfoderàre v. tr. to unsheathe; to make a display (of) (fig.)

sfoderàto agg. unlined

sfòglia s. f. puff pastry

sfogliàre v. tr. to skim (through), to leaf (through)

sfógo s. m. vent, outlet; vent (di sentimenti); rash (eruzione cutanea)

sfollagènte s. m. inv. truncheon, baton

sfoltìre v. tr. to thin

sfondàre v. tr. to break open; to stave in (rompere il fondo); to break through (mil.); to wear out (logorare)

sfondàto agg. bottomless

sfóndo s. m. background

sformàre v. tr. to stave in; to turn out (togliere dalla forma)

sfornàre v. tr. to take out of the oven

sfortùna s. f. bad luck

sfortunataménte avv. unluckily

sfortunàto agg. unlucky

sforzàto agg. forced, strained

sfòrzo s. m. effort, stress; strain (mecc.)

sfràtto s. m. eviction

sfregàre v. tr. to rub

sfregiàre v. tr. to slash, to gash; to deface, to disfigure (deturpare)

sfrégio s. m. slash, gash; defacement (deturpazione)

sfruttàre v. tr. to exploit; to profit by (approfittare di)

sfruttàto agg. exploited

sfruttatóre s. m. exploiter

sfumatùra s. f. shade; touch (fig.)

sfuocàto agg. blurred

sgabèllo s. m. stool

sgabuzzìno s. m. store-room

sgàrbo s. m. incivility

sgargiànte agg. showy, gaudy

sgelàre v. tr. e intr. to thaw

sghignazzàre v. intr. to guffaw

sgocciolàre v. intr. to drip

sgocciolatóio s. m. drip

sgombràre v. tr. to clear; to empty out (svuotare); to vacate (un alloggio)

sgómbro s. m. mackerel (zool.)

sgomentàrsi v. intr. pron. to quail

sgonfiàre v. tr. to deflate

sgónfio agg. deflated, flat

sgorgàre v. intr. to gush out

sgradévole agg. disagreeable, unpleasant

sgradìto agg. unwelcome

sgranocchiàre v. tr. to crunch

sgrassàre v. tr. to degrease, to scour

sgridàre v. tr. to scold, to rebuke

sguàrdo s. m. look, glance

shampoo s. m. inv. shampoo

si avv. yes

sia cong. whether... or, either... or (o...o); both... and (tanto... quanto)

siccità s. f. drought

sicurézza s. f. security, safety; certainty (certezza); confidence (fiducia); **uscita di** – emergency exit

sicuro agg. safe, secure, sure; certain (certo)

siderurgia s. f. iron metallurgy

sidro s. m. cider

siépe s. f. hedge

siéro s. m. whey; serum (biol.)

sieroterapia s. f. serotherapy

sièsta s. f. siesta, nap

sifóne s. m. siphon

sigarétta s. f. cigarette; **un pacchetto di sigarette** a packet of cigarettes

sigaro s. m. cigar

sigillo s. m. seal

sigla s. f. initials pl.; signature (mus.)

significativo agg. significant, expressive

significàto s. m. meaning

signóra s. f. lady, Mrs (davanti a nomi propri); madam (vocat. senza nome proprio)

signóre s. m. gentleman, Mr (davanti a nomi propri); sir (vocat. senza nome proprio)

signoria s. f. rule; dominion (dominio)

signorina s. f. young lady, girl; Miss (davanti a nomi propri)

silènzio s. m. silence

silenzióso agg. silent

sillaba s. f. syllable

silvèstre agg. wild, silvan

simbiòsi s. f. symbiosis

simbòlico agg. symbolic(al)

simbolista s. m. e f. symbolist

simbolo s. m. symbol

simile agg. similar, like, alike; such (di tal fatta); **un uomo** – such a man

similitùdine s. f. simile, similitude, similarity (geom.)

simmetria s. f. symmetry

simmètrico agg. symmetrically

simpatia s. f. liking, fancy, attraction

simpàtico agg. nice; sympathetic (anat.)

simpatizzànte s. m. sympathizer

simulazióne s. f. simulation, pretence

simultàneo agg. simultaneous

sinagòga s. f. synagogue

sincerità s. f. sincerity

sincèro agg. sincere, true

sincronia s. f. synchrony

sindacàto s. m. trade-union, (labour) union; syndicate (fin.)

sindaco s. m. mayor; auditor (di società)

sindrome s. f. syndrome

sinfonia s. f. symphony

sinfònico agg. symphonic

singhiózzo s. m. hiccup, sob; **avere il** – to hiccup

singolàre agg. singular (gramm.); rare (unico) • s. m. singular

singolo agg. single, individual, separate

sinistra s. f. left

sinistro agg. left • s. m. accident

sinònimo s. m. synonym

sintàssi s. f. syntax

sintesi s. f. synthesis

sintètico agg. synthetic(al); concise (conciso); **fibre sintetiche** synthetic fibres

sintomatologia s. f. symptomatology

sintomo s. m. symptom

sinusite s. f. sinusitis

sipàrio s. m. curtain

sirèna s. f. siren; – **da nebbia** foghorn

siringa s. f. syringe

sisma s. m. seism, earthquake

sismico agg. seismic

sismòlogo s. m. seismologist

sistemàre v. tr. to arrange, to fix, to settle; to accomodate (alloggiare)

sito s. m. place, locality

situazióne s. f. situation

slacciàre v. tr. to unlace, to loosen

slavina s. f. snowslide

slegàre v. tr. to untie, to unfasten; to release (liberare)

slip s. m. inv. panties pl., briefs pl.

slitta s. f. sleigh, sledge

slittàre v. intr. to sledge; to skid (autom.); to slip (mecc.)

slogàrsi v. intr. pron. to dislocate, to sprain, to strain

slogatùra s. f. dislocation, sprain, strain

smacchiàre v. tr. to clean

smacchiatóre s. m. stain-remover

smagliatùra s. f. ladder (di calza); stretch mark (della cute)

smaltatùra s. f. enamelling; glazing (ceramica)

smalto s. m. enamel; glaze (ceramica); nail-polish (per unghie)

smarriménto s. m. loss; miscarriage (di un pacco o lettera)

smarrire v. tr. to lose • intr. pron. to get lost; to be at a loss (fig.)

smarrito agg. lost; bewildered (fig.)

smentita s. f. denial

smeràldo s. m. emerald

smèrlo s. m. scallop

sméttere v. tr. e intr. to stop, to leave, to leave off; to pack up (fam.)

smistaménto s. m. shunting

smistàre v. tr. to shunt (ferr.); to sort (alla posta)

smontàbile agg. dismountable

smontàggio s. m. disassembly

smontàre v. tr. to disassemble, to dismount

smòrfia s. f. grimace

smottaménto s. m. landslip

snèllo agg. slender, slim

snervànte agg. enervating

snidàre v. tr. to rouse, to flush; to dislodge (fig.)

snobbàre v. tr. to snob

snobismo s. m. snobbery

snodàbile agg. jointed

snòdo s. m. articulated joint, pivot

sobbalzàre v. intr. to jerk, to jolt; to start (trasalire)

sobbàlzo s. m. jerk, jolt

sobbórgo s. m. suburb

sòbrio agg. sober

soccórrere v. tr. to help, to relieve

soccorritóre s. m. helper, reliever

soccórso s. m. help, aid, assistance; **pronto** – first aid

socialdemocràtico agg. Social Democratic

sociàle agg. social; **previdenza** – social security; **assistente** – social worker

socialismo s. m. Socialism

socialista agg. Socialist

società s. f. society; league (alleanza); company, partnership, corporation (di capitali)

sociévole agg. sociable

sòcio s. m. member; partner (di una società); fellow (di un'accademia)

sociologia s. f. sociology

sociòlogo s. m. social scientist

soddisfacènte agg. satisfactory

soddisfàre v. tr. e intr. to satisfy, to fulfil, to meet

soddisfàtto agg. satisfied

soddisfazióne s. f. satisfaction

sòdio s. m. sodium

sofà s. m. sofa

sofferènte agg. suffering • s. m. e f. sufferer

sòffice agg. soft

soffiàre v. tr. e intr. to blow

sòffio s. m. blow; breath; murmur (med.)

soffitta s. f. attic

soffitto s. m. ceiling

soffocaménto s. m. choking, suffocation

soffocànte agg. choking, stifling

soffocàre v. intr. to choke, to suffocate, to be stifled

soffrire v. tr. to suffer; to stand (tollerare) • intr. to suffer

soggettivo agg. subjective

soggètto s. m. subject; (subject) matter

soggiórno s. m. stay; **stanza di** – living-room

sòglia s. f. threshold, sill

sògliola s. f. sole

sógno s. m. dream

sòia s. f. soya-bean

solàre agg. solar; sun (attr.)

sólco s. m. furrow

soldàto s. m. soldier

sóle s. m. sun; sunshine (luce del sole)

soleggiàto agg. sunny

solènne agg. solemn

solennità s. f. solemnity

solfàto s. m. sulphate

solféggio s. m. solfeggio

solidarietà s. f. solidarity

solidità s. f. solidity

sòlido agg. solid

solista s. m. e f. soloist

solitaménte avv. usually

solitàrio agg. solitary, lonely

solitùdine s. f. solitude

sollecitàre v. tr. to urge; to speed up; to expedite

sollécito s. m. solicitation, request

sollético s. m. tickle, spur; prick (fig.)

sollevàre v. tr. to raise, to lift; to hoist (issare); to relieve (dare sollievo); to bring up (far sorgere)

sollièvo s. m. relief

soltànto avv. only, just

solùbile agg. soluble; **caffè** – instant coffee

soluzióne s. f. solution

solvènte agg. solvent

somàro s. m. ass, donkey

somigliànza s. f. resemblance, likeness

somigliàre v. tr. e intr. to resemble, to be like

sómma s. f. sum

sommàre v. tr. to add (up), to sum (up)

sommità s. f. top, summit, peak

sommòssa s. f. rising, revolt

sommozzatóre s. m. frogman
sonàglio s. m. bell, rattle
sondàggio s. m. poll, survey
sondàre v. tr. to sound; to poll, to survey (l'o-pinione pubblica)
sonettista s. m. e f. sonneteer
sonétto s. m. sonnet
sonnàmbulo agg. sleepwalker
sonnífero s. m. sleeping pill, sleeping potion
sónno s. m. sleep
sonnolènza s. f. sleepiness, drowsiness
sonorità s. f. sonority, acoustics pl.
sonóro agg. sonorous, resonant
sontuóso agg. sumptuous
soppàlco s. m. mezzanine floor
sopportàbile agg. endurable
sopportàre v. tr. to bear, to sustain (reggere); to endure, to stand, to put up with, to cope with (tollerare)
sopprìmere v. tr. to suppress, to put down, to abolish
sópra prep. on, upon, over; above (al di sopra di) • avv. above (precedentemente); up-stairs (al piano di sopra)
sopràbito s. m. overcoat
sopraccìglio s. m. eyebrow
sopraggiùngere v. intr. to arrive, to turn up
sopralluògo s. m. on-the-spot investigation, inspection
sopràlzo s. m. raising
soprammòbile s. m. knick-knack
soprannóme s. m. nickname
sopràno s. m. e f. soprano
soprattùtto avv. above all
sopravvalutàre v. tr. to over-estimate; to upvalue (fin.)
sopravvivènza s. f. survival
sordità s. f. deafness
sórdo agg. deaf
sordomùto agg. deaf and dumb
sorèlla s. f. sister
sorellàstra s. f. half-sister, stepsister
sorgènte s. f. spring, source
soriàno s. m. tabby (cat)
sorpàsso s. m. overtaking; divieto di – no ov-ertaking
sorprendènte agg. surprising
sorprèndere v. tr. to catch; to surprise (pren-dere di sorpresa); to surprise, to astonish, to amaze (meravigliare)
sorprésa s. f. surprise
sorrèggere v. tr. to support
sorridènte agg. smiling

sorrìdere v. intr. to smile
sorrìso s. m. smile
sorseggiàre v. tr. to sip
sórso s. m. sip, gulp, draught
sòrte s. f. fate, destiny, fortune; chance (caso)
sorteggiàre v. tr. to draw
sortéggio s. m. draw
sortilègio s. m. sorcery, witchcraft
sorvegliànza s. f. watch, surveillance
sorvegliàre v. tr. to guard, to watch; to look after (tenere d'occhio)
sorvolàre v. tr. e intr. to fly over, to pass over; to over look (fig.)
sòsia s. m. inv. double
sospèndere v. tr. to suspend
sospensióne s. f. suspension
sospéso agg. suspended
sospettàre v. tr. to suspect
sospètto s. m. suspicion
sospiràre v. intr. to sigh
sospiro s. m. sigh
sòsta s. f. halt, stop, stay (fermata); pause (pausa); break (interruzione); rest (riposo); divieto di – no parking
sostantivo s. m. substantive
sostànza s. f. substance, matter, material, stuff
sostanziòso agg. substantial
sostàre v. intr. to stop, to stay, to pause
sostégno s. m. support, prop
sostentaménto s. m. sustenance, mainte-nance
sostituìbile agg. replaceable
sostituìre v. tr. to replace
sostitùto s. m. substitute
sostituzióne s. f. replacement, substitution
sottacéti s. m. pl. pickles
sottàna s. f. skirt
sotterràneo s. m. cellar, vault
sottìle agg. thin
sottilizzàre v. intr. to subtilize
sottintèndere v. tr. to understand; to involve (implicare)
sottintéso s. m. implied reference
sótto avv. e prep. under, below, beneath, un-derneath
sottobicchière s. m. glass-mat; coaster; sau-cer (piattino)
sottobòsco s. m. underwood
sottocutàneo agg. subcutaneous
sottofóndo s. m. background
sottopassàggio s. m. underpass, subway
sottoprodótto s. m. by-product
sottoscàla s. m. inv. understairs

301

sottoscrizióne s. f. subscription
sottosópra avv. upside down
sottostànte agg. underlying, below
sottosvilùppo s. m. underdevelopment
sottovènto avv. downwind
sottovèste s. f. petticoat
sottovuòto avv. in a vacuum
sottràrre v. tr. to take away; to abstract, to pilfer (rubare); to deduct (detrarre); to subtract (mat.)
sottrazióne s. f. taking away; abstraction (furto); subtraction (mat.)
soviético agg. Soviet
sovraccaricàre v. tr. to overload, to overburden; to surcharge (autom.)
sovraespórre v. tr. to overexpose
sovraffollàto agg. overcrowded
sovràno s. m. sovereign
sovrapponìbile agg. superimposable
sovrastànte agg. overhanging
sovvenzióne s. f. subvention, aid
sovversìvo agg. subversive
spaccàre v. tr. to break, to split
spacciàre v. tr. to circulate (moneta); to peddle, to push drugs (droga) • rifl. to pretend (to be)
spacciatóre s. m. pusher
spàccio s. m. sale, shop; store (luogo di vendita); drug pushing (di droga)
spàda s. f. sword
spagnòlo agg. Spanish • s. m. Spaniard; Spanish (lingua)
spàgo s. m. string, twine
spalàre v. tr. to shovel
spàlla s. f. shoulder
spalliéra s. f. back
spalmàre v. tr. to spread; – di burro to butter
spànna s. f. span
sparàre v. tr. to shoot, to fire
sparecchiàre v. tr. to clear
sparéggio s. m. play-off
sparìre v. intr. to disappear, to vanish
sparizióne s. f. disappearance
spàro s. m. shot
spartiàcque s. m. inv. watershed
spartìto s. m. score
spartitràffico s. m. inv. traffic divider
spassóso agg. funny
spàstico agg. spastic
spàtola s. f. paddle
spaventapàsseri s. m. scarecrow
spaventàre v. tr. to frighten, to scare • intr. pron. to be scared

spavènto s. m. fright, fear
spaventóso agg. frightful, frightening
spàzio s. m. space; room (limitato)
spazióso agg. spacious
spazzanéve s. m. inv. snow-plough
spazzàre v. tr. to sweep
spazzatùra s. f. dust, rubbish
spazzìno s. m. street-sweeper
spàzzola s. f. brush; – da capelli hair-brush
spazzolàre v. tr. to brush
spazzolìno s. m. brush; – da denti tooth-brush
spazzolóne s. m. mop
specchiàrsi v. rifl. to look at oneself in a mirror; to be reflected (riflettersi)
specchiéra s. f. dressing-table
specchiétto s. m. looking-glass; driving mirror (autom.)
spècchio s. m. mirror
specialìsta s. m. e f. specialist
specialìstico agg. specialist (attr.)
specialità s. f. speciality
specializzàto agg. specialized; non – unskilled
spècie s. f. inv. kind, sort; species (scienza)
specificàre v. tr. to specify
specìfico s. m. specific
speculàre agg. specular
speculazióne s. f. speculation
spedìre v. tr. to send, to dispatch
spedìto agg. expeditious, prompt (sollecito)
spedizióne s. f. forwarding, dispatch (lettere, ecc.); expedition (scientifica, militare)
spedizionière s. m. forwarder; shipping agent (marittimo)
spégnere v. tr. to extinguish; to put out (fuoco); to turn off (luce, radio, ecc.)
spegnimènto s. m. extinction; turning off, switching off (di apparecchi); stopping (di macchine)
speleologìa s. f. spelaeology
speleòlogo s. m. spelaeologist
spellàre v. tr. to skin • intr. pron. to peel
spellatùra s. f. scrape, excoriation
spèndere v. tr. to spend
spensieràto agg. thoughtless
spènto agg. extinguished; out (pred.); switched off (pred.)
sperànza s. f. hope
speràre v. tr. e intr. to hope; to expect (aspettarsi)
spericolàto agg. reckless
sperimentàle agg. experimental
sperimentàre v. tr. to experiment, to test, to try; to experience (su di sé)

speronàre v. tr. to ram

speronàto agg. rammed

spésa s. f. expense, charge, cost; shopping (compere)

spésso agg. thick • avv. often

spessóre s. m. thickness

spettacolàre agg. spectacular

spettàcolo s. m. spectacle, sight; performance, show (teatro)

spettatóre s. m. bystander; witness (testimone); **gli spettatori** audience

spèzie s. f. pl. spices

spezzàre v. tr. to break

spezzatìno s. m. stew; – **di montone** Irish stew

spìa s. f. spy

spiacènte agg. sorry

spiacérsi v. intr. pron. to be sorry

spiacévole agg. unpleasant, regrettable

spiàggia s. f. beach, shore

spiàzzo s. m. open space

spiedìno s. m. skewer; – **di carne** skewer meat

spièdo s. m. spit; **allo** – on the spit

spiegàre v. tr. to explain; to unfold (stendere)

spiegazióne s. f. explanation

spìffero s. m. draught

spìga s. f. spike, ear

spìgola s. f. bass

spìgolo s. m. edge, corner

spìlla s. f. brooch

spìllo s. m. pin

spìna s. f. thorn; plug (elettr.); fishbone (lisca)

spinàci s. m. pl. spinach sing.

spinétta s. f. spinet

spìnta s. f. push, shove, thrust

spinterògeno s. m. distributor

spìnto agg. extremist (attr.); scabrous, risky (scabroso)

spintóne s. m. shove

spiovènte s. m. slope

spiràle s. f. spiral

spiritìsmo s. m. spiritualism

spìrito s. m. spirit; wit (brio)

spiritosàggine s. f. witticism

spiritóso agg. witty

splendènte agg. shining

splèndido agg. splendid

splendóre s. m. splendour

spogliàrsi v. rifl. to undress, to strip

spogliatóio s. m. dressing-room

spolveràre v. tr. to dust

spónda s. f. edge, border, bank, side; shore (riva); parapet (parapetto)

sponsorizzàre v. tr. to sponsor

spontaneità s. f. spontaneity

spontàneo agg. spontaneous, natural

sporadicità s. f. sporadicity

sporàdico agg. sporadic

sporcàre v. tr. to dirty, to soil, to stain • rifl. e intr. pron. to dirty oneself, to get dirty

sporcìzia s. f. filthiness

spòrco agg. dirty, filthy; stained (macchiato)

sporgènte agg. projecting, protruding, protuberant

sporgènza s. f. projection

sportèllo s. m. counter, window; ticket-window (di biglietteria)

sportìvo agg. sporting; sport (attr.)

spòsa s. f. bride

sposalìzio s. m. wedding

sposàre v. tr. to marry • rifl. e rifl. rec. to marry, to get married

spòso s. m. bridegroom

spostàre v. tr. to move; to delay (differire) • rifl. to move, to shift

spregiatìvo agg. contemptuous

prèmere v. tr. to squeeze

spremiagrùmi s. m. inv. citrus-fruit squeezer

spremùta s. f. squash, fruit juice

sproporzionàto agg. disproportionate

sproporzióne s. f. disproportion

sprovvìsto agg. unprovided

sprùzzo s. m. spray, sprinkle, splash

spùgna s. f. sponge; terry-cloth (tessuto)

spumànte s. m. sparkling wine

spuntìno s. m. snack

sputàre v. tr. to spit

spùto s. m. spit

squàdra s. f. team (sport); squad (mil.)

squalìfica s. f. disqualification

squàllido agg. bleak; squalid (misero)

squallóre s. m. squalor

squàlo s. m. shark

squàma s. f. scale; – **di pesce** fish-scale

squilibràto agg. unbalanced, (mentally) deranged

squillànte agg. shrill

squìllo s. m. ring; blare (di tromba)

squisìto agg. exquisite, delicious

srotolàre v. tr. to unroll

stabilimènto s. m. factory, plant, works pl.; establishment (edificio); – **balneare** bathing establishment

stabilìre v. tr. to establish; to fix (fissare); to settle (sistemare)

stabilità s. f. stability

staccàre v. tr. to take off; to tear off (strap-

pare); to unhook (sganciare); to disconnect (mecc., elettr.)
staccionàta s. f. fence
stàdio s. m. stadium (sport); stage (fase)
stàffa s. f. stirrup
staffétta s. f. courier; relay (sport)
stagionàle agg. seasonal
stagionàre v. tr. to season
stagionàto agg. seasoned
stagionatùra s. f. seasoning
stagióne s. f. season
stagnatùra s. f. tinning; soldering (saldatura)
stàgno s. m. pond, pool • tin (chim.)
stalagmìte s. f. stalagmite
stalattìte s. f. stalactite
stàlla s. f. stable; cowhouse (per bovini)
stallière s. m. stableman, groom
stamattìna avv. this morning
stambécco s. m. rock-goat
stàmpa s. f. print, printing; (the) press (giornali, giornalisti)
stampànte s. f. printer
stampàre v. tr. to print
stampatèllo agg. block letters
stampatóre s. m. printer
stampèlla s. f. crutch
stàmpo s. m. die, mould; stamp (indole)
stancàre v. tr. to tire, to tire out • rifl. to get tired
stanchézza s. f. tiredness, fatigue
standardizzàre v. tr. to standardize
stanòtte avv. last night (appena trascorsa); tonight (questa)
stànza s. f. room
stàre v. intr. to stay, to remain, to be, to live (abitare)
starnutàre v. intr. to sneeze
starnùto s. m. sneeze
staséra avv. this evening, tonight
statàle agg. state (attr.), government (attr.)
statìsta s. m. statesman
statìstica s. f. statistics pl. (v. al sing.)
stàto s. m. state
stàtua s. f. statue
statùto s. m. statute, charter
stavòlta avv. this time
stazionàrio agg. stationary
stazióne s. f. station
stécca s. f. stick, rod; cue (da biliardo); false note (mus.); carton (di sigarette)
steccàto s. m. fence
stecchìno s. m. toothpick
stèle s. f. stele

stélla s. f. star; – **di mare** starfish; – **filante** streamer
stellàto agg. starry
stèlo s. m. stem, stand (sostegno)
stèmma s. m. coat of arms
stendàrdo s. m. standard, banner
stèndere v. tr. to stretch (out), to spread; to lay (spiegare); to hang out (sciorinare)
sterilità s. f. barrenness, sterility
sterilizzàre v. tr. to sterilize
sterilizzatóre s. m. sterilizer
sterilizzazióne s. f. sterilization
sterlìna s. f. pound, sterling
sterminìo s. m. extermination
stèrno s. m. breast-bone
sterzàre v. intr. to steer, to turn
stèrzo s. m. steering-gear
stésso agg. e pron. same
stesùra s. f. drawing up
stìle s. m. style
stilìsta s. m. e f. stylist, designer
stilòbate s. m. stylobate
stilogràfica s. f. fountain pen
stìma s. f. valuation; appraisal (valutazione); esteem (buona opinione)
stimàre v. tr. to estimate; to value (valutare); to esteem (apprezzare); to consider (giudicare)
stìmolo s. m. sting, prick; stimulus (med.)
stìnco s. m. shin-bone; shank (alim.); – **di vitello** veal shank
stìngere v. tr. e intr. to fade
stipèndio s. m. salary
stìpite s. m. jamb
stiraménto s. m. stretching, sprain; strain (med.)
stiràre v. tr. to stretch (allungare); to iron (col ferro); to straighten (i capelli)
stiratùra s. f. ironing
stirerìa s. f. ironing-room
stìrpe s. f. stock, birth, family, race, escent
stitichézza s. f. constipation
stìtico agg. constipated
stìva s. f. hold
stivàle s. m. boot
stivalétto s. m. bootee, ankle-boot
stoccafìsso s. m. stock-fish
stòffa s. f. cloth, material, fabric
stoìno s. m. (door-)mat
stòmaco s. m. stomach
stonàto agg. out of tune, false
stoppìno s. m. wick
stordìre v. tr. to stun, to daze

stòria s. f. history, story; tale (racconto)

stòrico agg. historic(al) • s. m. historian

storièlla s. f. funny story, joke

storiografìa s. f. historiography

stórmo s. m. flight

stòrto agg. crooked

stovìglie s. f. pl. dishes (piatti); cutlery sing. (posate)

stràbico agg. squint

strabismo s. m. strabismus (med.); squint

stràccio s. m. rag, cloth

stracòtto s. m. stew

stràda s. f. road; street (di città); – **dissestata** uneven road; – **a senso unico** one-way street

strafalcióne s. m. blunder

stràge s. f. slaughter

stràllo s. m. stay

stranièro agg. foreign

stràno agg. strange, queer, weird

straordinàrio agg. extraordinary

strappàre v. tr. to tear, to rip • intr. pron. to tear, to get torn

stràppo s. m. tear, rent; sprain (med.)

strapuntìno s. m. quilt

straripaménto s. m. overflowing

stratèga s. m. e f. strategist

stràto s. m. stratum, layer; coat (rivestimento)

stratosfèra s. f. stratosphere

stravagànte agg. queer, extravagant

stravècchio agg. very old

strèga s. f. witch

stregóne s. m. wizard

stregonerìa s. f. witchcraft, sorcery

strènna s. f. gift, present

strepitóso agg. resounding, outstanding

stressànte agg. stressing

strètta s. f. grip; – **di mano** handshake

strètto agg. narrow; tight (di abiti); strict (rigoroso) • s. m. straits pl.

strettòia s. f. narrow passage, bottle-neck

strillóne s. m. news-man

strìnga s. f. lace; string (inf., ling.)

strìngere v. tr. to clasp, to grasp, to grip, to tighten

strìscia s. f. stripe, slip, strip • comic strip (fumetto)

striscióne s. m. banner

strizzàre v. tr. to squeeze, to wring

stròfa s. f. strophe

strofinàccio s. m. cloth; – **per spolverare** duster; – **per stovìglie** tea-cloth; – **per pavimenti** floor-cloth; – **per rigovernare** dish-cloth

strombatùra s. f. splay

stroncàre v. tr. to break off, to cut off, to slash; to slate (criticare); to crush (reprimere)

stroncatùra s. f. slating

stropicciàre v. tr. to rub, to crumple, to crease

struménto s. m. instrument, tool

strùtto s. m. lard

struttùra s. f. structure, frame

strutturalìsmo s. m. structuralism

strùzzo s. m. ostrich

stuccàre v. tr. to plaster, to putty

stùcco s. m. plaster; putty (per i vetri)

studènte s. m. student

studentésco agg. student (attr.)

studiàre v. tr. to study

stùdio s. m. study

studìolo s. m. study, private room

studióso agg. studious, diligent • s. m. scholar; researcher (ricercatore)

stùfa s. f. stove; heater (elettrica)

stufàto s. m. stew

stùfo agg. bored, fed up

stuòia s. f. mat

stupèndo agg. stupendous, marvellous, wonderful, terrific

stupidità s. f. stupidity

stùpido s. m. stupid, fool

stupóre s. m. amazement, wonder

stupratóre s. m. rapist

stùpro s. m. rape

stuzzicadènti s. m. inv. toothpick

su prep. on, upon, over, above (al di sopra di); at, about, around (verso, intorno a); towards (direzione) • avv. up; upstairs (ai piani superiori)

subàcqueo agg. subaqueous, underwater, submarine • s. m. skin-diver

subaffittàre v. tr. to sublet

subìre v. tr. to undergo, to suffer

sùbito avv. at once

sublìme agg. sublime

subùrbio s. m. suburb

succèdere v. intr. to succeed; to happen, to occur, to take place (accadere); to follow (seguire) • intr. pron. to follow one another

successióne s. f. succession; sequence (mat.); **imposta di** – inheritance tax

successivaménte avv. subsequently

successìvo agg. successive, following

successo s. m. success

successóre s. m. successor

succhiàre v. tr. to suck

sùcco s. m. juice

sud s. m. south
sudàre v. intr. to sweat, to perspire
sudàto agg. sweaty
sùddito s. m. subject
suddividere v. tr. to subdivide, to split up
sùdicio agg. dirty, filthy
sudóre s. m. sweat, perspiration
sufficiènte agg. sufficient
suggerimènto s. m. suggestion
suggerire v. tr. to suggest; to prompt (teatro, scol.)
suggeritóre s. m. prompter
suggestionàbile agg. suggestible
suggestivo agg. evocative
sùghero s. m. cork
sùgo s. m. gravy (di carne); sauce (salsa)
suicìda s. m. e f. suicide
suicidàrsi v. rifl. to commit suicide
suicìdio s. m. suicide
suìno s. m. swine
sulfamìdico s. m. sulphamide
sultanàto s. m. sultanate
sultàno s. m. sultan
suòcera s. f. mother-in-law
suòcero s. m. father-in-law
suòla s. f. sole
suòlo s. m. soil, ground, land
suonàre v. tr. to sound, to ring (campanello); to play (strumenti musicali); to strike (battere le ore)
suonatóre s. m. player, performer, musician
suòno s. m. sound
suòra s. f. nun; Sister (prima del nome)
superàre v. tr. to exceed, to surpass, to excel, to get over (oltrepassare); to overtake (con un veicolo); to overcome (sormontare)
superàto agg. old-fashioned
supèrbia s. f. pride, conceit
supèrbo agg. proud, haughty; superb, magnificent (magnifico)
superconduttività s. f. superconductivity
superficiàle agg. superficial; surface (attr.)
superficie s. f. surface
superfluo agg. superfluous
superióre agg. superior; higher (più elevato); upper (sovrastante); senior, higher (di grado superiore); advanced (più avanzato)
supermercàto s. m. supermarket
supèrstite agg. surviving • s. m. e f. survivor
superstizióne s. f. superstition
superstizióso agg. superstitious
superstràda s. f. motorway

suppellèttili s. f. pl. furnishings
suppergiù avv. about, nearly, roughly
supplementàre agg. supplementary, additional, extra
supplemènto s. m. supplement; addition (aggiunta); extra charge (sovrapprezzo)
supplènte agg. temporary, substitute
suppòrto s. m. support, stand, bearing
supposizióne s. f. supposition, assumption
suppòsta s. f. suppository
surgelàre v. tr. to deep-freeze
surgelàto s. m. deep-frozen food
surrealìsmo s. m. surrealism
surrealìsta s. m. e f. surrealist
surriscaldàto agg. overheated
surrogàto s. m. substitute
suscettìbile agg. susceptible
suscitàre v. tr. to stir up, to excite, to arouse
susìna s. f. plum
susìno s. m. plum-tree
sussìdio s. m. subsidy, grant; aid (aiuto)
sussistènza s. f. subsistence
sussurràre v. tr. to whisper
sussurrìo s. m. whispering
sutùra s. f. suture
suturàre v. tr. to suture
svàgo s. m. amusement, relaxation
svaligiàre v. tr. to ransack, to burgle
svalutàre v. tr. to devalue (fin.); to cry down (comm.); to depreciate (fig.)
svalutazióne s. f. devaluation
svantàggio s. m. disadvantage, drawback
svantaggióso agg. disadvantageous
svasatùra s. f. flare
svedése agg. Swedish • s. m. e f. Swede; Swedish (lingua)
svéglia s. f. call; alarm-clock (orologio)
svegliàre v. tr. to wake up, to awake • intr. pron. to wake up
sveltézza s. f. quickness, speed
svèlto agg. quick; smart (intelligente)
svéndere v. tr. to sell off
svéndita s. f. selling-off; (clearance) sale
svenimènto s. m. faint
svenìre v. intr. to faint
sventùra s. f. misfortune
svernàre v. intr. to winter; to hibernate (di animali)
svestìre v. tr. e rifl. to undress
svezzamènto s. m. weaning
svezzàre v. tr. to wean
sviluppàre v. tr. to develop
svilùppo s. m. development
svincolo s. m. turn-off

svista *s. f.* oversight, slip; **fare una** – to make a slip; **per una** – inadvertently
svitàre *v. tr.* to unscrew
svizzero *agg. e s. m.* Swiss

svogliàto *agg.* indolent
svòlta *s. f.* turn
svoltàre *v. intr.* to turn
svuotàre *v. tr.* to empty

T

tabaccàio s. m. tobacconist

tabàcco s. m. tobacco; snuff (da fiuto)

tabèlla s. f. table, schedule

tabellóne s. m. notice-board

tabernàcolo s. m. tabernacle

tabulàto s. m. printout

tàcca s. f. notch

taccàgno agg. miserly, stingy • s. m. miser

taccheggiatóre s. m. shoplifter

tacchino s. m. turkey

tàcco s. m. heel

taccuìno s. m. note-book

tacére v. intr. to be silent; to keep silent (mantenere il silenzio)

tachicardìa s. f. tachycardia

tachìmetro s. m. speedometer

tacitùrno agg. taciturn

tàfano s. m. horse-fly

tafferùglio s. m. brawl, scuffle

tàglia s. f. size; reward (premio)

tagliàndo s. m. coupon, slip (scontrino)

tagliàre v. tr. to cut

tagliàto agg. cut

tagliènte agg. sharp

taglière s. m. chopping-board

tàglio s. m. cut; edge (parte tagliente); haircut (capelli)

tagliòla s. f. trap

tàlco s. m. talc; – in polvere talcum powder

tàle agg. indef. such; this, that (questo/a, quello/a); so (così) • pron. indef. person, man, fellow, chap

talènto s. m. talent

talismàno s. m. talisman

tallóne s. m. heel

talmènte avv. so (con agg. e avv.); so much (con v.)

tàlpa s. f. mole

talvòlta avv. sometimes, at times

tamarìndo s. m. tamarind

tamburèllo s. m. tambourine

tambùro s. m. drum; tambour (arch.)

tamponaménto s. m. bump (autom.); plugging, stopping up (otturazione); tamponage (med.)

tamponàre v. tr. to bump into (autom.); to tampon (med.)

tampóne s. m. tampon (med.); ink-pad (per timbri), blotting-pad (di carta assorbente)

tàna s. f. den

tangenziàle s. f. tangent (geom.); by-pass, ring road (strada)

tàngo s. m. tango

tànica s. f. can, tank

tànto agg. indef. so much, so many pl., such, so great • pron. indef. so much, so many pl., enough (abbastanza) • avv. so (con agg. e avv.); so much (con v.) • cong. however, but, in any case; – quanto as much, as many

tappàre v. tr. to plug, to cork, to stop

tapparèlla s. f. roll-up shutter

tappéto s. m. carpet

tappezzerìa s. f. tapestry; wall-paper (carta)

tappezzière s. m. decorator

tàppo s. m. cork; plug (di lavandino); stopper (di bottiglia)

tàra s. f. tare (comm.); hereditary defect (med.); flaw (fig.)

tardàre v. tr. to delay • intr. to be late, to delay (indugiare)

tàrdi avv. late

tàrga s. f. plate

targhétta s. f. plate

tariffa s. f. tariff, rate, fare

tariffàrio s. m. tariff, price list

tàrlo s. m. woodworm

tàrma s. f. moth

tarmicìda s. m. moth-killer

taròcco s. m. tarot, tarok

tarsìa s. f. marquetry, inlaying

tartagliàre v. intr. to stutter, to stammer

tartarùga s. f. tortoise; turtle (di mare)

tartìna s. f. canapé

tartùfo s. m. truffle

tàsca s. f. pocket

tascàbile agg. pocket (attr.)

taschìno s. m. breast-pocket

tàssa s. f. tax, fee

tassàbile agg. taxable

tassàmetro s. m. meter

tassàre *v. tr.* to tax, to assess
tassazióne *s. f.* taxation
tàsso *s. m.* badger (*zool.*); yew (*bot.*); rate (*fin.*)
tastiéra *s. f.* keyboard
tastierista *s. m. e f.* keyboard operator
tàsto *s. m.* key
tàttica *s. f.* tactics *pl.* (*v. al sing.*)
tàtto *s. m.* touch; tact (*fig.*)
tatuàggio *s. m.* tattoo
tatuàre *v. tr.* to tattoo
tauromachìa *s. f.* bullfight
tavèrna *s. f.* tavern
tàvola *s. f.* table; plate (illustrazione); painting (quadro)
tavolàta *s. f.* table
tavolétta *s. f.* tablet, bar
tavolino *s. m.* small table
tàvolo *s. m.* table
tavolòzza *s. f.* palette
tàzza *s. f.* cup
tazzina *s. f.* coffee-cup
tè *s. m.* tea
teatràle *agg.* theatrical
teatrino *s. m.* puppet theatre
teàtro *s. m.* theatre
tèca *s. f.* reliquary
tècnica *s. f.* technique; technics *pl.* (*v. al sing.*)
tecnicaménte *avv.* technically
tècnico *agg.* technical • *s. m.* technician, engineer
tecnologìa *s. f.* technology
tedésco *agg. e s. m.* German
tegàme *s. m.* pan
tèglia *s. f.* baking-tin
tègola *s. f.* tile
teièra *s. f.* tea-pot
téla *s. f.* cloth, canvas
telàio *s. m.* loom, frame
telecabìna *s. f.* cable-car
telecàmera *s. f.* telecamera
telecomàndo *s. m.* telecontrol
telecomunicazióne *s. f.* telecommunication
telecrònaca *s. f.* newsreel
telecronista *s. m. e f.* TV commentator
teleférica *s. f.* cableway
telefonàre *v. tr. e intr.* to telephone, to phone, to ring up, to make a call
telefonàta *s. f.* (phone) call, ring
telèfono *s. m.* telephone; **elenco del –** telephone directory
telegiornàle *s. m.* news
telègrafo *s. m.* telegraph
telegràmma *s. m.* telegram, wire

telemàtica *s. f.* telematics *pl.* (*v. al sing.*)
telepatìa *s. f.* telepathy
teleschérmo *s. m.* telescreen
telescòpio *s. m.* telescope
teleselezióne *s. f.* direct dialling system; **telefonàta in –** (direct) dialled call
televisióne *s. f.* television
televisìvo *agg.* television (*attr.*)
televisóre *s. m.* television set, TV set; telly (*fam.*)
tellina *s. f.* clam
telóne *s. m.* tarpaulin
tèma *s. m.* subject, topic, theme
temére *v. tr.* to fear, to be afraid of
tèmpera *s. f.* tempera
temperamatìte *s. m. inv.* pencil-sharpener
temperaménto *s. m.* temperament, disposition
temperàto *agg.* temperate, moderate; sharpened (affilato)
temperatùra *s. f.* temperature
temperino *s. m.* penknife (coltellino); pencil-sharpener (temperamatite)
tempèsta *s. f.* storm, tempest
tempestàre *v. intr.* to storm, to rage
tempestività *s. f.* opportuneness, timeliness
tempestìvo *agg.* opportune, timely
tèmpia *s. f.* temple
tèmpio *s. m.* temple
templàre *s. m.* Templar
tèmpo *s. m.* time; season (stagione); weather (atmosferico); stage (fase); tense (*gramm.*)
temporàle *s. m.* storm
temporàneo *agg.* temporary
tenàce *agg.* tenacious
tenàglie *s. f. pl.* pliers
tènda *s. f.* tent; curtain (di finestra)
tendènza *s. f.* tendency; bent (attitudine); trend (orientamento)
tendenziàle *agg.* tendential
tendenzióso *agg.* tendentious
tèndere *v. tr.* to stretch (out); to strain (mettere in tensione) • *intr.* to tend, to aim
tendìna *s. f.* curtain
tèndine *s. m.* tendon, sinew
tendóne *s. m.* awning; tent (di circo)
tenènte *s. m.* lieutenant
tenére *v. tr.* to hold, to keep; to contain (contenere); to take (prendere) • *intr.* to be (for), to valve; to care (tenerci)
tenerézza *s. f.* tenderness
tènero *agg.* tender; soft (morbido)
tènia *s. f.* tapeworm, taenia

tennista *s. m. e f.* tennis-player
tenóre *s. m.* way; tenor (*mus.*)
tensióne *s. f.* tension
tentàre *v. tr. e intr.* to try, to attempt; to tempt (indurre in tentazione)
tentativo *s. m.* attempt, try
tènue *agg.* slender, tenuous
teologìa *s. f.* theology
teòlogo *s. m.* theologian
teorèma *s. m.* theorem
teorìa *s. f.* theory
teòrico *s. m.* theorician
tepóre *s. m.* warmth
teppista *s. m. e f.* hooligan
terapèutico *agg.* therapeutic
terapìa *s. f.* therapy
tergicristàllo *s. m.* windscreen-wiper
termàle *agg.* thermal; **sorgenti termàli** hot springs
tèrme *s. f. pl.* thermal baths; spa *sing.*; thermae (*archeol.*)
tèrmico *agg.* thermic, thermal
terminàle *s. m.* terminal; boundary (di confine)
terminàre *v. tr.* to end, to finish, to terminate
tèrmine *s. m.* end, close, expiry; term (condizione, *mat.*, *gramm.*); word (parola)
terminologìa *s. f.* terminology
tèrmite *s. f.* termite
termodinàmica *s. f.* thermodynamics *pl.* (v. al *sing.*)
termòmetro *s. m.* thermometer
termòstato *s. m.* thermostat
tèrra *s. f.* land; earth (pianeta e crosta terrestre); ground (terreno)
terracòtta *s. f.* terracotta; **vasellame di –** earthenware
terrafèrma *s. f.* mainland
terràglia *s. f.* earthenware
terrapièno *s. m.* bank; rampart (*mil.*)
terràzza *s. f.* terrace
terrazzaménto *s. m.* terracing
terremòto *s. m.* earthquake
terréno *s. m.* ground, land; soil (suolo); field (campo da gioco)
terrèstre *agg.* terrestrial; land (*attr.*)
terrìbile *agg.* terrible, awful, dreadful
territoriàle *agg.* territorial
territòrio *s. m.* territory
terrorìsmo *s. m.* terrorism
terrorìsta *s. m. e f.* terrorist
terziàrio *s. m.* tertiary; **il settore –** the services sector

terzino *s. m.* back
téschio *s. m.* skull
tesòro *s. m.* treasure
tèssera *s. f.* card, pass
tèssile *agg.* textile
tessitóre *s. m.* weaver
tessitùra *s. f.* weaving
tessùto *s. m.* fabric, material, cloth; **– di lana** woollen fabric; **– di seta** silk material
tèsta *s. f.* head
testacòda *loc. sost. m. inv.* about-face
testaménto *s. m.* will, testament
testàrdo *agg.* stubborn
testatóre *s. m.* testator
testìcolo *s. m.* testicle, testis
testimóne *s. m. e f.* witness
testimoniàre *v. intr.* to witness, to testify
testìna *s. f.* head
tèsto *s. m.* text
testùggine *s. f.* tortoise; turtle (di mare)
tètano *s. m.* tetanus
tètro *agg.* dismal, gloomy
tétto *s. m.* roof
tìbia *s. f.* tibia, shin-bone
tibùrio *s. m.* lantern
tièpido *agg.* tepid, lukewarm
tifàre *v. intr.* to be a fan of
tifo *s. m.* typhus (*med.*); fanaticism (*sport*)
tifóne *s. m.* typhoon
tifóso *agg.* fanatic • *s. m.* fan, supporter
tignòla *s. f.* moth
tìgre *s. f.* tiger
timbàllo *s. m.* timbale, pie
timbràre *v. tr.* to stamp; to punch (il cartellino)
tìmbro *s. m.* stamp; postmark (postale); timbre (*mus.*)
timidézza *s. f.* shyness
tìmido *agg.* shy
timo *s. m.* thyme (*bot.*); thymus (*anat.*)
timóne *s. m.* rudder, helm
timonière *s. m.* helmsman, steersman
timóre *s. m.* fear, dread
timoróso *agg.* fearful, timid
tìmpano *s. m.* tympanum, ear-drum (*anat.*); tympano (*mus.*); tympanum, gable (*arch.*)
tìnca *s. f.* tench
tìngere *v. tr.* to dye, to paint
tino *s. m.* tub, vat
tinòzza *s. f.* tub
tìnta *s. f.* paint, dye, colour
tintarèlla *s. f.* tan
tinteggiàre *v. tr.* to paint; to colour-wash (un muro)

tinto agg. dyed, coloured

tintóre s. m. dyer

tintoria s. f. dry cleaner's (shop)

tintùra s. f. dyeing; – **per capelli** hair dye

tipico agg. typical

tipo s. m. type, fellow, chap, guy (individuo); standard (campione)

tipografia s. f. typography

tipógrafo s. m. printer, typographer

tipologia s. f. typology

tiràggio s. m. draught

tirànno s. m. tyrant

tirànte s. m. connecting rod; tie-beam (edil.)

tiràre v. tr. to pull, to draw, to drag (trascinare); to throw (lanciare); to attract (attirare); to stretch (tendere)

tiratóre s. m. shot

tiratùra s. f. printing; edition, run, circulation (numero di copie)

tirchio agg. stingy • s. m. miser

tiro s. m. draught, throw, cast (lancio); pull (strappo)

tirocinio s. m. apprenticeship, training

tiroide s. f. thyroid

tisàna s. f. infusion, herb tea

titolo s. m. title; headline (di articolo sul giornale); qualification (qualifica)

toccànte agg. touching

toccàre v. tr. to touch

toccasàna s. m. inv. cure-all

tócco s. m. touch; stroke (di pennello)

tòga s. f. robe, gown

tògliere v. tr. to take away; to take (out, from, of); to take off, to remove • rifl. to get away (off, out); to clear off (andarsene)

tolleránte agg. tolerant

tolleràre v. tr. to tolerate, to bear, to stand

tómba s. f. tomb, grave

tombàle agg. tomb (attr.), grave (attr.)

tombino s. m. manhole cover

tómbola s. f. tombola; tumble (caduta)

tòmo s. m. tome, volume

tomografia s. f. tomography

tònaca s. f. cowl; frock (di frate); cassock, soutane (di prete)

tonalità s. f. tonality, tone; shade (sfumatura)

tonàre v. intr. to thunder

tóndo agg. round • s. m. circle, round; tondo (arte)

tónfo s. m. thud; splash (in acqua)

tonificànte agg. tonic

tonnellàta s. f. ton

tónno s. m. tuna, tunny

tòno s. m. tone

tonsilla s. f. tonsil

tonsillite s. f. tonsillitis

topàzio s. m. topaz

topicida s. m. rat-poison

tòpo s. m. mouse, mice pl.

topònimo s. m. toponym

tòppa s. f. patch; keyhole (della serratura)

toràce s. m. chest

tórba s. f. peat

tórcere v. tr. to twist, to wring

tórcia s. f. torch, brand

torcicòllo s. m. stiff neck

tórdo s. m. thrush

torménta s. f. snow storm

tornacónto s. m. advantage, interest

tornàdo s. m. inv. tornado

tornàre v. intr. to return, to go back (andare di nuovo); to come back (venire di nuovo); to become again (ridiventare)

tórnio s. m. lathe

tòro s. m. bull; Taurus (astr.)

torpóre s. m. torpor, numbness

tórre s. f. tower, castle; rook (scacchi)

torrènte s. m. stream, torrent

torrenziàle agg. torrential

torrióne s. m. keep

torsióne s. f. torsion

tórsolo s. m. core

tórta s. f. cake, pie, tart; – **di mele** apple-pie

tortièra s. f. baking-tin

tortino s. m. pie

tòrto s. m. wrong

tórtora s. f. turtle-dove

tortuóso agg. winding; tortuous, devious (fig.)

tortùra s. f. torture

tosàre v. tr. to shear, to clip

tòsse s. f. cough

tòssico agg. toxic

tossicodipendènte s. m. e f. drug addict

tossicodipendènza s. f. drug addiction

tossina s. f. toxin

tossire v. intr. to cough

tostapàne s. m. inv. toaster

tostàre v. tr. to toast; to roast (caffè)

totàle agg. total, utter

tòtano s. m. squid

tovàglia s. f. table-cloth

tovagliòlo s. m. napkin

tra prep. between (fra due); among (fra più di due); in the middle of, amid, amidst, through (in mezzo a); in, within (entro); of, among (partitivo)

311

trabiccolo *s. m.* rickety vehicle

traboccàre *v. intr.* to overflow

tràccia *s. f.* track; trail (striscia); trace (*fig.*); outline (linee principali)

tracciàre *v. tr.* to trace (out), to mark out, to draw, to plot, to lay out; – **a grandi linee** to outline

tracciàto *s. m.* tracing, lay-out

trachèa *s. f.* trachea, windpipe

tracòlla *s. f.* shoulder-belt, baldric; **borsa a** – shoulder-bag

tradiménto *s. m.* betrayal; treason (*leg.*); treachery (slealtà)

tradìre *v. tr.* to betray; to be unfaithful to (essere infedele); to fail (venire meno a); to deceive (ingannare)

traditóre *s. m.* traitor, betrayer

tradizionàle *agg.* traditional

tradizióne *s. f.* tradition

tradótto *agg.* translated

tradùrre *v. tr.* to translate

traduttóre *s. m.* translator

traduzióne *s. f.* translation

trafficàre *v. intr.* to trade, to deal; to bustle about (affaccendarsi)

tràffico *s. m.* traffic; trade (*comm.*)

trafila *s. f.* procedure

trafilétto *s. m.* paragraph

tràforo *s. m.* perforation, boring, tunnelling; tunnel (galleria)

trafugàre *v. tr.* to purloin, to steal

tragèdia *s. f.* tragedy

traghettàre *v. tr.* to ferry

traghétto *s. m.* ferry(-boat)

tràgico *agg.* tragic

tragicòmico *agg.* tragicomic(al)

tragìtto *s. m.* journey, passage; crossing (per mare)

tragguàrdo *s. m.* finishing line

traiettòria *s. f.* trajectory

tràina *s. f.* tow-rope

trainàre *v. tr.* to drag, to draw, to pull; to tow (rimorchiare)

tràino *s. m.* dragging, towing

tralasciàre *v. tr.* to leave out, to pass over

tralìccio *s. m.* pylon (*elettr.*); trestle (ponte)

tram *s. m.* tram, street-car

tràma *s. f.* weft (di tessuto); plot (macchinazione)

trambùsto *s. m.* confusion, bustle

tramezzìno *s. m.* sandwich

tramèzzo *s. m.* partition wall

tramontàna *s. f.* north wind

tramontàre *v. intr.* to set; to fade (*fig.*)

tramónto *s. m.* sunset; fading (*fig.*)

trampolière *s. m.* wading-bird, wader

trampolìno *s. m.* spring-board (per tuffi); ski-jumping board (per sci); – **elàstico** trampoline

tràncio *s. m.* slice

tranèllo *s. m.* trap, snare

trànne *prep.* except, save, but

tranquillànte *s. m.* tranquillizer

tranquillìtà *s. f.* quiet, stilness; tranquillity (di spirito)

tranquìllo *agg.* peaceful, calm, quiet

transatlàntico *s. m.* (trasatlantic) liner

transènna *s. f.* barrier; transenna (*arch.*)

transessuàle *s. m. e f.* transsexual

transètto *s. m.* transept

transitàre *v. intr.* to pass, to transit

trànsito *s. m.* transit; – **interrotto** road up; **divieto di** – no thoroughfare, do not enter

tranvière *s. m.* tram-driver

trapanàre *v. tr.* to drill, to bore

tràpano *s. m.* drill

trapèzio *s. m.* trapezium (*geom.*); trapeze (attrezzo ginnico); trapezius (*anat.*)

trapezìsta *s. m. e f.* trapezist

trapiànto *s. m.* transplant; transplantation (operazione)

tràppola *s. f.* trap

trapùnta *s. f.* quilt

trasalìre *v. intr.* to start, to jump

trasandàto *agg.* slipshod, careless, shabby

trasbòrdo *s. m.* transfer

trascinàre *v. tr.* to drag • *rifl.* to draw oneself (along); to drag (on) (andare per le lunghe)

trascórrere *v. tr.* to spend, to pass • *intr.* to pass, to elapse

trascrìvere *v. tr.* to transcribe; to register (*leg.*)

trascrizióne *s. f.* transcription; transcript (copia)

trascuràbile *agg.* negligible

trascuràre *v. tr.* to neglect, to disregard

trasferiménto *s. m.* transfer

trasferìre *v. tr.* to remove, to transfer • *intr. pron.* to move

trasfèrta *s. f.* transfer; **partita in** – away game

trasformatóre *s. m.* transformer

trasfusióne *s. f.* transfusion

trasgressióne *s. f.* transgression; infringement (*leg.*)

traslitterazióne *s. f.* transliteration

traslocàre *v. tr. e intr.* to move

traslòco s. m. removal, move

trasméttere v. tr. to transmit; to send (spedire); to broadcast (radio); to convey (comunicare)

trasmissióne s. f. transmission; – radiofonica broadcast

trasparènte agg. transparent

trasparènza s. f. transparency

traspirazióne s. f. transpiration; perspiration (cutanea)

trasportàbile agg. transportable

trasportàre v. tr. to transport, to carry, to convey; to move (spostare)

trasportatóre s. m. transporter, carrier; conveyor (mecc.)

traspòrto s. m. transport, conveyance, carriage; mezzi di – means of transport

trasversàle agg. transversal; cross (attr.)

trasvolàre v. tr. to fly across

trasvolàta s. f. flight, (air) crossing

tràtta s. f. trade; draft (comm.); section (percorso ferroviario)

trattàbile agg. tractable (persona); treatable (chim.); prezzo – price subject to negotiation

trattaménto s. m. treatment

trattàre v. tr. to treat, to deal with; to handle (maneggiare); to deal in (commerciare) • intr. to treat, to deal

trattatìva s. f. negotiation

trattàto s. m. treatise; treaty (accordo)

trattenùta s. f. deduction

trattóre s. m. tractor

trattorìa s. f. inn, restaurant

tràuma s. m. trauma; – psìchico mental shock

traumatòlogo s. m. traumatologist

travàglio s. m. trouble, pain, suffering; labour (parto)

travasàre v. tr. to pour off

tràve s. f. beam

traversàre v. tr. to cross

traversàta s. f. crossing, passage

travertìno s. m. travertin(e)

travestiménto s. m. disguise

travisàre v. tr. to distort, to alter, to misinterpret

travolgènte agg. overwhelming

travòlgere v. tr. to sweep away; to overwhelm (sopraffare); to run over (investire)

trazióne s. f. traction; drive (autom.)

tréccia s. f. plait, braid

trègua s. f. truce, respite; pause (fig.)

tremàre v. intr. to tremble, to shake, to quiver; – di freddo to shiver

treméndo agg. frightful, awful, terrible

trémito s. m. tremble, shake, quiver

tremóre s. m. trembling, shaking; shivering (per il freddo); tremor (med.)

trèno s. m. train; – accelerato slow train; – diretto through train; – direttìssimo fast train; – rapido express train; – in partenza da train departing from; – in arrivo a train arriving at

triangolàre agg. triangular

triangolazióne s. f. triangulation

tribù s. f. tribe

tribùna s. f. tribune; stand (sport); apse, tribune (arch.)

tribunàle s. m. court, tribunal

triciclo s. m. tricycle

triclìnio s. m. triclinium

tricòlogo s. m. trichologist

tricolóre agg. tricolo(u)r

tricuspìdale agg. tricuspid(al)

tridimensionàle agg. tridimensional, three-dimensional

trielìna s. f. trichloroethylene

trìglia s. f. mullet

trìglifo s. m. triglyph

trilobàto agg. trilobal

trimestràle agg. quarterly

trimotóre s. m. three-engined craft

trìna s. f. lace

trinità s. f. trinity

trìo s. m. trio

trionfàle agg. triumphal

trionfàre v. intr. to triumph

trionfo s. m. triumph

trìppa s. f. tripe

trìste agg. sad; bleak (di luogo)

tristézza s. f. sadness; gloom (di luogo)

tritacàrne s. m. inv. mincer, meat-grinder

tritaghiàccio s. m. inv. ice-crusher

tritàre v. tr. to mince, to chop

tritatùtto s. m. inv. mincer, food-grinder

trìttico s. m. triptych

trofèo s. m. trophy

troglodìta s. m. troglodyte, cave man

trómba s. f. trumpet

trombettìsta s. m. e f. trumpet (player)

trombòsi s. f. thrombosis

troncàre v. tr. to cut off, to break off

tronchése s. m. o f. (cutting) nippers pl., clippers pl.

trónco s. m. trunk; log (d'albero abbattuto); section (di strada)

tròno s. m. throne

tropicàle agg. tropical

tròppo *agg. e pron. indef.* too much, too many *pl.* • *avv.* too (con *avv. e agg.*); too much (con *v.*); too long (*avv.* di tempo)

tròta *s. f.* trout

trottatóre *s. m.* trotter

tròtto *s. m.* trot

tròttola *s. f.* spinning-top

trovàre *v. tr.* to find; to meet (incontrare); to see (visitare) • *rifl. rec.* to meet, to see

truccàre *v. tr.* to make up; to falsify • *rifl.* to make up

truccatóre *s. m.* make-up man, visagiste

trùcco *s. m.* make-up; trick (imbroglio)

trùffa *s. f.* fraud, swindle

truffàre *v. tr.* to defraud, to cheat, to swindle

tubétto *s. m.* tube

tùbo *s. m.* tube, pipe; – **di scappamento** exhaust-pipe

tuffàre *v. tr.* to plunge, to dip • *rifl.* to dive, to plunge

tuffatóre *s. m.* diver

tùffo *s. m.* dive, plunge

tùfo *s. m.* tufa

tùga *s. f.* deckhouse

tulipàno *s. m.* tulip

tumefazióne *s. f.* tumefaction

tumóre *s. m.* tumour; tumor (USA)

tùmulo *s. m.* tumulus; barrow (*archeol.*); mound (cumulo di terra); tomb (tomba)

tumùlto *s. m.* uproar; riot (sommossa)

tùndra *s. f.* tundra

tùnica *s. f.* tunic

tunnel *s. m. inv.* tunnel

tuonàre *v. intr.* to thunder

tuòno *s. m.* thunder

tuòrlo *s. m.* yolk

turàcciolo *s. m.* stopper; cork (di sughero)

turàre *v. tr.* to plug, to stop, to cork

turbaménto *s. m.* upset

turbànte *s. m.* turban

turbina *s. f.* turbine

turchése *s. m.* turquoise

tùrco *agg.* Turkish • *s. m.* Turk; Turkish (lingua)

turista *s. m. e f.* tourist

tùrno *s. m.* turn; shift (di lavoro); – **di guardia** watch

tùta *s. f.* overalls *pl.*; track-suit (sportiva); – **mimetica** camouflaged combat clothing

tutt'al più *loc. avv.* at the most, at worst

tuttavia *cong.* but, yet, still, however

tùtto *agg. indef.* all; whole (intero); every (ogni); any (qualsiasi) • *pron. indef.* all; everything (ogni cosa); anything (qualsiasi cosa); all, all people, everybody, everyone (ognuno); each one (ciascuno)

tuttóra *avv.* still

U

ubbidiènte *agg.* obedient
ubbidire *v. intr. e tr.* to obey
ubicazióne *s. f.* location, site
ubriacàrsi *v. intr. pron.* to get drunk
ubriachézza *s. f.* drunkenness
ubriàco *s. m.* drunk
uccèllo *s. m.* bird
uccidere *v. tr.* to kill; to shoot (con arma da fuoco)
uccisióne *s. f.* killing
udibile *agg.* audible
udiènza *s. f.* audience; hearing (*leg.*); interview (colloquio)
udire *v. tr.* to hear
udito *s. m.* hearing
ufficiàle *agg.* official; formal (formale) • *s. m.* officer
ufficio *s. m.* office, bureau; – turistico tourist office; – postale post office; orario d'– office hours
ugèllo *s. m.* nozzle, jet
ùggia *s. f.* boredom, nuisance
uguaglianza *s. f.* equality
uguagliàre *v. tr.* to equalize, to level; to equal (essere uguale)
uguàle *agg.* equal, like, identical
ugualménte *avv.* equally, alike; all the same (malgrado tutto)
ùlcera *s. f.* ulcer; – duodenale duodenal ulcer; – gastrica gastric ulcer
ùlna *s. f.* ulna
ulterióre *agg.* further
ultimaménte *avv.* lately
ultimàre *v. tr.* to complete, to finish
ùltimo *agg.* last; the latest (il più recente)
ultrasuòno *s. m.* ultrasound
ultraviolétto *agg.* ultraviolet
ululàto *s. m.* howl
umanésimo *s. m.* humanism
umanista *s. m. e f.* humanist
umanità *s. f.* humanity; mankind (genere umano)
umanitàrio *agg.* humanitarian
umàno *agg.* human; humane (gentile)
umidificàre *v. tr.* to humidify, to moisturize

umidificatóre *s. m.* humidifier
umidità *s. f.* damp, humidity
ùmido *agg.* damp, moist, humid
ùmile *agg.* humble
umiliànte *agg.* humiliating
umiliàre *v. tr.* to humiliate
umiliazióne *s. f.* humiliation
umóre *s. m.* humor, humour, temper; mood (stato d'animo); sap (linfa)
umorismo *s. m.* humour
umorista *s. m. e f.* humorist
umoristico *agg.* humorous, funny, comic
unànime *agg.* unanimous
unanimità *s. f.* unanimity
uncinétto *s. m.* crochet
ùngere *v. tr.* to grease
unguènto *s. m.* ointment
ùnghia *s. f.* nail; claw (artiglio)
unicaménte *avv.* solely
ùnico *agg.* only; unique (senza pari); sole (esclusivo)
unifamiliàre *agg.* one-family (*attr.*)
unificàre *v. tr.* to unify, to standardize (standardizzare)
unificazióne *s. f.* unification; consolidation (*fin.*)
uniformàre *v. tr.* to conform
uniforme *agg.* uniform
uniformità *s. f.* uniformity
unióne *s. f.* union; unity (accordo)
unire *v. tr.* to unite; to join, to connect (collegare); to add (aggiungere)
unità *s. f.* unity, unit
universàle *agg.* universal; world (*attr.*)
università *s. f.* university
universitàrio *agg.* university (*attr.*)
univèrso *s. m.* universe
univoco *agg.* univocal, unambiguous
ùnto *s. m.* grease
untuóso *agg.* greasy, oily
uòmo *s. m.* man
uòvo *s. m.* egg
ùpupa *s. f.* hoopoe
uragàno *s. m.* hurricane
urànio *s. m.* uranium

urbanista s. m. e f. urbanist, city-planner
urbanìstica s. f. urbanism, city-planning
urbanizzazióne s. f. urbanization
urbàno agg. urban; city (attr.)
urèa s. f. urea
urètra s. f. urethra
urgènte agg. urgent, pressing
urgènza s. f. urgency; emergency (med.)
urìna s. f. urine
urlàre v. intr. to howl, to shout
ùrlo s. m. shout, cry
ùrna s. f. urn; – elettorale ballot-box
urografìa s. f. urography
uròlogo s. m. urologist
urtàre v. tr. to bump into, to collide with; to shove (spingere); to irritate (provocare)
urticànte agg. urticant
ùrto s. m. bump, knock, collision
usànza s. f. custom; habit (abitudine)
usàre v. tr. to use; to act with (agire con)
usàto s. m. second-hand, used
uscière s. m. usher
ùscio s. m. door
uscìre v. intr. to go out
uscìta s. f. going out; exit (teatro); exit, way out (passaggio); – di sicurezza emergency exit

usignòlo s. m. nightingale
ùso s. m. use, custom; habit (abitudine); fuori – out of order
ustionàre v. tr. to scald, to burn • rifl. to scald oneself, to burn oneself
ustionàto agg. scalded
ustióne s. f. burn, scald
usuàle agg. usual, customary
usufruìre v. intr. to take advantage (of st.)
usufrùtto s. m. usufruct, right of use
utensìle s. m. tool, utensil, implement
utènte s. m. e f. user, consumer
utènza s. f. users pl., consumers pl.
ùtero s. m. uterus
ùtile agg. useful, helpful
utilità s. f. utility, usefulness; benefit (vantaggio)
utilitària s. f. compact car
utilizzàre v. tr. to use, to utilize
utilizzatóre s. m. utilizer
utilìzzo s. m. use, utilization
utopìa s. f. utopia
utopìsta s. m. e f. utopian
ùva s. f. grapes pl.; – passa raisin
uxoricìda s. m. e f. uxoricide

V

vacànte *agg.* vacant, empty

vacànza *s. f.* holiday, vacation; **vacanze estive** summer holidays

vàcca *s. f.* cow

vaccinàre *v. tr.* to vaccinate

vaccinazióne *s. f.* vaccination

vaccino *s. m.* vaccine

vagabondàre *v. intr.* to wander about, to rove

vagabóndo *s. m.* tramp

vagàre *v. intr.* to roam

vagìna *s. f.* vagina

vaginìte *s. f.* vaginitis

vàglia *s. m. inv.* money-order; **– postale** postal order; **– telegrafico** telegraphic money-order

vagóne *s. m.* wagon, coach

valànga *s. f.* avalanche

valére *v. intr.* to be worth; to count (essere valido)

valeriàna *s. f.* valerian

valicàre *v. tr.* to cross

vàlico *s. m.* mountain pass

validità *s. f.* validity; effectiveness (efficacia)

vàlido *agg.* valid; effective (efficace)

valigerìa *s. f.* leather-goods shop

valìgia *s. f.* suitcase

vallàta *s. f.* valley

vàlle *s. f.* valley

vallóne *s. m.* deep valley

valoróso *agg.* valiant, brave

valùta *s. f.* currency

valutàre *v. tr.* to value, to estimate, to appraise; to assess (determinare)

vàlvola *s. f.* valve; fuse (fusibile)

vampàta *s. f.* flush (di calore); blast (di aria)

vampiro *s. m.* vampire

vandàlico *agg.* vandalic

vàndalo *s. m.* vandal

vanésio *agg.* foppish • *s. m.* fop

vànga *s. f.* spade

vangàre *v. tr.* to spade

vangèlo *s. m.* Gospel

vanìglia *s. f.* vanilla

vanitóso *agg.* vain

vantàggio *s. m.* advantage; lead (distacco)

vantaggióso *agg.* advantageous, favourable

vantàre *v. tr.* to boast of

vànto *s. m.* boast; virtue (merito)

vapóre *s. m.* steam; **ferro a –** steam iron; **vapori di benzina** petrol fumes

vaporétto *s. m.* ferry, water bus

vaporizzatóre *s. m.* vaporizer, atomizer

vaporóso *agg.* flimsy

varàre *v. tr.* to launch

varcàre *v. tr.* to cross

vàrco *s. m.* opening, passage

variàbile *agg.* varying, changeable

variàre *v. tr. e intr.* to change, to vary; to differ, to vary (essere differente)

variatóre *s. m.* variator

varìce *s. f.* varix, varicose vein

varicèlla *s. f.* chicken-pox, varicella

variegàto *agg.* variegated, streaked, speckled

varietà *s. f.* variety • *s. m.* variety, vaudeville

variopìnto *agg.* multi-coloured

vàsca *s. f.* basin; bath tub (da bagno)

vascèllo *s. m.* vessel, ship

vaselìna *s. f.* vaseline

vàso *s. m.* vase; pot (di terracotta); jar (per conserve)

vassóio *s. m.* tray

vàsto *agg.* vast, wide

vecchiàia *s. f.* old age

vècchio *agg.* old • *s. m.* old man

vedére *v. tr.* to see; to look (at) (guardare)

vedétta *s. f.* look-out

védova *s. f.* widow

védovo *s. m.* widower

vedùta *s. f.* view, sight

vedutìsta *s. m. e f.* vedutista

vegetàle *agg. e s. m.* vegetable

vegetariàno *agg. e s. m.* vegetarian

vegetazióne *s. f.* vegetation

veggènte *s. m. e f.* seer, clairvoyant

véglia *s. f.* watch, vigil

vegliàre *v. intr.* to stay up late, to keep watch

vegliòne *s. m.* ball, dance; **– di fine d'anno** New Year's Eve dance

veìcolo *s. m.* vehicle; carrier (med., chim.)

véla *s. f.* sail; sailing (sport); **barca a –** sailing boat

317

veleggiàre v. intr. to sail
veléno s. m. poison
velenóso agg. poisonous, venomous
veliéro s. m. sailer
velista s. m. e f. sailor
velivolo s. m. aircraft
vellùto s. m. velvet
vélo s. m. veil; film (strato sottile)
velóce agg. fast, quick, swift
velocista s. m. e f. sprinter
velocità s. f. speed, velocity; **eccesso di –** speeding; **limite di –** speed limit
velódromo s. m. cycle-track
véna s. f. vein
venatùra s. f. vein
vendémmia s. f. vintage, harvest
vendemmiàre v. tr. to harvest
véndere v. tr. to sell
vendétta s. f. revenge, vengeance
vendibile agg. saleable, marketable
vendicàre v. tr. to revenge, to avenge
véndita s. f. sale; **in –** on sale; **– all'asta** auction
venditóre s. m. seller, vendor
veneràre v. tr. to revere; to venerate (relig.)
venerdì s. m. Friday
venire v. intr. to come
ventàglio s. m. fan
ventilàre v. tr. to air; to ventilate (fig.)
ventilàto agg. airy, ventilated
ventilatóre s. m. fan
vénto s. m. wind
véntola s. f. fire-fan, fan
ventósa s. f. sucker
ventóso agg. windy
véntre s. m. stomach, belly, tummy
véra s. f. wedding-ring
veraménte avv. really, truly
verànda s. f. veranda
verbalizzàre v. tr. to record, to minute
verbéna s. f. vervain, verbena
vérbo s. m. verb
vérde agg. green
verdeggiànte agg. green, verdant
verdétto s. m. verdict
verdùra s. f. greens pl., vegetables pl.
vérgine s. f. virgin; Virgo, the Virgin (astr.)
verginità s. f. virginity
vergógna s. f. shame; disgrace (disonore)
vergognàrsi v. intr. pron. to be ashamed; to be shy (per timidezza)
vergognóso agg. shameful, disgraceful; shy (timido)
verificàbile agg. verifiable

verificàre v. tr. to verify, to check
verismo s. m. verism, realism
verista s. m. e f. verist, realist
verità s. f. truth
vérme s. m. worm
vermíglio agg. vermilion
vernàcolo s. m. vernacular
vernice s. f. paint; varnish (trasparente)
verniciàre v. tr. to paint; to varnish (con vernice trasparente)
verniciatóre s. m. painter, varnisher
véro agg. true; real (reale)
verosimigliànte agg. likely, probable
verosimile agg. likely, probable
verrùca s. f. verruca, wart
versànte s. m. slope; versant (geog.)
versàre v. tr. to pour; to spill (rovesciare)
versàtile agg. versatile
versétto s. m. verse
vérso s. m. line, poem, verse; way (direzione)
vèrtebra s. f. vertebra
vertebràle agg. vertebral
vertebràti s. m. pl. vertebrates
vertènza s. f. controversy, dispute
verticàle agg. vertical
verticalménte avv. vertically
vérza s. f. savoy cabbage
vescìca s. f. bladder; blister (della pelle)
vescovile agg. episcopal, bishop's
véscovo s. m. bishop
véspa s. f. wasp
vespàio s. m. wasps' nest
véspro s. m. Vespers pl.
vessillo s. m. standard, banner
vestàglia s. f. dressing-gown
véste s. f. clothing, dress
vestiàrio s. m. clothing
vestibolo s. m. hall; vestibule (anat., archeol.); foyer (teatro)
vestìre v. intr. to dress, to wear • rifl. to dress (oneself); to get dressed, to put on, to wear (indossare)
vestìto s. m. suit (da uomo); dress (da donna)
veterinàrio s. m. vet(erinarian)
véto s. m. veto
vetràio s. m. glass-maker
vetràta s. f. glass-window; glass-door (porta a vetri)
vetrerìa s. f. glass works pl. (v. al sing.)
vetrina s. f. shop-window
vetrinista s. m. e f. window-dresser
vétro s. m. glass
vetrofanìa s. f. diaphanie

vettóre s. m. vector (geom., fis.); carrier (leg.)

vettura s. f. coach; car (automobile)

vetustà s. f. ancientness

vezzeggiàre v. tr. to fondle, to pamper

vézzo s. m. habit, affectation

vezzóso agg. charming

via s. f. road, street • avv. away, off; out, away (fuori)

viadótto s. m. viaduct

viaggiàre v. intr. to travel

viaggiatóre s. m. traveller; passenger (passeggero)

viàggio s. m. journey; tour (turistico); voyage (per mare); trip (gita); – **tutto compreso** package tour

viàle s. m. avenue, boulevard

viandànte s. m. e f. wayfarer, traveller

viavài s. m. inv. coming and going

vibràre v. tr. to brandish; to strike (assestare con forza)

vicàrio s. m. vicar

vicènda s. f. event; vicissitude; **a** – in turn

vicepresidènte s. m. vice-president

viceré s. m. viceroy

vicevèrsa avv. vice versa, conversely

vicinànza s. f. proximity

vicinàto s. m. neighbourhood

vicino agg. e avv. near, nearby • s. m. neighbour

vicolo s. m. alley

videocassétta s. f. video cassette

videocitòfono s. m. videointercom

videoregistratóre s. m. video recorder

vietàre v. tr. to forbid; to prevent (impedire)

vietàto agg. forbidden; **senso** – no entry

vigilànte s. m. e f. supervisor; guard (guardiano)

vigilànza s. f. supervision; vigilance; care, surveillance

vigilàre v. tr. to watch over, to supervise

vigile agg. vigilant, watchful

vigilia s. f. eve

vigliàcco agg. coward

vigna s. f. vineyard

vignéto s. m. vineyard

vignétta s. f. illustration, sketch; **umoristica** cartoon

vignettista s. m. e f. cartoonist

vigógna s. f. vicugna

vile agg. coward; base, vile (meschino)

vilipèndio s. m. scorn, contempt; public insult (leg.)

villa s. f. villa

villàggio s. m. village

villàno agg. rude, rough

villeggiànte s. m. e f. holiday-maker

villeggiatùra s. f. holiday, vacation; **luogo di** – holiday resort

vincénte agg. winning • s. m. e f. winner

vincere v. tr. to win; to overcome (sopraffare)

vincita s. f. win; winnings pl. (ciò che si vince)

vincitóre s. m. winning • s. m. winner

vincolo s. m. bond, tie

vino s. m. wine; **spumante** sparkling wine; – **secco** dry wine

vinto agg. beaten; overcome (sopraffatto)

viòla s. f. violet; viola (mus.)

violazióne s. f. breach

violentàre v. tr. to rape

violènto agg. violent

violènza s. f. violence; – **carnale** rape; **non** – nonviolence

violinista s. m. e f. violinist, fiddler

violino s. m. violin, fiddle

violoncellista s. m. e f. cellist

violoncèllo s. m. cello

viòttolo s. m. path, lane

vipera s. f. viper, adder

viràle agg. viral

viràre v. intr. to veer

viràta s. f. veer

virgola s. f. comma

virile agg. manly, masculine

virilità s. f. manliness, virility

virtuóso agg. virtuous; virtuoso (mus.)

virus s. m. virus

visagista s. m. e f. beautician

vischio s. m. mistletoe

viscido agg. viscid, slimy

viscónte s. m. viscount

viscontéssa s. f. viscountess

visìbile agg. visible

visibilità s. f. visibility; **scarsa** – poor visibility

visièra s. f. peak

visionàrio agg. visionary

visióne s. f. vision

visita s. f. visit; **biglietto da** – visiting card; – **medica** medical examination

visitàre v. tr. to visit, to call; to examine (med.)

visitatóre s. m. visitor

viso s. m. face

visóne s. m. mink

vista s. f. sight

vistàre v. tr. to visa

visto s. m. visa; – **d'ingresso** entry visa

vistóso agg. showy

319

visuàle *s. f.* view
vita *s. f.* life
vitalità *s. f.* vitality
vitalìzio *s. m.* life annuity
vitamìna *s. f.* vitamin
vite *s. f.* vine (*bot.*); screw (*mecc.*)
vitèllo *s. m.* calf; veal (*alim.*); calf (cuoio); arrosto di – roast veal
vitellóne *s. m.* fatted calf; veal (*alim.*)
viticoltóre *s. m.* vine-grower
vìtigno *s. m.* vine
vìttima *s. f.* victim
vitto *s. m.* food; board (pasti); – e alloggio board and lodging
vittòria *s. f.* victory; win (*sport*)
vittorióso *agg.* victorious, winning
vivàce *agg.* lively; bright (di colore)
vivacità *s. f.* liveliness; brightness (di colore)
vivàio *s. m.* nursery, garden centre (*bot.*, *agr.*); vivarium (di pesci)
vivaménte *avv.* warmly; keenly (con interesse)
vivànda *s. f.* food
vivandière *s. m.* sutler
vivènte *agg.* living
vìvere *v. tr. e intr.* to live
vìveri *s. m. pl.* food *sing.*; food-stuffs, victuals, provisions
vivisezióne *s. f.* vivisection
vivo *agg.* living; alive (*pred.*); live (*attr.*)
viziàre *v. tr.* to spoil
viziàto *agg.* spoilt; aria – stale air
vìzio *s. m.* vice; bad habit (cattiva abitudine)
vizióso *agg.* vicious, corrupt
vocabolàrio *s. m.* vocabulary; dictionary (volume)
vocàbolo *s. m.* word, term
vocàle *s. f.* vowel
vocalizzo *s. m.* vocalization
vocazióne *s. f.* vocation, calling
vóce *s. f.* voice; entry (di dizionario)
vogàre *v. tr. e intr.* to row
vogatóre *s. m.* rower, oarsman; rowing-machine (attrezzo)

vòglia *s. f.* longing, fancy
volàno *s. m.* badminton (gioco); fly-wheel (*mecc.*)
volànte *s. m.* wheel
volantìno *s. m.* leaflet
volàre *v. intr.* to fly
volàtile *s. m.* bird
volenteróso *agg.* willing
volentièri *avv.* willingly, with pleasure
volére *v. tr.* to want; to wish (desiderare)
volgàre *agg.* vulgar
volièra *s. f.* aviary
vólo *s. m.* flight
volontà *s. f.* will
volontariaménte *avv.* voluntarily
volovelìsta *s. m. e f.* glider
vólpe *s. f.* fox
vòlta *s. f.* time; vault (*arch.*)
voltàggio *s. m.* voltage
voltéggio *s. m.* vault, vaulting
vólto *s. m.* face
volùbile *agg.* fickle
volùme *s. m.* volume
volumetrìa *s. f.* volumetry
voluminóso *agg.* voluminous, bulky
volùta *s. f.* volute (*arch.*); spiral (spira)
vomitàre *v. tr. e intr.* to retch, to throw up
vòmito *s. m.* vomiting; vomit (ciò che è stato vomitato)
vóngola *s. f.* clam
voràgine *s. f.* chasm
vòrtice *s. m.* vortex; – d'acqua whirl pool; – d'aria whirlwind
votànte *agg.* voting • *s. m. e f.* voter
votàre *v. tr. e intr.* to vote
votazióne *s. f.* voting
votìvo *agg.* votive
vóto *s. m.* vote; mark (valutazione)
vulcàno *s. m.* volcano
vulcanòlogo *s. m.* volcanologist
vulneràbile *agg.* vulnerable
vuotàre *v. tr.* to empty; to drain (prosciugare)
vuòto *agg.* empty

X

xenofobia *s. f.* xenophobia
xerocòpia *s. f.* xerographic copy

xerografia *s. f.* xerography
xilofonista *s. m. e f.* xylophonist

Y

yacht *s. m.* yacht; – **a vela** sailing yacht; – **a motore** motor yacht

yarda *s. f.* yard
yògurt *s. m.* yogurt, yoghourt

Z

zabaióne *s. m.* egg flip
zaffàta *s. f.* whiff
zafferàno *s. m.* saffron
zaffiro *s. m.* sapphire
zàino *s. m.* backpack, knapsack, rucksack
zampa *s. f.* leg; paw; claw (di uccello)
zampillante *agg.* gushing
zampillo *s. m.* jet, gush
zampiróne *s. m.* fumigator
zampógna *s. f.* bagpipe
zampognàro *s. m.* piper
zanna *s. f.* tusk; fang (di carnivori)
zanzàra *s. f.* mosquito
zanzarièra *s. f.* mosquito-net
zappa *s. f.* mattock, hoe
zappàre *v. tr.* to hoe
zàttera *s. f.* raft
zavòrra *s. f.* ballast
zazzera *s. f.* long hair, mop

zèbra *s. f.* zebra (*zool.*); zebra crossing (passaggio pedonale)
zécca *s. f.* mint • tick (*zool.*)
zèlo *s. m.* zeal
zénzero *s. m.* ginger
zèppa *s. f.* wedge
zerbino *s. m.* door-mat
zia *s. f.* aunt
zibellino *s. m.* sable
zigomo *s. m.* cheek-bone
zinco *s. m.* zinc
zingarésco *agg.* gipsy (*attr.*)
zingaro *s. m.* gipsy
zio *s. m.* uncle
zircóne *s. m.* zircon
zitèlla *s. f.* spinster
zizzània *s. f.* darnel; discord (*fig.*)
zòccolo *s. m.* clog; hoof (di cavallo); base, plinth (di colonna); wainscot (di parete)

zodìaco *s. m.* zodiac
zólfo *s. m.* sulphur
zolla *s. f.* sod, turf
zollétta *s. f.* lump
zona *s. f.* zone
zoo *s. m. inv.* zoo
zoologìa *s. f.* zoology
zoòlogo *s. m.* zoologist
zoppicàre *v. intr.* to limp
zoppo *s. m.* cripple
zucca *s. f.* pumpkin

zuccheràre *v. tr.* to sugar, to sweeten
zuccheràto *agg.* sugared, sweetened
zuccherièra *s. f.* sugar-bowl
zùcchero *s. m.* sugar; – **a velo** icing sugar; – **in zollette** lump sugar; – **filato** candyfloss
zucchino *s. m.* courgette
zuffa *s. f.* brawl
zùfolo *s. m.* flageolet, flute
zuppa *s. f.* soup; – **di pesce** fish soup; – **di verdura** vegetable soup
zuppièra *s. f.* soup-tureen